PASTORAL DRAMA IN EARLY MODERN ITALY
THE MAKING OF A NEW GENRE

LEGENDA

LEGENDA, founded in 1995 by the European Humanities Research Centre of the University of Oxford, is now a joint imprint of the Modern Humanities Research Association and Maney Publishing. Titles range from medieval texts to contemporary cinema and form a widely comparative view of the modern humanities, including works on Arabic, Catalan, English, French, German, Greek, Italian, Portuguese, Russian, Spanish, and Yiddish literature. An Editorial Board of distinguished academic specialists works in collaboration with leading scholarly bodies such as the Society for French Studies and the British Comparative Literature Association.

MHRA

The Modern Humanities Research Association (MHRA) encourages and promotes advanced study and research in the field of the modern humanities, especially modern European languages and literature, including English, and also cinema. It also aims to break down the barriers between scholars working in different disciplines and to maintain the unity of humanistic scholarship in the face of increasing specialization. The Association fulfils this purpose primarily through the publication of journals, bibliographies, monographs and other aids to research.

Maney Publishing is one of the few remaining independent British academic publishers. Founded in 1900 the company has offices both in the UK, in Leeds and London, and in North America, in Boston. Since 1945 Maney Publishing has worked closely with learned societies, their editors, authors, and members, in publishing academic books and journals to the highest traditional standards of materials and production.

ITALIAN PERSPECTIVES

Series Editors
Professor Zygmunt Barański, University of Cambridge
Professor Anna Laura Lepschy, University College London

In the light of growing academic interest in Italy and the reorganization of many university courses in Italian along interdisciplinary lines, this book series, founded by Maney Publishing under the imprint of the Northern Universities Press and now continuing under the Legenda imprint, aims to bring together different scholarly perspectives on Italy and its culture.

Italian Perspectives publishes books and collections of essays on any period of Italian literature, language, history, culture, politics, art, and media, as well as studies which taken an interdisciplinary approach and are methodologically innovative.

BOARD OF ADVISORS

Patrick Boyde, UK	Millicent Marcus, USA
Patricia Brown, USA	Giuseppe Mazzotta, USA
Victoria De Grazia, USA	Martin McLaughlin, UK
John Gatt-Rutter, Australia	Lino Pertile, USA
Paul Ginsborg, Italy	Eduardo Saccone, Ireland
Guglielmo Gorni, Switzerland	Rebecca West, USA
Giulio Lepschy, UK	Diego Zancani, UK

APPEARING IN THIS SERIES

1. *The Letters of Giacomo Leopardi 1817-1837*, ed. by Prue Shaw
2. *Nelle Carceri di G. B. Piranesi*, by Silvia Gavuzzo-Stewart
3. *Speculative Identities: Contemporary Italian Women's Narrative*, by Rita Wilson
4. *Elio Vittorini: The Writer and the Written*, by Guido Bonsaver
5. *Origin and Identity: Essays on Svevo and Trieste*, by Elizabeth Schächter
6. *Italo Calvino and the Landscape of Childhood*, by Claudia Nocentini
7. *Playing with Gender: The Comedies of Goldoni*, by Maggie Günsberg
8. *Comedy and Culture: Cecco Angiolieri's Poetry and Late Medieval Society*, by Fabian Alfie
9. *Fragments of Impegno*, by Jennifer Burns
10. *Contesting the Monument: The Anti-Illusionist Italian Historical Novel*, by Ruth Glynn
11. *Camorristi, Politicians and Businessmen*, by Felia Allum
12. *Speaking Out and Silencing*, ed. by Anna Cento Bull and Adalgisa Giorgio
13. *From Florence to the Heavenly City: The Poetry of Citizenship in Dante*, by Claire E. Honess
14. *Orality and Literacy in Modern Italian Culture*, ed. by Michael Caesar and Marina Spunta
15. *Pastoral Drama in Early Modern Italy: The Making of a New Genre*, by Lisa Sampson

Managing Editor
Dr Graham Nelson, 41 Wellington Square, Oxford OX1 2JF, UK

www.maney.co.uk/series/italianperspectives
www.legenda.mhra.org.uk

Pastoral Drama in Early Modern Italy

The Making of a New Genre

Lisa Sampson

LEGENDA

Modern Humanities Research Association and Maney Publishing
Italian Perspectives 15
2006

Published by the
Modern Humanities Research Association and Maney Publishing
1 Carlton House Terrace
London SW1Y 5DB
United Kingdom

LEGENDA is an imprint of the
Modern Humanities Research Association and Maney Publishing

Maney Publishing is the trading name of W. S. Maney & Son Ltd,
whose registered office is at Hudson Road, Leeds LS9 7DL, UK

ISBN 1 904713 06 8 / 978-1-904713-06-7

First published 2006

All rights reserved. No part of this publication may be reproduced or disseminated or transmitted in any form or by any means, electronic, mechanical, photocopying, recording or otherwise, or stored in any retrieval system, or otherwise used in any manner whatsoever without the express permission of the copyright owner

© Modern Humanities Research Association and W. S. Maney & Son Ltd 2006

Printed in Great Britain

Cover: 875 Design

Copy-Editor: Dr Avery T. Willis

CONTENTS

	Acknowledgements	ix
	List of Illustrations	x
	Note on Transcription and Translation	xii
1	Introduction	1
2	The Earliest Examples of Pastoral Drama: The Self-Conscious Evolution of a New Genre	12
3	Tasso's *Aminta*: Raising the Profile of the Pastoral Play	61
4	Imitations and Innovations after Tasso's *Aminta*: Accommodating a Female Voice	98
5	Guarini's *Pastor fido*: The Establishment of an Ethical and Political Model of Pastoral Drama	129
6	Performing Pastoral Drama	169
7	Pastoral Drama in the Seventeenth Century and Beyond	195
	Bibliography	241
	Index	263

To Erik

ACKNOWLEDGEMENTS

This monograph represents the outcome of a research project begun several years back while a doctoral student at Cambridge. Along the way it has been influenced and helped by many academics, colleagues and friends. It is a great pleasure to be able to thank here those who have made a particularly significant contribution. I am deeply endebted to Virginia Cox for her inspiring guidance of my work since my graduate days and her insightful suggestions during the preparation of this monograph. I am sincerely grateful also to Richard Andrews for generously giving me the benefit of his expertise in his meticulous reading of the whole manuscript. My thanks go also to David Robey for his critical observations on a substantial part of the book, as well as to Abigail Brundin and my father, Rodney Sampson, for their comments on individual chapters. The publication of this monograph would not have been possible without the generous financial assistance of Reading University and the MHRA. I would also like to acknowledge with thanks the award of a British Academy post-doctoral fellowship (2000–03) and Small Research Grant which allowed me to embark on research that has contributed to the present study. I am grateful to the copy-editor, Avery Willis, for her thorough work, and to Graham Nelson for his attentive editing of this volume and his understanding of delays in the last phase of the project arising from the birth of my daughter. Lastly, I must thank my parents and especially my husband for their endless patience and support at all stages of the writing process.

Lisa Sampson
Oxford, June 2006

LIST OF ILLUSTRATIONS

Cover

Anonymous woodcut illustration of the narrated scene of the Satyr's attempted rape of Silvia (preceding Act III) in Torquato Tasso, *Aminta, favola boschereccia* (Venice: Aldo Manuzio, 1589; first printed in the 1583 edition). Reproduced by kind permission of the Bodleian Library, University of Oxford (Auct. 2. R. 4. 78, p. 61).

Illustrations

1. (p. 23) Woodcut of 'Scena satyrica', in *Il Secondo libro di perspetti[v]a di Sebastiano Serlio Bolognese, Le Second livre de perspective de Sebastian Serlio Bolognois, mis en langue francoise par Iehan Martin, Secretaire de Monseigneur Reverendissime Cardinal de Lenoncourt* (Paris: n. pub., 1545).
   Reproduced by permission of the Bodleian Library, University of Oxford (Douce S 848 (1), fol. 70^v).
2. (p. 66) Anonymous woodcut illustration of Amore (Cupid) in pastoral dress (preceding Prologue), in Torquato Tasso, *Aminta* (Venice: Aldo Manuzio, 1589; first included in the 1583 edition).
   Reproduced by permission of the Bodleian Library, University of Oxford (Auct. 2. R. 4. 78, p. 17).
3. (p. 78) Anonymous woodcut illustration of the Satyr's monologue in a pastoral scene with animals (preceding Act II), in Torquato Tasso, *Aminta* (Venice: Aldo Manuzio, 1589; first included in the 1583 edition).
   Reproduced by permission of the Bodleian Library, University of Oxford (Auct. 2. R. 4. 78, p. 44).
4. (p. 133) Engraving (by Francesco Val(l)egio?) from frontispiece of Battista Guarini, *Pastor fido, tragicommedia pastorale* (Venice: Giovanni Battista Ciotti, 1602).
   Reproduced by kind permission of Reading University Library (Overstone Shelf 19F/19).
5. (p. 144) Engraving (by Francesco Val(l)egio?) from Battista Guarini, *Pastor fido, tragicommedia pastorale* (Venice: Giovanni Battista Ciotti, 1602). The prologue delivered by the river god Alfeo (Alpheus), with pastoral perspective and a neo-classical temple in the backdrop.
   Reproduced by permission of Reading University Library (Overstone Shelf 19F/19, fol. b^v).
6. (p. 158) Engraving (by Francesco Val(l)egio?) preceding Act V of Battista Guarini, *Pastor fido, tragicommedia pastorale* (Venice: Giovanni Battista Ciotti, 1602). Reproduced by permission of Reading University Library (Overstone Shelf 19F/19, p. 350).

LIST OF ILLUSTRATIONS   xi

7. (p. 182) Engraving (by Francesco Val(l)egio?) preceding Act III of Battista Guarini, *Pastor fido, tragicommedia pastorale* (Venice: Giovanni Battista Ciotti, 1602), depicting Mirtillo in the foreground, with the 'Gioco della cieca' [game of blind-man's-buff] behind on the right.
   Reproduced by permission of Reading University Library (Overstone Shelf 19F/19, p. 138).

8. (p. 205) Engraving by F. Val(l)egio for the frontispiece of Guidubaldo [de'] Bonarelli, *Filli di Sciro, favola pastorale* (Ferrara: Vittorio Baldini, 1607), with the emblem of the printer for the Intrepidi academy.
   Reproduced by kind permission of The Warden and Fellows of All Souls College, Oxford (Codrington Library, mm.12.1).

9. (p. 207) Engraving preceding Act I of Guidubaldo [de'] Bonarelli, *Filli di Sciro, favola pastorale* (Ferrara: Vittorio Baldini, 1607).
   Reproduced by permission of The Warden and Fellows of All Souls College, Oxford (Codrington Library, mm.12.1, fol. †4^v).

10. (p. 214) Engraving for Act II of Guidubaldo [de'] Bonarelli, *Filli di Sciro, favola pastorale* (Ferrara: Vittorio Baldini, 1607).
    Reproduced by permission of The Warden and Fellows of All Souls College, Oxford (Codrington Library, mm.12.1, p. 38).

NOTE ON TRANSCRIPTION AND TRANSLATION

Where available, modern editions of early sources have been used, observing their respective transcription criteria. Otherwise, early modern Italian sources have been transcribed following the original as closely as possible, for example preserving the original spelling of double/single consonants unless marked. The following minor changes have, however, been made to facilitate the modern reader:

- *u* and *v* have been distinguished according to modern usage.
- *h* used only for (pseudo-) etymological purposes has been removed, though it is retained where it serves a diacritic function.
- *j* in intervocalic or initial position has been altered to *i*.
  In final position, *j* has been rendered by *î* if it indicates *–ii*; or *i* if it is purely a graphic feature.
- The sequence *–ti* and *–tti* followed by a vowel has been changed to *–zi*. (e.g. *servitio* → *servizio*; *attioni* → *azioni*).
- *Et* has been changed to *e*, except when preceding words beginning with an *e*, when it has been changed to *ed*.
- Word boundaries have in some cases been changed for clarity: conjunctions, and prepositions + definite article not requiring *raddoppiamento sintattico* have been joined together (e.g. *perciò*, *poiché*, *dai*).
- Ampersands have been expanded; other abbreviations have also been given in full (sometimes in square brackets), though they are left as in the original in the titles of works.
- Accents follow standard usage.
- Capitalization generally follows standard modern usage, except where it serves a rhetorical function in the original.
- Punctuation, including apostrophes for omissions, follows the original as far as possible, although some changes have occasionally been necessitated to aid comprehension.
- Variant spellings of first names have been standardized in the main text (e.g. Bartholomeo → Bartolomeo; Curtio → Curzio); and family names sometimes found with variable masculine/feminine forms (with *a* or *o* in final position) are consistently given in the masculine form (e.g. Isabella Pallavicino), except in titles of works.

Additional editorial interventions are indicated by square brackets.

Translations are my own, unless otherwise indicated. The overall aim has been for clarity and to assist comprehension of the original. For this reason, Italian verse is rendered in English prose, and a generally modern idiom is adopted.

CHAPTER 1

❖

Introduction

> Una favola nova pastorale
> Magnanimi, e illustri spettatori
> Oggi vi s'appresenta. Nova intanto,
> Ch'altra qui non fu già mai forse più udita
> Di questa sorte recitarsi in scena:
> Et nova ancor, perché vedrete in lei
> Cose non più vedute.[1]

[Today, generous and illustrious audience, you will see a new pastoral play; new in the sense that one of this kind has perhaps never before been heard performed on stage, and new too in that you will see in it things that you have never seen before.]

With these words, Agostino Beccari introduces his *Il Sacrificio* [The Sacrifice] (performed 1554), which is generally accepted as being the first example of an Italian pastoral play, a dramatic form that enjoyed enormous success with theatregoers and readers well into the seventeenth century. Since then, the genre has however undeservedly been consigned a relatively marginal place in theatre history. From the eighteenth century, and especially post-Romanticism, critics have accused it of artificiality, escapism and repetitiveness. In part, this can be related to negative views on literature generally from the later sixteenth and seventeenth centuries, which is described by De Sanctis, for instance, as being 'empty of ideas and feelings, a game of [ancient] forms and purely concerned with exteriors'.[2] The English critic Greg echoes such sentiments in relation to pastoral drama, agreeing that had it not been for Torquato Tasso's *Aminta* (probably first performed 1573; printed 1580/1), which today undoubtedly represents the most famous example, '[the genre] must almost necessarily have been stillborn'.

The modern reader cannot so easily dismiss what was one of the most characteristic dramatic genres of its time. Besides Tasso's *Aminta*, Battista Guarini's *Pastor fido* (printed 1589/90) has also widely been acknowledged as a landmark in theatre history, as the first significant example of pastoral tragicomedy. Moreover, studies conducted since the 1960s and my own investigations have uncovered around two hundred further examples, of which most are still relatively unknown, especially to Anglophone scholars.[3] These indicate not only the scale of the genre's popularity, which is well attested by contemporaries, but also its variety and broadening appeal over the period. While initially such plays tended to be composed for courtly circles in Italy, they increasingly found success with academic and less elite writers and audiences, especially as they began to appear more frequently in print. Given their romantic content and scope for decorous female roles, they also appealed to female audiences and even proved congenial to the first known women authors of secular drama. Like other kinds of Italian theatre, pastoral drama soon became known to dramatists abroad through translations, starting with Tasso's *Aminta* which first appeared in Croatian in 1580, then in French, English, Dutch, Spanish, Latin and German. This and other examples in turn sparked imitations, especially in France from the late 1580s, culminating in the plays of Racan and Mairet in the 1620s. The genre's impact was generally less widespread or directly felt in Spain and England, given the different socio-political conditions for theatre. Even so, certain tropes and examples were productively drawn upon by dramatists including Lope de Vega, Calderón and Shakespeare. More generally, its themes, ideas and lyric representation of love reveal that it played a significant part in forming a broader European tradition of pastoral literature and art.

This wide appeal of pastoral drama was in many ways due to its versatility and fundamentally mixed nature. Given its heterodox origins, ranging from classical eclogues to medieval romances and lyric poetry, and, later on, courtly pageants and rustic farces, it provided dramatists with a variety of motifs and traditions of spectacle which could be adapted to suit current tastes. Even when given a 'regular' or neo-classical five-act form (following Beccari), it therefore remained far less clearly defined than the neo-classical comedy, which had been restored to the Italian stage over a half century earlier by pioneering humanists. It is precisely this generic instability that in my view makes regular pastoral drama such a fascinating subject of investigation, especially since it coincided with significant changes within theatre and Italian culture generally. Although the period is typically associated with the restriction of possibilities for artistic expression following the convocation of the Council of Trent (1545–63), this was in many ways a formative time for modern theatre, with the consolidation of a professional tradition (*commedia dell'arte*), especially from 1560, and the first experiments with opera a few decades later. Pastoral drama to some extent stimulated the development of both these phenomena. In the later sixteenth century, professional *comici* performed and adapted popular pastoral plays according to their needs, occasionally writing their own. The genre's possibilities for plausibly incorporating spectacular stage effects, dance, music, and song, especially in the form of emotional outpourings, also meant it contributed to the development of new, mixed theatrical forms from the late sixteenth century — including the *melodramma*.

The present study represents the first comprehensive treatment in English of regular pastoral drama as it evolved over the sixteenth and seventeenth centuries, both on stage and in print. It explores something of the complexity of this genre, which presents the intriguing paradoxes of being in different ways both 'modern' and 'ancient', engaging in fantasy and yet obliquely reflecting reality, and representing a high as well as a popular art form. This study considers how writers of pastoral drama responded to social, cultural and intellectual pressures and innovations, especially regarding critical attitudes towards theatre and the arts. Through combining these approaches, it thereby aims to add new perspectives to the most extended explorations of Italian pastoral drama hitherto by Louise George Clubb and Marzia Pieri (see also the very recent study of Laura Riccò). Enrico Carrara's vast exploration of pastoral poetry including drama, though still an important point of reference is dated in its approach, while Robert Henke's wide-ranging comparative study focuses especially on aspects of Italian pastoral drama that relate to Shakespeare.[4] Notably, the present book provides a more nuanced historical and sociological understanding of the ways in which pastoral drama responded to external political and religious changes than is presented in Clubb's authoritative monograph on the three genres of Italian drama, which focuses rather on internal structures and imitative dramatic principles at work. My study also offers extended critical analysis of specific play-texts and discussion of the critical debates on the genre, which are largely avoided in Pieri's scholarly work in order to focus on the staging tradition of the genre from the fifteenth to the seventeenth centuries. In this way, I aim to investigate the ways in which the genre allowed dramatists to experiment with new ideas and combinations not envisaged by neo-classical conventions, which enabled the process of expanding the existing canon. This will help to cast a clearer light on the general panorama of Italian theatre and culture during a period which felt not only the conservative impact of Counter-Reformation sensibilities, but also, increasingly, the liberating effects of new scientific and other discoveries.

Some challenges to this task are presented from the outset due to the pastoral drama's elusiveness and inclusiveness. In contrast to the other major dramatic forms of the period, comedy and tragedy, one does not find anything like the ready availability of modern collections or series of plays. And in theoretical terms, it lacks the same kind of unequivocal classical models and authoritative definitions. Pastoral drama could in fact be taken to denote a vast, heterogeneous range of works dating from the late Middle Ages, to be performed or at least envisaged for performance. These could be scripted or unscripted, destined mainly to be enjoyed for their verbal content, or else heavily reliant for their effect on non-verbal, dramatic forms of expression. In many ways this resistance to definition remains part of its attraction, but for the present purposes it has been necessary to establish certain parameters and critical distinctions.

First of all, as mentioned, this study deals above all with 'regular' pastoral drama; that is, scripted plays that adopt the five-act form and neo-classical unities typically used for erudite comedy and tragedy. This will allow a more focused exploration of the genre during the period in which critical questions, especially relating to Aristotle's *Poetics*, became important to drama generally. It was more or less from this time that pastoral drama became considered as having its own distinct structure, characterization, style, and performance practices. Of course, as with any genre, variations are continually evident over time and between authors, and the conventions are at times stretched by individual works.[5] Even so, regular pastoral plays can be said to display certain broad traits, or 'theatergrams', to use Clubb's key dramaturgical concept — that is, structural units (themes, *topoi*, situations, character types), which can be repeated, transferred and transformed as they are shared and imitated between genres. Generally, these plays take place in a unified green setting, usually in a clearing with some trees and sometimes huts, a fountain or a temple. This space, often identified as Arcadia, evokes a remote pagan existence presided over by ancient Greco-Roman divinities like Pan, Venus and Diana, who are the object of cult worship and may appear on stage. Magic is also possible in this context. The cast consists mostly of pseudo-noble shepherds and nymphs (mainly understood as shepherdesses) who speak particularly about love and their emotional state in verse, though baser goatherds and satyrs may be introduced too. During such plays we follow the various tormented love affairs of the cast through to the conventional happy ending.

Close discussion of the wide range of earlier pastoral literature and mixed dramatic forms which contributed to such conventions regrettably falls outside the scope of this survey. However, some aspects of early modern 'pastoralism' (Greg's term) are inevitably used to throw light on developments in regular pastoral drama, since dramatists clearly drew much inspiration from other forms of pastoral, including verse, prose, and spectacle. It should be noted that I shall throughout understand the qualifying term 'pastoral' (*pastorale* or *boschereccia*) as referring to a *mode* rather than a specific genre. Following a useful and by now common critical distinction, a mode especially affects attributes such as tone, style and themes, and can apply across different genres (such as comedy, prose romance, novel), though it may be adapted in particular cases and over time. A mode therefore functions as a somewhat broader concept than genre, though, as Paul Alpers has argued, they share certain features.[6] The seminal study of William Empson and others have shown how the pastoral mode potentially encompasses an enormously diverse range of literary forms, tones, *topoi* and styles.[7] For this reason, it is difficult or even impossible to define this mode too categorically, especially since, as has been noted, it 'work[s] insistently against itself, problematizing both its own definition and stable definitions within its texts'.[8]

We shall not enter further into this definitional minefield, since concepts relevant to our enquiry will best be developed in context. However, it is worth noting some of the conflicting tendencies in early modern pastoral.[9] These allow it to reflect a greater range of concerns and values than might at first glance be expected, given its setting and apparently limited subject matter and style. Most commonly, the pastoral mode at this time implies an idealizing and sometimes elegiac perspective, heightened by mythological overtones. It evokes a simple and innocent existence, sometimes equated with a now lost Golden Age, in which shepherds and nymphs can freely discuss and engage in love affairs, hunting and poetic activities, removed from everyday preoccupations. This has frequently resulted in the reductive criticism of pastoral as escapist, since it privileges the aesthetic and sublimates real social and political tensions to portray an ordered harmony, often colluding with the desired image of ruling powers. In more positive terms, though, the less 'realistic' setting of pastoral drama in a secluded green world, less constrained by strict behavioural codes than the civilized cities and courts, meant that it could more plausibly represent certain areas of emotional and psychological experience than comedy and tragedy — including states of love, madness, and mourning. Furthermore, the pastoral could be used elegantly and self-consciously to explore literary issues, a feature of the mode since its inception with Theocritus' *Idylls*.[10] It thereby embodies the paradox of being theoretically simple, yet highly sophisticated and allusive — less about nature than about art, and related ideas of artifice, civilization, and human behaviour.

In addition, pastoral writings have long been recognized as offering possibilities for oblique social commentary. Since Virgil's eclogues (*Bucolics*), the Arcadian existence has provided a convenient veil under which to allude to real political situations or figures.[11] From the Middle Ages, moral and religious issues could be associated with the pastoral setting as well. This is evident in some miracle plays (*sacre rappresentazioni*) and in Latin pastoral eclogues, like the obscure, allegorical ones of Petrarch.[12] The pastoral mode therefore potentially offered a suitable vehicle for satire, especially when contrasted with an unacceptable reality. The related myth of the Golden Age, especially as used by Ovid, provided further opportunities for this kind of social criticism as well as eulogy.[13] Early modern pastoral drama, beneath its typical aspect of playful hedonism and idyll, may likewise contain criticism. This is usually voiced by humble goatherds, satyrs, or other characters who are in some way marginal or who represent 'outsiders' to the pastoral setting or love entanglements. Though the herdsmen are often treated rather patronizingly as comic figures, they may at the same time offer a glimpse of the real labours of country life and its simple pleasures.[14] Works that privilege the realistic and practical perspective should, however, more properly be considered as georgic (a mode in its own right, following Virgil's model) rather than pastoral.

Another counter-current to the idealizing aspect of the pastoral mode is the satyric vein — not to be confused with the idea of satire. This refers to the ancient Greek satyr-drama, categorized by Vitruvius as one of the three classical dramatic genres besides tragedy and comedy. This kind of drama (which still remains rather obscure) presents satyrs and other Dionysiac and divine beings, uncivilized by societal laws and norms, in the wild forests where mysterious rites could be celebrated with erotic, drunken and violent excess. Such evocations draw on longstanding collective cultural myths of man's primeval origins in the forests, and show their metaphorical importance for the formation of civic society.[15] For these reasons, pastoral drama may provide a valuable, if ambiguous, means of understanding broader ideas of society and what constituted civilized behaviour. However, its typically negative portrayal of satyric elements suggests the attempts of contemporary polite society to set limits to, and so repress, instinctual and animal kinds of behaviour that could be manifested in humans.

The exploration of such ideological and cultural issues in the pastoral mode generally, and the possibilities for staging that the mode offered, are important in the present study insofar as they influenced writers of pastoral drama. For the same reason other neighbouring genres are also considered. Most obviously, writers of pastoral drama often drew on comedy for plot structures and themes, and sometimes borrowed modified elements from tragedy too, which gives it its inherently tragicomic nature. In this form it was gradually consolidated alongside the two more established dramatic genres until it finally rivalled them in popularity. Pastoral dramatists also drew on the popular literary genres of chivalric romance and lyric poetry, as well as the classical epic and eclogues. An analysis of individual pastoral plays in relation to a larger sample shows that the genre could over the period variously be used to negotiate with pre-existing dramatic or literary 'kinds', a concept that Henke considers intrinsic to pastoral. Such generic experimentation, carried out more or less self-consciously, and decisions to imitate or adapt other conventions will form an important part of our investigation.

Where evidence survives and space permits, we also examine the broader external conditions that influenced the production of pastoral drama: the networks of patronage and the political, geographical and social connotations of the spaces in which plays were composed and performed (especially chapter 5). The various strategies used by authors, editors and critics to legitimize these works in print are considered too. These strategies include writing critical contributions to the debates that began from the late 1580s, polemical prefaces or prologues, histories of the genre, and allegories, as well as, more indirectly, the imitation of particular prestigious models. As many plays as possible have been included in this discussion, since the aim is to remedy the sometimes slanted picture of the genre presented by critics who focus too narrowly on the masterpieces by Tasso and Guarini with few other terms of comparison.[16]

Taking a broadly chronological approach, chapters 2 to 7 investigate examples from the mid-sixteenth (before *Aminta*) to the early seventeenth centuries, of which the latter especially represent a rather neglected area of study. Lack of space and a wish to avoid reduplication of the detailed analysis by Clubb and Riccò, and Pieri's wider more geographically organized survey, prevent an extensive examination of pastoral plays composed during the later 1570s and 1580s (between *Aminta* and *Pastor fido*) in chapter 4. However, this chapter goes on to discuss the surprising appearance of female-authored pastoral plays from the late 1580s which represents a fertile new area of study only so far briefly touched upon in specific relation to the genre by Riccò.[17] Chapters 3, 5 and 7 give detailed attention respectively to the high-profile plays of Tasso, Guarini and Bonarelli, because of their role in legitimizing the pastoral genre and documenting its fortunes, and the greater surviving evidence for their reception and performance. But by comparing them with other dramatic, intellectual and literary works, the intention is to see them less as 'fixed' models of the genre and, rather, to position them within a broader cultural context as significant milestones in the process of shaping pastoral drama.

In bringing together literary, performance, critical and sociological issues which are all relevant to pastoral drama, it has been useful to compare research on related genres such as comedy and tragicomedy as well as on the pastoral mode. The overall understanding of specific pastoral plays has further been aided by many specialized studies. These are especially numerous for Tasso and Guarini but, increasingly, less known writers are also attracting scholarly attention and some of their *favole pastorali* have in recent years appeared in critical editions.[18] These findings have been put into a broader context by countless valuable studies on critical and dramaturgical practices in Italy, especially by Italian scholars. Comparative work on the transformation of Italian pastoral drama in other national contexts (especially England), though at times rather sketchy on the historical background to the Italian production, has also raised many thought-provoking critical perspectives.[19]

One of the many questions that still surrounds pastoral drama is how to periodize it. When exactly did writers first begin to use it knowingly — was Beccari's *Sacrificio* really the first? Why did they adopt it? And can it really be termed a 'new' genre, given its substantial and self-conscious debt to a rich earlier tradition of pastoral writings? To understand this problem one needs to look back at least to the late fourteenth century, when early humanist writers became interested in imitating and adapting classical pastoral works, including especially Virgil's eclogues and Ovid's *Metamorphoses*, but also later the *Idylls* of Theocritus and Longus' prose romance *Daphnis and Chloe*, amongst other less well-known sources. In addition, they could draw on aspects of medieval vernacular poetry. Petrarch's lyric poetry provided a crucial model both for style and pastoral themes such as love, loss and poetic activity within an idealized landscape. Boccaccio too made a fundamental contribution to pastoral literature (though not directly to drama) by introducing a Greco-Roman mythological setting and gods into the vernacular Christian tradition in a number of his compositions, including *Caccia di Diana*, *Ninfale fiesolano* and *Comedia delle ninfe fiorentine* (or *Ameto*). These works notably featured nymphs as well as shepherds amongst their protagonists (unlike most eclogues), though such 'characters' are often heavily allegorized and veil allusions to contemporaries. Their amorous affairs become a pretext for analyzing the complex nature of love. Sannazaro was influenced by Boccaccio's idyllic landscape and Petrarchan themes and style, but also drew more explicitly on classical sources in his prose romance *Arcadia* (1504), which had an enormous impact on subsequent pastoral writings. Moreover, chivalric romances, notably Ariosto's *Orlando furioso* (final edition 1532), featured pastoral episodes that embroiled heroes in complex love affairs, involving madness and magic, and provided a major source of plots and scenarios.

Pastoral writings in Latin and the vernacular were cultivated particularly in fifteenth-century urban cultural circles such as Medicean Florence and Siena, as well as in Naples and the northern Italian courts. In these contexts, there also flourished a tradition of 'irregular' forms of dramatic pastoral: eclogues, semi-dramatic dialogues, interludes (*intermedi* or *intermezzi*), and hybrid dramas (*drammi mescidati*) mixing mythological pastoral, tragic and comic scenes (see chapter 2). There were also more popular rustic comedies, pageants and plays linked with religious and seasonal festivals such as carnival or Mayday. Many such works are now lost, though, suggesting their ephemeral nature and reflecting their occasional use. These traditions continued into the early sixteenth century and beyond, when certain writers and performers particularly associated with Venice, and to some extent Siena, began to take advantage of the press to cultivate a wider virtual audience as well.[20]

As pastoral drama was regularized around the mid-sixteenth century — a process that was clearly not achieved overnight with Beccari's *Sacrificio* — it continued to draw on themes, characterization, and scenarios from earlier 'irregular' examples, but with a more unified structure and a more consistently elevated and Petrarchan tone. This study begins in chapter 2 by examining the earliest known examples of 'regular' pastoral drama, which were composed at a time of broader experiments with mixed dramatic genres on the part of some progressive humanists — especially Giambattista Giraldi Cinthio from Ferrara. In response to the perceived vulgarization of comedy, and stimulated especially by his compatriot Ariosto's ground-breaking 'modern' romance *Orlando furioso*, Giraldi aimed to revive, codify and innovate existing genres. This experimentation was particularly aided by the resurgence of interest in Aristotle's *Poetics* in the 1540s, after its translation into Latin in 1536.[21] Though notoriously problematic to interpret, this authoritative text provided writers and theorists with a relatively systematic understanding of underlying poetic structures and principles, which was lacking in treatises previously used, such as Horace's *Ars Poetica*. Aristotle notably sets out the all important concept of imitation (*mimesis*) as the root of all art, and the need for artistic unity and coherence. A canon of genres and their relative hierarchy is also suggested. For this reason, many theorists used the *Poetics* to support a narrow view of literature that only recognized a limited number of strictly imitative classical genres. However, the example of Ariosto's recent success and various increasingly subtle re-interpretations of Aristotle's text enabled 'modernizing' critics to challenge this authority.[22] They used the *Poetics* to justify a wider canon, allowing for generic evolution, as well as to support less didactic and more hedonistic views on literature. All these issues became increasingly relevant as the pastoral drama became established on the literary landscape, especially as a result of the publication of Tasso's *Aminta* (see chapter 3).

The third dramatic genre therefore evolved at a time of broader theoretical ferment amongst intellectuals, though only a few practitioners of pastoral drama dealt with the question of poetics directly — and notably not Tasso. For many, the pastoral drama's popularity with contemporary audiences was justification enough. However, others were aware of the difficulties in reconciling its tragicomic form, fantastic scenarios and lengthy lyric outpourings with neo-Aristotelian norms of unity and verisimilitude. Such problems first became a matter of explicit concern in the late 1580s, with the debate that surrounded Guarini's *Il Pastor fido* (discussed in chapter 5). This pastoral tragicomedy stirred a series of polemics, just as the 'problematic' works of Ariosto's *Furioso*, Speroni's *Canace* and Tasso's *Gerusalemme liberata* had done previously, and in some cases continued to do.[23] The discussions on the *Pastor fido* dealt not only with specific issues regarding the play's tragicomic poetic structure, but also with broader questions on the possibility of combining or re-inventing genres. This led to wider speculation on the social and political function of art in general. Guarini argued for the acceptance of his pastoral tragicomedy within the modern neo-classical canon. Yet the porous genre boundaries of the pastoral mode and the dramatic genre's unstable position between comedy and tragedy, drama and lyric, meant that its status was always difficult to reconcile. Later this would prove useful, as it could more easily detach itself from the canonical genres and renew itself by synthesizing other literary and dramatic forms in order to adapt to altering audience tastes (see chapter 7).

Guarini's promotion of his 'modern' genre seems to have struck a chord with contemporaries — a fact equally suggested by the level of antagonism that his play provoked. Alongside other critics, Guarini responded to a perceived state of transition or even crisis in Italian theatre. The traditional genres of comedy and tragedy (like the epic), canonized with the enthusiastic 'Renaissance' revival of classical forms, were felt to be out of touch with current tastes and needing innovation. As Counter-Reformation sensibilities began to raise concerns about morality and decorum of the arts and their proper role in society, comedy of the risqué sort found earlier in the sixteenth century was considered too licentious. Tragedy, on the other hand, could be seen as broaching sensitive ideological issues such as tyranny, which could get too close to reality in an Italy that had for decades been almost entirely under foreign occupation (such questions would later be dealt with in a modified form in pastoral drama, see chapter 7). The underlying fatalism of tragedy was also hard to square with the Christian conception of providence. By contrast, pastoral drama could delight its audiences with seemly comic elements. The dangers it represented were only threatened rather than actual, and were resolved in a happy ending which could carry providential overtones. Furthermore, the ostensibly fictional setting and more oblique form of mimesis of the pastoral provided writers with a safer dramatic medium for artistic expression. Pastoral drama could thus be presented as providing artistic evasion, while also allowing an indirect imaginative response to real religious and political issues.

The mixed form of pastoral drama therefore helped to stimulate new enquiries into the possibilities and function of art. It also prompted questioning of the traditional Aristotelian canon, leading to the overturning of the traditional hierarchy of dramatic genres at the turn of the century and the ideological perspectives that these subtly reinforced.[24] So Guarini's analogy between the modern invention of pastoral drama and the opening up of new worlds and discoveries in astronomy that were then shaking traditional certainties may not be so far-fetched.[25] As another 'modern' later argued:

> Il non volere che la pastorale sia accettabile perché non fusse in uso appresso gli antichi, e perché Aristotele o altro buon filosofo non ne facesse parole, è proprio un volere che più sia commendabile la ignoranza degli antichi che il sapere dei nostri uomini. Gli antichi non ebber l'uso delle campane, della artigliaria, della carta degli stracci, non conobbero l'arte di mandar lettere intorno con quella agevolezza che oggidì si costuma; adunque non dobbiamo servirci di queste commodità noi, per non allontanarci dagli ordini, e dagli usi degli antichi?[26]

> [Not wanting pastoral drama to be accepted because it was not used by the ancients, and because Aristotle or other good philosophers never mentioned it, just shows the wilful belief that the ignorance of the ancients is more commendable than the wisdom of our [modern] men. The ancients did not know how to use bells, artillery, or rag paper, they didn't know the art of sending letters around with the ease that we do today. So should we too avoid using these commodities, so as not to stray from the provisions and customs of the ancients?]

At a time of perceived technical and intellectual innovations in all areas of early modern culture, the 'new' genre of pastoral drama should perhaps be regarded as enabling writers to make a similar challenge to the traditional dramatic canon and literature itself.

Notes to Chapter 1

1. Beccari, *Il Sacrificio, favola pastorale* (Ferrara: Francesco di Rossi, 1555), Prologo, fol. A5ᵛ. Note that *favola* (from Latin *fabula*) in this context means play or drama, not plot.
2. Francesco De Sanctis, *Storia della letteratura italiana*, ed. by Benedetto Croce, 2 vols (Bari: Laterza, 1949), II, 204. For citation below, Walter W. Greg, *Pastoral Poetry and Pastoral Drama* (London: Bullen, 1906), p. 177.
3. See Louise George Clubb, *Italian plays, 1500–1700, in the Folger Library* (Florence: Olschki, 1968); Marzia Pieri, *La scena boschereccia nel rinascimento italiano* (Padua: Liviana, 1983); and the list of plays in a 29 volume series in the Biblioteca Nazionale, Florence: Raffaele De Bello, 'Bibliografia della Collana Palatina delle Pastorali' (BNF, 12-2-0-3), in *Studi Secenteschi*, 5 (1964), 161–74; 6 (1965), 285–98; 7 (1966), pp. 145–54. Further examples can be found in Cambridge University Library, the British Library, the Biblioteca Nazionale, Florence, and elsewhere. I include amongst this group five-

act plays variously termed *favola*, *commedia*, *tragedia*, *tragicommedia*, *egloga* with the qualitative *pastorale*, *boschereccia* and, less commonly, *silvestre*, *pescatoria*.
4. See Louise George Clubb, *Italian Drama in Shakespeare's Time* (New Haven; London: Yale University Press, 1989), chapters 4–6 on pastoral drama; Pieri, *La scena boschereccia*; Enrico Carrara, *La Poesia pastorale* (Milan: Vallardi, 1909); and Robert Henke, *Pastoral Transformations. Italian tragicomedy and Shakespeare's Late Plays* (London: Associated University Presses, 1997). I thank Professor Laura Riccò for sending me an electronic version of her recent monograph, *'Ben mille pastorali'. L'itinerario dell'Ingegneri da Tasso a Guarini e oltre* (Rome: Bulzoni, 2004), however the timing of this publication during the last stages of my research has unfortunately prevented a detailed exploration of this work here.
5. For a useful overview of key critical perspectives on genre, see *Modern Genre Theory*, ed. by David Duff (Harlow: Longman, 2000).
6. Paul Alpers, *What Is Pastoral?* (Chicago: Chicago University Press, 1996); see chapter 2, 'Mode and Genre', for a useful overview of critical positions (especially pp. 45–50).
7. William Empson, *Some Versions of Pastoral* (London: Chatto and Windus, 1935) provides a very inclusive view of pastoral. For a study that addresses the multiplicity of pastoral, see Andrew V. Ettin, *Literature and the Pastoral* (New Haven: Yale University Press, 1984). For a succinct but wide-ranging study, which identifies three broad uses for pastoral, see Terry Gifford, *Pastoral* (London: Routledge, 1999). See also the anthology of nearly exclusively English-language criticism, *The Pastoral Mode: A Casebook*, ed. by Bryan Loughrey (London: Macmillan, 1984).
8. Judith Haber, *Pastoral and the poetics of self-contradiction: Theocritus to Marvell* (Cambridge: Cambridge University Press, 1994), p. 1.
9. See Marzia Pieri's chapter on 'Il terzo genere', in *La Nascita del teatro moderno tra XV e XVI secolo* (Turin: Bollati Boringhieri, 1989), pp. 156–78 (pp. 156–65 for the divergent tendencies in pastoral drama before 1560).
10. See the 'Introduction' to Theocritus, *The Idylls*, trans. by Robert Wells (Manchester and New York: Carcanet, 1988), pp. 9–52 (pp. 20–24, 29, 32).
11. For a fascinating exploration of the reception of Virgil's *Bucolics*, a cultural 'master-text' in Western culture, see Annabel Patterson, *Pastoral and Ideology. Virgil to Valéry* (Berkeley: University of California Press, 1988).
12. See *Petrarch's Bucolicum Carmen*, ed. and trans. by Thomas G. Bergin (New Haven: Yale University Press, 1974); and Patterson, pp. 42–59. On medieval pastoral eclogues modelled on Virgil's, including those of Petrarch and Boccaccio, see Helen Cooper, *Pastoral. Mediaeval into Renaissance* (Ipswich: Brewer, 1977), pp. 24–46.
13. See Harry Levin, *The Myth of the Golden Age in the Renaissance* (London: Faber and Faber, 1969).
14. This draws on what Cooper has described as the medieval French *bergerie* tradition (pp. 48–71).
15. Robert Pogue Harrison, *Forests: The Shadow of Civilization* (Chicago: University of Chicago Press, 1992), chapter 1.
16. This is true of much comparative work on English and Italian pastoral drama. Even Marvin T. Herrick concentrates only on the 'pastorals' by Giraldi, Beccari, Tasso and Guarini in *Tragicomedy. Its origins and development in Italy, France and England* (Urbana: University of Illinois Press, 1962).
17. Riccò, *'Ben mille pastorali'*, pp. 326–36 (on Torelli's *Partenia*). There are however various important shorter studies exploring Italian pastoral drama composed and performed by women by Richard Andrews, Julie D. Campbell, Virginia Cox, Lisa Sampson, and Lori J. Ultsch, as well as recent editions of the plays of Maddalena Campiglia and Isabella Andreini.
18. See for example Isabella Andreini, *La Mirtilla*, ed. by Maria Luisa Doglio (Lucca: Maria Pacini Fazzi, 1995), translated into English by Julie D. Campbell as *'La Mirtilla': A Pastoral*, Medieval and Renaissance Texts and Studies, 242 (Tempe, Arizona: Arizona Center for Medieval and Renaissance Studies, 2002); Antonio Ongaro and Girolamo Vida, *Favole*, ed. by Domenico Chiodo, with pref. by Giorgio Bárberi Squarotti (Turin: RES, 1998); and in the same Scrinium series, Agostino Beccari, Alberto Lollio, Agostino Argenti, *Favole*, ed. by Fulvio Pevere (1999); also Angelo Ingegneri, *La Danza di Venere* (Rome: Bulzoni, 2002), which I have not been able to access; and the bilingual edition of Maddalena Campiglia, *Flori*, transl. by Virginia Cox.
19. See for example Joseph Loewenstein, 'Guarini and the Presence of Genre', in *Renaissance Tragicomedy. Explorations in Genre and Politics*, ed. by Nancy Klein Maguire (New York: AMS Press, 1987),

pp. 35–55. This otherwise interesting article has some lapses in terms of the intellectual and historical background to the *Pastor fido*, and the theory on Italian pastoral is limited by only looking at Guarini's *Compendio* and briefly Jacopo Mazzoni. For English transformations of Italian models, see James, J. Yoch, 'The Renaissance Dramatization of Temperance: The Italian Revival of Tragicomedy and *The Faithful Shepherdess*', in Maguire, pp. 114–38; Henke, *Pastoral Transformations*, pp. 24–32, and *passim*; Robin Kirkpatrick, *English and Italian Literature from Dante to Shakespeare. A study of source, analogue and divergence* (London: Longman, 1995), pp. 254–59.
20. Marzia Pieri, *La Nascita*, pp. 158–59, and 164–65 on Andrea Calmo, whose *Le giocose moderne et facetissime egloghe pastorali...* (Venice, 1553) was printed five times until 1561 and then once in 1600.
21. Daniel Javitch, 'The Emergence of Poetic Genre Theory in the Sixteenth Century', *Modern Language Quarterly*, 59 (1998), 139–69 (pp. 139–40).
22. For the 'cultural emergency' caused by Ariosto's romance in the mid-century, and the simultaneous 'strategy of containment' by reactionary theorists, see Loewenstein, p. 39. On the expansion of the traditional Aristotelian canon of genres and on problem genres, see Rosalie Colie, 'Genre-Systems and the Functions of Literature', in Duff, pp. 148–66 (pp. 152–54).
23. On these debates, which also tied up with those on Dante's *Comedy*, see Bernard Weinberg, *A History of Literary Criticism in the Italian Renaissance*, 2 vols (Chicago: Chicago University Press, 1961).
24. Dominick LaCapra, 'Comment', *New Literary History*, 17 (1986), 219–21 (p. 221). For a similar conflict between a 'modern' and a conservative, classicizing perspective, in the quarrels over Marino and Chiabrera in the early to mid-seventeenth century, which preluded the full-blown *Querelle des anciens et modernes*, see Franco Croce, 'Critica e trattatistica del barocco', in *Storia della letteratura italiana. Il Seicento*, ed. by Emilio Cecchi and Natalino Sapegno (Milan: Garzanti, 1988), pp. 495–547 (pp. 497–500).
25. Battista Guarini, *Il Verato secondo, ovvero Replica dell'Attizzato Accademico Ferrarese in difesa del Pastor fido* (Florence: Per Filippo Giunti, 1593), p. 251.
26. Ludovico Zuccolo, *L'Alessandro, overo della pastorale, dialogo* (Venice: Andrea Baba, 1613), fols. 11^{r}-11^{v}.

CHAPTER 2

The Earliest Examples of Pastoral Drama: The Self-Conscious Evolution of a New Genre

> Le cose si vanno tuttavia avanzando di età in età, e [...] molte usanze antiche se ne cadono e se ne vanno in oblivione, e molte alla giornata di nuovo rinascono, le quali se portano seco il decoro del verisimile, non solamente non sono schifevoli, ma riescono grate nel cospetto de' giudiciosi.[1]
>
> [Things nonetheless progress from age to age, and [...] many ancient practices fall into disuse and sink into oblivion while, by the day, many others are once again revived; if these are accompanied by the decorum of verisimilitude, they are not only not unpleasant, but they appear pleasing to those with discernment.]

The Making of a New Genre

Perspectives on the origins of pastoral drama

Writings on the pastoral mode have long been bound up with issues of origins and processes of human and cultural development, construed both in a positive and negative sense. Similar concerns were raised about pastoral drama when it was first experimented with as a distinct 'new' genre in the mid-sixteenth century and in subsequent critical writings that sought to define it historically. These theoretical and practical questions are the subject of the present chapter, which deals with the few known 'regular' plays composed before the genre gained a higher profile with the composition and performance of Torquato Tasso's *Aminta* (1573). The plays will be explored in terms of their themes and structures. The different contexts of their production and reception will also be examined, during this time of significant cultural and social changes, especially for the Italian elites with whom the pastoral drama is closely associated.

The exploration of dramaturgical practice in these first 'regular' plays poses various difficulties as a result of the limited range and sometimes uncertain status of the sources available and their decidedly partial nature. Early historiography of the genre also tends to see the plays principally in relation to subsequent developments, thereby either unhelpfully ignoring these early beginnings or smoothing over the false starts. Battista Guarini, the most significant theorist of pastoral drama and first apologist, provides an instance of this. He takes the modernizing view that like all poetic genres the pastoral play was gradually perfected over time, developing organically from the short classical eclogue to its fully-fledged modern dramatic form.[2] Though an appealing account (and in part followed by more recent critics such as Carrara), it is unsatisfactory in that it fails to mention the dramatic eclogues that continued to be written or printed alongside pastoral drama later in the century. Nor does it adequately explain how the transition was made from the classical eclogue (for reading) to the staged five-act pastoral drama. In fact, closer inspection of the earliest 'regular' pastoral plays reveals that the genre developed in a way that was initially far from linear. Many early dramatists seem confused about how much it owed to the complex classical heritage or its relation to contemporary dramatic forms, and uncertain of the full implications of composing in such a genre.

Pastoral drama in its fully fledged form certainly appears more unified in structure and style, with a more consistently elevated tone, than earlier surviving 'irregular' examples of drama which integrated pastoral and sometimes rustic subjects. Yet it clearly continues to draw on themes, characterization, and scenarios found in these earlier kinds of 'mixed' drama, which as Pieri has shown, themselves drew both on classical motifs and on contemporary performance practices, used for example in sacred drama (*sacre rappresentazioni*). The best known *drammi mescidati* ('mixed' plays) are *Orfeo* (performed Mantua 1471/80; printed 1480) by the Florentine humanist Angelo Poliziano, and *Cefalo e Procri* (performed 1487) by the Ferrarese humanist-courtier Niccolò da Correggio.[3] Both use Ovid's *Metamorphoses* to different degrees — a work that would continue to be drawn on in regular examples of the genre. Also typical of later pastoral plays in *Orfeo*, is the opening dialogue on love between an older and a younger shepherd with a rustic 'servant', and the bard's sung eulogy of a patron (here unusually a Latin ode) and lament on hearing of the death of his beloved Euridice. However, the tragic and even violent ending, the brusque shifts in scene and tone, and great metrical variation (with substantial parts set to music) clearly mark it as belonging to an irregular tradition.[4] *Cefalo* reveals greater signs of unity: it requires a single pastoral set with a house and wood, and is in five acts with a happy ending, perhaps following the example of recent performances of Plautus' comedies in Ferrara.[5] The dialogic eclogue of Baldassar(r)e Castiglione and Cesare Gonzaga (*Tirsi*, performed in Urbino, 1506) provides a uniform pastoral setting for discussions on love, which allows graceful allusions to the patron and the performance context.[6]

More dramatic potential and less courtly allusion is offered in the eclogues of 'L'Epicuro Napolitano' (generally identified as Antonio Marsi, c. 1475–1555): *Cecaria* or *Dialogo di tre ciechi* ('Dialogue of Three Blind Men', performed 1523) and particularly *Mirzia* (composed c. 1523–28), which were also very popular in print, probably partly due to their complex metrical variation.[7] *Cecaria* falls into two parts; in the first, three unrequited 'blind' lovers variously describe their beloveds and their suffering, and finally decide to commit suicide together. In the second part a priest of Love intervenes and takes them to his temple to pray for divine illumination. Following an oracular pronouncement by the god of Love himself, the ladies seem to appear, after which the lovers' sight and proper understanding of love is restored. *Mirzia* similarly features three lovers, but this time also includes two principal nymphs (who became standard characters in regular pastoral) and the goddess Diana. This allows the development of three distinct plot strands, and more staged action including a game of blind man's buff between the nymphs, a practical trick on a nymph, and transformations of two of the characters, which points forward to the pastoral plays of Beccari and Guarini. Luigi Tansillo (1510–68), also from Naples — a city made famous as a centre for pastoral because of Sannazaro — substantially borrows from Marsi's plays in his *I due pellegrini* ('The Two Pilgrims', composed c. 1527, but not published until 1631). Like *Cecaria*, this represents rather stylized unrequited lovers who attempt suicide, but are finally dissuaded by the voice of a beloved dead nymph coming from within the very tree from which they were about to hang themselves. Rustic comedies performed and written by (semi-)professionals from the Veneto region and Tuscany, including Ruzante (Angelo Beolco) and Sienese dramatists like Niccolò Campani ('Lo Strascino') provide a livelier dramatic tradition. Their representations of 'realistic' peasants, often speaking in dialect with satirical and even obscene allusions, were popular with courtly audiences, though indecorous elements were later toned down when integrated into the regular pastoral play.

A further problem in analyzing the earliest examples of regular pastoral drama regards the genre's geographical origins and its frequent identification with Estense Ferrara, which continues to some extent even today.[8] This claim can partly be justified by the large proportion of early examples composed in Ferrara, to which we will return, and notably the masterpieces of Torquato Tasso (though born in Sorrento) and Battista Guarini. Given that the strongest initial proponent of this association was a Ferrarese nobleman (Guarini), it also needs questioning. Suspicions of regional patriotism and self-interest are raised particularly by the fact that, in his history of the genre, the major milestones are attributed exclusively to local dramatists. Guarini attributes its invention to Agostino Beccari with his *Il Sacrificio* [The Sacrifice] (1555), calling him 'onorato cittadin di Ferrara' [honoured citizen of Ferrara] and 'il primo de' moderni' [the first of the moderns] to present successfully pastoral dialogues in a complex plot structure modelled on regular comedy.[9] Tasso is credited with perfecting the genre by adding tragic-style choruses to his *Aminta*, while Guarini claims to have finally brought the genre to its culmination with his pastoral tragicomedy, *Il Pastor fido* (1589/90).

Guarini's contemporary and colleague, the Venetian dramatist-director Angelo Ingegneri (c.1550–1613), casts a somewhat different light on the development of pastoral drama at the start of his important treatise on dramatic poetry, *Della Poesia rappresentativa* (Ferrara, 1598). Not only is a less prominent role ascribed to the Ferrarese, but the earliest examples of pastoral drama, including Beccari's *Sacrificio*, are ignored altogether, since Tasso's *Aminta* is regarded as first legitimizing 'questa terza spezie di drama, prima o non ricevuta o non apprezzata od almeno non posta nella guisa in uso che s'è fatto d'allora in qua' [this third type of drama, which was previously either not received or appreciated, or which at least was not used in the way that it has been thereafter].[10] (This tribute to Tasso may also have reminded Ingegneri's readers of his role in editing and publishing several of the great poet's works.) While Guarini's *Pastor fido* is singled out for praise, it is followed by hopes for future great examples of varied provenance. Only in the dedicatory letter to the treatise, addressed to Cesare d'Este, are Ferrarese theatrical achievements specifically celebrated, though tactfully associated with the Este house, rather than the city from which the family had just been expelled (see Chapter 7, p. 203).

To assess properly the evolution of 'regular' pastoral drama, historiographical and critical questions will be balanced against an examination of the first known examples themselves, several of which were by authors from outside Ferrara. Here too our picture is bound to be somewhat incomplete since some plays are unfinished (Giraldi's *Favola pastorale*, Lollio's *Galatea*). Others only exist in later revised versions (those of Groto) or were printed without intervention from the author (Pasqualigo's *Intricati*). Apart from Giraldi's *Egle* (1545), none of the plays explored provide any explicit commentary on compositional principles, even though they depart from the kind of structures and metres associated with 'irregular' pastoral eclogues and rustic comedies. Notably, the metrical variety and mixed structures of the older forms are replaced by predominantly unrhymed hendecasyllable verse and a five-act structure, where the neo-classical unities of time, place, and action described by Lodovico Castelvetro are broadly observed. Even so, our exploration of the characters, style, and especially plot structures will give some sense of the intentions of the writers.

A significant proportion of the dramatists in question from this period were from Ferrara: Giambattista Giraldi Cinthio (Cinzio) (1504–1573) and the otherwise little known Agostino Beccari (before 1510–1590), Alberto Lollio (c.1508–1568), and Agostino Argenti (d. 1576). Pastoral plays were written also by the Venetian soldier, Count Alvise (Luigi) Pasqualigo (dates unknown), by the polymath and actor, Luigi Groto 'Il Cieco' [The Blind Man] from Adria in the Veneto region (1541–1585), and the Mantuan Jewish dramatist-director Leone de' Sommi (1525/7?–1590/2).[11] Examined comparatively, these works reveal many common features, but also suggest a particularly Ferrarese preoccupation with theoretical questions of verisimilitude and decorum, which will call for further explanation. It is with this cultural centre that our discussion will begin, focusing particularly on its dramatic culture and the important role played by Giraldi Cinthio.

Theatrical culture in mid sixteenth-century Ferrara

It is perhaps predictable that Ferrara should be associated with the emergence of pastoral drama in the mid-sixteenth century. Since the performance of Plautus' *Menaechmi* in 1486, patronized by Duke Ercole I d'Este, Ferrara had gained a distinguished reputation for its pioneering revival of classical theatre promoted by the ruling family, drawing on the services of humanist scholars trained in the tradition established by Guarino da Verona (from 1429).[12] It also had a reputation for splendid spectacles of a less strictly classical nature such as *sacre rappresentazioni*, mythological plays and pageants, and rustic *intermezzi*, as well as for the achievements of its poets especially in the field of the chivalric romance. Both the comic and romance traditions were superlatively adapted for contemporary audiences by Ludovico Ariosto (1474–1533), who notably gained international acclaim with his great romance epic, *Orlando furioso* (final version 1532). This vernacular masterpiece proved an important case for justifying 'new' artistic forms that were not mentioned in the supposedly 'universal' neo-Aristotelian canon (as Dante's *Comedy* had done before). The *Furioso* thus effectively sanctioned Ferrara's 'modern' attitude towards literature and an interest in generic experimentation, which helped prepare the way for pastoral drama.

The presence of Ludovico Ariosto dominated, though it did not entirely define, dramatic activities in Ferrara in the early decades of the sixteenth century. He was involved with theatrical activities on and off throughout his life, and is associated with many of the comic innovations in early sixteenth-century Italy. His *La Cassaria* (first version 1508) and *I Suppositi* (1509), written while in the service of Cardinal Ippolito d'Este, are amongst the earliest 'original' vernacular comedies and show an increasing divergence from Roman models. Under his new patron, Duke Alfonso I d'Este (from early 1518), Ariosto continued to compose and revise his plays as far as his substantial court duties permitted. Only in the second half of the 1520s, after returning to Ferrara from a difficult period as governor of the Garfagnana (recently brought under Estense control), was Ariosto finally able to devote more time to his literary activities. He took a leading role in court entertainment from 1528 and almost single-handedly reinvigorated the theatrical tradition after two decades marked by wars.[13] Ariosto's comedies were staged especially at carnival time with the collaboration of various court artists and actors, including the famous 'Ruzante' (Angelo Beolco) who was active in Ferrara with his company between 1528 and 1532.[14] The measure of Ariosto's success is clear from the fact that in 1531 the duke ordered a permanent theatre (*teatrino*) to be built in the main hall (*sala grande*) of the ducal palace according to the poet's specifications. Sadly, it was destroyed by fire shortly after (31 December 1532). One chronicler tellingly deduced that it was this disaster that precipitated Ariosto's death a few months later, demonstrating the extent to which the poet was popularly identified with Ferrarese theatre.[15]

Ariosto's plays enjoyed enormous appeal in performance. Courtly audiences delighted in his use of lively, complex intrigue plots and his attention to spectacular elements, local colour, and realistic contemporary details absent in early reworkings of Roman plays.[16] At the same time, intellectuals associated with the university and academic environments would have appreciated his erudite allusions and challenge to classical comedy, though it is less clear how far their own literary production was affected by his efforts. Notwithstanding the close connections between the Ferrarese Studio (university) and the courtly milieu, with which Ariosto was chiefly engaged, the two cultural centres promoted rather different values.[17] At this time, the Studio was still heavily dominated by the intellectual tradition founded by Guarino in the previous century, which had brought it European prominence. Its academic programme covering the humanities (rhetoric, history, geography) and sciences (cosmology, natural sciences) through the critical and philological study of classical authors meant that Latin and Greek culture held a privileged place, while the vernacular was slow to gain a hold.[18]

Many of the leading *letterati* of Ariosto's generation, like the professor of rhetoric at the Studio and canon Celio Calcagnini (1479–1541), Lilio Gregorio Giraldi (1479–1552) and Bartolomeo Ricci (1490–1569), disparaged the growth of a 'barbarous' vernacular culture, as they saw it. They considered the composition of secular verse in Tuscan to be properly a private or youthful leisure pursuit, marginal to more serious studies.[19] Lilio Gregorio Giraldi's *De poetis nostrorum temporum dialogi duo* (*On the poets of our time, two dialogues*, Florence, 1551) clearly demonstrates his linguistic conservatism. This dialogue comprises an earlier reported discussion (supposedly in Rome, 1513–15) of a broad range of works in Latin and Greek, reflecting the author's own prestigious literary acquaintances and the international quality of intellectual life at the Studio. By contrast, very few vernacular writers are mentioned (and most of these in the context of theatre), since the *volgare* lacked the dignity of Latin, being used even by 'barbers and common artisans'.[20] More space (pp. 212–15) is however devoted to vernacular literature in the later 'frame' dialogue (set in Ferrara in 1548), grudgingly reflecting its growing status from the 1530s after being sanctioned by Pietro Bembo (*Prose della volgar lingua*, 1525) and consolidated by the increased activity of the press.

Another significant cultural phenomenon that favoured the rise of the vernacular in Ferrara and, indirectly, the production of pastoral drama, was the rise of literary academies from the mid-sixteenth century.[21] These differed from literary circles loosely formed round leading cultural figures, which had existed since the fifteenth century, by being set up with formal statutes. The first in Ferrara was the Accademia degli Elevati [Academy of the Elevated Ones], which functioned for just under a year, disbanding on the death of its most distinguished member, Celio Calcagnini, in 1541. Other members included Lilio Gregorio Giraldi and Bartolomeo Ricci, the Florentine exile Bartolomeo Cavalcanti, and the aged Mantuan hellenist Marco Antonio Antimaco. A number of younger *letterati* were also admitted, possibly in some cases as the talented pupils or protégés of the above. For example, Alberto Lollio, the Ferrarese nobleman in whose house the Elevati met, studied in Ferrara with Antimaco.[22] The famous younger relative of Lilio Gregorio, Giambattista Giraldi (known as 'Cinthio' or 'Cinzio') was a pupil of Celio Calcagnini, as well as possibly of Antimaco.[23] Amongst the younger members was also Ercole Bentivoglio (1507–73), son of the Bolognese exile Annibale II and nephew of Alfonso I d'Este.[24]

Lollio's orations display a deferential attitude towards his elders in academic gatherings. Even so, he and other younger figures (particularly Giraldi Cinthio), diverge from their mentors in their enthusiasm for the burgeoning vernacular culture. This could in part be justified by Lollio's links with Florence (where he was born), while Giraldi's family also claimed distant Florentine forebears. More generally, though, it shows their support of 'modern' culture as reflected also in their interest in theatrical activities, following the illustrious Ariosto. This poet's example must in turn have tempered the reactionary attitude of the older generation. An enduring cult had formed around the great poet after his death in 1533, influencing the poetic choices of future generations.[25] The *Furioso* rapidly stimulated critical discussion and experimentation, including from 1554 the notorious literary quarrel between Giraldi Cinthio (himself the author of an unfinished epic, *Dell'Ercole*) and his former pupil, Giovanbattista Pigna.[26] Ferrarese critics consequently made an early contribution to the debate on the work that formally started in 1549, stimulated by the revival of interest in Aristotle's *Poetics* earlier that decade.[27]

However, Ariosto's Ferrarese successors mostly chose to imitate his comedies, probably because this genre presented fewer technical and theoretical problems, belonging clearly to the humanist canon. After all, even Ariosto's linguistically conservative friend Celio Calcagnini had translated Plautus' *Miles Gloriosus* for a carnival performance (1532) as requested by Alfonso I.[28] Bentivoglio, Lollio, and especially Giambattista Giraldi Cinthio emerge as protagonists of the post-Ariostan generation in terms of their theatrical endeavours. Bentivoglio, a friend and pupil of Ariosto, had been inspired by his teacher's more classicizing works: notably, he composed six satires as well as the comedies *I Fantasmi* and the more famous *Il Geloso* (both printed Venice 1544, though probably written in the late 1530s), as well as an unfinished tragedy and at least one more comedy. His theatrical skills and comedies were praised by Giraldi and the Mantuan Leone de' Sommi.[29] Alberto Lollio, besides his more famous academic orations (published during the 1550s and 1560s), also composed theatrical works. These include a translation of Terence's *Adelphi* (1554) with an additional prologue, another prologue for Ariosto's *I Suppositi*, an unpublished comedy, *I Nocchieri* (*The Helmsmen*) and, more adventurously, a pastoral comedy, *Aretusa* (Ferrara, 1564), and an undated manuscript sketch for another (*Galatea*).[30]

However, the most significant impact amongst the post-Ariostan generation in Ferrara was made by Giambattista Giraldi Cinthio (hereafter referred to as Giraldi). He stands out from his fellow dramatists for being far more prolific — his output includes nine tragedies, six of which have a happy ending, a satyr-play, and a rather unsuccessful comedy, *Eudemoni* — and for providing critical defences for his practices. Importantly, Giraldi marks the first move away from the standard practice of composing comedy in search of new dramatic forms that could better respond to his audience's tastes.

Theatrical production after Ariosto

Performance practices in Ferrara began to alter significantly after Ariosto's death. The accession of Duke Ercole II d'Este (1534–1559) the following year ushered in a period of relative peace for the duchy, though dominated by political and, notably, religious tensions. But by the mid-century, the status and authority of the Ferrarese court, like others in Italy, had been weakened after years of foreign invasions and wars. The Sack of Rome (1527) had definitively driven home to Italian potentates, including the papacy, their state of political subservience to the great European political and military powers of France and the Habsburg Empire. In order to secure their states, courtly rulers were therefore obliged to compete for the favour and protection of these foreign powers, which inevitably resulted in inter-state rivalry and petty struggles for precedence.

To compensate for their real political impotence, the Italian aristocracy increasingly felt the need to display their magnificence in cultural and ceremonial terms.[31] They became ever more sensitive to the observance of hierarchical order, where any improper deviation was considered a slight to their personal honour. For example, in 1541 the fact that Ercole rode at the more honourable right hand side of Charles V and handed the emperor his napkin at table was enough to spark off prolonged hostilities between the Este and Medici families.[32] The quarrel was not resolved until 1569, when Pope Pius V gave Cosimo de' Medici the title of Granduca, thereby raising his status above that of Duke Alfonso II d'Este. Elites responded ambivalently to these changes by seeking to define and fix their social and political role, which stimulated a flurry of printed conduct books. Castiglione's *Il Cortegiano* (final version 1528) particularly problematizes this conflict between the desire for order, as opposed to the nostalgia for intellectual freedom at least amongst educated aristocratics at court. This dialogue in many ways also illustrates the contemporary tendency of elites to produce apparently idealized and self-validating world views, as in Petrarchan poetry, neo-Platonic writings and myths of the Golden Age, though these still allowed possibilities for oblique political and social critique.

Ferrara under Ercole II was marked by an increased consolidation of ducal power through a clearly stratified social order and a skilful team of image-builders, including intellectuals and historians like Giovanbattista Pigna, Pirro Ligorio and Giambattista Giraldi Cinthio.[33] The Duke's political position had been strengthened by his marriage in 1528 to the daughter of King Louis XII of France, Renée, but his state was still in a delicate position due to his growing support for France's rival, Emperor Charles V, and the duchess's sympathies for protestantism shortly before the convocation of the Council of Trent.

Not surprisingly, the changing social and political climate affected theatrical practices in terms of what was performed. In particular, there was a noticeable shift in elite attitudes towards comedy from around the 1530s.[34] Despite Ariosto's innovations to 'modern' vernacular comedy, later Ferrarese writers experienced difficulties in maintaining the vitality and guaranteeing the exclusivity of the genre. From the 1530s, greater numbers began to be produced as the popularity of comedy increased, a demand that the press eagerly seized upon and fed. For instance, Ariosto complained in the prologue to his revised *Cassaria* (in verse, 1529) that the play had been prostituted in a defective version to public markets by insistent and greedy printers. He was probably concerned that his comedies, originally conceived for private courtly consumption, had not been subjected to the same careful revision process as the *Orlando furioso*, destined from early on for publication.[35] But there is also a class-oriented objection to the vulgarization of his comedy, reflecting the changing status of the genre from the 1530s as examples became more widely available in print. In 1551 the Venetian publisher Gabriele Giolito launched a series of comedies and Girolamo Ruscelli published a volume of selected vernacular examples (*Delle commedie elette*) in 1554 in response to growing demand.[36] This stimulated writers also from humbler social backgrounds to compose comedies and facilitated performances by private amateur groups, as well as by professional troupes from the 1550s and 1560s.[37]

Classical comedies were still apparently performed very privately starring children from the ducal family at the Ferrarese court during the late 1530s and 1540s (see Chapter 4, p. 105). More generally, though, Ferrarese intellectuals reacted to the comedy's perceived loss of cultural prestige around the mid-century by making their examples artificially academic, or by chosing not to engage with the genre at all. Not only snobbery was to blame for this attitude. As Andrews has argued, the spirit of comedy was gradually being stifled as writers became more anxious about the challenge it posed to prevailing moral values and to gender and class decorum — a concern that became particularly marked from the 1560s.[38] The discussion on humour in Castiglione's *Cortegiano* (Book II) already hints at some of these problems. For a fuller indication, we should turn to Giraldi Cinthio's *Discorso [...] intorno al comporre delle comedie e delle tragedie* [*Discourse [...] on composing comedies and tragedies*] (henceforth *Discorso*), printed together with his discourses on romances in 1554.[39] The *Discorso*, composed according to Horne between 1543 and 1554 while Giraldi was experimenting with comic structures with his *Eudemoni* (1548/49) and *Antivalomeni* (1548), presents a view of comedy which is both elitist and didactic.

He expresses concerns about the potential immorality of comedy given its cast of non-noble characters, its setting in a public piazza, and inclusion of *double entendres*, all of which are avoided in tragedy with its 'high and sublime' subjects and courtly setting. For this reason, Giraldi advises that:

> Serva [...] la comedia una certa religione che mai giovane vergine o polzella non viene a ragionare in iscena, e per contrario nelle scene tragiche vi s'introducono lodevolmente. E ciò m'estimo io che sia perché la scena comica, per lo piú è lasciva. (*Discorso*, p. 215)
>
> [Comedy religiously observes [...] a certain rule that young virgins or maids never speak on stage, while, by contrast, they can be introduced without blame on the tragic stage. This, I believe, is because the comic stage is mostly lascivious.]

It is also felt that licentious allusions in comedy should be veiled by honest words so that young women attending would not be ashamed (p. 223).[40]

In Giraldi's opinion, the aim of comedy is not simply to provoke laughter by indiscriminate means, such as by using 'modi sconci e sozzi, [...] atti e parole disoneste [...] degne piuttosto di ubbriachi e di tavernieri e d'infami persone' [sordid and dirty habits, [...] indecent words and acts [...] more suited to drunkards, tavern-keepers, and low sorts of people]; it is meant to uphold moral values too.[41] Terence, who figured large in Guarino's humanist educational programme, is for this reason proposed as the 'master author' for the genre whenever rules were in question, rather than Plautus, who was 'piú licenzioso del convenevole in molte cose' [more licentious than was proper in many things] (p. 199).[42] Giraldi's position (to some extent echoed by his Mantuan contemporary Leone de' Sommi) suggests insecurity about the act of laughing at risqué subject matter, which might be perceived as condoning such behaviour. This moralizing perspective, mostly realized in Giraldi's own single example of comedy (*Eudemoni*), points to the gradual involution of the genre later in the century as many intellectuals and elites preferred more 'serious' forms of comedy, or gradually disassociated themselves from its production, leaving it to emerging (semi-)professional groups.[43] Significantly, these views point to further changes in attitude towards drama during the years of the Council of Trent, though the religious and political demands implied by its convocation (1545) did not impinge directly on theatrical production until around the 1560s or after.

It was during this period of social and cultural transformation that very different kinds of spectacle began to be promoted by the Ferrarese court. Alternative forms of entertainment were sought by elites which would ensure the cultural exclusivity of the court and confer lustre upon it through splendid music, scenotechnics, and choreography, just as the *drammi mescidati* had done in the late Quattrocento. Favoured kinds of drama included regular Senecan tragedy, and tragedy with a happy ending (*tragedie di lieto fine*), both pioneered by Giraldi, and more explicitly spectacular 'irregular' forms like *intermezzi* and large-scale tournaments or *tornei* (see below). It is against the context of courtly experimentation with spectacular forms and the long-standing humanist interest in drama at the Studio that we should locate the early Ferrarese examples of regular pastoral plays. In this respect, they provided a suitable elite dramatic form to fill the void left by comedy.

Mixed Genres in the Mid-Sixteenth Century: Between Theory and Practice

The contribution of Giraldi Cinthio

The figure who most significantly contributed to reworking dramatic practices in mid-century Ferrara, and also beyond, was Giambattista Giraldi Cinthio. He not only composed the first successful Italian tragedy (the Senecan *Orbecche*, first performed 1541) and several other plays, whose staging he oversaw, but he was an important critic of drama. Besides discussing tragedy and comedy, as mentioned, Giraldi codified a new mixed form, the tragedy with a happy ending which had some impact on the development of romantic and tragicomic drama.[44] In broaching key critical issues relating to the combining of tempered forms of comedy and tragedy, it also indirectly influenced trends in pastoral drama in Italy. Furthermore, Giraldi provided an apparently more direct, though ultimately eccentric, contribution to the genre's development with his *Egle* (performed 1545). This is the result of the dramatist's humanist project of creating a modern version of an ancient Greek satyr-play, and was followed by a largely self-justificatory treatise on the form (*Lettera [...] sovra il comporre le satire atte alla scena* [*Letter [...] on composing satyr plays suited for staging*], dated 1554, unpublished). Probably some years later, Giraldi also wrote an incomplete pastoral play of a rather different kind.[45] These works, though never directly imitated, developed many of the main themes, characters, and scenarios used in pastoral drama.

Even so, Giraldi's contemporaries effectively removed him from their histories of pastoral drama. As mentioned, Guarini regarded Beccari's *Sacrificio* (1554) as the first example of regular pastoral drama, while in Ingegneri's treatise Giraldi's name appears only once, amongst the list of dramatists associated with the Estensi celebrated in the dedicatory letter.[46] Bruscagli plausibly attributes this neglect to the dramatist's polemical exclusion from the Ferrarese context after 1563.[47] Until this point, Giraldi had enjoyed a dominant cultural position, initially as a practising physician and then, primarily, as a distinguished humanist. He was awarded a chair in philosophy in 1534 and, in 1541, was elected to replace Celio Calcagnini as professor of rhetoric on the latter's death.[48] Like many distinguished *letterati* of his time, Giraldi was also employed at the court, being appointed in 1547 to the prestigious position of secretary to Duke Ercole II. This post was renewed with the succession of Duke Alfonso II in 1559, but Giraldi found less favour under this ruler. Worse still, an ambitious former pupil of his, Giovanbattista Pigna, rapidly made advances in his stead. The two men had recently been involved in a public altercation over their respective claims to priority in expounding a theory on chivalric romances, concerning Ariosto's *Furioso*, which resulted in mutual accusations of plagiarism.[49] Giraldi was ousted from his position at court on somewhat spurious grounds in 1561, after which Pigna quickly assumed his place. The older courtier was eventually compelled to leave Ferrara altogether for economic reasons. In 1563, he accepted an invitation from the Duke of Savoy to teach in the newly founded university of Mondovì, near Turin. He did not return to Ferrara until a few months before his death in 1573.

With his satyr-play, *Egle* (composed 1545), Giraldi attempted to modernize an ancient form following an established humanist practice. Indeed, it constitutes the first and only known regular example of this 'third' dramatic genre, which had been described by the ancient architectural authority Vitruvius and brought to modern attention (also in 1545) by Sebastiano Serlio (see fig. 1).[50]

The dedicatory letter to *Egle*, addressed to Bartolomeo Cavalcanti, clearly reveals this self-consciously pioneering stance, since Giraldi observes that his satyr-play is 'cosa non pur nuova, ma s'io non me 'nganno né anche conosciuta da molti a' tempi nostri' [not only something new, but (if I am not mistaken) not even known of by many people in our day] (p. 5).[51] (His bold attempt to reinstate Senecan tragedy on the Italian stage four years earlier with his *Orbecche* can be viewed in the same spirit). The author claims to have decided not to publish the play initially, to avoid attracting the envy and criticism that would, in his view, inevitably be directed at the first person to set foot on this terrain 'dopo mill'anni e più' [after a thousand years or more] (p. 5). He apparently resolved otherwise on recognizing the pleasure that his play might bring to learned readers ('dotti') and its capacity to enrich the vernacular tongue, which might perhaps spur other noble spirits to take this kind of writing even further.

This forward-looking attitude is abandoned in the prologue that follows, which questions the satyr-drama's ancient origins, later to be addressed in a more philological spirit in the *Lettera*. The prologue takes the form of a rather contrived debate between the pastoral goddesses Pales and Pomona, who dispute whether Nature (a metaphor for literary invention) is ever-expanding or becoming more restricted. The male narrator, who witnesses this, judges in favour of the former view. As proof of Nature's bounty, he points to the fact that ancient sylvans, satyrs, and fauns are not extinct but merely hidden in a large cavern (line 77).[52] The victorious goddess thereafter decides to correct popular opinion by presenting Arcadia with its inhabitants for all to see (93–134). By extension, the satyr play is represented as an original, natural form of 'life' that had gradually been rejected and seemingly extinguished with the arrival of other more 'civilized' (literary) forms (I. 1. 1–55). Thus, from its start *Egle* opens up issues that would become central to pastoral drama and its related theory concerning its relative modernity or ancient status, and tensions between nature and civilization.

The action of *Egle* is very simple, especially in comparison to most subsequent pastoral drama, and takes place in the wild forests of Arcadia, populated by sylvan deities and demi-gods. At the start, the satyrs and fauns (servants of Bacchus) have just discovered that the celestial gods are also in love with the various nymphs (dryads, hamadryads, nayads, oreads, and woodnymphs or *napee*) whom the sylvan inhabitants have long been wooing unsuccessfully. With the help of Silenus's lover, Egle (Aegle), the satyrs and fauns together devise a plan to preempt their rivals, who reportedly plan to descend upon the nymphs that night in a transformed state (II. 2. 93–94). The satyrs pretend to set off for Spain, leaving behind their young, whom Egle persuades the nymphs to adopt. The nymphs at this point feel secure enough to lay down their arms and engage in a dance with the young 'satirini'. However, they soon become aware of the group of satyrs together with Silenus on his donkey, hidden behind the trees and poised to attack. Fearful for their chastity, the nymphs flee with the satyrs in hot pursuit, but just as conquest seems imminent, the nymphs are turned (off-stage) into trees, rivers or flowers, recalling many such episodes from Ovid's *Metamorphoses*.

Figure 1. Woodcut of 'Scena satyrica', in *Il Secondo libro di perspetti[v]a di Sebastiano Serlio Bolognese, Le Second livre de perspective de Sebastian Serlio Bolognois, mis en langue francoise par Iehan Martin, Secretaire de Monseigneur Reverendissime Cardinal de Lenoncourt* (Paris: n. pub., 1545).

Reproduced by kind permission of the Bodleian Library, University of Oxford (Douce S 848 (1), fol. 70ᵛ).

The play concludes solemnly with the god Pan observing the folly of the sylvan deities in trying to defy the gods and bemoaning their collective loss, as well as his own particular grief at the transformation of his beloved Siringa (Syrinx) into a reed, now fashioned into a panpipe.

The play's mythological plot, based heavily on Sannazaro's Latin poem *Salices* and on Ovid's *Metamorphoses*, recalls the array of 'irregular' eclogues and *drammi mescidati* that had been performed since the late Quattrocento in northern Italian courts.[53] Its use of a festive satyric chorus specifically recalls Poliziano's *Orfeo*. Yet Giraldi ignores this more recent, popular performance tradition in his *Lettera*, where only the ancient Greek satyr-drama is regarded as a model for *Egle*. Unusually, too, the *Lettera* analyses the play in neo-Aristotelian terms, thereby providing an early example of interest in the *Poetics*. This text had been revived especially after its translation into Latin in 1536 by Alessandro Pazzi (de' Medici) and the first published commentary by Francesco Robortello (1548). Members of the Ferrarese Studio had engaged in discussions on this work from at least 1543, when Vincenzo Maggi was appointed professor of philosophy, having previously taught the *Poetics* in Padua. Giraldi himself lectured on Aristotle's *De anima* at the Studio from that year and his *Discorso* on comedy and tragedy is amongst the first critical treatises to adopt the methodology of the *Poetics*.[54] Even so, Giraldi does not observe a strictly Aristotelian position in his dramatic works. He was, for example, prepared to make modifications where there were conflicts with the tastes and wishes of his audience and patrons, as is clear from his preference generally for the 'less perfect' form of tragedy with a happy ending.[55]

In theorizing on the satyr-drama in the *Lettera* Giraldi was engaging with a very confusing genre. Today it is regarded as a comic, often bawdy, kind of play featuring a cast of satyrs, which provided light relief after a trilogy of tragedies at ancient Greek Dionysiac festivals.[56] There are, however, few surviving examples of the form and most are incomplete. In Giraldi's day only one was known, Euripides' *Cyclops*. This farcical retelling of the Polyphemus episode in the *Odyssey* (Book IX) had appeared in a Latin translation in 1503 (in a collection of Euripides' tragedies published by Aldus Manutius) and, in 1525, in an unpublished Italian translation by Alessandro Pazzi (de' Medici).[57] But as Giraldi noted, none of the ancients had provided clear rules or precepts about satyr-drama, except Horace in a few obscure comments in the *Ars Poetica* (lines 220–50).[58] In his *Lettera*, Giraldi chose to explore various different accounts of its origins, without taking a single authoritative position (pp. 227–32). He then provided an Aristotelian-style structural analysis (pp. 232–37), and finally examined the subject matter and verse forms (pp. 237–42). The author thereby for the first time helped to clarify the nature of the 'third genre', describing the plot, style, characters, melody (musical accompaniment) and stage-set (*apparato*), with observations on the chorus. At the same time, he also emphasized his own contribution to its re-establishment.

Giraldi succinctly defined the satyr-play thus:

> La satira è imitazione di azione perfetta di dicevole grandezza, composta al giocoso et al grave con parlar soave, le membra della quale sono insieme al suo luogo per parte, e per parte divise, rappresentata a commovere gli animi a riso ed a convenevole terrore e compassione. (*Lettera*, pp. 232–33)

[The satyr-play is an imitation of a perfect action of appropriate size, which is composed both in a playful and a serious manner with a sweet style [i.e. in verse]; its components are partly together in their correct place [the number and harmony of the verse] and partly separate [the song in the choruses], and it is staged in order to move the audience to laughter and appropriate terror and compassion.]

It therefore shares features of the 'perfect' tragedy defined by Aristotle (a single plot, unhappy ending, and chorus), but also contains comic, sensual aspects associated with the satyric cast (p. 233), as well as other characteristics that differentiate it both from comedy and tragedy. Notably, its cast is not human and it uses choruses which were normally omitted altogether in comedy, and differ from those of tragedy since they are danced and sung (p. 236).[59] Otherwise, the satyr-play is basically tragicomic in the affects it produces in the audience and in its style, which is meant to observe 'un certo convenevole mezzo tra la comedia e la tragedia' [a certain appropriate middle way between comedy and tragedy] (p. 235). The cast of *Egle* features a cast that is split between the predominantly comic, Bacchic characters (the satyrs, Egle and Silenus), and the more serious, pseudo-noble figures of Pan, Silvano, and the nymphs. Even the two 'messenger' figures (Egle and Pan) respectively display contrasting comic and tragic characteristics.[60] Finally, the festive and lascivious parts of the plot are offset by the tragic ending. This blend of tragic and comic elements in *Egle* recalls Giraldi's interest in 'mixing' dramatic genres also in his tragedies with a happy ending (though in a different way), as well as breaking down boundaries between other literary genres such as the epic, the tragedy, and the *novella*.[61] Yet, Giraldi disliked the term 'tragicomedy', perhaps because of its populist connotations, though he accepted it might be used to describe his *tragedia di lieto fine*, *Altile* (1543).[62]

To define the satyr-play Giraldi examined and drew on precepts and examples from various (mostly ancient) authorities, but his main cited model is Euripides' *Cyclops*. However, he acknowledges that some changes were made to the ancient play. He has notably substituted Ulysses and his companions with chaste nymphs from a recognizably Italian tradition (as in Boccaccio's pastoral works), and has introduced a new plot whereby the satyrs are in love with them. Interestingly, he has also created a distinction amongst the bacchic cast, between the more serious, noble characters of Silvano and Pan, and the humbler satyrs involved in their love intrigues.

> Onde si è veduta tra questi due e gli altri quella differenza che suole essere nelle civili azioni tra servi e signori nelle comedie [...]. E vi ho parimente quella gravità servata che alla pura ed onesta pudicizia delle ninfe è stata convenevole. E perché si conosca quanto sia il pregio della onestà e quanto si debbano ischifare i consigli delle lascive donne dalle vergini, ho fatto nascere I ragionamenti tra le ninfe che sono stati dicevoli a questo effetto. (*Lettera*, 237–38)

> [For this reason, the same distinction can be seen between these two characters and the other satyrs as there typically is between servants and masters in comic actions set in the city [...]. I have similarly given the nymphs a gravitas that matches their pure and chaste modesty. And in order to demonstrate how valuable decency is, and how necessary it is for virgins to avoid the advice of lascivious women, I have created discussions amongst the nymphs which could appropriately fulfil this aim.]

Giraldi's alterations to Euripide's *Cyclops* are far more radical than he admitted, though. In particular, while still maintaining a single plot structured around an *inganno*m (trick), he changed the nature of the ending of *Cyclops*, in which Ulysses and his companions triumph over the blinded monster, to a tragic conclusion in *Egle*.[63] Of Euripides' original cast, Giraldi only preserved the drunken Silenus with his chorus of satyrs. More generally, the crude farce and violence in the ancient *Cyclops* was removed and more moderate episodes of drunken revelry, sensual cavorting, and tragic Ovidian transformations were portrayed instead. The portrayal of nymphs also allowed the representation of decorous discussions on love and chastity which were popular in contemporary courtly contexts. These features make the *Egle* almost unrecognizable as a reworking of Euripides' satyr-drama. Indeed, Giraldi's end result bears closer resemblance to the kind of comedy that he advocated in his *Discorso*, which reflected the prevailing social hierarchy — the difference between masters and servants — and upheld contemporary moral and social values, in conformity with the expectations of an elite audience that included ladies. Furthermore, with its pastoral stage-set, and inclusion of music, dance, and even a donkey on stage, as well as a singing and dancing satyr chorus (see *Lettera*, pp. 234–36) this satyr-drama displays various similarities to pastoral eclogues and *intermedi* that were popular in courtly settings.

Despite this accommodation of the Greek satyr-drama to audience tastes, *Egle* still owes a clear debt to ancient traditions, as is evident in its heavy overlay of erudite, mythological allusions, and occasionally in terms of the sexual codes represented. For example, the god Pan is not censured for pursuing the nymph Siringa, although he is noted as being married to the less attractive Ega. The fleeing nymphs in the final act are also described by Silvano in their nakedness (typical during Roman festivals to Pan) as resembling Venus from the front and, from behind, Jove's boy-lover Ganymede (V. 5).[64] Though the *Lettera* occasionally objects to the 'abominable' lasciviousness of pagan religious customs (p. 230), it nonetheless examines a range of classical theories on the origins of the satyr-drama, ranging from Roman purification rituals and orgiastic fertility rituals to Greek Bacchic sacrifices. By this means, the author doubtless aimed to demonstrate his humanist credentials and the seriousness and novelty of his enterprise in composing a modern satyr-drama. As a final precaution, Giraldi refutes the association of the *satira* with the pastoral eclogue modelled on Virgil's *Bucolics*, as found in Sannazaro's *Arcadia* (pp. 238–42). Eclogues are said to differ from the satyr-play structurally, since they consist of a brief, undeveloped action (simple discussions between shepherds, a song contest or a funeral elegy) which would correspond to little more than an isolated scene of a play (p. 239). Furthermore, classical-type eclogues were not designed for staging. For good measure, the eclogue is presented as having totally antithetical origins from the satyr-play, since the former derives from Apollonian hexameter verse, and the latter from Bacchic dithyrambic verse (pp. 240, 229).

The motive for establishing this firm division between the satyr-drama and eclogues emerges only indirectly in the closing pages of the *Lettera*, where modern dramatic courtly eclogues are discussed. These consist of a plot divided into acts and/or scenes with a pastoral setting, and could also include nymphs. An unnamed example is referred to, written and performed by the highly reputed semi-professional actor, Sebastiano Clavignano (or Clarignano) known as 'il Montefalco'. This was staged first in Giraldi's own house with the collaboration of students from the Arts faculty and then at court before an audience that included the Duchess of Ferrara, Renée of France (pp. 241–42).[65] Despite recognizing the appeal of this tradition, and demonstrating his respect for Clavignano, Giraldi does not sanction this dramatic practice. Indeed, he advises his addressee to avoid composing this kind of courtly eclogue for the present, given the lack of ancient examples and firm rules which could guide a serious writer. With time, though, it is implied that the practice may gain enough authority to allow such compositions to be critically esteemed (p. 242).

As the first critical work to deal in this detail with satyr-drama, the *Lettera* bears out the cogent observations made by Javitch on the formation of genre theory from the mid-sixteenth century. He argues that this phenomenon corresponds especially to the desire by authors from this time for rules that would enable them correctly to use literary genres that lacked an obvious single 'master text' for imitation, as was the case especially with tragedy and the epic/chivalric romance.[66] At the same time, they could be used to justify a writer's own dramatic practices. Accordingly, Giraldi proposed his *Egle* as the only modern example to back his *arte* of the 'new' genre. The *Lettera* was intended for publication (1554) just after the first performances of Agostino Beccari's *Sacrificio* in Ferrara that same year. As Carla Molinari suggests, Giraldi may have sought thereby to direct audiences' attention to his earlier play, and to highlight his own role in initiating the dramatic process that developed into the *favola pastorale*.[67] Yet his stubborn emphasis on preserving a classical kind of drama, rather than assimilating it with forms sanctioned by modern tastes, would explain why this experiment was not repeated.[68] However, his unfinished sketch for a *Favola pastorale* suggests his later recognition of the different kind of drama being developed by his Ferrarese colleagues.

Early Ferrarese pastoral drama: Beccari, Argenti, Lollio

As discussed, various critics, and importantly Guarini, exclude Giraldi's *Egle* from their account of the development of pastoral drama. Writing in 1593, Guarini saw this as beginning rather with Agostino Beccari's *Il Sacrificio, favola pastorale* (performed twice in 1554, printed 1555), which is regarded as marking a clear break from the earlier eclogic tradition. He singles out Beccari's play for praise because of the way in which it grafts a neo-classical, comic plot structure onto the slender classical eclogue (without mentioning the more recent hybrid dramatic tradition). It is described as having an appropriate Aristotelian beginning, middle and end, 'col suo nodo, col suo rivolgimento, col suo decoro' [with its knotting of the plot and reversal, and decorum], and all the other attributes of comedy 'se non inquanto le persone introdotte sono pastori: e per questo la chiamò favola pastorale' [except for the fact that the characters introduced are shepherds; for this reason he called it a pastoral play] (*Verato secondo*, p. 207). In this way, Guarini expands on the comment by Alfonso Caraffa, the promoter of the revised 1587 edition of this play, that for a good thirty-four years before Beccari, one had only been able to read a few crude eclogues featuring two or three characters.[69]

In this section, we will be considering more critically the importance of this play alongside other early Ferrarese experiments with pastoral drama: Alberto Lollio's *Aretusa* (performed 1563, printed 1564) and his unfinished draft for *Galatea* (n. d., though after *Aretusa*) — notably both termed pastoral comedy (*comedia pastorale*); and Agostino Argenti's *Lo Sfortunato, favola pastorale* [*The Unfortunate Man*] (performed 1567, printed 1568).[70] The sizeable chronological gaps between these plays point to the fact that they were not composed in direct response or competition with each other, or with a common programmatic intention. However, despite their internal variations, some common trends emerge, doubtless as a result of being produced within a similar context for a similar courtly audience, which influenced the choice of themes, concerns and style of performance.

All three of the dramatists were involved with elite courtly circles to some extent as well as with the local university and/or academies. As we have already seen, Lollio played a key role in the academic life of Ferrara as well as elsewhere. Argenti is presumed to be the author of the formal printed account (1566) of three of the famous tournaments previously organized by the court and he was made 'cavaliere' by Duke Alfonso II.[71] The first preface to the play by Virginio Canani also portrays Argenti in a pseudo-academic discussion with members of the otherwise unknown Travagliati [The Tormented Ones] (p. 203). We know little about Beccari, apart from the fact that he had a humanist background, and that his brother (Nicolò) was a famous doctor and teacher at the Studio, later tried and exiled for heresy. No other works of his survive besides his *Sacrificio*, except for an occasional sonnet added to the 1587 edition. However, he did apparently compose other verse, and the 1587 preface to the reader mentions his forthcoming 'opera pastorale' [pastoral work] *Dafne*, of which no further trace survives.[72]

The circumstances of the staging of these writers' plays, and the paratextual additions to the printed editions, provide further evidence of this courtly and academic association. Like many aspiring *letterati* Beccari dedicated his play to members of the ducal family (the princesses Lucrezia and Leonora d'Este). It is also noted briefly (fol. Aiii[r]) that the two performances, on 11 February and 4 March 1554, were attended by members of the Estense dynasty and that it took place in Palazzo Schifanoia, the residence of the Duke's brother, Don Francesco d'Este, using some court artists and musicians.[73] Ivaldi argues that it was staged as part of the carnival activities that had long been organized by students at Schifanoia, though the Studio had suspended activities in the last seven years because of plague outbreaks.[74] The performance of Lollio's *Aretusa* in 1563 was similarly funded by students for an elite audience using ducal artists, though the exact date is unknown (see Chapter 6, p. 174). Argenti's *Sfortunato* was staged in part by students in an unknown location with 'degno apparato' [a worthy stage set] (p. 203), but apparently in July 1567 rather than during carnival. Some continuities appear therefore in the ways in which they were performed, which suggests a taste for such entertainments at court during this time. Their rarity (at least judging from available evidence) probably enhanced their appeal. This was doubtless reinforced by the fact that they upheld a consistently courtly perspective, by re-creating an apparently remote, mythological Arcadian existence in which noble-minded shepherds and nymphs could interact in accordance with moral and courtly norms, in contrast to baser characters. Explicit reference to delicate contemporary political and religious concerns could be avoided because of the less realistic setting, though as with earlier eclogues (such as Castiglione's *Tirsi*) the plays offer opportunities for the pleasing idealization of the court and veiled eulogy.

Specific themes and uses of pastoral *topoi* and characterization will be considered comparatively later in this chapter. For now we will merely outline some of the main characteristics of these early Ferrarese plays after Giraldi's *Egle*, especially relating to structure and cast. As suggested in Guarini's comment about Beccari's *Sacrificio*, the plays in this 'group' are influenced predominantly by regular comedy, though of the decorous and rather moralizing kind that Giraldi was arguing for, which evolved from around this time particularly in Siena amongst the Intronati academicians as *commedia grave*.[75] They therefore end happily with the lovers reconciled, and lack end-of-act choruses, in sharp contrast to *Egle*. The casts are also made up of only human rather than divine figures — apart from the ambiguous case of Beccari's satyr — which allows the exploration of contemporary and typically comic, urban concerns with wealth, social status, family, and marriage. Nonetheless, as Ivaldi has carefully demonstrated, Beccari and others following him still owe a significant debt to Giraldi's *Egle*. They particularly adopt his portrayal of psychological types, scenarios such as the recalcitrant nymph rejecting her lover, and the thematic contrast between love and chastity, as well as his use of scenes of comic drunkenness, the inclusion of dance or music, and polymetric passages amongst the unrhymed hendecasyllables.[76]

Unlike Giraldi, the other dramatists did not provide any accompanying critical reflection on the philological status of their experimentation with the 'third genre', for which their predecessor had opened the way. Their plays, however, evidently draw on the ancient and recent eclogic tradition that Giraldi explicitly rejected from his new elevated model of satyr-drama in his *Lettera* and warned writers of engaging with — although he showed that such plays were both possible and popular.[77] Beccari, for example, uses the kind of amorous intrigues involving nymphs, comic tricks (*beffe*), magical transformations and relatively loosely integrated songs found variously in the irregular pastoral plays of Epicuro, Tansillo and Castiglione, as well as in Correggio's elegant mixed drama, *Cefalo*, and romances. At the same time, Beccari, Lollio and Argenti show a new effort compared to their predecessors to observe the neo-Aristotelian unities within the five-act dramatic structure, and to respect neo-classical decorum and verisimilitude, undoubtedly influenced by intellectual discussions in Ferrara. For this reason these plays achieve a greater evenness of tone than some of the earlier eclogues. It is possible, though, that such concerns were in Beccari's case addressed mainly in the printed version of the play, in which he fears that the *Sacrificio* might be criticized by those used to comedy and tragedy ('cose civili, e reali'), because it is 'altramente divisa' [divided differently] from how it was staged (Dedicatory letter, fol. Aii^r). Pieri suggests this may indicate that he originally used a three-act form common in dramatic eclogues.[78] This would explain his very generic claim for the novelty of the play in his prologue, calling it simply 'favola nova pastorale' [new pastoral play] without providing further explanation.[79]

Following the model of many comedies and romances, as well as Epicuro's eclogue *Mirzia*, Beccari's *Sacrificio* features a complex plot with three pairs of lovers who are initially mismatched but finally happily reconciled each with their beloved — a pattern that would become popular with other writers of pastoral drama, including Argenti. Turico pursues the fickle nymph Stellinia, the villain of the piece, who has recently fallen in love with Erasto; Erasto is however in love with Callinome, who as a nymph of Diana prefers the single life. Meanwhile, Carpalio loves Melidia, who reciprocates this feeling but is inexplicably blocked from marrying by her violent twin brother (who never appears). The action is set against the mostly offstage celebration of the sacrifice and games in honour of Pan, which conveniently removes Melidia's evil twin so that she can consummate her love. (Her brother is later permanently removed by being turned into a wolf offstage after falling into a magic lake.) This occasion also provides a means for Stellinia to engineer a trick to have Callinome, her rival for Erasto's affections, caught at the games without her chastity belt which entails a dire punishment from Diana — a fight with a wild boar, which is won with the aid of a magic potion. On being expelled from Diana's group nonetheless, Callinome is persuaded to love Erasto. Before that, Stellinia had begun to love Turico again, after he saved her from the clutches of a violent and rather comically grotesque Satyr, who appeared at intervals during the play, trying to trap nymphs and trick the shepherds.

Lollio and Argenti's plays remove such evident magical and romance elements and present a more verisimilar kind of pastoral drama, closer to the conventions of urban comedy. For this reason, they do not feature a satyr, who represents the vestiges of a wild, primitive pastoral existence. Instead, unlike in Beccari's original *Sacrificio*, a rustic dimension is introduced by representing goatherds or shepherds who, especially in Argenti's play, provide the comic stage-action that is lacking from the static amorous complaints of the shepherds and nymphs.[80] *Aretusa* sounds a more idyllic note with its shepherd chorus. In this way, as we shall see, the pastoral plays of Lollio and Argenti present an Arcadian cast that is more socially mixed. This will allow them to reflect the values of city comedy transposed to an idealized country setting, as exemplified in the aristocratic villa.[81]

Differences emerge between Lollio and Argenti, however, in terms of the type of comic plot structure chosen. Argenti follows Beccari in using a complex plot structure that presents a patterned series of unreciprocated passions involving three shepherds and three nymphs, though of these the hunter Silvio and the chaste nymph Fiordiana remain committed to the single life until the end. Again, the action takes place on a sacred day marked by a great hunt devoted to Diana to rid the woods of wild beasts. In recompense, the goddess of chastity has granted the unlikely concession that a shepherd may marry his nymph that day, provided that his love is corresponded. This presents the opportunity for Silvio to devise a comic substitution trick which the shepherd lovers will practise on the nymphs, so that they find themselves unexpectedly alone with the shepherd who desires them. This ruse, condemned by the pro-feminist speaker in the discussions on comic tricks in Castiglione's *Cortegiano* (II. 93) proves effective with one nymph, but Dafne is only persuaded to love by the more pastoral scenario of witnessing Sfortunato's attempted suicide.

Lollio's *Aretusa* rather unusually rejects Beccari's complex triple plot in favour of a more linear one centred round the shepherd Licida's unrequited passion for the chaste nymph, Aretusa, which is finally resolved by a rather unconvincing recognition, drawing on a plot device found in comedy, tragedy and romance. When the aged Neapolitan shepherd, Palemone, arrives in Arcadia (V. 1), he reveals Aretusa to be Licida's long lost sister (Silvia), stolen from him in infancy, after which Licida ran away. Licida has meanwhile seen the error of his desperate passion, and has agreed to marry the (unseen) daughter of the wise, elderly Silvano, who saved him from suicide. The threat of incest alluded to in the prologue (58–60) is thus seen to be providentially averted, and Aretusa is free to consecrate herself to the service of Diana. Similar devices of recognition which prevent potential incest are explored also in *Galatea*, though this has a more complex plot involving two sets of separated lovers.

The early Ferrarese pastoral plays therefore present a variety of responses to the problem of how to create a regular plot structure for the essentially less dramatic, lyric and elegiac material of pastoral. Some of these solutions — and especially Beccari's complex plot structure — were variously used and adapted by later writers, though the plays themselves must have enjoyed a relatively limited and shortlived circulation. The *Aretusa* and *Sfortunato* only appeared in a single edition (Beccari's *Sacrificio* was revised and published 1587) and the early editions of all three plays are now quite rare.

Pastoral drama produced outside Ferrara

As mentioned in the preamble to this chapter, the emerging practice of composing regular pastoral drama may have been strongly associated with Ferrara, but was not exclusive to this centre. 'Mixed' and irregular dramatic forms, both pastoral and rustic, in a green setting had been popular in various parts of Italy from the turn of the century, especially in the northern Italian courts, Tuscany, and the Veneto region, and still continued to be produced during the 1550s and 1560s (see the eclogues of Andrea Calmo, 1553). But as dramatic forms became increasingly regularized from the early sixteenth century, with a more unified pastoral backdrop and plot, some dramatists also began to adopt the humanist five-act form that was by now common in comedy.

We will look at four plays of this kind apparently composed before the first performance of Tasso's *Aminta* (1573) and certainly before its print publication (1581). These are: Leone de' Sommi's *Irifile*, which was probably performed for carnival in Mantua after Beccari's *Sacrificio* (1555), from which it imitates several features;[82] Luigi Groto's *Calisto*, first performed in Adria in 1561 (revised for the printed version, 1583); and his *Pentimento amoroso* [*Lovers' regret*], composed and probably performed in 1565 at Palazzo Pretorio in Adria;[83] and Alvise Pasqualigo's *Gli Intricati* [*Love's Entanglements*], which was written and performed in 1569 at the Venetian naval base of Zara (Zadar, Istria).[84] Unlike the early Ferrarese examples, these plays were, however, not published until after 1573 (see bibliography for details), which complicates comparison as the existing texts may reflect revisions made after Tasso's *Aminta*. Even so, the exploration of their characterization, themes, style, or structure, and performance context may indicate important differences in the conception and reception of these plays as opposed to those produced in Ferrara.

These plays give evidence of practical experimentation with the pastoral genre that capitalizes on its performative possibilities. Little is known about the Venetian count and soldier Alvise (Luigi) Pasqualigo, but it is likely that he was involved in the probably amateur performance of his *Intricati*. The play has traces too of more popular comic 'masks' found also in his better known comedy (*Il Fedele*, performed Zara carnival 1575?; printed Venice 1576 and 1579).[85] However, Luigi Groto and especially Leone de' Sommi clearly contributed in significant ways to theatrical life in their respective regions. Biographical details on de' Sommi and the chronological status of his works are still somewhat uncertain, but there is otherwise considerable evidence regarding the activities of this remarkable figure — a Jewish theatre practitioner and critic, able to move between professional, courtly, and academic theatre.[86] Despite reservations about theatre in the Talmud, the *Università israelitica* in Mantua had staged and funded performances at court since the early sixteenth century. This represented a sort of 'taxation' in return for comparatively tolerant treatment by the ruling Gonzaga dynasty. De' Sommi was closely involved in these productions as director and costume designer, and also had an interest in professional theatre, which he sought to organize in the city.[87] In addition, he himself composed numerous plays, mostly in five acts, which included comedies in Hebrew, three pastoral dramas, and *intermedi*. More unusually, his talent earned him the protection of a prominent member of a cadet branch of the ruling family. Don Cesare Gonzaga of Guastalla had in 1562 founded the prestigious literary academy of the *Invaghiti* (the 'Desiring Ones') in his Mantuan palazzo, to which de' Sommi contributed as a writer.[88] As a Jew, he was not however entitled to the full privileges that such an association conferred. But, in recognition of his merits, Ferrante (son of Cesare Gonzaga) later sought permission from the Duke for de' Sommi to be exempted from wearing the distinguishing yellow sign (*sìman*).[89]

Luigi Groto (1541–1585), like de' Sommi, was also involved with various kinds of theatre at a time when distinctions between professionals and amateurs were becoming more rigidly observed. He originated from Adria, a provincial town on the Venetian mainland, but operated widely within the domains of the Republic. Despite going blind soon after birth (hence his assumed name 'Il Cieco' [The Blind Man]), Groto developed a remarkable range of professional skills during his life — as a lawyer, an accomplished musician, and teacher — as well as expertise in questions of hydraulic engineering and a less orthodox interest in astrology. From an early age he delivered public orations in his home town, acting as ambassador for Adria to Venice on many occasions from 1556, which must also have contributed to his talents as actor.[90] Groto experimented with all the main dramatic forms of his day: first composing a *sacra rappresentazione* (*Isaach*, 1558), then tragedies and comedies of different kinds, as well as two pastoral plays. He was a member of various academies, and in 1565 he founded one in his native Adria (the *Illustrati*, or the 'Illuminated Ones') in order to promote learning and intellectual activities.[91] Many of his plays were staged in this context, which meant that they would have lacked the kind of magnificent display associated with courtly performances. Though Groto never managed to secure lasting courtly patronage, he corresponded with and frequented many of the notable *literati* and aristocrats of his day, especially in Venice and neighbouring centres like Rovigo. Notwithstanding a brush with the Inquisition in 1567, he achieved a literary and dramatic reputation such that in the last year of his life he was asked to play the title role in the sumptuous performance of Sophocles' *Oedipus Rex*, to inaugurate the Olympic Theatre of Vicenza (1585).[92]

We should, however, be wary about overemphasizing the distinction between pastoral plays produced *within* the context of Ferrara and those from *outside* since the Ferrarese 'cluster' do not constitute an entirely homogeneous group, and there is some evidence of cross-fertilization between the dramatists. De' Sommi's *Irifile*, performed in the court of Mantua, suggests an awareness of contemporary developments in nearby Ferrara. This is not surprising given that the courts were closely connected, and the bond became especially close after 1579, when Vincenzo Gonzaga's sister (Margherita) married Duke Alfonso II d'Este.[93] Groto clearly also cultivated links with Ferrarese cultural figures: he gave the lecture inaugurating the academic year at the Studio in 1564, and dedicated some editions of his plays to Alfonso II d'Este in the early 1580s. His plays demonstrate the influence of Ferrarese as well as Venetian practices.

The prologues to these plays provide an important first indication of the dramatists' intentions for their pastoral plays and of their adherence to neo-classical principles of unity and decorum. De' Sommi's *Irifile* perhaps comes closest to Giraldi Cinthio's theory on mixed genres, in promising a harmonious balance between the two extremes of comedy and tragedy. A debate is staged between personifications of Comedy and Tragedy, in which each insists on their merits for a court audience, though a more moderate solution is finally proposed by the Mantuan poet, Virgil:

> VIRGILIO Lodo e vorrei che di pastori e ninfe
> tessendo bella et amorosa istoria,
> ma breve, una di voi le desse il grave
> e l'eroico sermon, l'altra il giocondo
> e piacevole stile, e fra gli estremi
> la maestà regal lasciar da un lato
> e da l'altro anco l'umiltà del volgo,
> senza passar a cose ond'abbia l'alme
> per troppa compassion affanno e tedio
> e senza cader anco in quel profuso
> e vano riso ond'han gli sciocchi gioia,
> stando nel mezzo ove virtù risiede. (Prologo, 89–100)[94]

> [VIRGIL: I praise and wish that in weaving a beautiful, but brief, love story about shepherds and nymphs one of you [Tragedy] would give it a grave and heroic style, the other [Comedy] a merry and pleasing style, and that between these extremes you would put regal majesty to one side and vulgar humility to the other, without dealing with things which would bring distress and tedium to the soul through excess compassion, and also without falling into that profuse and empty laughter which fools enjoy, by keeping to the middle way where virtue resides.]

In writing this, de' Sommi seems to have been aware of recent Ferrarese examples of pastoral by Beccari and Giraldi, as well as perhaps the latter's theory on mixed styles.[95] Yet, his views on mixed genres are not developed consistently in his *Dialoghi*, since he does not clearly distinguish between *satire* and *egloghe*. He is also open to gods being represented in such pastoral 'spectacles' (though they did not appear in the comic-type Ferrarese pastorals). This can be done 'senza scandalo della religione' [without scandal of religion] as in tragedies, though it is not possible in comedies (II, 35). Finally, de' Sommi's practical staging recommendations suggest a strong link between pastoral drama and the earlier 'irregular' tradition of pastoral *intermedi* (inter-act spectacles) and banquets (*conviti*).

Pasqualigo's *Intricati*, however, promises far greater diversity in style and subject matter in the prologue, spoken by a wild man (Salvatico):

> In fine, nel principio sentirete
> Lunghe istorie di pianti, e di martiri
> Strane mutazioni, diversi casi,
> Molte volubiltà d'uomini e donne,
> E dal principio al fin burle vedrete
> Assai nuove, e piacevoli. (*Intricati*, Prologo, fol. A6^r)

[In short, you will hear lengthy tales of laments and suffering at first, strange transformations, and various occurrences, great inconstancies of men and women, and from start to finish you will see entirely new and pleasing tricks.]

The play in fact mixes courtly pastoral and *villanesca* (rustic) elements with scenarios and popular masks found later in *commedia dell'arte* scenarios (see Chapter 7) without much attempt to find a dramatic balance between them. Its heterogeneous cast includes four shepherds and an equal number of nymphs, an enchantress with her infernal spirit Lucifero and three comic dialect-speaking characters: a braggart Spaniard (Calabaza), 'Doctor' Gratiano from nearby Francolino (in the Bologna region), and a peasant (Villano) from the Sienese Maremma. The main action concerns the Arcadian characters and tells how the recalcitrant nymphs are finally 'persuaded' through various magical, human, and divine means to reciprocate the love felt by the shepherds. A more farcical, though ultimately didactic, subplot is provided by the three baser characters who have arrived in Arcadia in the hope that the enchantress will grant them respite from their so-called love-sickness. Instead, she turns them into beasts to symbolize their inability as 'animals' to feel noble emotions, and only restores them to their natural form when they promise to relinquish all thoughts of love.[96]

Luigi Groto's first pastoral play, *Calisto*, also composed within a Venetian context, shows a similarly hybrid quality and wide stylistic range, encompassing low 'rustic' farce and erudite mythological allusions. The action draws heavily on Plautus' farcical tragicomedy, *Amphitryo*, and likewise features a cast of divine characters who interact comically with earthly ones, though this time in the pre-Arcadian setting of Parrasia (Pelasgia). The plot, based in part on Ovid's account in *Metamorphoses*, II, involves the gods Jupiter and his mischievous servant Mercury. These respectively cross-dress as the goddess Diana and the nymph Isse in order to seduce the chaste nymphs Calisto and Selvaggia. A secondary character, the comic but pathetic god Febo (Phoebus/Apollo) expelled from the heavens for the calamitous actions of his son Fetone (Phaeton), has more difficulties overcoming Isse. The play ends with the 'doubles' appearing together on stage, as in Plautus' *Amphitryo*, and with the restoration of order. Jupiter makes peace with his daughter Diana, who forgives the nymphs for their involuntary fall from grace. Calisto, it is explained, is to carry his child (Arcade, or Arcas) who will be the founder and ruler of Arcadia.[97] She and Selvaggia are then married to their shepherd lovers, Silvio and Gemulo, whilst Isse is bestowed on their goatherd Melio. *Calisto* therefore celebrates erotic and natural impulses paying less attention to courtly decorum — there are no fewer than three rapes.

The play evidently enjoyed some popularity with readers, since it was published twice more in that century (in 1586 and 1599), though it did not stimulate imitations, probably because of its rather risqué content both on- and off-stage. (In this way, it recalls somewhat Giraldi's earlier attempt to develop with his *Egle* a new form that partly went against courtly expectations.) Pieri has speculated that perhaps its satirical realism and sexual allusions, as found in rustic poetry of the Veneto region, for example by Ruzante, responded more to the tastes of the mainly bourgeois audience present at the performances in provincial Adria.[98] The relative lack of courtly emphasis in Pasqualigo's *Intricati* may similarly be explained by the original performance context. Yet Groto's inclusion in *Calisto* of a 22 octave eulogy of Alfonso II d'Este sung by Febo with his lyre (III. 1) in the 1580 version dedicated to the Duke indicates changing ambitions for the form.[99]

His later pastoral play, *Il Pentimento amoroso*, was extremely successful in Italy and outside, probably because of its more sentimental and decorous tone.[100] This play features complex, interlinking love plots with romance elements, as in Beccari's *Sacrificio*. The shepherds Nicogino and Ergasto are rivals for Dieromena, though she secretly loves Nicogino. Ergasto therefore resolves to win over his beloved through staging a false tryst between the nymph Panurgia and Nicogino (as Polinesso does in Ariosto's *Furioso*, V, 46–51), though this in fact only arouses the suspicions of Panurgia's lover. Meanwhile, Ergasto is pursued by Filovevia, whom he detests to the point of arranging to have her murdered by his goatherd, Melibeo. This part of the plot is resolved by the intervention of Pan, the god of Arcadia, who appears on stage with his suite of sylvans (*silvani*). His gravitas (I. 2; I. 6; V. 6) as executor of justice and restorer of harmony marks a notable departure from the scurrilous gods in *Calisto*. Groto thus indicates an increased conformity with the pattern of pastoral drama proposed by Ferrarese writers after Giraldi.

Themes and Structures of Early Pastoral Drama

Social relations in Arcadia

Clubb has clearly demonstrated that most regular pastoral plays composed in the 1550s and 1560s rely heavily on erudite comedy for their plot structure, characterization, and themes, despite growing reservations amongst the elite about this form.[101] Early authors generally tend to follow Beccari's example in adopting a complex comic structure typical also of romances, with various interweaving plots featuring mismatched couples, punctuated by episodes, and ending happily. The kind of linear comic plots found in Giraldi's incomplete *Favola pastorale* (as in his comedy *Eudemoni*) and Lollio's *Aretusa*, plays all resolved through recognition, are much more unusual, while dramatists avoided the more tragic-style plot of Giraldi's *Egle* altogether.[102]

Many early Ferrarese pastorals also show a distinctly comic influence in terms of their main themes. There is often an obsessive interest in social and moral issues of marriage and sexuality, as well as socio-economic ones of inheritance, wealth and property, which reflect ruling class ideology. However, these plays also show a new anxiety about authority, both 'paternal' and religious, that earlier comic writers like Ariosto had to some extent been able to challenge. Such concerns could be effectively explored through various ready-made character types and situations drawn from comedy, though some adaptation of these 'theatergrams' (Clubb's term, see Introduction, p. 3) was naturally required in light of the Arcadian setting.

Most obvious of these pastoral adaptations is that of comic *padroni* (masters) into wealthy, noble-spirited shepherds or *pastori*, well-versed in the appropriate courtly leisure pursuits of music, poetry, hunting, and love. Indeed, in Lollio's *Galatea* Silvano is actually referred to as 'padrone' (1. 4 and passim). More menial, agricultural labours, on the other hand, are left to their rustic herdsmen (*capraii* or *pecoraii*), who act like servants. Argenti's *Sfortunato* specifically draws this connection when, in reply to Gordino's comment that his master is likely to die soon and leave him his wealth, the goatherd Rustico observes: 'Questo è proprio costume di noi servi' [This is just the way with us servants] (IV. 6. 816). (In Giraldi's *Egle* this class distinction is also observed, despite its semi-divine cast, see p. 25 above.)

All the pastoral plays of the 1550s-60s observe the contrast between nobler and baser characters, but 'servant' types are viewed with varying degrees of sympathy. Dramatic representations of the lower orders were gradually changing over the sixteenth century, as the elite classes grew less secure about their own position. So whereas erudite dramatists like Ariosto in the early part of the century frequently represented ingenious servants outsmarting their masters, such an open challenge to social and 'paternal' authority was less tolerated from around the mid-century. The Terentian design became preferable to that of Plautus, since it reinforced prejudices against servant classes, who were deemed to be naturally inferior, and incapable of reasonable thought. Pastoral drama composed in courtly environs generally assumed this patronizing attitude — Lollio's draft *Galatea* is unusual in depicting an older shepherd-master repeatedly mocked by his servants. Plays not written specifically for elite audiences, or else for audiences with a more tolerant social outlook, could however allow for a relatively sympathetic representation of the peasant character in positive contrast to the rather vapid, love-sick Arcadian shepherds. The 'realistic' *capraio* in this case provided the opportunity for limited social criticism, as in the earlier rustic comedies of Ruzante and various Sienese dramatists.[103]

Groto's pastoral plays both feature Ruzante-type rustics who reflect cynically on their position as 'servants'. In the *Calisto*, Melio makes frequent comments on his hunger and comments ironically on the actions of the shepherds, as in his interruptions during the pseudo-magical ceremony to propitiate their love (IV. 2). He is also the only character to actually benefit economically by marrying (Isse), thereby becoming a *padrone* himself.[104] In the *Pentimento amoroso*, the equally sharp-tongued goatherd, Melibeo, observes bluntly on completing a task for his master (Ergasto) that his service is inspired purely by self-interest and not by a natural sense of duty. Indeed, on being offered a reward of two cows and a sheep he expresses the desire to achieve social independence from and even some kind of economic parity with his superior:

> MELIBEO   Non ti occupar in ringratiarmi, osservami
> Pur quel che m'hai promesso. Questo ufficio
> Non ho fatt'io per servir te, ma fattolo
> Ho sol per me.
> ERGASTO   come per te?
> MELIBEO   sperandone
> Quanto mi prometteste [...]

>   avrò da vendere
> E lana, e casio, e agnelle, e al tuo servizio
> Non vorrò più restar, ma viver libero,
> Farmi capane e tegge, comprar pascoli.
>   (*Pentimento amoroso*, IV. 1, fols 57^v-58^r).

> [MELIBEO   Don't bother thanking me, just do as you promised. I haven't carried out this duty to be of service to you, but only for myself.
> ERGASTO   What do you mean 'for yourself'?
> MELIBEO   I did it in the hope of getting what you promised [...] I will then be able to sell wool, cheese, and ewes, and I won't want to stay in your service any longer, but to live freely, to build huts and shelters for myself, and to buy pastures.]

Despite his rather crude and mercenary quality, Melibeo is seen to possess greater humanity than his master and a stronger sense of justice, since he refuses out of pity to follow Ergasto's orders secretly to kill the latter's desperate lover, Filovevia (IV. 3). Thus Groto uses this character to challenge the values typically ascribed to *pastori* and *capraii*, doubtless recalling the critical attitude towards oppressive masters expressed by Virgil's Melibeus (Eclogue I).

Otherwise, in most early pastoral plays the 'rustics' function as comic foils to the Arcadian shepherds, arousing derision through their uncouth actions and appearance, their ignorance and unrefined, dialectal speech. Following a long pastoral tradition, they merely attend to the material matter of pastoral life, tending the flocks and running errands, like the dialect-speaking Dalmatian shepherd in the opening of Poliziano's *Orfeo* (1480). Unlike the sophisticated shepherds with whom the elite attending such performances would naturally identify, they lack the ability to conceive of emotional and metaphysical matters (especially love and beauty) except in concrete terms, particularly with reference to food. (The other Ruzantian obsession with scatological details is decorously omitted in these plays.) Morally, the goatherds in early pastoral drama also fall far short of courtly ideals, often being represented as idle, lustful and gluttonous. They cheat, boast, steal, and display little loyalty towards each other or their masters. In Lollio's *Aretusa*, for example, Menalca neglects his duties and gets comically drunk (I. 4, II. 2); while asleep, Corimbo steals his flask and knapsack (II. 3), which later leads to fighting (III. 1). Later, two of the rustics express their distinctly jaded world view:

> CORIMBO   Che si de' far, se non darsi buon tempo
>   Quando si può? Noie non mancan mai.
> DAMETA   Il bello è viver lieto a costo altrui. (*Aretusa*, III. 2. 72)

> [CORIMBO   What should we do other than have a good time when we can? There's no shortage of bothersome things.
> DAMETA   The best thing is to live happily at others' expense.]

Social differences could be further emphasized by means of costumes, since shepherds (in de' Sommi's view) should wear a silk tunic draped with animal skins, while the *bifolco* (herdsman) had a coarse peasant's smock.[105]

Although *capraii* generally play a fairly peripheral part in the plots of the more regular pastoral plays, they also serve an important dramatic function besides an ideological one. Notably, they inject an active, comic dimension and their colloquial, realistic expressions break up the sometimes relentless Petrarchan monologues of the shepherds and nymphs.[106] For instance, a performance of Lollio's *Galatea* would have required the rustic Brusco to steal an ass on stage from his master (II. 2) and for another *capraio* to be smeared in mulberry juice while asleep (like Virgil's Silenus, Eclogue VI), having drunkenly stripped off most of his clothes (III. 6). The episodes featuring rustics (and satyrs) therefore recall the kind of pastoral or rustic *intermezzi* long popular at courts, which could feature choreographed fights (*moresche*), dancing satyrs, and singing nymphs.[107] Consequently, such scenes often appear at the end of scenes, like Menalca's drunken hallucinations concluding the first act of Lollio's *Aretusa,* or the quarrels at the end of Acts II and IV of Argenti's *Sfortunato*. Alternatively, they can function as comic 'padding' to what would otherwise be a static eclogic kind of play in the manner of Castiglione's *Tirsi*.

Masters may frequently display a rather contemptuous attitude towards rustics in courtly pastoral drama, as in Sfortunato's view that Gordino 'sempre spende da sciocco i giorni suoi' [always spends his days like a fool] (Argenti, *Sfortunato*, I. 1. 195). However, such a view is not systematically observed. Indeed, the *pastori* sometimes long wistfully for the simpler existence of their herdsmen, which allows them to enjoy the surrounding countryside without burdensome responsibilities, a sentiment famously expressed in Guarini's *Pastor fido* by the heroine Amarilli. For instance, the older shepherd (Silvano) in Lollio's *Aretusa* comments on Menalca's freedom to play his pipes and indulge in other pastoral pleasures: 'Senza pensier guidando la sua vita,/ Com'è costume d'uom c'abbia buon tempo' [leading his life without cares, like a man who can take his time] (I. 3. 140). Pastoral has repeatedly projected this kind of nostalgic and idealizing attitude towards the herdsman's life of honest toil caring for his flocks, punctuated by periods of rest and enjoyment of simple natural pleasures.[108] These could take the form of playing music, making improvised feasts of bread, cheese, and maybe a roast lamb, or competing in sports or singing, as depicted for example in Longus' *Daphnis and Chloe*, Virgil's *Eclogues*, and Sannazaro's *Arcadia*.

This sense of community and continuity of local practices and shepherd skills contrasts with the lovesick shepherds' alienation and solitude. As in the Petrarchan love-idiom, following a *topos* from troubadour poetry, these lovers perceive themselves as existing outside the rhythms of nature, which they only experience as a projection of their inner torment. The longing of the elite shepherds for an apparently simpler existence thus indicates a desire to return to harmony with nature, though it ignores all the less desirable aspects that the herdsmen's state would entail.

The multiple facets of love

The same ambiguous and conflicting 'double code' of the pastoral and the rustic has been seen to apply also to the representation of love.[109] Love constitutes the principal theme of early pastoral drama, just as it had done in most dramatic and many lyric eclogues. This can range from the shepherds' respectful, Petrarchan-style courtship to the crude sensuality of the peasants and the occasional satyr, which is sometimes accompanied by frustrated violence and misogynistic rage (see Gordino in *Sfortunato*,

I. 2). Plays in fact consist mainly of a succession of solo laments by lovers, narrated accounts of amorous adventures, and dialogic *contrasti* or debates on love, through which the shepherds, nymphs, and baser characters reveal their intrinsic nature.

Dramatists had at their disposal a wide range of sources on love within the pastoral context, including classical eclogues, mythological works (especially Ovid's *Metamorphoses*), as well as influential contemporary vernacular sources, including Petrarch's verse, Boccaccio's romances, and especially Sannazaro's prose and verse romance, *Arcadia*. This last not only depicted a refined pastoral lifestyle, but also various love stories, including the much imitated account of the suicidal Carino (Prosa VIII).[110] Another important precedent was the long tradition of debates on love in princely courts, which had stimulated a series of influential works, such as Pietro Bembo's *Asolani* (1505), Mario Equicola's *Libro de natura de amore* (1525) and especially Leone Ebreo's *Dialoghi de amore* (1535).[111] A sense of the courtly interest in the subject, which was related to the contemporary debate on women, is gained from Castiglione's *Cortegiano* in which various ideas on love — realistic, misogynistic, courtly, and neo-Platonic — are generated over the four days of discussion.

Many of the plays follow a *stilnovo* trope, whereby the capacity to feel true love is equated with innate nobility, understood particularly in class terms. Pasqualigo dramatizes this superior attitude in his *Intricati*, where the didactic enchantress (Maga) tells the three farcical characters that 'Non si convien l'Amor con gente vile/ Come voi sete' [Love is not appropriate to base people of your kind] (V. 5, fol. 66^v), a point highlighted by their transformation into beasts (a device reused in Shakespeare's *A Midsummer Night's Dream*). These non-Arcadian buffoons are later expelled after being restored to their original forms.[112] However, Arcadian and rustic codes are not always kept rigidly separate with regard to love. In *Aretusa*, after an angry fight with another goatherd, Corimbo momentarily switches to a lyric style on imagining an encounter with his beloved Amaranta (the name recalling the *senhal* of a nymph in Sannazaro's *Arcadia*, Eclogue III):

> CORIMBO   Andremo ratti
> All'ombra d'un bel pino, e quivi insieme
> Corcati in grembo a mille vari fiori,
> Or ghirlande tessendo, or lietamente
> I nostri amor cantando in dolci tempre,
> Empierem l'aria di sonori accenti. (*Aretusa*, III. 2. 38)

[We will go swiftly to the shade of a beautiful pine: and lying there together in the bosom of a thousand different flowers, now weaving garlands and now joyfully singing of our love in sweet tones, we will fill the air with resounding songs.]

Conversely, some of the supposedly noble-hearted *pastori* lapse into misogyny, an attitude perhaps sanctioned by Ovid's Orpheus. This can range from the milder expressions of Carparlio in the *Sacrificio* to Silvio's violent outbursts in Argenti's *Sfortunato* (though this attitude is at one point ambivalently criticized, IV. 3. 490–91).

Pastoral drama was heavily influenced by the style and imagery of the fashionable Petrarchan love lyric. Occasionally, writers of pastoral drama also included hints of neo-Platonism that had been brought to the idiom more recently in Bembo's *Asolani*

(1505) and by Castiglione, though they tended to gloss over the moral and Christian implications of this and of Petrarch's verse. Throughout most of the pastoral plays, the Arcadian characters are portrayed as traditional Petrarchan lovers, in a state of physical and mental suffering and decline.[113] Models of specifically pastoral melancholia could be found also in Sannazaro's *Arcadia* (Sincero, Prosa XII, and Clonico, Prosa and eclogue VIII), while the classical tradition was full of such figures: especially Corydon (Virgil, *Eclogue* II), Daphnis (Theocritus, *Idyll* I), and Narcissus and Echo (Ovid, *Metamorphoses*, III). Early pastoral playwrights often also noted the social disorder caused by private passion, such as the ruin of the lover's flocks and lands, thereby integrating the urban values of comedy with the elegiac pastoral mode.

However, Corimbo's words quoted above suggest one fundamental way in which pastoral drama departs from the lyric convention. Whereas the Petrarchan lover is doomed never to find earthly satisfaction from his distant or cruel beloved since union is impossible except on a transcendent level, pastoral drama (again like comedy) typically ends with the beloved's surrender to her suitor and the promise of marriage. In this respect, pastoral drama upholds the longstanding association of the natural landscape with sensual, earthly pleasure, as in the *topos* of the *locus amoenus*. Such tendencies may be linked with the fact that such plays were popularly performed during carnival celebrations, celebrating the triumph of the flesh and nature. It also explains why they became popular as entertainments for courtly weddings in the later years of the century when there was increased concern with moral norms.[114] In fact, pastoral drama may well have been influenced by a literary form intimately associated with marriage, namely the classical epithalamium. This was revived with great success by humanists from the mid-fifteenth century, especially in northern Italian courts, with Ferrara characteristically at the forefront.[115] By 1561, it was codified in Julius Caesar Scaliger's *Poetices libri septem* (1561) as a distinct sub-genre. It followed the Petrarchan model of courtship, but could also integrate erotic and aggressive elements typical of Ovid's *Ars Amatoria* and Catullus' verse that were normally excluded from the kind of lyric poetry sanctioned by Bembo. For this reason, Forster describes the epithalamium as functioning as a 'safety-valve' for petrarchism throughout the duration of the convention, until around the early eighteenth century.[116]

Some aspects of the epithalmium emerge in Beccari's *Sacrificio*, in which a pair of lovers is anxious to consummate their union. Otherwise courtly pastoral plays mostly confine allusions to sensual enjoyment to the 'lower' characters, or until the happy *dénouement*, as in Pasqualigo's *Intricati*.

> FILEMONE   mi par che per ciascun fia buono
> Il ritornar alle capanne, dove
> Avintticchiati alle fidel compagne
> Potem spegner d'Amor la sete ardente. (V. 5, fol. 70^v)

> [I think that it would be good for all of us to go home to our shepherd huts, where, in the tight embrace of our faithful nymphs, we may quench the burning thirst of Love.]

Amongst the 'noble' characters erotic sentiments normally surface less directly (the earthy sensuality of Groto's *Calisto* is exceptional). But the idyll of reciprocated love in most early pastoral plays still appears relatively unrestricted by scruples about its moral and religious legitimacy, which would later affect the pastoral.

A sense of concern about hedonistic love is however sometimes raised in the Ferrarese plays in the popular debates or *contrasti* on sensual love versus chastity. Giraldi presents a problematic exploration of this question in his *Egle* (III. 1), which unevenly pits four choruses of chaste nymphs against a single female representative (Egle) of the pleasure-loving followers of Bacchus. This 'fallen' nymph stimulates the action of the play and also provides much of the comedy by fooling around with her consort Silenus and making veiled sexual allusions through the metaphors of food and appetite. She also, strikingly, becomes the spokesman of the pagan value of pleasure in human existence, a position rebuffed by the other nymphs:

> EGLE al mondo non è ben senza diletto
> E [...] solo il piacere è che condisce
> Di dolcezza ogni amar di questa vita;
> Tal che la vita istessa che viviamo
> Saria una morte espressa, se privata
> Fosse di quel piacer che la conserva;
> Ond'io conchiudo che di ciò che vive
> Il diletto sia fine e tra i diletti
> Quel di Venere e Bacco il maggior sia. (*Egle*, II. 1. 21–29)

[In this world there is no good without pleasure, and [...] it is only pleasure that sweetens all the bitterness of this life; in that our life itself would be like death if it were deprived of that pleasure which preserves it. For this reason, I conclude that delight must be the purpose of everything that lives and, of these delights, the greatest are those of Venus [i.e. love] and Bacchus [i.e. wine].]

Giraldi was evidently uneasy about such aspects of his play and, as Horne has demonstrated, practised some fairly strict self-censorship when revising the earlier manuscript version for publication.[117] Lines were not only deleted to create greater stylistic homogeneity, but also for moral purposes. For instance, Giraldi removed a vulgar, slapstick episode between Egle and the Satyr and purged Egle's soliloquy (cited above in its printed form) of other potentially problematic allusions to sexual pleasure, the determining role of Fortune in human affairs, and the Epicurean idea of plurality of worlds. Giraldi's excisions therefore uphold his moralizing views on drama, but were doubtless also prompted by the religious tensions in Ferrara during the 1540s (see below) and by his efforts to promote his hitherto untried genre. At all events, he takes care to close off Egle's hedonism by representing the failure of her plan, with the nymphs' transformation and the permanent frustration of the satyrs. The play ends tragically with Silvano's maxim emphasizing the need for chastity and obedience to the gods.

Argenti's *Sfortunato* further minimizes the mention of any sensual enjoyment in his debate on love between the two nymphs of Diana (Dafne and Fiordiana, I. 3) and upholds a consistently moralizing and courtly perspective. Fiordiana, the proponent of chastity, piously refuses love as a 'desiderio insano' [mad desire] (I. 3. 345) associated with *otium* and suicidal tendencies. Her opponent, Dafne decorously represents a *stilnovo* and even neo-Platonic conception of love as a refining and ennobling force, experienced only by the noble-hearted (and upper class): 'amor' è solo/ ordinato desio d'alma gentile' [love is only the orderly desire of a gentle soul] (350–51; see also 377–80), as exemplified by Cimone in Boccaccio's *Decameron*, V. 1, and the young hunter Iulio in Poliziano's *Stanze*. Characteristically, this kind of 'true and holy' love is clearly distinguished from the lascivious kind, which she sees as typical of foolish lovers who lack 'il ben dell'intelletto/ E la ragion sommettono al talento' [the good of the intellect and subordinate their reason to passion] (I. 3. 369). This explicit allusion to the lustful in Dante's *Inferno*, adds a religious dimension to the condemnation, echoed elsewhere in the play's imagery of pagan hell (II. 3; V. 3).

Discussions of this kind are typical in pastoral drama, which often hinges on persuading a chaste young nymph to yield to love. The persuasive armoury used can range from gentle arguments, trickery, threats (of the lover's suicide), and occasionally even rape (as in Groto's *Calisto*), to divine intervention. In the case of Beccari's Callinome (and later Guarini's Amarilli), a trick makes it appear that the nymph has compromised her chastity, after which she is expelled from the chaste all-female community by the harsh and unforgiving Diana (*Sacrificio*, V. 8, fol. H3^{r-v}). After this, she must shed her former 'wild' independence (symbolized by her enjoyment of hunting) and be integrated into pastoral society through love and marriage — a pattern that became typical in pastoral drama, especially after it was dramatized by Tasso. Pastoral drama therefore shows a significant concern with female characters and their psychological development. Indeed, their resistance to, or final acceptance of love frequently forms much of the drama of such plays, though the more comic device of overcoming external blocking figures may also be found. It is also noticeable how pastoral drama allows the representation of seemly young female characters on stage, who were usually absent from early sixteenth-century regular comedy. Decorum typically prevented young, wealthy virgins from taking part in the action of comedy because of its public street setting and unseemly intrigues. The secluded pastoral setting, however, allowed such characters in the guise of nymphs to appear in considerable numbers — nearly balancing the male characters of the cast — and to participate fully in the action. Such characteristics would account for the female interest in the genre later in the century (see Chapter 4).

Occasionally, some early pastoral plays (especially those composed in Ferrara) feature exceptional nymphs who manage to resist all persuasion to love and maintain their vow of chastity, renouncing secular pleasures in conformity with contemporary ideals of female celibacy. For instance, Fiordiana in *Sfortunato* ignores numerous attempts to sway her resolve, and consistently promotes chastity and the pure pleasures of hunting and bathing associated with the devotees of her goddess. Thereby she so impresses even the misogynistic Silvio that he swears he would give his life to please her (V. 5. 720–23). Lollio's Aretusa is similarly committed to chastity and refuses to marry her suitor Licida despite the insistence of family and friends. While initially condemned for her 'unnatural' desire for the single life, like Fiordiana, she is finally admired for her 'incorrotta mente' [uncorrupted mind] (I. 6. 280) and firm resolve to serve her goddess. Her resolution not to marry in this case is also retrospectively justified in that it serves to prevent incest. In Giraldi's *Egle* too, the rejection by the chaste nymphs (this time not human characters) of sensual love and wine, associated with the cults of Pan and Bacchus, is central in structuring the plot, in that they choose to preserve their chastity and thwart their lovers at the cost of their very identity.

It should be noted, though, that it is very rare to find nymphs who remain devoted to the single life in pastoral drama. Normally, they are represented as progressing from this secluded chaste existence to the 'natural' end of marriage, mirroring contemporary practices for elite girls. In early Ferrarese plays, the institution of marriage is given a further secular slant, typical of comic plots, by introducing economic and political concerns that would have been very familiar to their aristocratic audiences. In Lollio's *Aretusa, comedia pastorale* marriage is treated throughout as a commercial transaction or 'negocio' (IV. 1. 52) which should be negotiated carefully to secure the family's patrimony and create new inter-familial bonds. As Silvano observes about the young Licida's obstinate love for Aretusa, it should not be confused with blinding passion, but entered into only if it will profit him (IV. 1). That is, Licida should accept the offer of marrying Silvano's daughter so that he will inherit the older shepherd's 'sostanze' [assets] (III. 3. 126). The elderly Palemone, on the other hand wanted his daughter Aretusa to marry 'Perch'io sperava pur, che la sua prole/ Della vecchiezza mia fosse il sostegno' [because I was hoping too that her children would support me in my old age] (*Aretusa*, V. 5. 328–29). Such practical and domestic concerns are also represented in Giraldi's unfinished *Favola pastorale*, where unusually, the *mother* of Viaste pleads with her son's reluctant beloved to marry him and consider what will be advantageous ('utile') to her (I. 131 [there is no scene division]).[118] Viaste's supposed father (Dino), however, finally suggests he forget his mad passion and instead marry the nymph of his family's choice (V. 19), a view again justified by the later discovery that his beloved is a first cousin.

Shepherds in early pastoral drama are by contrast usually portrayed as committed lovers, so it is rare to find them undergoing similar transformations from chastity to love, as Iulio does in Poliziano's *Stanze* and, later, Silvio in Guarini's *Pastor fido*. *Lo Sfortunato* is uncharacteristic, therefore, in presenting a shepherd (Silvio) who is inexplicably opposed to love and its potentially debasing effects (IV. 2. 284–99) — though an autobiographical reason is hinted at in a *capitolo* following the play.[119] In Silvio's view (I. 4), a wife and children would only disturb the happiness to be found in the simple pastoral life, characterized by hunting, making cheeses, and feeding the flocks in solitude. In this character's case, his attitude towards love is used to imply an anti-courtly stance, since he claims to prefer 'rozze canzoni' [rustic songs] (I. 4. 469) to ornate courtly verse 'Che ne' pieni teatri, e ne' palagi/ (Dove l'ambition suo regno tiene)/ Soglion cantar poeti illustri e chiari' [which illustrious and famous poets often sing in packed theatres and palaces (where ambition reigns)] (470–73). Although such an attitude is not maintained consistently, *Sfortunato* is notable, even so, for using this character to re-introduce to pastoral drama the conflict between city/court and country that was intrinsic to the mode since antiquity.[120]

The question of authority

Through its exploration of love, early pastoral drama therefore raises various important questions about gender, social order, and even spirituality. The dramatization of the conflict between individual and paternal/social desires also points to another important question raised, namely the appropriate representation of structures of authority. In mid sixteenth-century Ferrara the gradually weakening power of the nobility and religious conflicts involving the ducal family made this question particularly controversial, especially given the courtly context of the production of pastoral drama. Elsewhere too, during the years of the Council of Trent (1545–63), and particularly afterwards, writers register a greater anxiety about the proper representation of moral issues and patriarchal, secular and religious authority. As we have seen, the emerging 'new' pastoral drama, like other literary forms of this period and especially comedy, reflects this uncertainty and perceived crisis by observing social distinctions between shepherd-masters and their goatherds, and upholding generally patriarchal views of marriage.

Existing social hierarchies were further reaffirmed by portraying a deferential attitude towards elders in many early Ferrarese pastoral plays, including Giraldi's *Favola pastorale*, though *Egle* was necessarily somewhat unusual with its cast of divine and semi-divine characters. Relations between youths and their elders were depicted very differently from how they were in earlier comedies. In the latter, much dramatic capital had been made from the inter-generational clash, where impetuous younger heroes triumph over older rivals or father figures, who are often ridiculed or tricked in the process. Youth is seen as the optimum time for daring, virile erotic conquest — a situation that seems to be given a political subtext in Machiavelli's *Mandragola*. Even so, Ariosto's comedies show a less marked challenge to conventional views on age decorum and, implicitly therefore, to political and social hierarchy. Later, Giambattista Giraldi explicitly condemned the disrespectful representation of ridiculous, senile passion (as in Bibbiena's *Calandria*) with costume changes and inappropriate behaviour, which are considered to set a bad example to the audience (*Discorso*, p. 218). Terence is held up as an example of how to portray filial respect and paternal benevolence, and propriety even when dramatizing disagreements (p. 282 n. 92).

Especially in the Ferrarese pastoral plays and de' Sommi's *Irifile*, younger and older shepherds are usually clearly distinguished in the casts of pastoral plays — even to the extent of labeling them 'giovane' or 'vecchio'. Youth is equated with folly and lack of responsibility, since the younger shepherds (like many a comic lover) are typically driven by amorous passion rather than reason. Consequently, they cannot govern their emotions, their property or their servants. However, for advice they tend to turn not to cunning servants but to prudent elders. The latter's previous experience of love, from which they are themselves now distanced, makes them able to counsel and wisely correct their younger counterparts. Little or no challenge is presented to their authority. Even the irreverent description of Ofelio as a 'vecchio ubbriaco' [old drunkard] by the Satyr in *Sacrificio* can be discredited on account of the latter's marginal, comic status, and his annoyance that the old man accidentally disturbed his trick on Melidia (II. 4, fol. D2^r; see also fol. D^r). Pastoral drama tends to display a far greater emphasis on age decorum therefore, compared with comedy earlier in the century, indicating a perceived anxiety about maintaining the status quo.[121] Youthful opposition has been replaced by deferential dependence. Cox has shown a similar trend around the same time in the literary dialogue, where possibilities for challenging age decorum as represented in the open discussions of Castiglione's *Cortegiano* with 'angry young men' like Gaspar Pallavicino, were increasingly closed off.[122] Instead, a hierarchical relationship is set up between reverent younger speakers and undisputed older authorities.

However, not all early pastoral drama features elders: there are none for instance in the plays of Argenti, Pasqualigo, and Groto, though the latter two dramatists portray various wise and powerful magical or divine figures and ministers. In the pastoral plays which do feature older authority figures, there is a further divergence from comic conventions in that the elders are not exclusively presented as parents and are certainly not rivals in love. Moreover, they have less direct influence and control over the youthful Arcadians. Lollio's *Aretusa* and Giraldi's *Favola*, which are more heavily influenced by comedy show only limited attempts by (adopted) fathers to try to influence their offspring, which are not always successful. The only family obstacle in Beccari's *Sacrificio* is posed by Melidia's brother to some extent, though he never actually appears on stage. In de' Sommi's *Irifile* the older shepherd Veridico merely comments on and gives pious, moral advice to the lovers. Meanwhile, pastoral lovers are freer to express their emotional states and pursue their passions relatively unchecked, apart from their variable sense of decorum and morality. Such a situation could offer attractive opportunities for dramatists to explore the feelings and actions of lovers of both sexes with greater depth and seriousness than was possible in comedy.[123] The possibilities this offered for innovative female characterization were notably taken up later by Maddalena Campiglia (see Chapter 4). However, later in the century and particularly with Guarini's *Pastor fido* (1589/90) pastoral drama became marked by an increased emphasis on paternal and patriarchal authority, as the moral imperatives of the Counter-Reformation became unavoidable also in this genre.

Older shepherds are also used in early Ferrarese pastoral plays after *Egle*, and in de' Sommi's *Irifile*, to uphold practical and social religious customs. For example, in Beccari's *Sacrificio* Orenio (paradoxically) advises Erasto to observe the purity of the cult of Pan on the god's feast day and that of Love the rest of the year to resolve his conflicting duties (I. 1, fol. B2^v).[124] In Lollio's *Aretusa* Silvano and Micone comment approvingly on the religious fervour shown by the Arcadians during the sacrifice to Venus:

SILVANO   I santi sacrifici
Secondo il mio parer, con maggior zelo,
Con più divote e belle cerimonie,
Non furon fatti già molt'anni sono.
MICONE   Quest'è il debito mezzo e proprio modo,
Di placar l'ira delli giusti dei,
Et mostrarsi de' molti benefici
Riconoscenti e grati. (*Aretusa*, III. 3. 82–89)

[SILVANO   In my view, the holy sacrifices have not been performed with greater zeal and more devoted and beautiful ceremonies for many years.
MICONE   This is the right and proper way to assuage the anger of the just gods, and to show that we recognize and are grateful for the many divine gifts.]

The pagan religion implied by the Arcadian setting is treated fairly superficially, but with intended erudition in these plays. It provides a mythologizing frame to the action in the form of sacrifices, hunts, and feast days dedicated to pastoral gods and goddesses like Pan, Venus, and Diana. In Beccari's *Sacrificio*, the sacrifice in question unusually legitimates the representation of a lyric interlude at the exact midpoint of the play (III. 3). In this scene, a priest (played in the 1554 performances by Andrea Dalla Viola) sings three strophes accompanied by a 'lira' (presumably a lute or *lira da braccio*), to which a four-part chorus of 'pastori nudi' [naked shepherds] responds in pseudo-liturgical fashion by repeating the invocation of the last line: 'O Pan liceo' [O Pan of Liceum].[125] This represents the earliest known example of an entire scene of a play set to music and thus marks an important precedent for the development of opera, though it is unclear how the same scene was performed in the revised 1587 version where the text was changed. Besides the scene's obvious performative value, it also marks the moment when the chaste Callinome first begins to experience love for Erasto. Interpreted in neo-Platonic terms, the music suggests the mysterious movement of her soul. The rather abstracted and sacred quality of this scene, and the fact that it is the only point at which the priest appears, makes it distinct from the rest of the action. None of the other early Ferrarese writers of pastoral drama chose to represent a priest.

In this respect, Beccari could be regarded as continuing to use the same broad mix of characters, divine and secular, that had long been traditional in 'irregular' tragicomic genres and continued to be used later in professional pastoral performances (see Chapter 7). Priests or divine, magical presences had also been integrated into the pastoral mode since its classical origins, and were variously used in Sannazaro's *Arcadia* (*Prose* IX, X) and in verse romances to convey a sense of awe and marvel, especially when practising their mysterious rituals. In pastoral drama they provide opportunities for fantastic scenarios with evident dramatic appeal. For example, in de' Sommi's *Irifile* the plot is resolved after the blind prophet Tiresia transforms two nymphs back to their original state (V. 1). Pasqualigo's *Intricati* features various transformations reversed by an enchantress with her 'infernal spirits'. The Arcadian lovers are then represented on stage offering up prayers and gifts in the temple of Venus (IV. 2). The allusion by one of the nymphs at this point in the pagan ceremony to an unspecified deity and 'la croce degli ombrosi mirti,/ Ove afflitto pendesti' [the cross of shady myrtles where you hung in pain] (fol. 48ʳ) is striking in this instance.

Though not unusual in earlier pastoral drama and other humanist fiction, syncretism increasingly caused concern from the 1560s with the implementation of Tridentine reforms.[126] This becomes apparent through a comparison of commentaries on Sannazaro's *Arcadia*. Those by Tommaso Porcacchi (1558) and Francesco Sansovino (1578) gloss references to 'pagan' religion or ritual without further comment, though Porcacchi does advise some circumspection in a note to Eclogue VII (p. 179).[127] By 1596, however, Giovan Battista Massarengo carefully distinguishes these from orthodox Christian beliefs. For example, the representation of the afterlife in Eclogue V is glossed as being pagan rather than Christian: 'e sempre intendiamo di parlare secondo l'uso della gentilità, eccetto quando facciamo particolar menzione della Chiesa Santa' [and throughout we intend to speak in terms of gentile customs, except when we make particular mention of the Holy Church].[128]

Perhaps it was for this reason, as well as for personal motives, that Groto represents a hint of caution about mixing sacred and less orthodox elements in his *Calisto*, revised in the early 1580s. Notably, the priest Eugenio (together with his minister,

Montano) asks after their rituals are finished that 'la strada sgombrisi./ Non vo' che queste cose si risapiano' [the path be cleared. I don't want people to know about these things] (*Calisto*, IV. 2, fol. 56ᵛ). Early Ferrarese writers after Beccari may have abandoned the priest figure and the semi-divine satyr and gods (which appear in de' Sommi's *Irifile* and Groto's *Pentimento*) for this same reason, as well as to achieve greater verisimilitude.[129] (The inclusion of a priest in Guarini's *Pastor fido* marks a new and deliberate re-integration of religious, and specifically Christian, issues into pastoral drama.)

Allusions to sacred matters in these plays are limited to rather generalized expressions of piety such as Erasto's notion that 'ben per mal render si dee' [one must return good for evil] (*Sacrificio*, IV. 1, fol. E7ʳ). The most frequent allusions to religious subjects in the early Ferrarese examples come in the form of references to fate. As Clubb comments, all dramatic genres in Italy after the mid century were affected in some way by Counter-Reformation quietistic moralism, reflecting a lack of confidence in human reason or power to act, and ability to perceive the truth.[130] Beccari's Turico, for instance, observes that one has to trust in heaven since 'Il ciel sa fare,/ [...], quando vuol mirabil cose' [Heaven knows how to do [...] marvellous things when it so wants] (*Sacrificio*, V. 7, fol. H2ᵛ). This vision proposes that human affairs are governed by a benign Providence controlled ultimately by God, to which all must resign themselves — an attitude that at times seemed to border dangerously on the Calvinist idea of Predestiny. Finally, as Lollio's shepherd chorus observe, it should be remembered that all mortal things are transient and pass 'like a rushing stream' (*Aretusa*, I. 2. 15).

It is tempting to see even these cautious religious suggestions against the background of the polemics in mid-sixteenth century Ferrara. During the late 1530s to mid 1550s, the Estense capital had become a hotbed of reformist activities due to the presence of Renée of France, the consort of Duke Ercole II. Visitors to her sizeable court from around 1535 included Clément Marot her poet-secretary and, briefly in Spring 1536, the notorious Protestant exile, Jean Calvin (her spiritual adviser, under the pseudonym Charles d'Espeville), and Léon Jamet, as well as the reformist sympathizer Vittoria Colonna (1537–38).[131] The discussions in her circle stimulated wider religious debate, leading to the formation of 'heretical' groups in Ferrara and elsewhere in the state. In Modena particularly there was a notoriously pro-Protestant academy, which Ercole II practically closed down in 1546. Even more seriously, the rift within the ducal household put Ercole in a difficult, not to say dangerous, position with regard to his feudal overlord, the Pope. In 1554, the Duke's increasing intolerance of his wife's practices led to him to take the extreme measure of removing their daughters from her care and inviting to Ferrara a French inquisitor who duly charged her with heresy. Temporarily isolated from her entourage, she abjured and formally re-converted to Catholicism, though subsequently continued to frequent protestant reformers.[132] The situation was eventually defused with Ercole II's death, after which Renée in 1563 finally left Ferrara for France where she died (1575).

Such religious ferment stirred vigorous reactions by Catholic apologists within the court and Studio. There was much preaching and writing on the institutions, sacraments, and dogma of the Church, notably affirming the central doctrine of free will in opposition to the Calvinist position. Alberto Lollio took action to eliminate heretical tendencies amongst fellow academicians as well as making a celebratory oration on the occasion of England's return to Catholicism under Mary Tudor.[133] Yet Horne has observed that intellectuals from the Studio tended to take a more moderate Catholic position in religious debates.[134] Giambattista Giraldi Cinthio for instance wrote important anti-Lutheran works dealing with practical virtue rather than metaphysical speculation on Catholic doctrine, and seems to have believed in persuasion rather than repression as a means of ensuring orthodoxy. His private correspondence also reveals his sympathy for the reformists Pole and Morone, and he defended Ludovico Castelvetro from heresy.

Giraldi's religious views to some extent inform his views on theatre. Notably, his idea of a beneficial Christian Providence guiding the tortuous affairs of men to a happy outcome was conflated with the new dramatic structure adopted in his second tragedy *Altile* (1543), which ended happily with virtuous characters being rewarded and sinful ones punished. In this way, Giraldi created a secular counterpart to the sacred tragicomedy developed during the sixteenth century, particularly in the Protestant countries of northern Europe, by the writers collectively known as the 'Christian Terence'.[135] The didactic quality applied in Giraldi's tragedies pertains in his *Egle* too, despite the play's flirtation with hedonistic ideas. So, whereas later Ferrarese pastorals follow Beccari's comic model in which the single transgressor is finally forgiven and socially reintegrated, in *Egle* the Bacchic characters' collective transgression of divine laws produces tragic consequences. It thus exemplifies the moral maxim that:

> SILVANO   Non si dee desiar cosa che nieghi
> Il ciel, né cosa all'onestà contraria,
> Che non sen può veder felice fine. (*Egle*, V. 5. 396)

[One should not desire anything that Heaven denies, nor anything that is contrary to honesty, as a happy ending can never follow from this.]

The fragments of Giraldi's *Favola pastorale* demonstrate that he could not resist introducing a providential design when using a comic plot structure either. For instance, on perceiving a favourable outcome to the seemingly disastrous events, the authoritative Montano concludes that 'mai disperare/ Non si dee l'uom de la bontà divina' [man must never despair of divine goodness] (V. [3]. 139–40). When the young Viaste is saved in time from making an incestuous marriage, Montano again sententiously notes that 'Dio ha voluto/ Proveder che non cadi in error tale' [God wanted to ensure that you don't fall into such error] (V. [4]. 207–08). This emphasis on providence is, however, not nearly so evident in the other Ferrarese pastorals. Indeed, Beccari's subplot involving Melidia and Carpalio is resolved in the manner of more irregular plays, through a magical transformation of Melidia's brother into a wolf, off-stage (V. 6), possibly ordained by pagan deities. Characters in these plays often still refer to astrological determinism or the unpredictable goddess Fortune turning the heavens with her wheel, blind to human fates. Carpalio for instance laments his difficulty in uniting with his lover:

> CARPALIO   Poi che l' infima parte de la rota,
> Onde scorger si ponno i gradi umani,
> Mi preme' l piede, e a la sublime 'l braccio
> Quasi vittorioso in parte stendo. (*Sacrificio*, I. 3, fol. B5^v)

[Since the lowest part of the wheel, from which people of all levels of fortune can be seen, presses my foot, while with my arm I reach almost victorious for the sublime.]

This concept of fortune to some extent parallels Providence, though, in that humans are unable to resist or alter its course. For example, Stellinia later in *Sacrificio* realizes that her 'bella industria' [ingenious efforts] to ruin her rival, Callinome, have failed because of Orenio's intervention with a magical potion (IV. 4, fol. F2^v), and she regrets not having left things to fortune.

Deceptions or *inganni* are used to structure the plots of other early pastoral plays too following comic practice (though not Lollio's *Aretusa* or Giraldi's *Favola*), but the possibilities for human agency are questioned in practical and moral terms. In *Sfortunato*, the misogynistic Silvio's trick to have two nymphs seduced by their desperate lovers (III. 4; IV. 1) only succeeds with one nymph (the other is converted to love later by a threatened suicide). He also admits that 's'acquisti/ Poca lode a ingannar'una fanciulla' [there is little praise to be gained from deceiving a young girl] (IV. 2. 279). Giraldi's *Egle* more spectacularly dramatizes the failure of an ingenious *inganno* instigated by a Machiavellian Satyr and Faun, who respectively advocate the use of brute force and cunning, together with Egle's persuasion, to gain their ends. Their crushing defeat highlights the insufficiency of their values, but the violence and chaotic movement of these scenes would probably have left a more lasting impression on the audience than the recitation of woes and moral messages at the end. Such problematic issues were rejected in Giraldi's subsequent *Favola pastorale* which, like the other pastoral plays following *Egle*, presents characters whose more limited and tempered actions are brought to a happy conclusion according to a benign providential design.

Innovation in Pastoral Drama: A Reassessment

A strong sense of the novelty of the regularized 'third' genre emerges from Giraldi's *Lettera* justifying his *satira*, and the preface and prologue to *Egle*, as it did later in Guarini's historiography of the pastoral. The same cannot be said of other early Ferrarese dramatists. They provide no similar theoretical defences of, or commentary on, their practice; indeed, references to their plays suggest that they were not self-consciously breaking with an earlier irregular tradition. For instance, the dedicatory letter of Argenti's *Sfortunato* (to Luigi d'Este, 1 August, 1567) mentions 'questa mia favola pastorale, overo egloga che ella si sia' [this pastoral play of mine, or rather, eclogue as it may be], and the prologue connects it with the illustrious and varied tradition of Ferrarese courtly spectacles. Its happy ending is said to be a function of this performance context and the need to delight, rather than an underlying concern with moral or structural design:

> E sì perché gli par che i gran trionfi,
> I spettacoli alteri e i bei conviti
> Che tutto dì con gran piacer si fanno
> In quest'alma città degna e regale,
> Comportino ch'in scena liete genti
> Si veggano, e sì pur dolenti e tristi

> Siano amorosi effetti, e che il suo dolo
> Tenda a felice e avventuroso fine,
> E non pianti, e singulti iniqui e gravi
> Di tragiche sventure e sangue e morti
> Che turbarian tanta letitia in voi.
> (*Sfortunato*, Prologo, 52–62)

[As [the author] thinks that the great triumphs, the proud spectacles, and fair banquets that are held every day with our great pleasure in this noble and most worthy royal city mean that only happy characters should appear on stage; and that, even though the effects of passion may be sad and mournful, the grief should result in a happy and prosperous end, and not terrible and unjust weeping and sobbing from tragic mishaps, blood and death, which would cloud your great happiness.]

Similarly, the dedicatory letter of Lollio's *Aretusa* (to Laura Eustochia d'Este) merely points out that the aim of the play is to please and be honoured by its onlookers.

Apart from Giraldi, early Ferrarese dramatists tend to refer to the novelty of their pastoral plays in very generic terms. Thus, while the *Sfortunato* is described as a 'spettacol nuovo/ D'un'opra non più udita' [new spectacle of a work as yet unheard] (Prologo, 66–67), the author only considers that its anti-courtly qualities might be potentially polemical. Beccari observes three times that his *Sacrificio* is new in the prologue to the 1555 edition (see the incipit to the Introduction), but does not specify the changes made or justify his work theoretically as Giraldi had done — though the revised 1587 prologue of the *Sacrificio* provides an almost programmatic description. The emphasis on novelty in the earlier version does, however, partly imitate Plautus' prologue to *Amphitryo* (the earliest 'tragicomedy') and may refer to Beccari's new method of laying out the pastoral material performed.[136] This claim therefore seems more like a conventional device to arouse audience attention and advertize the fact that it does not simply rework existing plots. Furthermore, it is significant that there are no known formal or even private accounts of the performances of the early Ferrarese pastorals. This may simply be explained by the fact that they were performed for intimate courtly occasions (except perhaps Argenti's *Sfortunato*), and so would not have required the kind of formal descriptions provided for the five high-profile *tornei* (tournaments) staged in Ferrara 1561–70.[137] At the same time, it might suggest that the audience failed to perceive any radical innovations to existing traditions in these plays. As mentioned, Beccari's *Sacrificio* may in fact first have been performed in a three-act form and 'regularized' retrospectively for printing.[138] In that case, it would reflect an older humanist practice, as exemplified by the anonymous, five-act reworking of Poliziano's *Orfeo* (between 1480 and 1486). This raises the unsolvable question of whether the procedure was also adopted for the other plays examined in this chapter, especially those composed outside Ferrara and published some time after.

Little is known of pastoral performances in Ferrara before 1545, which included eclogues by Ruzante and 'il Montefalco', so we cannot assess how radically Beccari departed from this practice. Even so, the pastoral plays performed after this time in Ferrara must have differed from the kind of mixed and undifferentiated dramatic forms performed elsewhere. Leone de' Sommi's *Dialoghi* gives some indication of the fluid perception of forms of pastoral drama in Mantua in the mid to later sixteenth century. In keeping with his less rigid bias towards classical values and perhaps his less rigorous humanist training, he acknowledges that while regular five-act plays are more complex structurally, three-act ones are most suitable for farces or eclogues with a simple plot (*Dialoghi*, II, 33). Later, he fails to distinguish between eclogues and satyr-plays, since both are said to represent 'sotto abiti di pastori et di dei o dee, quella semplicità, purità et piacevolezza de' primi secoli di che favolosamente si fa menzione da' nostri celebrati poeti' [under the guise of shepherds and gods or goddesses, the simplicity, purity, and pleasing quality of those earliest years which are mentioned in the fables of our celebrated poets] (34).

Despite much practical experimentation with pastoral drama after Giraldi's examples, his philological defence and modern reworking of the 'third' genre was not explicitly developed further until Guarini's contribution from the late 1580s. Guarini in fact tended to diminish the pastoral drama's debt to the ancient genres of the satyr-drama and eclogue, claiming it as an intrinsically modern form:

> Hassi dunque a sapere che la poesia pastorale, benché, 'n quanto alle persone introdotte, riconosca la sua primiera origine e dall'egloga e dalla satira degli antichi, nulladimeno, quanto alla forma e ordine, può chiamarsi cosa moderna, essendo che non si truovi appresso l'antichità di tal favola alcuno esempio greco o latino. (*Compendio*, pp. 271–72; see also *Verato secondo*, p. 206)

> [It should be noted that although pastoral poetry recognizes its earliest origins in the ancient eclogue and satyr-drama as far as the characters are concerned, nonetheless, as regards the form and structure, it can be termed a modern creation, since there are no ancient examples of plays of this kind in Greek or Latin.]

This is because, in his view, the form and structure of this modern dramatic form is on a much larger scale than the ancient eclogue (*Verrato*, p. 800). Furthermore, Guarini tends to downplay the influence of the satyr-play, despite its influence at least on Beccari's *Sacrificio* (doubtless via *Egle*) and the authority of Euripides' *Cyclops* as a model of tragicomedy. This is perhaps because he perceived it as 'dissolute' and lacking decorum, as well as being 'mista di due nature tanto contrarie, quanto è il ridicolo e 'l grave' [a mixture of two natures as contrary as the ridiculous and the grave] (*Verrato*, p. 782). His final definition of the development of the *favola pastorale* in the *Compendio* (pp. 271–76) barely mentions the contribution of the satyr-drama.

Our consideration of early examples of regular pastoral drama has therefore exposed some broad differences between the dramatists based in Ferrara and those from outside. Notably, Ferrarese dramatists of the post-Ariosto generation tend to be more concerned with neo-classical issues of verisimilitude and decorum, reflecting their humanist values. It is this classicizing tendency that stimulated Giraldi in particular to provide a historical justification for the third classical genre and to attempt to revive it in the vernacular. Following through this impulse, later writers gradually abandoned the representation of magic, and toned down extremes of tragic or comic style and exaggerated contrasts in character. All the writers integrated aspects of erudite comedy into the new dramatic form, including themes, characters, and, most importantly, structural principles. The model of Terence for which Giraldi and others expressed a theoretical preference was especially favoured. Yet the Ferrarese writers only superficially engaged with Giraldi's serious experiments to introduce a Providential and moralizing structure to the pastoral play, or else ignored them altogether. In this respect at least, it would appear that the early pastoral drama continued to fulfil a hedonistic function similar to that of the long-established courtly eclogue, which it still resembled in various ways beneath the veneer of a 'regular' structure.

Giraldi therefore explicitly makes a radical departure from contemporary thinking about the 'third genre'. But his exclusion of a thriving, if still 'irregular' eclogic tradition and introduction of a rather disturbing, pre-civilized satyric community in his new example evidently did not win over his courtly audiences as his *tragedie di lieto fine* (and Senecan tragedy) did. In practice the *Egle* appears less innovatory than his theory would suggest, since it includes many typical pastoral ingredients which continued to be used subsequently, as well as proposing a rather conventional moral message. Even so, Giraldi's example was ultimately to occupy an anomalous position within the history of the genre. With Tasso's *Aminta*, however, a tragic plot-structure was once more introduced into the pastoral, reflecting the author's concern with neo-Aristotelian poetics. It was this poet's combination of a self-consciously mixed structure, so intrinsic to pastoral, with the pleasing aspects of the courtly eclogue designed for a Ferrarese audience that was to ensure the *Aminta*'s lasting success.

Notes to Chapter 2

1. G. [B.] Giraldi Cinzio, *Discorso over Lettera di Giovambattista Giraldi Cinzio intorno al comporre delle commedie e delle tragedie a Giulio Ponzio Ponzoni* [1554], in *Scritti critici*, ed. by Camillo Guerrieri Crocetti (Milan: Marzorati, 1973), pp. 171–224 (p. 283 n. 94); all further references to this edition.
2. Guarini, *Il Verrato, ovvero difesa di quanto ha scritto M. Giason Denores contra le tragicomedie e le pastorali in un suo discorso di poesia* [1588], in *Opere di Battista Guarini*, ed. by Marziano Guglielminetti (Turin: UTET, 1971), p. 811; all further references to this edition.
3. Antonia Tissoni Benvenuti, *L'Orfeo del Poliziano, con il testo critico dell'originale e delle successive forme teatrali* (Padua: Antenore, 1987). On the context and musical dimension of *Orfeo*, see Nino Pirrotta and Elena Povoledo, *Music and Theatre From Poliziano to Monteverdi*, trans. by Karen Eales [from *Li due Orfei*, Turin: Eri, 1969] (Cambridge: Cambridge University Press, 1982), pp. 3–36. Niccolò da Correggio, *Fabula de Cefalo*, in *Teatro del Quattrocento. Le corti padane*, ed. by Antonia Tissoni Benvenuti and Maria Pia Mussini Sacchi (Turin: UTET, 1983), pp. 208–55; see also Tissoni Benvenuti's introduction, pp. 199–207. On the Ferrarese tradition of 'irregular' pastoral drama and eclogues, see Angelo Solerti, *Ferrara e la corte Estense*, 2nd edn (Città di Castello: Lapi, 1900), pp. lxxxi-lxxxii.
4. For the non-unified stage set of *Orfeo*, which includes a pastoral set, a mountain and a hell, see Pirrotta and Povoledo, pp. 283–84.
5. Tissoni Benvenuti, *Teatro*, pp. 201–02, 204–06. She suggests *Cefalo* may also have drawn on an anonymous five-act version of *Orfeo*, as well as other vernacular sources.
6. Baldesar Castiglione, *Tirsi*, in *Il Libro del Cortegiano con scelta di opere minori*, ed. by Bruno Maier (Turin: UTET, 1964), pp. 549–71.
7. *I Drammi pastorali di Antonio Marsi detto l'Epicuro Napolitano*, ed. by Italo Palmarini (Bologna: Romagnoli-Dall'Acqua, 1888). See Richard Andrews, 'Theatre' in *The Cambridge History of Italian Literature*, ed. by Peter Brand and Lino Pertile (Cambridge: Cambridge University Press, 1999), pp. 277–335 (p. 293). For the identification of *Cecaria* as Francesco Cherea's *Orba*, see Pieri, *La Nascita*, p. 165.
8. For the argument that the definitive form of the *pastorale* originated in Ferrara and was not influenced by the earlier eclogues of Ruzante and Epicuro, see Arnaldo Di Benedetto, 'L'*Aminta* e la Pastorale Cinquecentesca in Italia', *GSLI*, 173 (1996), 481–514 (p. 488).
9. Guarini, *Compendio della poesia tragicomica tratto dai duo Verati* [1601], in *Il Pastor fido e Compendio della*

poesia tragicomica, ed. by Gioachino Brognoligo (Bari: Laterza, 1914), pp. 219–88 (pp. 272–73). The same point is made in *Il Verato secondo, ovvero Replica dell'Attizzato Accademico Ferrarese in difesa del Pastor fido* (Florence: Per Filippo Giunti, 1593 [1592]), pp. 206–07; all further references are to these editions. The prologue to the revised version of Beccari's *Sacrificio* (1587), which Guarini staged with a new prologue only months later, similarly observes the difference between the former 'poema pastoral' and modern dramatic forms, though does not detail the transition process (lines 1–35). For a reconsideration of the importance of Beccari's pastoral to the overall development of the genre, see Laura Riccò, 'Sassuolo 1587: Viene Imeneo', in *Rime e Lettere di Battista Guarini, Atti del Convegno internazionale* (Padova, 5–6 Dec. 2003), forthcoming; I am grateful to the author for sending me an electronic copy of this essay.

10. Angelo Ingegneri, *Della Poesia rappresentativa e del modo di rappresentare le favole sceniche*, ed. by Maria Luisa Doglio (Modena: Panini, 1989), p. 4; all references are to this edition. On Ingegneri, see A. Siekiera, 'Ingegneri, Angelo', in *DBI*, 62 (2004), 358–60; Marina Calore, 'Angelo Ingegneri "devotissimo e obbligatissimo servitore". Società, teatro e musica nel tardo rinascimento', *Il Flauto dolce. Rivista per lo Studio della Musica Antica*, 16 (1987), 3–7; and Stefano Mazzoni, *L'Olimpico di Vicenza, un teatro e la sua 'perpetua memoria'* (Florence: Le Lettere, 1998), especially pp. 113–16. For detailed discussion of Ingegneri's role in the theorizing on pastoral drama, also in comparison with Guarini, see Riccò, *'Ben mille pastorali'. L'itinerario dell'Ingegneri da Tasso a Guarini e oltre* (Rome: Bulzoni, 2004).

11. This chapter examines *La Calisto* and *Pentimento amoroso* by Luigi Groto; *Gl'Intricati* by Alvise Pasqualigo, and Leone de' Sommi's *Irifile*. For further references to non-Ferrarese pastoral plays pre-*Aminta*, see Pieri, *Scena boschereccia*, pp. 166–67.

12. On early 'regular' comedy, see Andrews, *Scripts*, pp. 31–39. Specifically on the Ferrarese context, see Fabrizio Cruciani, 'Gli attori e l'attore a Ferrara. Premessa per un catalogo', in *La corte e lo spazio, ferrara estense*, ed. by G. Papagno and A. Quondam, 3 vols (Rome: Bulzoni, 1982), II, 451–66 (pp. 451–57); Thomas Tuohy, *Herculean Ferrara: Ercole d'Este, 1471–1505, and the invention of a ducal capital* (Cambridge: Cambridge University Press, 1996), pp. 257–64; also, Günter Berghaus, 'Stagecraft in the service of statecraft: political aspects of early Renaissance theatre in Ferrara', in *Scenery, Set and Staging in the Italian Renaissance*, ed. by Christopher Cairns (Lewiston: Edwin Mellen, 1996), pp. 1–38.

13. On Ariosto's theatrical career and works (still a comparatively neglected area of study), see Stefano Bianchi, 'The Theatre of Ariosto' (trans. by Hiroko Fudemoto), in *Ariosto Today. Contemporary Perspectives*, ed. by Donald Beecher, Massimo Ciavolella, and Roberto Fedi (Toronto: University of Toronto Press, 2003), pp. 176–94 (with useful bibliography); Antonio De Luca, *Il Teatro di Ludovico Ariosto*, with preface by Walter Binni (Rome: Bulzoni, 1981); Andrews, *Scripts*, pp. 35–47, 77–87. On the few recorded dramatic performances in Ferrara between 1508 and 1528, see P. R. Horne, *The Tragedies of Giambattista Cinthio Giraldi* (Oxford: Oxford University Press, 1962), p. 6 n. 1; and Elena Povoledo, 'Ferrara', in *Enciclopedia dello Spettacolo*, V (Rome: Le Maschere, 1958), cols 173–85.

14. Raimondo Guarino, 'Beolco e Ruzante. Tra due élites', in *Il Teatro italiano nel rinascimento*, ed. by Fabrizio Cruciani and Daniele Seragnoli (Bologna: Il Mulino, 1987), pp. 149–75 (pp. 156–57); Cruciani, 'Gli attori', p. 465; also Michele Catalano, *Vita di Ludovico Ariosto, ricostruita su nuovi documenti*, 2 vols (Geneva: Olschki, 1930–31), I, 579–95; II, 319.

15. De Luca, p. 29. The chronicler is Mario Equicola de Alveto (*Genealogia delli signori estensi*, cod. Ferrarese II, 349, c. 113 [6 June 1533]), quoted in Catalano, II, p. 339.

16. See Bernardino Prosperi's enthusiastic description of the performance of *Cassaria* to Isabella d'Este (8 March 1508), in contrast with the Marchioness's bored reaction to Plautus' *Bacchides* (letter to Marchese Francesco Gonzaga, 5 February 1502), cited in *Il teatro italiano, II: La Commedia del Cinquecento*, ed. by G. Davico Bonino, 2 vols (Turin: Einaudi, 1977–78), I (1977), 413–14.

17. On the Ferrarese Studio, see Francesco Tateo, 'Guarino Veronese e l'Umanesimo a Ferrara', in *Storia di Ferrara*, ed. by Luciano Chiappini, Walter Moretti, and Antonio Samaritani (Ferrara: Corbo, 1987-), VII: *Il Rinascimento. La letteratura*, ed. by Walter Moretti (1994), 16–57. On Ariosto's ambivalence towards the classics in his drama, see Dennis Looney, 'Ariosto and the Classics in Ferrara', in Beecher, Ciavolella and Fedi, pp. 18–31 (pp. 25–26).

18. See Tateo, especially pp. 18, 23 n. 5, 25–26, 32 (on humanist interest in Plautus and especially Terence); E. Garin, 'Guarino Veronese e la cultura a Ferrara', in *Ritratti di umanisti* (Florence: Sansoni, 1967), pp. 69–103.

19. Horne, *Tragedies*, pp. 13–15. See also S. Foà, 'Giraldi, Lilio Gregorio', in *DBI*, 56 (2001), 452–55.
20. *Due dialoghi sui poeti dei nostri tempi*, ed. by Claudia Pandolfi ([Ferrara]: Corbo, 1999), I, 116–17.
21. See the useful volume of essays ed. by D. S. Chambers and F. Quiviger, *Italian Academies of the Sixteenth Century* (London: Warburg Institute, 1995); Eric Cochrane, 'Le Accademie', in *Firenze e la Toscana dei Medici nell'Europa del '500*, ed. by Giancarlo Garfagnini (Florence: Olschki, 1983), pp. 3–17; and Amadeo Quondam, 'L'Accademia' in *Letteratura italiana, I: Il letterato e le istituzioni* (Turin: Einaudi, 1982), 823–98. On the *Elevati*, see Michele Maylender, *Storia delle Accademie d'Italia*, 5 vols (Bologna: Licinio Capelli, 1926–30), II (1927), 260–61.
22. See Giannandrea Barotti, *Memorie Istoriche di Letterati Ferraresi, Opera postuma*, 2nd edn, 3 vols (Ferrara: per gli eredi di Giuseppe Rinaldi, 1792–1811), I (1792), 365–75, 384–85.
23. See Giovan Battista Giraldi Cinzio, *Carteggio*, ed. by Susanna Villari (Messina: Sicania, 1996), pp. 11–12 (henceforth *Carteggio*); also S. Foà, 'Giraldi, Giovan Battista (Giovan Battista Cinzio)', in *DBI*, 56, 442–47 (pp. 442–43).
24. N. De Blasi, 'Ercole Bentivoglio', *DBI*, 8 (1966), 615–18.
25. For a taste of the retrospective glorification of the poet's life and works, see G. B. Pigna's *La Vita di M. Lodovico Ariosto, tratta in compendio dai Romanzi* prefacing an edition of Ariosto's *Furioso* (Venice: Valgrisi, 1565), fols ★4^v-A1^r.
26. On the quarrel, see p. 21 and n. 49 below. Giraldi's *Dell'Ercole* (dedicated to Ercole II) was started around 1551; the first 26 cantos were published in Modena, 1557.
27. For the debate on Ariosto's *Furioso*, see Bernard Weinberg, *A History of Literary Criticism in the Italian Renaissance*, 2 vols (Chicago: Chicago University Press, 1961), II, 954–1073; see also Daniel Javitch, *Proclaiming a Classic. The Canonization of 'Orlando Furioso'* (Princeton: Princeton University Press, 1991).
28. See Giraldi Cinthio, letter to Ercole II d'Este [1541], *Carteggio*, pp. 155–56. Ariosto had translated Terence's *Andria* and *Eunuch* for the court stage.
29. See Marina Calore, *Pubblico e Spettacolo nel Rinascimento. Indagine sul territorio dell'Emilia Romagna* (Bologna: Forni, 1982), pp. 103–04; De Blasi, pp. 616–17; Philip Horne, 'Introduction' to G. B. Giraldi, *Gli Eudemoni. An Italian Renaissance Comedy* (Lewiston: Edwin Mellen Press, 1999), pp. lxv-lxix. See also Giraldi, *Discorso*, in *Scritti Critici*, p. 171 (see n. 1); and Leone de' Sommi, *Quattro dialoghi in materia di rappresentazione scenica*, ed. by Ferruccio Marotti (Milan: Il Polifilo, 1968), I, 21; see also IV, 60.
30. On *Aretusa* and *Galatea*, see below. See also Barotti, pp. 378–82. It is unclear for what use Lollio intended his manuscript 'Prologo in difesa d'una Comedia fatta in prosa' [Prologue in defence of a prose comedy], n. d., in *Scritti Inediti di Daniello Bartoli, Fulvio Testi, Alberto Lollio* (Ferrara: Negri alla Pace, 1838), pp. 41–45.
31. On the court's idealizing self-representation, see Sydney Anglo, 'Humanism and the Court Arts', in *The Impact of Humanism on Western Europe*, ed. by Anthony Goodman and Angus Mackay (London: Longman, 1990), pp. 66–98. For similar tendencies amongst new *signori* since the late fourteenth century, see Denys Hay and John Law, *Italy in the Age of the Renaissance 1380–1530* (London: Longman, 1989), pp. 36, 238–39.
32. G. Benzoni, 'Ercole II d'Este', in *DBI*, 43 (1993), 107–26 (p. 115); see also Eric Cochrane, *Italy 1530–1630*, ed. by Julius Kirshner (London: Longman, 1988), p. 168.
33. See Letizia Lodi, 'Immagini della genealogia estense', in *L'Impresa di Alfonso II. Saggi e documenti sulla produzione artistica a Ferrara nel secondo Cinquecento*, ed. by Jadranka Bentini and Luigi Spezzaferro (Bologna: Nuova Alfa, 1987), pp. 151–62. On Ercole II's marriage negotiations, see Luciano Chiappini, *Gli Estensi* ([Milan]: Dall'Oglio, 1967), pp. 249–50; on the consolidation of his absolutist power, through reform to the statutes (1534) and increased tax burdens, see Lino Marini, 'Lo stato estense', in *I ducati padani, Trento e Trieste*, ed. by Lino Marini and others, *Storia d'Italia*, 17 (Turin: UTET, 1979), pp. 3–211 (pp. 51–52, 61–62); and Benzoni, p. 121; though for a more apologetic perspective, see Chiappini, *Gli Estensi*, p. 251.
34. Povoledo, 'Ferrara', col. 178.
35. *Cassaria* (1529), Prologue, 4, 7–15. On Ariosto's comedies, see Laura Riccò, 'Testo per la scena — testo per la stampa: Problemi di edizione', *GSLI*, 173: 2 (1996), 210–66 (pp. 211, 213); and Brian Richardson, *Printing, Writers and Readers in Renaissance Italy* (Cambridge: Cambridge University Press, 1999), pp. 79, also 85–89 (on the publication of Ariosto's *Furioso*).

36. Andrews, *Scripts*, pp. 64–65.
37. Professional troupes are first documented in Ferrara in 1565, see Angelo Solerti and Domenico Lanza, 'Il teatro ferrarese nella seconda metà del secolo XVI', *GSLI*, 18 (1891), 148–85 (pp. 154–56).
38. Andrews, *Scripts*, pp. 208–26.
39. The edition used is from *Scritti critici*. For the dating see Horne, 'Introduction' to *Eudemoni*, p. xxii. On the ideological and sociological associations of comedic practice compared with tragedy, see Marco Ariani, 'Introduzione' to *Il teatro italiano, II: La tragedia del Cinquecento* (Turin: Einaudi, 1977), I, VII-LXXXII (pp. X-XVI).
40. For similar ideas, see De' Sommi, *Dialoghi*, I, 18 and II, 36; and the *Annotations* to Guarini's *Pastor fido*, II. 2 (Venice: Ciotti, 1602), fol. 65^v.
41. *Discorso*, p. 221.
42. For the idea of 'master authors', see Daniel Javitch, 'The Emergence of Poetic Genre Theory in the Sixteenth Century', *Modern Language Quarterly*, 59 (1998), 139–69 (pp. 157–60). On Terence's importance, see also Calore, *Pubblico e Spettacolo*, p. 99; and Riccardo Bruscagli, 'Ancora sulle pastorali ferraresi del Cinquecento: la parte del Lollio', in *Sviluppi della drammaturgia pastorale nell'Europa del Cinque-Seicento*, ed. by M. Chiabò and F. Doglio (Viterbo: Union Printing, [1992]), pp. 29–43 (pp. 40–41).
43. On theories of laughter and the changes in the aristocratic conception of comedy over the sixteenth century, see Andrews, *Scripts*, pp. 10–21, 208–33. During the 1560s and 1570s only one comedy was definitely composed by a Ferrarese writer (*Il Prigione*, by Borso Argenti, brother of Agostino), though Battista Guarini wrote a comedy (*L'Idropica*) in 1584. From 1580, comedies in Ferrara tended to be performed only by professionals, see Alain Godard, 'La Première Représentation de l'*Aminta*: La Court de Ferrare et son double', in *Ville et Campagne Dans la Littérature Italienne de la Renaissance, II: Le Courtisan Travesti* (Paris: Université de la Sorbonne Nouvelle, 1977), pp. 187–301 (p. 192).
44. Herrick, pp. 63–124.
45. See Giambattista Giraldi Cinzio, *Egle, Lettera sovra il comporre le Satire atte alla scena, Favola pastorale*, ed. by Carla Molinari (Bologna: Commissione per i testi di lingua, 1985); all references to *Egle* and the *Favola pastorale* are to this edition. The rare Cinquecento edition of *Egle* [n. p., n. publ., n. d.] is reproduced in the 'Il Narciso' series, ed. by Giorgio Cerboni Baiardi (Urbino: Edizioni 'Quattro venti', 1980). For the convincing view that *Egle* was printed in Venice by Nicolò Boscarini, c.1545–1547, see D. E. Rhodes, 'The printer of Giraldi's *Egle*', *Italian Studies*, 41 (1986), 82–84. The *Lettera* was apparently prepared for publication (between 1549 and 1554?) with Giraldi's other critical works, but was first printed 1864; for its composition date, see Molinari, 'Introduzione' to *Egle*, pp. VII-XLIX (pp. XVI-XIX). More broadly on Giraldi's contribution to emerging genre theory, see Daniel Javitch, 'Self-justifying Norms in the Genre Theories of Italian Renaissance Poets', *Philological Quarterly*, 67 (1988), 195–217.
46. Ingegneri makes no reference to Giraldi's *Egle*, although this play almost certainly influenced his own pastoral drama (*Danza di Venere*, 1584), especially the satyr attack during the central dance episode (III. 3–4), as in Sannazaro's *Salices*. See Jane Tylus, 'Purloined Passages: Giraldi, Tasso and the Pastoral Debates', *Modern Language Notes*, 99 (1984), 101–24 (pp. 103–06).
47. Riccardo Bruscagli, 'G. B. Giraldi: comico, satirico, tragico', in *Il teatro italiano del rinascimento*, ed. by Maristella de Panizza Lorch (Milan: Edizione di Comunità, 1980), pp. 261–83 (pp. 263–65).
48. Besides Foà, 'Giraldi', see the still useful study by Louis Berthé de Besaucèle, *J.-B. Giraldi, 1504–1573. Étude sur l'Évolution des Théories Littéraires en Italie au XVIe siècle* (Paris, [n. pub.], 1920; repr. Geneva: Slatkine Reprints, 1969), pp. 1–36.
49. The polemic, one of many during Giraldi's career, was sparked by the publication of his discorso on romances (*Discorso intorno al comporre dei romanzi*, 1554). For a close discussion, see the introduction to G. B. Giraldi, *Eufimia. An Italian Renaissance Tragedy*, with introduction, notes and glossary by Philip Horne (Lewiston: Edwin Mellen Press, 2003), pp. 2–19; Weinberg, *Literary Criticism*, II, 957–71; see also 918–29 for Giraldi's previous comments on Speroni's experimental tragedy *Canace*. For the letters exchanged between Giraldi and Pigna, see Giraldi, *Scritti critici*, pp. 245–53; see also more broadly *Carteggio*, pp. 224–33, 269–76, 280–341.
50. Serlio described and illustrated the 'scena satirica' alongside scenes for comedy and tragedy, all consolidating existing stage practice, see fig. 1; also, Vitruvius, *Ten Books on Architecture*, ed. by Ingrid D. Rowland and Thomas Noble Howe (Cambridge: Cambridge University Press, 1999), V. 6. 8, p. 70.

51. Though for the precedent of Poliziano's *Orfeo*, see Bruscagli, 'Ancora sulle pastorali', p. 33. Compare Giraldi's comment on tragedy being neglected for many centuries so that there is scarcely much trace of them, in the dedicatory letter to *Orbecche* (1543, though dated 1541), see *Carteggio*, p. 179.
52. *Egle*, Prologue, 73–87.
53. See Pieri, *Scena boschereccia*, pp. 1–29.
54. On early interest in neo-Aristotelian poetics, see Weinberg, *Literary Criticism*, I, pp. 349–423; and Javitch, 'Emergence', pp. 148–62 and 'Self-Justifying Norms', pp. 195–96, 202–05.
55. *Discorso*, pp. 184, 222. Compare Giraldi's earlier acknowledgement of having strayed from Aristotle's rules in his tragedy *Didone* 'per conformarmi co' costumi de' tempi nostri [...] ed oltre a ciò lo mi ha concesso il medesmo Aristotile' [to conform to the practices of our times [...] and furthermore Aristotle himself allowed me to do this], letter to Ercole II d'Este [1541], in *Carteggio*, p. 169.
56. Umberto Albini, 'Il dramma satiresco greco', in Chiabò and Doglio, pp. 15–27.
57. Pazzi's *Tragedia Cyclope [...] secomdo [sic] il contexto di Euripide poeta greco* (including a preface dedicated to Filippo Strozzi detailing the poetic principles) was first printed in Alessandro Pazzi de' Medici, *Le tragedie metriche*, ed. by Angelo Solerti (Bologna: Romagnoli dall'Acqua, 1887), pp. 137–200.
58. *Lettera overo Discorso di Givambattista Giraldi Cinzio sovra il comporre le satire atte alla scena a Messer Attilio dall'Oro*, in *Scritti critici*, pp. 227–53 (p. 227); all references to this edition. Giraldi notes a similar absence of critical writings on romances in his *Discorso [...] intorno al comporre de i romanzi* [1554], in *Scritti critici*, p. 1. Giraldi lectured on Horace's *Ars Poetica* and apparently wrote a (now lost) commentary on it. A letter to Ercole II d'Este [1541] refers to this work in connection with satyr-drama, *Carteggio*, p. 163). On Robortello's essay on satyric poetry (1548), not mentioned by Giraldi, see Herrick, *Tragicomedy*, pp. 8–9.
59. Pazzi stressed the 'festive' aspect of satyr-drama, but viewed it as the 'lighter' of two forms of tragedy identified by Aristotle (rather than as a comedy, tragicomedy or dithyramb) (*Tragedia Cyclope*, p. 140).
60. See Tylus, 'Purloined Passages'.
61. Javitch, 'Emergence', pp. 149–52.
62. See G. B. Giraldi's *Altile: The birth of a new dramatic genre in Renaissance Ferrara*, ed. by Peggy Osborn (Lewiston: Edwin Mellen, 1992), prologue, pp. 54–58, 78. Giraldi considered that Plautus' irreverent farce *Amphitryo*, styled a 'tragicomedy' in the prologue, should more properly be termed a tragedy with a happy ending (*Discorso*, pp. 203, 281–82 n. 88; Osborn, pp. 18–19).
63. Carrara, pp. 322–23; Herrick, pp. 11–13. See also the alternative comparative reading of *Cyclops* and *Egle*, associating Egle with the 'civilizer' Ulysses, Tylus, 'Purloined Passages', pp. 106–10.
64. Silvano's description is longer and more sensuous in the autograph manuscript version of the play, see Carla Molinari, 'Dall'"Arcadia" alla favola pastorale', *Studi e problemi di critica testuale*, 26 (1983), 151–67 (p. 158 n. 13).
65. For contemporary admiration of Montefalco's acting skills, see Giraldi, *Discorso*, p. 198; De' Sommi, *Dialoghi*, III, 42. He performed in Giraldi's *Egle* and *Orbecche* as well as in Ariosto's *La Cassaria* and *La Lena*, see Cruciani, 'Gli attori', pp. 465–66; and the anon. entry in *Enciclopedia dello Spettacolo*, III (1956), cols 954–55.
66. 'Emergence', pp. 139–42, 147.
67. 'Introduzione', to Giraldi, *Egle*, p. xviii.
68. Bruscagli, 'Ancora sulle pastorali', p. 32; though for the suggestion that Giraldi was proposing a type of drama reworking the highly sucessful model of 'evasive', purely literary pastoral proposed in Sannazaro's *Arcadia*, see Molinari, 'Dall'"Arcadia"', pp. 151–61.
69. *Agostino Beccari, Alberto Lollio, Agostino Argenti, Favole*, ed. by Fulvio Pevere (Turin: RES, 1999) [henceforth *Favole*], p. 3 (dedication to Marco Pio of Savoy). See also n. 9 above.
70. References to Beccari's *Sacrificio* will be to the rare edition by Francesco di Rossi da Valenza (Ferrara, 1555), held in Florence, Biblioteca Nazionale, Palat. E. 6.6.46. References to Lollio's *Aretusa* (Ferrara: Valente Panizza Mantoano, 1564) and Argenti's *Sfortunato* (Venice: Gabriel Giolito de' Ferrari, 1568) will be to the recent editions in *Favole*, which give line numbers, pp. 131–99; 201–350. For *Galatea*, see Angelo Solerti's edition of the fragment, 'La *Galatea* di Alberto Lollio', *Il Propugnatore*, n.s. 4 (1891), 199–212. It has been suggested (*Favole*, p. 345) that the *Sfortunato* was also performed in 1570 as part of the celebrations for the ill-fated marriage of Lucrezia d'Este, but without supporting evidence (Riccò, 'Sassuolo 1587', n. 44).
71. M. Quattrucci, 'Argenti (Arienti), Agostino', *DBI*, 4 (1962), 116–17; and see n. 137 below.

72. Armando Fabio Ivaldi, '"Il Sacrificio" di Agostino Beccari. Per l'edizione critica del testo', *Atti e Memorie della Deputazione Provinciale Ferrarese di Storia Patria*, s. 3, 24 (1977), 87–136 (pp. 93–94, 102; 103, 116 (on Nicolò)). For the preface to the 1587 edition (presumably by Caraffa), see *Favole*, p. 5.
73. For a possible, though undocumented performance of *Sacrificio* for Henry II of France in Paris, 1555, see A. Migliori, 'Beccari, Agostino', in *DBI*, 7 (1965), 426–27 (p. 427).
74. Ivaldi, '"Il Sacrificio"', pp. 87–88, 90.
75. See Bruscagli, 'Ancora sulle pastorali', pp. 40–41 (the possible influence on Lollio by the Intronati); and 29–36 (the problem of finding a suitable plot for pastoral drama).
76. Armando Fabio Ivaldi, 'L'esordio del dramma pastorale: fra sperimentazione e mimetismo', in Panizza Lorch, pp. 381–86 (especially pp. 384–86).
77. Riccardo Bruscagli, 'L'*Aminta* del Tasso e le pastorali ferraresi del '500', in *Studi di Filologia e Critica offerti dagli allievi a Lanfranco Caretti*, 2 vols (Rome: Salerno, 1985), I, 279–318 (pp. 284–85).
78. Pieri, *Scena boschereccia*, pp. 157, 160–61.
79. See the incipit to the Introduction. Compare, however, the explicit claims made for the novelty of this pastoral play in the prologue to the 1587 edition, in *Favole*, p. 12. On the other significant changes made in the revised edition, see Ivaldi, '"Il Sacrificio"', pp. 112–36.
80. Bruscagli, 'L'*Aminta*', pp. 288–91; and see n. 107 below.
81. See Clubb, *Italian Drama*, p. 103.
82. For the view that *Irifile* was performed carnival of 1555/6, see Abd-El-Kader Salza, 'Un dramma pastorale inedito del Cinquecento (L'*Irifile* di Leone De Sommi)', *GSLI*, 54 (1909), 103–19 (pp. 118–19). For a later composition date, though before Tasso's *Aminta*, see Ferruccio Marotti's introduction to Leone de' Sommi, *Quattro dialoghi*, pp. xv–lxxiii (p. xlix). For a further discussion, largely in agreement with Marotti's dating, see Giuseppe Dalla Palma 'L'*Irifile* e la cultura letteraria di Leone de' Sommi (con un'edizione critica del testo)', *Schifanoia*, 9 (1990), 139–225 (pp. 139–47). All references to the play text are to this edition.
83. On the problematic chronology of Groto's pastoral plays see Marzia Pieri, 'Il "Laboratorio" Provinciale di Luigi Groto', *Rivista italiana di drammaturgia*, 14 (1979), 3–35 (pp. 6–7 n. 10); though for contradictory evidence about the 1561 performance of *Calisto*, and doubts about the record that Groto's *Pentimento* was performed in Adria in 1565, see V. Gallo, 'Groto (Grotto), Luigi (detto il Cieco d'Adria)', *DBI*, 60 (2003), 21–24 (p. 23). The *Pentimento* was definitely performed in 1575 under the loggia of Palazzo Civico (see the first printed edition by Bolognino Zaltiero 1576). See also the modern version of the *Pentimento* by Antonio Lodo, in *Luigi Groto e il suo tempo*, ed. by Giorgio Brunello and Antonio Lodo, 2 vols (Rovigo: Minelliana, 1987), II, 195–375.
84. I follow Pieri's dating of the performance (*Scena boschereccia*, p. 167); though for the view that the *Intricati* was composed in the late 1570s, see Clubb, *Italian Drama*, p. 100. In the preface, dedicating the play to Count Pietro Porto of the Accademia Olimpica of Vicenza, Evangelista Ortense mentions the Zara performance but not the date (Venice: Francesco Ziletti, 1581), fol. A2^v. For further examples of plays composed before Tasso's *Aminta*, see Pieri, pp. 166–67.
85. *Il Fedele* was adapted into Latin by Abraham Fraunce (*Victoria*, before 1583?; printed 1906) and into English by Anthony Munday (*Fedele and Fortunio. The Deceits in Love*, 1585) and may have influenced Shakespeare's *Two Gentlemen of Verona*. *Fedele* was reprinted several times that century. See Clubb, *Italian Drama*, pp. 43–44, 50 n. 3.
86. See Marotti's introduction to *Dialoghi*; and *Leone de' Sommi and the Performing Arts*, ed. by A. Belkin (Tel Aviv: Yolanda and David Katz Faculty of the Arts, Tel Aviv University, 1997). On de' Sommi and Jewish theatre in Mantua, see Claudia Burattelli, *Spettacoli di corte a Mantova tra Cinque e Seicento* (Florence: Le Lettere, 1999), pp. 146–48; Iain Fenlon, *Music and Patronage in Sixteenth-Century Mantua*, 2 vols (Cambridge: Cambridge University Press, 1980), I, 40–42; Emilio Faccioli, 'Cronache e personaggi della vita teatrale', in *Mantova. Le Lettere*, 3 vols (Mantua: Istituto Carlo d'Arco per la Storia di Mantova, 1959–63), II (1962), 553–612 (pp. 553–64); and Alessandro D'Ancona, *Origini del Teatro Italiano*, 3 vols (Turin: Loescher, 1891), Appendix II, 5, 398–429.
87. De' Sommi is commonly identified with the most authorial speaker in the *Dialoghi* (Veridico), who is described as having 'guidate più comedie, che composte' [directed more comedies than (he has) composed], III, 37. See also the request by Count Francesco Gonzaga to Duke Guglielmo Gonzaga of Mantua (15 April 1567) that de' Sommi be allowed a monopoly for ten years to stage performances by travelling professional actors (in Marotti, *Quattro dialoghi*, p. xliv).

88. On the Invaghiti, see Fenlon, *Music and patronage*, I, 36–37; Maylender, III, 363–66.
89. Letter from Ferrante Gonzaga to Duke Guglielmo, 7 May 1580, cited in Davico Bonino, p. 439.
90. See Luigi Groto, ed. by Brunello and Lodo, especially Lodo's 'Cronologia grotiana', I, 15–21; See also Giovanni Sega, 'Vita di Luigi Groto, Cieco d'Adria', in Luigi Groto, *Lettere famigliari* (Venice: G. Brugnolo, 1601), fols A3^r-A4^r; and Groto's introductory letter to his *Orationi*, 20 December, 1585 (Venice: A[press]o li Zoppini, 1598), fols a2^r-a4^r.
91. Groto gave the inaugural oration as president of the Accademia degli Illustrati [more literally: 'The ones who have been made illustrious'], 1 January 1565, *Orationi*, fols. 19^v-26^v.
92. Groto had first (appropriately) been cast in the role of the blind prophet Tiresias (Pieri, 'Il "Laboratorio"', p. 4; Mazzoni, p. 141). On Groto's 'heresy', see G. Mantese and M. Nardello, *Due processi per eresia. La vicenda religiosa di Luigi Groto, il 'Cieco di Adria', e della nobile vicentina Angelica Pigafetta Piovene* (Vicenza: Officine grafiche Sta, 1974); Franco Rizzi, 'Le socialità profonde: la famiglia di Luigi Groto, il Cieco d'Adria', in Brunello and Lodo, I, 23–60 (pp. 39–48).
93. Marotti, *Quattro dialoghi*, p. XXXII. On Groto's connections with Ferrara, see Gallo, pp. 21, 23.
94. All citations from Dalla Palma's edition based on the original, partly fire-damaged manuscript held in the Biblioteca Nazionale of Turin (N. IV. 18). *Irifile* is the only one of de' Sommi's three or more pastoral dramas to survive more or less intact from the fire in this library. His others include: *I Doni, favola pastorale* (1575); *Drusilla, favola tragica pastorale* (pre 1575?).
95. On the similarities between the pastorals of de' Sommi and Beccari, see Salza, pp. 115–18; for de' Sommi's allusions also to Giraldi's works and possibly Tasso's *Aminta*, see Dalla Palma, 'L'*Irifile*', pp. 140–47.
96. For further detail on the plot, see Clubb, *Italian Drama*, pp. 93–96.
97. Groto brings a happy ending to the Greek legend as told by Pausanias (*Description of Greece*, Book VIII), in which Zeus (Jupiter) seduces Callisto, whose pregnancy was later discovered by Artemis (Diana) as she was bathing with her nymphs. The angry goddess then turned Callisto into a she-bear and shot her, at which Zeus transformed the dead nymph into the constellation of the Great Bear and had Hermes (Mercury) rescue their unborn child (Arcas).
98. 'Il "Laboratorio"', pp. 7–9.
99. On Groto's aims to publish his *Calisto*, see his letter thanking Antonio Beffa Negrini for an accompanying sonnet (27 November 1580), *Lettere famigliari*, fols 118^v-119^r.
100. The *Pentimento* was published eight times from 1576 (i.e. before the *Calisto*); and three times in France from 1592. On its influence on English writers of pastoral drama, see Violet M. Jeffery, 'Italian and English Pastoral Drama of the Renaissance III: Sources of Daniel's *Queen's Arcadia* and Randolphe's *Amyntas*', *MLR*, 19 (1924), 435–44.
101. *Italian Drama*, p. 48.
102. Lollio's *Galatea* involves a double recognition, brought about by a Dryad (V. 4). On the hybrid structural mix of early Ferrarese pastoral plots, see Bruscagli, 'L'*Aminta*', pp. 285–91.
103. For a reading of Ruzante's plays as a demystification of the exploitation of the peasants by the patriciate and the clergy, see Sergio Bullegas, 'Cultura ed emarginazione in Ruzante', *Rivista Italiana di Drammaturgia*, 11/12 (1979), 3–16. On the sympathetic and more realistic treatment of the Sienese peasant in plays by members of the Sienese Congrega dei Rozzi, see Jane Tylus, 'Colonizing Peasants: The Rape of the Sabines and Renaissance Pastoral', *Renaissance Drama*, n. s., 23 (1992), 113–38 (pp. 124–31).
104. Pieri, 'Il "Laboratorio"', pp. 10–11.
105. De' Sommi, *Dialoghi III*, 52–53. On the adaptation of the real peasant's smock for the stage, see Pieri, *Scena boschereccia*, p. 106 n. 53; on pastoral costumes see also chapter 6, pp. 178–79.
106. More dramatic scope is given to rustics in less unified plays, as in Bartolomeo de' Rossi's *Fiammella pastorale* (Paris: Abell'Angeliero, 1584), as with Shakespeare's 'rude mechanicals' in *A Midsummer Night's Dream*.
107. See, for example, the description of a comic *intermedio* with four rustic porters who performed a choreographed fight in *moresca* time; and another one in which four satyrs emerged from a giant ball and danced a *moresca* (De' Sommi, *Dialoghi*, IV, 70–71). On the *moresca*, see Pieri, *Scena boschereccia*, p. 16. Beccari added an interlude with the goatherd Brusco's drunken picnic to his revised *Sacrificio* of 1587 (IV. 8); see Ivaldi, '"Il Sacrificio"', pp. 130–34.
108. See Terry Gifford, *Pastoral* (London: Routledge, 1999), pp. 8–9; more specifically on the medieval

bergerie tradition, see Helen Cooper, *Pastoral. Mediaeval into Renaissance* (Ipswich: Brewer, 1977), pp. 50–67.
109. Marzia Pieri, *La Nascita del teatro moderno tra XV e XVI secolo* (Turin: Bollati Boringhieri, 1989), p. 157.
110. The Carino episode of Sannazaro's *Arcadia* was imitated in Epicuro's *Mirzia*, Groto's *Calisto* (I. 3–4), and de' Sommi's *Irifile* (I. 1).
111. See generally Pieri, *Scena boschereccia*, pp. 101–10.
112. See Henke, *Pastoral Transformations*, pp. 189–91.
113. On the commonplace of love as a wasting disease, see Leonard Forster, *The Icy Fire. Five Studies in European Petrarchism* (Cambridge: Cambridge University Press, 1969), p. 115.
114. For an interesting analysis of the changes to the representation of love by performing pastoral drama at a wedding rather than during carnival, see Riccò, 'Sassuolo 1587'.
115. Forster, pp. 94–120. Epithalamia were for example delivered for the ruling family of Ferrara by Guarino (1445), Ludovico Carbone (1473); and by Ariosto (1501). On fifteenth-century wedding spectacles exploiting the themes of love and nature, see also Pieri, *Scena boschereccia*, pp. 10–12.
116. Forster, pp. 106–15, 118–20.
117. P. R. Horne, 'The Three versions of G. B. Giraldi's Satyr-Play *Egle*', *Italian Studies*, 24 (1962), 32–43 (pp. 34–35, 38, 39–40).
118. The fragments of the play (Acts I and V) are incomplete and undated, but its subject matter and inclusion of 'pastori' suggest that it was written after the *satira*. Molinari hypothesizes that it was probably composed after the first performance of the *Sacrificio* (1554), when Giraldi wanted to try a version of the new genre himself (*Egle*, pp. XXI-XXV).
119. See Argenti's *capitolo* to Paolo Quaresima, where the author apologizes for his former misogyny, caused by a mad youthful passion, and presents a reparatory praise of women (*Sfortunato*, pp. 339–42). The contentment with the single life may also have a literary precedent in romances, such as Bernardo Tasso's *Amadigi*, and some Sienese plays, see Carrara pp. 330–31.
120. The country-city polemic is either not directly explored in earlier plays (Groto) or is little commented on (Beccari's *Sacrificio*, IV. 6. fol. F5ᵛ; De' Sommi, *Irifile*, III. 4. 169–72). However, in the prologue to *Egle*, poetry is described as developing from the 'incolti boschi' [uncultivated woods] while the 'città altieri' [proud cities] are criticized for their scorn of this humble past. On Tasso's development of this theme, see chapter 3, pp. 71–72, 76–79, 87–90.
121. See the explicitly political significance given to the concept of age, in Battista Guarini, *Trattato della politica libertà* [1600], ed. by Gaetano A. Ruggieri (Venice: per Francesco Andreola, 1818), p. 35.
122. Virginia Cox, *The Renaissance Dialogue. Literary dialogue in its social and political contexts, Castiglione to Galileo* (Cambridge: Cambridge University Press, 1992), p. 67.
123. This arguably inspired Shakespeare to allow his lovers freedom in the 'green world' in *Midsummer Night's Dream* and *As You Like It*. I thank Richard Andrews for drawing my attention to this point.
124. On the incongruity of associating Pan with chastity, see Richard Andrews, 'The Dilemma of Chastity and Sex in Pastoral Drama', unpublished paper for a Symposium at University College, London (1997). The other older shepherd in *Sacrificio* (Ofelio), however, recommends that Melidia consummate her love during the sacrifice to Pan (II. 4, fol. D2ʳ).
125. The music for *Sacrificio* (III. 3) was composed by the performer's brother, the ducal *maestro di cappella* Alfonso Dalla Viola. The manuscript score is appended to the 1555 edition in Florence, Biblioteca Nazionale (Palat. E. 6.6.46). See Jessie Ann Owens, 'Music in the Early Ferrarese Pastoral: A Study of Beccari's *Il Sacrificio*', in Panizza Lorch, pp. 583–601 (pp. 592–93, 595).
126. For the mixing of classical pagan and Christian traditions in Galeotto del Caretto's *Tempio d'Amore* (1504, first published 1518), see Pieri, *Scena boschereccia*, pp. 26–27.
127. *Opere Volgari di Jacopo Sanazzaro cavaliere napoletano, cioè l'Arcadia, Alla sua vera lezione restituita, colle Annotazioni del Porcacchi, del Sansovino, e del Massarengo...* (Padua: Giuseppe Comino, 1723), p. 179.
128. Sannazaro, *Opere volgari*, p. 251. See also pp. 280 (on the 'wake' of Massilia, *Prosa* XI), and 283 (on Eclogue XI).
129. See Ornella Garraffo, 'Il satiro nella pastorale ferrarese del Cinquecento', *Italianistica*, 14 (1985), 185–201.
130. *Italian Drama*, pp. 13, 110.

131. On Renée's large court and religious (and political) inclinations, see Chiappini, *Gli Estensi*, pp. 254–56; for links also with contemporary religious affairs in France, see Anne Puaux, *La huguenote Renée de France* (Paris: Hermann, 1997), pp. 134–40, 143–62.
132. Chiappini, *Gli Estensi*, pp. 260–61. The religious crisis can be said to have finally ended only with the execution for heresy of the university teacher and doctor, Francesco Severi (1570). On the serious political implications of the Ferrarese situation, see Benzoni, pp. 112–18; Adriano Prosperi, 'L'eresia in città e a corte', in *La corte di Ferrara e il suo mecenatismo 1441–1598*, ed. by M. Pade, L. W. Petersen, and D. Quarta (Copenhagen: Forum for Renaessancestudier; Ferrara: L'Istituto di Studi Rinascimentali, 1990), pp. 267–81; P. R. Horne, 'Reformation and Counter-Reformation at Ferrara: Antonio Musa Brasavola and Giambattista Cinthio Giraldi', *Italian Studies*, 13 (1958), 62–82 (pp. 64–65, 67).
133. Alberto Lollio, *Orazione nel ritorno dell'Inghilterra all'obbedienza della Sede Appostolica a' Principi del Consiglio di quel regno* (1552).
134. Horne, 'Reformation', pp. 65–70; Foà, 'Giraldi, Giovan Battista', p. 445.
135. Herrick, pp. 61–62.
136. Carrara, p. 325. *Amphitryo* was well known to Ferrarese audiences and had been frequently performed since 1487 (Povoledo, 'Ferrara', cols 175–76).
137. *Il Castello di Gorgoferusa* (March 1561), *Il Monte di Feronia* (March 1561), *Il Tempio d'Amore* (December 1565), *L'Isola Beata* (May 1569) and *Il Mago Rilucente* (February 1570). Accounts of the first three are published in [Argenti?], *Cavalerie della Città di Ferrara* (Ferrara: Francesco Rossi il Giovane, 1566). See also Ercole Estense Tassone, *L'Isola Beata* (Ferrara 1569); anon., *Il Mago rilucente* [Ferrara, 1570]; and, more generally, Alessandro Marcigliano, 'Cavallerie a Ferrara: 1561–1570', in *Italian Renaissance Festivals and their European Influence*, ed. by J. R. Mulryne and Margaret Shewring (Lewiston: Edwin Mellen Press, 1992), pp. 75–94; and Andrea Gareffi, 'Cavallerie ferraresi', in Papagno and Quondam, II, 467–87.
138. Pieri, *Scena boschereccia*, pp. 157, 160–61.

CHAPTER 3

Tasso's *Aminta*:
Raising the Profile of the Pastoral Play

> Vennero l'antepaste buone assaie
> E d'Egroche e de Farze e Pastorale,
> De li quale a bezeffa se mangiaie,
> Perch'erano bazzoffia prencepale;
> De Mertillo le deta se leccaro,
> De Fille e Filarmino, che cchiù bale
> Ed Aminta ch'è cosa da Segnure;
> L'autre lassaro pe li servirure.[1]

[First came the excellent appetizers consisting of eclogues, farces and pastorals which were eaten in great quantities, as they formed the main dish; they licked their fingers with Mirtillo, and Filli and Filarmino (which is better), and Aminta, which is a dish fit for lords; the others they left for the servants.]

Tasso's *Aminta* and its Courtly Context

Ferrarese courtly performances

Tasso's *Aminta* enjoyed immediate success both in performance and in printed form and was instrumental in securing the reputation of the genre. Contemporaries were quick to recognize the *Aminta*'s importance to the establishment of regular pastoral drama and even today it represents the best known example of the genre. Yet the play remains extremely problematic. There are only very incomplete records of its first performance (probably in 1573) and almost nothing is known of the original play text or how it was adapted for publication seven years later. Its printed version lacks any supplementary prefaces by the author and, unusually, Tasso provides no related theoretical explanation. All this has led to enormously diverse critical interpretations of the play and of its relation to the earlier pastoral tradition as well as to the genre's overall development.[2]

This chapter will explore these issues with a view to providing a speculative understanding of the author's intentions for the work and its implications for the genre as a whole. In the absence of a clear theoretical programme, it will be productive to read the play as an intertextual dialogue with Tasso's own and others' literary and critical works.[3] At the same time, it needs to be considered against the Ferrarese dramatic tradition within which Tasso was operating and in terms of the audience for whom it was originally destined (which will be dealt with in more detail in Chapter 6).

By 1573, Tasso would already have been well acquainted with the varied Ferrarese tradition of spectacle and entertainment.[4] He had in 1565 entered the service of Cardinal Luigi d'Este, formerly the patron of his father, which marked the start of a long and later difficult association with the court. On his returning from a visit to France with the cardinal (1570–71) and dissatisfied with his service, Tasso was invited in early 1572 to join the court of Duke Alfonso (1559–97) on very favourable terms. He was required only to write occasional verse and granted various privileges, including a generous salary, his own rooms, and permission to dine at the ducal table.[5] Romantic criticism has linked the rapturous description in *Aminta* of Tirsi's happy state of leisure granted by his 'god' (II. 2. 174–75) to this relatively happy time in Tasso's life.[6] However, the poet's rather anomalous position at court, compared with that of other *letterati* like Guarini, later caused him some frustration, as is evident from the ambivalent attitude in his letters.[7]

During Tasso's early years in Ferrara, the court was regularly entertained with various theatrical performances of comedies, pastorals or eclogues, and tragedies by the *scolari* of the university and semi-professionals. From 1565, professional *zanni* and acting groups also visited Ferrara on their way from Venice to Rome.[8] There were frequent *tornate* (tourneys), jousts, musical events, banquets, hunts, and balls, in which the ducal family and the courtiers could participate too. These could range from the most private entertainments to huge-scale, choreographed public events like the five *tornei* (tournaments) staged in Ferrara between 1561 and 1570 (see Chapter 2, n. 137; Chapter 6, p. 173). The *tornei* gave the duke the occasion to display his princely virtues of liberality and magnificence to his citizens, using costly ephemeral sets. They also allowed him, together with his noblemen, to demonstrate his skill in arms, acquired during his stay at the French court before his accession. Though the outcome of these mock battles was of course predetermined, with virtue triumphing over vice, they nonetheless displayed the virtuoso skill of the performers. The chivalric ideals of the nobility were thereby reaffirmed by aesthetic and symbolic means at a time when Ferrara was experiencing limited involvement in real war, as well as growing political difficulties with the papacy.[9]

A famous passage in Tasso's dialogue *Il Gianluca, overo delle maschere* [*Gianluca, or On Masks*] (1585) gives an idea of his first impressions of the magical, theatrical quality of the city during carnival, or possibly during the staging of the *torneo*, *Il Tempio d'Amore*, in December 1565 in honour of Duke Alfonso II d'Este's second bride, Barbara of Austria.[10]

> Mi parve che tutta la città fosse una maravigliosa e non più veduta scena dipinta, e luminosa e piena di mille forme e di mille apparenze, e l'azioni di quel tempo simili a quelle che son rappresentate ne' teatri con varie lingue e con vari interlocutori; e non bastandomi l'esser divenuto spettatore, volli divenire un di quelli ch'eran parte de la comedia, e mescolarmi con gli altri.[11]

> [It seemed as though the whole city was a marvellous and entirely new painted stage-set, all lit up and full of countless shapes and semblances, and the actions at that time were like those performed in theatres, in many languages and with many speakers. Not satisfied with having become a spectator, I wanted to become one of those taking part in the comedy and to mix with the others.]

Amongst those involved in devising the elaborate programmes for the *tornei* was Agostino Argenti, whose pastoral play, *Lo Sfortunato*, was the last to be staged in Ferrara before *Aminta* (in 1567), and could even have been attended by Tasso. Its performance, which may have continued practices of the earlier pastoral plays by Beccari and Lollio, was commemorated soon after in a printed edition.

However, in *Aminta* (first generally believed to have been staged 31 July 1573) Tasso seems to develop new ways of combining stage practice with a changed idea of pastoral dramaturgy.[12] Like Ariosto's comedies, it seems to have been conceived more specifically as an occasional court entertainment, staged directly at the duke's request rather than for posterity. It also apparently used professional actors from the Gelosi troupe then present in Ferrara, rather than the usual amateurs or semi-professionals. Tasso is thought to have supervised the first performance himself, in the exclusive gardens of Belvedere, one of the famous Estense pleasure palaces on a small island in the Po close to Ferrara. This location may have suggested itself because Ferrara had been affected by terrible earthquakes from the end of 1570 to 1572.[13] During these years, the deaths of various members of the ducal family, notably that of Alfonso II's second wife, Barbara of Austria, also made most types of spectacle inappropriate; the performance of *Aminta* in fact marks the recommencement of court entertainments after a period of mourning.[14]

The tiny island of Belvedere, measuring no more than a mile across, had been bought and developed by Ariosto's patron, Alfonso I d'Este, and was greatly admired by both Ferrarese and foreign visitors.[15] It had a palace with beautiful gardens, fountains, woods, and lawns filled with all sorts of unusual birds and animals, as well as 'vaghissime prospettive e pitture eccellentissime' [most delightful perspective scenes and excellent paintings].[16] It thus served as a miniaturized and transposed courtly space, with all the typical ingredients of the pastoral scene, integrating natural and artistic beauty. In this idyllic place, enclosed by walls and the Po river, the courtly audience was temporarily removed from urban responsibilities and the exercise of power, in a kind of intimate haven of *ozio* (leisure) of the sort pictured in the frame of Boccaccio's *Decameron*. Belvedere similarly allowed space for self-contemplation, games and debate, all of which occur in Tasso's pastoral as in the earlier examples of such plays. *Aminta* also draws on a rich tradition of courtly and academic discussions on love in Ferrara, stimulated by the proliferation of academies from the 1560s. These could sometimes take a theatrical form: Tasso himself sustained fifty theses on the subject (*Conclusioni amorose*) in 1570 before the Duke and the court wearing masks on the last of three days of wedding festivities for Lucrezia d'Este.[17]

Through its relationship to the court and its values, Tasso's *Aminta* differs significantly from previous examples of pastoral drama. While earlier Ferrarese plays take place in a remote fictional Arcadia (though still obliquely reflecting the values of the courtly audiences), *Aminta* lacks a clear sense of place. There is no mention of Arcadia or of any identifiable topographical features, perhaps because its original outdoor performance setting made it unnecessary, in contrast to earlier plays which probably used perspectival, painted backdrops. For this and other reasons, *Aminta* has been seen as instead alluding covertly to contemporary events, figures and places under pastoral guise. For example, the wise shepherd Elpino is identified with the ducal secretary, Giambattista Nicolucci (known as Pigna); Batto with Battista Guarini; and the teasing nymph Licori represents the noblewoman and singer Lucrezia Bendidio, to whom Pigna dedicated his verse collection *Ben divino*.[18] The poet-shepherd Tirsi has frequently been related to Tasso himself, also aged twenty-nine as Tasso was at the time of the performance, and employed by 'colui che Dio qui può stimarsi' [the one who can be viewed as God here] (II. 2. 175). The 'qui' [here] in this case, like other adverbs of place and demonstratives elsewhere, further encourages the audience almost unconsciously to conflate the idealized stage-space with the real place of the performance.[19]

Yet, the play does not serve consistently or unproblematically as a *drame à clef*. Some of the places evoked are so unspecific that they could reflect the courtly context as well as a mythical pastoral one: like the 'isoletta' [little island] near the city, where Silvia goes to admire her reflection (II. 2. 36) and the 'solito fonte' [usual fountain] dedicated to Diana in which Silvia bathes. Furthermore, the associations are continually distorted through idealization and satire, and some characters (Dafne, and the lovers Aminta and Silvia) and places elude identification altogether. The (off-stage) wild woods populated by wolves (III. 2) and the steep precipice from which Aminta jumps (IV. 2) appear remote from the known courtly reality.[20] Tellingly, these settings are described in the play with scarcely any deictic markers.

Love and Pastoral Disguise

The play thus in part draws on a long and ambiguous tradition of pastoral 'disguising' which goes back to Virgil's eclogues, in which eminent figures are alluded to in the form of shepherds and nymphs, and actions transposed to a green setting. This could on the one hand allow graceful flattery and commemoration, provoking amused self-recognition in a known audience, as in Sannazaro's *Arcadia*, where the author evokes himself and members of his intellectual circle in Naples. Alternatively, it could provide a safe fictional 'veil' with which to cover criticism of society or individuals or to 'insinuate and glaunce [*sic*] at greater matters' (as Puttenham put it), as in Petrarch's complex allegorical eclogues and, later, those of Boiardo and Ariosto.[21] The three-act dramatic eclogue *Tirsi* by Castiglione and Cesare Gonzaga (first performed 1506), with its discreet flattery of the court of Urbino, may in this respect have provided an important precedent for Tasso, who spent part of his adolescence there.

Tasso was also fascinated by Castiglione's *Cortegiano*, which explores complex views of masking and social role-playing within a courtly context, and includes some consideration of the mechanisms of pastoral disguise.[22] On the second day of discussions, one of Castiglione's speakers suggests that a knight might appear in the guise of a simple shepherd on an elegantly decorated horse (*Cortegiano*, II. 11). In keeping with the ideal of *sprezzatura*, the 'cavaliere' will demonstrate appropriate modesty and apparent unconcern with appearances, while his actual superior status is clear to onlookers.[23] Indeed the juxtaposed signs of high and low status and his assumed attitude of humility should provide a pleasing sight for his audience, while stimulating them to imagine his concealed magnificence. At the same time, the disguise allows a prince to mix on apparently equal terms with his inferiors, and to show that his virtues and skills are 'natural' and innate, rather than a consequence of his position: 'Col rifutare la grandezza piglia un'altra maggior grandezza, che è il voler avanzar gli altri non d'autorità ma di virtù, e mostrar che'l valor suo non è accresciuto dallo esser principe' [in laying aside his grandeur he gains an even greater stature, since he strives to surpass others not by authority but by prowess and to show that his reputation is not increased just because he is a prince] (II. 11, p. 116).

Disguising in this context is said to allow 'una certa libertà e licenzia' [a certain freedom and licence] (p. 116), though it needs to be practised with great caution and requires an initiated audience to perceive the underlying reality. It is therefore more suitable for a private courtly setting, like that of Castiglione's fictional dialogue, where the elite audience would be aware of the subtle implications. In such spaces, removed from the highly controlled display of hierarchy and decorum required in the public arena, noblemen and ladies could interact more freely, since their noble status supposedly guaranteed their voluntary restraint of immoral or anti-social impulses. However, unresolved doubts are still raised at intervals in Castiglione's dialogue about the ethical implications of disguise and the enhancement of personal qualities through *sprezzatura*, which can be used for deceptive purposes. This is associated with a general pessimism amongst some speakers about the limitations of human perception and true knowledge of self and others.

These moral aspects of literary and particularly dramatic 'masking' are explored in Tasso's open-ended dialogue *Il Gianluca*, mentioned above, composed some years after the *Aminta*. By this time the author's relations with the court of Ferrara had deteriorated irrevocably following his imprisonment by the duke from 1579 (see below). Tasso's changed attitude towards masking or masquerading is reflected through his fictional persona of the Forestiero Napoletano [Neapolitan Stranger]. While this carnival activity is initially associated with youthful pleasurable and amorous pursuits, it is later considered in terms of its ethical connotations. Masks of the *commedia dell'arte* in this case seem inappropriate to someone of the Forestiero's standing. Doubts are even raised about the practice in general: 'l'ammascherarci, s'è degno di scusa, non è meritevol di laude' [if masking is excusable, it does not merit praise].[24] The dialogue thereby calls into question the very fabric of courtly life with its masked balls and mock tournaments. More importantly, it challenges the subtle use of pleasing appearances and deceptive manners to mask its intrinsic corruption.[25]

However, in 1573, Tasso still seems to use the masking idea inherent to pastoral in its more light-hearted carnivalesque function, and there is little sense of the serious moral questions that would later be raised. The ludic and transgressive potential offered by pastoral disguise is in fact exploited from the very start of *Aminta* where Amore (the god of Love) is presented as having escaped the authority of his mother Venus to follow his own inclinations: 'voglio dispor di me come a me piace' [I want to live my life as I please] (Prologue, 25).[26] Like the courtly audience in attendance, this powerful god has left his usual sphere of influence in the court for the humble domain of the 'genti minute' [common people] (32), normally presided over by lesser divinities (see fig. 2). His stated intention is to remain there disguised as one of the group of 'pastori festanti e coronati' [shepherds who are crowned and celebrating] (70) who are gathered for the pleasures of the 'dí solenni' [solemn festive days] (72).

Amore, in habito Paſtorale.

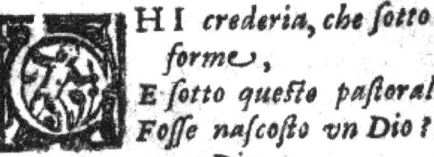 HI crederia, che ſotto humane
forme,
E ſotto queſte paſtorali ſpoglie,
Foſſe naſcoſto vn Dio? non mica
vn Dio.
Seluaggio, ò de la plebe de gli Dei,
Ma tra grandi, e celeſti il più potente,
Che fà ſpeſſo cader di mano a Marte
Lo

FIGURE 2. Anonymous woodcut illustration of Amore (Cupid) in pastoral dress (preceding Prologue), in Torquato Tasso, *Aminta* (Venice: Aldo Manuzio, 1589; first included in the 1583 edition). Note the visual distinction made between the courtly and the pastoral settings. Reproduced by permission of the Bodleian Library, University of Oxford (Auct. 2. R. 4. 78, p. 17).

The text does not clarify how far he is to be seen by the audience to intervene in the action, but he has clearly played an instrumental role in overturning divine and social hierarchies. It is left open-ended, though, as to when his 'normal' functions and values will be resumed. Even in the 'Amor fuggitivo' [Love, the fugitive], which perhaps served later as a framing epilogue to the play, his mother Venus does not succeed in finding him and restoring order.

As in Castiglione's description of the nobleman disguised as shepherd, Amore assumes the typical pastoral accoutrements of a spear and staff, but his humble appearance conceals an invisible and greater essence which only the initiated audience can fully appreciate. Love is in fact intrinsically linked to the idea of deceptive appearances, since even in his 'natural' state as a young, blindfolded boy he conceals age and experience. These ideas are neatly summed up in his concluding conceit which describes his power and perception in contrast to his mother's vain ambition: 'è cieca ella [i.e. Venus], e non io,/ cui cieco a torto il cieco volgo appella' [she is blind, not I, though the blind common people wrongly call me blind] (90–91).

The very act of writing in the pastoral mode of course implies the same paradoxical dynamic of enhancing one's status through voluntary self-abasement, which links Tasso-poet with the figure of Amore.[27] The pastoral had long been identified with the lowest of the three poetic styles, its unadorned simplicity matching its humble subject matter. Yet, it is also associated with the highest artistic tradition and poetic inspiration itself, symbolized by the mythological figures of Orpheus and Apollo, and the Judaeo-Christian shepherd-psalmist David. Virgil's *Bucolics* (a collection of ten eclogues) provided an important example of the stylistic ambiguities in the pastoral mode. Though often seen as marking the first stage in the author's progression from a modest low style, to the middle (*Georgics*) and then high style (*Aeneid*), the eclogues clearly display elegant rhetorical devices and conceits. At times they also verge on a more elevated style, as at the start of the famous fourth Eclogue predicting the return of the golden age ('paulo maiora canamus' [I would try now a somewhat grander theme]) and in the humorous slippage between the heroic and pastoral modes prefacing Eclogue VI (1–8).[28]

Likewise, in the *Aminta*, the powerful god Amore prepares the audience for a breach of stylistic conventions, by noting how he will level the differences between himself and the pastoral inhabitants: 'Spirerò nobil sensi a' rozzi petti,/ raddolcirò de le lor lingue il suono' [I shall inspire these crude breasts with noble sentiments, and sweeten the sound of their rustic speech] (Prologue, lines 80–81). Elsewhere, Tirsi (the character identified with Tasso) also threatens to break away from the 'simple' pastoral style by lapsing into an epic-style encomium of his godlike patron and ruler (II. 2. 204–05), as in Virgil's Eclogue I, line 6. Tirsi notes how he will try to honour the ancestors of this Apollo or great Jove' (a modest allusion to the epic *Gerusalemme liberata* on which Tasso was then working), even though his verse is inspired by an 'agreste Musa' [rustic muse] (II. 2. 192). However, Dafne quickly draws Tirsi back down to the proper pastoral mode after his momentary and seemingly casual display of greater talent. In practice, this idiom with its connotations of simplicity and humility therefore provided an elegant, indirect way for the poet to flatter his duke and to draw his audience's attention to his apparently natural art, without incurring the slur of affected self-praise.[29]

Adapting the Ferrarese Model of Pastoral Drama

Tasso and the theoretical tradition

The style, characterization and original performance dynamics of *Aminta* indirectly suggest a variety of poetic intentions for the play. But what can be deduced more concretely from Tasso's theoretical writings and literary practice in general? He began his literary activities from an early age, having been closely involved with the composition of the romance *Amadigi* by his father, Bernardo (published 1559). Torquato thereby became interested in neo-Aristotelian discussions of the work with the Paduan, Sperone Speroni.[30] As Tasso later observed, he often frequented the private chamber of this critic in his youthful days in Padua, perhaps at the start of his studies at the university (1560–62) or a couple of years later when he returned as a guest of his student friend, Scipione Gonzaga.[31] But while his relationship with Speroni was later to sour during the process of revising the *Gerusalemme*, Tasso remained close throughout his life to Gonzaga, who became an important critic, patron, and literary agent. This association was firmly consolidated early on within the context of the short-lived Accademia degli Eterei (Academy of the Ethereal Ones) formed by Gonzaga in Padua (1564), where some of the leading young poets of the day (including Battista Guarini) discussed literary and critical questions, and honed their compositional skills.[32]

By the time he started composing his *Aminta* (probably in 1572), Tasso had already established his credentials with the publication of his chivalric romance (*Rinaldo*, 1562) and some lyric verse. A letter penned to Ercole Rondinelli by Tasso in 1570, before the latter's journey to France with Cardinal Luigi d'Este, gives a further indication of the variety of Tasso's unpublished compositions and the importance to him of critical theory. In the event of the poet's death, Rondinelli is instructed what to do with Tasso's lyric sonnets and madrigals, his inaugural oration for the Ferrarese academy, various *canti* of his *Gottifredo* (later entitled *Gerusalemme liberata*) and, importantly, 'quattro libri del poema eroico' [four books on the heroic poem].[33] These writings on the epic or heroic poem (finally published in 1587 as *Discorsi dell'arte poetica*) indicate an already mature interest in neo-Aristotelian literary theory, which had been burgeoning in Padua, and also in Ferrara, since the 1540s. As Javitch has argued, this responded to a perceived need to understand the formal and intrinsic norms for classical genres, particularly by writers trying to revive the tragedy and epic.[34] Given the sketchy knowledge of Greek tragedies at this time and lack of significant modern examples and unquestionable 'master authors', Aristotle's *Poetics* offered would-be practitioners a vital means of understanding this art as well as a method of technical analysis that was both genre-specific and applicable to other genres. Theoretical works using the *Poetics* thus differed significantly from earlier ones based on Horace's *Ars Poetica*, which were descriptive rather than prescriptive.

In the previous chapter, we have seen how Giraldi made a vital early contribution to neo-Aristotelian criticism in Ferrara before he left in 1563. He was instrumental in sparking controversy on Ariosto's *Orlando furioso* (together with Pigna) in 1554, as well as being the first theorist to provide a theoretical justification of the ancient *satira* in order to legitimize its revival and justify changes made to suit modern tastes.[35]

Yet his rather conservative stance on this 'third' genre contrasts with the generally modernizing perspective in his discussions on the *tragedia di lieto fine* and especially the *romanzo*. He considers the romance as an intrinsically new genre, distinct from the classical epic (of Virgil and Homer), though it still adheres to universal poetic principles of verisimilitude and decorum. Given the absence of a single authoritative model for classical epic, he suggests that rules should be created whereby 'severe ancient *gravitas*' is combined with the 'pleasure' of the contemporary *romanzi*.[36]

The enormous prestige that Ariosto had conferred on Ferrara, followed by the cultural domination by Giraldi in the 1550s, must have stimulated intense interest in theory on the epic as well as about literary genres generally. On arriving in Ferrara in 1565, the younger Tasso already knew of Giraldi's views on the epic through letters exchanged with Bernardo in 1556 and 1557. Torquato was soon involved in the Ferrarese literary scene within the Accademia ferrarese, for which he gave the inaugural oration in 1567 as well as later performing his *Conclusioni amorose*.[37] Tasso flatteringly evokes these circles in the *Aminta* through the figures of Guarini, and Giambattista Pigna who is elliptically described as the poetic successor of Ariosto.[38] However, Tasso's position as something of an outsider to Ferrarese culture may explain his departure from Ariosto's model in his own theory and practice.[39] (This stance was complicated though by the felt need to defend his father's *Amadigi*, which was closer in structure and romance content to Ariosto's model.[40])

In Tasso's first theoretical treatise, *Discorsi dell'arte poetica* (henceforth *DAP*), composed some time in the mid-1560s, he dealt explicitly with the epic poem, a subject that engrossed him for most of his life.[41] Here and elsewhere he also discussed other major literary forms with which he engaged (tragedy, lyric verse and dialogue). His letter to Rondinelli of 1570 clearly shows that he was deeply engrossed in theoretical issues around the time of the pastoral's composition, as does another letter from 1574: 'ai discorsi non posi più mano: ma ho studiato e pensato molto per arricchirli e fortificarli' [I have not touched my *Discorsi* for some time, but I have studied and thought considerably about adding to them and justifying them further].[42] Importantly, between *Aminta*'s first performance (1573?) and its publication (in 1580/81), Tasso was intensely contemplating theoretical issues relating to his *Gerusalemme liberata*, as well as embarking on his tragedy *Galealto*, begun 1573, but abandoned and published incomplete at around 1,000 lines in 1582. It is therefore perplexing that no commentary or legitimization is given for *Aminta* or pastoral drama.[43] In the very few references to the work in his letters, it is simply referred to as 'l'egloga mia' [my eclogue]. Could this be because the play was originally meant only as an ephemeral entertainment for a particular courtly audience and therefore would not require a critical explanation? Or perhaps Tasso, like previous pastoral dramatists except for Giraldi, did not view the play as departing significantly from a recent eclogic tradition and was not claiming to revitalize an ancient tradition with the intellectual seriousness that this implied?

Tasso's lifelong concern with critical issues of verisimilitude, imitation and unity in poetry, and his observance of the authoritative *Poetics* in his practice, makes it more likely, as Bruscagli argues, that he consciously detached himself from the debate on the 'third' genre initiated by Giraldi because of its still controversial status.[44] An underlying poetics emerges indirectly, however, from the way in which the *Aminta* is structured, as well as from its themes and characterization, which differ considerably from earlier pastoral plays. It is important in the first instance to focus on the plot, since this was seen in Aristotelian terms as the 'forma ed anima del poema' [form and soul of the poem].[45] More precisely, the arrangement of the plot (*dispositio*) was considered to be even more important to the reception of epic and tragedy than the choice of the 'materia nuda' [raw material] itself, since it was this that provided its desired novelty and suspense. So what do Tasso's theories on plot structure regarding these other genres imply about the dramaturgy of *Aminta*?

The surprisingly simple plot of *Aminta* portrays the travails of the eponymous young shepherd as he tries to woo the chaste nymph, Silvia, and the process of her gradual conversion to love. The action is precipitated when Aminta is encouraged by the cynical Tirsi (with the help of the older nymph Dafne) to seize the 'opportunity' that will be offered when Silvia later bathes at a fountain. However, events begin to take a tragic turn when a Satyr is reported to have been encountered there, tying up the naked nymph by her hair to a tree (III. 1). Aminta is described as fending off the semi-bestial aggressor (as depicted in the cover illustration to this volume), but the cold response of his beloved drives him to attempt suicide with a spear off-stage, stopped in time by Dafne. On hearing the false report of how Silvia was killed by a wolf soon after, Aminta throws himself off a cliff, again off-stage.[46] When Silvia learns of her lover's actions she finally begins to feel pity for him, a feeling that matures into love, as promised in the prologue. The play ends with the description of her discovery that Aminta is still alive and the prospect of their marriage.

By using a single, unified plot with two (false) recognitions and reversals, Tasso polemically rejects the structure of most earlier pastoral plays, following Beccari's *Sacrificio* (1555), in which various intertwining love plots involving mismatched lovers are punctuated by often unrelated episodes.[47] Even the satyr's attack, which had in Beccari's play provided repeated opportunities for 'pleasing tricks' (Argomento, fol. A3^v), is intrinsic to *Aminta*'s main plot, acting as a catalyst for its reversal according to Love's design. Tasso also omits the kind of comic, rustic *lazzi* (gags) commonly used in earlier plays and excludes *capraii* figures, thereby creating a more uniformly elevated cast, with the ambiguous exception of the satyr. This suggests that he was observing a tragic-style structure, in which episodes are kept simple and to a minimum (see also Aristotle's *Poetics* 5.6, 8.4).[48] In this way, less confusion will be generated: 'se ben la tragedia ama molto la subita ed inopinata mutazion delle cose, le desidera nondimeno semplici e uniformi, e schiva la varietà degli episodi' [even though tragedy benefits greatly from a sudden and unexpected reversal of affairs, it still prefers these to be kept simple and uniform, and without great variety in the episodes] (*DAP*, II, 45).

Tasso's systematic rebuttal of arguments for a multiple plot in the 'modern' *romanzo* is also of some relevance to his pastoral drama. While recognizing the undeniable appeal of Ariosto's *Furioso* with its many plot strands, Tasso argues that this practice cannot be justified by claiming that the modern *romanzo* was unknown to Aristotle and therefore not subject to his rules, since Aristotle had elucidated the very essence of poetry which applies universally (*DAP*, II, 33). Furthermore, the apparent appeal of the romance is due not so much to its structure, but to its inclusion of 'accidental' features of modern customs and decorum. Although Tasso agrees with defenders of the genre about the importance of variety, which is 'in sua natura dilettevolissima' [by its nature most pleasing] (40), he concludes this should be controlled within a unified plot structure, which demands far greater poetic skill but thereby brings greater 'novelty' and *meraviglia* [wonder] (42).

Tasso may have rejected the complex pastoral plot structure for the same reason, in favour of a more Aristotelian tragic model. He seems to have been inspired in different ways by tragedies such as Euripides' *Hippolytus* and possibly by Speroni's *Canace*, from which two lines were taken.[49] Scarpati has also argued for the importance of Ovid's tale of Pyramus and Thisbe as a model, with its two specular moments of recognition and reversal.[50] However, *Aminta* does not maintain a perfectly tragic design, since the signs and recognition prove to be false and there is a happy ending. Although Aristotle recognized such traits in 'inferior' tragedies and, in Giraldi's view, such tragedies were even preferable for modern audiences, it meant that the play could not fully inspire the archetypal tragic affects of horror and pity, or produce catharsis. Even so, the *Aminta* arguably contains enough *catastrophe* (horrifying events and laments) for it to represent an example of the 'affettuoso' [pathetic] type of tragedy, one of the four tragic plot structures that Tasso identifies (*DAP*, II, 44).

The tempered tragicomic structure of Aminta

The tragic action of the protagonists in *Aminta* is, however, continually undermined by being doubled, fragmented and distorted by the 'intermediary' characters of Tirsi, Dafne and Elpino. These characters obliquely evoke the Ferrarese court through discreet allusions to a known reality and verisimilar discussions of love and poetry. Tirsi and Dafne play an important role in the first two acts, where they appear either singly or together in every scene except for the satyr's monologue (II. 1), and suggest a 'realism' more typical of comedies and *novelle*.

Dafne initially attempts unsuccessfully to persuade the stubbornly chaste Silvia to fall in love, following a pattern established in earlier pastoral plays. Yet, unlike some prototypes, such as Beccari's Stellinia, she is not motivated by base feelings of jealousy or rivalry. Rather, she wishes that Silvia should taste the more satisfying pleasures of Venus, compared to those of hunting, and in this way better harmonize with the natural world. In this way, her persuasive speech recalls that of Giraldi's Egle (*Egle*, III. 1), though it is less explicitly morally deviant. Dafne's greater maturity both in terms of age and experience makes her a contrastive figure to Silvia, like the *balia* [nurse] type in comedy and tragedy; though a certain continuity is also suggested between the two nymphs: 'qual tu sei, tal io fui' [as you are now, I once was] (I. 1. 48).[51] Dafne can recognize in Silvia her own youth spent hunting and cruelly rejecting her lovers, after which she was conquered by the rituals of courtship (I. 1. 69–70). This identification posits a paradigm for Silvia's development in the play, but is at the same time problematized by Dafne's introduction of broader ideas of temporal change.

At first, Dafne proposes a positive model of evolution, whereby humankind progresses from primitivism to greater sophistication. This is linked to a courtly view of love as civilizing and, hopefully, taming Silvia in her present 'wild' state, as implied in the sylvan connotations of her name.

DAFNE   Così la gente prima, che già visse
         nel mondo ancora semplice ed infante,
         stimò dolce bevanda e dolce cibo
         l'acqua e le ghiande, ed or l'acqua e le ghiande
         sono cibo e bevanda d'animali,
         poi che s'è posto in uso il grano e l'uva. (I. 1. 20–25)

[Thus the first people, who lived on earth earlier while it was still simple and in its infancy, considered water and acorns to be sweet food and drink; now water and acorns are food and drink for beasts, since it has become our custom to use grain and grape.]

However, the older nymph later appears more doubtful of these benefits of civilization, sensing a parallel loss in innocence. Through a long narrated anecdote, she observes that even the apparently naïve Silvia is not free from narcissistic coquetry, and concludes:

DAFNE   Non erano pria le pastorelle
         né le ninfe sí accorte; *né io tale*
         fui in mia fanciullezza. Il mondo invecchia,
         e invecchiando intristisce. (II. 2. 69–72, italics mine)

[Neither shepherdesses nor nymphs were as shrewd previously; *nor was I like this in my girlhood*. The world is growing older and, in doing so, is going into decline.]

In part, this attitude may be linked with her semi-tragic nostalgia for a youth full of amorous promise from which she is now excluded (II. 2. 105), though she still clings to the accompanying illusions.[52] At the same time, she disassociates herself from Silvia's conduct, perhaps to avoid insinuations about her own former behaviour, and her unscrupulous actions within the play

Like Dafne, Tirsi at first seems to act as an experienced adviser to Aminta following earlier models (see chapter 2, p. 44). He listens sympathetically to the younger shepherd's account of how he was initiated to love, significantly promising a '*miglior fin* che tu non pensi' [*happier end* than you might think] (I. 2. 63, emphasis mine) while Aminta, like many a young lover, entrusts Tirsi with his fate.[53] Even so, the Tirsi-Aminta relationship in many ways subverts the established model, since Aminta has reservations about his friend's capacity to unite him with Silvia (II. 3, 1–2) and subsequently takes charge of the situation himself, his tragic solution of suicide proving more effective. Tirsi is also still relatively young (not yet thirty) and his authority on matters of the heart is distinctly questionable, since he surprisingly rejects love. In this respect (though not in his pastoral indolence), he recalls the young shepherd Silvio in Argenti's *Sfortunato*. However, Tirsi's stance is explained in the play by more than just misogyny. According to Dafne, it results from his mad love for Licori, which led him to roam the forests like Ariosto's Orlando, moving onlookers to pity and laughter (I. 1. 221–31). As Tirsi later observes himself (II. 2. 146–47), he now wishes to avoid similar suffering, favouring (like chorus V) more facile pleasures gained quickly and without pain.

TIRSI   I diletti di Venere non lascia
         l'uom che schiva l'amor, ma coglie e gusta
         le dolcezze d'amor senza l'amaro. [...]

> Periglioso è cercar quel che trovato
> trastulla sí, ma piú tormenta assai
> non trovato. (II. 2. 127–29; 139–41)

[The man who avoids love does not give up the pleasures of Venus; instead he gathers and savours the sweetness of love without its bitterness. [...] It is perilous to seek what will indeed bring delight if it is found, but which produces far greater torment if it is not.]

He is therefore the only character (besides the chorus) to be removed from the economy of love that subtends the play.

In devising a trick (*inganno*) by which Aminta will be united with Silvia, Dafne and Tirsi recall comic intermediaries like Egle in Giraldi's *Egle* and Silvio in Argenti's *Sfortunato*. They also present an unsettling and morally ambivalent antitype to the protagonists with their provocative and cynical banter about love, courtship and human nature. For instance, Tirsi speaks of his distrust of the feminine art of appearing beautiful (II. 2. 15). Dafne advises that lovers should do away with the prescribed courtly ritual if it proves insufficient, and even resort to force to obtain from women what they actually want: 'se questo non basta, anco rapisca' [if this is not enough, then ravish her] (88). (Ironically, she begs Tirsi not to repeat or to publicize her comment in his verse, 94–95.) In the plan that they devise for their charges, it is in fact implied but never directly stated that rape may be used if necessary to 'persuade' the beloved (as in *Egle* or *Sfortunato*). A dramatic tension is conveyed by the edgy quality of the dialogue with its broken lines and repetition. Even so, they express some doubts beforehand about the inflexible nature of their charges, since Silvia is rigorously set against love, while Aminta is too respectful (83).

TIRSI	Ma che però?
DAFNE	Ma che però? Da poco intenditor! s'hai senno, tanto basti.
TIRSI	Intendo; ma non so s'egli avrà tanto d'ardir.
DAFNE	S'ei non l'avrà, stiasi, ed aspetti ch'altri lui cerchi.
TIRSI	Egli è ben tal che'l merta. (II. 2. 115–20)
[TIRSI	But what then?
DAFNE	What do you mean 'what then'? You don't understand much! If you've got any sense that should be enough.
TIRSI	I understand; but I don't know if he will be daring enough.
DAFNE	If not, then let him stand and wait until someone seeks him out.
TIRSI	He's the sort that deserves that.]

Dafne's proposal thus disturbingly echoes that of the satyr in the previous scene, who also plans to leave aside verbal persuasion for force ('Sforzerò, *rapirò* quel che costei/ mi niega' [I'll force, I'll *ravish* what she denies] (II. 1, 81–82, my italics).[54]

We learn in Act III, however, that the satyr was driven away by Aminta, who for the first time takes charge of the situation himself. From this point in the play there is an abrupt transition to the tragic mode, which Bruscagli argues reinforces the pastoral's fragile plot structure and gives it greater dignity.[55] The role of both the 'advisers' changes significantly. The now lamenting Dafne is reduced to asking for help when the satyr unexpectedly attacked her charge (III. 1. 47–49); and Aminta ignores her prudent injunctions to wait for further news about whether Silvia is dead (III. 2. 116–19). Tirsi, after the failure of the plan for daring and virile action, finally leaves the stage altogether (III. 1), hoping to find Aminta with Elpino, and is only mentioned thereafter in V. 1. Meanwhile, Aminta takes on greater depth as a character. While previously hesitant about acting on his love, he is now described as showing real heroism in defending his beloved. However, his frenzied acts of suicide, first after his rejection by Silvia and the second time on hearing of her supposed death, though heroic in their extreme self-sacrifice, reveal a still somewhat immature appreciation of love.

The tragic dimension of Acts III-IV is strengthened by the introduction of a chorus of shepherds (from III. 1) and, later, the separate appearance of two tragic messengers. From this point the stage space no longer appears reconcilable with the enclosed space of the court. It is described as a 'luogo di passo' [place of passage] (III. 1. 30), in which news may be brought from messengers about wider, uncharted areas beyond.[56] These more explicitly 'tragic' characters evoke the classic *affetti* (affections) of horror and pity. For instance the shepherd chorus comment on Tirsi's anxious appearance, his sweating and breathlessness, provoked by his fear that Aminta may have committed suicide (III. 1. 16–19). The two messengers who report the (apparent) deaths of Silvia and Aminta, bearing 'tokens' to strengthen the inferences, emphasize similar tragic emotions. Nerina notes the terrifying discovery of Silvia's bloody veil with seven wolves nearby near some naked bones (III. 2). Ergasto describes at greater length how, after having sworn not to restrain Aminta, with 'scongiuri orribili' [horrible supplications] (IV. 2. 51) to the woodland gods and Hecate, he witnessed the young shepherd jump from a cliff so high that it made him shudder to look down. Silvia responds to this second account with the equally tragic view that vengeance is required 'de l'empio mio rigore/ e del suo amaro fine' [for my wicked severity and for his bitter end] (IV. 2. 129–30). The chorus, however, responds with compassion and a more stoic stance: 'Consòlati, meschina,/ ché questo è di fortuna e non tua colpa' [O wretched girl, take heart, for this blow comes from fortune and not from you] (145). This preludes a transition to a more balanced perspective in the final act.

Act V (a single scene) begins with a new character (Elpino) unexpectedly describing Aminta's happiness to the on-stage chorus, whose perplexity at this news partly mirrors and rationalizes the audience's reaction.[57] Events are now described as unfolding within a providential scheme dictated by Love rather than by blind fortune. This causality may have been further reinforced by non-verbal signs, including the god's 'invisible' presence amongst the shepherd chorus (as noted in the prologue):

> ELPINO Veramente la legge con che Amore
> il suo imperio governa eternamente
> non è dura, né obliqua; e l'opre sue,
> piene di providenza e di mistero,
> altri a torto condanna. Oh con quant'arte,
> e per che ignote strade egli conduce
> l'uom ad esser beato, e fra le gioie
> del suo amoroso paradiso il pone,
> quando ei piú crede al fondo esser de' mali! (V. 1. 1–9)

[Truly the law with which Love eternally governs his kingdom is neither harsh nor adverse; and his works, which are full of providence and mystery, are wrongly condemned by some. Oh with what art and through what unknown paths this god leads man to blessedness, and places him amongst the joys of his amorous paradise, when he believes himself sunk most deeply in his woes!]

Elpino's late appearance on stage from the removed space of his 'speco' [cave], after having been invoked on various occasions as poet and lover, perhaps suggests the kind of magical figure or divine interpreter found for example in de' Sommi's *Irifile* or Pasqualigo's *Intricati*.[58] There is, however, nothing overtly supernatural about this character. Instead, he plays a mediating role in terms of seeking social sanction for the lovers' union through marriage, and he connects the off-stage tragedy with the earlier 'realistic'/courtly aspect of the play. Most importantly, he perceives the underlying mysterious order of Love's ways. As such, he is clearly superior to the 'blind masses' that Amore condemned, as well as other characters in the play, who believed they could determine events themselves through their ingenuity or were driven by tragic fatalism.

Unlike the messengers' stories, Elpino's account of the unexpected 'spettacolo' [spectacle] of Aminta's near-fatal fall followed by the union of the lovers shows a detachment, coming from a full knowledge of events. On a dramaturgical level, Elpino achieves a tragicomic balance by tempering the tragic elements (death is avoided) and introducing a more intimate and sentimental quality. This is realized through the use of a middle, lyric style, which Tasso notes elsewhere: 'con un soave temperamento maggiormente diletta' [provides greater pleasure with a sweet temperament] (*DAP*, 55). Thus Silvia's Baccante-like frenzy (V. 1. 100) on finding her apparently dead lover (which Scarpati links to the last part of Ovid's tale of Pyramus and Thisbe) is described as giving way to a pathetic and sensual scene. Aminta's deathly pallor is likened to a sweetly faded violet, while the effect of Silvia's tears in reviving him and their sighing kiss is expressed in lyric *settenari*. By the end, Aminta has realized that love is more than purely physical possession, and has been saved from its excessive and destructive tendencies, while Silvia has understood that her proud independence verged upon cruelty and needed to be tempered by pity (IV. 2, 176–78).[59] The lovers have undergone an inner transformation: their rigid perspectives on love have been tempered to an Aristotelian 'golden mean'. Love, as exemplified in the play itself, may appear both tragic and comic, but ultimately it reconciles the tensions between scenes and acts, genres, characters, and styles. As the god Amore promises from the start: 'la disagguaglianza de' soggetti/ come a me piace agguaglio' [the inequality of my subjects, as I desire, I equalize] (Prologue, 84–85).

Realism and idealism

Yet Elpino's narrated account of the lovers' reunion suggests some wishful thinking on his part, since it is used as grounds to hope for *pietà* (pity) from his own cruel beloved, Licori. There is no external confirmation of the happy ending by the lovers either, which means that the anxiety about death that haunts the play is never fully allayed.[60] The lovers in fact never meet on stage and only appear in the presence of the mediating, pseudo-courtly characters of Dafne and Tirsi, suggesting that the ideal love that they achieve may be unrepresentable. Finally, the chorus challenges Elpino's idealizing stance, rejecting the kind of love Aminta has suffered at such a price (Chorus V, 8–9). It would rather win a nymph's love after a brief courtship with 'soavi disdegni/ e soavi ripulse' [sweet acts of scorn and sweet rejections] (15–16) — a hedonistic perspective which echoes Tirsi's earlier rejection of courtly love. Likewise, the shepherd chorus demythologizes Aminta's heroic self-sacrifice to gain Silvia's love: 'Caro prezzo a chi 'l diede; a chi 'l riceve/ prezzo inutile, e infame' [A high price for him who paid it; and a useless and disgraceful price for the one who receives it] (IV. 1. 150–51).

The continual and unresolved tension in Tasso's *Aminta* between idealism and realism on issues of love and chastity, and concerning the pastoral location itself, marks the play off from earlier Ferrarese examples and recalls the same author's inconclusive, 'open' dialogues.[61] The audience is confronted by a continual clash of perspectives without any single authoritative position. Notably, even the end-of-act choruses (of which only those of I and V were probably used in the first performance) fail to uphold moralizing ideals, and consider sophisticated poetry and courtship rituals inappropriate in the pastoral context. The shepherd chorus that appears on stage in the tragic second half of *Aminta* maintains a similarly sceptical dimension, for example, deflating the Petrarchan idea of the suicidal lover: 'E' uso ed arte/ di ciascun ch'ama minacciarsi morte:/ ma rade volte poi segue l'effetto' [It is common and a ploy for all lovers to threaten suicide; but the act rarely follows the words] (III. 1. 131–33).

Questions about idealization and realism are raised most famously in *Aminta* in the chorus that concludes Act I. This explicitly alludes to the ancient *topos* of the Golden Age (taken especially from Ovid's *Metamorphoses*, but going back to Hesiod) as an early period of natural abundance, happiness and justice for mankind, which was later followed by a corrupt age of iron. The idea of temporal, and implicitly spatial, difference which underpins the *topos* therefore makes it useful for encomium and nostalgic idyll, as well as for satire of current practices.[62] Although the Golden Age was frequently evoked in pastoral eclogues (following especially Virgil's *Eclogue IV*), and sometimes used for encomiastic purposes in early Ferrarese pastorals, Tasso was the first to incorporate it to such effect within regular pastoral drama. However, he alters Ovid's version of the *topos* by ignoring its more political ingredients, like the absence of war and invasion, and the edenic implications of eternal spring and fruitfulness, to focus explicitly on the issue of love within a temporal existence.[63] With the disjunction between 'then' and 'now' clearly emphasized through the chorus's structure, the Golden Age is described polemically as being a time when sensual love could be expressed spontaneously, unrestricted by shame or guilt, and the deceptive rituals of courtship and decorum. The chorus thus dramatizes the clash between individual nature and the limits imposed on it by social restraints, which require 'unnatural' and artful duplicity. These restraints are contained within the umbrella term 'onore' [honour]:

> Tu prima, Onor, velasti
> la fonte dei diletti,
> negando l'onde a l'amorosa sete; [...]
> tu i dolci atti lascivi
> fésti ritrosi e schivi;

> ai detti il fren ponesti, ai passi l'arte;
> opra è tua sola, o Onore,
> che furto sia quel che fu don d'Amore.
> (Chorus, I, 40–42, 48–52)

> [You, Honour, first veiled the fount of pleasures, denying its waters to slake the lover's thirst; [...] you made sweet, lascivious acts coy and bashful; you restrained open speech, and made movements contrived; this is solely your doing, Honour, so that what was previously a gift of Love is now theft.]

The sensuality of the nostalgically recalled primitive world is reflected in the balanced lyricism of the rhymed verse and the playful use of *concetti*, especially in stanza 3 which alludes to the naked nymphs' 'fresche rose' [dewy roses] and 'le poma del seno' [the apples of her breast].[64] The last lines of the chorus (64–68) further provocatively recall Catullus' call to love and the *carpe diem* motif, drawing attention to the transience of life and thus negating the Christian view of redemption in the afterlife. They also contain a tantalizing suggestion of Epicurean beliefs in the mortality of the soul, and the necessity of seeking pleasure as the highest good.[65] Thus the chorus with its pagan ethic may do more than simply propose a courtly in-joke. As Scarpati argues, it may represent an antithesis or a 'hypothesis' that the *favola* in its entirety is trying to disprove.[66] Characteristically, the problem is left unanswered. Only a vague hint of doubt about the chorus's proposed 'golden and happy law' sculpted by nature: 'S'ei piace, ei lice' [It is right if it pleases you], may be suggested by its resonance with Dante's description of the lustful Semiramis' licentious law (*Inferno*, V. 56).[67]

Similar tensions between the real and the ideal, an original nature and civilization are embodied within the figure of the satyr, who appears only once, immediately after the Golden Age chorus (see fig. 3). Given the unusual absence of rustic 'servant' figures in the *Aminta* compared to earlier pastoral plays (apart from Beccari's 1555 edition of *Sacrificio*), the satyr provides the greatest contrast to the noble shepherds and their ideal pastoral existence, characterized by love, poetry and hunting, unfettered by obligations — though as we have seen, both Dafne and Tirsi problematize this identification in other ways. The satyr is in fact implicitly associated with this pastoral underclass since he mentions his discussion with a 'caprar' [goatherd] (II. 1. 83) and Tirsi describes him as 'villan' [peasant/base] (III. 1. 64). This is the first time that a satyr has been used in a Ferrarese pastoral play since Beccari's *Sacrificio* and Giraldi's *Egle*, and so suggests Tasso's reversion to the more humanistically inspired satyric mode. However, there is no concomitant mention of the satyr's divine status as a follower of Bacchus. He appears instead without the festive, comic and magical qualities of Beccari's counterpart, at the margins of the courtly pastoral existence, which triggers his frustrated violence and misogyny.[68]

By comparison to his earlier counterparts, Tasso's satyr goes further in exploring the satirical possibilities considered intrinsic to this character.[69] He undermines the nostalgic view of a 'natural' kind of love presented by the Golden Age chorus with his critique of a contemporary venal 'golden age' that recalls Ovid's *Ars Amatoria*, II:

> SATIRO   Ahi, che le ville
> seguon l'essempio de le gran cittadi;
> e veramente il secol d'oro è questo,
> poiché sol vince l'oro e regna l'oro. (II. 1. 55–58)

ATTO SECONDO.

SCENA PRIMA.

Satiro solo.

PICCIOLA è l'Ape, e fa col
   picciol morso
Pur graui, e pur moleste le ferite;
Ma, qual cosa è più picciola
d'Amore,
Se in ogni breue spatio entra, e s'asconde
In ogni breue spatio? hor, sotto a l'ombra
                                          De

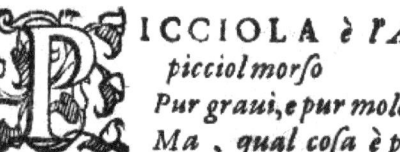

FIGURE 3. Anonymous woodcut illustration of the Satyr's monologue in a pastoral scene with animals (preceding Act II), in Torquato Tasso, *Aminta* (Venice: Aldo Manuzio, 1589; first included in the 1583 edition). Reproduced by permission of the Bodleian Library, University of Oxford (Auct. 2. R. 4. 78, p. 44).

[Alas, even the rural villages follow the example of the great cities; and this is rightly called the golden age, since gold alone conquers and reigns.]

He deplores the encroachment of the city (or court) with its vices on the countryside (a polemic picked up in the following scene by Tirsi, II. 2. 72–77), which has led to his exclusion from the commerce of love by dint of his poverty and distance from courtly ideals.

Meanwhile, the Satyr promotes his own virility and strength by contrast to the more 'sophisticated' but effete, courtly shepherds: 'femine nel sembiante e ne le forze' [feminine in their appearance and strength] (II. 1. 49–50) — a position later echoed in Tirsi's exhortation to Aminta: 'ma fa d'uopo/ d'esser *un uom*, Aminta, *un uom* ardito' [but you must be a man, Aminta, a daring man] (II. 3. 17–18). But in presenting this rivalry, the Satyr exposes his comic, even pathetic, delusions about his physical charms, recalling Theocritus' monstrous Cyclops (Idyll, 11) and a host of other unfortunate, crude pastoral lovers.[70] His elegant Petrarchan and classicizing style is also increasingly disturbed by suggestions of indecorous violence and sexual desire, which highlights the hypocrisy and insincerity of this pose. In fact, he demonstrates how primitivism risks declining into egocentricity and violence, perverting the golden age ideal of love as a freely given gift, to one of theft and rape (II. 1. 81–82) — a view which as we have seen is, perhaps more shockingly, replicated in Tirsi's advice to Aminta (II. 3. 88–91).

Compared to most earlier pastorals, *Aminta* also develops ideas on Nature and Art in a more nuanced and sometimes polemical fashion. While previous examples tend to follow some of Virgil's eclogues in describing a beautiful nature enhanced by art, Tasso presents a call for rustic simplicity in Chorus II, which is seen as a guarantee of sincerity.[71] This is wittily represented in the 'harsh' style of the final lines:

> Amor, leggan pur gli altri
> le socratiche carte,
> ch'io in due begli occhi apprenderò quest'arte;
> e perderan le rime
> de le penne piú saggie
> appo le mie selvaggie,
> che rozza mano in rozza scorza imprime. (Chorus II, 36–42)

[O Love, let others read Socratic writings [i.e. of Plato], for I will learn this art from two beautiful eyes; and verse from more learned pens will be judged inferior to my rustic rhymes, which are carved by a coarse hand on coarse bark.]

The second chorus proposes that love is more fully understood through direct experience than through the study of poetry or ancient philosophy. It is also expressed more eloquently through simple, confused phrases and even silence than by 'voci adorne e dotte' [ornamented and learned words] (33). The fact that this sentiment is voiced by a tragic-style chorus for an elite audience, and that the play is replete with erudite allusions, points to the deliberate paradox of this pose of naturalness. Yet, it is precisely in this intimate courtly context that the nostalgic ideal of living simply, according to natural dictates, will resonate so powerfully.

Tasso's *Aminta* in Print and its Challenge to Decorum

Aminta immediately enjoyed enormous success: it was quickly staged in various centres and from 1581 it became available to a wider audience in print. By 1600 it had appeared in at least twenty-five editions and was translated into French (1584), and reworked in English (1591). In the following century there were twenty-eight editions in Italian, as compared to only eleven editions of *Orlando furioso*.[72] However, its textual status remains surprisingly problematic. There is no definitive autograph manuscript and — unlike the earlier Ferrarese plays published soon after their performance with commemorative prefaces — over seven years elapsed before the first (unauthorized) printed edition.[73] Even modern editions of *Aminta* vary as to what parts of the play are included, since changes were apparently made between the shorter original version for performance and later printed editions.[74] By 1581, Tasso's status at court had altered significantly. He had lost Duke Alfonso d'Este's favour probably because of his insistent consultation with the Inquisition in Rome and Bologna, and perhaps his indiscreet accusations of leading figures at court. In June 1577 Tasso attacked a servant he suspected to be spying on him, but managed to escape from arrest and left Ferrara. On returning to the court in 1579 as Alfonso II was preparing for his third marriage to Margherita Gonzaga, the poet hoped to be restored to the Duke's grace again. But his cold treatment provoked another outburst of rage. This time Tasso was confined in the hospital of St. Anna, on grounds of insanity, until his release in July 1586 through the intervention of Duke Vincenzo Gonzaga of Mantua.[75]

It is unclear too what form the probable first performance of *Aminta* in 1573 would have taken. It is likely that it was performed without at least some of the inter-act choruses, since a nobleman who attended a later performance requested by Lucrezia d'Este in Pesaro in 1574 observes:

> Quel che di grazia s'è aggiunto a quest'Egloga e c'ha piaciuto più che mediocremente è *la novità del coro fra ciascuno atto* che rendeva maestà mirabile, e recava con piacevolissimi concetti infinito diletto agli spettatori e ascoltatori. (Emphasis mine)[76]

> [What has favourably been added to this eclogue, bringing greater than average pleasure, is *the novelty of choruses between each act*, which brought marvellous majesty and infinite delight to the audience watching and listening with their most pleasing conceits.]

It is not clear whether Tasso considered all the choruses intrinsic to the play. Those for Acts III and IV had originally been composed for other purposes and appeared in print separately in the late 1580s, while the Aldine edition of 1581 only contains choruses for Acts I and V, as in all the manuscripts. Furthermore it is not certain that Tasso wrote the *intermedii* for *Aminta*. Aldo Manuzio's first 1581 edition also lacks the curious episode reporting Mopso's almost hallucinatory critique of the court followed by its hyperbolic praise by Tirsi (I. 2. 215–311). This episode was almost certainly added some time after Tasso's relations with the Ferrarese court had deteriorated, and has been understood as alluding to Speroni. The postlude 'Amore Fuggitivo' (published initially with Tasso's *Rime* and first added to the play in Baldini's edition, 1581), in which Venus appears in search of her missing son Amore, is not always considered an authentic part of *Aminta* either. These alterations therefore seem to indicate changed views of the play by the author or editors during the 1570s and '80s.

Tasso apparently prepared a manuscript of the play for publication around 1577,[77] but its abandonment may indicate his diffidence about the appropriateness of such a gesture. Given that the *egloga* was meant for private courtly occasions, any implication of *industria* or diligent study as associated with print publication would have undermined the desired effect of improvised *sprezzatura*.[78] In this respect, Tasso seems to have adopted a wholly different agenda for his eclogue from his epic *Gerusalemme liberata* (printed 1581), with which he intended to excel poetically and break new ground. Tasso's correspondence between the time of *Aminta*'s composition and its publication show that all his energies were focused on revising the epic, while his play is barely mentioned. In a letter to Scipione Gonzaga of 26 March 1575, though, Tasso begs his friend to take precautions so that manuscript copies of cantos from his epic poem are not read or disseminated against his wishes by falling into the wrong hands 'com'avvenne de l'egloga' [as happened to the eclogue] (*Lettere*, I, 21, 55). The poet is perhaps referring to the circulation of copies by actors or others after the recent performance of the play in Urbino.

While seemingly uninterested in publishing his *Aminta*, Tasso was desperate around this time to have his epic printed in order to gain recognition as well as financial independence which could free him from his service in Ferrara.[79] Exchanges with printers particularly in Ferrara and Venice testify, however, to his problematic relationship and increasing disenchantment with the press.[80] From 1576 there were attempts by unscrupulous publishers to pirate his works, despite Alfonso d'Este's intervention that year to prevent an unauthorized edition of the *Gerusalemme liberata* being sold and Tasso's own purchase of a twenty-year privilege from Florence. It must have been partly the poet's mania for extensive correction of his work that induced printers to publish without his consent and often inaccurately, since they sought priority in the fiercely competitive market for his new works. Even so, Tasso frequently lamented that he was paid little for publications, despite their enormous popularity. After his confinement in Sant'Anna from 1579, there was even less that he could do to control this situation. Indeed, the Florentine ambassador (Orazio Urbani) observed mockingly that this madman's caprices 'sono stati rubati e stampati da ciascuno che gli è tornato comodo' [have been stolen and printed by everyone who found it useful to do so].[81] In fact, the epic first appeared in an incomplete pirated version (Venice, 1580), and the title by which it became publicly known was chosen by Angelo Ingegneri, the editor of the first complete editions in Parma and Casalmaggiore (1581), though the poet had considered *Gerusalemme racquistata* [reconquered] or *Goffredo*.[82]

Tasso's seems to have changed his mind about publishing *Aminta* in the face of his own changes in circumstances and his recognition of the possibilities offered by the press, which was by now eager for his works. This would reflect a general pattern of 'vulgarization' of courtly forms, as witnessed earlier with regular comedy (see chapter 2) and later, for example with the publication in 1601 of Luzzasco Luzzaschi's madrigals written originally for Duke Alfonso's exclusive and private *concerto delle dame*.[83] In a letter to Scipione Gonzaga (undated, but September 1580?), Tasso asks him if he would print the first twelve canti of his epic poem 'ed oltre ciò l'egloga mia' [and besides that, also my eclogue] (*Lettere*, II, 136, 29), since nothing had come of his many requests to Duke Alfonso to publish these works and two volumes of verse. He thereby hoped to gain financial benefits, though he was otherwise not enthusiastic about publishing his play, possibly due to uncertainties about how to present it.

Aminta seems to have been printed first in 1580 by Cristoforo Draconi in Cremona, with a dedication to Duke Vespasiano Gongaza Colonna of Sabbioneta dated 15 December. However, the Venetian edition of *Aminta* by Aldo Manuzio (Aldus Manutius) may have been prepared around the same time if not before, since Tasso had already received a copy by early December.[84] As with his epic, the poet lacked full control over the play's publication. Manuzio denied him any choice about the important matter of the dedication, which could have been useful to him in financial terms: 'avrei nondimeno avuto caro che la dedicazione fosse stata lasciata a me. [...] sono infermo, e prigione, ed oppresso da tutte le calamità' [even so, I would have appreciated it if the dedication had been left to me. [...] I am ill, and a prisoner, oppressed by all kinds of calamities].[85] The edition was in fact dedicated by Manuzio to Don Ferrante Gonzaga of Guastalla (dated 20 December 1580) and lacks any supplementary material by the author, whose unfortunate condition is referred to. Later, Tasso was evidently also unhappy with the form in which the play itself appeared. In a letter to Manuzio (18 March 1581) acknowledging the receipt of a printed copy of *Aminta* and his *Rime*, Tasso asks the printer to delay sales so that he can send a revised and corrected volume of verse and also 'la favola pastorale molto migliorata, con quelle parti ch'ancor le mancano' [the pastoral play in a greatly improved state, with those parts that are still missing from it].[86]

The Ferrarese ducal printer, Vittorio Baldini, quickly responded to the Venetian edition of *Aminta* by producing a version that claims to be based on a good original by the author ('a' Lettori', 1 February 1581). Besides implicitly establishing his own and the duke's claim on the local celebrity author, Baldini testifies to the rapid demand for Tasso's play.[87] Numerous editions were produced in 1581 and soon after, especially in courtly centres of northern Italy (Parma, Mantua, Piacenza, Ferrara), Venice, as well as abroad. Although *Aminta* underwent some slight alterations for publication, it does not seem to have been subjected to the kind of close linguistic amendment that his *Rime* and particularly his epic received. Nor does it seem to have undergone theoretical revision, though Scipione Gonzaga was asked to supervise its publication, and there is no suggestion of doubts about its potentially subversive aspects.

Tasso's rather more carefree attitude may perhaps partly be related to the fact that *Aminta* was first published in Venice and Cremona, rather than Rome, where the *Liberata* was extensively and rigorously revised. As Tasso observes to Scipione Gonzaga with regard to his epic (24 April 1576), these centres differed significantly in the restrictions they imposed:

> Io son sicuro di far stampare il mio poema in Venezia, e in ogni altro luogo di Lombardia con licenza de l'Inquisitore, senza mutar cosa alcuna, con la mutazion sola d'alcune parole: ma mi spaventa l'esempio del Sigonio, il quale fe' stampare con licenza de l'Inquisitore, e poi il libro li fu sospeso: mi spaventa un altro esempio del Muzio, narratomi dal Borghesi: mi spaventa la severità di ... , imaginandomi che molti siano in Roma simili a lui: temo assai d'alcun cattivo offizio del ... .[88]

[I feel sure that I can have my [epic] poem printed in Venice and in all other parts of Lombardy with a licence from the Inquisitor, without changing anything or only a few words. But the example of [Carlo] Sigonio frightens me, as he went into print with an Inquisitor's licence and then the book was suspended; I am also worried by another case involving [Girolamo] Muzio that [Diomede] Borghesi [an inquisitor] told me about; I am fearful of the severity of [the reviser Silvio Antoniano?], since I imagine that there are many people in Rome like him: I am also very afraid of some unpleasant action by [Speroni?].]

Tasso's letter points to his general concern with the observance of moral and religious orthodoxy in printed secular works. Such feelings were becoming widespread and institutionalized in the second half of the century, with the more severe enforcement of Indexes by the Roman Inquisition, especially after that of Paul III (1559) which for the first time proscribed works deemed immoral as well as heretical. Drama attracted serious consideration because of its social and public status. This is particularly evident in changed attitudes towards comedy and its practitioners. We have seen how already in the 1540s, Giraldi was preoccupied with moral decorum in theatrical works, emphasizing how authority figures and female characters should properly be represented, and the need for a didactic message. By the 1570s, critics like the clergyman Bernardino Pino da Cagli were even more anxious to limit inappropriate material and to emphasize the genre's didactic qualities.[89] Professional *comici*, who had become more established since the 1560s, were also widely condemned for immorality and licentiousness. Carlo Borromeo barred them from Milan in 1565, and Pius V did the same in Rome 1566, though companies continued to find support from courtly institutions and private individuals after this time.

As a result of such attitudes, writers, editors and publishers took various precautions to prevent works from being banned or slated for expurgation. Besides avoiding potentially risqué subjects, they could add paratexts which would encourage a moralizing interpretation of a work. These could include annotations and allegories, such as those composed by Tommaso Porcacchi for the popular 1568 Guerra edition of the *Orlando furioso* which was widely imitated.[90] In revising his epic for publication from 1575, Tasso was keenly aware of the 'prohibitions' encountered by various poets.[91] His letters increasingly register his own and others' doubts about the *Liberata* from a moral and religious point of view.

Forse anco io non ho avuto tutto quel riguardo che si doveva al rigor de' tempi presenti, ed al costume c'oggi regna ne la corte romana: del che è buon tempo ch'io vo dubitando: ed ho temuto talora tant'oltre, che ho disperato di potere stampare il libro senza gran difficultà.[92]

[Perhaps I too have not paid due and sufficient attention to the rigour of our times and to the climate now prevailing in the Roman court, about which I have been having my doubts for some time. Sometimes my fear has reached such a point that I have despaired of being able to print the book without great difficulty.]

He worried, for instance, about the appropriateness of including in his Christian epic love episodes, which generally came under increasing investigation by papal authorities from 1576. The 'miracoli del bosco' [miracles of the (enchanted) forest] especially concerned him, though these could be justifiable in poetic terms as providing the 'maraviglia' [wonderment] required in the genre.[93]

Tasso's concern with moral and religious orthodoxy in his *Gerusalemme* does not seem to have extended to his *Aminta*. In this respect, Tasso may be considered as continuing in the tradition of earlier writers of Ferrarese courtly pastorals who, with the exception perhaps of Giraldi, aimed to please their spectators above all, without too much concern about potential criticism of immorality or unorthodox syncretism. Indeed, Tasso proposes even more provocative sensuality in the voyeuristic description of the naked Silvia in the satyr's clutches (III. 1) and in his Golden Age chorus, which touches also upon questions of individual liberty and social morality.

The dramatization of social authority described in earlier pastoral plays, especially those composed in Ferrara, likewise appears surprisingly attenuated in the *Aminta*. The slightly older 'adviser' figures (Dafne and Tirsi) are, as we have seen, distinctly ambiguous. No other uncontroversially authoritative or divine characters are represented on stage. Elpino remains a somewhat aloof and idealizing commentator on the action. The chorus (both as character and between acts) fails to impart an impartial moralistic commentary or to uphold the values of the ruling elite. Meanwhile, the authority of the god Amore is problematic too, since he has shed his usual insignia and left his sphere of power. While apparently determining the course of the action, he remains 'invisible' and transformed on stage. Unlike various earlier pastoral plays, there is no clear sense of his struggle against the usually uncompromising goddess of chastity, Diana. Instead, Amore quarrels only with his ineffectual mother, Venus, who does not appear in the play itself.

Aminta also lacks the religious 'frame' of earlier pastorals. It seems to take place on some undefined festive occasion, but the hunt that is prescribed for that day (I. 1. 233–35) has no divine or ritual significance like that in *Sfortunato*. There is no allusion to a temple either, which would increasingly become a visually and dramaturgically important backdrop in pastoral plays, since the lovers in *Aminta* are reconciled offstage, outside Elpino's 'cave'.[94] The nymphs are disassociated from their usual function as votaries. Dafne is not dedicated to Amore or Bacchus, and her previous renunciation of the single life as a servant of Diana (or Cynthia) appears more like a 'natural' process of development than a conversion: "'Eccoti, Cinzia, il corno, eccoti l'arco,/ ch'io rinunzio i tuoi strali e la tua vita'" ["Here, Cynthia, is your horn, and here your bow, for I renounce your arrows and your way of life"] (I. 1, 76–77). Indeed, Bruscagli views the goddess as functioning more on a metaphorical or symbolic level, being invoked as a talisman when Silvia fears Aminta's proximity ('Pastor, non mi toccar: son di Diana' [shepherd, do not touch me; I am a devotee of Diana] (III. 1. 105)) or as a tag by Dafne to describe the fountain where Silvia usually bathes (II. 2. 110).[95] Given that the play hinges on Silvia's conversion from chastity to love, it is significant that Dafne does not persuade her by invoking religious authority and family duties, but rather by positing the example of nature and recalling the passing of time.

Thus Tasso rejects various pseudo-religious components evident in earlier pastorals and fundamental to Sannazaro's *Arcadia*, creating instead a more verisimilar, secular or even pagan context for the discussion of love. The exploration of this subject in *Aminta* amongst a restricted group of sophisticated characters (the satyr is excluded) perhaps also means that, rather like in Castiglione's *Cortegiano*, risqué questions on social and sexual behaviour and human nature can be explored more freely while still maintaining decorum. By including veiled but titillating sensual elements, Tasso would also have been satisfying a recognized courtly demand, as witnessed by the popularity of madrigals full of sexual innuendos (such as Guarini's notorious 'Tirsi morir volea') and the nearly naked figures in courtly *intermedi*, though these could be justified in neo-Platonic terms.[96]

Even so, Tasso was conscious that such material was frowned upon in published works. For this reason, he was prepared in 1576 to excise from his *Gerusalemme liberata* some stanzas deemed lascivious and even some of the enchantments and marvellous episodes. However, he begs the stern critic, Silvio Antoniano, to be indulgent in consideration of 'il costume del paese nel quale io vivo, e quella che sin'ora giudico mia natural inclinazione' [the customs of the country in which I live, and what I have until now considered my natural inclination].[97] Strikingly, Tasso confides shortly after to Scipione Gonzaga that he intends to circulate the problematic cantos of *Gerusalemme liberata* in their uncensored form amongst a private readership:

> Le più lascive [...] sono le più belle: e perchè non si perdano affatto, farò stampare duplicati questi due canti [IV and XVI]; e a diece o quindici al più de' più cari e intriseci padroni miei darò gli canti intieri; a gli altri, tutti così tronchi, come comanda la necessità de' tempi: ma di questo non occorre far motto. (*Lettere*, I, 66, 162 (24 April 1576))

> [The more lascivious ones [...] are the best, and so that they are not totally lost, I will have these two cantos [IV and XVI] printed in duplicate; and will give the whole versions to ten or fifteen at most of my dearest and closest patrons. To others I will give the cut versions which reflect the necessity of the times. But there is no need to mention this to anyone.]

'Moralizing' the Pastoral

Poetics and morality

The critical writings surrounding the *Gerusalemme liberata* and pastoral episodes from the epic itself provide some useful means of exploring Tasso's evolving views on the end of poetry from the 1570s, throwing further light on *Aminta*. In particular, they reveal in interesting shift in the author's attitudes towards hedonistic literature. Tasso states at various points in his *Discorsi* that the purpose of poetry is to please (for example, *DAP*, II, 39). As mentioned also in his letters, he felt this to be necessary to secure the *Gerusalemme liberata*'s appeal to a courtly and general reading audience, as Ariosto had done before him, and to avoid the fate of Trissino's unpopular epic (17, 38, 39–40). When Tasso felt surer of the theoretical and stylistic aspects of his poem, he therefore asked Scipione Gonzaga to help him canvas opinion amongst 'cortigiani galanti' [galant courtiers] and 'uomini mezzani' [average people]:

> Resta solo ch'io dubiti del diletto. Io non mi proposi mai di piacere al vulgo stupido; ma non vorrei però solamente soddisfare ai maestri de l'arte. Anzi sono ambiziosissimo de l'applauso de gli uomini mediocri; e quasichè altrettanto affetto la buona opinione di questi tali, quanto quella de' più intendenti. (*Lettere*, I, 40, 100 (16 July 1575))

[I am only concerned now about how pleasing the poem is. I never intended to please the ignorant masses, but I do not solely wish to please experts in the art of poetry. Indeed, I am most ambitious for the approval of the average man; and I am almost as keen to gain the good opinion of such men as of those who are more knowledgeable.]

Pleasure is to be achieved in poetry, according to Tasso, through a careful balance between verisimilitude (or plausibility) and 'il maraviglioso' [wonder], which pleases both common and more learned readers (*DAP*, I, 8–9). While the poet should operate according to the universalizing poetic rules set out by Aristotle, he is also accorded some creative autonomy, or 'la licenza del fingere' [licence to invent] (I, 12), which distinguishes him from the historian who is to represent the truth (II, 21–22).[98] Even as Tasso was having his epic scrutinized by revisers in Rome, he continued to insist (citing the authority of Aristotle) that poetry is not concerned with theological or ontological truth, but only with what is 'probable' or apparently true (verisimilar), as sanctioned by opinion.[99] Furthermore, Tasso argued in his *DAP* (I, 10) that the poet is obliged to serve a didactic function (political or moral) only insofar as he is a member of a civic society and subject to its laws.

This hedonistic view of poetry as being principally for pleasure and not instruction was undoubtedly influenced by the theories of Speroni, with whom we have noted the poet had contacts in his youth and was later accused of plagiarizing.[100] Lodovico Castelvetro's similar position in his *Poetics* (published 1570) also attracted Tasso's attention.[101] However, as will be discussed in more detail in chapter 5, such a view was becoming polemical around this time. Tellingly, Tasso's more radical opinions in the *DAP* (published 1587) are modified in his expanded and amended *Discorsi del poema eroico* (published 1594). This was composed while Tasso was reworking his *Gerusalemme liberata*, which later appeared as the *Gerusalemme conquistata* (1593). This time, the poet argues that pleasure should be subordinated to 'giovamento' [instruction], which is determined by the higher art of politics (I, 498). He does not discount the necessity of pleasure as an end, when it is morally useful (500), though the poet's end is considered now not as being to represent 'dilettosa verosimiglianza' [delightful verisimilitude], but rather 'il vero meraviglioso' [marvellous truth].[102]

Already by 1575, Tasso was concerned with making the published poem more morally acceptable also by composing an accompanying allegory, following a still popular medieval practice, as witnessed by various recent moralizations of Ovid, Boccaccio's *Decameron* and Ariosto's *Furioso*.[103] Although Tasso expresses some doubts about allegories not being sanctioned by Aristotle's authority, he recognizes that they are expedient for making the 'marvellous' episodes and other problematic parts acceptable in religious terms (*Lettere*, I, 48, 114), so that they conform outwardly with the 'temper of the times' (*Lettere*, I, 79, 187 (June 1576)). As he notes cynically to his friend Luca Scalabrino around this time, he only composed this 'caprice'

> per dare pasto al mondo. Farò il collo torto, e mostrerò ch'io non ho avuto altro fine che di servire al politico; e con questo scudo cercherò d'assicurare ben bene gli amori e gl'incanti. (*Lettere*, I, 76, 179 (n.d.))

> [to satisfy the world. I will be a pious hypocrite and show that I have had no end in mind except to serve a political function; and with this shield I shall try to protect completely the episodes of love and enchantment.]

Tasso was now prepared publicly to revoke his earlier stance on the poet's autonomy by having his allegory printed before his poem with a letter declaring the poet's political role.

Pastoral transformations in the Gerusalemme liberata

Comparison between the play and the epic poem is bound to be problematic given the different purposes and audiences for which they were intended, and their very different generic conventions. After all, the *Gerusalemme* was destined from the start for publication for a broad reading audience, and composed in a predominantly high style or 'stile eroico' (*DAP*, III, 48). This reflects the genre's serious purpose and religious, historical subject matter (the eleventh-century crusade to liberate the Holy Land). By contrast, the *Aminta* appears a more lightweight form of entertainment, as a work of pastoral fiction still of uncertain poetic status. It seems to have been conceived for an intimate elite performance rather than for public dissemination, which would explain its potentially subversive elements and style that combines the simplicity of tragedy with a pleasing lyric quality.[104] Even so, certain key issues left tantalizingly open in *Aminta* seem to be taken up and polemically recast in the epic, thus inviting comparative reading.

In particular, both works question the concepts of pleasure and love, human 'nature' and instinct, and artifice as opposed to 'naturalness', though the epic at least superficially seems to resolve the play's ambiguities in accordance with moralizing Christian principles. Love in the poem is explicitly associated from the start with 'artful', false appearances and deviance, represented in moral, spiritual, and poetic terms, and it lacks the providential function it had in *Aminta*. The intrinsic weakness of the Christian heroes Tancredi and Rinaldo, which puts at risk the Christian crusade against Jerusalem, stems almost entirely from their unruly passions, not properly controlled by reason and dedication to the true cause.[105] Pagans are subject to the same folly: the princess Erminia is condemned by the narrator for deciding to pursue the illusory hopes of Amore, rather than observing Onore's prudent counsel to safeguard her chastity (VI. 78. 1–2). Even so some ambivalence about its role in the poem is suggested in her *psychomachia*, where Love presents a longer and more complex persuasive speech than Honour.

The pagan temptress and magician, Armida, in particular embodies the dangerous attraction of love and the arts, since by ably manipulating appearances, words and actions to seduce her audience, she almost succeeds in undermining the Christian cause. Her perversion of the impulse for *virtù* is represented most potently in her enslavement and effeminizing of the principal Christian warrior, Rinaldo, through love in Cantos XIV-XVI. This forms the most famous of the pastoral episodes in the epic, and in many ways seems to challenge the subtle and witty blend of nature and art in *Aminta*, by associating the mode with 'error' and deviation from Christian duty. The seduction of Rinaldo away from his cause notably begins with his invitation to go alone to an 'isoletta' [little island] in the middle of the river Oronte (XIV. 57), a place that recalls the scene of Silvia's narcissism in *Aminta* (II. 2. 36). In the epic this 'isoletta' has all the typical ingredients of the pastoral stage-set — a gurgling stream, flowers, grasses and caves (XIV. 59–60), as well as a naked 'donzella' [maiden] emerging sensuously from the water, who is described in explicitly theatrical terms:[106]

> Così dal palco di notturna scena
> o ninfa o dea, tarda sorgendo, appare.
> Questa, benché non sia vera Sirena
> ma sia magica larva, una ben pare
> di quelle che già presso a la tirrena
> piaggia abitàr l'insidioso mare. (*Gerusalemme*, XIV. 61. 1–6)[107]

[Just as, from the set of a night-time stage, a nymph or goddess slowly rises up, this figure appears. Though she is no true siren but a magic apparition, she truly seems like one of those creatures who, by the Tyrrhenian shores, used to haunt the treacherous seas.]

Rinaldo, already charmed and literally disarmed by the beauty of the surrounding nature, is serenaded by this artful creation of Armida's. The siren promotes the ethic of living for pleasure alone in one's youth, according to the dictates of nature: 'Solo chi segue ciò che piace è saggio' [Only those who follow what is pleasurable are wise] (XIV. 62. 5). In terms that even more explicitly echo the wording of the Golden Age chorus of *Aminta*, she also condemns worldly fame and honour as a vain shadow: 'Nome, e senza soggetto idoli' [Just a name, and idols without substance] (XIV. 63. 3).[108] Finally, Rinaldo's senses are taken over by this song and he falls asleep in a 'queta imagine di morte' [still image of death] (XIV. 65. 6), perhaps recalling the closing line of the *Aminta* chorus, where the listener is enjoined to love now since ''l sonno eterna notte adduce' [sleep points to our eternal night].

Compared to *Aminta*, there is a strong attempt to control the sensual pastoral in the epic, though this does not seem to be consistently achieved. For instance, the siren's song is recounted by the authoritative and censorious Mago d'Ascalona, a sage or natural magician and convert to Christianity, who is said in the *Allegory* to stand for natural reason, as a counterpart to theology represented by Peter the Hermit. The Mago concludes his description with the comment: 'Sì canta l'empia' [Thus sings the wicked creature] (XIV. 65.1). However, his remark is notably confined to the frame of the siren's song, which is not otherwise mediated. Armida, the creator of this scene, is also seen to be unexpectedly seduced by it, so that her original desire for revenge on Rinaldo is turned to amorous desire. This perhaps symbolizes the poet's own susceptibility to the pagan charm of his creation.

The enchantress now jealously removes Rinaldo to another 'isoletta' (XIV. 69. 8) on top of a remote, rugged mountain amongst the 'Fortunate Isles' ('isole Felici'). Here she conjures up a pseudo-natural golden age realm of the senses, with a perpetual spring climate, abundant nature, and the possibility of sensual fulfilment. What in *Aminta* was a nostalgic, unrecoverable ideal of the past is thus actualized through 'art' in the present of the epic. But it carries with it a polemical moral and religious charge. Again the reader (like the Christian soldiers Carlo and Ubaldo listening to the Mago) is prepared to distrust the pleasant appearances and false inhabitants, by being instructed about Rinaldo's succumbing to temptation. As the warriors journey subsequently towards the Fortunate Islands, they are given a further warning by their guide (Fortune). These islands were given this name by the 'prisca etate' [earliest age] (XV. 35. 4) because of their natural fertility and delights: 'ma pur molto di falso al ver s'aggiunge' [but, even so, much falseness is mixed with the truth] (XV. 37. 6).

When Carlo and Ubaldo see these things for themselves they, like the reader, are supposed to have internalized the Christian taboo on sensuality and pleasure. In fact, they do not allow themselves to respond to the calls of the surrounding pastoral context and its inhabitants to follow nature and abandon thoughts of fame and honour.[109] They rigidly suppress their desire for food and drink, beauty, and love (XVI. 17), as offered by one of the two semi-naked maidens they see, who for the first time explicitly likens the place to the Golden Age world:

> Questo è il porto del mondo; e qui è il ristoro
> de le sue noie, e quel piacer si sente
> che già sentì ne' secoli de l'oro
> l'antica e senza fren libera gente. (XV. 63. 1–4)

[This is the harbour of the world; here you may assuage its sorrows and feel that pleasure that the ancient peoples, unfettered by restraints, felt in the age of gold.]

The warriors' voyeurism (shared by the reader), however, suggests that they do not fully succeed in their struggle against these 'diaboliche tentazioni' [diabolical temptations] as they are termed in the *Allegoria* (fol. a5ʳ). It even raises criticism of the 'unnaturalness' of this restraint (XV. 65).[110] The scene in this way contrasts negatively, but somewhat ambiguously, with Dafne's attempt to persuade Silvia to give in to nature's course and abandon her rigid shame and enjoy love before her youth passes (*Aminta*, I. 1).

Various echoes from *Aminta* may therefore be sensed in the magically created pastoral of the epic, though they acquire a stronger sense of sensuality, artificiality and decadence in the poem, especially within the enclosed garden of Armida's palace. Here, the ideal of eternal spring and freedom from duties (*ozio*) is associated with Rinaldo's lascivious, vain lifestyle and neglected Christian obligations. The *carpe diem* motif is proposed by a parrot, a bird that counterfeits the human voice, and its closing call to love (XVI. 15) recalls both the *commiato* of the Golden Age chorus and Dafne's message to Silvia. The description of the animals and plants responding to this sentiment and enjoying love (XVI. 16. 4) also directly recalls Dafne's speech (I. 1. 131). But the whole scene in the epic is described in a style that is, like the garden itself, hyperbolic and self-consciously fictional, filled with a super-abundance of lyric *concetti*. This episode is therefore meant to show a debased pagan ideal of life dedicated to love and nature in contrast with Christian values. On a poetic level, this struggle could also be representative of tension between ancient/pagan and romance traditions, and the modern Christian epic. This, Chiodo argues, may even suggest that the poetic focus of the work is found less in the conquest of Jerusalem than in Armida's enchanted garden.[111]

The 'artificial' pastoral is represented as dangerous precisely because of its seduction through the subtle and almost indistinguishable blending of art and nature. It paradoxically appears that nature is contriving to imitate art in Armida's garden:

> Stimi (sì misto il culto è co 'l negletto)
> sol naturali e gli ornamenti e i siti.
> Di natura arte par, che per diletto
> l'imitatrice sua scherzando imiti. (*Gerusalemme*, XVI. 10. 1–4)

[You would think (since the polished and the uncultivated seem so mingled) that both the ornaments and places were all natural. It appears an artifice of nature, which for pleasure playfully imitates art, its imitator.]

By contrast, true 'nature' is generally inhospitable and wild, as in the dense and frightening forest of Saron (VII. 23. 3; XIII. 2–4) or the dry plains of the battlefield. The lonely dwelling of a shepherd and his family at least provides a more pleasant pastoral setting, complete with trees, flowers and river (VII. 5). Yet, its humility and poverty make it an example of 'hard' pastoral. The shepherd family here needs to work to survive, by tending their flocks and weaving baskets. By contrast to Armida's garden, nature is not abundant here, but it is free from erotic desire and excess. The shepherds sing in a humble style with: 'un chiaro suono [...]/ che sembra ed è di pastorali accenti/ misto e di boscareccie inculte avene' [a clear sound [...] that seems, and is, a mixture of pastoral voices and of rustic oaten reeds] (VII. 6. 2–4). In this remote pastoral space, appearances do not belie reality.

It is in this context that the pagan princess Erminia arrives and takes refuge after fleeing the Christian camp, where she had searched for her beloved Tancredi — an episode that remained extremely popular despite being removed by Tasso in his *Conquistata*.[112] The pastoral setting thus functions here as an opposite pole to the war that is raging beyond. It also contrasts with the court, which is marked by ambition and avarice. This is indicted by an elderly shepherd, himself an erstwhile courtier seduced by the illusory promises of the 'inique corti' [wicked courts] (VII. 12. 8). Seeking solace for her impossible love, Erminia takes up a simple shepherd's lifestyle and coarse dress, though this cannot disguise her inherently noble manners. As with Castiglione's imagined knight in pastoral disguise,

> Non copre abito vil la nobil luce
> e quanto è in lei d'altero e di gentile,
> e fuor la maestà regia traluce
> per gli atti ancor de l'essercizio umile. (VII. 18. 1–4)

[Her humble garb does not conceal her noble beauty, nor her proud and courteous qualities, and her royal dignity shines forth even when at her lowly tasks.]

The pastoral mode in the epic thus appears inseparable from the world of the court, as in *Aminta*, where contradictory views about it and its values are presented by Tirsi, the satyr and in the later added Mopso episode. The mode is used in both works to project varyingly critical, celebratory and illusory perspectives. Otherwise, *Aminta* in many ways appears to allow a freer treatment of more risqué themes of pastoral regarding human liberty, sensuality and pagan antiquity, since it lacks the framing Christian perspective and public dimension of the epic. Different views are allowed to conflict openly in the play without the control of a narrator or single authoritative speaker.[113] However, after *Aminta*, writers of pastoral drama seem to have been less willing or able to follow this model. Their plays reflect a greater concern with the moral, religious and in some cases poetic preoccupations that Tasso was forced to confront in his *Gerusalemme*.

Notes to Chapter 3

1. Giulio Cesare Cortese, *Viaggio di Parnaso, poema* (Naples: Novello de Bonis, 1666), V, 15, p. 54; quoted in Vittorio Rossi, *Battista Guarini ed il 'Pastor fido'. Studio biografico-critico con documenti inediti* (Turin: Loescher, 1886), p. 251. This farcical verse in Neapolitan dialect probably refers to Guarini's *Pastor fido* (1589/90), Bonarelli's *Filli di Sciro* (1607) and perhaps Ridolfo Campeggi's *Filarmindo* (1605), besides *Aminta*.
2. Suggested dramatic sources for *Aminta* include: Beccari's broadly comic *Sacrificio* (Guarini, *Compendio*, p. 273); Sperone Speroni's mythological tragedy, *Canace*, composed 1542, printed 1546, which similarly uses mixed 7- and 11-syllable verse and does not stage a meeting between the protagonists (see Ingegneri, *Della poesia*, p. 4; Guarini, letter to Speroni, 10 July 1585, in *Opere*, ed. by Guglielminetti, p. 109); Giraldi's satyr play *Egle* (Carrara, pp. 334–37); also ancient tragedy, notably Euripides' *Hippolytus* and Seneca's *Phaedra* (Arnaldo Di Benedetto, 'L'*Aminta* e la Pastorale Cinquecentesca in Italia', *GSLI*, 173 (1996), 481–514 (p. 498)). For further classical and contemporary pastoral, lyric and romance sources, including Tasso's own *oeuvre*, see Hermann Grosser, '*Aminta*: lo stile della pastorale', in *Il merito e la cortesia. Torquato Tasso e la Corte dei Della Rovere*, ed. by Guido Arbizzoni and others (Ancona: Il lavoro editorial/Cassa di Risparmio di Pesaro, 1999), pp. 237–71 (pp. 237–38).
3. This approach is partly suggested by Bruscagli, in 'L'*Aminta*', pp. 279–82.
4. For spectacles preceding *Aminta*, see Solerti and Lanza, pp. 154–64.
5. Tasso's monthly salary is listed in the *libro di bollette* as 58 lire, 10 soldi (unchanged until his imprisonment in 1579); he also had an honorarium of just over 110 lire per month, see *Le Lettere di Torquato Tasso, disposte per ordine di tempo*, ed. by Cesare Guasti, 5 vols (Naples: Gabriele Rondinella, 1857), I, 24; Giosué Carducci, 'Su l'*Aminta* e il *Torrismondo*. Saggi di Giosué Carducci', in Angelo Solerti, *Torquato Tasso, Operi minori in versi*, 3 vols (Bologna: Zanichelli, 1895), III, iii-xli (p. x). By comparison, during the period 1574–82 the *maestro di cappella*, Ippolito Fiorino, earned 21 lire a month (Anthony Newcomb, *The Madrigal at Ferrara 1579–1597* (Princeton: Princeton University Press, 1980), Appendix I, pp. 155–90).
6. All references to *Aminta* from the edition by Marco Ariani, in *Il teatro italiano*, II: *La tragedia del Cinquecento* (Turin: Einaudi, 1977), II, 641–72; line numbering restarts each scene and chorus. On Tasso's attitude to the court and that of intellectuals generally, see Giovanni Da Pozzo, *L'Ambigua armonia. Studio sull'*Aminta *del Tasso* (Florence: Olschki, 1983), pp. 73–75. For an alternative reading of *Aminta* in the light of Tasso's diplomatic function at court, see Elisabetta Graziosi, *Aminta 1573–1580. Amore e matrimonio in casa d'Este* (Pisa: Maria Pacini Fazzi, 2001).
7. Compare for example Tasso's letter of complaint about his idle existence to the Duke of Urbino, n.d. [1578] (*Lettere*, I, 109, 273), with the later nostalgic mention to Scipione Gonzaga of his previous life of literary ease at court (n. d. [February/March 1587?]), *Lettere*, III, 770, 157). All references to Tasso's *Lettere* are, unless otherwise stated, from Guasti's edition (see n. 5), and give volume, letter number and page number.
8. Solerti and Lanza, pp. 154–56.
9. Relations with the papacy worsened with the promulgation of a Papal bull in 1567 to the potential disadvantage of the still childless Alfonso II d'Este, since it prohibited succession in ecclesiastical feuds of illegitimate heirs or distant relations. Pius V may thus have seen a way to regaining the papal feud of Ferrara, having heard rumours of Alfonso's impotence (Paul Larivaille, *Poesia e ideologia. Letture della 'Gerusalemme Liberata'* (Naples: Liguori, 1987), pp. 14–16).
10. On this *torneo*, see Margaret McGowan, 'Adventure and theatrical innovation at Ferrara and Mannheim', in *The Renaissance in Ferrara and its European Horizons*, ed. by J. Salmons (Cardiff: University of Wales Press, 1984), pp. 61–81 (pp. 66–70); Alessandro Marcigliano, 'Cavallerie', pp. 81–83.
11. Torquato Tasso, *Il Gianluca, overo delle maschere*, in *Dialoghi*, ed. by Ezio Raimondi, 3 vols (Florence: Sansoni, 1958), II/2, 671–82 (p. 675).
12. The date, proposed by Angelo Solerti (*Vita di Torquato Tasso*, 2 vols (Turin: Loescher, 1895), I, 181–85), based on indirect, circumstantial evidence, has been repeated so much in subsequent criticism that it has almost become accepted as fact. Though for the hypothesis of a first performance given 23 March 1573, following Pierantonio Serassi (*La Vita di Torquato Tasso*, 2 vols, ed. by Cesare Guasti

(Florence: Barbèra, Bianchi, 1858), I, 237–39), also based on circumstantial evidence, see Grazioso, especially pp. 44–45, 49–50 (n. 89 for other doubtful critics). Tasso may have met the Gelosi in France while serving Cardinal Luigi d'Este there in 1571. On his staging of a series of *intermezzi* for a comedy by his father (Bernardo Tasso) in Sassuolo, 1568, see Solerti, *Vita*, I, 124–25, II, no. 39, 97; Marcigliano, 'Verato', p. 89.

13. See Solerti, *Ferrara*, pp. CLXI-CLXXIII. Tremors continued to occur until 1579 (Da Pozzo, pp. 66–69).
14. Godard 'Première Représentation', p. 208. Duchess Barbara of Austria died Sept. 1572, Cardinal Ippolito d'Este in Dec. 1572 and Laura Eustochia Dianti (mistress and perhaps wife of Alfonso I d'Este), in June 1573. During the period of mourning for the Duchess only one tragedy was performed by university students (April 1573). No *comici* performed in Ferrara in 1571 (Solerti and Lanza, p. 159); in February 1572 the Florentine ambassador, Bernardo Canigiani wrote to the Granduca that the *comici* performed less frequently and less appealingly than usual, because of the deaths and earthquakes, while he noted later that Carnival ended without any entertainments at all (Florence, Archivio di Stato [henceforth ASF], Archivio Mediceo, filza 2893, letters from 8 and 23 Feb. 1572).
15. Anton Francesco Trotti, 'Le delizie di Belvedere Illustrate. Raccolta di documenti editi ed inediti', *Atti della Deputazione Ferrarese di Storia Patria*, 2 (1889), 3–32; for Belvedere's political significance in relation to *Aminta*, see James J. Yoch, 'Renaissance Gardening and Pastoral Scenery in Italy and England', *Research Opportunities in Renaissance Drama*, 20 (1977), 35–43 (pp. 37–38).
16. M. A. Guarini, *Compendio historico dell'origine, accrescimento, e prerogative delle Chiese [...] di Ferrara* [1621], cited in Trotti, p. 9 (on S. Giacopo). The gardens did not survive long after the city's devolution to the papacy in 1598.
17. Antonio Montecatini had previously publicly defended 1090 philosophical theses; Tasso's *Conclusioni* may also have been influenced by Flaminio de' Nobili's *Trattato dell'amore umano* [*Treatise on human love*] (1567) (Solerti, *Vita*, I, 128–32; Aldo Manetti, 'Le Conclusioni amorose', *Studi tassiani*, 24 (1974), 33–45). Later discourses to deal with love by Ferrarese intellectuals include those of Francesco Patrizi (*L'amorosa filosofia*, 1577), Annibale Romei (*Discorsi*, 1585), and Guidubaldo Bonarelli (see Chapter 7).
18. See Godard, 'Première Représentation', pp. 226–51; also Louise George Clubb, 'The Pastoral Play: Conflations of Country, Court and City', in Panizza Lorch, pp. 65–73 (p. 69). On Lucrezia Bendidio, the lady-in-waiting of Leonora d'Este (addressed as 'Licori' in a Latin epigram by Pigna) and the commentary on Pigna's elite manuscript edition of *Ben divino* (1572) by the young court poets Tasso and Guarini, see Grazioso, pp. 34–36.
19. Daniela Quarta, 'Spazio scenico, spazio cortigiano, spazio cortese. L'*Aminta* e il *Torrismondo* di Torquato Tasso', in Pade, Petersen, and Quarta, pp. 301–27 (pp. 308, 313).
20. Antonio La Penna, 'Note all'"Aminta" del Tasso', in *Omaggio a Gianfranco Folena*, ed. by Pier Vincenzo Mengaldo and others, 3 vols (Padua: Programma, 1993), II, 1171–82 (pp. 1176–80).
21. For the Puttenham citation (from *The Arte of Poesie*, 1589), see *The Pastoral Mode: A Casebook*, ed. by Bryan Loughrey (London: Macmillan, 1984), p. 34.
22. See Emilio Bigi, *Poesia Latina e Volgare nel Rinascimento italiano* (Naples: Morano, 1989), pp. 319–21, 338. On Tasso's dialogue *Malpiglio* as a reworking and subversion of Castiglione's *Cortegiano*, see Virginia Cox, 'Tasso's *Malpiglio overo de la corte*: The Courtier Revisited', *MLR*, 90 (1995), 897–918.
23. Baldassarre Castiglione, *Il Cortegiano*, ed. by Ettore Bonora, 2nd edn (Milan: Mursia, 1976), II. 11, p. 116 (all references to this edition, giving book, chapter and page numbers). For Castiglione's formulations on *sprezzatura* and *grazia*, see I. 25–27, pp. 60–64. On how these values are linked to the pastoral setting, see Bigi, *Poesia latina*, p. 323.
24. *Il Gianluca*, in Tasso, *Dialoghi*, p. 681. Compare Sperone Speroni's changing views on the decorum of the writer and the proper subjects of imitation, in his *Apologia dei dialoghi*, in *Opere [...] tratte da' MSS. originali*, 5 vols (Venice: Domenico Occhi, 1740), I, 637–82 (pp. 267–68, 272–73, 330–31, 334–35). See also Andrews, *Scripts*, p. 214, and Cox, *Renaissance Dialogue*, pp. 70–77.
25. Cox, 'Tasso's *Malpiglio*', p. 911; see also the Tasso's later criticism of the court added to *Aminta* (the Mopso episode), p. 80 below.
26. Translations mine, though reference has been made in part to the recent verse translation with facing text: *Aminta: A Pastoral Play by Torquato Tasso*, ed. and trans. by Charles Jernigan and Irene

Marchegiani Jones (New York: Italica Press, 2000). On the characterization of Amore in the prologue as compared to the later added epilogue, see Nelia Saxby, 'Amore e Venere nell'*Aminta*', *Studi e problemi di critica testuale*, 36 (1988), 103–14.

27. For the Platonic implications of this association, see Angela Andrisano, 'Il Satiro dell'*Aminta*', in *Torquato Tasso e l'Università*, ed. by Walter Moretti and Luigi Pepe (Florence: Olschki, 1997), pp. 357–71 (p. 362–63 n. 20). On Amore as an 'agency of transformation', see Tylus, 'Purloined Passages', pp.111–12.
28. Virgil, *The Eclogues. The Georgics*, trans. by C. Day Lewis (Oxford: Oxford University Press, 1983), p. 18. On pastoral and style, see Cooper, *Pastoral*, pp. 127–33.
29. For a further subtle allusion to Tasso's 'natural' poetic activity, see *Aminta* I. 1. 227–31. See *Cortegiano*, I, 18 on the difficult art of self-praise. On the influence on Tasso of the artfully simple style of Castiglione's *Tirsi*, see Bigi, *Poesia latina*, pp. 325–38.
30. See Giuseppe Toffanin, *Il Tasso e l'età che fu la sua (L'età Classicistica)* (Naples: Libreria Scientifica n.d. [1945/6?]), pp. 41–43; Solerti, *Vita*, I, 40.
31. Torquato Tasso, *Discorsi dell'Arte Poetica, ed in particolare sopra il poema eroico* [1587], in *Scritti sull'arte poetica*, ed. by Ettore Mazzali (Turin: Einaudi, 1977), I, 3–64 (p. 18); all references to this edition. Speroni famously accused Tasso of plagiarizing his ideas in this treatise before it was published in a letter to Felice Pacciotto, 29 January 1581 (Speroni, *Opere*, V, 272). For an outline of Tasso's life 1560–65, see C. P. Brand, *Torquato Tasso. A Study of the Poet and of his Contribution to English Literature* (Cambridge: Cambridge University Press, 1965), pp. 9–11. See also Maria Teresa Girardi, 'Tasso, Speroni e la cultura padovana', in *Formazione e fortuna del Tasso nella cultura della Serenissima*, ed. by Luciana Borsetto and Bianca Maria da Rif (Venice: Istituto Veneto di Scienze, Lettere ed arti, 1997), pp. 63–77.
32. On the Eterei, see Maylender, II, 319–23; on their collected verse publication, Ginetta Auzzas, 'La "raccolta" delle "Rime de gli Academici Eterei"', in Borsetto and da Rif, eds, pp. 97–109. On Scipione Gonzaga, created a cardinal in 1587, d. 1593, see G. Benzoni's entry in *DBI*, 57 (2001), 842–54 (especially pp. 843–45, 849 [relations with Tasso], 852 [relations with Guarini]). Though focused more on Gonzaga's musical interests, see also Iain Fenlon, 'Scipione Gonzaga: A "Poor" Cardinal in Rome', in *Music and Culture in late Renaissance Italy* [first printed 1988] (Oxford: Oxford University Press, 2002), pp. 93–117 (pp. 98–100).
33. Tasso, *Lettere*, I, 13, 21. Notably, none of his works were to be published without the approval and revision of Scipione Gonzaga, Domenico Venier and Battista Guarini.
34. Javitch, 'Emergence', pp. 139–42, 147.
35. For discussions on Ariosto's *Orlando furioso* before Tasso's *Liberata* (1549–81), see Weinberg, *Literary Criticism*, II, 954–83.
36. 'Lettera a Bernardo Tasso sulla poesia epica' (7 October 1557), reprinted in, *Trattati di poetica e retorica del Cinquecento*, ed. by Bernard Weinberg, 4 vols (Bari: Laterza, 1970–74), II, 453–76. On Giraldi's treatise *Discorso intorno al comporre dei romanzi* (dated 1549), see Weinberg, *Literary Criticism*, I, 433–39. See also Javitch, 'Emergence', p. 164.
37. Maylender, II, 365. See also Vittorio Zaccaria, 'Le accademie padane cinquecentesche e il Tasso', in Borsetto and da Rif, eds, pp. 35–61 (p. 52).
38. *Aminta*, I. 1. 192; see also I. 2. 295–96; and III. 1. 135–42.
39. Paul Larivaille, 'Dall'Ariosto al Tasso. Poeta, principe, pubblico nel "Furioso" e nella "Liberata"', in *Studi in onore di Bortolo Tommaso Sozzi*, ed. by Aldo Agazzi (Bergamo: Centro di Studi Tassiani, 1991), pp. 169–82 (pp. 172–73).
40. See Margaret W. Ferguson, *Trials of Desire. Renaissance Defenses of Poetry* (New Haven: Yale University Press, 1983), p. 55 (for a psychoanalytical interpretation of the later critical debate).
41. Tasso's *DAP* was first published (unauthorized) in Venice 1587 by Giulio Vasalini (Solerti, *Vita*, I, p. 121). The three parts were read to the Accademia ferrarese some time before 1571, but were written earlier; either in Ferrara 1567–70 (Solerti) or, more likely, in 1564 (Serassi), during Tasso's second stay in Padua.
42. Letter to Bartolomeo di Porzia, nunzio in Germany, 13 November 1574, *Lettere*, I, 18, 47–48. The attribution of the comedy *Intrichi d'Amore* (first performed 1598) to Tasso in the first printed edition (1603) is still disputed.
43. For a rare comment on *Aminta*'s composition, see Tasso's sonnet to Antonio Vandali (12 July 1586): 'Ardite sì, ma pur felici carte/ vergai di vaghi pastorali amori,/ e fui cultor de' Greci antichi allori/

ne le rive del Po con novell'arte' [I traced daring but fortunate pages with delightful pastoral loves, and I cultivated ancient laurels of the Greeks on the banks of the Po with new art] (in Solerti, *Vita*, I, 185). For the view that this responds to Guarini's criticism that *Aminta* imitates Speroni's *Canace*, see Andrisano, 'Il Satiro', p. 360 n. 13.

44. Bruscagli, 'L'*Aminta*', pp. 279–80, 92. Note that Tasso ultimately entitles his play 'favola boscareccia' avoiding any mention of comedy or tragedy. Compare the reluctance by writers of nineteenth-century novels to refer to this non-classical genre in the title of their works (Gérard Genette, *Paratexts. Thresholds of interpretation*, trans. by Jane E. Lewin, foreword by Richard Macksey [1st published as *Seuils* (Paris: Editions du Seuil, 1987)] (Cambridge University Press, 1997), pp. 96–97).
45. *DAP*, I, 16 (see n. 31 above on the edition).
46. The issue of the appropriateness and dramatic effect of representing deaths on stage had been raised in the debate over Speroni's *Canace* (which avoids them) by Giraldi in his *Giudizio*, n.d. (published 1550), reproduced in *Sperone Speroni, Canace e Scritti in sua difesa. Giambattista Giraldi Cinzio, Scritti contro la Canace, Giudizio ed Epistola Latina*, ed. by Christina Roaf (Bologna: Commissione per i testi di lingua, 1982), pp. 97–182 (pp. 125–28). Giraldi had himself represented deaths for tragic effect in *Orbecche*.
47. *Aminta* only includes a passing reference to such mismatched loves (I. 1. 90–94), see Bruscagli, 'L'*Aminta*', pp. 287–93. For earlier plot structures, see chapter 2.
48. Tasso uses tragic theory (more fully developed than that on epic in Aristotle's *Poetics*) comparatively throughout his *Discorsi* to develop prescriptions for epic.
49. *Aminta* I. 1. 70 and III. 2. 71 respectively echo Speroni's *Canace*, IV, II. 244 and IV. I. 10. See Da Pozzo, p. 208, though he describes the comparison between the two plays as 'absurd'.
50. Claudio Scarpati, 'Il nucleo ovidiano dell'*Aminta*', in *Tasso, i classici e i moderni* (Padua: Antenore, 1995), pp. 75–104 (pp. 75–78); also La Penna, pp. 1171–74. On the interference of non-tragic elements in *Aminta*, see Quarta, p. 311. On thematic borrowings from ancient Greek romances (Achilles Tatius, *Leucippe and Clitophon* and Longus, *Daphnis and Chloe*), see Graziosi, pp. 139–44, 148.
51. On Dafne's correspondence with the 'theatergram' [transferable type] of the *balia*, see Clubb, *Italian Drama*, p. 15.
52. See Douglas Radcliff-Umstead, 'Structures of Conflict in Tasso's Pastoral of Love', in *Studi tassiani*, 22 (1972), 69–83 (pp. 78–79); and his 'Love in Tasso's *Aminta*: A Reflection of the Este court', in Panizza Lorch, pp. 75–84 198 (pp. 80–81). For conflicting views on the primitive age, see chapter 5. Compare also Castiglione's ambiguous exploration of the *topos* of decline over time in *Cortegiano*, II. 1–3.
53. See also Tirsi's assurance to Aminta that Mopso's prediction of his cruel fate is, paradoxically, a guarantee of a 'felice fine' [happy conclusion] (I. 2. 225).
54. Similarly, the satyr's reference to female 'armi' [arms] of beauty (II. 1. 76), followed by his sexual threat to dip his 'arms' into her blood (II. 1, 97), is echoed by Dafne's mention 10 lines later of Silvia's 'armi' (II. 2, 10). Compare the polemical question of the legitimacy of rape posed by Gaspar Pallavicino in *Cortegiano*, II. 94–95 (especially pp. 201–02). On the idea of rape as underpinning 'civilization', see Tylus, 'Colonizing Peasants'; also, in relation to mythological *cassoni* paintings, see Susanne L. Wofford, 'The social aesthetics of rape: closural violence in Boccaccio and Botticelli', in *Creative Imitation. New Essays in honour of Thomas M. Greene*, ed. by David Quint and others (New York: Binghamton, 1992), pp. 189–238.
55. Bruscagli, 'L'*Aminta*', pp. 313–15. On the accommodation of tragedic experience in the pastoral, see Henke, *Pastoral Transformations*, pp. 88–92.
56. See Quarta, p. 309.
57. Riccardo Scrivano, 'Tasso e il teatro', in *La norma e lo scarto. Proposte per il cinquecento letterario italiano* (Rome: Bonacci, 1980), pp. 209–48 (pp. 237, 240).
58. For a reading of Elpino's role in connection with Pigna's interpretative function in the Ferrarese *tornei*, see Godard, 'Première Représentation', pp. 273, 279–80.
59. Scarpati, 'Il nucleo ovidiano', p. 80. See also Radcliff-Umstead's useful concepts of 'pastoral of self' and 'pastoral of love' ('Love in Tasso's *Aminta*', pp. 76–78).
60. Quarta, pp. 310–11; Di Benedetto, p. 500.
61. On Tasso's dialogue structure and the general transition to a 'closed' kind in response to Counter-Reformation scruples, see Cox, *Renaissance Dialogue*, pp. 66, 68, 93–96). On the 'open' form, see also Speroni, *Apologia*, I, 275–85.

62. See Harry Levin, *The Myth of the Golden Age in the Renaissance* (London: Faber and Faber, 1969) and Gustavo Costa, *La leggenda dei secoli d'oro nella letteratura italiana* (Bari: Laterza, 1972). For the use of the Golden Age *topos* to praise the courtly audience and the Duke of Ferrara, see Lollio's *Aretusa*, Prologue, 1–16; for its more critical use, to reprehend the ambition and envy of the courts, see Argenti, *Sfortunato*, Prologue, 22–47. See also Chapter 5 for this *topos* in Guarini's *Pastor fido*.
63. See Claudio Scarpati, 'Il nucleo ovidiano', pp. 87–88. On the influence of Tibullus, Ovid and Virgil, see Domenico Chiodo, 'Il mito dell'età aurea nell'opera tassiana', *Studi tassiani*, 35 (1987), 31–58 (pp. 31–37); also Costa, pp. 64–70, 96–98.
64. Tasso and Guarini used similarly sensual conceits in a pastoral context in their popular madrigals, see Tim Carter, *Music in Late Renaissance and Early Baroque Italy* (London: Batsford, 1992), pp. 126–30.
65. Chiodo, 'Il mito', p. 47. For the reception of Epicurean ethics in the Renaissance, see Jill Kraye, 'Moral Philosophy', in *The Cambridge History of Renaissance Philosophy,* ed. by Charles Schmitt and others (Cambridge: Cambridge University Press, 1988), pp. 303–86 (pp. 374–86); also, focused especially on the reception of Valla's *De Voluptas* and courtly views on Epicureanism, Stephen Kolsky, 'Theorizing Pleasure in the Renaissance', *Spunti e ricerche*, 4–5 (1988/9), 33–49.
66. Scarpati, 'Il nucleo ovidiano', p. 92; though compare Grazioso's reading of the golden age *topos* in *Aminta* as an indirect eulogy of Alfonso's rule (pp. 61–63, 65–71).
67. Compare Guarini's treatment of this dictum, chapter 5, p. 152.
68. See Ornella Garraffo, 'Il satiro nella pastorale ferrarese del Cinquecento', *Italianistica*, 14 (1985), 185–201, Bruscagli 'L'*Aminta*', pp. 300–01, Scarpati, 'Il nucleo ovidiano', pp. 80–81 (for the satyr's asymmetry within the Ovidian nucleus), and Andrisano, p. 361 (on the satyr's key structural function and fundamental ambiguity).
69. For the link between satyrs and satire, see Giraldi Cinzio, *Lettera*, in *Scritti critici*, pp. 228, 230; and the *Annotazioni* to Battista Guarini, *Il Pastor Fido* (Venice: Giovanni Battista Ciotti, 1602), fol. 46^v.
70. For example Silenus in Euripides' *Cyclops*, Corydon in Virgil's Eclogue II; also Poliziano's Polyphemus in *Stanze*, I, 115–17, and Pan in Giraldi's *Egle*, IV. 2. Note also the rich tradition of sophisticated, mock-rustic verse parodying the Petrarchan love lyric, as explored by Lorenzo de' Medici (see for example *Nencia da Barberino*) and others in his circle.
71. See the descriptions of beautiful gifts in Beccari's *Sacrificio*, III. 2, and Lollio's *Aretusa*, III. 4; gifts in Argenti's *Sfortunato* are however natural objects. Compare the Prologue to Sannazaro's *Arcadia*, which explicitly prefers rugged nature and style to the cultivated kind, though this position is not consistently maintained in practice.
72. Lorenzo Carpané, *Edizioni a stampa di Torquato Tasso 1561–1994. Catalogo breve*, 2 vols (Bergamo: Centro di Studi Tassiani, 1998), I, 125–232; and 'La fortuna editoriale tassiana dal '500 ai giorni nostri', *Italianistica*, 25 (1995), 541–57 (pp. 546–47). The French translation was by Pierre De Brach (*Aminte, fable bocagère*), dedicated to Marguerite de Navarre; it was adapted into English by Abraham Fraunce in 1591. On the fortunes of *Aminta* in France, see Daniela Dalla Valle 'Il Mito dell'età dell'oro e la concezione dall'amore dell'*Aminta* alla pastorale barocca francese', in *La frattura. Studi sul barocco letterario francese* (Ravenna: Longo, 1970), pp. 21–84. For early performances of *Aminta*, see Chapter 6.
73. For details of manuscript editions of *Aminta*, see Angelo Solerti, *Torquato Tasso, Opere minori in versi*, 3 vols (Bologna: Zanichelli, 1895), III, XCI–XCIII.
74. Tasso's early biographer, G. B. Manso, notes that the play's brevity was designed to suit the tastes of Duke Alfonso, see his *Vita di Torquato Tasso*, ed. by Bruno Basile (Rome: Salerno, 1995), p. 39.
75. See Tasso, *Lettere*, I, 116–20, pp. 288–90 (February 1579: hoping initially for reconciliation), and I, 123, pp. 299–332 (n.d., Holy Week 1579; after the rupture); also Chiappini, *Gli Estensi*, p. 303. Tasso's treatment in prison became more lenient over time.
76. Letter by Tiberio Almerici, 28 February 1574, cited in A. Saviotti, 'Torquato Tasso e le feste pesaresi del 1574', *GSLI*, 12 (1888), 404–17 (p. 413). See Chapter 6.
77. Solerti *Vita*, I, 345–46.
78. On the stigma attached to print, see Cox, *Renaissance Dialogue*, pp. 42–44; and Brian Richardson, *Printing, Writers and Readers in Renaissance Italy* (Cambridge: Cambridge University Press, 1999), pp. 79–80.
79. See Tasso's letters to Scipione Gonzaga of 20 July 1575 and 1 Oct. 1575 (*Lettere*, I, 41, 101, and 47, 111). The latter notes his need to publish soon to 'uscire di miseria e d'agonia' [escape from wretchedness

and agony], though anxiety about its success made him want to delay. On the financial rewards expected from its publication, see *Lettere*, I, 22, 57 [31 March 1575]; see also I, 59, 137 (24 March 1576).

80. See Richardson, *Printing*, pp. 98–99; also the same author's *Print Culture in Renaissance Italy. The editor and the vernacular text, 1470–1600* (Cambridge: Cambridge University Press, 1994), pp. 13–14. On Tasso's difficulties in getting the *Gerusalemme* printed in 1576, for reasons of censorship, privileges and external factors, and its unauthorized publication, see Solerti, *Vita*, I, 219–21, 250.
81. ASF, AM, filza 2901, 16 August 1583 (also in Solerti, *Vita*, I, 367). See also Brand, pp. 24–26; and Solerti *Vita*, I, 332–50. Though for a helpful qualification of the romantic view of Tasso as victim of the press, see Mariella Magliani, 'Stampatori veneti del Tasso', in Borsetto and da Rif, pp. 121–39.
82. Angelo Ingegneri, 'A Gl'Intendenti lettori' (Parma, 1 Feb. 1581) in *Gerusalemme liberata del Sig. Torquato Tasso* (Casalmaggiore: Apresso Antonio Canacci, & Erasmo Viotti, 1581), fols †v^r–†vii^r (†vi^{r-v}). See Solerti, *Vita*, I, 328–33.
83. See Carter, *Music*, pp. 132–36.
84. Solerti *Vita*, I, 324, 344–45. For details, see Carpané, *Edizioni a stampa*, I, pp. 125–27. I have been unable to consult the apparently lost Draconi edition of *Aminta*, in Parma, Biblioteca Palatina (BPP) (Cons. Bened. 5261); or the one held in Bergamo, Biblioteca Civica.
85. Tasso to Manuzio, 3 Dec. 1580, in Solerti *Vita*, II, I, xxiii, 22. For relations between the two men (relating to the *Rime*), see Magliani, pp. 137–38.
86. Solerti, *Vita*, II, 24.
87. For biographical details on Baldini, see Alessandra Chiappini's entry in *Dizionario dei tipografi e degli editori italiani. Il Cinquecento*, ed. by Marco Menato, Ennio Sandal, and Giuseppina Zappella (Milan: Editrice Bibliografica, 1997), I, 57–62; also Giuseppina Zappella, *Le marche dei tipografi e degli editori italiani del Cinquecento. Repertorio di figure, simboli e soggetti e dei relativi motti*, 2 vols (Milan: Editrice Bibliografica, 1986), I, 346–47. See also Paul F. Grendler, *The Roman Inquisition and the Venetian Press, 1540–1605* (Princeton N.J.: Princeton University Press, 1977), pp. 3–24 (on Venetian printing); and Diego Cavallina, 'L'editoria ferrarese nei secoli XV e XVI' in *Il Rinascimento nelle corti padane. Società e cultura*, ed. by Paolo Rossi (Bari: De Donato, 1977), pp. 341–62.
88. Tasso, *Lettere*, I, 66, 160–61.
89. Bernardino Pino da Cagli, *Breve considerazione intorno al componimento de la comedia de' nostri tempi* (written 1572, published 1578). On comic theory in late sixteenth-century Italy, see Andrews, *Scripts*, pp. 211–16; and Nicola Mangini, 'Il teatro veneto al tempo della controriforma', in Brunello and Lodo, pp. 119–37 (p. 133). On publishing restrictions during the period of Trent, see Richardson, *Printing*, pp. 44–46.
90. Richardson, *Print Culture*, p. 148. Compare the moralization of Ovid's *Metamorphoses* in the 1580s, see James J. Yoch, 'The Renaissance Dramatization of Temperance: The Italian Revival of Tragicomedy and *The Faithful Shepherdess*', in *Renaissance Tragicomedy. Explorations in Genre and Politics*, ed. by Nancy Klein Maguire (New York: AMS Press), pp. 114–38 (pp. 122–23).
91. Tasso to Scipione Gonzaga, 14 April 1575, *Lettere*, I, 25, 65.
92. *Lettere*, I, 47, 111. See also Tasso to Scipione Gonzaga, I, 51, 121 (24 Jan. 1576).
93. On the problem of love in the *Liberata*, see Tasso's defence of Eustazio's hyperbolic address to Armida (IV. 35. 1), *Lettere*, I, 31, 76–77 (24 May 1575); on *maraviglia*, *Lettere*, I, 47, 111 (1 Oct. 1575). On the Inquisition's restriction of vernacular works on love, see Richardson, *Print Culture*, p. 150.
94. On the tradition of neo-classical temples in the pastoral stage-set, see Adriano Cavicchi, 'Imagini e forme dello spazio scenico nella pastorale ferrarese', in *Sviluppi della drammaturgia pastorale nell'Europa del Cinque-Seicento*, ed. by M. Chiabò and F. Doglio (Viterbo: Union Printing, [1992]), pp. 45–86 (p. 50). A neo-classical temple was used in Giambattista Aleotti's set for Beccari's *Sacrificio* (1587), and probably appeared in some performances of Guarini's *Pastor fido* (see also the engravings in the 1602 edition preceding the Prologue and Acts III and V, figs 5–7.
95. Bruscagli, 'L'*Aminta*', p. 306.
96. See, for example, Guarini's recommendation for a nymph to appear 'totally naked, apart from a fine, light green silk veil covering her private parts' in the first *intermezzo* of his *Pastor fido* (ed. by Ariani, p. 1053). The naked figure of the aged Saturn (covered discreetly by a mantle) required for the fourth *intermezzo* (p. 1056) should be considered more in the mythological, Platonic tradition. On the use of skin-coloured stocking in pastoral costumes, see chapter 6, p. 179. See also Richard Cody,

The Landscape of the Mind. Pastoralism and Platonic Theory in Tasso's Aminta *and Shakespeare's Early Comedies* (Oxford: Clarendon Press, 1969), p. 53.
97. *Lettere*, I, 60, 140 (30 March 1576).
98. On the limits to poetic licence, however, see *DAP*, II, 833. For Paolo Beni's similar argument for fictional autonomy as opposed to historical truth in the literary quarrel over Guarini's *Pastor fido*, see chapter 5, pp. 143–45. See also Weinberg, *Literary Criticism*, II, 1097–98.
99. Tasso, *Lettere*, I, 52, 124 [11 Feb. 1576]; and I, 46, 108 (17 Sept. 1575).
100. See pp. 68 and 93 n. 31; also chapter 5, pp. 135–37 (Speroni and hedonistic literature).
101. On the Modenese philosopher Castelvetro, who fled to Switzerland in 1561 after being condemned to death by the Inquisition, see the entry by V. Marchetti and G. Patrizi in *DBI*, 22 (1979), pp. 8–21. For Tasso's criticism of Castelvetro's daring interpretation and corrections to Aristotle's *Poetics*, see Baldassarri, 'Introduzione ai "Discorsi dell'arte poetica" del Tasso', *Studi Tassiani*, 26 (1977), 5–38 (p. 10).
102. All citations from Torquato Tasso, *Discorsi del poema eroico*, in *Prose*, ed. by Ettore Mazzali, with preface by F. Flora (Milan; Naples: Ricciardi, 1959). See also Mazzali's 'Introduzione', pp. xvii-xliv (pp. xxviii-xxx).
103. On allegory as a strategy of poetic legitimization, see Daniel Javitch, *Proclaiming a Classic. The Canonization of 'Orlando Furioso'* (Princeton N. J.: Princeton University Press, 1991), p. 6. For Tasso's view that allegory, though persuasive, is less authoritative than a poetic defence, see *Lettere*, I, 79, 188.
104. For Tasso's views on the lyric style (based on analysis of Petrarch and Ariosto), described as far more 'lascivious', 'flowery' and 'ornate' than the majestic, heroic style of the *Aeneid*, see *DAP*, pp. 49, 60–64.
105. This point is emphasized in the *Allegory*, see Torquato Tasso, *Il Goffredo, overo Gierusalemme Liberata …Con l'Allegoria universale dell'istesso & gli Argomenti del Sig. Horatio [Orazio] Ariosti* (Venice: Presso Gio. Battista Combi, 1576), fol. a5^r.
106. See Scrivano, pp. 212–23.
107. All citations from Tasso, *Gerusalemme liberata*, ed. by Marziano Guglielminetti, 10th edn, 2 vols (Milan: Garzanti, 1996). Translations mine, though I have consulted the translation by Edward Fairfax of 1600 (Torquato Tasso, *Jerusalem Delivered* (New York: Capricorn Books, n.d. [1963]).
108. Compare *Aminta*, Chorus I. 14–16: 'quel vano/ nome senza soggetto,/ quell'idolo d'errori, idol d'inganno' [that vain name without substance, that idol of errors and of deception].
109. Scarpati, 'Il nucleo ovidiano', pp. 90–91.
110. Chiodo, 'Il mito', pp. 50–51. The delights of the pastoral landscape, music and nymphs are described in the *Allegory* as 'i fallaci sillogismi, che ci mettono innanzi gli agi, e i diletti del senso, sotto apparenza di bene' [false syllogisms which present to us the ease and pleasures of the senses under the guise of goodness] (fol. a5^v).
111. Chiodo, 'Il mito', p. 49.
112. On the fortunes of Erminia in pastoral drama and other art forms, see chapter 7, n. 25.
113. Compare with the differences noted between dramatic dialogues and the more authorially controlled and censored narrated ones, in Cox, *Renaissance Dialogue*, pp. 73–76.

CHAPTER 4

Imitations and Innovations after Tasso's *Aminta*: Accommodating a Female Voice

In quelle allegrezze [...], alcuni furbacchiotti poeti ruppero lo scrigno più secreto del Tasso, ove egli conservava le gioie delle composizioni sue più stimate, e ne rubarono l'*Aminta*, la quale poi si divisero tra essi: ingiuria, che tanto trafisse l'anima del Tasso, che gl'inamarì tutte le sue passate dolcezze; e perchè gli autori di così brutto furto subito furono iscoperti e dagli sbirri fu data loro la caccia, essi, come in sicura franchigia, si ritirarono nella casa dell'Imitazione: onde dal bargello di espresso ordine di Apollo furono sùbito estratti e vergognosamente condotti prigioni. E perché ad uno di essi fu trovato addosso il prologo di essa pastorale, conforme ai termini della pratica sbirresca, subito fu torturato e interrogato *super aliis et complicibus*: onde il misero nella corda nominò quaranta poeti tagliaborse suoi compagni, tutta gente vilissima, e che, essendosi data al giuoco ed a tutti i piú brutti vizi, non ad altro mestiere piú attendono che a rubare i concetti delle altrui fatiche, facendo tempone, avendo in orrore il sudar ne' libri e stentar nei perpetui studi per gloriosamente vivere al mondo con le proprie fatiche.[1]

[During those festivities [...], some rascally poets broke open Tasso's most private safe in which he kept his most precious and valued compositions, and they stole the *Aminta* and divided it amongst themselves. This injurious act wounded Tasso so keenly that all his past pleasures were turned sour. The authors of this appalling theft were immediately discovered and pursued by the constables, so they took refuge in the House of Imitation, which seemed a safe haven. At this, the chief of police [*bargello*], on Apollo's express orders, had them removed forthwith and brought to him in shame as prisoners. When one of these thieves was found to be carrying the prologue of Tasso's pastoral, he was immediately tortured, according to police customs, and interrogated about his aiders and abetters. Stretched on the rope, the wretch named forty pickpocket poet companions of his, who were all of the lowest sort. These men had given themselves over to a life of gambling and all the worst kind of vices, so their only occupation was to steal conceits from others' labours and thereby have a good time of it, as they were horrified by the idea of sweating over their books and struggling in endless study so as to be able to bask in the glory of their own work.]

Pastoral Drama after Tasso's *Aminta*

Traiano Boccalini's anecdote, though clearly facetious and metaphorical, gives some idea of the extent to which Tasso's *Aminta* was generally revered and often crudely imitated by subsequent authors. This situation is not surprising given the prestige attached to Tasso's name, and *Aminta*'s rapid success in performance and especially in print. After its publication in 1580/81, over 250 printed editions appeared in Italian in the following centuries, stimulating a demand for new plays of this kind. It was also popular abroad; for a long time *Aminta* was even used as a teaching text for Italian in France.² However, Tasso's play was not imitated systematically. An exploration of ways in which it was used — or not used — by writers in the decade after its publication, focusing particularly on the first female authors of pastoral drama, will help to provide a more complete picture of *Aminta*'s reception and importance within the genre's overall development.³

Increasingly, writers from all over Italy wanted to associate their own pastorals with Tasso and his *Aminta*. This may be apparent on a rather superficial level, for example, by the addition of a prefatory verse to Pietro Lupi's *I Sospetti, favola boschereccia* (Florence, 1589) by a fellow member of the Svegliati academy of Pisa, which describes the work as closely imitating Tasso's example, playing with the names Tasso [badger] and Lupo [wolf]. In Marco Montano's *T(h)eonemia* (1584), Tasso is actually evoked on stage contending with Ariosto.⁴ It has been suggested too that the foreign shepherd Alessi in Maddalena Campiglia's *Flori, favola boschereccia* (Vicenza, 1588), who is eventually joined in a spiritual and poetic union with the eponymous protagonist, may represent a pastoral disguising of Tasso. Indeed, Campiglia (to whom we will return) evidently had a copy of her play sent to the poet in 1589, hoping for some favourable comment, which came a couple of months later in the form of a polite letter paradoxically praising *Flori* as outshining his own *Aminta*.⁵ The inclusion of prefatory verse by Tasso in Giovan Donato Cucchetti's *La Pazzia, favola pastorale* (first printed Ferrara, 1581) doubtless represents a further bid to boost the reputation of his pastoral play.⁶

Internal textual evidence shows that many writers were influenced by episodes or scenarios from the *Aminta*, such as the false reports of suicides or deaths based on tokens and Tirsi's rescue of his beloved nymph from a satyr's clutches (though the latter scenario also occurred in a more comic guise in Beccari's *Sacrificio*). In addition, Tasso's lyric style quickly became popular with writers of pastoral drama after 1581.⁷ This combined shorter, seven-syllable lines (*settenari*) with the more common dramatic metre of the hendecasyllable to signal moments of heightened emotion and pathos, perhaps following the example of Speroni's tragedy *Canace*. As Ingegneri commented, many tried to reproduce Tasso's 'dilicatezza' [delicacy] of style. This, in the Venetian's view, made pastoral plays generally more pleasant to read, but also had the negative effect of making writers and audiences more attentive to the 'fiorita locuzione' [ornate expression] than to the dramatic content, namely the disposition of the plot and decorum.⁸ The madrigalistic quality of *Aminta*'s lyric monologues also made it fairly popular with musicians from 1594, when Simone Balsamino set whole scenes independently to music.⁹ Gierolamo Vida, an imitator of Tasso, already picks up on the genre's musical potential in his *Filliria, favola boscareccia* (Padua, 1585).¹⁰ However, this association became much more evident with Guarini's *Pastor fido*, which proved an enormously popular text for musicians after it was printed in 1589/90.¹¹ Its publication coincided with the intense theorizing and experimentation to realize music drama (*melodramma*) then ongoing, especially in Florence.

By contrast, Tasso's innovation (as Guarini saw it, see p. 14), of inserting tragic-style choruses between the acts was not so consistently imitated during the 1580s, perhaps partly because of the technical difficulties involved. Those found in Cristoforo Castelletti's *L'Amarilli, pastorale* (Ascoli 1580, revised in later editions) and Vida's *Filliria* appear very short — more like madrigals to be sung (offstage in *Filliria*). Those in Antonio Ongaro's *Alceo, favola pescatoria* (Venice, 1582) and in Ingegneri's *Danza di Venere, pastorale* (Vicenza, 1584) are however more like Tasso's. Ingegneri ensures that his are carefully integrated dramaturgically within the action, as he would later recommend in his theory. He also stated that choruses were generally not necessary in pastorals (or comedies), given the private nature of their action.[12]

Very few dramatists chose to imitate the simple, tragic structure of *Aminta* either. Indeed, from a sample of twenty pastorals written between 1573 and 1590, Clubb identifies only one (Ongaro's *Alceo*) that follows Tasso's model, though the action is now transposed to a marine setting.[13] At least one more written during this period features a single plot, Cesare Cremonini's *Pompe funebri, favola silvestre* (Ferrara, 1590), while other writers opted for a tragic bias, such as Barbara Torelli Benedetti (*Partenia, favola boschereccia*, MS, 1587?) and Ferrante Gonzaga, ruler of Guastalla, whose lost *Enone* (begun 1584, unfinished) Ingegneri considered a tragedy with a happy ending. But generally writers continued to adopt the complex intrigue structure used by Beccari, Groto and others, with comic features, sometimes including clowning and magic which provided more opportunities for varied stage effects. Even the Aristotelian philosopher Cremonini's predominantly serious and mythologically inspired *Pompe* includes two episodes of cross-dressing (III. 9 and V. 1) and a hamadryad speaking from within a tree (III. 4).[14] Most writers of pastoral plays after Tasso chose to exploit the performance potential of pastoral drama more fully, by dramatizing a larger proportion of the action on stage. Notably, rather than relying solely on narrations by messengers, they chose to represent the drama of the lovers interacting, as even Ongaro does (*Alceo*, III. 4, V. 3). Various dramatists also included lower-class characters, or even rustic clown figures to add variety to the action and tone. Interestingly, it was around the same time that the first pastoral plays by professional *comici* appeared, including Bartolomeo de' Rossi's *Fiammella pastorale* (Paris, 1584) and Isabella Andreini's *La Mirtilla, pastorale* (Verona, 1588).

Moreover, few dramatists grappled with the provocative issues of authority and eroticism to the same degree as Tasso. For instance, from the prologue of *Aminta* many imitated the idea of a disguised god descending to the pastoral world, in which he/she will remain an invisible guiding presence, but it is rare to find a figure as ambivalent and critical of courtly mores as Tasso's Cupid (see Chapter 3).[15] Some played self-consciously with Tasso's formula, though. Guazzoni in his *Andromeda, tragicomedia boscareccia* (Venice, 1587) paradoxically reverses the respective attitudes of Cupid and Venus towards court and country in *Aminta*, so that here Venus angrily sends her son away from the sensual courts to deal with the excessive chastity of the humble Arcadian nymphs. In Ongaro's prologue Venus takes on Cupid's role after stealing his bow and golden arrow, while Ingegneri's Venus opens almost with a polemic rebuttal of her representation by Tasso's Amore.[16] However, Andreini's prologue notably features a moralized Amore with his mother Venus *after* he has returned to her; and describes him facilitating marriage and celestial happiness, as opposed to the devious 'furore' that impersonates him and denigrates his reputation on earth.

Imitations of *Aminta* nearly all omit the other more polemical, anti-courtly elements expressed by Tirsi (especially II. 2 and in the Mopso section). This is even more noticeable in the case of Tasso's Golden Age chorus. While many writers evoke its suggestions of erotic innocence and freedom, they do not go so far as to attack contemporary courtly conventions dominated by the false and inhibiting demands of honour.[17] Cremonini is unusual in retaining the polemic against 'Onore' after his sensual description of reciprocal love which renews the Golden Age:

> SILENO Andavan, la fanciulla delicata,
> E lo scaltro garzon, nudi le membra;
> Riamava l'amata, [...]
> Amor gli congiungeva, e morian' cheti
> Su l'erba, e rinascean' festanti, e lieti.
> Sciocca ignoranza, e vilmente superba
> Avelenò la purità d'Amore;
> Fè il garzon' rozo, e la fanciulla acerba
> Dietro a una vanità, c'ha nome Onore,
> E formando un suo rustico decreto,
> Che s'accresca gran prezzo il bel ritroso,
> Fè i sospir' col divieto,
> E profanò legislatrice infame
> L'ordin' d'amor, che l'amata riame. (IV. 3, pp. 88–89)

[The delicate maid and the sly lad wandered bare of limb; and the beloved returned her lover's love, [...] Love united them and they 'died' softly on the grass and were joyfully and happily revived. Foolish and rudely proud ignorance poisoned the purity of Love; it made the boy crude and the maiden hostile in the name of a vain thing called Honour and, by forming a rustic decree that reluctant beauty be more highly prized, its prohibitions resulted in laments. This wicked legislator profaned love's order, by which a maid returns her lover's love.]

Yet this message is undercut by being sung in strophic verse by Silenus, the drunken servant of Bacchus, as a forfeit for being caught in the snare laid by his 'satirini' (recalling Virgil's Eclogue VI). It is also introduced as a retelling of the 'wondrous song of Love' that was written semi-seriously in the sand by the 'gran pastor' [great shepherd], who knew so much that he went mad (IV. 3, p. 86) — presumably an allusion to Tasso. This song therefore appears more of an academic, carnivalesque exercise than a serious polemic, as indicated by the direction that precedes it in the text: 'Sileno canta d'Amore à l'Epicurea' [Silenus sings of Love in an Epicurean style].[18]

Cremonini's *Pompe* is otherwise marked by a spiritual and moral dimension conspicuously absent from *Aminta*, though which had been hinted at obliquely in other plays under the veil of pagan mythology (as in Ingegneri's *Danza* and Cucchetti's *Pazzia*). The action of *Pompe* is framed by a sacrifice and games in honour of the dead shepherd-lover, Dafni (Daphnis), whose shade recites the prologue, and it features a priest and his minister who note at length the necessity of religion in pastoral life (I. 2). Even the satyr, Rustico, comments on the importance of piety (V. 9, p. 127). More unusually, philosophical and theological ideas are raised independently of the plot, such as the affirmation of the immortality of the soul and of Free Will. The introduction of such questions, and especially of moralizing and pious *sententiae*, became more noticeable in later pastoral drama, particularly after the publication of Guarini's *Pastor fido* (1589/90). This significant development was however anticipated by some female writers of pastoral drama, which represents an unusual aspect of the history of the genre.

Women and Pastoral Drama

Composition and performance

Such changes towards a moralized pastoral reflect a general shift that we have already noted occurring in polite Italian literature and drama from the Tridentine period. This has been described as a move away from 'realistic', erotic modes typical of literary forms like the *novella* and the comedy, to more sublimated, decorous ones which use the language of Petrarchism and neo-Platonism.[19] These changes had important effects on the extent to which women were able to engage in literary activities in the later sixteenth century. Cox argues against the view put forward by Carlo Dionisotti (amongst others) that opportunities for women writers resulting from the burgeoning of vernacular culture in the 1530s, the increased activity of the press and the legitimating example of Vittoria Colonna, were restricted as a result of Counter-Reformation sensibilities. Instead, this climate is demonstrated to have fostered more adventurous and even pioneering literary activity by women from around 1580 to 1620. As the range of literary genres engaged with during this period generally became more seemly, the usual barriers on female writers posed by sexual decorum were to some extent lifted. They could therefore engage more freely with a far greater and more ambitious range of genres available to their elite male contemporaries — including the chivalric romance and, importantly, pastoral drama.

However, for women to venture publicly into composing secular drama marks a particularly striking departure from the traditional lyric and devotional literary forms typically preferred by women before then.[20] This was all the more surprising given the typical conception of secular theatre as a 'public' and therefore a 'masculine' preserve, as highlighted in the famous hypothetical scenario of Shakespeare's sister in Virginia Woolf's *A Room of One's Own* (1929). Contemporary reactions to women's attendance of theatrical performances especially of comedy, and above all to their appearance on stage, give some sense of the ambivalence and anxieties felt about gender decorum where theatre was concerned. There were fears of its potentially corrupting effects on impressionable female spectators, though mixed audiences — albeit usually observing gender separation in the seating — had long been the norm in courts. The new phenomenon of actresses being showcased in professional troupes especially from the 1560s stirred up particularly strong feeling. Though 'leading ladies' were an undeniable success both with commercial audiences and in more restricted courtly environments, moralists and churchmen like the seventeenth-century Jesuit Giovan Domenico Ottonelli, decried this phenomenon. They viewed actresses as a threat to public decency and family values because of the way they spoke openly and displayed their body in a way that was deemed sexually provocative.[21] In England, actresses drew an even more hostile reception, and they are generally regarded as appearing on the commercial stage only in 1660.

It is therefore no surprise that examples of women *writing* secular drama are quite rare, especially in the more 'public' dramatic genres of comedy or tragedy. The first known Italian tragedy by a woman was not published until 1611 (*Celinda* by the Paduan Valeria Miani Negri) and the only known example of a female-authored comedy in the early modern period is significantly by a courtesan, Margherita Costa (*Li buffoni*, 1641).[22] However, the picture looks very different for pastoral drama. In the above discussion on imitators of Tasso's *Aminta* we have already mentioned three examples composed by female writers in the late 1580s, making them the earliest known ones of this kind anywhere in Europe. These are Barbara Torelli Benedetti's *Partenia*, which today exists only in a single, undated manuscript in Cremona (c. 1587), and the published ones of Maddalena Campiglia (*Flori, favola boschereccia*, Vicenza, 1588) and Isabella Andreini (*Mirtilla*, Verona, 1588). (Both the latter two have recently been edited and translated into English, reflecting a renewed interest especially among Anglo-American scholars in early modern women's writings.) These plays were all celebrated in their day, though with the exception of Andreini's *Mirtilla* they did not have a very long-lasting or wide geographical impact.[23] Even so, they may have stimulated later women to compose pastoral plays, such as Valeria Miani Negri (*Amorosa speranza*, Venice, 1604) and Isabetta Coregli(a) of Lucca (*Dori*, Naples, 1634, and *Erindo*, 1650). In addition, other examples now untraceable or lost may have been written by Margherita Asinari Valperga (possibly inspired by Torelli's example), and by Eleonora Bernardi Bellati (perhaps entitled *Clorindo*).[24] It is also clear that three pastoral ballets (now lost) were composed by Laura Guidiccioni Lucchesini for the Medici court. Taken together these give a sense of a broader tradition of female-authored pastoral drama which could be connected to theatrical activities by women also beyond Italy, and would merit further investigation than is possible in this context.[25]

The remaining part of the chapter will focus on the first three known female-authored pastoral plays, which represent the examples of greatest literary interest, especially compared to the 'workaday genre exercises' of Coreglia and Miani.[26] Moreover, they together provide a general sense of themes and concerns raised by women in writing secular, fictional drama, given the prescriptive gender norms of the day. All three writers faced common difficulties in gaining access to and acceptance within literary circles, as well as in 'publishing' their plays, whatever form this took. Campiglia and Torelli also lacked the more obvious routes for performance in (semi-) public arenas that were available to Andreini. However, they all approached these difficulties in varying ways, which in part reflect the writers' differing social, geographical and personal backgrounds. Our analysis of these plays will therefore explore the contexts of their production, and the ways in which the authors worked selectively with existing pastoral conventions to suit their own particular agendas. It will be seen that female writers of pastoral drama, like those of vernacular love lyric from the mid-sixteenth century studied by Ann Rosalind Jones, similarly had to 'negotiate' the previously male-oriented tradition by adopting strategies which could range from adaptive imitation to more overtly oppositional stances.[27]

The first question that must be posed is why did women feel able to engage with pastoral drama as opposed to comedy and tragedy? Pastoral fiction and verse had after all, like the neo-classical dramatic forms, been dominated by a 'male' canon, which stretched back to classical antiquity via Sannazaro and others. This influenced the prevailing pastoral discourse on questions of love, authority and inter-social relations. Nonetheless, it still proved amenable to female writers for various reasons. In particular, its ostensible focus on *private* emotions and the inner life connected it with typical female literary concerns. Its portrayal of a secluded, idealized pastoral existence, away from the city streets of comedy and the courts of tragedy, allowed the representation of subjects removed from political affairs and characters less bound by (patriarchal) social and familial restraints. The apparently 'unrealistic' quality of the pastoral mode also made it an ideal medium for women discreetly to voice veiled complaint or criticism, and flattery of patrons and cities, as well as to explore alternative polemical ideas of a female-oriented society, in ways that were less likely to compromise their reputation. Similar issues are evident in the pastoral verse of Gaspara Stampa and the eclogue of Laura Battiferri in the mid-century, and later in the little known pastoral prose romance of Lucrezia Marinella (*Arcadia felice*, published 1605).[28] Most importantly, the more romantic and serious (tragicomic) representation of love in pastoral *drama* meant that decent female characters could unusually appear on stage decorously expressing their feelings, drawing on a literary tradition of female laments. As Ingegneri comments: 'admettendo le vergini in palco e le donne oneste, quello che alle comedie non lice, danno luoco a nobili affetti, non disdicevoli alle tragedie istesse' [by allowing virgins and chaste women on stage, which comedies do not allow, they give rise to noble emotions not inappropriate to tragedies themselves].[29]

Pastoral drama with its Petrarchan and neo-Platonic discourse was accordingly more elevated in tone than much comedy, but it lacked the sublimity and unrelenting gravitas of tragedy. (It should be noted though that the more decorous form of *commedia grave* which developed around the same time, similarly presented 'serious' female characters and greater emotional depth.) Furthermore, the pastoral mode was stylistically appropriate for female writers, since it was considered as belonging theoretically to the lowest of the three styles and therefore suitable for inexperienced writers wishing to demonstrate humble poetic ambitions. Andreini for instance presents her *Mirtilla* to the Marchioness of Vasto, Lavinia della Rovere, as: 'la prima fatica dell'ingegno mio che sia venuta in luce' [the first labour of my intellect which has been brought out publicly] and the product of poetic endeavours which began 'quasi da scherzo' [almost as a joke] (p. 33). Similarly, Campiglia in her dedicatory letter to the Marchioness of Soragna, Isabella Pallavicino Lupi, calls her *Flori* a 'rozzo parto' [unsophisticated offspring] (p. 44), and describes it as a mere prelude for greater things that she will offer her patron. The use of this modesty topos observes a convention frequently also adopted by young male pastoral dramatists (see for example Tirsi's speech in *Aminta*, II. 2. 192–96). However, when used by female dramatists it takes on a different emphasis given their greater need to observe gender decorum. At the same time, of course, their use of the pastoral mode with its scope for sophisticated literary allusions and rhetorical play allowed them to display their literary credentials in a form recently sanctioned by Tasso himself.

Ingegneri commented that the decorous nature and elegance of this kind of drama made it suitable for performances before noble audiences of both sexes (*Della poesia*, p. 7). More surprisingly, there is evidence that elite women themselves actively patronized such spectacles from the 1580s. Ingegneri was in fact asked to finish his *Danza di Venere* by Isabella Pallavicino Lupi, the dowager Marchioness of Soragna, a small feud near Parma so that she could have it performed privately at her court (see the dedicatory letter, 31st December, 1583). A few years later, she arranged for the staging of the Venetian Giovan Donato Cucchetti's pastoral play *La Pazzia* in Parma by the amateur Compagnia dei Pellegrini (as mentioned in the dedicatory letter to the 1586 edition). It is not clear whether Maddalena Campiglia dedicated her *Flori* to the Marchioness also with a view to a performance. Other female patrons with similar interests include Marchioness Marfisa d'Este Cybo of Scandiano, who seems to have planned a private performance of Guarini's *Pastor fido* in 1595 funded by local aristocrats.[30] Agnese Argotta, Marchioness of Grana and mistress of Vincenzo Gonzaga of Mantua from around 1587, was instrumental in attempting to have Guarini's *Pastor fido* staged there in the early 1590s. An acquaintance of hers, the notorious Barbara Sanseverino Sanvitale, Marchioness of Colorno (near Parma), besides attending an early recitation of Guarini's *Pastor fido* in Guastalla in 1583, intriguingly also patronized a private performance of the mythological tale of Perseus and Andromeda in 1580, starring Vincenzo Gonzaga together with the noblelady Ippolita Torelli Simonetta.[31]

This shows that on extremely private occasions elite women could also participate in amateur theatrical performances, especially in courtly environments. Such performances are in fact documented as taking place in Italy from at least the late fifteenth century.[32] The young Anna d'Este, sister of the future Duke Alfonso II of Ferrara, for instance appeared in a private staging of Terence's *Andria* in 1539; and also with her siblings in *Adelphi* before Pope Paul III in 1543.[33] For the Soragna performance of Ingegneri's *Danza*, Isabella Pallavicino Lupi arranged for her unmarried, fourteen-year-old daughter, Camilla Lupi, to star as the lead nymph, alongside a group of her own and her mother's ladies-in-waiting (it is not clear if male performers were involved).[34] The Marchioness apparently aimed to display her daughter's deportment, memory, and oratorical skills to the prestigious audience present, which included the young Duke of Parma and Piacenza, Ranuccio Farnese. She may thereby have hoped to present Camilla as an attractive marriage partner — the girl was in fact married three years later to Mario Farnese, Duke of Latera.[35] It is, however, unclear how far high-class women continued this practice beyond marriage and what training they received for this kind of performance. Aristocratic girls may have gained some acting experience through a convent education, or else they may have learnt dramatic skills alongside brothers in the private schoolroom as part of a general humanist training including elocution and public speaking.

This type of spectacle should probably be related to a wider tradition of noble ladies performing to delight their peers by singing and dancing, as described in Castiglione's *Cortegiano* and which evidently continued throughout the century. The Ferrarese court during the 1570s was known for its private displays of virtuoso singing by three or four female aristocrats, which developed into the more regulated and semi-professional phenomenon of *musica secreta* in the early 1580s.[36] For similarly exclusive gatherings, the young bride of Duke Alfonso II d'Este (Margherita Gonzaga) also arranged elaborately choreographed dances for herself and her ladies. Strikingly, on one occasion, the Duchess appeared in a pastoral ballet in which four of the eight ladies were cross-dressed as shepherds despite contemporary taboos about such practices.[37] It seems that some pastoral plays were intended for a similar kind of production. For instance, the minor nobleman and dramatist, Muzio Manfredi, suggested in the dedication of his *Il Contrasto amoroso* [*The Lovers' Quarrel*] to Vittoria Doria Gonzaga, the consort of the ruler of the Mantuan satellite court of Guastalla, that the play could be staged by Doria's own ladies-in-waiting. Its cast, he notes, is almost exclusively female and the single shepherd (Fileno) is so young that a lady could play him cross-dressed. Perhaps this style of performance would then avoid any potential indecorum involved in having performers of both sexes:

> Volendo voi, Signora mia, per sorte vederla rappresentare; con le vostre proprie donne, e donzelle, fare il potreste, e senza adoperarvi uomo veruno, sendo anche Fileno sì giovane, che una donna fingere commodamente il potrebbe, e un'altra Amore per lo Prologo quando il Prologo mutar non le voleste, o non recitarvelo.[38]

> [If perchance your Ladyship should wish to see it performed, you could do so with your own ladies and maidens, without using a single man, since Fileno is so young that a woman could easily play this role, and another could play Love in the prologue, if you didn't want to change this or leave it out.]

Restricted all-female performances of pastoral drama involving some cross-dressing roles evidently also took place outside Italy too, at least from the early seventeenth century. Bonarelli's *Filli di Sciro* (1607) was apparently performed by the Duchess of Savoy with her ladies some time before 1640. Henrietta Maria, queen consort of Charles I of England, who is described as bringing a French tradition of performances by royal females to the English court, played alongside her ladies in a production in French of *Artenice* (a pastoral drama based on Racan's *Les Bergeries*) in 1626, and in an English production of Walter Montagu's *The Shepherds Paradise* (1633).[39]

For obvious reasons of decorum this kind of performance by female elites was not described in printed treatises, but a sense of what they must have been like may be gleaned from dedicatory prefaces and correspondence. It is likely that such performances presented a practical form of in-house entertainment for smaller courts. Yet the fact that they were also popular in larger courts alongside more 'professional' performances (as in the French court of Maria de' Medici) suggests that they were perceived as an alternative and possibly more prestigious form of entertainment. This hypothesis is supported by the observation of Muzio Manfredi, that the *intermedi* for plays using men and boy actors needed only to be 'belli sì ma puri, e senza bisogno di macchine' [beautiful but simple, and without machines], whereas for productions involving ladies they needed to be 'bellissimi e rari' [most beautiful and rare] in order to reflect appropriately the social status of the performers and of the elite audience attending.[40]

Barbara Torelli's Partenia *and elite female-authored pastoral drama*

As argued elsewhere, the *Partenia* of Barbara Torelli (1546-post 1603) — the earliest known female-authored pastoral play — in part needs to be evaluated against this tradition of courtly female interest in theatre and pastoral drama.[41] Torelli originated from one of the leading aristocratic families of Parma (though her father was illegitimate at birth), and she was the cousin of the celebrated dramaturge Pomponio Torelli, Count of Montechiarugolo. Some time before 1580 she married the otherwise unknown Cavaliere Giovanni Paolo Benedetti and it appears that she lived as a widow after his death in 1592. During the 1580s she must have been well integrated into local courtly spheres and familiar with the traditions of music, poetry and spectacle, as suggested by her inclusion amongst a series of ladies interested in such practices in Manfredi's verse collections of 1580 and 1587 (in the latter of which *Partenia* is praised).[42] Torelli's own flattering allusion to Isabella Pallavicino Lupi, under the literary pseudonym of Calisa (*Partenia*, V. 3, fol. 66^r) points to a closer connection to this important local patron, although there is unfortunately no evidence that *Partenia* was ever staged by the Marchioness. The setting of the play at the Farnese villa of Collecchio, a few miles from Parma, and frequent veiled allusions to important courtly figures (including probably Duke Ottavio Farnese as the venerated elder shepherd Ottinio) only suggests that it was originally meant for a local aristocratic audience, like Tasso's *Aminta*.[43]

The single undated Cremona manuscript of the play provides no further clues as to Torelli's links with female courtly circles. Indeed, this manuscript, which is perhaps identifiable as the one gifted by Manfredi some time before September 1591 to Duke Carlo Emanuele of Savoy (the original dedicatee of Guarini's printed *Pastor fido*, 1589/90), lacks any prefatory material or a prologue by the author herself. It is framed instead by dedicatory sonnets by twelve male *letterati*.[44] Many of these were fairly distinguished locally in their day: some were aristocrats, such as Marchese Camillo Malaspina, Marco Pio of Savoy (ruler of Sassuolo), and Don Ferrante Gonzaga of Guastalla, a satellite court of Mantua, which had until 1539 been ruled by the Torelli family. All were connected with the courts round Parma and Mantua, and local literary circles or academies frequented by Manfredi. Seven were members of the academy of the Innominati ['The Unnamed Ones'] of Parma (founded c.1574), which Manfredi headed in 1580 and amongst whom Pomponio Torelli was a leading figure.[45] Surprisingly, no trace of literary connections between the Torelli cousins has hitherto been found, though it is reasonable to suppose that Barbara's family status as well as her literary connection with Manfredi from 1580 (who was friendly also with her brother Guido), enabled her access to this circle. Such an association — necessarily an informal one as women were not admitted to the academy at this time — may have prompted her decision to write a pastoral play and determined the form that she gave it.

The Innominati were clearly interested in pastoral writings, inspired especially by their most famous member, Torquato Tasso, as well as by Sannazaro and Virgil.[46] They also cultivated a largely academic interest in drama, especially through the efforts of Pomponio Torelli, who lectured on Aristotle's *Poetics* from around 1586, and composed a series of academic tragedies beginning with *Merope* in 1587. Yet, although an early version of Guarini's *Pastor fido* was discussed in this context, academicians generally tended to produce pastoral drama only after the printing of Guarini's play (1589/90) and in manuscript, perhaps due to its still controversial theoretical status. It does not appear that they themselves had such plays performed.[47] However, some

Innominati members evidently took a more practical interest in the staging as well as in the writing of pastoral drama, including Muzio Manfredi and his patron Ferrante Gonzaga of Guastalla. Marco Pio, another contributor of verse to the manuscript, also commissioned a performance of Beccari's revised *Sacrificio* in 1587 for his wedding to Clelia [*sic*] Farnese. This contemporary aristocratic interest in the genre also by *male* courtly elites who contributed to the manuscript may further have encouraged Torelli's choice of this genre.

The only existing evidence regarding the performance of *Partenia* is in fact connected with Ferrante's court in Guastalla. Torelli seems to have had quite close contacts with the prince from at least the mid 1580s. She may perhaps be identified as the 'S[igno]ra Barbara gentiliss[im]a' who was eagerly awaiting a copy of Ferrante Gonzaga's pastoral tragicomedy, *Enone* (25 July, 1585).[48] Private correspondence between Manfredi and his princely patron further reveals that Gonzaga had a copy of the *Partenia* already by February 1586. Writing from Mantua on 18 March 1587, Manfredi mentions that Torelli's *Partenia* was by then rehearsed and could be performed for the ruler's arrival from Genoa with his bride, since the prince's own *Enone* was still not finished and nor was Manfredi's *Semiramis, boscherecchia*:

> So che la *Partenia* della S[igno]ra Barbara è già imparata. Se V[ostra] E[eccellenza] I[llustrissima] me'l comandasse, io scriverei alla S[igno]ra Barbara e la potessimo fare recitare alla venuta della S[igno]ra [Vittoria Doria], poichè le scene pastorali si fanno tosto e vi va poca spesa, e la cosa è bella, e onorata.[49]
>
> [I know that Lady Barbara's *Partenia* has already been learnt. If your Excellency so wished, I could write to Lady Barbara and we could have it performed for the arrival of your wife [Vittoria Doria], since pastoral stage-sets can be prepared quickly and with little expense, and the effect is beautiful and honourable.]

The proposal was again made in similar terms on 8 April, but there is no evidence that Torelli's pastoral was finally performed in Mantua or elsewhere. This may have been for reasons of decorum relating to the performance of a female-authored play on the occasion of a dynastic wedding. It may also have had something to do with Manfredi's marginal status at the court around this time, since he was not even invited to the wedding.[50] Nonetheless, it is notable that the play was at least considered and rehearsed for performance rather than purely for private recitation or reading, as some of the plays produced by the Innominati seem to have been.

Torelli's play may also have been discounted because its content was considered unsuitable for the occasion. Like Tasso's *Aminta*, it observes a streamlined plot structure with a rather tragic tone, and avoids staging much of the dramatic action. The lovers' meeting, Tirsi's suicide attempt, and Partenia's death-like swoon all take place off-stage (V. 2). However, Torelli goes even further by twice avoiding an encounter between the satyr Cromi and the nymph he pursues, which could potentially lead to unseemly descriptions of sexual violence. Instead, in *Partenia* the drama tends to be evoked through long narrated accounts or through long monologues which focus on the inner emotional conflicts of the characters.

The play otherwise differs in various respects from *Aminta*. It features the courtship of the chaste nymph Partenia by Leucippo and Tirsi, who are simultaneously friends and rivals in love. Importantly, the resolution is achieved through a staged recognition scene rather than the protagonist nymph's gradual change of heart (V. 3). Unlike Tasso's Silvia, Partenia remains consistent in her preference for chastity, and lacks any indication of nascent sensuality. What expressions of love she does voice remain innocently directed only towards her father, since she has no interest in her suitors. It is to satisfy his wishes for her marriage and an heir that she is reported as dutifully consenting (off-stage) to renounce her service of Diana and marry the wealthy shepherd Leucippo, though the audience learns directly of her private regret at this outcome (III. 4). Even in the final scene, it is noted that Partenia only wants to marry Tirsi to fulfil a divine vow that she unknowingly made to him that day during a festival in the temple of Diana (again off-stage). Providentially, this means that she avoids marrying her father's chosen suitor, who is finally recognized to be her long-lost brother abducted by a wolf in infancy (V. 3). This revelation ironically appears to have come too late, as both Partenia and Tirsi are by then believed dead. But with the news of the restoration of the lovers to life in the final scene a happy ending is possible. Tirsi is now free to marry Partenia, thereby upholding his divine vow, with the assent of her father and Leucippo.

The play's noticeable interest in questions of marriage, family and economic matters, and filial piety introduces a domestic dimension that is largely absent in *Aminta* and which, in Manfredi's view, justified Torelli's lack of choruses.[51] Such themes (and the device of recognition) are however found in earlier pastoral plays like Lollio's *Aretusa*, Giraldi's unfinished *favola* and, importantly, also in Ingegneri's *Danza di Venere*. This last play is relevant to Torelli since Ingegneri was also a member of the Innominati from around 1580 and, as we have seen, his *Danza* was performed under the aegis of Isabella Pallavicino Lupi and then printed probably only shortly before the composition of *Partenia*. Ingegneri's pastoral similarly presents a single plot which revolves around an advantageous marriage arranged by a father for his daughter (Amarilli) to a wealthy (unseen) shepherd, while another shepherd (Coridone) of unknown origins and believed mad is in love with her. The resolution is precipitated, after Amarilli is reported dead, by the recognition of Coridone's identity and disqualification of the other suitor, though this time there is no threat of incest.

However, as with *Aminta*, Torelli makes certain changes to Ingegneri's play which may be linked with her status as a married noblewoman wishing to legitimize her literary engagement with a still relatively new genre, as yet never attempted by a woman. Notably, she avoids the more spectacular and potentially indecorous aspects of Ingegneri's play, which includes a dance by a group of nymphs and one of shepherds during which Amarilli is abducted by Coridone with some satyrs (III. 3–4). As mentioned, Partenia never encounters the lustful satyr, who terms himself as a 'semidco' [demigod] (III. 5, fol. 45^r) and is finally described as simply disappearing over the hill (IV. 4, fol. 54^r). She follows Ingegneri and Tasso, though, in avoiding representing other baser rustic characters who would lower the tone of the play, as found for example in Cucchetti's *Pazzia* (performed in Parma in 1585).

The introduction of the shepherd Lice also adds a tragic tone to Torelli's play from the first act. This character creates a strangely inconclusive episode, which Riccò speculates may have been added after Torelli was widowed. He appears only once (I. 4), when he is encountered by Partenia's companion, Talia, mourning the sudden death of his unnamed beloved who is buried in a nearby tomb (off-stage). They together then visit and duly honour the tomb (as described III. 1), which thereafter plays a symbolic role in the main plot, marking the site of Partenia and Tirsi's supposed deaths and their restoration to life by Talia. In her use of this motif, Torelli shows the influence of Sannazaro's *Arcadia*, V, X and XI and Tasso's *Gerusalemme liberata*, XII. 96–99 in which the tomb and funeral rituals have a significant part in the pastoral landscape.[52] However, while Lice's own tragedy remains unresolved, his example serves a spiritual and positive end by reminding Talia and her beloved Coridone of the brevity and value of earthly love, dissuading them from petty misunderstandings and jealousy.

Torelli further ensures the decorum of her pastoral play by having the chaste goddess Diana function as the presiding deity of the action, rather than Venus, as in Ingegneri's *Danza* (and Andreini's *Mirtilla*). Partenia's resistance to marriage is thereby justified by her chaste devotion to her goddess, in contrast to Amarilli's feeling merely that she is not yet ready for this institution (*Danza*, II. 3, p. 43). More strikingly, a spiritual dimension is added to the characterization of the pure and pious Partenia, which goes further than in most pastoral drama of this time — though it is discernible also in Campiglia's *Flori*. First of all, her name points to the Greek term for the Virgin, as well as perhaps the mythological Parthenos, who on her death was turned into the constellation Virgo. Secondly, in the scene where Partenia is reported to submit obediently to her father's will for her marriage, there are even hints of the Annunciation scene:[53]

> [ELPINO] 'Sia pur come si voglia', ella rispose [...]
> soggiungendo Ergasto:
> 'Sian benedette', disse, 'le fatiche,
> C'ho per te fatte, col sudor c'ho sparso,
> E benedetta sia tu, figlia cara
> Dai sommi Dei'. (*Partenia*, IV. 2, 50^v-51^r)

> ['Let it be as you wish', she replied [...], to which Ergasto replied, 'Blessed be the labours that I have undertaken for you, and the sweat I have expended, and may you be blessed, dear daughter, by the gods on high'.]

Such allusions to the Virgin and the avoidance of provocative representations of female characters and potentially sensual subject matter, indicate Torelli's observance of recognized legitimizing strategies adopted by female writers of lyric verse and other literary genres. By this means she may also have sought to suggest a link between her work and an earlier tradition of female-authored convent theatre.[54]

In *Partenia*, Torelli may have sought to critique the patriarchal and mercenary view of marriage commonly presented in pastoral drama, bound up with patrimony and the generation of heirs, sometimes with a misogynistic tone (as in Ingegneri's *Danza*, II. 3). The pastoral idiom was well suited to such a polemic, with its setting apparently removed from the power politics and avarice of the city and underpinned by Golden Age values of simplicity and purity. Torelli seems to have broadly split attitudes towards marriage along gender lines in her play. Partenia consistently disdains earthly love and the pursuit of wealth: 'Che donna è quella sol che'l ciel onora,/ E le terrene cose have in dispregio' [For a true woman only honours the heavens and holds worldly things in disdain], (I. 3, fol. 9ᵛ), while Talia believes in the force of chaste and constant earthly love ('Amore vince ogni cosa' [Love conquers all], III. 1, fol. 37ᵛ). Meanwhile, the male characters (apart from Lice and the offstage Ottinio) at various points affirm the importance of wealth in marriage and its persuasive power on the beloved. Such positions are crystallized especially in the relationship between Partenia and her more materialistic father. Ergasto may claim to be different from wealthy city-dwellers, who are prepared to marry their daughters at all costs and even by force to infirm, elderly and monstrous men to gain 'ereditadi e onori' [inheritance and honours] (II. 6, fol. 29ᵛ), but he still aims to secure a prosperous marriage for Partenia despite being aware that she would prefer a life of chastity. He reminds his daughter that: 's'aman [le ricchezze] per servirsene in onore/ Degli Dei, di sè stesso, e degli amici' [one should love riches to use them honourably in the service of the gods, for oneself and one's friends] (IV. 2, fol. 50ᵛ).

However, while a somewhat critical, female-oriented perspective may be detected in *Partenia* in the standard pastoral debate on the relative values of chastity and (marital) love, this does not emerge as the main theme of the play. Equal if not greater emphasis is given to the contrast between love and friendship between the two male shepherds, Leucippo and Tirsi (a theme often dramatized both in tragedy and serious comedy). In fact, the central scene of the play (III. 2) dramatizes Tirsi's shocked discovery that his friend Leucippo is also secretly in love with Partenia and has been favoured by the nymph's father Ergasto. This sets in train Tirsi's jealous suspicion and despair, later provoking his suicide attempt. Furthermore, the three female characters (out of a cast of ten) appear little on stage, and in less than half of the total of twenty-three scenes. In particular, Partenia only appears in four scenes (I. 3, II. 4, III. 4, IV. 4), in which she is either alone or with another female companion (Talia or Clori), as befitting a virtuous, unmarried nymph. Her realization of the prescribed female values of chastity, obedience, and piety also denies her much scope for dramatic agency or development of character.[55] The older female character, Talia, is by contrast a more rounded and independent character. Talia — whose name refers to the comic muse who carried a shepherd's staff, and was used as a pseudonym for the author herself — displays not only the conventional feminine virtues of piety, empathy, and constancy in love, but also literary skills (she is the only character to carve on trees, III. 1, fol. 37ʳ) and a knowledge of natural medicine (V. 4, fol. 69ᵛ). She is also portrayed in a mutual loving relationship with Coridone and interacts with male characters on an equal footing, sometimes offering pious counsel.

Nonetheless, Partenia does acquire a certain tragic and moral depth in the play. In IV. 4 the young nymph is visited by a horrifying vision of Diana with the furies, which Clori deduces may be due to the goddess's anger about Partenia marrying Leucippo and thereby breaking her vow to Tirsi. Partenia's subsequent terror and conflict about whether to observe her filial duty or her religious vow finally drives her to attempt suicide. Off-stage she becomes a more heroic figure: accusing Tirsi of his unworthy trick, and then repenting after his suicide, and arranging for his burial (like Tasso's Silvia), before herself collapsing out of compassion (V. 2). Even Partenia's acceptance of marriage and consequently of earthly love over a life of spiritual devotion, which is presented as passive submission to the 'paterno giogo' [paternal yoke] (IV. 2, fol. 49^r), may thus be read as a heroic 'feminine' preparedness to renounce her own desires to fulfil those of others — and finally to satisfy a divine will.

Maddalena Campiglia: developing a feminine pastoral poetics

Many of the literary strategies used to legitimize Torelli's pastoral play may be identified also in Maddalena Campiglia's *Flori* (printed Vicenza, 1588). Although *Flori* differs substantially in structural terms from *Partenia*, since it has a complex triple plot with numerous subplots and episodes, it shares with Torelli's example a noticeable tragic bias (especially in the first half) and a strong concern with spiritual values and chastity. *Flori* similarly decorously limits the representation of sensual love typically associated with the genre, though she does stage an encounter between two nymphs and a predatory Satyr and Wildman [Silvano] (I. 6), and surprisingly presents a nymph from a secondary plot (Licori) contemplating the beauty of her beloved (I. 5). Campiglia also deals with the question of marriage as opposed to the single life, giving unusual emphasis to the theme of chaste, spiritual love and sounding a note of condemnation against contemporary marriage practices. Given these similarities and the literary connections the two women had in common (see below), one wonders — in the absence of any firm documentary evidence — whether Campiglia was acquainted with Torelli's play before beginning her own.

However, Campiglia's treatment of these motifs, while pre-empting certain future changes to pastoral drama as with Torelli, departs far more polemically from the conventions of the genre than *Partenia* does in order to promote a more radically pro-feminist stance on love and literary activity. The different use made of the genre is especially notable given the dramatists' similar class backgrounds. Campiglia (1553–95) was also of noble descent, though compared to Torelli, her family was of less exalted pedigree in its local context of Vicenza (then part of the Venetian republic). From the little we know of her life, she was educated in letters and music, and was married in 1576 to a local nobleman, Dionisio Colzé, perhaps more for financial reasons than out of choice. The marriage soon proved unsuccessful, possibly connected with the fact that the couple remained childless or perhaps as a consequence of Campiglia's preferred lifestyle. By the early 1580s she was living separately from her spouse, though the marriage was apparently never formally dissolved. This left her in a rather anomalous social position, outside the conventional female estates of marriage or widowhood. Unusually, it seems that she did not become a tertiary in a religious order either, but lived instead as a laywoman devoted to spiritual concerns ('dimessa nel mondano conspetto'), a way of life that was in those years becoming more common for elite women.[56] It is from this time of social independence that all her literary compositions can be dated.

Campiglia's unconventional lifestyle attracted some comment already in her first printed work, *Discorso [...] sopra l'Annonciatione della Beata Vergine* [Discourse on the Annunciation of the Blessed Virgin] (1585), where she is described as: 'donna celeste più che terrena, e unica fra questo sesso, seguendo ella l'orme d'uomi[n]i dotti, vivendo al tutto diversamente, con gran stupore altrui, dal costume donnesco' [a lady more heavenly than earthly, and unique of her sex, since she follows the footsteps of learned men, living to the amazement of all in a manner that is totally different from other women]. This alerts the reader to additional difficulties that she would have to overcome in gaining literary acceptance amongst her contemporaries. For this reason, it is understandable that Campiglia chose to present edifying spiritual subject matter in embarking on her literary path, although, as one of the earliest extended works of devotional prose, following the example of Vittoria Colonna, the *Discorso* is remarkably ambitious. Furthermore, its praise of the chaste marriage of the Virgin to a youthful Joseph, and corresponding condemnation of many contemporary abusive unions and the vain preoccupation by some women with earthly things (pp. 5–7, 40) introduces polemical themes to which Campiglia later returns in her pastoral play. The *Discorso* was dedicated by Campiglia to a nun (Vittoria Trissina Frattina) and the prefatory letter mentions other female religious. Yet the work strikingly includes poetic tributes and framing material by seventeen male literati, including various members of the prestigious Accademia Olimpica [Olympic academy] of Vicenza. Already by this time, Campiglia therefore seems to have been known by a surprisingly large circle of acquaintances, which expanded during her lifetime also beyond her native city and reflects the increasing adventurousness in her literary activities.

    As with Torelli, Campiglia's choice to write a pastoral drama may have been informed by her connections with members of her local academy. The Accademia Olimpica was famed for its theatrical and literary activities particularly in the years surrounding the inauguration in 1585 of the new theatre building initially designed by Andrea Palladio. From 1579 there had been plans to stage a pastoral play for this event. Important dramatists and critics from the academy and outside were consulted in the following years as to the choice of an appropriate play and later for advice on its performance. These included Sperone Speroni and others important to the history of Italian pastoral drama, such as Ingegneri (who had originally begun to compose his *Danza di Venere* in 1580 for performance at the academy) and Guarini, who presented his *Pastor fido* at an academic gathering in 1584. Ferrante Gonzaga and Manfredi joined the Olimpici in the same year.[57] But by 1583 general opinion had swung in favour of tragedy — although Tasso's *Aminta* still seems to have been considered a possible contender.[58] Eventually, the choice fell to a translation of Sophocles' *Oedipus Rex*, which was performed by (semi-)professional actors who included Luigi Groto, Guarini's friend Giovan Battista Verato and the latter's daughter.

    It is unclear to what extent Campiglia associated directly with the academicians and knew of their discussions. Noblewomen were invited to attend special performances such as the inaugural one (celebrated in *Flori*, III. 6. 171–98), but were excluded from membership. Two female musicians were however employed in a more professional capacity to perform for public and private occasions.[59] Campiglia nevertheless at least had contacts with certain prominent members of the academy, such as Ingegneri, and Paolo Chiappino (the secretary from 1582), whom she notes provided her with critical feedback on her pastoral play.[60] At the time of writing *Flori*, the genre was only just becoming the subject of open debate, stimulated by the example of Guarini's *Pastor fido* (see Chapter 5). Though it still lacked the theoretical baggage of the other classical dramatic genres, it was evidently a hot topic of debate alongside tragedy, especially in the Veneto region. Campiglia's letter dedicating *Flori* to Curzio Gonzaga explicitly shows her awareness of dramaturgical issues discussed amongst local academicians, such as unity of plot, and the relative length of episodes and speeches, which would also concern pastoral drama. But she fears modestly that she may be reproached by certain male critics for not fully observing Aristotelian precepts, and asks for Gonzaga's understanding if, as a *woman*, she deviates from them somewhat and follows her own tastes (p. 46–48). However, her apparently self-deprecating reference to her sex hints more daringly at her justification for adopting an alternative, female poetics.[61] In this respect, Campiglia differs significantly from Torelli and Isabella Andreini, who provided no explanation for their poetic practices.

Campiglia may well also have established more informal cultural contacts at the local library founded in the 1580s by the bookseller Perin Libraro. (Perin was jointly responsible for the publication of Campiglia's *Discorso*, while *Flori* was printed jointly by his successors, including his widow, Anna.[62]) Users of this establishment included people associated with the bookselling business from various parts of the Veneto region, as well as two of the contributors to the edition of Campiglia's *Discorso* (Vespasiano Giuliani and Ingegneri). This context may explain Campiglia's surprising contribution of four sonnets in rustic dialect to a collection marking the death of the famous Vicentine dialect poet Agostino Rava (printed 1584), together with three other local women poets. As has been discussed elsewhere, her adoption here of a more earthy language as opposed to the customary refined Tuscan demonstrates her extraordinary versatility of style and literary range. She did not however transgress the bounds of female decorum so far as to adopt a peasant persona, as male contemporaries did.[63] Evidence of such literary activity by Veneto women may be linked to other ambitious literary endeavours on the Venetian mainland in the field of romance (Giulia Bigolina, Lucrezia Marinella) and drama (Isabella Andreini and Valeria Miani Negri), and suggests that this particular geographical context proved a fertile environment for women writers.

A further stimulus to Campiglia's dramatic creativity may have been gained by her connections with courtly circles, especially around Parma and Mantua. These exclusive environments offered possibilities in terms of freedom of movement and cultural associations — as well as theatrical activities — to women of an elevated social class which were denied their equals in republican Venice.[64] Vicenza had been subject to the republic since 1404, but its local feudal aristocracy were keen to display their independent cultural identity and values which brought them closer to other *terraferma* dynasties, especially ones with imperial ties like the Gonzagas.[65] Campiglia evidently cultivated extensive contacts with a wide variety of *letterati* outside Vicenza, especially in Venice, Genoa, and Mantua, sometimes sustained by correspondence alone, as was probably the case with Tasso (see p. 99). The marriage of her cousin Elena to Marchese Guido Sforza Gonzaga in 1584 may also have enabled her association with members of the Gonzaga entourage, including Muzio Manfredi, and especially with Curzio Gonzaga, who became an important patron and literary contact until her death.[66] How Campiglia became acquainted with Isabella Pallavicino Lupi, the other dedicatee of *Flori* besides Gonzaga, is less clear. Possible intermediaries who may have facilitated this connection include Muzio Manfredi and Angelo Ingegneri, who were both close to Barbara Torelli.

Flori (like *Partenia*) therefore appears to draw on Campiglia's experience both of academic and courtly contexts, as indicated by various allusions within the play, the dedicatory letters, and the appendix included in some editions.[67] This appendix contains an array of verse by twenty-seven male writers from Vicenza and other cultural centres, demonstrating Campiglia's expanded range of contacts and literary ambitions since writing the *Discorso*. Even so, there is no evidence to suggest that she was sufficiently integrated into a context that enabled *Flori* to be performed. As argued previously, it is intriguing to imagine that the play was staged in private female circles, such as that of Isabella Pallavicino Lupi, and that what we now have is the version polished for publication.[68] Compared with Torelli's *Partenia*, *Flori* certainly displays more action that could be effective on stage, such as the central choral sacrifice (III. 5), the attempted abduction of two nymphs by a satyr and Silvano (I. 6), some mad scenes, and two songs (III. 3; V. 3). However, it lacks choruses or *intermedi*, and rarely demonstrates the kind of lively dialogue or sung and danced interludes that are found for instance in the pastoral plays of Ingegneri and Andreini, which were clearly written with performance in mind. In fact, other aspects of Campiglia's play suggest that, as it stands, it was more likely to have been designed for reading aloud or private study, like many an academic tragedy (and some later pastorals). For example, it contains numerous lengthy monologues (as Campiglia herself notes in the preface to Gonzaga, p. 48), the linguistic style is complex and dense with conceits, and, most tellingly, an acrostic in the second song reveals that this text was destined for readers. Perhaps Campiglia's greater distance from the courtly environments favourable to female endeavours and her more problematic social status compared to Torelli, encouraged her to use the medium of the press instead to extend her work to a virtual audience. This would explain the setting of *Flori* in Arcadia rather than in a transfigured courtly context like the examples of Tasso and Torelli. The published version of Andreini's play could perhaps be seen as taking this tendency further still, given its minimal allusions to an external reality.

Of the three female-authored pastoral plays explored in this context, *Flori* in many ways appears the most unconventional in terms of its content, which may be related to Campiglia's social status as well as her personal tastes. As mentioned, this is signalled already in critical terms in the preface to Curzio Gonzaga, and it is apparent also in the prologue. Here *Flori* explicitly alludes to Tasso's *Aminta* by featuring the all-powerful god Amore, who has descended in invisible form to the humble pastoral setting, thereby ennobling the pastoral style of the inhabitants (Prologue, lines 97–102). He similarly threatens to pierce the heart of the lead nymph Flori, who is rebellious to love and committed to the service of Diana. However, the protagonist's resistance is uncharacteristically shown to be caused also by her morbid and mad attachment to her beloved dead female companion, Amaranta. This has driven Flori to frequent the nymph's tomb (*Flori*, I. 1. 20–52; I. 5. 261–65), recalling Lice in Torelli's *Partenia*. In order to cure Flori's madness and that of her unrequited shepherd suitor (Androgeo), a societal sacrifice will be arranged at an altar erected over Amaranta's urn (III. 5). During this event, Love promises to make Flori fall in love with a foreign shepherd (Alessi) then passing through Arcadia, who had also foresworn love since he was mourning the death of his beloved (unnamed) nymph. However, the god observes that his divine arrows which normally inspire the mutual mortal love so desired in pastoral drama, will in the case of Flori and Alessi bring about a transcendent spiritual passion that distinguishes them from the usual pastoral lovers:

> Ameranno, arderan, ma il fine ond'altri
> Ogni lor brama appaga, non fie mai
> Da lor pensato pur, non che bramato.
> Virtute occulta inusitata, e nova
> In somma avran gli dardi, che ferita
> Faran profonda, ma sì onesta e santa,
> Che meraviglia altrui porran nel core
> Spesso lor voglie, ardenti sì ma caste.
> Tal vo' che sia l'emenda del lor fallo
> Che s'amin sì, sì ch'ardano, ma'l fine
> De' fidi Amanti, vero pregio mai
> Non aggian, quando pur chiamar si voglia
> Emenda grazia a nullo ancor concessa. (Prologo, 78–90)

[Flori and Alessi will love, they will burn, but that end to which other lovers' burning desires are directed, and which can alone assuage their pain, will be by this pair not even contemplated, still less desired. Rather, my arrows will have a strange and unwonted hidden virtue, which will make their wounds deep, yes, but so honest and pure that others will marvel to see their desires, at once ardent and chaste. In this way I will have them make amends for their offence against my power, that, though loving with true ardour, they will never attain that end and true prize sought by faithful lovers — if it is right to speak of making amends when a grace is being granted that no other mortal has received. (trans. by Virginia Cox)]

The prologue thus highlights the unusual outcome of the principal plot, omitting mention of the two other interwoven plot strands and the vaguely comic subplot which end more conventionally in marriage. In this way, the audience is from the start made aware of Campiglia's singular emphasis in her pastoral play on chaste love over marriage. This was of course a familiar theme in Petrarchan and especially neo-Platonic lyric verse, which combines ascetic Christian principles with the values of courtly love and was used extensively by women writers. But it is extremely rare to find it given such prominence in pastoral drama, which typically presents the innocent pleasures of sensual love. The conflict between these different kinds of love is dramatized particularly in the second part of the play. After the sacrifice, Flori has fallen in love with Alessi (III. 5–6), but desires a chaste spiritual union with him rather than marriage in the 'normal' sense. She perceives this as distinguishing her from the 'sciocca plebe' [foolish, vulgar hordes] (V. 1. 115) that love only transient earthly things.[69] However, her faithful companion, Licori, cannot understand Flori's 'pensieri insoliti' [strange thoughts] (V. 1. 51). For Licori, herself until recently a nymph of Diana but now in love with Androgeo, all honest lovers yearn to be united with the objects of their desire (V. 1. 89–95). According to her Aristotelian and earth-bound perspective, this entails marriage and procreation. Such a view is however presented as inferior to the neo-Platonic love that Flori desires, inspired by the beauty of the lover's soul and predicated on mutually respectful and de-sensualized companionship — perhaps akin to that of Talia and Coridone in *Partenia*, though here explicitly realized in the service of Diana.

While the prologue implies that it is Love's divine force that determines Flori's fate, the action of the play suggests that it also results from the providential outcome of the sacrifice and, importantly, from Flori's own choice after her sanity and agency are restored. Unlike other rare examples where the heroine nymph decides to continue serving Diana rather than marry, as in Lollio's *Aretusa* (see ch. 2, p. 42) and the Vicentine Livio Pagello's *Cinthia* (undated MS), this preference of Flori's is not retrospectively justified by the discovery that it will avoid incest. Rather, her decision is more reminiscent of the rational choice to adopt a celibate, independent lifestyle by the shepherd Silvio as well as by the chaste nymph Fiordiana in Argenti's *Sfortunato* (see ch. 2, pp. 42–43), and perhaps by Tirsi in Tasso's *Aminta*. Flori is presented as being able to pursue this path unencumbered by considerations of an economic, familial nature. Her father is dead and her brother (Fronimo) presents no obstacles to her wishes, being anxious only for his sister's cure (II. 5, III. 2–3). Indeed, Fronimo elsewhere comments on the misguided contemporary obsession with wealth over true love (IV. 2) and describes money as the root of all evil (V. 5. 55–57). It is for this reason that he agrees to help the young shepherd Leggiadro marry his beloved Gelinda (never presented on stage) — though ultimately this is facilitated by the recognition of Leggiadro's noble birth.[70] Flori's autonomy is further underscored by contrast to Licori, whose marriage to Androgeo depends on the consent of her father (Melampo). Even so, it is notable that in this play it is the nymphs who fulfil their desires rather than their shepherd suitors.

Campiglia's female lead thus allows a surprising exploration of the possibilities inherent in pastoral drama of representing individual self-determination. Yet it is the representation of Flori's first love for her dead companion Amaranta which probably strikes the modern reader as being Campiglia's greatest innovation to pastoral conventions. Lesbianism is very rarely mentioned in early modern writings of any kind. It is almost unprecedented to find the theme foregrounded to this extent in a pastoral play, though it is hinted at for titillating effect in Guarini's *Pastor fido* (the narrated kissing competition, II. 1. 122-249) and Groto's *Calisto* (II. 4, fol. 27^r), which both feature cross-dressed males insinuating themselves into all-female groups. Flori's love for Amaranta is, by contrast, consistently described as being pure and chaste. In this way, it appears closer to the protagonist's friendship with Licori, her other inseparable companion since childhood. Campiglia's play in fact gives unusual prominence to the theme of loyal and disinterested friendship between the nymphs (II. 1), in positive contrast to the selfishness and rivalry displayed by the shepherd Serrano (II. 3). This portrayal of female-female love could thereby challenge the conventional Renaissance idea of friendship being realized only amongst men. More radically, it potentially invoked a model of erotic female self-sufficiency and female empowerment, which was also implied in the representation of Diana bathing and hunting with her nymphs.[71] These suggestions would, however, seem to be defused somewhat by the chaste nature of Flori's desire and its final re-orientation toward a male subject.

Although Flori's love for Amaranta is de-sensualized in the play and further distanced through death, it still aroused bewildered unease and the moral condemnation of some of the male writers who contributed verse to the printed edition of the play.[72] They saw it as 'unnatural' or frankly even impossible that a woman could feel this way about another woman. As argued elsewhere, the play itself offers no clear single interpretation of this female-female love. On the one hand, it could be read in a moralizing or normalizing way as an irrational and excessive passion for an aberrant object. In this case, it reflects Flori's initial state of madness, which is 'corrected' by the societal sacrifice under the auspices of a priest and the gathered Arcadians, by being redirected towards a proper and sane (male) object of desire. According to this interpretation, Flori's love can also been seen as reflecting her neo-Platonic progression from an attachment to the mortal, physical body (symbolized by Amaranta's ashes) to a spiritual love of the soul (Alessi's). On the other hand, the play-text invites more complex interpretations when one considers that it is not solely the societal gods of Pan and Pales who bring about this conversion, but also the mischievous god Amore, who claims to be able to disrupt human rationality and undermine social and gender hierarchies (Prologue, 9–29). Furthermore, certain continuities are suggested between Flori's two loves. Both are described by Licori as being a desire for what is 'impossible' (V. 1. 51–60), since they refuse to accept the conventional norms of female behaviour. She had in fact earlier considered that Flori's madness was a punishment by the gods for refusing to accept her status as a woman and for aspiring to literary glory (I. 1. 100–12). In addition, Flori does not wholly reject her previous love for Amaranta after the sacrifice, but continues to recognize her companion's chastity and honour. It is suggested that Flori's earlier madness lay more in her refusal to accept the fact that her love object was dead than in the fact that she loved someone of her own sex.

Another link between Flori's two loves may be drawn in terms of their effects on the protagonist's literary development, following a consolidated tradition in lyric verse in which love and literary creativity are symbolically interlinked. Amaranta is described as first inspiring Flori to write, which stimulated her to 'leave the vulgar crowd' (III. 5, p. 167), while her love for Alessi holds the promise of future creativity. Alessi in fact declares that he loves not only the 'sun' in her eyes, but also the 'armonia soave/ De l'accorte parole' [the sweet harmonies of her sage words] (V. 2. 63–64); and he admires Flori's earlier intention to produce only intellectual offspring (V. 3. 90–93), which marks her off from other nymphs. The two lovers are finally represented singing together a eulogy of their patrons Pallavicino Lupi and Gonzaga (V. 3. 340–55). It is therefore tempting to read this union as an ideal staging of the equal literary relations that Campiglia sought between males and females.[73] So while her depiction of female-female love in her pastoral play can be read as an explicit challenge to canonical (patriarchal) representations of love and friendship, and as presenting a strong model of female self-sufficiency, it does not appear to call for a separatist feminist poetics (as suggested in Moderata Fonte's near contemporary *Il Merito delle donne*). Instead, it uses the genre to represent equal social and literary relations between women and men (and sometimes female superiority), and to stage the possibility of a 'bisexual' female poetic voice, inspired by both male and female models, and addressing both sexes.[74]

Isabella Andreini's Mirtilla

In comparison with the pastoral plays of Campiglia and Torelli, Isabella Andreini's *Mirtilla* (also printed 1588) contrasts markedly in tone, themes and characterization. In particular, it has a much stronger comic bias and promotes a distinctly earthy attitude to love. To a great extent, this should be linked with the author's very different social status, as one of the most distinguished virtuoso actresses of her day. This would explain the greater popularity and renown of her play in her time and today. Nonetheless, despite the availability of a recent edition in Italian by Maria Luisa Doglio and an English translation by Julie D. Campbell, *Mirtilla* has not received as much critical attention within the context of pastoral drama as one might expect.[75] Indeed, while theatre scholars have become increasingly interested in Andreini's dazzling performance career and the part played by actresses in the development of professional theatre, her play is often given only passing mention within this broader context.

Nothing precise is known of the early life of Isabella Canali (her maiden name) or of her presumably humble family origins in Padua until she joined the famous Gelosi acting company, possibly in 1576. Importantly for her career, she married Francesco Andreini, an actor from the same troupe. In becoming an actress, Isabella was entering a profession that was, as we have noted, socially ambiguous and often linked with the idea of sexual availability, as with the talented 'honest' courtesan. However, Taviani comments that Andreini was the first to succeed in offsetting these associations, and to create an image of the noble, beautiful actress who was not only a virtuoso in her stage-art, but also a virtuous wife and mother.[76] Such qualities are highlighted in the fulsome tributes that she received during her lifetime and also on her premature death in childbirth in Lyon in 1604.

Probably in order to dispel the idea of the actor as an illiterate improviser or whore and to transcend the evanescent fame of the theatrical world, Andreini sought to secure a more lasting name for herself. This was achieved in part by engaging in literary dialogue with eminent nobles and intellectuals of her day — including Gabriello Chiabrera, Angelo Ingegneri, and most notably Torquato Tasso — who celebrated her in verse and to whom she in turn dedicated occasional poetry.[77] As a result of her artistic success, she also gained access to elite male literary circles. She was evidently connected with the small coterie of Cardinal Cinzio Aldobrandini in Rome in the early 1590s, which included Tasso.[78] In 1601, most unusually, she was invited to join the Intenti academy of Pavia, where she adopted the name 'L'Accesa'. Importantly, she also strategically exploited the press to promote her fame through her writings, with the help of numerous male friends and admirers both from within the acting profession and outside. Prominent amongst those who contributed to glorifying her name (and thereby indirectly their profession) were her husband and oldest son, Giovan Battista, who continued publishing her works also after her death.[79]

Mirtilla represents Andreini's first literary venture published under her own name, probably at the age of twenty-six. Although some of her occasional verse had appeared in edited miscellanies before then, her own collection of *Rime* was not printed until 1601. According to a (posthumous) dedication to her *Lettere*, her *Mirtilla* was written 'a pena sapea leggere (per dir così)' [as soon as I could read, in a manner of speaking].[80] Though clearly making use of a conventional modesty topos here (as she does in the original dedication of the play, see p. 104), Andreini thereby draws further attention to the unusualness of an actor producing a 'literary' work. *Mirtilla*, as mentioned, represents a very early example of erudite pastoral drama composed by a professional actor. It is also the first and only known one by a female actor.[81] However, as Henke has recently demonstrated, virtuoso female actors had been playing the roles of *innamorate* (lovers) in tragicomedies and pastoral drama with great success since their prominent emergence on the stage in the 1560s. Such genres, often adapting plots from high literature, offered new possibilities for displaying a wider emotional range than was possible in comedy, including lyric and tragic scenes.[82]

From the outset it seems that Andreini intended *Mirtilla* to be appreciated not merely as the work of an actress meant to recall theatrical practices, but as a dramatic text of 'literary' value. So while the play makes use of certain standard theatrical devices reminiscent of professional techniques, and certainly brings more action to the stage than the examples of Torelli and Campiglia, there is surprisingly no reference to its performance. Indeed, this is not even mentioned in the dedicatory letter of the first edition of *Mirtilla*, addressed to Lavinia della Rovere, Marchioness of Vasto (24 February 1588), where the author refers only to her literary development. Unlike Campiglia's dedicatory letters to *Flori*, Andreini makes no allusion here to her sex or that of her patron either. Instead, she notes generically that this pastoral is the rather daring result of her sense of obligation to employ her intellect and pursue her studies, since 'l'ingegno umano' [human intellect] must be used properly; those who fail to do so are unsuited to be included 'tra gli uomini' [amongst men] (p. 33). This hints already at Andreini's less evidently pro-feminist aims in writing pastoral drama, although, as we will see, she enjoys playing ambiguously with existing conventions of gender.[83] In this respect, there is some continuity with her theatrical performances, where she frequently adopted masculine roles and personae. This practice is noted in the opening sonnet of her *Rime* and is suggested by the representation of the 'Isabella' character in Scala's collection of *commedia dell'arte* scenarios (1611), as well as being repeated in rhetorical terms in her *Lettere*.

The action of *Mirtilla* features a very conventional plot, with three couples of entangled lovers, as in Beccari's recently performed and revised *Sacrificio* (1587), who are eventually all happily paired off. It also draws on a series of episodes and motifs found in various earlier pastoral plays and irregular eclogues.[84] As mentioned, the prologue clearly alludes to that of Tasso's *Aminta*, featuring the god Amore who has come to Arcadia, where he will remain invisible in order to take revenge on those who scorn his power. In this case, though, he is accompanied by his mother Venus and targets two adversaries. The first is the shepherd-hunter (Tirsi) — a possible reference to Tasso's model, though probably closer to Silvio in Guarini's *Pastor fido* which Andreini knew by 1585 (see Chapter 6, p. 186) — who will feel the pangs of unrequited love for Mirtilla before she is finally persuaded to love him. However, for Ardelia, the chaste nymph of Diana, Cupid proposes a more bizarre punishment: 'avvampi/ per sua pena maggior di se medesma' [let her burn with self-love, as greater punishment] (Prologue, 157–58).

This scenario compares interestingly to Campiglia's form of 'deviant' love, since there is a suggestion of female-female desire initially in the naïve Ardelia's passion for the beautiful 'goddess' she appears to see in a fountain (IV. 4). By self-consciously altering the gender of the protagonist in the myth of Narcissus in Ovid's *Metamorphoses* III, Andreini gives a parodic and erotic twist to the familiar Petrarchan tropes about female beauty and its destructive effects.[85] But the potential offered by this display of narcissism for exploring gender relations and states of madness remains limited to this single scene. The prologue further suggests moralizingly that Ardelia's deviant passion is meant as punishment for her arrogant defiance of love. The scene functions also as a representation of the nymph's awakening to love, through her appropriation of Petrarchan topoi, but lacks the subtle sensual ambiguity found in Dafne's account of Silvia's self-admiration at a pool in *Aminta* (II. 2).[86] This is because Ardelia's gradual awareness of her predicament is exteriorized in way that was probably more comic than tragic in practice, since she is staged gesturing and talking to her own reflection. Furthermore, although she hopes that her desperate love will end in her death, as it did for Narcissus, she (unlike the boy) is able to walk away from the pool at the end of the scene. The situation is later normalized when Ardelia's suitor Uranio observes the 'strana meraviglia' (V. 5, 1840) of her self-love, and persuades the nymph to surrender to his love instead, with the conceit that she will in this way still be loving herself.

Mirtilla thus conforms to established conventions of pastoral drama, by having the independent nymph be gradually 'tamed' through love. Meanwhile, the other nymphs, Filli (or Fillide) and Mirtilla, who are initially rivals for the love of Uranio, are later moved with unconvincing haste by their rejected lover's promise of suicide (V. 3; V. 6) to reciprocate their feelings, following a much used pastoral device. Andreini therefore proposes a vision of love that is unthreateningly oriented towards the fulfilment of male desire, as found in most pastoral drama (though notably not Campiglia's *Flori*). Her acceptance of a conventionally patriarchal perspective is reinforced by having Tirsi refer to his wealth and lineage in persuading Mirtilla to love him (IV. 3. 2393–403), and by representing a wise, elderly shepherd (Opico) counselling the rival nymphs to abandon their suit of Uranio and re-establish friendship (III. 5).

Unlike the two other early female pastoral dramatists, whose social position made them more vulnerable to implications of sexual impropriety, the actress could acceptably favour a sensual view of love, rather than a chaste neo-Platonic union. As Ardelia finally declares to Uranio: 'amare il corpo voglio, e non più l'ombra' [I want to love the body and no longer the shadow] (V. 5. 2906). This stance is staked out already in the prologue, where Amore in its true form is described as being accompanied by honour, fidelity, prudence and the torch of Hymen, the god of marriage (102–08). In the play this view is supported by Amore's sage devotee, Coridone (Prologue, 191–92), who exemplifies and provides a lengthy eulogy for the pleasures of reciprocated sensual love in marriage (IV. 2). Andreini therefore appears to propose a more bourgeois view of love that would appropriately reflect her cultivated image as a respectable wife and mother.

At the same time, her less elevated social status allowed her the freedom to represent more frankly erotic and buffoonish episodes excluded from *Aminta*, drawing on the precedent of earlier pastoral dramatists like Groto, Beccari, and Cucchetti (who also had acting experience) as well as *commedia dell'arte* style gags. This is apparent in the scenes which involve the sensual, gluttonous goatherd Gorgo and the bestial but foolish Satyr. In Act III scene 2 Andreini stages an episode full of opportunities for comic action, where the Satyr seizes Filli by force threatening to tie her to an oaktree, as Tasso's Satyr did to Silvia, but ends up himself being tricked by the nymph. Filli plays on his deluded ego as a lover in order to humiliate him (like Corisca with the satyr in Guarini's *Pastor fido*). With the promise of a kiss, he allows himself to be tied to a tree so that he will not crush her, whereupon she pulls his beard, manhandles him, and gives him bitter aloe to eat before leaving him to his shame. In this respect, Filli's actions recall various earlier *beffe* in comedies, as well as in pastoral plays, including Melidia's cunning ruse to get out of the satyr's trap in Beccari's *Sacrificio* (II. 4), and Isse's trick of secretly tying the satyr-like god Apollo to a tree with her chastity belt to save herself from rape in Groto's *Calisto* (III. 5). Filli's ingenuity cannot therefore justifiably be described as challenging in terms of its depiction of feminine agency as suggested by Campbell ('Introduction', pp. XVIII–XX). The fact that the scene was meant to be acted — possibly by Andreini herself, since she was often referred to under the pseudonym of Filli — explains her adoption of such comic formulae in sharp contrast to the pathos of the off-stage attempted rape of the passive Silvia, described so voyeuristically in Tasso's *Aminta* (III. 1, see cover illustration).[87]

Besides the failed rape scene, *Mirtilla* includes other pastoral scenarios that would be effective in performance, such as a comically patterned dialogue between mismatched lovers (II. 3), and a final scene where all the lovers make offerings at the temple of Venus, punctuated by Gorgo's incongruous behaviour (V. 8). The most notable, though, is the song contest between two nymphs to win their beloved Uranio, which is wisely resolved by their forming a friendship (III. 5). This last scenario is closely modelled on Virgil's third eclogue, as MacNeil demonstrates, though it again alters the gender of the performers. In this way, a staged performance of *Mirtilla* could showcase the musical talents of the two leading ladies of the acting company — presumably in this case Andreini with her real stage rival Vittoria Piissimi — while also demonstrating the author's awareness of classical pastoral prototypes.[88] Otherwise the play appears less evidently 'dramatic' than might be expected, since it abounds with lengthy set-piece speeches and exchanges by the pastoral lovers. Yet these may well draw on the fragments of scenes or dialogues which formed part of the oral repertoire of an actor playing male or female lovers, which were rehearsed separately to adopt where needed. These re-usable elements, which included arguments for or against love, Petrarchan laments, threats of suicide, and descriptions of the beauty of nature, could then be inserted in the appropriate part of improvised pastoral or other drama. Presumably, the same procedure could also have been used by Andreini to construct her scripted play, after the set-pieces were rewritten in lyric unrhymed verse and garnished with references to classical mythology and neo-Platonism.[89] For this reason, pastoral drama must have appeared an effective starting point to launch her literary career, since it still enjoyed a relatively 'open' form, dependent less on theoretical precepts than on the imitation and adaptation of various recyclable scenarios — for which her profession equipped her well.

Conclusion

Despite their great variety, the earliest known female-authored pastoral plays here explored all reveal the importance in different ways of Tasso's *Aminta*, which served as a prestigious model from which to borrow selectively. All three women — including a socially mobile actress and two elite women dramatists — found additional ways of altering the genre, so as to maintain social and literary decorum while negotiating access to and acceptance in (semi-)public literary circles. They show that pastoral drama not only allowed the authors to project accepted gender values for their particular social position and to allude to patrons and other socially legitimizing figures, but it also had the potential to accommodate more challenging explorations of feminine concerns and critiques of patriarchal ideology.

Torelli and Campiglia's plays are also significant in that they prefigure some of the changes that occurred in pastoral drama from around the last decade of the century, with their general reduction of indecorous material and introduction of a moralizing and spiritualizing strain. Such changes have typically been associated with Guarini's *Pastor fido* (printed 1589/90), the most famous 'reworking' of *Aminta* of all. This brought the more serious model of the genre with Christian overtones initiated by the female dramatists to popular attention, but at the same time maintained its comic performance potential. As we will see in the next chapter, Guarini follows other dramatists in drawing self-consciously on *Aminta*, while rejecting its structure and some of the ideological positions. Moreover, he breaks new ground for the genre in developing a sophisticated theoretical justification for it, linked to tragicomedy. In doing so, he harks back to the more complex, comedic model established by Beccari's *Sacrificio*, a play that Guarini helped to stage with some additions of his own in 1587. Guarini thus seems to propose an alternative path for the development of pastoral drama from that taken by Tasso — one in which he could be considered as playing a more instrumental role, and which would bestow it with clearly defined poetic objectives and monumental aspirations.

Notes to Chapter 4

1. Traiano Boccalini, *Ragguagli di Parnaso, e scritti minori*, ed. by Luigi Firpo (Bari: Laterza, 1948), Cent. I, LVIII, p. 209.
2. Carpanè, 'fortuna editoriale', pp. 543–44, 546–48. For a sense of the numbers of writers of pastoral after *Aminta*, from different geographical centres, see Pieri, *Scena boschereccia*, pp. 167–74.
3. For further studies, see Louise George Clubb's valuable 'The Making of the Pastoral Play: Some Italian experiments between 1573 and 1590', in *Petrarch to Pirandello, Studies in Italian Literature in honour of Beatrice Corrigan*, ed. by Julius A. Molinaro (Toronto: University of Toronto Press, 1973), pp. 45–73 (which appears in a slightly different form in Clubb's *Italian Drama in Shakespeare's Time* (New Haven; London: Yale University Press, 1989), chapter 4); Domenico Chiodo, 'Tra l'"Aminta" e il "Pastor fido"', *Italianistica*, 24: 2–3 (1995), 559–75 [this has appeared more recently in *Torquato Tasso, poeta gentile* (Bergamo: Centro di Studi Tassiani, 1998)]; Di Benedetto; Giuseppe Dalla Palma, 'Aminta, Alceo, Tirena: Una serie pastorale', in *La Poesia pastorale nel rinascimento*, ed. by Stefano Carrai (Padua: Antenore, 1998); and Riccò, 'Ben mille pastorali'.
4. Chiodo, 'Tra l'"Aminta"', pp. 559–61. *Teonemia* (unpublished during the author's lifetime) appears to be one of the earliest imitations of *Aminta*, influenced by the performance of the play in Urbino in 1574.
5. Tasso, *Lettere*, IV, 1160, 234 (see also IV, 1123, 196, and IV, 1131, 203); Maddalena Campiglia, *Flori, a pastoral drama*, ed. by Virginia Cox and Lisa Sampson, trans. by Virginia Cox (Chicago: University of Chicago Press, 2004), pp. 32, 322 n. 92 (identification of Alessi).
6. Cucchetti's *Pazzia* (Ferrara: Vittorio Baldini, 1581) includes one sonnet by Tasso.
7. See for example Dalla Palma's close analysis of linguistic borrowings from *Aminta* by Antonio Ongaro and Pietro Cresci ('Aminta'). However, a few plays published after *Aminta* still used older metres such as the *terzina* and octave, such as Camillo Della Valle's *Fillide, egloga pastorale* (Ferrara: Vittorio Baldini, 1584). On Tasso's use of metre in *Aminta*, see Scrivano, 'Tasso', pp. 228–35.

8. Ingegneri, *Della Poesia*, pp. 4, 5, see also 15.
9. See Andrea Chegai, *Le Novellette a sei voci di Simone Balsamino. Prime musiche su* Aminta *di Torquato Tasso* (1594) (Florence: Olschki, 1993). He notes, however, the belatedness of the fifty-two musical settings of the play, which only appeared in eleven publications, using few sections of the text (p. 24 n. 58). For details, see Antonio Vassalli, 'Il Tasso in musica e la trasmissione dei testi: alcuni esempi', in *Tasso, la musica, i musicisti*, ed. by Maria Antonella Balsano and Thomas Walker (Florence: Olschki, 1988), pp. 45–90 (pp. 59–90).
10. See Domenico Chiodo, 'Introduzione' to Antonio Ongaro and Girolamo Vida, *Favole* (Turin: RES, 1998), pp. VII–XXV (pp. XXIII–XXIV).
11. See James Chater's preliminary list of musical compositions based on or inspired by Guarini's pastoral play: '*Il Pastor fido* and music: A bibliography', in *Guarini, La musica, I musicisti*, ed. by Angelo Pompilio (Lucca: Libreria Musicale Italiana, 1997), pp. 157–84.
12. *Della poesia*, p. 11. This point was made also by Muzio Manfredi, see n. 51 below.
13. Clubb, 'The Making'. For a critical evaluation of the borrowings from *Aminta* in *Alceo*, though focusing on style, see Giuseppe Dalla Palma, 'Un capitolo della fortuna dell'*Aminta*: L'*Alceo* di Antonio Ongaro', *Rivista di letteratura italiana*, 12 (1994), 79–128; Chiodo, 'Tra l'"Aminta"', pp. 567–69; and Chiodo, 'Introduzione', pp. VII–XXV (pp. XIV–XVII).
14. For a comparison between the pastoral plays of Cremonini and Tasso, see Elena Bergonzi, 'Cesare Cremonini scrittore, il periodo ferrarese e i primi anni padovani, la pastorale *Le Pompe funebri*', *Aevum*, 67 (1993), 571–93 (pp. 581–87). See also C. B. Schmitt, 'Cremonini, Cesare', in *DBI*, 30 (1984), 618–22.
15. See, however, the prologue to Campiglia's *Flori*, discussed below, p. 115–16.
16. For the view that Ingegneri reuses the subject of the prologue of Sannazaro's *Farsa di Venere* (performed 1488/1490), see Pieri, *Scena boschereccia*, p. 65 n. 1; for further comparisons with Tasso's prologue, see Riccò, 'Sassuolo 1587'.
17. Chiodo, 'Tra l'"Aminta"', p. 566; also his 'Introduzione', pp. VIII, X, XV–XVI (on the *Alceo* choruses).
18. Scarpati, 'Il nucleo ovidiano', pp. 94–97.
19. Virginia Cox, 'Fiction, 1560–1650', in *A History of Women's Writing in Italy*, ed. by Letizia Panizza and Sharon Wood (Cambridge: Cambridge University Press, 2000), pp. 52–64 (pp. 52–54). Compare Carlo Dionisotti, 'La letteratura italiana nell'età del Concilio di Trento' in *Geografia e storia della letteratura* (Turin: Einaudi, 1967), pp. 227–54 (pp. 238–39).
20. Sacred drama was however composed by Antonia Tanini Pulci (1452–1501), Raffaella de' Sernigi (c. 1473–1557) and Beatrice del Sera (1515–85), see Elissa Weaver, *Convent Theatre in Early Modern Italy. Spiritual fun and learning for women* (Cambridge: Cambridge University Press, 2002), pp. 67 n. 50, 96–127.
21. See Richard Andrews, 'Isabella Andreini and others: women on stage in the late Cinquecento', in *Women in Italian Renaissance Culture and Society*, ed. by Letizia Panizza (Oxford: Legenda, 2000), pp. 316–33 (p. 317).
22. Cox, 'Fiction', p. 53. By comparison, the first original female-authored play in England is Elizabeth Cary's *The Tragedy of Mariam* (composed c.1603–09, printed 1613), itself influenced by Ludovico Dolce's *Marianna* (1565). (I thank Richard Andrews for this point.) On Costa and the pro-feminist subtext to her three-act comedy, see Marcella Salvi, '"Il solito è sempre quello, l'insolito è più nuovo": *Li Buffoni* e le prostitute di Margherita Costa fra tradizione e innovazione', *Forum Italicum*, 38/2 (2004), 376–99.
23. *La Mirtilla* was published ten times in a variety of centres between 1588 and 1620 and also translated into French in 1602. See the edition by Maria Luisa Doglio (Lucca: Maria Pacini Fazzi, 1995), pp. 23–29. On the reception of Torelli's *Partenia*, see my '*Drammatica secreta*: Barbara Torelli's *Partenia* (c. 1587) and women in late sixteenth-century theatre', in *Theatre, Opera, and Performance in Italy from the Fifteenth Century to the Present: Essays in Honour of Richard Andrews*, ed. by Brian Richardson, Simon Gilson and Catherine Keen (Society for Italian Studies, Occasional Papers, 2004), pp. 99–115 (pp. 99–100, 110). On the fortunes of Campiglia's *Flori*, see Cox and Sampson, pp. 31–35.
24. For Asinari Valperga, see Ireneo Affò, *Memorie degli Scrittori e Letterati Parmigiani*, 7 vols (Parma: Dalla Stamperia Reale, 1793; repr. Bologna: Forni, 1969), IV, 295.
25. See especially the recent wave of research on the patronage, performance and composition of theatre by female elites in England, which includes pastoral drama and masques: for example, Alison Findlay,

'Gendering the Stage', in *A Companion to Renaissance Drama*, ed. by Arthur F. Kinney (Oxford: Blackwell, 2002), pp. 399–415 (pp. 411–13); and, in the same volume, Margaret Ferguson, 'Sidney, Cary, Wroth', pp. 482–506 (on Mary Wroth's unpublished pastoral tragicomedy *Love's Victory*, composed c. 1615–18). See also *Renaissance Drama by Women: Texts and Documents*, ed. by S. P. Cerasano and Marion Wynne-Davis (London: Routledge, 1996); and Alison Findlay and Stephanie Hodgson-Wright with Gweno Williams, *Women and Dramatic Production 1550–1700* (Harlow: Longman, 2000).

26. Cox, 'Fiction', p. 56.
27. Ann Rosalind Jones, *The Currency of Eros: Women's Love Lyric in Europe, 1540–1620* (Bloomington and Indianapolis: Indiana University Press, 1990), especially pp. 1–10 for the concepts of imitation, 'negotiation' and appropriation.
28. See Jones, *Currency*, pp. 122–41 (on Stampa, though this somewhat overemphasizes the 'fantasy' dimension of Italian pastoral and the idea that women are normally denied a voice in this mode). For Laura Battiferri degli Ammannati's encomiastic eclogue and other verse, of which some contains pastoral tropes, see *Il Primo Libro delle Opere Toscane* [Florence, 1560], ed. by Enrico Maria Guidi (Urbino: Accademia Raffaello, 2000); Guidi's introduction (pp. 5–26) emphasizes the spiritual themes latent in her poetry, but does not discuss her use of the pastoral mode. See also the introduction by Françoise Lavocat to her edition of Lucrezia Marinella, *Arcadia felice* (Florence: Olschki, 1998), pp. vii–lx. I am indebted to Virginia Cox to bringing this edition and Battiferri's verse to my attention.
29. *Della poesia*, p. 7. The word 'palco' is here understood as stage, rather than as the seats for the audience. For a wide-ranging critical discussion of the appearance of women on stage, see Richard Andrews, 'L'attrice e la cantante fra Cinquecento e Seicento: la presenza femminile in palcoscenico', in *Teatro e Musica. Ècriture vocale et scénique*, Actes du Colloque, 17–19 February 1998 (Toulouse: Presses Universitaires du Mirail, 1999), pp. 27–43. See also Giraldi on representing women in comedy and tragedy, chapter 2, p. 20.
30. Solerti, *Ferrara*, p. CLX.
31. See Sampson, '*Drammatica secreta*', pp. 106–07; Anna Ceruti Burgio, 'E' una Torelli l'Hippolita amata da Vincenzo Gonzaga', *Aurea Parma*, 84 (2000), 39–46; and Gambara, Pellegri and De Grazia, pp. 181–84. On the still understudied figure of Pallavicino Lupi, see Stefano Andretta, *La Venerabile Superbia, Ortodossia e trasgressione nella vita di Suor Francesca Farnese (1593–1651)* (Turin: Rosenberg & Sellier, 1994), pp. 56–60; Carlo Ossola, *Dal Cortegiano all' "Uomo di mondo". Storia di un libro e di un modello sociale* (Turin: Einaudi, 1987), pp. 113–20. On Argotta, see Fenlon, *Music and Patronage*, pp. 33, 149.
32. For a private performance in Ferrara in 1492 involving various court ladies, see Richard Andrews, 'Isabella Andreini', p. 330 n. 6. Around the same time Alessandra Scala (daughter of the Florentine chancellor) played the lead role in a private performance in Greek of Sophocles' *Electra* (Anthony Grafton and Lisa Jardine, *From Humanism to the Humanities. Education and the Liberal Arts in Fifteenth- and Sixteenth-Century Europe* (London: Duckworth, 1986), pp. 53–56 (especially p. 54)).
33. Povoledo, col. 178.
34. See the dedicatory letter, commemorating the performance in Soragna, 1583; also Muzio Manfredi, *Cento Madrigali di Mutio Manfredi, Il Fermo Academico Innominato, Invaghito, e di Ferrara* (Mantova: Francesco Osanna, 1587), p. 63.
35. Sampson, 'Drammatica secreta', p. 109. Compare the display by the Queen Regent of France, Maria de' Medici, of her unmarried daughters in dramatic performances at court, when marriage negotiations were underway, as described in Melinda J. Gough, 'Courtly *Comédiantes*: Henrietta Maria and amateur Women's Stage Plays in France and England', in *Women Players in England, 1550–1660. Beyond the All-Male Stage* (Aldershot: Ashgate, 2005), pp. 193–215 (pp. 195–96, 201–03).
36. Elio Durante and Anna Martellotti, *Cronistoria del Concerto delle Dame principalissime di Margherita Gonzaga d'Este* (Florence: SPES, 1979), pp. 16–17; Newcomb, pp. 7–14, 35–44.
37. Weaver, p. 85; Newcomb, pp. 36–37. At the English court, Queen Henrietta Maria also appeared in a pastoral play with her ladies, some cross-dressed with beards (Gough, p. 207; Nancy Cotton, 'Women playwrights in England: Renaissance noblewomen', in *Readings in Renaissance Women's Drama. Criticism, history, and performance 1594–1998*, ed. by S. P. Cerasano and Marion Wynne-Davies (London: Routledge, 1998), pp. 32–46 [p. 38]).
38. Muzio Manfredi, *Il Contrasto amoroso, pastorale* (Venice: Giacomo Antonio Somascho, 1602), dedicatory letter to Vittoria Doria Gonzaga, Ravenna, 1 October 1601, fols A5^{r-v}.

39. On the performance of *Filli*, see Francesco Ronconi's dedicatory letter to Cardinal Antonio Barberino, in Guidubaldo Bonarelli dell Rovere, *Opere* (Rome: Ludovico Grignari, 1640), fol. 2ᵛ. On Henrietta Maria, see Findlay, 'Gendering', p. 411, and especially Gough, pp. 198–99, 203–10 (though she considers the female royal performers in France as being indebted to the example of Italian virtuoso actresses). On a performance of Guarini's *Pastor fido* (trans. by Sir Richard Fanshawe, 1648) in a private house, performed and directed by Lady Elizabeth Delavel, see Findlay, Hodgson-Wright, with Williams, pp. 144–45; and more generally pp. 52–55, 59–66, 70–76.
40. Letter to Duke Vincenzo Gonzaga (2 April 1596), cited in Marina Calore, 'Muzio Manfredi tra polemiche teatrali e crisi del mecenatismo', *Studi romagnoli*, 36 (1985), 27–54 (p. 50).
41. Sampson, 'Drammatica secreta'. For biographical details on Torelli, see p. 100, and Affò, IV, 292–97 (though not wholly reliable).
42. *Cento donne cantate da Mutio Manfredi, Il Fermo Academico Innominato di Parma* (Parma: Nella Stamperia d'Erasmo Viotti, 1580), p. 35 (see also p. 257, where she is described as writing verse and being close to the author); and *Cento Madrigali*, p. 43. Despite Manfredi's reference in 1580 to Torelli's verse composition, her earliest datable literary work is the *Partenia*. Some occasional verse of hers appears later in works published by male acquaintances.
43. 'Drammatica secreta', p. 106.
44. Preceding the play, there are verses by Muzio Manfredi, Bernardino Baldi (2), Girolamo Pallantieri, and Marchese Camillo Malaspina. Following it, there is one anonymous verse (by Torelli?), then others by Don Ferrante Gonzaga, Prospero Cataneo, Curzio Gonzaga [Curtio Gonzzagi], again by Muzio Manfredi, Silvio Calandra, Marco Pio di Savoia, Fortuniano Sanvitale, and Antonio Beffa Negrini. On the gifting of the *Partenia* manuscript, see Manfredi, *Lettere brevissime* (Venice: Roberto Meietti, 1606), p. 214 (letter no. 263 to Carlo Emanuele, 20 Sept. 1591).
45. Maylender, III, pp. 292-98. See also the recent study by Lucia Denarosi, *L'Accademia degli Innominati di Parma: teorie letterarie e progetti di scrittura (1574-1608)* (Florence: Società Editrice Fiorentina, 2003), which I have unfortunately not been able to consult.
46. See Bernardino Baldi's eclogues and Girolamo Pallantieri's translation of Virgil's *Bucolics* (printed posthumously with the intervention of Manfredi in 1603).
47. Pastoral plays printed in Parma before 1587 (such as that of Cucchetti) were not explicitly associated with the academy. Unprinted examples by academicians include one by Crisippo Selva (by 1591, see Manfredi, *Lettere*, p. 182) and Eugenio Visdomini's *Erminia* (based on Tasso's *Gerusalemme liberata*, XIX, dedicated to Pomponio Torelli). Several were printed and dedicated to the Farnese family after Manfredi's *Semiramide, boscareccia* (1593) (Pieri, *Scena boschereccia*, p. 170; Sampson, 'Drammatica secreta', p. 105). For interesting recent analysis of the theorizing on pastoral drama within the Innominati academy, see Riccò, 'Ben mille pastorali', especially pp. 309-19, 324-27, which draws on Denarosi's *L'Accademia degli Innominati*.
48. Parma, Archivio di Stato [ASP], Epistolario scelto, b.11 'Manfredi', fasc. 2; Sampson, 'Drammatica secreta', pp. 108, 114 n. 39.
49. ASP, Epistolario scelto, b. 11, fasc. 3; see also Calore, p. 42 (which has one minor mistake in the transcription). On Manfredi's relations with Ferrante Gonzaga, see Lucia Denarosi, 'Il Principe e il letterato: due carteggi inediti di Muzio Manfredi', *Studi italiani*, 17 (1997), 151–76. On pastoral staging, see Chapter 6.
50. Denarosi, p. 158, Calore, 'Muzio Manfredi', pp. 42–43.
51. In attempting to dissuade Torelli from her apparent desire to add choruses (four *canzonette*) to her play, Manfredi writes: 'La Partenia, bellissima pastorale, di V[ostra] S[ignoria] da prima fu senza il coro composta, e fu ben fatto; conciosia che contenendo la Pastorale azion private, non è capace del coro' [Your Ladyship's beautiful pastoral play, Partenia, was first composed without a chorus and was well done; for as pastoral drama represents private actions, a chorus is not suited to it], *Lettere brevissime*, 11 January 1591, no. 11, pp. 10–11. For Manfredi's views on pastoral and further analysis of *Partenia*, see Riccò, 'Ben mille pastorali', pp. 326–36 (p. 335 n. 63 on the lice episode).
52. Pastoral verse had been associated with elegy and funeral celebrations since classical times (see Virgil, Eclogue, V; Bion, Idyll 1; Moschus, Idyll III).
53. On the Christian subtext to pastoral drama, especially following Guarini's *Pastor fido*, see Andrews, 'Theatre', p. 297; Clubb, *Italian Drama*, pp. 110–12.
54. 'Drammatica secreta', p. 103. Prior to the *Partenia*, only sacred plays are known to have been written by Italian women, see n. 20 above. The links between convent and secular drama in the context

55. Tasso's Silvia appears in a greater proportion of scenes in *Aminta* (three of ten), and more significantly positioned ones (I. 1; both scenes of act IV).
56. Vespasiano Zugliano (Giuliani), preface to Maddalena Campiglia *Discorso* [...] *Sopra l'Annonciatione della Beata Vergine* (Vicenza, Appresso Perin Libraro, & Giorgio Greco compagni, 1585), fol. †6ᵛ. (The quotation below is by Gregorio Ducchi and prefaces the concluding celebratory verse.) For an interesting exploration of Campiglia's social position and the polyvalent term 'dimessa', see Lori J. Ultsch, 'Maddalena Campiglia, "dimessa nel mondano cospetto"?: Secular Celibacy, Devotional Communities, and Social Identity in Early Modern Vicenza', *Forum Italicum*, 39/2 (2005), 350-77; and, especially on the 'dimessa' movement, Adriana Chemello, '"Donne a poetar esperte": la "rimatrice dimessa" Maddalena Campiglia, *Versants*, n. s. 46 (2003), 65-101 (I am grateful to Virginia Cox for this reference). For further biography on Campiglia, see also Cox and Sampson, pp. 2-7; Giovanni Mantese, 'Per un profilo storico della poetessa vicentina Maddalena Campiglia: aggiunte e rettifiche', *Archivio veneto*, 81 (1967), 89-123; and Bernardo Morsolin, *Maddalena Campiglia, poetessa vicentina del secolo XVI, episodio biografico* (Vicenza: Paroni, 1882). On Campiglia and her oeuvre, see also Chemello; and Ultsch, 'Epithalamium Interruptum: Maddalena Campiglia's New Arcadia', *Modern Language Notes*, 120/1 (2005), 70-92.
57. Vicenza, Biblioteca Bertoliana (BBV), Atti dell'Accademia Olimpica, 2. fasc. 10 ('L'), fol. 28ᵛ, p. 54.
58. Mazzoni, pp. 94–105.
59. Cox and Sampson, p. 320 n. 74. All references to *Flori* are to this edition. For speculation that Campiglia may have performed some madrigals informally for the Olimpici, see Ultsch, 'Maddalena Campiglia', p. 353.
60. *Flori*, Dedicatory letter to Curzio Gonzaga, p. 48; Cox and Sampson, p. 7.
61. Cox and Sampson, pp. 14–15.
62. Giovanni Mantese, *I mille libri che si leggevano e vendevano a Vicenza alla fine del secolo XVI* (Vicenza: Accademia Olimpica, 1968), pp. 7–16.
63. Cox and Sampson, p. 10; Marisa Milani, 'Quattro donne fra i pavani', *Museum Patavinum*, 1 (1983), 387–412 (pp. 393–95, 408–09).
64. Cox and Sampson, pp. 4–5, 22–23 (Campiglia's lifestyle compared to the secluded existence of Moderata Fonte, an upper-class Venetian married woman). Though on the cultural possibilities that Venice offered to Marinella later, see Lavocat, pp. XIII-XIV.
65. Mazzoni, pp. 88–93; see also Bruno Brizi, 'Le feste e gli spettacoli', in *Storia di Vicenza*, ed. by Girolamo Arnaldi and others, 4 vols (Vicenza: Neri Pozza, 1987–93), III/2 (1990): *L'Età della repubblica veneta (1404–1797)*, ed. by Franco Barbieri and Paolo Preto, pp. 183–210.
66. Mantese, 'Profilo', p. 97; Cox and Sampson, pp. 4, 11, 32.
67. On the editions, see Cox and Sampson, Appendix A, pp. 305–06.
68. Cox and Sampson, pp. 29–31.
69. The priest, Damone, suggests that Flori's madness was caused initially by her own excessive attachment to earthly beauty (of a woman), I. 2, 17–18. On Campiglia's unconventional treatment of the themes of love and marriage in pastoral drama and her oeuvre generally, see also Ultsch, 'Epithalamium'. However, the union between Flori and Alessi is here read as an unusual form of marriage rather than as an alternative to it.
70. Fronimo's dialogue with Leggiadro carries echoes of the speech of Tasso's satyr (*Aminta*, II. 1) and especially Torelli's *Partenia* (I. 2, II. 6, III. 2). However, no mention is made here of the associated pastoral topos of the Golden Age.
71. Patricia Simons, 'Lesbian (In)visibility in Italian Renaissance Culture: Diana and Other Cases of 'Donna con Donna', *Journal of Homosexuality*, 27 (1994), 81–122 (pp. 94–109). Otherwise, on the omission of lesbianism in different kinds of writing, see Judith C. Brown, 'Lesbian Sexuality in Medieval and early Modern Europe', in *Hidden from History. Reclaiming the Gay and Lesbian Past*, ed. by Martin Duberman and others (New York: Dover, 1989), pp. 67–75; also Cox and Sampson, p. 23.
72. See especially the verse of Chiappino, Manfredi and Prospero Cattaneo (Cox and Sampson, pp. 23–24; and for different interpretations of the female-female love, pp. 24–28).
73. Cox and Sampson, p. 22.
74. Cox and Sampson, p. 26. Compare too the representation of female-female love for the more conventional purpose of symbolizing the poet's relationship with her patron (Isabella Pallavicino

Lupi) in Campiglia's pastoral eclogue *Calisa* (pp. 27–28). See also Carlachiara Perrone, *'So che donna ama donna': La* Calisa *di Maddalena Campiglia* (Galatina: Congedo, 1996), p. 44–45 and Ultsch, 'Epithalamium' for a different reading of the theme in *Calisa*.

75. See note 23. Notably, Clubb does not include *Mirtilla* in her survey of plays composed between *Aminta* and *Pastor fido*, but includes a separate section on Andreini at the end of her *Italian drama*, pp. 257–73. Amongst recent studies which specifically mention *Mirtilla*, see Franco Vazzoler, 'Le pastorali dei comici dell'arte: La *Mirtilla* di Isabella Andreini', in Chiabò and Doglio, pp. 281–99; Richard Andrews, 'Isabella Andreini', pp. 324–35; and Julie D. Campbell's 'Introduction' to her translation of *Isabella Andreini, La Mirtilla: A Pastoral* (Tempe AZ: Center for Medieval and Renaissance Studies, 2002), pp. xi-xxvii, and her '*Love's Victory* and *La Mirtilla* in the Canon of Renaissance Tragicomedy: an examination of the influence of salon and social debates', *Women's Writing*, 4: 1 (1997), 103–24. For analyses of specific scenes in *Mirtilla*, see also Anne MacNeil, *Music and women of the commedia dell'arte in the late sixteenth century* (Oxford: Oxford University Press, 2003), pp. 37–46 (III. 5), 122–25 (III. 2). All references to *Mirtilla* are to Maria Luisa Doglio's edition (Lucca: Maria Pacini Fazzi, 1995).
76. Ferdinando Taviani, 'Bella d'Asia. Torquato Tasso, gli attori e l'immortalità', *Paragone letteratura*, 35 (1984), 3–76 (p. 5, 45), see also Andrews, 'L'attrice'. For biographical details, see also Nancy Dersofi, 'Isabella Andreini (1562–1604)', in *Italian Women Writers. A Bio-Bibliographical Sourcebook*, ed. by Rinaldina Russell (Westport CT: Greenwood, 1994), pp. 18–25.
77. For a detailed exploration of the real and suggested ways in which Isabella's association with Tasso was forged during her lifetime and posthumously, see Taviani, 'Bella d'Asia'. See also MacNeil, *Music and Women*, pp. 41 (Ingegneri), 62–64 (Chiabrera).
78. Taviani, 'Bella d'Asia', pp. 29–30, 36
79. Andrews notes the consequent difficulty in interpreting Andreini's posthumous works ('Isabella Andreini', pp. 320, 323–24, 326–27).
80. *Lettere d'Isabella Andreini* (Venice: Sebastiano Combi, 1612); the dedicatory letter (dated 14 March 1607) is quoted in MacNeil, *Music and Women*, pp. 292–94 (p. 293).
81. While it has been suggested that the actress Vittoria Piissimi wrote a pastoral play entitled *Fillide* besides a comedy (Jolanda De Blasi, *Le scrittrici italiane dalle origini al 1800* (Florence: 'Nemi', 1930), pp. 105–13), it is more likely that *Fillide* was dedicated to the actress by Bernardino Lombardi as noted by Taviani ('Bella d'Asia', p. 19 n. 44).
82. Robert Henke, *Performance and Literature in the Commedia dell'Arte* (Cambridge: Cambridge University Press, 2002), pp. 85–105.
83. Campbell's argument for Andreini's challenge to idealizing, Petrarchan portrayals of female characters does not take into account the long tradition of representing pro-active, resourceful nymphs in pastoral drama. For the view that *Mirtilla* displays limited evidence of a personal or female perspective, see Andrews, 'Isabella Andreini', pp. 324–25. On Andreini's adoption of male personae, see pp. 326–27 (I thank Andrews for his observation on Scala's scenarios); and Taviani, 'Bella d'Asia', pp. 7–8 (Andreini playing Aminta in Tasso's *Aminta*), p. 57.
84. On the links with Calmo's eclogues, see Marzia Pieri, 'Il "Pastor fido" e i comici dell'Arte', *Biblioteca teatrale*, 17 (1990), 1–15.
85. For further readings and a possible prototype for this transformation in the *arte* scenario *Li Tre Satiri*, see Campbell, 'Introduction', pp. xxi-xxii.
86. Compare, however, the comic scenario in Campiglia's *Flori* (IV. 3), where the foolish nymph Urania tries to admire herself in a pool and seems to see her beloved with Love, which raises questions about female vanity and self-delusion.
87. Though for the argument that Andreini's attempted rape scene acts as a parody of Tasso's, see MacNeil, *Music and Women*, pp. 122–23. Note that the device of a nymph's counter-trick on a satyr was also used in Valeria Miani's *Amorosa speranza*. (I thank Virginia Cox for this point.)
88. On Andreini's erudition and the musical performance implied in *Mirtilla* III, 5, see MacNeil, *Music and Women*, pp. 36–46.
89. For neo-Platonic elements to Andreini's work, see Anne MacNeil, 'The divine madness of Isabella Andreini', *Journal of the Royal Musical Association*, 120 (1995), 193–215. For the suggestion that Andreini's *Lettere* (1612) demonstrate how collections of rhetorical commonplaces could be reworked as literary exercises, see Andrews, 'Isabella Andreini', pp. 327–28.

CHAPTER 5

Guarini's *Pastor fido*: The Establishment of an Ethical and Political Model of Pastoral Drama

> [Aristotile] ubbligò ben i poeti moderni alle regole delle spezie da lui addotte, ma non vietò che sul tronco della poetica naturale non si possano far nuovi innesti.[1]
>
> [[Aristotle] may have obliged modern poets to follow the rules of the poetic genres that he defined, but he did not forbid new grafts from being made onto the trunk of natural poetics.]

Guarini's *Pastor fido* and the Critical Debate on Pastoral Tragicomedy

Within the history of regular pastoral drama, Battista Guarini's *Pastor fido* and related theoretical writings occupy a central position. Through these works, the dramatist sought to legitimize the pastoral tragicomedy (so termed with a clear dramaturgical intent for the first time) in relation to other dramatic forms, and to propose his own authoritative model for future authors to imitate. Guarini's careful blending of selected dramatic, literary and stylistic ingredients in his play, in a manner calculated to appeal to contemporary audiences, and his skilful definition of his practice according to Aristotelian poetic theory — and later moral justification of it — contributed to the extraordinary success of the *Pastor fido*. It became one of the most popular works of secular literature in Europe during the seventeenth century as attested to by the many imitations and literary allusions to it.[2]

This chapter explores Guarini's experiments with pastoral drama to expand its scope, and the strategies by which he subsequently defended his *Pastor fido* from accusations that it lacked verisimilitude as well as moral and literary decorum. Given the great number and variety of existing studies on Guarini's masterpiece, we shall examine questions and works that remain less explored. For this reason, discussion of Guarini's poetic style and performance-related issues is deferred to later chapters. The focus of this chapter will fall on the critical debate surrounding the pastoral tragicomedy, which raised important questions about the social role of poetry and drama. This will be considered in relation to contemporary thought in the context of Paduan circles which Guarini frequented for much of his life. Reflections on the ideological connotations of the Arcadian space and community evoked in the *Pastor fido* will further enable the evaluation of how Guarini altered pastoral poetics since the time of *Aminta*'s composition. In particular, his vision of an Arcadian society is shown to reveal a striking debt to contemporary thought on social and human evolution, as well as suggesting conflicting new ethical and religious perspectives.

Battista Guarini (1538–1612) was well placed to make a seminal contribution to the development of pastoral drama. He originated from a prominent Ferrarese family, distinguished by his namesake Battista Guarini, son of the more famous Guarino of Verona; and from 1567 he was employed for several years as a courtier in the service of the Estensi.[3] While fulfilling a more stable career at court than his slightly younger contemporary Tasso — first being entrusted with various important embassies and then as ducal secretary between late 1585 and 1588 — Guarini too experienced mounting frustration with Alfonso II and became increasingly critical about princely service. This led to him resigning his post temporarily in Ferrara in 1583 and later to his definitive break with the Duke in 1588. Intermittently, Guarini attempted with limited success to find more satisfactory employment elsewhere, particularly at the courts of Turin (1585) and Florence (1588, succeeding in 1599–1601), as well as serving in Mantua (1592–93) and Urbino (1602–04). Some intellectual stimulation and freedom from his often fraught lifestyle was found in Padua, where he had been a student and later participated in the academies of the Eterei (1564–67) and Ricovrati. Here he was also near to his villa 'La Guarina' in the Polesine (San Bellino), which gave him the opportunity to conduct his family business and engage in literary activities. However, Guarini frequently stressed that poetry for him, unlike Tasso, represented only a pastime and was difficult to reconcile with his courtly obligations.[4]

It was probably in this Paduan context that Guarini carried out much of the long and complex process of composing his *Pastor fido*. He began working on it in 1580/81 around the time that the Aldine edition of Tasso's *Aminta* appeared. By April 1584 the play still lacked the whole of Act V, and the choruses, which were still incomplete in January 1586 and possibly not fully finished until publication.[5] Detailed philological examination by Carla Molinari of the three surviving manuscripts of the play alongside Guarini's letters has revealed that significant alterations continued until at least 1585–86, which show the dramatist's changing theoretical conception of structure and characterization.[6] Yet, even while incomplete, the play was circulating in manuscript form and discussed in literary circles in Padua and elsewhere in the Veneto and northern Italian courts. In 1586, Guarini turned his attention to the revision of stylistic aspects. He sent his play to the leading linguistic authority in Italy, Lionardo Salviati of the Florentine Accademia della Crusca, who had recently been so critical of Tasso's *Gerusalemme liberata*. In a letter of 1 April, 1586, Guarini asked the critic to correct the play freely: 'e ciò s'intenda in ogni parte di lei, ma più nella favella, che non sia lorda di lombardesimi' [and this applies to all parts of the play, but especially the language, so that it is not sullied by Lombard expressions] [7] Scipione Gonzaga, another former adviser of Tasso and mutual friend since the days of the Eterei academy, also helped with the correction of the *Pastor fido*. Even after the play was first printed by Giovanni Battista Bonfadino in Venice, 1589 (though dated 1590), Guarini continued polishing it. Indeed, it was not until 1602, a staggering twenty-one editions or so later, that the *Pastor fido* appeared in its definitive, authorized version published in Venice by Giovanni Battista Ciotti.[8]

With his *Pastor fido* Guarini clearly set out to challenge and outdo his predecessors: Tasso particularly, but, as Selmi demonstrates, also a variety of other models both ancient and modern. The play is noticeably much longer than any earlier examples and features a double plot, superficially similar to the model used by Beccari and others, but much more rigorously constructed, using the Aristotelian devices of recognition and reversal. These had been used previously in tragedy and *commedia grave* but, until then, they had only been experimented with occasionally in pastoral drama, for instance by Giraldi, Lollio and Ingegneri. As Guarini later theorized, the action follows a pattern established in Terence's *Andria*, consisting of a principal, complex plot and a secondary one which is 'grafted' onto it and dependent upon it, observing necessity and verisimilitude.[9] The main action represents the love of Mirtillo (the 'faithful shepherd' of the title) for Amarilli, who reciprocates this feeling, but tragically cannot express it because an oracle has dictated that she must marry the son of the Arcadian ruler, presumed to be the love-shy Silvio. Only by this marriage will the divine curse be lifted on Arcadia that Diana had placed long ago following a nymph's infidelity towards her lover, the goddess's priest (intriguingly named Aminta). The plot begins to develop when the dutiful Amarilli reveals her feelings to a supposed friend Corisca — a nymph herself with lascivious designs on Mirtillo — and is tricked into a compromising situation, as a result of which Amarilli is condemned to death for adultery. In the final act, Mirtillo heroically offers to die in Amarilli's place, but the sacrifice is halted dramatically by the chance arrival of his foster father (Carino). After a Sophoclean-style investigation, Mirtillo is discovered to be the long-lost first son of the Arcadian ruler, Montano, believed drowned in a flood. However, it is only after the oracle is fully interpreted that tragedy is finally averted. Mirtillo and Amarilli are then free to marry, demonstrating the conformity of divine laws with those of nature.

Amarilli never actually encounters her betrothed, the hunter Silvio, on stage during the play. Instead, he appears in conjunction with the nymph Dorinda in a related, but almost entirely separate, pastoral context. Despite his initially stubborn rejection of her love, he is surprisingly converted after mistakenly shooting Dorinda with an arrow (Act IV). By contrast to the popular, tragic Ovidian tale of Procris and Cephalus, the wound proves not to be fatal and the couple are united. It is in this secondary action that we find the more typical ingredients of pastoral drama: evocations of the hunt, rituals to the goddess Diana, a prophetic echo, and a rather sensual and vaguely comic kind of love. Finally, a Satyr, enamoured of Corisca, provides comic intrigue and even slapstick episodes in the first half of the play (especially II. 6). As Selmi notes, these two characters recall types that Guarini used in his comedy *L'Idropica* (completed in 1583), which was being composed around the time of his early work on *Pastor fido*.[10] Nevertheless, they gain a weightier ideological significance through their function within the play's tragicomic structure with its providential outcome.

The protracted process of composing this work testifies partly to the ambitions of the author as he attempted to produce an example that could consolidate the status of pastoral drama and present a counter-model to Tasso's popular *Aminta*. Crucially, in the later 1580s Guarini sought also to alter conceptions of pastoral drama, by codifying for the first time the malleable and inherently mixed structure, and exploring the sociological implications of the pastoral mode. Like many of the critical discussions in the sixteenth century over genres, this activity was undertaken in a debate. It was apparently triggered by the publication of a treatise by Giason Denores, a professor of moral philosophy at the university of Padua (1570–90), entitled: *Discorso [...] intorno a quei principii, cause et accrescimenti che la Commedia, la Tragedia, ed il Poema Eroico ricevono dalla Filosofia Morale e Civile* [*Discourse* [...] *on the principles, causes and amplification that Comedy, Tragedy and the Heroic poem receive from moral and civil philosophy*] (1586, though dated 1587). This concluded with a short section generally condemning tragicomedy and the *pastorale* (and particularly the pastoral tragicomedy) on moral and artistic grounds.[11] Guarini construed this as an unprovoked and personal attack on his play, arguing that: 'in tutta l'arte poetica, da poi che'l mondo è mondo, non troverete più d'una tragicomedia pastorale' [in the whole art of poetics, since the world began, you will only find a single pastoral tragicomedy] (*Verrato*, p. 818). In this regard, he was particularly anxious to deny Denores's later claim that other tragicomedies had been written previously and were associated with the practice of the despised 'commedianti della gazzetta' [professional comic actors] (*Verato* [sic] *secondo*, pp. 25–31).[12]

As Guarini noted, Denores had every chance to know of his play even while it was in manuscript form, since by 1586 it had already been widely read and discussed in Padua and Venice and 'corso per le bocche di tutti, e letterati, e stampatori, e librai, non altramenti, che se fosse stato in pubblica forma' [mentioned by everyone — literati, printers and booksellers — as if it were already published] (*Verato secondo*, pp. 19–20). Besides circulating privately in academic circles, the play was also possibly known through unauthorized manuscript copies pirated by actors after an early attempt to stage the *Pastor fido*.[13] For this reason, Guarini felt justified to publish a vitriolic defence of the new genre, under the pseudonym of a distinguished Ferrarese semi-professional actor and colleague, Giovan Battista Ver(r)ato (*Il Verrato*, 1588). This was followed by Denores's *Apologia contro l'auttor del Verrato* (1590, the year that the *Pastor fido* appeared in print), which added little of further interest, except to connect the play to the mongrel tragicomedies of professionals.[14] Guarini thereafter produced another lengthy reply (*Verato* [sic] *secondo*, 1592/3) this time under the pseudonym of 'l'Attizzato Accademico Ferrarese' ['The Incited One' of the Ferrarese Academy] to the now deceased Denores. The debate resumed in the late 1590s with a new set of critics, and argument continued over the *Pastor fido* well into the following century, which doubtless helped to stir general interest in the work.[15] After the definitive edition by Ciotti (Venice, 1602), over thirty appeared in Italy and the rest of Europe during the rest of the seventeenth century.[16]

The final authorized edition of the *Pastor fido* is of particular interest since it contains the author's last two critical interventions on his work. It appears in a lavish quarto with copper engravings illustrating each act, as opposed to the cheaper octavo (or smaller) formats frequently used for pastorals (see fig. 4). A dedicatory letter by the author to Duke Vincenzo Gonzaga commemorates the prestigious 1598 performance of the play before the Queen of Spain. Also included are Guarini's *Compendio della Poesia Tragicomica tratto dai duo Verati* (written in 1599, first published in Venice, 1601) and a new commentary on the play (*Annotationi*).[17] All this gives the impression of a work of *gravitas*, meant for close study rather than leisure reading, perhaps emulating the 1590 edition of Tasso's *Liberata*.[18]

The *Compendio* is presented as a treatise summing up the theories expressed at greater length and more caustically in Guarini's earlier pseudonymous polemical works, *Verrato* and *Verato secondo*. While the two *Verati* (as we shall call them hereafter)

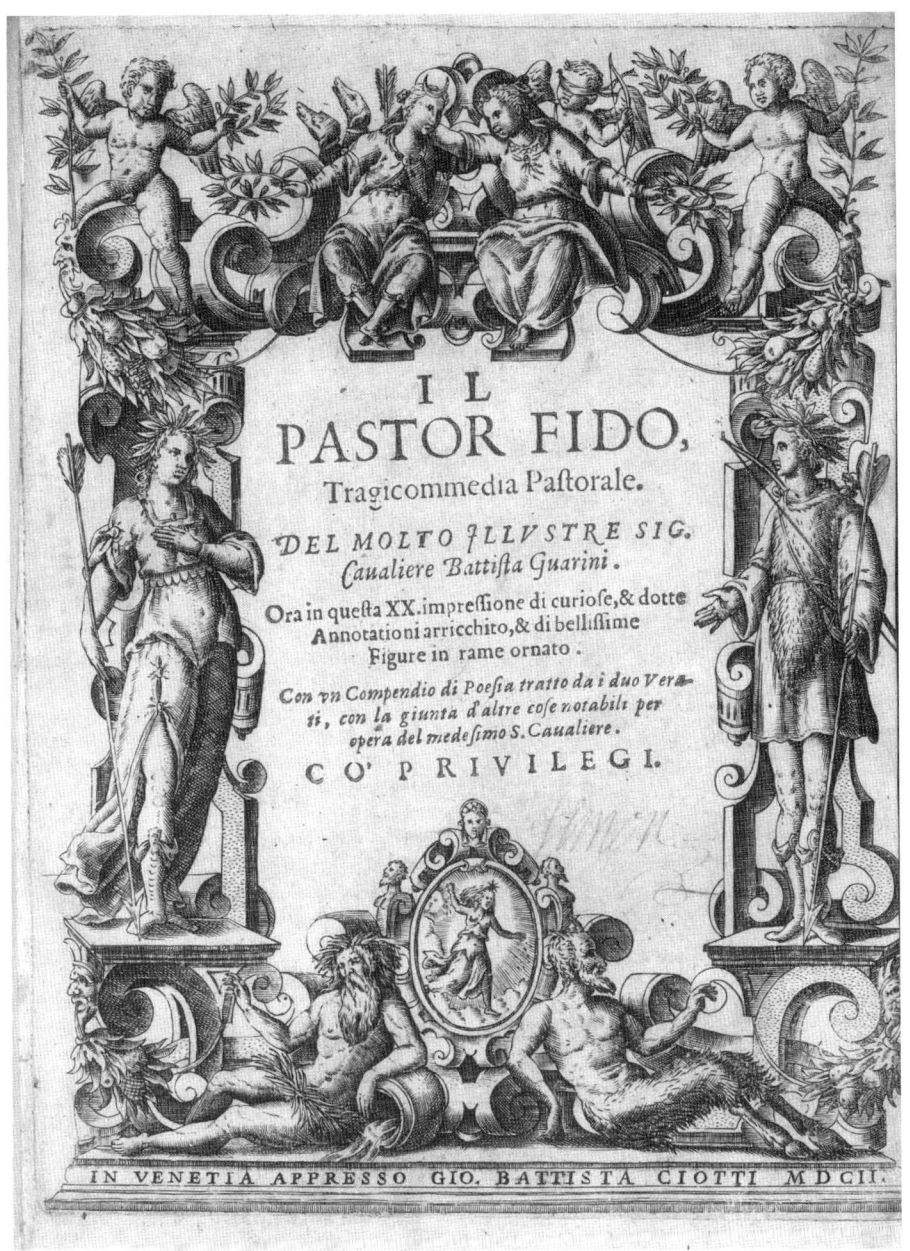

Figure 4. Engraving (by Francesco Val(l)egio?) from frontispiece of Battista Guarini, *Pastor fido, tragicommedia pastorale* (Venice: Giovanni Battista Ciotti, 1602), depicting the key character types in the play: Diana and Venus at the top centre, presumably Amarilli and Mirtillo on the two side columns and, below centre, Alfeo (Alpheus) and the Satyr. Reproduced by kind permission of Reading University Library (Overstone Shelf 19F/19).

provide a point by point response to Denores's objections, the author evidently sought to distance himself publicly from the debate when composing his *Compendio*. This consequently appeared under the author's own name, omitting personal allusions to his detractors and some other problematic issues — especially regarding the hedonistic end of poetry.[19] Yet, as Ciotti's prefatory letter to his 1602 edition reveals, Guarini hesitated about publishing this work, completed already by 1599, in case it seemed to be replying to the fresh critiques of the *Pastor fido* (fol. A2^v). Publication was apparently only agreed to in 1601 after two other critics had taken on the defence of his play.[20]

The (anonymous) *Annotationi* or commentary on the *Pastor fido* — an extremely unusual addition to a contemporary printed play — only engages in critical issues intermittently and indirectly. It consists of glosses on individual words or phrases which appear after the prologue, every scene and chorus, drawing on an encyclopaedic range of mostly classical works of history and moral philosophy, literary and juridical texts. While specific techniques of stage-writing and occasionally practical experience are sometimes alluded to, explanations of key dramaturgical concepts, such as catharsis, are relegated to the subsequent *Compendio*. With their bulk, authoritative weight, and intrusive positioning within the text, the annotations necessarily impose themselves on its interpretation, despite being set out in an apparently neutral manner. As Guarini is referred to throughout in the third person, it is unclear whether he actually penned the *Annotationi* himself. Many critics (including Rossi and Herrick) have unproblematically assumed this to be the case. However, Molinari has argued convincingly that while the dramatist probably prepared most of them, another not very proficient or up-to-date (anonymous) editor must have worked on them before printing.[21] By this means the author probably hoped to rehabilitate his play unobtrusively, following a long-established practice that was then enjoying some vogue, as with commentaries on Boccaccio's *Decameron* by Salviati (1582) and especially on Tasso's *Liberata* (1590).[22] Read alongside the other critical works it sheds further light on the process of retrospectively shaping the reception of Guarini's masterpiece.

The Political and Poetic Background to the *Pastor fido*: the Paduan Inheritance

Even before its publication, the *Pastor fido* became associated with questions of imitation, generic legitimacy and decorum, and ethical values in relation to the pastoral setting. To understand these points better, it will be helpful to set them against the traditions of civic and moral philosophy, rhetoric and poetics in Padua, a cultural centre with which many participants in the debate were associated.[23] This city, subject since 1405 to the Venetian republic, was principally famous for its long established university, as well as some leading humanist educators.[24] During the later sixteenth century, the Studio attracted many distinguished Italian Aristotelians, including the first commentator on the *Poetics*, Francesco Robortello. It became famed for its rigorously secular and rationalistic Aristotelian tradition of speculative sciences which, by the end of the century, was increasingly even perceived to border on atheism.[25] The early debate on the *Pastor fido* resonated in university circles, most notably because of the intervention of Giason Denores, though professors like Antonio Riccobono and Jacopo Zabarella also took an interest. Later others participated directly, such as Faustino Summo and Paolo Beni. However, discussion seems to have taken place particularly within the informal setting of the academies and bookshops. In these spheres professors, promising students and other local intellectuals had for some decades explored ideas on rhetoric and poetics, which would prove highly influential with regard to pastoral drama.[26]

Speroni Speroni: changing views on rhetoric

One of the key cultural figures in Padua from the mid- to late-sixteenth century was Sperone Speroni (1500–1588), a figure already encountered in connection with Tasso (Chapter 3). Speroni's wide-ranging works stand at the vanguard of contemporary debates, often occupying a polemical and ambiguous position. Speroni had initially taught philosophy at the university, but had stopped in 1528, after which he held some public offices in Padua.[27] His influence was felt principally in the city's avant-garde academic life, most notably within the short-lived Accademia degli Infiammati (founded 1540), famous for its discussions on language and philosophy, as well as the successive Elevati (founded c. 1557, where Speroni defended his tragedy *Canace*) and the Animosi (founded 1573).[28] His academic activities were to introduce him to many younger *letterati* on whom he was to exert a lasting influence, including significantly Tasso, Denores, Guarini, and Summo. Even though Speroni left Padua definitively for Rome in 1573 his works continued to be familiar to his protégés through discussion or the circulation of manuscript copies, many of which remained unpublished at his death.

Speroni's dialogues testify to important shifts in his views on rhetoric and poetics during his lifetime, which make interesting comparison with subsequent discussions in the debate on pastoral drama. Significantly, in the mid-century there is a move away from the humanist, Ciceronian position on rhetoric as a means of persuading men to participate virtuously in civic life according to reason (*Del modo di studiare*, composed c. 1530), in favour of a new technical and hedonistic definition of the art. Speroni's incomplete *Dialogo della retorica* (written c. 1538–40, published posthumously) testifies to the need to redefine the social role of rhetoric and requalify its professional specificities. The civic and moral function previously attributed to rhetoric is now played down, and it acquires a more circumscribed autonomy in the separate field of aesthetics. As the principal speaker argues, rhetoric serves above all to please, which is what makes it so persuasive and beautiful.[29] This end is to be achieved by privileging *elocutio* (traditionally a less important part, relating to language and style) over *inventio* (governing the choice of subject matter) and *dispositio* (its arrangement so as best to move and teach). For this reason demonstrative (or epideictic) rhetoric, for praise and blame, is judged the most suitable of the three classical genres, since it is less concerned with teaching virtue or representing truth than with delighting its audience.

The acceptance of this hedonistic view of rhetoric coincides with a changing conception of literature and the increased professionalization of the *letterato* from the fourth decade of the sixteenth century, with the major expansion of print culture. Particularly within the printing capital of Venice, this led to a vastly increased demand for vernacular works and facilitated the emergence of a new breed of writer (the *poligrafo*), who lived by their pen or contacts with the press. Pietro Aretino epitomized the success of such independent professionals, rising to literary prominence despite his humble origins and relative lack of humanistic erudition.[30] Nevertheless, this freer literary climate was destined to be re-evaluated towards the later part of the century when, as we have seen, there was a growing sense that 'public' literature needed to promote political and even religious norms. While Tasso presents a somewhat extreme case of this tendency, Speroni reflects similar concerns in his extraordinary and complex dialogue, *Apologia dei dialoghi* [Apology for Dialogues], composed 1574–75, but printed posthumously 1596. This was completed ostensibly in reply to the church's accusations of immorality of his earlier dialogues (also printed 1596), and the last section was actually written while the author was being investigated in Rome by the Inquisition.

Over the four dialogues of the *Apologia*, a highly contradictory evaluation of the role of rhetoric (and literature) in relation to politics emerges.[31] The first two parts still favour a rather hedonistic conception of rhetoric to justify the apparently immoral content of Speroni's early dialogues. However, the third part, which appears in the form of a confessional conversation between the author and his conscience, marks an abrupt retraction of this position. The liberal arts of rhetoric and poetry are at this point considered subordinate to the principal rational and civil art of politics (p. 347), with the city being exalted as the means for fully realizing man's nature and happiness (Aristotle's *eudaimonia*). All arts are consequently judged as good only if they fulfil a political purpose. Therefore demonstrative rhetoric is now considered inferior to the deliberative (or political) kind which '[ha] l'occhio al suo populo, lo quale intende di costumare e conservar costumati' [is conceived with a view to the people, whose behaviour it means to correct and keep seemly] (p. 349).[32] Furthermore, demonstrative rhetoric and poetry (as in his own earlier dialogues) is considered to be intrinsically problematic, since it can air sinful opinions without proposing a final incontrovertible truth. The various forms of classical rhetoric are at this point valued only in terms of their moral function, and ability to distinguish truth from lies. It has thus assumed an end associated in the earlier parts of the *Apologia* with philosophical rather than poetic enquiry, while its characteristic concern with the pleasing manipulation of words is tainted by the suspicion of sophistry (p. 359).

During the fourth dialogue, the use of rhetoric in the service of civic life is itself gradually questioned along with the value of this existence. While it is initially considered necessary for mankind to live in the city to satisfy material and sensual needs and as a basis for spiritual life (p. 399), this is viewed later as being not fully compatible with religious values: 'non possendo ad un tempo istesso filosofare e negoziare, esser boni uomini virtuosi, e non inutili cittadini' [as one cannot at the same time both practise philosophy and civic business, nor be both good, virtuous men and valuable citizens] (p. 414). Civic values are increasingly found to be imperfect and merely auxiliary to religious ones, which all writers should seek through philosophy and, it would seem, cannot truly exist in imperfect republics unless they have virtue as their *raison d'être* (pp. 412–15). Therefore, it is concluded that an explicitly modern kind of republic is required, ruled by God's laws and absolute truth: 'quella è bona repubblica, ove è signore il religioso, cioè dove è reina la nostra vera religione' [a good republic is one that is ruled by a man of religion, or rather where our true religion is queen] (p. 420). In line with Counter-Reformation thinking, civic virtues *per se* are seen merely as a condition for transcendent religious ones. In his *Apologia*, Speroni therefore explores a wide spectrum of views on the end of poetry as well as its intrinsic properties, which would variously influence subsequent writers on pastoral drama.

The debate on pastoral drama: Giason Denores

From the start, the debate over the *Pastor fido* may be seen to reflect differing approaches to literature explored within the Paduan context, though Denores and Guarini both refer to Speroni during the quarrel.[33] As mentioned, Guarini had studied in Padua in his youth and since participated in academies there, and he was friends with the professors Riccoboni and Zabarella. But by the 1580s he was associated more with practically oriented literary and elite theatrical circles in Padua, Venice, and Vicenza, as well as with courtly circles in Ferrara, Parma, and the Mantuan territories.[34] Denores, meanwhile, was one of many Greek Cypriots exiled after the Turkish invasions of 1570 and granted political asylum by the Venetian government. Soon after, he was awarded a lectureship; and then, in 1577, Robortello's chair in moral philosophy at the Studio of Padua.[35] This would account for his essentially theoretical and moralizing approach to theatre. For instance, in his *Poetica* (1588) he ignores all performative aspects of drama, in order to concentrate solely on the art of the dramatist-writer, interpreted in political and ethical terms.[36]

Denores raised various objections to the tragicomedy and the pastoral in his *Discorso* (1586, published 1587) which were repeatedly re-examined thereafter. These concerned particularly the poetic legitimacy of tragicomedy and the ethical and socio-political status of pastoral drama. He regarded tragicomedy as a 'mostruoso, e disproporzionato componimento, misto di due contrarie azion, e qualità di persone' [monstrous and ill-proportioned composition, mixed in kind, with two completely different actions and types of characters] (*Discorso*, p. 200). Its combination of the distinct genres of comedy and tragedy, in opposition to Cicero and Plato's injunction against mixed forms, for him meant that it breached the classical ideals of unity and decorum. The long and complex modern pastoral play was also judged to contravene the proper bounds of the form, which was in his view exemplified by the eclogues of Virgil and Theocritus' *Idylls*. Particularly with its inclusion of noble characters and situations from tragedy it was felt to exceed the decorum of the humble pastoral mode.

For Denores, only the three approved Aristotelian genres of tragedy, comedy, and epic were capable of teaching virtuous, civic conduct, which was the principal aim of poetry. For this reason, Aristotle did not mention some 'minor' poetic forms, including epigrams, odes, and elegies, which are considered unable to fulfil this end, since they are non-imitative and 'pertinenti piuttosto al grammatico, che al filosofo morale, e civile' [more pertinent to the grammarian, than to the moral and civil philosopher] (p. 199). Although eclogues do not fall into this category, being imitative of pastoral life, they were similarly neglected by the philosopher, as the subject matter they represented was inappropriate for city audiences and might undermine their sense of civic obligations.[37] Denores considers the 'turbulent' beginning and 'prosperous' ending in pastoral plays as presenting 'un tacito invitar gli uomini a lasciar le città, ed ad innamorarsi della vita contadinesca' [a tacit invitation for men to leave the cities and fall in love with country life] (p. 202). They are therefore described as being 'inappropriate, or even contrary to the principles of moral and civil philosophers' (p. 204).

Such objections to tragicomedy and pastoral poetry/drama reflect Denores's opinion that all mimetic arts should serve the utilitarian end of promoting the unity and glory of the republic, stimulating the citizens to live virtuously, obeying the laws of the state or fighting for its preservation. This view was doubtless partly influenced by Denores's personal background and obligations to the Venetian state, but it can also be compared to that which is explored in the third part of Speroni's *Apologia*. Denores's particular brand of Aristotelianism also combines Platonic principles, whereby poetry and rhetoric should be subject to the strictures of moral and civil philosophy and only properly produced within this ethical framework, with Horace's dictum that poetry should both instruct and delight.[38] He held that the poet should use the pleasurable aspects of his art in order to seduce the audience into learning useful precepts about civic life, so as to fulfil art's primary political function.

> All'auditore, il principal fine della poesia per il più non è altro, che il diletto, ma in quanto all'intenzione del buon poeta [...] è la utilità, comandata da' filosofi, e da' governatori delle repubbliche. (Denores, *Discorso*, p. 190)
>
> [As far as the audience are concerned, the main purpose of poetry is normally just to please, but for the good poet [...] the intention is to instruct, as ordered by the philosophers and governors of the republic.]

Poets who put *diletto* [pleasure] before *utilità* [profitable instruction] are denounced as sophists, concerned only with appearances, since the 'vero ufficio delle loro arti [...] non [ha] altro per mira che il ben vivere della lor patria' [the sole true purpose of their arts [...] is to bring about the health of their country] (p. 205).

Towards a poetics of poetry for pleasure

In response to Denores, Guarini adopted an aggressively 'modern' stance in the *Verati*, exploring a wide range of issues raised by the supporters of Ariosto in the debate over the merits of *Orlando furioso*, especially as against Tasso's *Gerusalemme liberata*, which were central to the so-called quarrel of the Ancients and the Moderns from the late sixteenth century.[39] In summary, Guarini broadly argues against the Platonic idea of poetry being founded entirely on immutable universal principles, as proposed also by Tasso in his *Discorsi dell'arte poetica*, printed 1587. Guarini favours a broadly relativistic view of poetry which takes into account changes over time according to contemporary tastes. However, he importantly maintains that new genres still to some extent depended on Aristotle's universal poetic rules, especially regarding imitation, unity, and verisimilitude. In this respect, Guarini departs from Giraldi's theory on new genres in defence of the modern *romanzo* (never directly alluded to), though he follows the earlier critic's view that poetic genres were in a state of organic growth and constantly evolving over time. Guarini is convinced that new genres would have been discussed by Aristotle had they existed then (see the epigraph to this chapter).[40] The view that Aristotle's *Poetics* limits the number and determines the hierarchy of genres is therefore called into question. After all, Guarini observes that the ancient treatise, besides being inconsistent and obscure, is incomplete. It lacks the promised discussion on comedy as well as analysis of other important poetic forms, such as the dithyramb, hymns and Davidic psalms (*Verrato*, pp. 737–39, 743), which were then being experimented with. It also necessarily cannot account for genres established much later, as exemplified by Dante's *Commedia*, Petrarch's *Trionfi* and Ariosto's *Furioso* (pp. 751–52, 754).

Most importantly, Guarini made a major contribution to the debate on the autonomy of art, alluded to in the early part of Speroni's *Apologia* and championed by the radical Lodovico Castelvetro, the first vernacular translator of Aristotle's *Poetics* (1570).[41] Drawing on Castelvetro's rigorously technical reading of the *Poetics*, Guarini denied Denores's claim that art should be subordinated to political and moral objectives, which probably represented the more widely held critical position in his age based on the Ciceronian rhetorical tradition.[42] In the dramatist's view, poetry primarily aims to please and move rather than to teach its audience, though its didactic function is not entirely disregarded. This position was particularly polemical at the time, given that from around 1570 the Roman Inquisition had begun to impose increasingly severe limitations on artistic freedom in Italy, aided by civil authorities. Venetian printers began to observe the 1564 Tridentine index more zealously from 1569 to the early 1570s, and in 1571 Pius V established a separate Congregation of the Index to regulate publication and handle censorship.[43] The effects are noticeable in all forms of art after this time and especially in drama, either through revisions and expurgations of texts which were allowed to be published or in writers' conscious conformity to moral orthodoxy.[44]

Guarini's rather hedonistic stance is ingeniously supported with references to Aristotle's *Poetics*, as well as the philosopher's other writings. Guarini writes in response to Denores: 'Io per me non so veder in tutto il corpo delle *Morali*, e particolarmente nella *Politica*, dove sarebbe stato il suo luogo che il legislatore aristotelico ci prescriva leggi di poesia' [I myself am unable to find any point in the *Ethics* and particularly in the *Politics* in which the Aristotelian legislator is supposed to have prescribed rules on poetry] (*Verrato*, p. 740).[45] Although the author allows that poetry may dispose its citizen audience towards civic virtues such as temperance, it does not itself directly teach them. Indeed, he observes witheringly: 'infelice comune che non ha altro maestro de' costumi che la poetica, la qual non ha per fine l'insegnare, ma il dilettare, e dilettando giovare' [what an unfortunate state whose only instructor in good behaviour is poetry, the purpose of which is not to instruct, but to please, and through pleasing to provide benefit] (p. 747). The poet's primary role is to provide entertainment; instruction, on the other hand, is the main aim of the philosopher who is under no obligation to please his audience (p. 750).

Denores and Guarini's conceptions of poetry differ therefore in terms of the relative value placed on the Horatian ends of pleasure and utility. This informs their views on Aristotelian devices to achieve this, especially on the vexed questions of imitation and *catharsis*. For the civic-minded Denores, the imitation of scenes of horror in tragedy has the effect of diminishing the citizens' fear and compassion and spurring them on in battle to defend the *patria*. By contrast, Guarini's definition of purgation forms part of a more sophisticated aesthetic consideration of the affective power of drama on its audience (*Verrato*, pp. 765–80). He argues that tragic actions need not instruct audiences directly, but should rather dispose the souls of the spectators 'a quel temperamento, ch'è utile a chi vuol apprender buoni costumi e bene operare' [to that temper which is useful if one wants to learn seemly manners and how to act virtuously] (p. 780).[46] Importantly, tragic catharsis is no longer considered necessary for modern, Christian theatre audiences, since they more appropriately derive their instruction from the Gospel. Such catharsis is even undesirable, when understood in Denores's terms, since it could make them cruel and pitiless. 'Purgation' in tragedy should in his age more appropriately be understood not as *removing* pity and fear, but as *moderating* these affects to a virtuous mean (p. 768), or better still as dissipating the socially harmful effects of melancholy through pleasing imitation, as in comedy (pp. 765, 775–78). Guarini's tragicomedy therefore appears ideally suited for modern times, since it fulfils the overall end ('fine architettonico') of comedy through the subordinate end ('fine [i]strumentale') of imitating selected comic and tragic subjects:

> [Il] fine [...] della tragicomedia, [...] è d'imitare con apparato scenico un'azione finta e mista di tutte quelle parti tragiche e comiche, che verisimilmente e con decoro possano star insieme corrette sotto una sola forma dramatica, per fine di purgar col diletto la mestizia degli ascoltanti; in modo che l'imitare, ch'è fine istrumentale, è quel ch'è misto, rappresentando egli cose comiche e tragiche giunte insieme, ma il purgare, ch'è fine architettonico, non è se non un solo, riducendosi il misto delle due qualità sotto un soggetto solo: di liberar gli ascoltanti dalla malinconia. (*Verrato*, p. 779)

> [[The] end [...] of tragicomedy [...] is to imitate on stage a fictional action, mixed with all the parts of tragedy and comedy which can exist together observing verisimilitude and decorum, adapted to a single dramatic form, in order to purge the melancholy of the audience through delight. In this way the imitation, which is the instrumental end, is mixed, since it represents comic and tragic subjects together; but the purgation, which is the architectonic end, is unified, since it brings together the mixture of the two qualities into a single aim: to free the audience from melancholy.]

Both ends serve to delight through imitation rather than to instruct and, as such, are attuned to contemporary tastes of audiences, as well as the current religious and political situation.

On discussing the *pastorale* later in the *Verrato*, Guarini again makes a clear separation between poetics (and all arts) as a branch of speculative thought, and ethics, which is a habit of the active intellect (p. 794). While drama may represent various virtues and vices, this is because of its essential function as imitation (an idea insisted on from the start of the *Compendio*), rather than because of any explicitly didactic intention. It is conceded, though, that drama may have more or less licence according to the type of political context in which it is performed (p. 795). After all, poets like other citizens — philosophers, theologians, and artisans — are subject to the laws of their city, as Denores also observed with reference to Plato (*Discorso*, pp. 157–58). But this is the sole extent to which artistic activity is controlled by politics: 'in quanto ai suoi princìpi intrinsechi e formali non ha che fare con esso lui, ma è membro della sofistica e della ritorica' [as regards its intrinsic and formal principles, poetry has nothing to do with [politics], as it is a branch of sophistry and rhetoric] (*Verrato*, p. 795).[47]

Thus, through his rigorous analysis of Aristotle's works and relativizing historical perspective on the *Poetics*, Guarini presents in his *Verrato* a strong challenge to Denores's narrow view of poetry. He argues for a broader, more technical definition of the art, championing its aesthetic autonomy. Even so, he does accept that the artist-poet is subject to political regulations to a limited extent, and that art may dispose the audience to ethical teachings as a by-product of its main aim to please. In this way, Guarini's earliest theoretical defence of pastoral tragicomedy hints at grounds for arguing both for its conformity to moral and political standards, and for its hedonistic end — a stance which became increasingly widespread in the seventeenth century.

Placing the Pastoral

The Arcadian society of the Pastor fido

Denores' condemnation of the new mixed kinds of drama that were appearing, whether in the form of tragicomedy or *pastorale* (understood as a distinct dramatic form rather than a mode), suggests an anxiety about their lack of a clear and controlled ideological message like that implied in neo-classical comedy and tragedy. Renaissance genres carry strong social, ethical and even political connotations through their association with particular places and social classes. As Henke observes, their conventions typically serve a mediating function between the play and the audience, preparing expectations and recognition.[48] Therefore the transformation of classical genres, or creation of new ones, as Guarini polemically set out to do, would indicate a challenge to the traditional hierarchy linked with a changing perception of social structure and practices. This would explain the hostility of more reactionary critics to generic variation or mixture, and the polemics surrounding popular new works that did not conform to the traditional kinds. As LaCapra notes, this attitude 'often occults or conceals an attempt to retain or reinforce a dominant position or an authoritative perspective'.[49]

During the debate on Guarini's *Pastor fido* the pastoral setting posed a particular problem to critics because it challenged the traditional mimetic relationship of drama, which was considered the most direct means of artistic imitation.[50] When the action takes place outside the city (or court), it is less clear how 'realistic' it is or how one should understand the relative status of the pastoral characters. Such concerns prompted discussions on the nature of the pastoral community, raising questions about its ethical, political and historical status. These had only been vaguely touched upon in relation to the themes of nature/art or civilization/primitivism in earlier pastoral plays apart from Tasso's *Aminta*. Now they became important in defending the unity and verisimilitude, and even the dramatic viability of the *Pastor fido*. No consistent presentation of the pastoral context emerges either within the play or in the criticism. However, the divergent readings point to various layers of meaning associated with pastoral drama that problematize some of the very aims for the genre first presented by Guarini.

The *Pastor fido* is set in a by now conventional Arcadia, but this is no imaginary never-never land for erotic encounters, nor simply a disguised version of the court as a *drame à clef*. From the start it is imbued with mythical overtones, and given a moral dimension, being presented as a fallen society, cursed like Oedipus's Thebes for an earlier act of divine and moral transgression. This is however eventually remedied by a human sacrifice (prepared, but not realized, in line with tragicomic principles) which restores Arcadia to its original Golden Age values. A cyclical pattern of history is thus established, which brings an atemporal universalizing quality to the action. At the same time, a serious providential design clearly underpins the action of the play, which cannot as in *Aminta* and its many imitations be ascribed to the machinations of the mischievous god Amore. Disruptions to this pattern occur at various key points, though, by means of oblique allegorical satirical or encomiastic references, which link the play to contemporary reality and the context of its intended performance. These are concentrated especially in the prologue and in the Carino episode (V. 1).

The Terentian-style prologue appears to have been written originally to mark the marriage of Duke Carlo Emanuele of Savoy (for whom the play was apparently intended from the start) to Catherine of Austria in 1585.[51] It is delivered by the Arcadian river-god Alfeo (Alpheus), famously represented amongst others by Virgil (*Aeneid*, III, 694–95) and Ovid (*Metamorphoses*, V, 573–641) as amorously pursuing the chaste nymph Aret(h)usa, which led him from Arcadia to Sicily. However, on this occasion Alfeo notes that he has left his usual underground course and joined the waters of the Po. On arriving in Turin (where the Po meets the river Dora) he seems to see his old home of Arcadia, a circumstance which naturally provides an opportunity for courtly encomium.

> ALFEO Ecco, lasciando il corso antico e noto,
> per incognito mar l'onda incontrando
> del re de' fiumi altero,
> *qui* sorgo, e lieto a riveder ne *vegno*
> qual esser *già solea* libera e bella,
> *or* desolata e serva,
> *quell'*antica mia terra ond'io derivo. [...]
> *Queste* son le contrade
> sì chiare un tempo, e *queste* son le selve
> ove'l prisco valor visse e morío.
> In questo angolo sol del ferreo mondo
> cred'io che ricovrasse il secol d'oro,
> quando fuggìa le scelerate genti. [...]
> Ma chi mi fa veder dopo tant'anni
> *Qui* trasportata, dove
> Scende la Dora in Po, l'arcada terra?
> (Prologo, 17–23, 28–30, 79–81, italics mine)

[Behold! Leaving behind my well-known, ancient course and flowing into the waters of the mighty king of rivers across an uncharted sea, I rise *here*, happy again to see *that* ancient land of my birth, which *once* was beautiful and free, and *now* languishes in desolate servitude. [...] *This* is the region which was once so famous, and *these* are the woods where ancient virtue lived and died. I think that solely in this corner of the corrupt iron world did the golden age take refuge when fleeing human wickedness. [...] But who allows me after so many years to see Arcadia transported *here*, where the river Dora flows into the Po?]

By contrasting the river's former and new course, the author may be hinting at his own turning away from the classical mythological pastoral for an altered modern kind. In any case, it introduces a strong sense of temporal and spatial disjunction as Alfeo views what appears to be his former country, miraculously transported to this contemporary site. Through the repeated deictic markers ('qui', 'queste') and emphasis on his recognition of Arcadia (24–26), he encourages the audience to identify the real stage space — complete with groves, cave and temple to Diana (82–85) — with Arcadia in its former glory, in contrast to its present wretched state (see fig. 5).[52] The speaker's amazement at this 'miracolo stupendo' [wondrous miracle] (86), points to the effect of wonderment (*meraviglia*) which the dramatist sought to inspire through his dramaturgy. However, it is immediately afterwards ascribed to the 'insolito valor' [exceptional power] (87) of Catherine of Austria and the Habsburg family, drawing a flattering parallel between the Savoy court and golden age Arcadia, as seen in previous courtly pastorals and eclogues.[53]

Guarini's prologue thus tends to conflate courtly and pastoral space, in distinct contrast to that of Tasso's *Aminta*, which polemically contrasts the hierarchical, tyrannical courts and the freer space of the woods (as represented visually in fig. 2).[54] Unlike Tasso's anarchic Amore, Guarini's god, this time unambiguous in his identity (Prologue, 14–16) and probably presented as a venerable elder deity as in the engraving to the 1602 Ciotti edition, makes no attempt to mediate between these worlds or to explain apparent contradictions.[55] The shepherds are described as being virtuously engaging in scientific pursuits, arts and other aristocratic pastimes despite their pastoral condition, and none are 'né di pensier né di costume rozzo' [coarse either in thought or conduct] (61). Furthermore, the Arcadians are described as dwelling in peaceful relations with their warring neighbouring Greek states, free from envy and greed (43–57), an analogy that must have seemed somewhat discordant to contemporaries familiar with the belligerent policies of Carlo Emanuele I (1580–1630).

The representation of Arcadia and its inhabitants in the *Pastor fido* therefore displays both allegorical and mythical/fictional qualities. Various critics objected to Guarini's apparent lack of verisimilitude, and his departure from historical sources by Polybius, Thucydides, and Pausanius, and the model of Virgil's *Bucolics*. Giovanni Pietro Malacreta for instance complained amongst other things that Guarini's Arcadia is too 'delicato e vago' [delicate and delightful], the shepherds too 'dotti e sentenziosi' [learned and sentenious], and that the variety of actions (sacrifices, oracles, hunts, *inganni*) is more typical of cities.[56] Paolo Beni in his critical reply to Malacreta (composed shortly afterwards in 1600) similarly notes the implausibility of the over-sophisticated setting and complains about the licentiousness of the Arcadians. However, he makes an important justification for the use of poetic licence to adorn ancient historical facts:

Mentre si conviene nella regione, sito, monti, fiumi, e genti, il resto sta in arbitrio del poeta: il quale tutta volta che non esca del verisimile, può andare alterando e

FIGURE 5. Engraving (by Francesco Val(l)egio?) from Battista Guarini, *Pastor fido, tragicommedia pastorale* (Venice: Giovanni Battista Ciotti, 1602). The prologue delivered by the river god Alfeo (Alpheus), with pastoral perspective and a neo-classical temple in the backdrop. Reproduced by permission of Reading University Library (Overstone Shelf 19F/19, fol. b^v).

> fingendo oracoli, sacrifizii, giuochi, essercizii, amori e costumi a suo piacere. [...] basta che tali costumi e accidenti siano possibili, e non repugnino al verisimile.[57]
>
> [While [representations of] the region have to include the appropriate sites, mountains, rivers and inhabitants, the poet can decide upon the rest himself. As long as he continuously observes verisimilitude, he can alter things and invent oracles, sacrifices, games, activities, love stories and customs as he wishes. [...] These customs and accidental features just have to appear possible and not be incompatible with verisimilitude.]

In common with many critics (like Tasso), Beni distinguished between history, which was to present true events, and poetry or drama, which was only to present the probable and universal. The latter should therefore be judged on its artistic merits, on its *dispositio* and the *elocutio*, rather than on the exact truth of its subject matter.[58]

Guarini had already argued in his *Verrato* (p. 758) that tragicomedy, like tragedy and comedy, need only be verisimilar, but he further emphasized its fictional autonomy in the commentary to the prologue of *Pastor fido*:

> La Scena è figurata in Arcadia provvincia del Peloponesso, che oggi Morea si chiama. Et hassi d'avertire, che'l sito di essa è tutto finto, si come è finta tutta la favola, e finte tutte le cose, che sono in essa, che di così fare a poeta comico, e tragicomico si concede: sì come per lo contrario nel tragico non è lecito. (*Annotationi*, fol. 6[v])
>
> [The scene is set in Arcadia, a province of the Peloponnese, which is now called Morea. And, it should be noted that the setting is totally fictional, as is the plot and everything in it, since a writer of comedy and tragicomedy is entitled to do this, whereas the tragedian is not.]

By this means the dramatist could include various staged elements calculated to delight the audience, as well as a suitable political order (fol. 14[r]), as long as they seemed plausible in the context. Importantly, he could also avoid potential accusations of flattery or unorthodoxy — something that Guarini would have been careful about given the criticism that Tasso's *Liberata* had attracted for mixing religious history with sensual episodes.

The question of verisimilitude was especially contentious with regard to the pastoral characters, since social status carried generic implications. Supposedly following Aristotle, comedy was linked to socially and (incorrectly) to morally inferior characters, while tragedy was associated with noble ones, who were equal to, or better than, contemporaries, and the epic with characters of excellent virtue. On the basis of Virgil's eclogues, Denores held that country-dwellers were therefore inappropriate characters for comic or tragic action. Their chaste and virtuous lifestyle, uncorrupted by the vices found in the city, made it unsuitable for them to experience frenzied, tragic loves or to show 'urbanity' in the form of comic *motti* and *facezie* (*Discorso*, p. 203). They should also be represented as uniformly poor and 'vivendo senza alcuna delicatezza' [living in a totally unrefined state'] (*Apologia*, p. 322).[59] Given that Guarini's *Pastor fido* includes a broad range of characters, from a shepherd ruler and priests to a base satyr, the author was understandably anxious to disprove this view. He countered that tragicomedy allows the mixing of comic and tragic characters (*Verrato*, p. 759–61), for which equivalents existed in the pastoral mode. (The idea of 'pastoral' being used to qualify the term 'tragicomedy', rather than as a substantive, is clarified in *Verato secondo*, pp. 207–09.) Guarini also codified the well established distinction between simple, comic *contadini* and noble, pseudo-courtly *pastori*:

> Non tutti i pastori sono simili a' contadini, ma tutti i contadini sono ben vili e tutti i pastori non furon al tempo antico sucidi e rozzi, come voi vi pensate, ma molti di loro e di nascita e di costumi e d'animo [...] non pur gentili, ma grandi. (*Verrato*, pp. 796–97)

> [Not all shepherds are like peasants, for while the latter are indeed all of low origins, not all shepherds were dirty and coarse in ancient times as you imagine; in fact, many of them were by birth, custom and spirit [...] not only noble, but great figures.]

Crucially, to elevate the new pastoral tragicomedy, Guarini maintained that *pastori* were in ancient times capable of virtuous government and philosophical wisdom, and of the kind of tragic actions and emotions reserved for noble characters in neo-Aristotelian theory (*Verrato*, pp. 806, 811).[60] To justify this view he points to mythological precedents such as Apollo, Diana and Minerva, as well as other demigods and the founders of Rome (pp. 811–14). The matter is clinched in the *Verrato* by associating the Jewish Patriarchs and even Christ himself with the pastoral existence.[61] Strikingly, the pastoral drama is therefore explicitly assimilated to the Judeo-Christian way of life for the first time in sixteenth-century literary criticism, harking back to an association common in medieval versions of pastoral. This analogy shows a remarkable departure from the conception of most earlier Ferrarese writers of pastoral drama. These, as we have seen, tended to favour a mythological, pagan setting with only vague allusions to contemporary religious sentiments, while Tasso's *Aminta* presents a pastoral world apparently removed from secular and religious authority.

Guarini was, however, more ambivalent about Denores's view (itself inconsistent) that pastoral figures were by nature good, leading 'una vita semplice, senza inganni, contenta di poco, casta, religiosa' [a life that is simple, without deceit, content with little, chaste and religious] (*Discorso*, p. 202). The dramatist first describes eclogues as representing 'la natura nostra quasi vergine' [our almost virgin nature] (*Verrato*, p. 750), but later specifies the nature of rustics as being simple rather than purely good, since they, like *pastori*, can vary in degrees of morality (pp. 796, 798). He suggests that they feel the same mixture of emotions as urban audiences and display intrinsic human failings. Even so, drawing on a *topos* of the mode, pastoral characters are described as being less corrupted and their loves purer (pp. 801, 803) than their urban counterparts in comedy and tragedy. The shepherds demonstrate 'la simplicità de' costumi in quella natura non alterata dal desiderio d'avere e dal pestifero morso dell'ambizione' [the simplicity of customs in that nature not corrupted by the desire for gain and the cursed gnawing of ambition] (*Verrato*, p. 750). So while Guarini argues that the pastoral like all poetry merely imitates 'costumi' [behaviour] rather than teaching it, there is a suggestion of its concern with morality.

The city-pastoral polemic in the *Pastor fido* is especially developed through the figures of Corisca and Carino. Both are in different ways 'outsiders' to Arcadia and central to the development of the tragicomic plot, respectively triggering the complication of the *inganno* and the pseudo-tragic recognition. The broadly comic character of the lustful nymph, Corisca, is described by the Satyr as coming from 'le contrade scelerate d'Argo,/ ove lussuria fa l'ultima prova' [the wicked land of Argos, known for its extreme lustfulness] (I. 5. 84–85).[62] The accompanying gloss states that this was mentioned to demonstrate that this wicked woman is not an Arcadian but originating from 'una terra la quale aveva il suo Re, e consequentemente la corte' [a land with its own King and therefore a court] (*Annotationi*, fol. 47ʳ). Within the pastoral context, she functions as the prime example of the degradation of the city or court, though this is notably explored more in moral than political terms.

Unlike the Arcadians, she is motivated entirely by her own selfish desires and lacks a proper awareness of her place within the social and divine order. In choreographing the *inganno* against Amarilli and tricking the satyr, she believes that her own *virtù* and 'industry' can control *fortuna*, echoing her counterparts in earlier pastorals (Giraldi's Egle, Beccari's Stellinia). Her virtuoso use of disguise and illusion, and immoral, hedonistic persuasion of Amarilli to forget fidelity, shame and *onestà* [chastity] (II. 5; III. 5) may be interpreted in light of her basically comic roots.[63] However, as Guarini noted (*Compendio*, pp. 280–81) her malice in seeking to destroy her rival exceeds the proper bounds of comedy, and within the providential structure of the tragicomedy her plot is doomed to failure. Although Guarini toyed in the early stages of composition with having this character transformed punitively into a cow at the end (recalling similar transformations in Pasqualigo's *Intricati*, and Beccari's *Sacrificio*), her final more verisimilar gaining of moral understanding, repentance, and forgiveness by her victims serves to demonstrate the way in which comedy could be rendered serious and decorous in tragicomedy (p. 286).[64]

Carino (a name drawn from Terence's *Andria*), by contrast, embodies a different perspective on the urban/country dichotomy. This aged shepherd appears at the start of Act V, returning to his native Arcadia after a long time spent in various cities and courts. His appearance sets in motion the recognition sequence, demonstrating Guarini's point that shepherds could appropriately trigger this, as in Sophocles' *Oedipus* (*Verrato*, pp. 801–02), despite Denores's objection (*Discorso*, p. 202).[65] Because of this part in the underlying literary design, Foster interprets him as embodying a meta-theatrical role pointing to the authorial presence.[66] This adds further resonance to his polemical account of his travels, which appears to be a fairly thinly veiled allegory of the author's disillusionment with Ferrara, modelled on his compatriot Ariosto's complaints. It is described in the commentary as the point in which some have judged the dramatist to be referring similarly to the lack of recognition of his poetic muse. Nothing further is said to affirm or deny it, though it is added that 'potendo molto ben essere, che anche questo sia finto, come son tutte l'altre cose del presente episodio' [it could well be that this too is purely fictional like everything else in this episode].[67]

In the first scene of Act V, which significantly follows the Golden Age chorus, Carino relates how he left Arcadia in his youth driven by worldly ambition to 'acquistar fama ov'è più chiaro il grido' [gain fame where reputation is greatest] (85). After a happy period in Elide (Elis) and Pisa (generally regarded as the time Guarini spent with the Eterei in Padua), Carino moved to Corisca's homeland of Argos and Mycenae where he became 'adorator di deità terrena' [one who adores earthly gods]

(V.1.104). There follows a famous account of Carino's unhappy period of servitude there (108–87), which Molinari notes was omitted from all the existing manuscript versions except the Turin one.[68] Following a long satirical tradition, the court is indentified as a place of illusion and idolatry, dominated by the struggle for honours and possessions and antithetical to conventional morality: 'quel ch'altrove è virtù, quivi è difetto' [what is considered virtuous elsewhere, is a fault there] (V.1.144). For this reason Carino's pastoral innocence and simplicity made him a target for envious deception. Furthermore, his muse and industry went unrewarded as he was forced to play the morally ambiguous role of the court servant (V.1.113). Through this character Guarini thus reverses the encomiastic stance of Tirsi (Tasso) in *Aminta* (I. 2), aligning himself more with Tasso's Mopso (Speroni?) and even to some extent the Satyr. By contrast to *Aminta*'s pastoral setting, which shows signs of contamination by the city, Carino presents the unambiguously positive values of the pastoral life, described in Guarini's theory as being 'più natural[e], non alterat[o] […] ne' viziat[o] dalle tre miserabili corrutele della città: ambizione, lusso, avarizia' [more natural, and not ruined […] nor corrupted by the three wretched vices of the city: ambition, extravagance and avarice] (*Verrato*, p. 801).

The Ciceronian evolutionary model as a pattern for Arcadia

Guarini's positive view of the pastoral life as representing an original state of natural innocence clashes with sanctioned views of the city as the ideal form of human society. Civic humanists and moralists like Denores, following Aristotle (*Ethics*, I), held that the city represents the only place in which humans could fully realize their natural potential and enjoy the highest form of earthly happiness, while beyond it dwelt only gods and beasts. This conception of the city was based on a long tradition of seeing world history in terms of a gradual progression from primitive beginnings towards greater sophistication.[69] From this perspective, the pastoral life represented an earlier, imperfect type of society compared to the city. In this myth of origins men were originally coarse and bestial, roaming the woods without reason, religion, or law. They later began to gather together into groups to guarantee their protection and provide for their needs. In these primitive social gatherings they responded to the laws of nature alone. Only through reason or, in Cicero's model a combination of wisdom and eloquence, were these men 'humanized' and civilized, and their social groups elevated to the status of cities, with their own laws, religion and morality.[70] Humans were then able to express themselves to their full capacity through their actions in the community using their intellect.

This long-used aetiological fable or 'cave myth' (Arthur Ferguson's term) was drawn on in a consistent way by a range of Renaissance European political thinkers and became particularly appealing after the discovery of primitive peoples in the New World. As Ferguson observes, the success of the myth lay in its ability to lead the imagination 'beyond the point where empirical evidence leaves off yet remaining in accord with reason and experience, an essentially secular myth, uncommitted to the traditions of pagan theology, and only indirectly committed to "historia sacra"'.[71] The myth as presented by Cicero was not developed much further, but for centuries it provided a logical point of departure for enquiries into political and social history.

This generally optimistic view of the potential of human nature to develop from its primitive mentality stands in opposition to Hesiod's myth of human development, which begins with the Golden Age and posits a universal decline to an age of iron. Usually developed over four ages, this historical paradigm was more or less condensed by Ovid to an antithesis between gold and iron. This made it possible to synthesize with the Christian model of the pre- and postlapsarian world, and offered scope both for eulogy and satire. For this reason the Golden Age myth was re-used time and again by moralists, court artists and poets (notably for the Medici), for nostalgic, elegiac and political ends.[72] The myth's praise of simplicity reflects essentially a sophisticated, urban state of mind, the same type that was attracted to the closely related pastoral mode. Compared with the 'cave myth', it attaches a radically different value to man's initially simple condition, which is considered not as primitive or uncivilized, but as a 'natural' and pristine state to which mankind longs to return.

We have seen that the Golden Age myth is used in the ideological frame of the *Pastor fido*. However, this perspective is complicated by the description of the pastoral society in terms of the alternative evolutionary model in Guarini's theoretical works. In order to explain the verisimilitude of the Arcadians' differentiated social roles it is suggested that this pastoral world represents a pre-urban community: ''n quel tempo ancor non erano le città, ma si reggevan da sé, e chi valeva per avventura piú, comandava' [there were at that time no cities yet, but the people governed themselves, and those who happened to be more worthy were in command] (*Compendio*, p. 268; compare *Verrato*, p. 798). Intriguingly, it is suggested that this itself represents a historical evolution from an earlier primitive state:

> Può esser per avventura che nel primordio del mondo, pastoralmente vivendo, gli uomini tutti pascessero indifferentemente le gregge; ma in progresso di tempo, avendo essi bisogno e di governo e di capo, è molto verisimile che tra lor pullulasse la forma e'l nome d'alcun governo, e che quella, quantunque assai semplicemente in quel rozzo secolo, fosse anch'ella onorata col preservarla dall'uso di quel sordido ministero, onde poi ne seguisse che 'l pascer degli armenti restasse cura, parlando all'aristotelica, de' peggiori e'l governar de' migliori. E, perché tutti, e migliori e peggiori, altra vita né conoscevano né menavano che quella prima lor pastorale, il nome di 'pastore' indifferentemente ritennero. (*Compendio*, p. 269; almost verbatim from *Verato secondo*, pp. 193–94)

> [It is possible that, when the world began, people lived a pastoral life where everyone without distinction took their herds to pasture. Over time, however, as they increasingly needed a system of government and a leader, it is very probable that some form and name of government arose. Although it would have been a very simple form in that primitive period, it is likely that it was honoured by being exempted from practising that menial task. This would have meant that the duty of herding would be left to the inferior people, in Aristotelian terms, while the better people would govern. Yet, as they all led or knew no other lives than the original pastoral kind, whether inferior or superior, they used the term 'shepherd' indiscriminately.]

This model gains further ethical and political (if not religious) resonances, relevant to the interpretation of the *Pastor fido*, when compared with some passages in Guarini's less known *Trattato della politica libertà* [Treatise on political liberty], composed in Florence 1599.[73] This starts its exploration of so-called free states with a description of the first phases of the ancient Jewish 'republic', a comparison already linked to the pastoral life in the *Verrato*, as we have seen. In the very first period, from Adam to Moses, the people are said to have been free but without awareness of political freedom:

> Tutti vissero da pastori, e senza forma di governo alcuno abitavano sparsi per le campagne, nè altra legge aveano, che quella della natura illuminata da Dio. Furono sopra tutti eminentissimi i Patriarchi, amici grandi di Dio, che meritarono di godere quell'ineffabil colloquio che promise loro la benedizione delle genti, e destinolli ad essere fondatori dell'umana redenzione, e primi padri in quanto alla carne del Redentore figliuol vero di Dio. (p. 32)

> [They all led the life of shepherds, dotted around the land, without any form of government or law, except that of nature illuminated by God. The Patriarchs were eminent above all the others, and great friends of God, so they merited the enjoyment of that ineffable dialogue which promised them the blessing of their peoples and destined them to be the founders of human redemption, and the first fathers to form the flesh of the Redeemer, the true son of God.]

However, the Jewish peoples are said only to have properly realized this political liberty (later abused and lost) in a second phase, under the rule of law instituted by Moses. At this point it formed a sort of oligarchy in the guise of a republic, where tribes and families were headed by a Patriarch and a political system was created with a senate and elected governors known as judges or elders (p. 34).

This description not only highlights the way in which the pastoral setting could be related to questions of law, political order, ethics and to some extent religion, to which we will return, but also points to an alternative way of reading the characters in the *Pastor fido*. Namely, they may be seen to embody different stages along the evolutionary social model — from the primitive and bestial, through the 'natural' to the enlightened (and paradoxical) state of Arcadian citizen. The *Annotationi* in particular draw on this kind of reading, but present it more in abstract moral terms (to do with reason and free will) than in historical, temporal ones, which would undermine the unity and verisimilitude insisted on in the *Compendio*.

The figure of the satyr typifies this ambiguity. Like many Ferrarese precedents, he follows the brutish laws of nature in his conduct towards his deceptive beloved Corisca (I. 5. 117–18, 125–26). However, his primitive status is confounded by his use of learned *topoi*, especially in the long misogynistic polemic against the female use of cosmetics, and his sophisticated perception of Corisca's insincere use of Petrarchan rhetoric: '(La perfida m'ha mosso; e s'io credessi/ solo a l'affetto, a fè che sarei vinto!)' [(This treacherous nymph has moved me; and if I trusted in my emotions alone, in faith I would be overcome)] (II. 6. 79–80). Malacreta was therefore not altogether unjustified in criticizing the satyr for speaking 'tanto cittadinescamente' [so like a city-dweller] (*Considerazioni*, p. 97). In dramaturgical terms, this urbane quality can of course be related to the satyr's comic status within the play, as seen particularly in the farcical episode with Corisca (II. 6), and structurally from the part he unwittingly plays in Corisca's *beffa*, by enclosing Amarilli in a cave (III. 9).[74]

The *Annotazioni*, on the other hand, draw attention to the satyr's moral status: 'parla da Satiro com'egli è, cioè da lascivo, petulante, e sfacciato, e degno amante di Corisca, che non ha altro fine nell'amor suo che la carne' [he speaks like the Satyr he is; that is lascivious, petulant and brazen, and therefore a suitable lover for Corisca whose only end in love is to satisfy the flesh] (fol. 47^r; see also 104^r). The satyr's equation with the equally bestial Corisca therefore disregards their distinct social origins, reaffirming the idea of pastoral as a reflection of human nature. The critical works omit any mention of the satyr's possible religious significance, which Selmi identifies in his last (reported) role: the betrayal of Corisca (as he believes) to the authorities and leading of the priestly ministers to the cave, which sets in motion the tragic events (IV. 3. 151–64). His portrayal as a Judas figure and description as 'malvagio' [wicked], indicate a significant transformation of the comic type within the pastoral tragicomedy.[75]

The pure and innocent pastoral state apparently seems to be best exemplified through the two younger characters of the subplot: the love-sick nymph Dorinda and the rigorously chaste hunter, Silvio. Their love-story delicately combines gentle humour with pathos, in a predominantly lyric tone, full of madrigal-style, erotic double entendres, which Guarini described as proper to pastoral and appropriate to please audiences (*Compendio*, pp. 254–55). However a shadow of barbarity and excess lingers over these characters. For this reason, the lovers have been read as a self-consciously debased and almost parodic version of Tasso's lovers in *Aminta*.[76] For instance, Silvio's cruel unresponsiveness to love — less delicately nuanced than that of Tasso's Silvia — is likened to the monstrous beast that he is hunting in the woods outside civilization (I. 1. 54–57, 63–65). His arrogant but naïve attitude drives the passionate Dorinda to beg a kiss from him (albeit indirectly) and to resort to undignified tactics to woo him. Animal imagery is frequently associated with the nymph: she envies the affection lavished by Silvio on his beloved hunting dog (II. 2), compares herself with a beast of prey, and later literally turns herself into one after dressing in the 'rozze, orride spoglie' [coarse, shaggy skins] of a wolf (IV. 2. 4; see also lines 31–48).

Dorinda's unseemly behaviour, and Linco's persuasion of Silvio to love Amarilli (I. 1), was strongly condemned in 1600 by the moralizing Faustino Summo, precisely because they seemed in his view to betray the purity of the pastoral mode. While he accepted that comedy may provide both positive and negative examples of private citizens, 'nelle tragicommedie, e specialmente nelle pastorali, in cui si serva un sol tenor di vita semplice, pura, e innocente, fondata e stabilita sopra l'istessa natura […] far il simile non conviene' [in tragicomedies and especially in pastorals in which only a simple, pure and innocent tenor of life is represented, based and founded on nature itself […] it is unseemly to do so].[77] Such concerns are addressed in the *Annotationi*, where it is argued that different customs pertained in this early period, which justified Dorinda's amorous ruses (fol. 144^r) and Linco's speech:

> Nè questo è sconvenevole, essendo'l fine onestissimo; senza che *in quel primo secolo, nel quale si viveva alla natura, l'esser casto non era come oggi virtù tanto stimata. Sì come anco molti congiungimenti che sono illeciti a noi si concedevano allora.* (*Annotationi*, fol. 23^r, my italics)

> [This [persuasion to love] is not inappropriate either, since the end is completely legitimate; especially considering that *in that first age, in which people lived according to nature, chastity was not such a highly prized virtue as it is today. For this reason, many couplings that we now deem illicit were allowed at that time.*]

Dorinda and Silvio therefore seem to exist within a sort of pastoral state still ruled by the more hedonistic law of nature, as in the Golden Age. While Silvio almost fanatically observes the traditional rituals to Diana (see IV. 6), the couple are otherwise unaffected by the kind of religious and family obligations found in the more tragic main action of the play. Nonetheless, despite the sensuality of the 'grafted' plot, an underlying concern with morality does emerge, as the lovers are finally unified with the promise of marriage (IV. 9. 223–26), in sharp contrast to the violent end to the adulterous passions in Euripides' *Hippolytus* and Seneca's *Phaedra* on which the plot is partly modelled.

By staging the lovers' reconciliation, a clear contrast is made with the narrated finale of the *Aminta*. The Golden Age chorus that immediately follows more famously highlights Guarini's self-conscious allusion to Tasso's model and departure from it, representing the only point at which the *Aminta* is explicitly referred to in the *Annotationi* (fol. 191^r). Whereas in Tasso's play a bygone human condition is envisaged in which desires are accommodated with the law of nature: '*S'ei piace ei lice*' [It is allowed if it is pleasing], Guarini changes this to: '*Piaccia, se lice*' [Let it be pleasing if it is allowed]. A Golden Age state has, in his version, been achieved through the voluntary curbing of natural desire to accord with moral and social norms (*onestà* and *fede*). This original condition is likened in the fourth chorus (lines 2–3) to a state of childlike innocence, when the world drank milk and was cradled by the forest. The commentary further associates it with an Edenic existence, when the land was fertile and 'purgato' [purged] (*Annotationi*, fol. 189^v). The inhabitants lived in a state of prelapsarian grace according to the laws of nature, free from virtue or vice; and 'se non eran perfetti gli animi umani, almen non erano pravi, nè commettevano alcun delitto contra natura, com'è quello dell'adulterio' [men may not have been perfect but at least they were not depraved, nor did they commit any crimes against nature such as adultery] (*Annotationi*, fol. 189^r).[78]

Within the play and his critical writings, Guarini therefore seems to accept apparently contradictory visions of the pastoral age: as an age of purity and childishness (an association often made with the primitive mentality by the end of the sixteenth century), as well as of primitive barbarism.[79] However, these values are only fully understood by comparison with the main plot which, as Residori suggests, develops the tragic expressions from *Aminta* in order to present a superior model of pastoral. Set in a more evolved society governed by laws, religion and honour, Guarini's principal action presents divinely ordained characters who are removed from the simpler state of nature (see Amarilli's famous lament, II. 5. 1–68). Only in this context are true virtue (and sin) possible, because of the rule of law which gives humans the crucial attribute of free will.[80]

Accordingly, the main plot displays heroic and marvellous human actions, which climax in Act V with Montano's resolve knowingly to kill his own son and Mirtillo's voluntary self-sacrifice to save Amarilli and thus Arcadia. This demonstrates the way in which horrific and sublime qualities typically associated with tragedy or epic are in Guarini's model infused and modified in the modern pastoral drama.

Political Thought and the City

> Delle cose di stato niuna altra sorte di uomini meglio [sa] discorrere e deliberare che i pastori; e [...] beati sarebbono i prencipi, se nel governare i sudditi loro usassero la medesima carità che praticano i pecorai nel pascere la greggia loro: felicissimi i popoli, se nell'ubbidire i loro prencipi imitassero le pecore. (Boccalini, *Ragguagli di Parnaso*, Cent. I, XLVII, p. 170)
>
> [No one is better able to discuss and deliberate on affairs of state than shepherds; and [...] princes would be blessed if they used the same charity in governing their subjects as shepherds use in feeding their flock: and the people would be most happy if, in obeying their princes, they imitated sheep.]

The pastoral state

By contrast to the subplot of the *Pastor fido*, which focuses on the tempering of the characters' emotions removed from social necessity, the main action unfolds against the backdrop of a tightly ordered political society. Unusually for a pastoral drama, Arcadia is governed by a priestly ruler (Montano), who heads a hierarchy of priests and ministers of justice entrusted with observing and enforcing the laws of Diana, as interpreted through oracles.[81] This pious society thus in some ways recalls the second phase of the Jewish pastoral 'republic' under the rule of law instituted by Moses described in Guarini's *Trattato della politica libertà* (see also *Annotationi* to prologue, fol. 14^v). Certainly, there is little evidence of Arcadia's historical roots at the margins of the Greek democratic *polis*, and it appears more like an absolutist theocracy in line with Counter-Reformation aims to unite the temporal and spiritual realms.[82]

Despite the claim of fictional autonomy, various contemporary political concerns are obliquely raised in the *Pastor fido* and developed in the critical writings. Notably, the form of tragicomedy is itself compared to a mixed republic, combining democracy and oligarchy, as described by Aristotle.[83] This may reflect Guarini's practical involvement in and thought on politics following the radical alterations within the Italian peninsula over the past three centuries or so. By the late sixteenth century, the humanist vision of the city-state as an autonomous space for wide-based political engagement and morality was a vanishing ideal. From 1559, most states were firmly under princely control and all relied on support from greater European powers (see Chapter 2). Furthermore, the reinvigorated Catholic Church was increasingly claiming the role of moral guardian of political life in cooperation with civic rulers, especially of the emerging nation states, as well as trying to stir the individual conscience.[84]

The political order in Guarini's *Pastor fido* hints significantly at some of the issues later explored in his *Trattato*, written for Grandduke Ferdinando de' Medici in 1599. This treatise proposes the commonplace in sixteenth-century courtly writings that an enlightened principality is needed to guarantee the safety and economic security of its citizens.[85] The princely legislator will ensure the health of the body politic by tempering disordered private passions which keep the will enslaved and unable to act honestly, and which cause sedition in the 'malsane e stemperate' [sick and untempered] republics (p. 130). The moral and social benefits of political liberty are best realized (following Aristotle, it is said) through the firm but just enforcement of law, which the prince can do better than a communal government, since: 'come legge viva supplisce con l'arbitrio là dove manca la legge, e ne forma di nuove quando bisogna, e l'osservanza loro difende con mano regia' [like the law in person he adds his will to the law where it is wanting, and forms new ones when necessary, and defends their observation with his royal hand] (p. 28). His authority stems from the fact that he is '*sopra le leggi*, che nel farle osservare non tema le vicende, né le repulse civili, e *possa far giustizia senza rispetto*' [*above the law*, so that in ensuring its observance he does not fear reprisal or civil disobedience, and can administer justice without restraint] (pp. 126–27, my emphasis).

Such ideas on authority, justice, virtuous rule of self and others, and social responsibility are particularly explored in the main plot of the *Pastor fido*, concerning Mirtillo and Amarilli. It thereby introduces a public, political dimension that was new to pastoral drama and explicitly avoided in the *Aminta*.

The theme of justice

The main plot of Guarini's *Pastor fido* is underpinned by a divine law imposed by Diana, which entails a yearly sacrifice from the Arcadians of a virgin, and orders that women caught committing adultery or even breaking the 'fede' [faith] sworn to their betrothed are condemned to death. As such, the goddess here appears noticeably more severe than she typically does in earlier pastoral plays, though in Beccari's *Sacrificio* (IV. 3) she sentences a fallen nymph to fight a vicious boar. In being directed against all women rather than just her devotees, this law supports a rigid patriarchal social order and enshrines a double standard like Ariosto's 'aspra legge di Scozia' [harsh law of Scotland] (*Orlando furioso*, IV. 59. 1). As such it evokes contemporary social and increasingly also religious anxieties about sexuality which was not contained within marriage.

Adultery had long presented a serious threat to the status quo, which was dependent on the predominantly patrilineal inheritance of titles, class affiliation and patrimony. Illicit sexual acts were consequently punished severely, especially in the case of women.[86] During, and particularly after, the Council of Trent the Church began to take stronger measures to regulate the sacrament of marriage, and to monitor sexual deviance such as homosexuality, sodomy and adultery as well as public immorality. This stance, aimed at safeguarding social order, was backed by demands for state legislation which could in some cases be extremely harsh. For instance, Sixtus V (1585–90) called for the death penalty for adultery, incest and abortion amongst other things in a virulent campaign launched in 1586. Church and State control therefore became increasingly intertwined within the domain of personal morality. It was of course in practice impossible fully to enforce the penalties established, especially against members of the nobility, but even so it is indicative of the blurring of the secular and spiritual in law that Italian statutes were increasingly transforming sexual 'sins' into 'crimes'.

Within the economy of the play, episodes of adultery have a special significance, twice marking the moment of reversal of both private and social fortunes. As described in the *antefatto* (I. 2. 149–57, drawn from Pausanias), the infidelity of the nymph Lucrina towards her lover Aminta, Diana's priest, explains the institution of the divine law, which continued to be applied after Lucrina's suicide following Aminta's self-sacrifice for her. The Arcadians' only hope for salvation now lies in the prophesied marriage of the semi-divine Amarilli, although her father fears that she will contravene her vows to her betrothed (Silvio) under the sway of her unreciprocated natural sexual urges (I. 4) — a general male suspicion that is exploited by Corisca (II. 5). Amarilli's heroic observance of chastity ultimately proves a condition for the resolution of the complication. However, it is finally realized through Mirtillo's magnanimous offer of self-sacrifice in accordance with the divine law. This outdoes the earlier gesture of Aminta bringing about a happy outcome, since this time Mirtillo is voluntarily submitting to justice; his free will harmonizes with the providential order.

During the course of the play numerous appendices to Diana's law are referred to which restrict its application, and which Malacreta criticized as being inappropriate in a play (*Considerazioni*, p. 64). These of course serve to explain plausibly how it is that Mirtillo can be publicly sacrificed in place of his beloved Amarilli (V. 2. 145–47), outdoors (V. 2. 160–67), where his putative father (Carino) will see him, but cannot in turn substitute him (IV. 4. 104–05); and where the fact of Mirtillo's origins as an Arcadian prompts questions that will lead to his recognition and eventually the reversal of fortunes. The processes of the law in the form of a trial and cathartic ritual punishment in Acts IV-V also provide important opportunities for visual spectacle, inspiring near-tragic affects of pathos and fear (see fig. 6). Furthermore, they allow the exploration of ideas on justice and error within the pastoral tragicomedy. This is particularly noticeable in the scene of Amarilli's trial by the priest Nicandro (IV. 5), and in the discussion between Carino and Montano, the priestly ruler of Arcadia (V. 4–5), which raises the question of the relationship of the ruler with his subjects.

On his arrival in Arcadia, Carino has discovered to his horror that the victim being sacrificed is his long-sought son, Mirtillo. Having interrupted the ritual so that it has to be postponed, Carino reminds the angered Montano of his duty to observe the mutual bond of obligations with his subject:

> CARINO   Dunque se grazia non impetro, almeno
> fa' che giustizia i' trovi, e ciò negarmi
> per debito non puoi,
> ché chi dà legge altrui,
> non è da legge in ogni parte sciolto;
> e quanto se' maggiore
> nel comandar, tanto più d'ubbidire
> se' tenut' anco a chi giustizia chiede. (V. 5. 23–30)

[So though I do not beg for grace, at least grant me justice, since by right you may not deny me this. For he who legislates over others is not fully exempt from the law himself; and the greater your superiority in command, the more you are bound to obey those who ask for justice.]

This obligation is glossed as the 'first law' that a good prince must follow: 'sì come l'uno [il soggetto] è ubbligato a ubbidire il sovrano, così il sovrano è ubbligato a far giustizia al soggetto; e non facendola, il soggetto non è tenuto a ubbidirlo' [just as the subject is obliged to obey the sovereign, so the sovereign must provide justice for the subject; and should the ruler fail to do so, the subject is not required to obey him] (*Annotationi*, fol. 225ʳ). Carino's request for justice therefore raises the interesting question of whether the ruler should be above the law. Understandably, the commentator remains cautious on this matter, referring to authoritative sources, but it is suggested that the prince is subject to divine and natural laws, but retains some scope for deciding how far some of his own laws are enforced (fol. 224ᵛ).

The political relationship depicted between the shepherd ruler and subject however soon appears more like the autocratic kind theorized on in the *Trattato*, where the prince rules his subjects with the natural authority that reason holds over the unruly senses or passions.[87] In such a political regime upheld by spiritual authority — as was being realized at that time particularly in the Habsburg territories — the prince is set apart from his people and his magistrates as the supreme earthly executor of justice, a position that gave him the sole right (following God) to grant pardon or remission as he wished.[88] For this reason, Carino ultimately needs to rely more on 'mercede' [mercy] and 'grazia' [grace] (V. 5. 10, 23) than on justice alone. Montano is no tyrant, though, since he is committed to upholding justice and protecting the common good.[89] With tragic irony, he states to Carino that if necessary, he would himself be prepared to sacrifice his own son (referring to Silvio) for Arcadia:

> MONTANO   Ché sacro manto indegnamente veste
> chi, per publico ben, del suo privato
> comodo non si spoglia. (V. 4. 126–28)
>
> [For the ruler who does not divest himself of his private convenience for the public good is unworthy of wearing the sacred mantle.]

This affirmation ends up being spectacularly tested when Montano discovers that he has to sacrifice his newly re-discovered older son, Mirtillo, to observe the divine law, recalling the biblical example of Abraham.[90] This response to the recognition demonstrates Montano's moral integrity, but also his limitations. Only through divine illumination can Mirtillo's preordained role as the 'pastor fido' be understood, true justice be carried out, and Arcadia saved.

The Establishment of an Ethical Pastoral Model

The limitations of the law (in terms of human understanding of it) are perhaps most effectively dramatized in Amarilli's trial by the chief minister, Nicandro (IV. 5), which is described in the commentary as being 'tutta tragica, in modo che s'ella non fosse in favola tragicomica, mista di persone, azioni, scherzi, risi, ed ordine, e fine comico, sarebbe atta a purgare il terrore, e la commiserazione che in lei si muove' [totally tragic, so that if it was not part of a tragicomedy with its mixed characters, actions, jokes and laughter, and comic structure and ending, it would be able to purge the fear and pity that it arouses] (fol. 160ᵛ). This scene is prepared by the messenger Ergasto's account of the discovery of the lovers in the cave by Nicandro and the 'chorus' of minor ministers (IV. 3. 178–79), which leads to Amarilli being charged with adultery. During the interrogation itself, Nicandro assumes Amarilli's culpability from the start, as Ergasto did, on the basis of the evidence: 'dove/ il fatto accusa, ogni difesa offende' [where the facts point to guilt, any defence is wrong] (IV. 5).[91] In his view, she has voluntarily contravened Diana's law by breaking her faith to Silvio and giving way to her desires. Her carefully reasoned protestations of innocence of intent and conduct are therefore passed off merely as technical quibbling or even blasphemy:

> NICANDRO Non incolpar le stelle,
> ché noi soli a noi stessi
> fabbri siam pur de le miserie nostre. (IV. 5. 80–82)

[Do not blame the stars, for we alone forge our own misfortunes.]

Although the priest is aware that the true state of the heart cannot be known externally (IV. 5. 3) and that Amarilli's plight will affect all of Arcadia, he rigidly observes Diana's law. Yet he is not without compassion and humanity: 'chi sa questo, e non piange, e non sen duole,/ uomo non è, ma fera in volto umano' [he who knows this and does not weep is no man but a beast in human guise] (IV. 5. 23–24).

In judging Amarilli's actions, Nicandro makes an important distinction beween the law of nature, which is in part dictated by necessity and is intrinsically good, and superior human and divine laws, which presuppose free will:

> NICANDRO Contra la legge di natura forse
> non hai, ninfa, peccato: 'Ama, se piace';
> ma ben hai tu peccato incontra quella
> degli uomini e del cielo: 'Ama, se lice'. (IV. 5. 66–69)

[Nymph, you may not have sinned against the law of nature: 'Love if you so wish'; but you have sinned against human and divine law: 'Love, if it is permitted'.]

This point is glossed as follows:

> Due sono le leggi, una della natura, che instiga e permette di seguitare l'oggetto dilettevole; l'altra che regola la natura secondo i tempi, i casi, le persone, le forme dei governi, ed altre circostanze, che vi concorrono. La prima s'adempie col piacere: e la seconda col dovere, che vien da Dio per mezzo degli uomini, e però dice degli uomini e del cielo. Questo per cagion di Diana, che diè la legge: quelli, per cagion dei ministri, che la maneggiano.[92]
>
> [There are two laws: one is dictated by nature, which stimulates and allows a person to follow the object of desire; the other regulates this nature according to the time, situation, persons, forms of government and other relative circumstances. The first law is fulfilled according to pleasure; the second according to obligation, which derives from God by means of men and is therefore said to be made by men and the heavens, since Diana made the law, while it is enforced by ministers.]

The tragic conflict between these laws in Amarilli's trial strikingly points to Guarini's revision of Tasso's Golden Age dictum. A parallel is also created in the secondary plot where Silvio chooses not to run away, but to submit to Dorinda's retributive justice after unintentionally shooting her (IV. 8–9), thereby fulfilling the oracular prophecy of the god of Love (IV. 8. 63–120). The young hunter feels compelled to confess his cruelty towards the nymph, and even kneels down before her reverently to beg her forgiveness (IV. 9. 138–40), offering his breast for her vengeance. This personal acceptance of responsibility marks Silvio's passage to a more evolved state of consciousness, characterized by moderated individual emotions and regard for others. In this way he demonstrates a natural and internal sense of justice, rather than having

Figure 6. Engraving (by Francesco Val(l)egio?) preceding Act V of Battista Guarini, *Pastor fido, tragicommedia pastorale* (Venice: Giovanni Battista Ciotti, 1602). The upper two scenes represent the sacrifice of Mirtillo at an altar with a chorus of shepherds and one of priests. To the upper right is the crucial scene of Montano's interrupted execution of Mirtillo. Reproduced by permission of Reading University Library (Overstone Shelf 19F/19, p. 350).

it imposed by formal belief, which chimed with the post-Tridentine emphasis on repentance rather than satisfaction of an offence.[93] The closing scene where Corisca confesses to her victim Amarilli (V. 9) further establishes this pastoral tragicomedy as a drama of penitence and reconciliation, where willingness to make amends is rewarded by forgiveness and exemption from the penalties otherwise entailed.

The apparent conflict between 'natural' justice and Diana's law in Amarilli's case serves to demonstrate the limitations of the law when exercized punitively by humans. For a perfect harmony between the two orders one must look far above the sphere of its pale human imitation to infallible Divine justice, which ultimately remains almost unknowable and inexplicable. Only the ancient, blind sage (Tirenio), who represents the spiritual life and, significantly, dwells outside the 'state' of Arcadia, is privileged with some divine knowledge. This character, clearly modeled on Tiresias from Sophocles' *Oedipus Rex* as well as perhaps Pier l'Eremita (Peter the Hermit) in Tasso's *Gerusalemme liberata*, acts as a medium to interpret properly the riddle of the oracle (rather than let the protagonist understand it for himself as in the classical version).[94] Only by surrendering to God's will in the face of human spiritual blindness, is the providential significance of the sacrifice resolved, resulting in the happy ending. Through Tirenio's intervention, Mirtillo's sentence to death in place of Amarilli is miraculously reversed (recalling the episode of Sofronia and Olindo in Tasso's *Liberata*, II). The marriage of the lovers seems to herald the return of the Golden Age, where potentially anarchic individual desires are tempered and contained, and apparent conflicts resolved. Now as then 'era un nome sol marito e vago' [husband and lover was one and the same word] (Chorus, IV. 39) — a situation that perfectly resonated with the intended occasion of the play's performance at the dynastic wedding in Turin.

The question of divine justice is only cautiously touched upon in the commentary, with careful avoidance of potentially theological issues. This office would after all be inappropriate for a poet dealing with ostensibly fictional, pagan subjects and is relegated to priests or his readers' individual judgement. The author merely alludes to the indisputable good of providence, though he is tantalizingly reticent as to the proof of his argument, in which one might see a reference to Christ:[95]

> [La] divina providenza e giustizia, [...] bramosissima del ben nostro, tutto'l mal che ei manda è sol per fin di giovarci. Potrei di questa tal providenza e giustizia dare un'esempio sì concludente, e tanto sublime, che piena sodisfazione potrebbe dare a chiunque imputasse quest'atto per ingiusto, e biasimasse il Poeta nostro, che come cosa di male esempio l'avesse usata; ma voglio anzi che la difesa di questo resti nella considerazione e prudenza delle persone dotte e sincere, che valermi dei Sacrosanti misteri della nostra relligione per esempio delle profane novelle dell'antica gentilità (*Annotationi*, fol. 214ᵛ)

> [Divine providence and justice [...] desire what is good for us so much that all the misfortunes sent our way are only meant to help us. I could provide such a conclusive and sublime example of this providence and justice that it would fully satisfy anyone who considered this act to be unjust and blamed our Poet for using it as a bad example; but I would rather relegate this defence to the judgment and prudence of those who are wise and sincere, than use the sacrosanct mysteries of our religion as an example for profane tales from the time of the ancient gentiles.]

The *Pastor fido* as an Authoritative Model for the Pastoral Genre

Various retrospective defensive strategies can therefore be seen to have been adopted in an effort to legitimize the play. Within the tragicomic structure itself the more sensual secondary plot is subordinated to an explicitly decorous, even heroic or semi-tragic, main plot, featuring lovers who appear as models of virtue for their sex. The pastoral setting is generally idealized, with cruder comic or sensual elements being carefully modified in line with the tragicomic ethos. Subsequent theoretical works further exploited the genre's allusiveness and capaciousness to justify its orthodoxy. This approach was probably used in order to forestall or deflect the kind of criticism that dogged Tasso's *Liberata*, especially for its blending of religious history with 'implausible' marvels and erotic episodes. Guarini notably sought in his polemical works to emphasize the purely fictional status of his play and its aim of pleasing its audiences.

While the idea of drama's hedonistic function became more widely accepted by the end of the century (for example by Summo), some critics continued to attack the perceived lack of verisimilitude and immorality of the *Pastor fido*. They targeted the very aspects that were considered pleasurable by courtly audiences, such as Dorinda's lyric speeches and the description of the kissing game amongst the nymphs with the cross-dressed Mirtillo (II. 1. 59–271). Guarini's theoretical writings accordingly suggest more orthodox ways of understanding the pastoral state: in historical and moral terms, as a condition of innocence in which eros was justifiable or as a space in which human nature could be most perfectly realized. Furthermore, the representation of pastoral life was justified by Biblical precedents, though only explicitly in historical terms, as was appropriate for this context.

With the definitive edition of the *Pastor fido* in 1602, Guarini offered a final justification for his dramaturgical practice and, in the commentary, specifically clarified points of the text that had been considered morally or theologically dubious by detractors. This also gives orthodox explanations for political and legal questions referring to respected classical authorities, and especially to Aquinas and Aristotle's *Ethics*. Doctrinal questions that could cause difficulties are conspicuously avoided. Similarly, the insistence on a hedonistic end for poetry made explicitly in the *Verati* is less evident in Guarini's later justifications of his *Pastor fido*.[96] Indeed, the *Annotationi* conclude with an extraordinary moral allegory by which the *Pastor fido* is read as symbolizing the moral journey of man (Mirtillo) towards a state of human happiness or virtue (Amarilli) on the Aristotelian model. In this way, it could be held up as an exemplary secular myth for modern times. Discussion of the daringly syncretic elements of the play could thereby be neutralized or avoided: these inlude the cataclysm of the flood and saving of a first-born male, the sacrifice of a beloved son to appease God, which takes on Eucharistic symbolism, and the self-sacrifice of an innocent male shepherd for the salvation of others, redeeming an earlier female sin.[97]

Guarini's retrospective 'institutionalization' of his play through allegory may in part have been in response to the new wave of polemics following the publication of Ingegneri's *Della poesia* (1598). Or it could have been connected with his hopes of becoming a secretary to the College of Cardinals (he applied in 1595 and 1598). On a more personal level, he may have been seeking to vindicate the honour of his family after the brutal murder of his daughter, Anna, by her husband (Count Ercole Trotti) in 1598 on the grounds of adultery.[98] According to the eighteenth-century biographer Barotti, some moralists indirectly suggested a connection between her death and the pernicious effects of the pastoral tragicomedy.[99] Guarini's play also came under attack from religious authorities, including possibly Cardinal Bellarmino, who was said to have blamed the *Pastor fido* for corrupting countless women and having caused greater harm to the Catholic Church than Luther and Calvin.[100]

Despite moral objections to the play's 'excessive' lyricism and erotic subject matter, the neutral-sounding theoretical works that were added to the definitive edition (1602) must have helped to establish a model of pastoral drama that apparently at least conformed to orthodox ethical and political values. At the same time, Guarini developed a daring aesthetic justification for his work, which balanced Aristotelian poetic rules (on imitation, verisimilitude, unity) with the demands of modern audiences for variety, novelty and 'diletto', preluding significant developments in seventeenth-century poetics. Thus the Ciotti edition of the *Pastor fido* may be seen as marking a key stage in the pastoral play's legitimization, enabling subsequent examples to be granted printing privileges at a time when the publication of secular drama was no easy matter.

Notes to Chapter 5

1. Battista Guarini, *Il Verrato* [1588], in *Opere di Battista Guarini*, ed. by Marziano Guglielminetti (Turin: UTET, 1971), pp. 731–821 (p. 754), hereafter *Verrato*. This edition will be referred to as Guarini, *Opere*, ed. by Guglielminetti.
2. On the play's fortunes from the seventeenth to the twentieth centuries, see Nicolas J. Perella, *The Critical Fortune of Battista Guarini's 'Il Pastor Fido'* (Florence: Olschki, 1973).
3. For biographical details on Guarini, see Elisabetta Selmi, 'Guarini, Battista', in *DBI*, 60 (2003), 345–52; Guglielminetti, 'Introduzione' to his edition of Guarini, *Opere*, pp. 9–69; and the still important monograph by Vittorio Rossi, *Battista Guarini ed Il Pastor Fido. Studio biografico-critico con documenti inediti* (Turin: Loescher, 1886). On the relative status of Guarini and Tasso in Ferrara, see Guido Baldassarri, 'Introduzione', in Battista Guarini, *Il Pastor fido*, ed. by Elisabetta Selmi (Venice: Marsilio, 1999), pp. 9–24 (pp. 12–13).
4. See for example letters to Cornelio Bentivoglio, 25 Jan. 1582, and Francesco Maria Vialardi, 22 July 1583, in Guarini, *Opere*, ed. by Guglielminetti, pp. 97–101, 103–07; Rossi, pp. 41–49, 73, 75.
5. See Guarini's letter to Vincenzo Gonzaga, 7 April, 1584, in which the dramatist politely refused to send a copy of the unfinished *Pastor fido* for performance at the prince's wedding (Mantua, Archivio di Stato (ASM), Archivio Gonzaga, 1514; D'Ancona, *Origini*, II, 539–40). Also the letter to Eugenio Visdomini (secretary of the Duke of Parma), 7 Jan. 1586, which mentions that the choruses still lacked 'alcuni pochi versi' [a few lines], in Battista Guarini, *Lettere* (Venice: Giovanni Battista Ciotti, 1598), p. 214.
6. Carla Molinari, 'Per il "Pastorfido" di Battista Guarini', *Studi di filologia italiana*, 43 (1985), 161–238; Rossi, pp. 189–222. Manuscript versions of the play include one incomplete, mostly autograph, and one complete autograph, untitled final version, besides some other draft versions of scenes (Biblioteca Marciana, Venice, cod. Zanetti Ital. LXV (=4782)); and a complete copy in Biblioteca Comunale Ariostea, Ferrara, Classe I H, probably made at an intermediary stage. Only fragments remain of the Turin manuscript in the Biblioteca Nazionale dedicated to Duke Carlo Emanuele of Savoy, destroyed by fire in 1902 (see Rossi, pp. 192–93). For an excellent study of the interrelated process of textual revision and developing theoretical ideas, see the 'Introduzione' and notes to Elisabetta Selmi's edition of the *Pastor fido*; and her exhaustive *'Classici e Moderni' nell'officina del 'Pastor fido'* (Alessandria: Edizioni dell'Orso, 2001).

7. *Opere*, ed. by Guglielminetti, p. 113. Guarini became a member of the Accademia della Crusca in 1587. For Salviati's comments *Sopra la Tragicomedia del Guarini Censure e correzioni* (in the Ferrarese ms cited n. 6, fols 77^r-109^v), see the transcription by Silvio Pasquazi, 'Le annotazioni al "Pastor fido" di Leonardo Salviati', in *Poeti estensi del Rinascimento* (Florence: Le Monnier, 1966), pp. 191–233. Scipione Gonzaga's recommendations have not survived.
8. The frontispiece to the first Ciotti edition of 1602 claims to be the twentieth edition, though 21 earlier ones are known of. A second Ciotti edition of 1602 states it is the twenty-seventh (Carla Molinari, 'La parte del Guarini nel Commento al "Pastor fido"', *Schifanoia*, 15–16 (1995), 141–50 (p. 148 n.2); 'Per il "Pastorfido"', pp. 227–38).
9. The plot structure of *Andria* is mentioned briefly in *Verrato*, pp. 786–87 (on double plots); but compared at much greater length in his treatise *Il Verato* [sic] *secondo, ovvero Replica dell'Attizzato Accademico Ferrarese in difesa del Pastor fido* (Florence: Per Filippo Giunti, 1593 [1592]), pp. 279–84, and re-used in Guarini's *Compendio della poesia tragicomica* (1601).
10. See Selmi, *Pastor fido*, pp. 41–44, 308–09, 325–26, 355–58 (comparison with Beccari's *Sacrificio*) and 'Classici e moderni', pp. 68, 86–87; and Rossi, pp. 79–82. Guarini sent his manuscript of *L'Idropica* to Vincenzo Gonzaga in 1584, but it was lost for some years, and only performed in Mantua in 1608, printed 1613.
11. Henceforth *Discorso*; all references to Battista Guarini, *Opere*, 5 vols (Verona: Tumermani, 1737–38), II (1738), 153–206 (the section mentioned is at pp. 199–204). These volumes include most of the significant contributions to the debate on the *Pastor fido*.
12. All quotations from *Verato secondo* from the 1592/3 edition (see n. 9). The treatise also appears in the cited Tumermani edition of Guarini's *Opere*, III, 1–384; there is no modern edition. Denores's claim was not wholly unjustified. Though most previous pastoral plays were termed *favola, egloga* or *comedia*, with the complement *pastorale* or *boschereccia*, so-called tragicomedies had been composed by this time by Diomisso Guazzoni (*Andromeda, tragicomedia boscareccia* (Venice: Appresso Domenico Imberti, 1587)); and by Anello Paulilli (*Il ratto d'Helena, tragicomedia* (Naples: Gio. Maria Scotto, 1566); *Il giuditio di Paride, tragicomedia* (Naples: Gio. Maria Scotto, 1566)). Epicuro's *Cecaria* was also entitled *tragicommedia* in many editions from the 1530s onwards. On similarities between Guarini's dramaturgy and that of the *commedia dell'arte*, see Henke, *Pastoral Transformations*, pp. 186–87; also, Marzia Pieri, 'Il "Pastor fido" e i comici dell'Arte', *Biblioteca teatrale*, 17 (1990), 1–15.
13. Henke, *Pastoral Transformations*, pp. 21–22; Rossi, pp. 179–89, 223–38.
14. *Apologia [...] contro l'Autore del Verato*, in Guarini, *Opere* (Verona: Tumermani, 1737–38), II (1738), II, 313–75 (p. 325).
15. For the aesthetic premises to the debate and a chronological account of the works, see Weinberg, *Literary Criticism*, I, 26–31; II, 1074–1105; Herrick, pp. 135–42; also Perella, *Critical Fortune*, pp. 10–39 (focusing especially on ethical aspects and the aesthetic reception in Italy till 1671). For bibliography on the actor Ver(r)ato, see chapter 6, n. 48.
16. Rossi mentions thirty-nine editions from 1602–1700 (pp. 314–15, 236–37; see 315–23 for further editions and translations). The *Pastor fido* was translated into French in 1593, Spanish and English in 1602, and later a Cretan dialect of Greek (pre 1611?), Swedish, Polish, and various Italian dialects amongst other languages. On the play's early reception abroad, see Perella, *Critical Fortunes*; pp. 39–64 (France), 64–79 (England); also Rosemary Bancroft-Marcus, 'The Pastoral Mode', in *Literature and Society in Renaissance Crete*, ed. by David Holton (Cambridge: Cambridge University Press, 1991), pp. 79–102 (pp. 89–96). I thank Richard Andrews for this reference. For the play's fortunes in performance, see chapter 6.
17. All quotations here will refer to the 1602 edition. A later edition of the *Annotationi sopra il Pastor fido* (Verona: Tumermani, 1737) is reproduced in Andrea Gareffi (ed.), *La questione del "Pastor fido". Giovan Battista Guarini* Annotazioni. *Faustino Summo. Due Discorsi* (Manziana: Vecchiarelli, 1997). All references to the *Compendio* from Giambattista Guarini, *Il Pastor fido e Compendio della Poesia Tragicomica*, ed. by Gioachino Brognoligo (Bari: Laterza, 1914), pp. 219–88.
18. Richardson, *Printing*, p. 133. Tasso's *Liberata* appeared with engravings and two sets of annotations by Scipione Gentili (1586) and Giulio Guastavini in 1590. The Bonfadino edition of the *Pastor fido* (dated 1590), by contrast, includes only an 'argomento' by way of paratexts.
19. On the connotations of adopting a pseudonym, see Genette, pp. 46–54.
20. Giovanni Savio, *Apologia in difesa del Pastor fido* (Venice: Per Horatio Larducci, 1601); Orlando

Pescetti, *Difesa del Pastor fido tragicommedia pastorale del molto illustre Sig. Cavalier Battista Guarini* (Verona: Nella Stampata di Angelo Tamo, 1601).
21. Molinari, 'La parte'. Genette is unaware of authorial notes on plays; and recalls the slur of presumption attached to epitextual self-commentary in this period (pp. 333, 367). On the critical tradition surrounding Speroni's polemical tragedy *Canace* (1542), see Roaf.
22. On Salviati's edition, see Richardson, *Print Culture*, pp. 171–72.
23. Paduan critics involved in the debate on *Pastor fido* include: Denores, his pupil Faustino Summo (lecturer in logic), and Paolo Beni (lecturer in humanities). Orlando Pescetti was based in nearby Verona, while an opponent, Giovanni Pietro Malacreta was originally from Vicenza (though his treatise is set in Padua). For Guarini's connections with Padua, see Rossi, pp. 11, 16–20, 78, 97–98; and Guarini, *Opere*, ed. by Guglielminetti, pp. 65–69 ('Nota biografica'). On Padua university, see Paul F. Grendler, *The Universities of the Italian Renaissance* (Baltimore and London: Johns Hopkins University Press, 2002), pp. 21–40.
24. Pier Paolo Vergerio and Vittorino da Feltre, trained in Padua, were important in promoting the study of rhetoric (and therefore literature) in their schools. The university was a little slower than some others (notably Florence), though, in developing humanist studies.
25. Antonino Poppi, 'Il prevalere della "vita activa" nella Paidea del Cinquecento', in *Rapporti tra le università di Padova e Bologna. Ricerche di filosofia medicina e scienza*, ed. by Lucia Rossetti (Trieste: Lint, 1988), pp. 97–125 (pp. 98, 112).
26. Grendler, *Universities*, pp. 225, 234; on the interconnections between the University of Padua and the Infiammati academy, see V. Vianello, *Il Letterato, l'accademia, il libro. Contributi sulla cultura veneta del Cinquecento* (Padua: Antenore, 1988), pp. 64–70. See also Brian Vickers, 'Rhetoric and Poetics', in *The Cambridge History of Renaissance Philosophy*, ed. by Charles B. Schmitt and others (Cambridge: Cambridge University Press, 1988), pp. 715–45 (p. 729); and his *In Defence of Rhetoric* (Oxford: Oxford Clarendon Press, 1988), pp. 264–66, 270–76.
27. Poppi, pp. 99–108; Maria Rosa Davi, 'Filosofia e retorica nell'opera di Sperone Speroni', in *Sperone Speroni: Filologia Veneta. Lingua, letteratura, tradizioni*, ed. by A. Daniele and others (Padua: Programma, 1989), pp. 89–112; R. Scrivano, 'Cultura e letteratura in Sperone Speroni', in *Cultura e letteratura nel Cinquecento* (Rome: Edizioni dell'Ateneo, 1966), pp. 119–41.
28. On the Infiammati, Elevati and Animosi, see respectively Maylender, III (1929), 266–70 (p. 268–69); II (1927), 263–65; I (1926), 197–200.
29. Sperone Speroni, *Dialogo della retorica*, in *Trattatisti del Cinquecento*, ed. by M. Pozzi (Milan: Ricciardi, 1978), pp. 637–82 (pp. 641, 658). On the context of this dialogue, see Giancarlo Mazzacurati, *Il Rinascimento dei moderni. La crisi culturale del XVI secolo e la negazione delle origini* (Bologna: Il Mulino, 1985), pp. 237–43. On the general privileging of *elocutio* from around 1540, see Vickers, *In Defence*, pp. 282–85; also Davi, pp. 93, 97–98, where the hedonistic end of rhetoric is linked with its civic use.
30. See Speroni, *Dialogo della retorica*, pp. 658–59; also Mazzacurati, *Il Rinascimento*, pp. 242–43, 252–56; and on Speroni's modernizing position (with Aretino, Ludovico Dolce and others) within the Infiammati academy, Vianello, *Il Letterato*, pp. 78–79. See also more generally Dionisotti, 'Letteratura italiana', pp. 237–42.
31. Sperone Speroni, *Apologia dei dialoghi*, in *Opere [...] tratte da' MSS. originali*, 5 vols (Venice: Domenico Occhi, 1740), I, 266–425 (all references to this edition). See Cox, *Renaissance Dialogue*, pp. 70–76. For the view that Speroni tended to conflate oratory and poetry, see Baxter Hathaway, *The Age of Criticism: The Late Renaissance in Italy* (Ithaca: Cornell University Press, 1962), pp. 67, 82–83 (pp. 68–69).
32. However, Speroni wistfully comments on the diminishing role and prestige of rhetoric in the civic context (even in Venice), see *Apologia*, pp. 358–60.
33. See Denores, Dedicatory letter, *Discorso*, p 152; and Guarini, *Verato secondo*, pp. 35–39 (denying that Denores was following Speroni), 74–75 (on the moral and political end of poetry), and 263 (on Denores not mentioning Speroni amongst great modern tragedians). Speroni appears to have influenced Denores's theories on Aristotelian *peripezia*, verisimilitude and necessity, which are used to contest the poetic legitimacy of the *pastorale* (see Giancarlo Cavazzini, 'Padova e Guarini: la *Poetica* di Aristotele nella teoria drammaturgica prebarocca', in *Il diletto della scena e dell'armonia. Teatro e musica nelle Venezie dal Cinquecento al Settecento*, ed. by Ivano Cavallini (Rovigo: Minelliana, [1990]), pp. 137–88 (pp. 142–43)).

34. Guarini states that his tragicomedy was read and reread many times in Venice (*Verato secondo*, p. 28); and that he had sometimes attended Denores's lectures out of respect (*Verrato*, pp. 818–19).
35. G. Patrizi, 'Denores, Giason', *DBI*, 38 (1990), 768–73. See also Cavazzini, p. 138. On the Venetian-Turkish conflicts, see Eric Cochrane, *Italy 1530–1630*, ed. by Julius Kirshner (London: Longman, 1988), pp. 166, 253–54.
36. *Poetica [...] Nella qual per via di Definitione, & Divisione si tratta secondo l'opinion d'Aristotele Della Tragedia, del Poema Heroico, & della Comedia* (Padova: Appresso Paulo Meietto, 1588), fols 8^r, 119^v.
37. The contrast between urban and country values is intrinsic to the pastoral mode, see Gifford, p. 2 and *passim*.
38. Denores, *Discorso* (p. 154); see also Cavazzini, pp. 140–42; and Claudio Scarpati, 'Poetica e retorica in Battista Guarini', in *Studi sul Cinquecento italiano* (Milan: Vita e Pensiero, 1982), pp. 201–38 (pp. 205–06, 218–20). For a helpful overview of Plato's complex and shifting views on poetry, see G. R. F. Ferrari, 'Plato and Poetry', in *The Cambridge History of Literary Criticism*, ed. by Peter Brooks and others (Cambridge: Cambridge University Press, 1989-), I: *Classical Criticism*, ed. by George A. Kennedy (1989), pp. 92–148.
39. For an outline of the Italian quarrel between Ancients and Moderns, see Weinberg, *Literary Criticism*, II, 988–90, 1103–05; and 983–1073 (debate over Ariosto and Tasso). See also Marga Cottino-Jones, 'Literary-critical developments in sixteenth- and seventeenth-century Italy', in *Cambridge History of Literary Criticism*, III: *The Renaissance*, ed. by Glyn P. Norton (Cambridge: Cambridge University Press, 1999), 566–77 (pp. 571–77); and, in the same volume, Terence Cave, 'Ancients and Moderns: France', 417–25.
40. *Verrato*, pp. 738–39, 748. See also Marvin Carlson, *Theories of the Theatre. A Historical and Critical Survey, from the Greeks to the Present* (Ithaca: Cornell University Press, 1984), pp. 53–56; Selmi, 'Classici e Moderni', pp. 16–19 (Guarini's debt to Giraldi).
41. On Castelvetro's unconventional interpretation of the *Poetics*, see Marchetti and Patrizi, pp. 18–20, and chapter 3, n. 101. See also Bernard Weinberg, 'Castelvetro's Theory of Poetics', in *Critics and Criticism Ancient and Modern*, ed. by R. S. Crane (Chicago: Chicago University Press, 1952), pp. 349–71 (pp. 354–55); and Luisa Avellini, 'L'eredità di Castelvetro: Guarini', in *Letteratura italiana*, ed. by Alberto Asor Rosa, 6 vols (Turin: Einaudi, 1982-), II/I: *Storia e geografia. L'età moderna* (1988), 578–82.
42. Weinberg, *Literary Criticism*, pp. 31–37; Hathaway, pp. 67, 82–83; though for the suggestion of a hedonistic end for epideictic rhetoric in some works of Cicero and by Quintilian, see Vickers, *In Defence* pp. 57–58. Carlson notes that this moralizing position responded to the objections of Plato on poetry (*Theories*, pp. 51–52). See also chapter 3 on Tasso.
43. Antonio Rotondò, 'La censura ecclesiastica e la cultura', in *Storia d'Italia*, V: *I Documenti*, 2 (Turin: UTET, 1973), pp. 1399–1492 (pp. 1401–03, 1406–11); Paul F. Grendler, 'The Roman Inquisition and the Venetian Press, 1540–1605', in *Culture and Censorship in Late Renaissance Italy and France* (London: Variorum Reprints, 1981), pp. 48–65 (pp. 56–60); Dionisotti, 'La letteratura italiana', pp. 235, 247–49.
44. On the effects of Church and state control on the theatre and especially comedy, see Andrews, *Scripts and Scenarios*, pp. 220–26. On Tasso's response to these limitations, see chapter 3.
45. See also Guarini's dialogue *Il Segretario* (1594), in which rhetoric is related to dialectics and distinguished from politics; and Scarpati, 'Poetica e retorica', pp. 201–05.
46. For Garini's different definitions of 'purgation', see also *Compendio*, pp. 234–46. For Denores and Guarini's views on catharsis, see also Perella, *Critical Fortune*, pp. 12–13; and Selmi, 'Classici e Moderni', pp. 42–46.
47. This point is less developed in *Verato secondo*. For the view that Guarini derived from Zabarella and other Paduan intellectuals his idea that poetics and rhetoric were related to logic rather than politics, see Scarpati, 'Poetica e retorica', p. 225 and passim.
48. Henke, *Pastoral Transformations*, pp. 69–76, 166–68, 173–75 and *passim*. On the historical, social and aesthetic nature of these generic 'markers', and the 'horizon of expectations' that they create, see for example Ralph Cohen, 'History and Genre', *New Literary History*, 17 (1986), 203–18 (pp. 206–11, 216).
49. Dominick LaCapra, 'Comment', *New Literary History*, 17 (1986), 219–21 (p. 221).
50. On the ideological nature of tragedy and comedy in terms of the social and political connotations

of the stage-space and the procedures of mimesis and catharsis, see Marco Ariani, 'Introduzione' to *Il teatro italiano*, II: *La tragedia del Cinquecento* (Turin: Einaudi, 1977), VII-LXXXII (also pp. VII-XV; LXVII-LXVIII on the 'civic and ideological vacuum' of the pastoral). For a detailed comparison of contemporary theory on artistic imitation, see Hathaway, pp. 23–64 (pp. 40–42).

51. On the proposed Turin performance, which coincided with Guarini's attempts to gain a permanent position at the court, see chapter 6, n. 73.
52. The engraving for the prologue in Ciotti's 1602 edition of *Pastor fido* (fig. 5) may suggest Giambattista Aleotti's set designed for the 1598 performances, see Adriano Cavicchi, 'Imagini e forme dello spazio scenico nella pastorale ferrarese', in *Sviluppi della drammaturgia pastorale nell'Europa del Cinque-Seicento*, ed. by M. Chiabò and F. Doglio (Viterbo: Union Printing, [1992]), pp. 45–86 (pp. 59–60).
53. See also Elisabetta Selmi's close reading of the prologue as embodying Guarini's poetics of *meraviglia* and fictional autonomy for epistemological purposes, in her edition of *Pastor fido*, pp. 279–85 (p. 279).
54. Domenico Chiodo, '"Soavi licor" e "succhi amari": Guarini e Baldi emuli del Tasso', *Lettere italiane*, 45, 116–28 (pp. 119–24).
55. For the possible representation of Alfeo, see also the description of the god of the Sebeto in Sannazaro's *Arcadia*, Prosa XII, pp. 219–20.
56. Giovanni Pietro Malacreta, *Considerazioni intorno al Pastor fido* [1600], in Battista Guarini, *Opere*, IV (Verona: Tumermani, 1738), pp. 1–222 (pp. 33, 38–40).
57. Paolo Beni, *Risposta alle considerazioni o dubbii dell'eccellentissimo signor Dottor Malacreta Accademico Ordito Sopra il Pastorfido*, in Guarini, *Opere*, IV (Verona: Tumermani, 1738), pp. 125–300 (pp. 144–45).
58. See P. B. Diffley, *Paolo Beni: A Biographical and Critical Study* (Oxford: Clarendon, 1988), pp. 71–73 (on the *Risposta*); 124–26 (on his distinction elsewhere between poetry and history, also to defend Tasso's *Liberata*), pp. 172–76, 195–97; Giancarlo Mazzacurati, 'Beni, Paolo', in *DBI*, 8 (1966), 494–501; and Hathaway, pp. 24, 33, 43, and 50 (on Tasso).
59. See also Malacreta, *Considerazioni*, pp. 30–31. For Aristotle's much debated ideas on characters, see *Poetics*, 2.2–3, 3.2–4, 7.2, 8.1; also Hathaway, pp. 35–36.
60. See also *Verato secondo*, pp. 230–31. On the political hierarchy of the pastoral community mirroring that of the city, see *Verato*, p. 798. This question is expanded more in the later critical works (*Compendio*, pp. 268–70) and described rather intriguingly also as reflecting the priestly hierarchy in *Verato secondo*, pp. 192–93.
61. This point is repeated in *Verato secondo* (pp. 204, 230) and *Compendio* (pp. 270–71).
62. See also the gloss on I. 3. 104: 'nelle città, [...] per ordinario i vizii sono maggiori, e le persone in esse molto più licenziose' [in the cities ... vices are usually greater and the inhabitants are far more licentious] (*Annotationi*, fol. 35^r).
63. Corisca (a name used in Ariosto's *Cassaria*) can be linked to the courtesan Loretta in Guarini's *Idropica*, see Selmi, *Pastor fido*, pp. 309, 346–47 (on her conception of fortune); and Franca Angelini, 'Il *Pastor fido* di Battista Guarini', in *Letteratura italiana*, ed. by Alberto Asor Rosa, 6 vols (Turin: Einaudi, 1982–). *Le Opere*, II: *Dal Cinquecento al Settecento*, 705–24 (pp. 713–16).
64. For a summary of the earlier plot in the Marciana manuscript (see n. 6 above), where Corisca is named Licori, see Rossi, pp. 196–98; and Selmi, *Pastor fido*, pp. 469, 471.
65. Guarini stresses his close imitation of the recognition scene in Sophocles' *Oedipus*, without mentioning earlier examples in pastoral plays: Lollio's *Aretusa*; and particularly Ingegneri's *Danza di Venere*. See Baldassarri, pp. 17–18; also Raphael Lyne, 'English Guarini: Recognition and Reception', *Yearbook of English Studies*, 2006 (forthcoming).
66. Verna A. Foster, *The Name and Nature of Tragicomedy* (Aldershot: Ashgate, 2004), pp. 45–46.
67. *Annotationi*, fol. 199^r. Compare Guarini's letter to Luigi Zenobi, 14 July 1590 (in *Opere*, ed. by Guglielminetti, pp. 125–26). On the poet's conflictual feelings towards the court, see Luisa Avellini, '"Pelago" e "Porto": la corte e il cortigiano nell'epistolario del Guarini', in *La Corte e lo spazio, Ferrara estense*, ed. by Giuseppe Papagno and Amadeo Quondam, 3 vols (Rome: Bulzoni, 1982), II, 683–96.
68. A long passage from this scene is found also amongst the draft fragments of the Marciana manuscript (fols. 174^r-177^r). Molinari speculates that it marks a late, extra-textual addition, easy to remove where appropriate. The early Marciana version also includes Carino's polemical mention of

changes in the present-day Arcadia (fols 118ᵛ-119ʳ) which were later removed ('Per il "Pastorfido"', pp. 183–84).
69. Anthony Pagden, *The Fall of Natural Man: The American Indian and the origins of comparative ethnology* (Cambridge: Cambridge University Press, 1982), pp. 18–19. On the ubiquity of the idea of primitive beginnings, see Arthur B. Ferguson, *Utter Antiquity: Perceptions of Prehistory in Renaissance England* (Durham, NC: Duke University Press, 1993), p. 62. On its visual representation, see also Erwin Panofsky, 'The Early History of Man in Two Cycles of Paintings by Piero di Cosimo', in *Studies in Iconology: Humanistic Themes in the Art of the Renaissance* (London: Harper and Row, 1962; repr. 1972), pp. 33–67.
70. 'For there was a time when men wandered at large in the fields like beasts and lived on wild fare; they did nothing by the guidance of reason, but relied chiefly on physical strength; there was as yet no ordered system of religious worship nor of social duties; no one had seen legitimate marriage' (Cicero, *Rhetorici Libri duo. Qui vocantur de inventione*, trans. by H. M. Hubbell as *Two Books on Rhetoric [...]* (London: Heinemann, 1968), I, §2.2).
71. Ferguson, *Utter Antiquity*, p. 61. For a discussion of how Cicero's thought was conjoined with the Christian (and especially Augustinian) view of man's inherently sinful nature, see C. J. Nederman, 'Nature, sin and the origins of society: the Ciceronian tradition in medieval political thought', *Journal of the History of Ideas*, 49 (1988), 3–26.
72. Levin, pp. 5–7, 13–15, 22, 37–43. (Note that Hesiod's *Works and Days* presents five stages of social development.) On the cultivation of the Golden Age myth by Lorenzo and Cosimo de' Medici, see E. H. Gombrich, 'Renaissance and Golden Age', in *Norm and Form: Studies in the Art of the Renaissance* (London: Phaidon, 1966), pp. 29–34; by Alfonso d'Este, see Graziosi, *Aminta*, pp. 60–63; 65–71; by Tasso, chapter 3, pp. 76–79.
73. All references are to the only complete edition: Battista Guarini, *Trattato della politica libertà*, ed. by Gaetano A. Ruggieri (Venice: per Francesco Andreola, 1818). Sections of this treatise are found in Guarini, *Opere*, ed. by Guglielminetti, pp. 855–84. Guarini apparently also wrote a *Trattato sulla ragione di Stato* (now lost), see Selmi, 'Guarini, Battista', p. 348.
74. *Compendio*, pp. 280, 265, and 279 (on the satyr's necessity in the action). Selmi sees the satyr as a pastoral development of the pedant (Zenobio) in Guarini's comedy *Idropica* ('Guarini, Battista', p. 349; *Pastor fido*, pp. 321–23, 355–59). For Guarini's defence of the use of Petrarchan style in pastoral (implausible in 'urban' drama), see *Compendio*, pp. 248–55.
75. Selmi, *Pastor fido*, p. 412; compare a similar scenario of betrayal of a nymph to a priest, though by a shepherd, in Campiglia's *Flori*, II. 4.
76. Matteo Residori, '"Veder il suo in man d'altri": Note sulla presenza dell'*Aminta* nel *Pastor fido*', *Chroniques italiennes*, 5 (2004), 1–15 (pp. 4–7). The article only appears in the electronic version of the journal (http://www.univ-paris3.fr/recherche/chroniquesitaliennes). See also Robin Kirkpatrick, *English and Italian Literature from Dante to Shakespeare. A study of source, analogue and divergence* (London: Longman, 1995), pp. 264–65.
77. *Due Discorsi l'uno contra le tragicommedie, e le pastorali, L'altro contra il Pastor Fido tragicommedia pastorale [...]*, in Battista Guarini, *Opere*, 5 vols (Verona: Tumermani, 1737–38), III (1738), 545–96 (pp. 588–89, also p. 592). This is reprinted in an edition by Gareffi with the same page numbering (see n. 17 above). See also Malacreta, p. 96. Perella notes that the *Pastor fido* attracted an unusual degree of condemnation for its 'wilfully persuading to dissoluteness' (*Critical Fortune*, pp. 16, 19–21, 28).
78. See also the philosophical and theological glosses to Chorus I on nature. Malacreta censured Guarini's use of choruses in *Pastor fido* for introducing a Christian perspective while the rest of the play appears 'etnica' (*Considerazioni*, p. 121).
79. See Ferguson, *Utter Antiquity*, pp. 55–56. On childhood as a form of pastoral, read from a Darwinist and non-sentimental perspective, see William Empson, *Some Versions of Pastoral* (London: Chatto and Windus, 1935), chapter 7. For below, Residori, p. 4.
80. *Annotationi*, fol. 104ᵛ. See P. Nolan, 'Free Will', in *New Catholic Encyclopedia* (New York: McGraw-Hill, 1967-), VI, pp. 89–93.
81. See also *Verrato*, pp. 796–98. Guarini concedes, though, that the title of prince for Montano may suggest a rather more advanced order than actually existed (*Compendio*, p. 269; *Annotationi*, fol. 223ʳ).
82. Guglielminetti, 'Introduzione', p. 45. For a similar merging of the temporal and spiritual in the figure

83. *Compendio*, pp. 228–29; and see Yoch, 'Renaissance Dramatization', p. 115.
84. On the increased merging of political institutions and Church, also in Protestant regions, from the later sixteenth-century, see Robert Bireley, *The Refashioning of Catholicism, 1450–1700. A Reassessment of the Counter Reformation* (London: Macmillan, 1999); Wolfgang Reinhard, 'Reformation, Counter-Reformation, and the Early Modern State: A Reassessment', in *The Counter-Reformation*, ed. by David M. Luebke (Oxford: Blackwell, 1999), pp. 107–28; and Cochrane, *Italy 1530–1630*, pp. 186, 191–92.
85. Quentin Skinner, *The Foundations of Modern Political Thought*. I: *The Renaissance* (Cambridge: Cambridge University Press, 1978), pp. 124–25. Compare also Castiglione's *Cortegiano*, IV. 17–18. On the aristocratic and Platonic political ideal of temperance, see Yoch, 'Renaissance Dramatization', pp. 116–17.
86. For Ferrarese statutes which allowed adulterous women to be burnt alive, see Nicholas Davidson, 'Theology, nature and the law: sexual sin and sexual crime in Italy from the fourteenth to the seventeenth century', in *Crime, Society and the Law in Renaissance Italy*, ed. by Trevor Dean and K. J. P. Lowe (Cambridge: Cambridge University Press, 1994), pp. 74–98 (pp. 89–90, also 97).
87. See Vittor Ivo Comparato, 'A Case of Modern Individualism: Politics and the Uneasiness of Intellectuals in the Baroque Age', in *The Individual in Political Theory and Practice*, ed. by Janet Coleman (Oxford: Clarendon Press, 1996), pp. 149–70 (pp. 160–61). For a further pessimistic picture of citizens' capacity for self-government, see *Trattato*, pp. 128–29, 137–39, 146; and *passim* from p. 31.
88. Marie-Sylvie Dupont-Bouchat, 'Guilt and Individual Consciousness: The Individual, the Church and the State in the Modern Era, Sixteenth-Seventeenth Centuries', in Coleman, pp. 123–48 (p. 128). For similar views of the ruler's ability to grant pardon and clemency, transcending justice, see Tasso's letter to Scipione Gonzaga regarding Alfonso d'Este (Easter week, 1579), *Lettere*, II, 123, 312.
89. *Annotationi* (V. 5. 29), fol. 190^v.
90. Precedents for this plot include: Euripides' *Iphigenia in Aulis*, Sophocles' *Oedipus Rex* (with reversal of father/son role); and *Decameron* (IV. 4), see Selmi, 'Classici e Moderni', pp. 53–54. On the popular theme of Abraham's sacrifice of Isaac (*Genesis* 22. 1–18) in medieval and Renaissance religious drama, especially in northern Europe, see Foster, pp. 36–39, 41. For Guarini's process of syncretistic blending, see Scarpati, 'Poetica e retorica', pp. 237–38; also Selmi, *Pastor fido*, pp. 450, 455.
91. Compare with the type of prosecution instituted by Catholic absolutist states, as described by Dupont-Bouchat, pp. 129–34.
92. *Annotationi*, fol. 161^v. See also *Trattato*, pp. 4–7.
93. Kirkpatrick, pp. 261, 267. On Silvio's gesture as a tragicomic reworking of Oedipus' acceptance of punishment in Sophocles' tragedy, see Selmi, 'Classici e Moderni', pp. 41–42; also 44. See also John Bossy, 'The Counter-Reformation and the People of Catholic Europe' [first published 1970], in Luebke, pp. 86–104 (pp. 97–99). Compare the confession of the deviant Branco in Cucchetti's *Pazzia* (V. 3, fol. 47^r).
94. See Selmi, *Pastor fido*, p. 463; Nicolas J. Perella, 'Fate, Blindness and Illusion in the *Pastor fido*', *Romanic Review*, 49 (1958), 252–68 (pp. 258–59).
95. Note also the cautious denial that earthly suffering by the innocent would disprove divine providence, *Verato secondo*, p. 231. On Christian allegory in *Pastor fido*, see Andrews, 'Pastoral Drama', p. 297; also Scarpati, 'Poetica e retorica', pp. 237–38, which relates the issue to broader ideas on the intrinsically philosophical function of the *exemplum* in poetics; and Selmi, *Pastor fido*, pp. 448–50 and *passim*.
96. The *Compendio* does not mention the end of poetry very specifically except to say that it is meant to imitate, which is pleasing, but may also teach 'ben vivere' [correct behaviour] (pp. 220–21); see also p. 243.
97. Andrews, 'Theatre', p. 297.
98. Rossi, pp. 113, 115–18.
99. Giannandrea Barotti, *Memorie Istoriche di Letterati Ferraresi, Opera Postuma*, 2nd edn, 3 vols (Ferrara: per gli eredi di Giuseppe Rinaldi, 1792), I, 215.

100. The anecdote appears in Alessandro Guarini III, 'Vita del Cavalier Battista Guarini, autore del Pastor fido, scritta dal Sig. Alessandro Guarini, suo pronipote, al Sig. Dott. Ludovico Antonio Muratori', in *Supplementi al Giornale de' Letterati d'Italia* (Venice, 1722), II, 179–80; see Perella, *Critical Fortune*, pp. 28–31.

CHAPTER 6

Performing Pastoral Drama

> Chiara cosa è che, se le pastorali non fossero, si potria dire poco men che perduto a fatto l'uso del palco e 'n conseguenza reso disperato il fine dei poeti scenici, il quale deve essere che i loro componimenti vengano rappresentati.[1]
>
> [It is clear that if it were not for pastorals, you could say that the stage had almost totally stopped being used and that therefore the dramatists' purpose, which must be to have their works performed, had been made hopeless.]

Reconstructing Pastoral Performances

Although he may be somewhat overstating his case, this comment by the theatre director and critic Angelo Ingegneri gives a sense of how far public interest in pastoral drama had increased since the first handful of 'regular' pastoral plays were performed for fairly small-scale courtly audiences in the 1550s and 1560s (see chapter 2). By 1613, another apologist, Ludovico Zuccolo would add: 'se n'empiono le scene, e se ne veggono da ogni parte fornite le botteghe, e le panche de' librari' [the stages are filled with them and printers' shops and stalls everywhere are stocked with them].[2] The rapid rise in popularity may to a great extent be accounted for by the availability in print of numerous examples from the 1580s, and especially the authoritative models of Tasso and Guarini. The growing body of theoretical writings in defence of the genre, and particularly of the *Pastor fido*, from the late 1580s further contributed critical legitimization and guidance on its aims and structure. However, as Ingegneri's above statement indicates, the appeal of the genre at this time also needs to be understood in terms of its potential to appeal to audiences in performance.

This was something that Guarini understood well. We saw in the previous chapter how attentive he was to structural features and critical questions in composing and theorizing on his *Pastor fido*, which, together with its great length, suggest that it was intended as a text for reading. The play did in fact become extremely popular with readers, as noted amongst others by Ingegneri, and Zuccolo whose dialogue on pastoral drama (*L'Alessandro*) is initiated by the sight of one of the speakers holding a copy of the work.[3] However, Guarini was also very concerned with the technical and practical aspects of stagecraft, as is revealed especially in his letters, as well as in the *Annotations* (1602) to his play. It is in these terms that regular pastoral drama will be examined in the present chapter, to explore the forms that performances could take during the second half of the sixteenth century. Surprisingly, this subject has not hitherto been dealt with fully in broad terms since Marzia Pieri's authoritative monograph of 1983 on various forms of pastoral drama across the fifteenth to the early seventeenth centuries.[4] There are however numerous useful shorter studies especially on particular performances or pastoral plays (such as the still valuable ones of Rossi and D'Ancona, and those of Ivaldi, Cavicchi, Riccò, Taviani, Vazzoler, Henke, Sampson), or which relate these to certain aspects of sixteenth century theatre (Henke, MacNeil). This chapter attempts to provide further exploration of this subject, which will be touched upon to some extent in the next chapter too. Inevitably, the focus here falls on performances of Tasso's *Aminta* and Guarini's *Pastor fido*, for which more extensive documentation survives, but a variety of sometimes little known critical texts and accounts will be used to widen the general picture. These give a sense of the kinds of audiences and occasions for which the plays were performed, and the agendas of both writer and patron in choosing such a play. This will allow an investigation of how far the pastoral could reflect or project ideals and aspirations of its mainly courtly audiences during this period.

The task is, however, complicated from the outset by some methodological problems which present perennial difficulties for theatre historians. As always, the most immediate problem is how to relate existing play-texts to what was actually performed. Not only are we confronted with many versions of the *Aminta* and *Pastor fido*, both in printed editions and in manuscript, but we cannot know for sure if any of these correspond to the actors' parts used (none of which survive to my knowledge). Actors' copies were probably more rough and ready and were almost certainly less 'literary' than the texts prepared for readers, which could be worked at for some time — years in Guarini's case — in order to refine the language and style. Play-texts prepared for reading were often longer too, including more monologues, digressions and episodes, which would have made the play less dramatic on stage.[5] It was for this reason, the critic Giovanni Pietro Malacreta argues, that around 1,600 lines of the *Pastor fido* were cut from the total of c.6,700 for the Mantuan performance in November 1598, since they were deemed 'unnecessary' ('oziosi').[6]

During this period, unauthorized copies were sometimes circulated, often drawing on actors' parts, causing authors considerable frustration.[7] Not only did they then lose control over the audiences to whom their plays were presented, but the pirated texts could also be of inferior quality. In addition, the 'performance texts' no doubt included more frequent audience-specific allusions, such as references to contemporary events and persons present (especially in prologues). They may even have had satirical or risqué sections which writers wished to prune from the authorized printed/published versions, as seems to have been the case with Giraldi's satyr-play, *Egle*.[8] The performance text was therefore potentially more provocative and more labile than the 'fixed' printed version, in that alterations could be made to suit the conditions of each unique performance. For example the Mantuan ducal secretary, Annibale Chieppio, commented that the prologue of a planned performance of the *Pastor fido*: 'doveva regolarsi, sì come si costuma, dall'occasione con la quale ella [Duke Vincenzo Gonzaga] disegna di far recitare questa pastorale, essendo il Prologo cosa del tutto separata dalla favola' [should be governed, as is customary, by the occasion for which your lordship plans to have this pastoral performed, since the prologue is a wholly separate part of the plot].[9]

Furthermore, as theatre critics both from the late sixteenth century, such as Ingegneri, and more recently have observed, the play-text itself only constitutes one part in a whole dialogue of different 'voices' or codes that contribute to the overall meaning.[10] These include signifying spectacular and extra-textual features such as physical movements, stage-set, spatial arrangement of the stage, costumes, and other non-verbal sounds, especially music. Attitudes towards the relative importance of spectacle were however changing during the later sixteenth century amongst some elite theatre practitioners. While many saw the potential of winning audiences with the development of new, showy stage techniques (especially used for *intermedi*) within specially created theatrical spaces, writers and critics with academic pretensions still considered the written text (of tragedy) to be superior to spectacular elements. They followed Aristotle's view that:

> The plot is the source and (as it were) the soul of tragedy [...]. Spectacle is attractive, but is very inartistic and is least germane to the art of poetry. For the effect of tragedy is not dependent on performance and actors.[11]

Accordingly, the poet should be concerned principally with the composition of the written text, which is differentiated from the art of performance. The text should make what is to be shown to the audience clear to the reader too, without the need for stage directions. Guarini, for instance, notes how he achieved this in his *Pastor fido* in the scene of the *Gioco della cieca* (a sort of choreographed game of blind man's buff, see fig. 7). Amarilli is described by Mirtillo as coming on stage with her eyes covered (III. 2, 7–8), thus obeying an Aristotelian precept for drama that:

> Quello che si fa in Scena venga si bene espresso con le parole, che al lettore paia d'essere spettatore; da che si vede quanto ridicoli sian coloro, che gli atti malagevoli da esprimer con le parole, s'ingegnano di far notti a chi legge con la postilla in margine che dice, quì si fa la tal cosa.[12]
>
> [What is done on stage is expressed so well in words that the reader appears to be a spectator. From this we see how ridiculous those writers are who try to make marginal notes to the readers saying 'here such and such is done' for actions which are awkward to express in words.]

A reconstruction of the relationship between the 'verbal text' and the spectacular/non-verbal content is particularly necessary in the case of pastoral drama. As Pieri has demonstrated, spectacular features, including solo or choral song and instrumental music, dance, echo effects, and sometimes staged transformations and sacrifices are inherently and historically bound up with the genre in its broadest sense. However, she argues that regular pastoral drama only coincided with this well developed performance tradition for a relatively brief period, after which a split is once again discernible between more 'irregular' spectacular plays, and regular, less 'stagey' ones.[13] As we will see in the next chapter, many later regular pastoral plays (such as Bonarelli's *Filli di Sciro*, 1607) in fact appear more suitable for readers to linger over than for staging, due to their great length, their numerous lyrical sections and predominantly narrated as opposed to dramatic action.[14] Even so, pastoral drama clearly continued also to be written for performance into the seventeenth century.

Any attempt to assess fully the staging of pastoral drama, as with any sort of drama, also needs to take its reception into account, and the motives for which it was written and commissioned. In trying to do this, one needs to evaluate different kinds of accounts all posing different critical problems. These range from commissioned formal descriptions in festival books, which tend to celebrate the magnificence of the occasion thus indirectly flattering the patron(s), to private written communications, which often reveal a very different story. In these, we sometimes learn of practical failures, conflicts amongst organizers, and how audiences were not always able to see or hear properly in the usually packed halls or theatres — or capable of understanding the full significance of the plays. One wonders for example what the audience made of the Mantuan performance of Guarini's *Pastor fido* in November 1598? For this occasion only 'foreigners' (that is non-Mantuans) were admitted, and a German translation or summary of the play and of the *intermedi* had to be prepared for the royal guests in attendance (Margaret of Austria and her mother, Archduchess Maria).[15] It is therefore likely that many of the spectators were struck more by the non-verbal, spectacular effects and the rather obvious political message of the *intermedi*, while many of the play's subtler verbal inflections were lost on them.

In discussing erudite drama of this period, it is sometimes also difficult to distinguish between recitations and performance. This is because plays were often circulated in manuscript form, and read aloud or discussed alongside other literary works in small academic or elite gatherings, as tragedies had been since the early sixteenth century. For example, before it was published and staged in a high profile way the *Pastor fido* was read to a select group of intellectuals and nobles in the tiny court of Guastalla in 1583, and again probably at the Accademia Olimpica in Vicenza in 1584, and also around then in Padua in the bookshop of Meietti and at the house of the professor of logic, Jacopo Zabarella. In 1586 it was apparently shown to members of the Accademia degli Alterati by Salviati.[16] As mentioned in Chapter 4, Ingegneri's pastoral drama, *Danza di Venere* was performed by some elite females in 1583 at the small court of Soragna before Prince Ranuccio Farnese of Parma. It is not known how fully it was staged but, for reasons of decorum, one imagines it must have been a very private affair.[17] These cases demonstrate how 'performance' can shade into semi-public reading, and how the degree of audience participation and the gender and status of the players varied between public and private performances.

Bearing these general difficulties in mind, we shall now turn to aspects of the performances of some of the earliest pastoral dramas in Ferrara and Mantua, and particularly to those of Tasso and Guarini's masterpieces.

Spectacle and Theatre in Ferrara and Mantua

These courts are characterized by a long-standing interest in theatre and were amongst the first to stage regular pastoral plays, besides a rich array of pastoral banquets, *intermedi* and dramatic eclogues. As we have seen, many of the earliest writers of regular pastoral drama hail from Ferrara, and Tasso and Guarini were associated with the court of Alfonso II d'Este (1559–97) for most of their creative lives. In later years, they also frequented Mantua which was justly famed for its theatrical tradition under the patronage of Duke Vincenzo Gonzaga (1587–1612), and had a record of promoting pastoral drama since the 1560s.[18]

Both these rulers were enthusiastic patrons of secular theatre and invested heavily in splendid, novel and costly performances for political occasions. Especially in Vincenzo's case, they spent far beyond their actual means and what the size of their state should dictate. However, at a time when minor Italian potentates were largely dependent on protection and favours of the greater political powers of France, the Empire or the Papacy, cultural patronage provided a way of displaying their due deference, while also reaffirming their status and superiority to other dynasties. Despite privately expressed disapproval at the Gonzaga Duke's excessive spending on festivities, this may in part have contributed to the successes that he did manage to obtain in international politics and marriage negotiations, and to the recognition of his state amongst other much larger or more important states for official occasions.[19] Similarly, in 1589 the Medici resident in Ferrara, Orazio Della Rena, noted the political expediency of Alfonso II's artistic patronage:

> Si dee avvertire che il Duca di Ferrara, se si misura dalla potenza et dallo stato suo, non è se non principe mediocre; con tuttociò con questo artificio, che in lui è mirabile, apparisce tanto grande, di tanto grido e di tanta stima che è posto sempre nel numero de' maggiori.[20]

> [It should be pointed out that if one judges the Duke of Ferrara by his power and [the size of] his state, he is only a middle ranking prince; however, through his use of artifice, which is wondrous, he appears so powerful and of such renown and esteem that he is always placed amongst the great princes.]

During the 1560s and '70s the Ferrarese nobility ensured their exclusivity particularly by cultivating two new dramatic forms: the *torneo* (choreographed tournament) and the pastoral drama. In all, five huge-scale *tornei* were publicly staged in Ferrara with unprecedented extravagance during the period 1561–70 to celebrate important court occasions.[21] Unlike earlier tournaments, the combats were woven into an elaborate, romance-style plot which could last over several days, involving the main nobles of the court. For example, in *Il Castello di Gorgoferusa* a 'queen' appeared with her herald at a dance in the Duchess's apartments one Sunday in carnival in 1561, asking for a group of knights to help her free her husband from the lascivious sorceress, Gorgoferusa. She was then accompanied in pomp along a main thoroughfare (the Giudecca) and followed by some fighting between small groups of armed noblemen, though the assault on the castle was delayed until the arrival of the Duke of Mantua and 'Prince' of Florence (presumably Francesco de' Medici) on the second Sunday in Lent.[22] To achieve the desired magnificence and project an idealized grandiose and chivalric image of the court and duke to a large audience (in this case apparently 10,000 spectators), the most prestigious painters, architects, engineers, writers, actors, musicians and scenographers available in Ferrara were called upon to realize the elaborate outdoor sets. The event was officially commemorated afterwards in detailed printed accounts, which explained the significance of the action, drew attention to the splendour of the costumes and sets, and named the participants, though rarely the artists involved.[23]

By contrast, there is little concrete evidence about the few earliest performances of regular pastoral drama in Ferrara during the same period (see Chapter 2). These plays tended to be printed locally soon after their first performance, with a brief preface noting which members of the ducal family were present, and sometimes who the main actor, architect, and musician were. We know little else about how they were produced or received. One of the fullest prefaces to an early pastoral drama (Alberto Lollio's *Aretusa*), for example, gives us only this bald statement regarding its performance situation:

> Fu rappresentata in Ferrara nel palazzo di Schivanoia [Schifanoia] l'anno MDLXIII. All'illustriss[imo] e eccellentiss[imo] signore il S. Alfonso da Esti Duca di Ferrara V. E all'illustriss[imo] e reverendiss[imo] signore il Cardinale Don Luigi suo fratello e a molti altri S[ignori]. La rappresentò M. Ludovico Betto, fece la musica M. Alfonso Vivola [Dalla Viola], fu l'archit[etto] e dipint[ore] della scena M. Rinaldo Costabili, fece la spesa l'università delli Scolari delle leggi.[24]

> [It was performed in Ferrara in Palazzo Schifanoia in 1563 before the most illustrious and excellent Lord Alfonso d'Este, fifth Duke of Ferrara, and before the most illustrious and reverent Lord Cardinal Don Luigi his brother and many other nobles. Mr Ludovico Betto performed in the play, Mr Alfonso Dalla Viola wrote the music, Mr Rinaldo Costabili was the architect and painter of the stage, and the performance was paid for by the law students of the university.]

To fill out some information on the artists involved in this production: Alfonso Dalla Viola was the leading composer and instrumentalist in the ducal household at this time. He directed the *musica da camera segreta* (music of the private chamber) from 1528, the year when Ercole II d'Este and Renée of France were married, and later became *maestro di cappella* at Ferrara cathedral (c. 1563-c. 72).[25] Besides *Aretusa*, he composed the music for Beccari's *Sacrificio* (1554), Giraldi's tragedy, *Orbecche* (1541), and Argenti's pastoral, *Lo Sfortunato* (1567) amongst other dramatic works. All the music is now lost apart from settings for a couple of scenes from Beccari's *Sacrificio* (III. 3 and V. 8 [the concluding *canzone*]). The painter Rinaldo Costabili designed the stage-set for Argenti's play and had previously collaborated as 'apparatore' on the ephemeral constructions for the entry of the newly crowned duke Alfonso II to Ferrara in 1559 and for the entry of the duke's first wife, Lucrezia de' Medici, the following year. Later, he contributed to painting the set for the great chivalric tournament-*naumachia*, *L'Isola beata* in 1569 (with Pasi da Carpi and Pirro Ligorio).[26] It would seem therefore that pastoral drama drew on a fairly consolidated tradition of court spectacle, including festive entries, *tornei*, and musical and theatrical displays, which did not require further explanation. With the same artists being drawn upon for pastoral productions during the period, quite a consistent performance style was almost certainly achieved. Indeed, one wonders whether the same sets were in fact re-used or adapted for the pastorals of Lollio and Argenti, and possibly later plays too.

The earliest pastorals in Ferrara, like many comedies, were staged in private houses of members of the ducal family or of important families closely related to the court. Giraldi's *Egle* was performed twice in 1545 and possibly again in 1547 (Solerti's hypothesis) at his house, when he was secretary of Ercole II.[27] Beccari's *Il Sacrificio* was performed twice in 1554 at Palazzo Schifanoia, the home of Don Francesco d'Este (uncle of Alfonso II), as were both *Aretusa* and *Sfortunato*. In 1564–65 two comedies were staged in the house of the Bevilacqua family, one of the leading Ferrarese families.[28] This may have been partly due to the fact that from 1532 (when Ariosto's theatre was destroyed by fire) to 1583 there was no permanent space equipped for theatrical activities within the ducal palace. The use of the newly restored Sala Grande [great hall] for the festivities marking Alfonso II's wedding to Barbara of Austria in 1565 was a short-lived exception.[29] However, the Sala Grande may have been used at other times (though no records survive for 1565–80) with a semi-permanent theatrical structure. Outside the court, a theatre was set up in 1577 by the ducal stables, apparently exclusively for chivalric exercises and *tornei*. In 1580–83 another space was set aside within the ducal palace for professional comic performances, probably directly under the Sala Grande. The earthquakes that shook Ferrara from 1570 would have been to a large part responsible for this lack of permanent theatrical space.

Pastoral plays performed in Ferrara before its devolution to the papacy in 1598 therefore principally relied upon ducal and aristocratic resources to provide artists and architects to design and mount the stage-sets, and supply musicians and dancers if necessary. The intimacy of the form and close rapport between contributors and audience is suggested by the sparse way in which the performances are commemorated in the printed versions.

The pastoral stage-set

Unfortunately, there are few precise indications of what the *scena boschereccia* looked like in the early performances of Ferrarese pastorals. Some non-related visual material (sketches, tapestries, paintings) by artists involved with theatre in Ferrara, such as Giralomo da Carpi, gives an idea of themes and styles used.[30] The play-texts provide other clues. Beccari's prologue to *Sacrificio* (1555), for instance, refers to trees and mountains faintly visible in the background, and some architectonic features were evidently added to the stage-set as well.[31] In Act II scene 2 the satyr strings a net between two poles concealed by grass and flowers, and hides behind a bush to wait for a nymph to be trapped. The tall oak tree under which Melidia wants to sleep (II. 3), may be the same one that is later split open by the satyr in order to create a trap for Stellinia (V. 1–2). The set of *Sfortunato* would probably have featured two huts (either painted or constructed), since these form the setting for the substitution trick played on the nymphs by the shepherds that love them.

Further information can be found in treatises or dialogues on theatre, or descriptions of specific performances. A starting point is provided in a brief description in Giambattista Giraldi Cinthio's treatise on satyr-drama:

> Essendo principalmente composta la favola per la rappresentazione, non si puote ella, senza l'apparato, convenevolmente rappresentare. E contiene l'apparato la fabbrica della scena, gli istrioni e i loro vestimenti e le macchine [...]; e vuole essere la scena boschereccia, ed avere in sé e selve, e grotte, e monti, e fontane, e le altre parti quali voi vedeste nella scena sulla quale si rappresentò la satira mia [*Egle*], la quale vi fe' solennemente rappresentare la università degli scolari delle leggi.[32]

> [As a play is principally composed for performance, it cannot be appropriately performed without the apparatus. This includes the construction of the stage-set, the actors and their costumes, and the machines [...]; and the set should be pastoral and have woods, grottos, mountains, fountains and the other features which you saw in the one used for the performance of my satyr-play [*Egle*], which was solemnly staged by the university law students.]

Although he takes pains to distinguish his own modern version of the satyr-drama from the 'irregular' courtly pastoral drama, a continuum is nonetheless evident between the two forms as far as the staging is concerned, as Pieri has shown. This is more explicit in Sebastiano Serlio's discussion and depiction of the satyric scene (also in 1545) (see fig. 1). In his description of the three ancient types of drama (tragedy, comedy and satyr-play), Serlio noted that Vitruvius wanted the satyric scene to be 'ornata di arbori, sassi, colli, montagne, erbe, fiori, e fontane: vuole ancora che vi siano alcune capanne alla rustica' [ornamented with trees, rocks, hills, mountains, grasses, flowers and fountains, and he also wants there to be some rustic style huts].[33] It is then assimilated to the lavish sets used for pastoral eclogues of his time which, Serlio writes, were mainly shown during the winter using trees and flowers made of silk. These were 'ancora più lodate che le naturali' [even more praised than the natural ones] (fol. 51^r), since they were more costly, and therefore more appropriate for generous and wealthy lords. A detailed description follows of a rich and varied pastoral and marine stage-set designed by Girolamo Genga for his patron the Duke of Urbino:

> Che magnificenzia era quella di veder tanti arbori e frutti, tante erbe e fiori diversi, tutte cose fatte di finissima seta di variati colori, le ripe e i sassi copiosi di diverse conche marine, di lumache e altri animaletti, di tronchi di coralli di più colori, di madre perle e di granchi marini inserti ne' sassi, con tanta diversità di cose belle che a volerle scrivere tutte io sarei troppo longo [sic] in questa parte. Io non dirò de' satiri, delle ninfe, delle sirene, e diversi monstri o animali strani, fatti con tal artificio che acconci sopra gli uomini e fanciulli, secondo la grandezza loro, e quelli andando e movendosi secondo la sua natura, rappresentavano essi animali vivi. (fol. 51^v)

> [What magnificence it was to see so many trees and fruits, so many different grasses and flowers, all made of the finest silk of varied colours, the shores and rocks full of different marine shells, snails and other small creatures, branches of coral of many colours, mother-of-pearl, and marine crabs inserted in the rocks, with such diversity of beautiful things that if I wanted to write about them all here it would take me too long. I will not mention the satyrs, nymphs, sirens and various monsters or strange animals, which were made with such artifice that, when these were arranged on men and boys according to their size, who then moved around imitating their nature, they looked like live animals.]

This highlights the delightful interplay between art and nature involved in pastoral sets. The mention of silk, coral and mother-of-pearl (probably fictive) also emphasizes the paradoxical contrast between pastoral's theoretical status as a 'low' genre, dealing with humble characters, and the evident expense or elaborate artifice that such sets could require.

However, pastoral plays, regular or not, were not consistently staged with this kind of ostentatious display. As Ingegneri commented, they could be performed with or without choruses and *intermedi* (which required greater cost and casts), and they could serve as 'diporti da state, passatempi da verno, trattenimenti d'ogni stagione, dicevoli ad ogni età, ad ogni sesso' [diversions for the summer, pastimes for the winter and entertainments for all seasons, appropriate for all ages and both sexes].[34] Notably, they could be staged more cheaply and easily than tragedies and comedies, both indoors and especially *outdoors* during the summer in the gardens of palaces or villas. Indeed in Mantua in the 1560s, pastorals were evidently more commonly staged outdoors in natural settings. Our most informative source on this is the four-part dialogue on dramatic performances (*Quattro dialoghi in materia di rappresentazione scenica* [*Four Dialogues on Dramatic Performances*], composed 1589?) by the Jewish theatrical director, Leone de' Sommi (see Chapter 2). His fictional mouthpiece (Veridico) in fact observes that he had never put on such a play indoors with artificial lighting.[35] In his view, performances should most appropriately take place outside in the summer, during the day where:

> Bastarà che la sua scena sia eminente et verdeggiante, et che, nello scoprirsi, porga vaghezza a' veditori. Et questo si fa agevolmente, rappresentando con le frondi e co i fiori, et con gl'arbori fruttuosi, le staggioni piú alegre, ponendo tra' rami di varii uccelli, che co 'l canto incitano la letizia, facendo anco alle volte erarvi sopra conigli o lepri, et altre cose simili, che rappresentino il naturale delle campagne gioconde, et de' boschi solitarii; et che con giudicio siano finti quei monti, quelle valli, quei tugurii, quei fonti e quegli antri od altre cose tali che vi occorrono facendo i lontani con le osservazioni prospettive, et lasciar dinanzi tanto loco piano, a guisa di un prato fiorito, per recitarvi sopra ordinariamente, quanto è larga una gran scena. (*Dialoghi*, IV, 66–67)

> [The stage has only to be raised and green, and to bring delight to the spectators on first being seen. This can easily be done by representing the most joyful seasons with leafy fronds and flowers and trees in fruit, by placing various birds amongst the branches which encourage happiness through their song, and by making rabbits or hares and other similar animals wander there every now and then, which represent the natural state of the pleasant countryside and the solitary woods. And let the mountains and valleys, the huts, fountains and caves or other such things required be carefully created through artifice, by making the distant views perspectival, and leave a large flat space in front like a flowery meadow, on which to act in the usual way, which is as wide as a large stage.]

De' Sommi demonstrates that even outdoor performances of pastoral plays continued to make use of artistic techniques to perfect and recreate nature. In this respect they could draw on the practice of banquet entertainment, which was well-developed in Ferrara and in Mantua. However, he warns that it takes great skill and experience to achieve this *effect* of naturalness: 'è molto piú difficile condur una sí fatta rappresentazione che stia bene, che non è a condurre una comedia, et, per la verità, fa anco molto piú grato et bello spettacolo' [it is far more difficult to bring off such a performance successfully than it is to bring off a comedy, and in truth, it also produces a far more pleasing and beautiful spectacle] (*Dialoghi*, III, 53).

Pastorals continued to be staged for smaller gatherings, indoors and outdoors, towards the end of the century, but they were also affected by innovations in the practice of staging large-scale comedies (*commedie grandi*), with *intermedi*, elaborate machines and sets, especially as developed in Florence in the 1580s.[36] This shift is clearly demonstrated by a performance of Beccari's *Sacrificio* in Sassuolo in 1587, for which Guarini wrote the prologue and *intermedi* and the Ferrarese architect, Giambattista Aleotti (known as 'L'Argenta'), designed an impressive stage-set.[37] This play, revised since its first staging in 1554, was performed for the dynastic wedding of Benedetta Pio and Gerolamo Sanseverini Sanvitale in Ferrara in summer 1587, and then the following December in the castle of Sassuolo for the wedding of Benedetta's brother, Marco Pio, the ruler of the Ferrarese feud of Sassuolo, and the pope's daughter, Clelia Farnese.[38] An anonymous Ferrarese eye-witness of the latter performance notes how the audience marvelled at the extreme variety and fantasy of this spectacle, although such observations were something of a *topos* in festival accounts. He admires the music, the lighting, costumes, machines, and neo-classical octagonal temple, and describes the painted backdrop with mountains and fields with various animals and birds, and woods with bears and wild boars, and even lions and elephants.[39] Such elements would of course have been inappropriate in the 'realistic' city and court settings of comedy and tragedy, and the variety in any case flouts verisimilitude. Yet even Ingegneri, who is something of a stickler for decorum in pastoral too, grants at one point that: 'quando il tutto sia rustico, ogni cosa servirà, avegna che anco quivi sia bene l'accostarsi il meglio che si possa alla similitudine del sito di quella regione [...] dove si presuppone che il fatto succeda' [as long as it is rustic anything will do, though even here it is best to keep as close as possible to the verisimilitude of the site of that region [...] where it is envisaged that the action takes place] (*Della Poesia*, p. 26).

However pastoral drama is staged, it clearly explores the contrast between the artificial and the apparently natural. Art perfects and surpasses Nature through the use of sophisticated stage techniques, though it may itself be challenged ideologically in the content of the play. By the end of the century, this complex interplay between Art and Nature was taken even further by Bernardo Buontalenti in his arrangement of the Uffizi hall in Florence for de' Bardi's comedy, *Amico fido* (1586). In this case the relationship was wittily reversed by making the hall and stage-set look and even smell like a garden within a theatre. This theatre engineer apparently devised a masterpiece of *trompe l'oeuil* round the walls, combining illusionistic architecture (a gallery of artificial marble balusters, elegantly designed doors) with beautiful images of nature: an espalier of flowering myrtle, trees laden with fruits of different ripeness, and wild animals and birds.[40] Live birds were later released to complete the impression of a 'third nature', a mixture of art and nature in which the two parts are indistinguishable. Around the same time, different combinations of nature and art were developed by Buontalenti, Aleotti and Vincenzo Scamozzi amongst others, for ornamental princely gardens, using complex hydraulic and architectural devices — which echo curiously with Tasso's morally ambiguous vision of Armida's garden.[41]

Costumes

As with the stage-sets, descriptions of costumes used for pastoral performances raise issues about verisimilitude, nature and art, and simplicity as opposed to magnificence. For instance, in the prologue to his *Sfortunato*, Argenti states pointedly that his shepherdesses are 'di natia beltade, a cui/ la vaghezza dell'arte non s'aggiunge' [of natural beauty, to which the delights of art add nothing'] (37–38). This would mark them off from the kind of splendid costumes that Serlio describes for some shepherds in Genga's performance (pre 1545), made of 'ricchi drappi d'oro e di seta, foderati di finissime pelli d'animali selvatici' [rich cloths of gold and silk, lined with very fine skins of wild animals] (fol. 51^v). By the end of the century, Ingegneri notes that sumptuous costumes were still often used, especially for shepherdesses who were made to look more like nymphs, superior to them in status. In his view, this was understandable given audience tastes, but inappropriate for the lowly cast, who should rather be dressed in a humble yet delicate style, which was as pleasing as pomp, a point that perhaps obliquely criticized the recent performance of Guarini's *Pastor fido*.[42]

For more precise detail about costumes, we must again turn to Leone de' Sommi, who may be considered something of an authority. Besides directing several pastorals himself during the 1550s–80s, including probably his own three (of which two are lost), he seems to have been closely involved with the design and provision of costumes for court productions, a task that frequently fell to the Jewish community in Mantua.[43] He recommends that a shepherd should wear a light silk, sleeveless undershirt ('camisciola') covered in front and behind by animal skins, and that his arms and legs could be bare if he was young and good-looking, or covered with a skin-coloured body stocking if not (III, 52). He could wear a wig and a crown of ivy or laurel, and his props might include a small flask or decorated wooden bowl tied to his belt, a knapsack, or a staff — and the more 'extravagant' this was the better.[44] The nymphs, who were usually played by boys, required a fairly elaborate, long-sleeved tunic, covered by a brightly coloured skirt fastened by a gold or coloured belt, and a rich cloak over one shoulder. Their thick blond hair (probably a wig) could be covered by a veil and worn loose, as long as it appeared natural. Their costume was completed by a bow and quiver and a single spear, as seen in the illustrations to the 1602 Ciotti edition of Guarini's *Pastor fido* (see figs 4 and 7), thus emphasizing the strong mythologizing and classicizing flavour of courtly pastoral.

Actors and the performance of pastoral drama

Most early performances of pastoral drama in Ferrara seem to follow the practice of using mainly amateur actors as for Lollio's *Aretusa* (see above), although the presence of professional *comici* in Ferrara is documented from 1565.[45] For this reason, pastorals tended to follow the practice for erudite comedy and tragedy in continuing to use boys to play the female parts after the 1560s, although by this time actresses commonly appeared in Italian professional troupes and elite women were also occasionally involved in exclusive courtly theatrical performances (see chapter 4). The notable exception to this pattern appears to be the first performance of Tasso's *Aminta* in 1573, which is generally believed, according to circumstantial evidence, to have been performed by the Gelosi troupe, who were active in Ferrara at the time.[46] As we have seen, Giraldi's *Egle*, Argenti's *Sfortunato* and Lollio's *Aretusa* were staged by university students, while the latter also featured one named, probably semi-professional actor (Ludovico Betto).[47] According to Marcigliano, 'semi-professional' actors, or excellent amateurs called upon to act for particular occasions, were a peculiarly Ferrarese phenomenon, since professionals preferred the more remunerative centres of Mantua and Florence. Notable examples include Sebastiano Clavignano da Montefalco — who performed in *Egle*, and possibly also in Beccari's *Sacrificio*, and was admired by Giraldi — and Giovan Battista Verato, who was highly regarded by Tasso and Guarini amongst others, and whose fame later extended beyond Ferrara. He acted in *Sfortunato* (1567), *Sacrificio* (1587, playing the part of the satyr), as well as in various *tornei* (those of 1561, 1569, and 1570), and he played Tiresias in the famous performance of Sophocles' *Oedipus* to inaugurate the theatre of the Accademia Olimpica in Vicenza (1585).[48]

However, suitable amateur actors were not always easy to come by and, for more high profile events, could require extensive searches throughout the Ferrarese state and beyond. This is evident from a series of letters written towards the end of 1584 surrounding the attempts of a Ferrarese ducal secretary (Giovanni Battista Laderchi) to recruit an older man and three boys of sixteen or seventeen with some theatrical experience to perform in Guarini's *Pastor fido*. (This seems to be the first in a long series of unsuccessful attempts to stage the play.) The story appears to begin 27 November 1584, when the secretary records how he has written to request actors:

> Conforme alla police che io ebbi per la tragedia [*sic*] del Sig[no]r Cav[alie]re Guarini ne ho scritto a tutti gli ufficiali acciò veggano di ritrovar que' giovani che si desid[era]no; io ho ordinato loro che trovati che siano ne diano subito aviso, acciò si possano sceglier quelli de' quali la vista (?) sia migliore, che il far venir così grosso n[umer]o di gente oltre che sarebbe di grossa spesa partorirebbe confus[ion]e....[49]

> [In accordance with the mandate that I had for the tragedy [*sic*] of the Cavaliere Signor Guarini, I have written about it to all the officials so that they can set about finding the youths that are required. I have ordered them to give immediate notification once these have been found, so that those who [look most appropriate?] can be chosen, because, besides costing a lot, getting such a large number of people to come would cause confusion....]

The Estense official in Modena, Ferrante Estense Tassoni, replied on 5 December that he was unable to find anyone of the right age or suitably skilled for the 'tragicomedia' [*sic*].[50] However, (H)ercole Zinzani, the governor of the Garfagnana (Estense territory bordering on Lucca) penned an interesting letter to Laderchi the day before from Castellonovo (Castelnuovo), recommending a local older man, and three boys to play the nymphs for the Ferrarese production:

> Ho fra gli altri trovati tre fanciulli di 16 o 17 anni d'assai bel'viso e buon garbo, e se bene non hanno più recitato altra volta, nondimeno credo che riusciranno assai bene, e saranno atti a fare la parte di ninfa come mi scrive, poiché nella pastorale del Tasso che feci mettere all'ord[i]ne l'anno passato per farla recitare, se bene l'occ[asio]ne de rumori con [i] lucchesi l'impedì, li detti fanciulli, nel provare ch'ella si fece molte volte, riuscivano benissimo. Quanto poi all'uomo d'età, di buona presenza, che abbia buona voce e lingua, e sappia recitare, qua non è alcuno che sia meglio e tanto buono come è m[esser] Baldassare Mentessi, quale credo che V[ostra] S[ignoria] lo conosca, e ha tutte le qualità ch'ella mi scrive, se il non essere molto grande non disdice [...], e ho detto sì ad esso come ai fanciulli che stiano in pronto per venirsene a Ferrara se saranno richiesti, sì come faranno tutta volta che S[ua] Alt[ezz]a si compiacerà di comandare che venghino; e se fra tanto le paresse bene che s'avessero qua d'essercitare potrà avvisarmene.[51]

> [Amongst others I have found three boys of sixteen or seventeen years of age with a very handsome face and pleasing manners, and although they have not yet performed, I nevertheless think that they will do very well, and will be able to play the part of a nymph, as you write. For in Tasso's *pastorale*, which I got rehearsed last year to have performed, although it was stopped by the outbreak of political troubles with the people of Lucca, the said boys were very good during the rehearsals which took place several times. As for the older man with strong presence, and who is to have a good voice and diction and be able to act, there is

nobody here who is better or as good as Mr Baldassare Mentessi, whom I believe your lordship knows and has all the qualities that you write about, if not being very tall is not inappropriate [...], and I have told him, like the boys, to be ready to come to Ferrara if they are required, as they will do each time it pleases his Highness [the Duke] to command them to come; and if, in the meantime, you thought it right for them to rehearse here please inform me.]

The boys may not have been that satisfactory though, despite previously having been involved in this intriguing-sounding planned (but cancelled) production of Tasso's *Aminta*, or they may not have been sufficient in number for this purpose. For only a few days later, Guarini wrote from Ferrara to Don Ferrante Gonzaga, ruler of the Mantuan satellite court of Guastalla, asking him if he knew of a boy who could play the part of a nymph.

> Sono intorno al *Pastor fido*, che queste Ser[enissi]me A[ltezze] fan tuttavia con molta diligenza mettere all'ordine per vederlo in scena questo carnevale. Et già tutte le parti son fuori, et si darà oggi o domani principio alla scena. Se V[ostra] Ecc[ellenz]a Ill[ustrissi]ma avesse qualche fanciullo in cotesti contorni, che fosse atto a far una Ninfa di sedeci in dicissette anni, oh quanta grazia me ne farebbe! et questo quanto più tosto.[52]

> [I am busy with the *Pastor fido*, which the members of the ducal family are still preparing with great diligence in order to stage it this carnival. The parts are all distributed already, and today or tomorrow we will start work on stage. If your illustrious Lordship has some boys aged sixteen or seventeen in your area who were suitable to play a nymph, what a favour you would do me! and especially if they were sent as soon as possible.]

Besides the problems caused by lack of talent, especially amongst boys who had to play the emotionally intense and lengthy female parts, rehearsals were thwarted by actors not turning up or refusing to co-operate. At one point, the voice of a boy playing Amarilli in Guarini's *Pastor fido* broke in between periods of rehearsal.[53] Yet, despite widespread complaints about amateurs during the period, they were still preferred for court performances in many instances due to a prevailing snobbish attitude towards professional actors, backed by clerical intolerance especially towards actresses.[54]

Many of the problems with performing pastoral drama stemmed from the fact that since its earliest irregular manifestations it had often included complex spectacular features such as choral, danced, and musical episodes, as well as echo scenes and rustic clowning. Magic and transformations were also common in earlier irregular pastorals and *commedia dell'arte* scenarios, though replaced in some later plays by elaborate pseudo-religious ceremonies with sacrifices and priests. For hunting scenes and to create a pastoral ambience live animals could sometimes be introduced to the stage too. In fact, a manuscript list of the props needed for a performance of the *Pastor fido* (Turin 1585?) includes 'Un cane grande, bello, domestico' [a large, attractive, tame dog]. Guarini, in his commentary to the play, described this as creating a very pleasing as well as realistic episode when Dorinda tries to win Silvio (II. 2).[55]

The music for pastorals was, it seems, written and sometimes performed by (semi-) professionals, while the choreography too was probably designed, though not always executed, by experts. Danced, and musical episodes undoubtedly offered great potential for spectacular display which appealed to audiences (as in *intermedi*),

FIGURE 7. Engraving (by Francesco Val(l)egio?) preceding Act III of Battista Guarini, *Pastor fido, tragicommedia pastorale* (Venice: Giovanni Battista Ciotti, 1602), depicting Mirtillo in the foreground, with the 'Gioco della cieca' [game of blind-man's-buff] behind on the right.
Reproduced by permission of Reading University Library (Overstone Shelf 19F/19, p. 138).

especially if they employed new techniques. They could however present considerable difficulties for actors who may well have had some knowledge of court dancing, but were otherwise relatively inexperienced. This is particularly highlighted in the case of Guarini's *Gioco della Cieca*, the choreographed game of blind man's buff at the centre of the *Pastor fido* (III. 2), which involved a novel combination of speech, dance, solo madrigals, and choral song (see fig. 7). This episode, along with the staged sacrifice (Act IV) was regarded, as the most dangerous part of the play in terms of its performance.[56] The dramatist therefore singled it out amongst the parts of the play that are full of 'novità' [novelties] and movement, and which needed to be 'con lungo studio provati e riprovati in scena' [rehearsed and re-rehearsed with lengthy preparation on stage].[57]

Musical and choreographed interludes like encomiastic songs or fights between peasant clowns may sometimes have been inserted more for effect than for truly artistic reasons, though a more serious motive for their inclusion may be suggested too. For example, in Isabella Andreini's *Mirtilla* the song contest between two nymphs (III. 5) was probably principally meant to show the author's own virtuoso talents as well as perhaps those of fellow Gelosi actress, Vittoria Piissimi, though it can be justified as demonstrating the harmonious reconciliation of female rivalry through their friendship, as well as displaying her learned adaptation of Virgil's third eclogue.[58] In some cases, such interludes could further symbolize a higher order of 'invisible reality' through the addition of neo-Platonic associations.[59] For example, the song by a priest of Pan with a chorus of 'pastori nudi' [naked shepherds] at the centre of the 1555 edition of Beccari's *Sacrificio* (III. 3) accompanies and reflects the nymph Callinome's conversion from chastity to love. In Giraldi's *Egle* (performed 1545) and Ingegneri's *Danza di Venere* (performed 1583) the dances are closely integrated into the plot, and can be read as making visible the dialectic between order/harmony/chastity and disorder/chaos/passion which runs through the plays. The deeper significance of Guarini's *Gioco della Cieca* and its necessity within the plot of the *Pastor fido* are also emphasized in the commentary, though the author cannot resist also drawing attention to his novel technique of composition and earlier experience of composing even more difficult ballets in Ferrara.[60]

Performing Tasso's *Aminta* and Guarini's *Pastor fido*

> E veramente se le publiche rappresentazioni son fatte per gli ascoltanti, bisogna bene che, secondo la varietà dei costumi e dei tempi, si vadano eziandio mutando i poemi. (Guarini, *Verrato* [1588], p. 778)
>
> [And in truth, if public performances are staged for the audience, plays too have to change according to the variety of customs and the times.]

The discussion so far has identified certain tendencies in staging pastoral drama in the second half of the sixteenth century, at least within the courtly circles of Ferrara and Mantua, without much specification of changes that occurred in these practices over time. In fact, one might well expect there to have been developments, given the growing status and popularity of the genre, and the general innovations to scenography and theatre design. Within the remaining pages of this chapter, we will briefly consider this question by looking at some of the early performances of Tasso's *Aminta* and Guarini's *Pastor fido*, which reveal to some extent how staging practices altered in the later decades of the sixteenth century.

The exploration in chapter 3 of the possible dynamics of the first hypothesized performance of Tasso's *Aminta* in 1573, and the descriptions of pastoral sets by de' Sommi and previously of Serlio suggest that pastoral drama represented an ideal medium to reflect courtly concerns. It is highly stylized yet apparently natural and unassumingly graceful, whether staged in elaborately prepared halls or outside. Indeed, cheaper outdoor performances could even enhance this effect, since they could then exploit the natural beauties of the gardens and give at least an illusion of effortlessness or *sprezzatura* created by their rapid organization.[61] Significantly, in late May 1581 the Duke of Ferrara ordered an unspecified 'pastorale' by Tasso (presumably *Aminta*) to be prepared 'con poca manifattura' [with few props] when he learnt of the arrival within a matter of days of Cardinal Farnese, hoping that his guest would defer his stay for it. It was to be staged during the day at the Montagnuola, a hill within a pleasure park, with fruit trees and artificial fountains, 'in uno di quei boschetti che servirà per scena e per teatro [in one of those groves which will serve as a stage and theatre].[62] Despite the simplicity of the staging, there was not in fact enough time available to mount it. However, only shortly before, another private garden performance of *Aminta* was successfully arranged as an after-lunch entertainment by some young members of the Accademia dei Filarmonici [Philarmonic Academy] of Verona, also using a nearby natural 'scena pastorale'.

As may be imagined, changes are evident in the pastoral's overall message and even content when it appeared *outside* the elite circles of court and academy. We have already seen Tasso's concern with adapting the content of his epic, *Gerusalemme liberata*, for print publication so that it conformed to his agenda and the tastes of his intended audience (Chapter 3). It is worth speculating also on possible alterations to performance styles and content when the pastoral play was staged more publicly, though, of course, the author was bound in such cases to have far less control over his work, especially after its publication.

In February 1574, less than a year after its probable first performance, *Aminta* was staged in Pesaro, where the court of Urbino had been based since 1536. It was performed in a hall that was made for the 1571 entry of the new Duchess, Lucrezia d'Este (sister of Alfonso II).[63] She had married Francesco Della Rovere in 1570, though still maintained strong links with her native Ferrara and with Tasso himself, who may have attended this performance. *Aminta* formed the last in a series of carnival festivities, perhaps organized by Lucrezia, which aimed to regain popular support for the ruling dynasty. These included also a *sbara* (tournament), performed in the *cortile grande* (great courtyard) of the court, and a sumptuously staged comedy (Sforza d'Oddo's *Erofilomachia*) with *intermedi*, which both involved local nobles participating. *Aminta* was performed by a different group of young men (and possibly women) from Urbino; it is unclear whether these were amateurs or professionals. There were now choruses after each act, following the convention, if not the overall spirit, of tragedy, though we cannot be sure whether they were all composed by Tasso. As Almerici remarks, the novelty of these delighted the spectators above all and created an effect of 'maestà mirabile' [wondrous majesty].[64] An epilogue spoken by

Venus (*Amor fuggitivo*), balancing the initial prologue by Amore, may also have been added in this performance of the play.[65] Such exterior additions (which may have differed from those in printed versions) would have brought greater symmetry and *gravitas* to *Aminta*, reflecting its use as part of a more formal and politically motivated programme of entertainments.

Later on, inter-act spectacles or *intermedi* also seem to have been added for performances, though none of these appear in the surviving manuscripts or editions from Tasso's time.[66] For instance, beautiful 'visible' ('apparenti') *intermedi* with various animals were added to one performance of *Aminta* (termed an 'egloga') given after an outdoor pastoral banquet in Ferrara, hosted by the nobleman Cornelio Bentivoglio for the Duke and Duchess some time before 1584.[67] By the 1580s, *intermedi* had increasingly become *de rigueur* for formal courtly productions, particularly after Buontalenti's magnificent ones produced in Florence for the comedies of Giovanni de' Bardi (*L'amico fido*) in 1586 and Girolamo (de') Bargagli (*La Pellegrina*) in 1589. In terms of theatrical innovation and impact, these far outweighed the comedies with which they appeared. *Aminta* may also have been performed on this grand scale in Florence in 1590 for the Grand Duke Ferdinando de' Medici, 'coll'accompagnatura delle macchine e prospettive' [with machines [for *intermedi*?] and perspectival scenes] designed by Bernardo Buontalenti amongst others.[68] If such a performance did indeed take place (Baldinucci's account, the single source for this, was first printed in 1681 and has a rather anecdotal and suspiciously eulogistic tone) it would no doubt have used some of the many new techniques for scenography, music and machines developed for the much celebrated recent Florentine *intermedi*. In this way, it would have displayed the magnificence and well-ordered power of the ruler-patron to a suitably awe-inspired audience. Thus any potentially ambiguous and anarchic material within the play could be controlled by the splendid frame.[69]

Compared to his rival Tasso, Battista Guarini had far greater ambitions for his *Pastor fido*, both in terms of its performance and particularly its publication, by which he hoped to earn great literary prestige. Already during the long gestation of the play and particularly after it began circulating privately from 1583, it began to be sought out as part of the widespread search for suitable and preferably new play-texts for courtly and other elite festivities. In 1584 Vincenzo Gonzaga requested a copy, though Guarini refused, protesting that the play was still unfinished and that there would not be time to perform it as splendidly as he desired.[70] As we have seen, a performance was planned by the ducal family in Ferrara for carnival 1585, though it failed for reasons that are still unknown. The same year, the play was presented to the Duke of Savoy, Carlo Emanuele I, for whom Guarini had apparently written it from the start,[71] to form part of the festivities celebrating the Duke's marriage to Catherine of Austria that August. At this time, Guarini was keen to secure a post at the court of Turin, so offering his still unpublished, but already known, play in person, must have seemed a good means of gaining the duke's favour. Rehearsals for the performance evidently advanced a long way; copies of the play were distributed to actors on the order of the Duke of Savoy and the prologue by Alfeo in all the printed editions retains allusions to the Savoy wedding.[72] There is some debate, though, about whether it ever actually took place.[73] At all events, Guarini received a valuable gold chain from the Duke for his efforts. Guarini also went in person to present a copy of the *Pastor fido* to the

Grand Duke of Tuscany in 1588. Presumably, he hoped this would smooth the way for him to obtain a position at this rival court, after again leaving the service of Duke Alfonso d'Este. He did not succeed.

The fact that Guarini's play was evidently intended for courtly audiences of the highest level and for an audience of readers, would explain his chagrin on learning that the play's reputation may have been damaged while still unprinted. It had apparently been circulated in a corrupted form by actors from the Gelosi troupe (the company of 'Isabellina') working on the Turin performance in 1585, who had plundered its *concetti*.[74] As mentioned in the previous chapter, Guarini strongly opposed any association between his play (and tragicomedy generally), with *commedia dell'arte* practices, which he claimed to despise while actually drawing upon them to some extent. His aim that the *Pastor fido* should achieve a public profile and readership to secure his own position, would explain its more overtly moralizing content compared to the *Aminta*, as well as its dramatic representation of clearly visible authority figures, and a pseudo-religious sacrifice meant to uphold the common good. Its closing portrayal of the harmonious reconciliation of the laws of nature, state and religion through divinely sanctioned marriage would also make the play a suitable accompaniment for dynastic wedding festivities.

Of the various critics who still condemned the *Pastor fido*, and pastoral generally, for being unedifying, and even dangerous to the social fabric, nearly all failed to take into account the play's function as drama. They continued to approach it only as a text for reading, though Guarini (at least in his earlier treatises) had justified the new dramatic form largely on its appeal and usefulness to contemporary audiences.[75] Faustino Summo was unusual in recognizing the vocation of pastoral drama (and tragicomedy) for the stage, though this was viewed as further grounds for criticism. Firstly, it posed difficulties in terms of a suitable stage set — since it could require that of tragedy or comedy, or both together, and pastoral too (*Due discorsi*, pp. 562–63). Secondly, the fact that it was to be performed only increased the persuasiveness of its 'corrupting' message:

> Le disonestà rappresentate ad onesta brigata dispiaciono, e sono odiose, là dove che nel leggersi sono ricevute con minor molestia per l'artificio e leggiadria del buon poeta, e perciò ancora alcune volte tollerate e laudate. Ma delle pastorali non è così, le quali vogliono la rappresentazione e i teatri al modo che oggi sono usate di farsi. (p. 589)

> [Immoral things performed before an honest company of people are disliked and hated, although when they are read they do less harm due to the artifice and elegance of good poets, and for this reason they are sometimes even tolerated and praised. But with pastorals this is not the case, as these require performance and theatres of the kind that are usually designed today.]

Guarini certainly exploited the genre's performance potential to the full in writing his *Pastor fido* and, as we have seen, incorporated complicated new dramatic techniques. He had considerable practical experience of theatre, having directed actors, and worked closely with choreographers and musicians. He also collaborated over many years with the much admired stage-designer, architect, and engineer, Giambattista Aleotti, of whom Guarini noted to his own son: 'molte cose vedrà egli nella pratica, che non posso veder io nella mia teorica' [he will see many things in practical terms, which I am not able to with my theoretical knowledge].[76] Before coming to Mantua, Guarini had also, crucially, played a key role in preparing the elaborate inaugural performance of the Teatro Olimpico in Vicenza (1583–85). This, as Mazzoni notes, brought him into contact with a great number of leading theatrical experts of the day, including Ingegneri, as well as involving him in the whole theatrical process, from the choice of text to its staging.[77] Despite all this experience, however, the *Pastor fido* proved extraordinarily difficult to perform. Apart from two fairly minor productions — in Crema with a costly stage-set for carnival 1596, and for a private academic performance in Ronciglione — there seems only to have been one other performance of the play (Siena, carnival 1593), before the watershed ones of 1598, despite many attempts to do so previously.[78]

Guarini steadfastly refused to compromise the *gravitas* and splendour of the performance by putting it on in a hurried and low-budget way. His letters to the ducal secretaries and to Duke Vincenzo Gonzaga during the period of rehearsals and projected performances in the 1590s reveal his detailed attention to the standard of the acting, especially in the dance and sacrifice, and to the stage-set. Initially, Guarini appears reluctant for *intermedi* to be added, since these would distract audiences from the overall beauty and perfection of the play with their showiness. In 1592, he wrote to the Duke advising him to omit them:

> Sì come necessari là dove solo si dubiti che la favola senza loro non sia per essere dilettevole. Ma perché forse essendo questo spettacolo di gran prencipe, può parere che non convenga rappresentarlo senza questo ornamento.
>
> [As they are only necessary when there are doubts that the play will not be delightful without them. But perhaps, as this spectacle is hosted by a great prince, it may seem inappropriate to perform it without this ornament.][79]

They were evidently later incorporated to satisfy the Duke, showing the dynamic nature of theatrical production. Aleotti was enlisted at Guarini's request to prepare some on the 'Harmonies of the four elements', a subject which recalls the Florentine *intermedi* of 1586 by Giovanni de' Bardi, which Guarini studied carefully.[80]

Guarini, however, dismissed a suggestion to reduce costs by not using artificial lighting (21 May 1592), arguing that this was a false economy since:

> La scena non allumata è priva d'ogni ornamento; et sopratutto di quello degli intramezzi, i quali a lume di sole riescono insipidissimi, ancorché fossero i più ricchi e i più belli del mondo. Oltre a ciò la spesa si diminuisce assai allumandola, poiché quelle finte vaghezze che ingannano la vista a lume finto non si potrebbero rappresentare se non con grandissima et ricca spesa.[81]
>
> [The stage that is not [artificially] lit lacks all ornament, and especially that of the *intermedi*, which appear very insipid in daylight alone, even if they are the richest and most beautiful in the world. Besides, the cost is reduced substantially by lighting the stage, since the artificial delights that deceive the eye in artificial light could not be represented except with very great and lavish expense.]

The performance could then also take place later in the day, when the hall was cooler — an important consideration as the play was expected to last six hours with the *intermedi*. A letter written the previous December to the Duke from the ducal secretary Annibale Chieppio, then entrusted with the arrangements, further suggests that Guarini was very aware of the decorum of the space used for the performance. For the dramatist reportedly felt that the only the ground floor hall where comedies used to be performed before the fire would be suitable to accommodate the large numbers of foreign guests expected, and to stage the play with 'quella onorevolezza che convenga alla grandezza di V[ostra] A[ltezza]' [the honour that is appropriate for your lordship].[82] Guarini would no doubt therefore have rejected the secret plan by Chieppio to perform the play *outside* after Easter, so as to form 'con l'aiuto della natura un teatro veramente pastorale, con minor spesa et disturbo' [with the aid of nature a truly pastoral theatre, with less expense and disturbance].[83]

It was not until 1598 that the *Pastor fido* was finally staged in the magnificent way that Guarini desired. That year there was a performance in June, and another in September, which evidently included *intermedi* since the Governor of Milan who attended was very impressed by the machines. However, the highpoint of the play's performance history was its staging in 22 November as part of the celebrations to honour Margaret of Austria as she passed through Mantua on her journey through Italy to join her husband, Philip III of Spain, to whom she had just been married (by proxy) by Pope Clement VIII in Ferrara.[84] For this occasion she was accompanied by her cousin Archduke Albert and mother, Archduchess Maria, and a very large suite of perhaps 3,000. For such a key political occasion, all the parts of the play, including the performance space, *intermedi* and prologue, would have contributed to the overall message that the Duke was promoting. It was performed with splendid stage-sets and machines by the prefect of the Ducal Fabric, Antonio Maria Viani of Cremona, in the theatre of the castle before a large audience possibly of 1,000 people, all of them visitors to the city.[85]

Eye-witnesses are however notably silent about how the play itself was performed. This may be partly explained by the fact that the play was already very well known by that time, having been available in print for almost nine years, and the subject of critical discussion for even longer. There is also a possibility that the performance of the play was rather mediocre, in which case it would have been politic to omit a description from the otherwise celebratory and idealizing accounts of the festivities. The most extensive by Giovanni Battista Grillo (*Breve trattato*) focuses instead almost exclusively on the spectacular *intermedi*, which doubtless overpowered the impression of the more finely nuanced play. Their description could better fulfil the propagandistic aim of a formal account too, by presenting a blatantly political message and conveying the magnificence and momentous quality of the event. As Grillo spells out, these *intermedi* told the simple mythological story of the *Marriage of Mercury and Philology*, providing a pretext for flattering analogies with the royal couple, and the recently deceased Philip II of Spain (as Jove, father of Mercury).[86] They also allowed the virtuoso scenographic display of the city of Mantua, the Elysian fields and a mouth of hell with a flaming city of Dis, a stormy sea-scape, a Mount Parnassus, and Fame rising up on a tower, in each case with elaborate cloud machines and rich costumes, all by now recognized ingredients in princely *feste*. Finally, it is presaged that, through the union of Mercury and Philology, peace and harmony will return again to the cosmos as in the Golden Age, re-emphasizing a theme from the play and echoing its refrain, 'Vieni santo Imeneo' [Come holy Hymen], ending with the appearance of the god of marriage himself.[87]

Afterthoughts

This sumptuous performance, glowingly commemorated in the definitive 1602 edition of the play (dedicated to Duke Vincenzo), can therefore be said to mark the highpoint of Guarini's career and perhaps of pastoral performances as a whole.[88] The genre had indeed in this case changed considerably since its earliest private performances to become a central part of princely festivities. This was partly as a result of the number of examples of pastoral drama available by writers of social and literary distinction by the end of the sixteenth century, and its critical justification as a dramatic genre worthy to be placed alongside the canonical tragedy and comedy. The apparently apolitical and ancient Arcadian setting which could now on Guarini's model be used to present moralizing views on love and marriage, also made it a suitable dramatic form for public performance at that time.

Such concerns undoubtedly affected the attitudes of intellectuals from academic or university circles towards the genre, and stimulated the interest of bookmen and potential patrons. Yet, courtly audiences were probably just as, if not more, interested in the possibilities for innovative and varied spectacle that pastoral drama offered. Besides being decorative and apparently decorous (erotic subjects could be elegantly veiled), pastoral plays were useful because of the extreme flexibility of their staging requirements. They could for instance be sumptuously staged so as to display princely magnificence, as Zuccolo comments that many princes and rulers had done recently.[89] On the other hand, pastoral plays could still be used for elegant low-budget entertainments too, at a time when several courts (and academies) were experiencing severe economic difficulties, which Ingegneri notes made the staging of tragedies prohibitive for most.[90] Following Guarini, pastorals could also be made to emphasize publicly the court's allegiance to moral and political norms, while allaying deeper anxieties about courtly identity by demonstrating its innate grace, simplicity and naturalness.

It is significant and perhaps typical of the extrovert and innovative Vincenzo Gonzaga that he should have chosen to patronize the still controversial *Pastor fido* in November 1598, when international attention was focused on Mantua.[91] At this time he would have felt the need to reaffirm the family's strong political, military and family links with the Empire, especially after the devolution of Ferrara (where his sister had been Duchess) to the papacy only a few months earlier. It was therefore crucial that he convey the correct blend of personal magnificence, and deference for the young Austrian monarch, as well as demonstrating his moral and Christian values, and entertaining his guests.[92] Guarini's pastoral, in its shortened state, with its splendid *intermedi* and presumably an altered prologue, would have been expected to fulfil all of these aims. The capacity to adapt pastoral performances to meet economic contingencies, as well as to reflect both private tastes and public values, may therefore be seen as a major reason for their continued popularity on the Italian court stage at this time.

Notes to Chapter 6

1. Angelo Ingegneri, *Della Poesia rappresentativa e del modo di rappresentare le favole sceniche* [1598], ed. by Maria Luisa Doglio (Modena: Panini, 1989), p. 6.
2. Ludovico Zuccolo, *L'Alessandro, overo della pastorale, dialogo* (Venice: Andrea Baba, 1613), fol. 6ᵛ.
3. Ingegneri remarks that the *Pastor fido* 'è poi stato con insolito giubilo letto e riletto' [was later read and reread with exceptional joy], *Della poesia*, p. 4. Zuccolo states in his *Della eminenza della Pastorale* (in *Dialoghi*, Venice, 1625) that pastorals were meant only for reading by this time, see Marzia Pieri, '"Il Pastor fido" e i comici dell'arte', *Biblioteca teatrale* 17 (1990), 1–15 (p. 10). I have been unable to consult a copy of this later dialogue by Zuccolo.
4. See the forthcoming monograph by Maria Galli Stampino for detailed research on various performances of *Aminta*: *Staging the Pastoral: Tasso's* Aminta *and the Emergence of Modern Western Theater* (Tempe: Medieval & Renaissance Texts & Studies). I thank the author for making certain chapters of this available to me. In writing this chapter it was not, however, possible to take into account the recent monograph by Laura Riccò, *'Ben mille pastorali'. L'itinerario dell'Ingegneri da Tasso a Guarini e oltre* (Rome: Bulzoni, 2004).
5. See Richard Andrews's section on pastoral drama in 'Theatre', pp. 292–98 (p. 296); Jonas Barish, 'The Problem of Closet Drama in the Italian Renaissance', *Italica*, 71 (1994), 4–31 (pp. 26–27).
6. Malacreta *Considerazioni*, p. 70; see pp. 69–73 for the cuts made on this occasion. He criticizes the inclusion in *Pastor fido* of more than one plot, an overly complex action, too many episodes, monologues and descriptions. Salviati also suggested cutting speeches in the play (Pasquazi, pp. 202–03). On the nature of the cuts made for the 1598 performance, see Sampson, 'The Mantuan Performance of Guarini's *Pastor fido* and Representations of Courtly Identity', *Modern Language Review*, 98 (2003), 65–83 (pp. 72–73).
7. See Guarini's letters to Salviati (1 April 1586) and to Filippo Da Este [1586] in Guarini, *Opere*, ed. by Guglielminetti, pp. 112–14; also Muzio Manfredi's preface to his *La Semiramis boschereccia* (1593). More generally, see Riccò, 'Testo per la scena'. The lack of authorial control is well illustrated also by the history of Guarini's comedy, *Idropica*, see chapter 5, n. 10.
8. See Chapter 2, p. 41.
9. Letter from Annibale Chieppio to Vincenzo Gonzaga, 23 Dec., 1591, quoted in D'Ancona, II, 545. On the impermanent status of the dramatic text see also Stephen Orgel, 'What is a Text?', in *Staging the Renaissance. Reinterpretations of Elizabethan and Jacobean Drama*, ed. by David Scott Kastan and Peter Stallybrass (London: Routledge, 1991), pp. 83–87.
10. See for example Cesare Segre, 'Il teatro del Rinascimento e la semiotica', in *Il Teatro italiano del Rinascimento*, ed. by Maristella de Panizza Lorch (Milan: Edizione di Comunità, 1980), pp. 389–401; and Peter Birch, *The Language of Drama. Critical Theory and Practice* (London: Macmillan, 1991), p. 11. On sixteenth-century poetics of stage-practice generally, see Cesare Molinari, 'Scenografia e spettacolo nelle poetiche del cinquecento', *Il Veltro*, 8 (1964), 885–902.
11. Aristotle, *Poetics*, trans. by Malcolm Heath (Harmondsworth: Penguin, 1996), 4.4, 50b, pp. 12–13, and 9.1, pp. 31–32.
12. Guarini, *Annotationi*, in *Pastor fido* (1602), fol. 90ᵛ. See also Ingegneri, *Della poesia*, pp. 42–43.
13. Pieri, *Scena boschereccia*, chapter 9 ('La breve stagione della drammaturgia').
14. For a similar reduction of a sense of orality in the Ferrarese chivalric romances/epics during the sixteenth century, as a wider audience of readers was targeted, see Paul Larivaille, 'Dall'Ariosto al Tasso. Poeta, principe, pubblico nel "Furioso" e nella "Liberata"', in *Studi in Onore di Bortolo Tommaso Sozzi*, ed. by Aldo Agazzi (Bergamo: Centro di Studi Tassiani, 1991), pp. 169–82 (especially pp. 177–79). Though on the taste for spectacular, declamatory recitative in late sixteenth-century music and theatre, see also Ferdinando Taviani, 'Teatro di voci in tempi bui (riflessioni brade su "Aminta" e pastorale)', *Teatro e storia*, 16 (1994), 9–39 (pp. 22–25).
15. See the accounts of this performance by G. B. Vigilio, *L'insalata: cronaca Mantovana dal 1561 al 1602*, ed. by D. Ferrari and C. Mozzarelli (Mantua: Arcari, 1992), fol. 42v/p. 89; and Giovanni Battista Grillo, *Breve trattato di quanto successe alla maestà della regina D. Margarita d'Austria N.S.* (Naples: Appresso Costantino Vitale, 1604), pp. 30–57 (pp. 55–56). Grillo's description of the *intermedi* for this performance is also quoted in *Il teatro italiano*, II: *La tragedia del Cinquecento*, ed. by Marco Ariani (Turin: Einaudi, 1977), II, 1056–63 (all references to the 1604 edition, unless stated). See also Ferrante

Persia, *Relatione de' ricevimenti fatti in Mantova alla Maestà della Regina di Spagna Dal Sereniss. Sig. Duca, [L]' Anno MDXCVIII del Mese di Novembre* (Mantua, repr. in Ferrara by Vittorio Baldini, [1598]). For other sources, see Sampson, 'Mantuan Performance', p. 68 n. 8; and D'Ancona, II, 570.

16. See Guarini, letter to Francesco Maria Vialardi (Turin, 22 July 1583), in *Opere*, ed. by Guglielminetti, p. 107; BBV, Atti dell'Accademia Olimpica, 2, fasc. 10 ('L'), fol. 30^v, p. 58 [September 1584], also Mazzoni, p. 99. On the blurred boundary between plays for acting and for reading by the late sixteenth century, see Barish, p. 25.
17. See Ingegneri's dedicatory letter to Camilla Lupi, Vicenza, 31 Dec. 1583, in *Danza di Venere* (Vicenza, Nella Stamperia Nova, 1584).
18. Sampson, 'Mantuan performance', pp. 70–71. On the near exclusive Gonzaga patronage of the arts in Mantua, Fenlon, *Music and Patronage*, pp. 43–44. Tasso left Ferrara for Mantua under the protection of Vincenzo Gonzaga in 1586; Guarini tried to stage his *Pastor fido* there during the 1590s, and was in the Duke's service 1592–93. For the chronology of the performances, see Rossi, *Guarini*, pp. 181–89, 224–35; D'Ancona, II, 535–75; Fenlon, *Music and Patronage*, pp. 149–52.
19. Claudia Burattelli, *Spettacoli di corte a Mantova tra Cinque e Seicento* (Florence: Le Lettere, 1999), pp. 9, 29–30 n. 17, 229–30 n. 71.
20. *Relazione dello Stato di Ferrara* [1589], cited in Solerti, *Ferrara*, pp. CCXVII–CCXXXVII (p. CCXXV). However, by 1589 Alfonso appeared to have lost interest in *giostre*, *tornei* and other festivities (p. CCXXII).
21. For details, see chapter 2, n. 137; see also chapter 3, p. 62.
22. Anon. [Agostino Argenti?], *Il Castello di Gorgoferusa et il Monte di Feronia, ne' quali si contengono le cose d'arme fatte in Ferrara nel Carnevale del MDLXI* (Ferrara: Francesco Rossi il Giovane, 1566).
23. Unlike in Florence, Ferrarese artists tended only to be named when this would increase the prestige of the patron, or disassociate him from disasters (Alessandro Marcigliano, 'Giovan Battista Verato: un attore nella Ferrara del Cinquecento', in *Scenery, Set and Staging in the Italian Renaissance*, ed. by Christopher Cairns (Lewiston: Edwin Mellen, 1996), pp. 81–99 (pp. 81–82)). On festival books see Roy Strong, *Art and Power. Renaissance Festivals 1450–1650* (Bury St. Edmunds: Boydell, 1984), p. 47.
24. Alberto Lollio, *Aretusa, comedia pastorale* (Ferrara: Valente Panizza Mantoano, 1564).
25. See James Haar, 'Dalla Viola, Alfonso', *The New Grove Dictionary of Music and Musicians*, 2nd edn., ed. by Stanley Sadie (London: Macmillan, 2001), VI, 862; and N. Balata, 'Dalla Viola, Alfonso', in *DBI*, 32 (1986), 59–61. Dalla Viola is listed as head of the ducal instrumentalists in the court records from February 1560 to December 1569, earning a good salary of 21 lire per month (Newcomb, App. 1, pp. 156, 164, 180–81).
26. A. Moneta, 'Costabili, Rinaldo', in *DBI*, 30 (1984), 262–63. Rinaldo Costabili (c. 1535–85) served as painter and scenographer for various spectacles and ducal entries at least between 1559 and 1581. He may also have been involved with the first performance of Tasso's *Aminta* in 1573 (see Cavicchi, p. 56).
27. See Solerti, *Ferrara*, pp. LXXIII, LXXVII (for a possible 1565 performance); also Cavicchi, p. 64. On the semi-private, suburban Palazzo Schifanoia, see Charles M. Rosenberg, 'Courtly Decorations and the decorum of interior space', in *La corte e lo spazio: Ferrara estense*, ed. by G. Papagno and A. Quondam, 3 vols (Rome: Bulzoni, 1982), II, 537–40. On Schifanoia as performance space, see also Grazioso, p. 50.
28. Solerti, *Ferrara*, p. LXXXVIII. The Bentivoglio family also patronized theatre, including a performance of Tasso's *Aminta* (see p. 185 below) and later *tornei*, see Janet Southorn, *Power and Display in the Seventeenth Century: The arts and their patrons in Modena and Ferrara* (Cambridge: Cambridge University Press, 1988), pp. 75–86.
29. Monica Bolzoni, 'Materiali sullo sviluppo del luogo teatrale ferrarese', in *L'Impresa di Alfonso II: Saggi e documenti sulla produzione artistica a Ferrara nel secondo Cinquecento*, ed. by Jadranka Bentini and Luigi Spezzaferro (Bologna: Nuova Alfa, 1987), pp. 225–33 (p. 225).
30. See the illustrations in Pieri, *Scena boschereccia*; and Cavicchi, pp. 65–66.
31. The prologue points out the mythical mountains of Menalus, Erymanthus and Parthenius, which are concealed by the tall trees (*Sacrificio*, 1555, fol. A5^v).
32. *Lettera [...] sovra il comporre le satire atte alla scena* [1554], in *Scritti critici*, pp. 234–35. See also Chapter 2, pp. 21–27.
33. Sebastiano Serlio, 'Della scena satirica', in *Il Secondo libro di Prospettiva, di Sebastiano Serlio Bolognese*, in *Tutte l'opere* (Venice: Francesco de' Franceschi Senese, 1584; 1st edn Paris, 1545), fol. 51^r (all textual

references to this edition). See also the description of the satyric stage-set by Pellegrino Prisciani (librarian of Ercole I d'Este), which requires 'arbori, spelunche, silve, monti et altre simile parte agreste' [trees, caves, woods, mountains and other similar rustic features], *Spectacula*, MS, quoted in F. Marotti, *Storia documentaria del teatro italiano. Lo Spettacolo dall'Umanesimo al Manierismo. Teoria e tecnica* (Milan: Feltrinelli, 1974), p. 63.

34. Ingegneri, *Della poesia*, p. 7.
35. De' Sommi, *Dialoghi*, IV, p. 67. On tragedies being only suitable for princes prepared to spend lavishly, though also for some practical tips for cutting down on expenditure, see III, p. 51. On the possible dating of the dialogues, of which the third was certainly written after 1561, see pp. XVII, 61 n. 42, 69 n. 48.
36. See for example Sara Mamone, *Il teatro nella Firenze medicea* (Milan: Mursia, 1981), pp. 62–77; and Cesare Molinari, 'Premesse cinquecentesche al grande spettacolo dell'età barocca', in *Studi sul teatro veneto fra rinascimento ed età barocca*, ed. by Maria Teresa Muraro (Florence: Olschki, 1971), pp. 97–117. On the rapid imitation, especially in Mantuan circles, of Florentine theatrical innovations and performance styles (themselves imitative of practices in Ferrara and France), see Fenlon, *Music and Patronage*, pp. 146, 157–61.
37. See Ivaldi, *Le Nozze Pio-Farnese*; also the detailed essay by Riccò, 'Sassuolo 1587'. Guarini's *intermedi* on the four elements written for this occasion imitated the subject of the 1586 Florentine *intermedi* for Giovanni de' Bardi's *L'Amico fido*. On Aleotti, see also A. O. Quintavalle and E. Povoledo, 'Aleotti, Giovan Battista', in *DBI*, 2 (1960), 152–54; Cavicchi, pp. 58–59, 62–63; and Ivaldi, *Le Nozze Pio-Farnese*, pp. 17–18; on his partnership with Guarini, see Mazzoni, pp. 62–64.
38. On the novelty of a pastoral play being performed for a wedding as opposed to for carnival celebrations as customary previously, see Riccò, 'Sassuolo 1587'.
39. The anonymous account (*Narratione delle Feste Sontuosissime et Superbissimi apparati* [Ferrara: Vittorio Baldini, 1587]) is transcribed in Ivaldi, *Le Nozze Pio-Farnese*, pp. 7–14 (see p. 9; and on the temple, pp. 21, 29–30 n. 10, 63).
40. Filippo Baldinucci, *Notizie dei professori del disegno da Cimabue in qua*, ed. by F. Ranalli, 5 vols (Florence, Batelli e Compagni, 1846), II [1681], 510–11; also quoted in Mamone, *Il teatro*, p. 64. This play was staged for the wedding of Cesare d'Este and Virginia de' Medici in 1586.
41. The term 'third nature' is first found in a letter of Jacopo Bonfadio of 1541, see Claudia Lazzaro, *The Italian Renaissance Garden: From the Conventions of Planting, Design, and Ornament to the Grand Gardens of Sixteenth-Century Central Italy* (New Haven; London: Yale University Press, 1990), pp. 9–10; see also chapters 1–3 on the dialectic between Art and Nature; and, on Buontalenti, Scamozzi and Aleotti, pp. 5, 16–18.
42. Ingegneri, *Della Poesia*, p. 29; and Mazzoni, p. 142.
43. De' Sommi, *Dialoghi*, III, pp. 52–53; Marotti, 'Introduzione' to *Dialoghi*, p. XXIX; Sampson, 'Mantuan performance', p. 70. For bibliography on the Jewish theatrical tradition in Mantua, see chapter 2, n. 86. For de' Sommi's pastoral plays, see chapter 2, n. 94.
44. *Dialoghi*, III, 52; Sampson, 'Mantuan performance', p. 80; more generally, see Pieri, *Scena boschereccia*, pp. 224–25.
45. Solerti, *Ferrara*, p. LXXXIX.
46. See chapter 3, n. 12.
47. See chapter 2; and for the performers of *Egle*, Giraldi, *Lettera*, p. 235. I have been unable to find further information on Betto.
48. Marcigliano, 'Giovan Battista Verato', pp. 82–83; Mazzoni, pp. 145–48; and Riccò, 'Sassuolo 1587', nn. 7, 15. Also, F. Cruciani, 'Gli attori e l'attore a Ferrara: Premessa per un catalogo', in Papagno and Quondam, II, 451–66; G. Calendoli, *L'attore. Storia di un'arte* (Rome: Edizioni dell'Ateneo, 1959), p. 194; and Solerti and Lanza, 'Il teatro ferrarese', pp. 149, 151 n. 2, 157–58. On Clavignano da Montefalco, see chapter 2, n. 65.
49. Modena, Archivio di Stato (ASMod), Cancelleria Ducale, 'Letterati', Letter from an Estense secretary [Laderchi] to Paolo Brusantini, 27 Nov. 1584; and in Rossi, Doc. XXVII, p. 298.
50. ASMod, Archivio per materie, 'Comici', Letter from Ferrante Estense Tassoni (Modena) to Giovanni Battista Laderchi in Ferrara, 5 Dec. 1584; also Solerti, *Ferrara*, p. CVI.
51. 4 December, 1584, ASMod, A. mat., 'Comici'; Solerti, *Vita*, II, letter CLXXXVI *bis*, 454–55.
52. 11 December, 1584, in D'Ancona, II, 535.

53. See the letters from Annibale Chieppio to Duke Vincenzo Gonzaga, 26 November 1591, and 23 December, 1591 (D'Ancona, II, 542, 545).
54. See chapter 4; and generally, Andrews, *Scripts and Scenarios*, pp. 213–14, 221–24; and Henke, *Pastoral Transformations*, pp. 182–88.
55. *Annotationi*, fol. 65^v; see also 'Lista di attrezzi per una rappresentazione del "Pastor fido"', in the Marciana MS (fol. 178^r), quoted in Rossi, p. 299 (for dating see p. 184 n. 3).
56. Guarini, letter to Duke Vincenzo, Mantua, 21 May 1592 (D'Ancona, II, 554).
57. Guarini, letter to Vincenzo Gonzaga, Padua, 7 April 1584 (D'Ancona, II, 540). See also Chieppio's description of the dance rehearsals in a letter to Duke Vincenzo Gonzaga, 23 December 1591 (D'Ancona, II, 545). On the composition of choreographed ballets and Ferrarese precedents for Guarini's dance, possibly drawing on his experience of an earlier (undocumented) performance, see Fenlon, *Music and Patronage*, pp. 150–61.
58. See chapter 4, p. 122.
59. Louise George Clubb's term (see *Italian Drama*, for example p. 162).
60. [Guarini], *Annotationi*, fol. 91^r; on the whole episode see fols 90^v–91^v. See also Iain Fenlon, 'Guarini, de' Sommi and the Pre-History of the Italian Danced Spectacle', in *Leone de' Sommi and the Performing Arts*, ed. by Ahuva Belkin (Tel Aviv University: The Yolanda and David Katz Faculty of the Arts, 1997), pp. 49–65.
61. On courtly grace being intrinsic to pastoral, see Bigi, *Poesia latina*, p. 233. See also Manfredi's comment on staging Barbara Torelli's *Partenia*, chapter 4, p. 108.
62. ASF, AM, filza 2900, Letter from Orazio Urbani to Grandduke of Tuscany, 22 May 1581; Solerti, *Vita*, II, CXLIX, 453. For the Filarmonici's performance, see the letter from Alberto Lavezzola (Verona) to Diomede Borghesi (Mantua), 23 May 1581, in Solerti, *Vita*, II, CL, 158.
63. For a detailed description, see Tiberio Almerici's letter to his cousin, Virginio Almerici, Pesaro, 28 February 1574, cited in Alfredo Saviotti, 'Torquato Tasso e le feste pesaresi del 1574', *GSLI*, 12 (1888), 404–17. For further discussion of sources (of which, regrettably, only Almerici's provides reliable evidence), and a fresh analysis of this performance in context, see Galli Stampino's chapter 'Pesaro, 1574: Carnevale', in her forthcoming *Aminta*, pp. 51–95 (pp. 73–78 [the hall used]; pp. 67–73 [the actors for the three performances]).
64. Saviotti, p. 413, on the choruses, see chapter 3.
65. For this hypothesis (following Solerti), see Tasso, *Opere*, ed. by Bruno Maier, 5 vols (Milan: Rizzoli, 1963–65), I (1963), 197. On the status and function of the epilogue, see Taviani, 'Teatro di voci', pp. 9–19.
66. *Intermedi* were first published in the edition by Giacomo Dragonelli (Rome, 1666), see Tasso, *Opere*, ed. by Maier, I, 205; and Solerti, *Tasso, Opere minori*, III, CXXI-CXXII.
67. Giovanni Battista Rossetti, *Dello Scalco* (Ferrara: Mammarelli, 1584), quoted in Solerti and Lanza, pp. 173–74. On *intermedi*, see Nino Pirrotta and Elena Povoledo, *Music and Theatre From Poliziano to Monteverdi*, trans. by Karen Eales (Cambridge: Cambridge University Press, 1982), I, ch. 5; II, ch. 4; and pp. 46–48 on 'visible' ones (performed on-stage).
68. Baldinucci, II, 493.
69. For this idea, see James J. Yoch, 'A Greater Power Than We Can Contradict: The Voice of Authority in the Staging of Italian Pastorals', in *The Elizabethan Theatre*, 8, ed. and intro. by G. R. Hibbard (Ontario: P. D. Meany, 1982), pp. 164–87.
70. Guarini to Gonzaga (7 April 1584), see chapter 5, n. 5. See also Fenlon, *Music and Patronage*, p. 149; Rossi, p 181.
71. See Guarini's letter to Francesco Maria Vialardi, Turin, 2 July, 1583, in *Opere*, ed. by Guglielminetti, pp. 103–07.
72. Guarini, letter to Filippo Da Este, Turin [1586?], ibid., p. 113. For the prologue, see chapter 5, pp. 142–43.
73. For the view that it was not performed in Turin, see Rossi p. 184; for the same view, though for slightly different reasons, see Franca Varallo 'Nota Introduttiva' to Anon., *Da Nizza a Torino. I festeggiamenti per il matrimonio di Carlo Emanuele I e Caterina d'Austria* (Turin: Centro Studi Piemontesi, 1992), pp. 11–87 (pp. 81–84). For the general view that it was staged there in some form in 1585, see Fenlon *Music and Patronage*, p. 149. See also the gloss on Turin as the place where the royal wedding was celebrated 'e si rappresentava la favola' [and the play was performed], *Annotazioni* [Prologue], fol. 13^v; and Francesco Cognasso, *I Savoia* ([Milan]: Dall'Oglio, 1971), p. 371.

74. Pieri, 'Il "Pastor fido"', p. 11; Mazzoni, p. 68.
75. See chapter 5, pp. 140, 145.
76. Letter to Alessandro Guarini, n. pl., n. d. [1598] in Rossi, p. 311; see also p. 231 n. 1. On Aleotti, see n. 37 above.
77. Mazzoni, pp. 70–74, 98–102.
78. D'Ancona, II, 563–65; Rossi, pp. 228–29. For the Siena performance, see C. Corso, *Carteggio inedito fra Battista Guarini e Belisario Bulgarini* (Siena: Accademia degli Intronati, 1951), pp. 10, 34–35; this is an offprint from *Bullettino senee di storia patria*, 57 (1950), 55–106. I am indebted to Laura Riccò for this reference. The first definite record for a performance in Ferrara was in 1602 by the Intrepidi academicians, though another was planned for 1595 (Bolzoni, p. 230; see also above and chapter 4, p. 105). On the repeated unsuccessful attempts to perform the *Pastor fido* in Mantua from November/December 1591-June 1592 and briefly in 1593, see Fenlon, *Music and Patronage*, pp. 149–50; D'Ancona, II, 535–61.
79. 14 April, 1592, in *Opere*, ed. by Guglielminetti, p. 132.
80. Letter to Vincenzo Gonzaga, 22 March 1593, in D'Ancona, II, 560; see also the letter of Annibale Chieppio to Duke Vincenzo, 23 December 1591, on Guarini's proposed *intermedi* (p. 545). Guarini's recommendations for the *intermedi* are found in *Opere*, ed. by Guglielminetti, pp. 719–23. See also Sampson, 'Mantuan performance', p. 78; Ivaldi, *Le nozze*, p. 101; and on Guarini's contribution of three (unperformed) compositions for the 1586 Florentine performance, which he did not attend, see Riccò, 'Sassuolo 1587', nn. 12, 38, and 39 (bibliography on the *feste*).
81. Letter to Duke of Mantua, in D'Ancona, II, 553.
82. For the letter dated 23 December, 1591, see D'Ancona, II, 545. Mantua was unusual in having a permanent hall used for theatre (the 'salone della Cavallerizza del Castello'), comissioned by Cardinal Ercole Gonzaga and completed in 1551 by the architect Giovan Battista Bertani on an ornate humanistic design. Fires damaged the theatre in 1588 and 1591, though it was definitively restored in 1596 (Giovanni Attolini, *Teatro e spettacolo nel Rinascimento* (Bari: Laterza, 1988), pp. 73–74).
83. D'Ancona, II, 546.
84. For further analysis of this performance, see my 'Mantuan performance'.
85. On Viani, see Burattelli, p. 96; Mazzoni, pp. 72–73; Fenlon, *Music and Patronage*, p. 122. Mazzoni attributes the 1598 designs in part also to Aleotti's earlier designs.
86. Grillo, p. 44 (see n. 15 above). The *intermedi* were probably composed by Gasparo Asiani, who assisted Federico Follino in directing the rehearsals of the *Pastor fido* in 1598 and had composed *intermezzi* on this theme in 1588 (Burattelli, pp. 86, 77 n. 106).
87. On the symbolism of Imeneo, god of 'legitimate [married] love', and connections with earlier representations in Beccari's *Sacrificio* (1587) and the 1586 Florentine *intermedi*, see Riccò, 'Sassuolo 1587'.
88. G. B. Ciotti, Dedicatory preface to Vincenzo Gonzaga (12 January), in Guarini, *Il Pastor fido* (Venice: Ciotti, 1602), fol. 2^v.
89. Zuccolo, fol. 11^r. He is no doubt alluding to the November 1598 performance of the *Pastor fido*.
90. *Della poesia*, p. 7; and see n. 35 above.
91. Fenlon, *Music and Patronage*, p. 147; and my 'Mantuan performance', p. 82.
92. Jewish performers were therefore probably not used for this performance, though at least one Jewish actor and one dancer, and the choreographer Isachino Massarano were involved in the earlier rehearsals in 1592. Otherwise, the Jewish community frequently performed comedies in Mantua during the 1590s providing an economical and skilled alternative to professionals. See Sampson, 'Mantuan performance', pp. 81–82; Fenlon, *Music and Patronage*, p. 40; Burattelli, pp. 147–48.

CHAPTER 7

Pastoral Drama in the Seventeenth Century and Beyond

Ora avvien dunque che sì piaccia la Pastorale, per essere nel più bel fiore degli anni suoi: là dove la Comedia, e la Tragedia, per essere oramai giunte alla decrepità, poco meno che a fastidio venir sogliono il più delle volte. (Zuccolo, *L'Alessandro*, 1613, fol. 20^v)

[Now it is the case that the pastoral play is so popular, since it is in its prime, whereas comedy and tragedy, having now reached a state of decrepitude, tend to be considered almost tedious most of the time.]

Developments in Post-Guarinian Pastoral Drama

From the end of the sixteenth century, and especially after the publication of Guarini's *Pastor fido* (1589/90), there was a sharp increase in the number of published pastoral plays in Italy. Zuccolo in his dialogue in defence of pastoral drama (*L'Alessandro*), noted that over eighty such plays had been written, while Ingegneri in 1598 mentioned 'over a thousand', and both critics alluded to distinguished writers and intellectuals who had written or were writing in this genre.[1] Around this time, it became influential abroad too, especially in France, and to a more limited extent, England, Spain and elsewhere. Tasso and Guarini's examples quickly proved very popular in translation with foreign audiences and were also performed alongside others by acting companies, especially in France, prompting writers abroad to imitate Italian models for themselves.

Yet, despite the widening interest in pastoral drama well into the seventeenth century, examples after the *Pastor fido* have not attracted much critical interest or approval. Those who have discussed such later plays, with a few exceptions, have tended to see them as lacking innovation in content and structure.[2] To some extent, this negative view could be linked to a longstanding critical distaste for Italian literary culture of this period that began in France around the mid-seventeenth century and spread to Italy with the Arcadia movement at the end of the century. Many intellectuals since then perceived poetry of this time as being decadent or too concerned with sheer virtuosity and rhetorical artifice, marking a decline from — or even perversion of — simpler, neo-classical values.[3] However, others have modified and called into question this view, drawing attention instead to progressive and 'modernizing' attitudes especially during the first half of the seventeenth century. These included the questioning of ancient authorities and search for modern forms and technical devices, as well as turning back to old models to create new syntheses and forms of expression, all tendencies foreshadowed in Guarini's theories from the later 1580s. This period is also valued for significant cultural and intellectual innovations particularly in theatre, music, architecture and the sciences, which inevitably affected literary and dramatic works.[4] Our re-evaluation of pastoral drama after Guarini's *Pastor fido* will therefore consider how far the genre can be said to have further evolved, and how dramaturgy was affected by broader cultural changes.

Some noticeable differences also result from the fact that seventeenth-century pastoral drama was composed by writers of a widening social spectrum and appeared increasingly outside the conventional geographical centres of production of the Northern Italian courts, the Veneto and parts of the Papal States. It rapidly came to be performed, and especially published, throughout the peninsula, from the heavily Spanish controlled South (Palermo, Macerata, Aquila, Naples) to Turin, as well as in Dalmatia and Crete.[5] Increasingly, plays were produced not only for private noble circles but for wealthy bourgeois spheres, and in the various academies that were proliferating all over Italy by the turn of the century, many of which admitted intellectuals of varying social levels, including some exceptional professional actors.[6] The greater social heterogeneity of writers resulted in plays of differing levels of conformity to neo-Aristotelian principles, and which proved varyingly receptive to contemporary developments in performance styles.

This chapter will draw attention to the increasing diversity and dispersion within the genre, responding to changing social environments and dramatic practices, and the evolving tastes and concerns of its audiences. At the same time it will trace some continuities within Italian pastoral drama as authors responded to Tasso and Guarini's rapidly canonized models. My investigation has revealed at least 150 pastoral (or piscatorial) plays of various kinds printed in the century after the publication of Guarini's *Pastor fido*, of which most are little known and very few are available today in modern editions. Exceptional in this respect is Guidubaldo Bonarelli's *Filli di Sciro* (printed 1607, henceforth *Filli*), whose great popularity in its day has ensured its modest survival in the modern canon.[7] Other writers of pastoral plays still recognized today, though not typically for these works, are the poet Gabriello Chiabrera and the actor-dramatist, Giovan Battista Andreini. It is on a small number of pastoral plays by these three writers that the following exploration focuses, while a broader sense of overall developments emerges from comparison with others. These include plays by the minor nobleman and dramatist-academician Muzio Manfredi (*La Semiramis, boschereccia*, 1593; *Il Contrasto amoroso, pastorale*, 1602) encountered already in relation to female dramatists (chapter 4), the prominent tragedian, Count Pomponio Torelli (*La Galatea, tragedia pastorale*, 1603) and Francesco Bracciolini (*L'amoroso sdegno* [The Lovers' Scorn], 1597), who was better known for his mock-epic poem *Lo scherno degli dei* [The Mocking of the Gods] (1618). Also mentioned are *favole pastorali* by the virtually unknown Giovanni Capponi (*Orsilla*, 1615), Count Gasparo Cesana (*La prova amorosa* [The Test of Love], 1606), and Count Marc'Antonio Ferretti (*Mirinda*, 1612), as well as Pietro Antonio Toniani's pastoral tragicomedy *Floriano il fido* [The Faithful Floriano] (1616). Though necessarily somewhat limited, this sample will indicate some of the important trends in pastoral drama in the early decades of the seventeenth century, especially the changing attitudes to 'canonical' models and increasing heterogeneity of the tradition.

Imitation or Innovation? Adapting to changing tastes

> Ora [...] si vedono a gara gli uomini comporre o appastricciar pastorali; chi mescolandovi due o tre compiute azioni; chi riempendole di alti e filosofici concetti; chi appicandovi qualche giunta, e chi per fornirla, recandosi a gloria in questi e simili particolari di parer simia del Pastorfido. (Malacreta, *Considerazioni* [1600], pp. 121–22)

> [Now [...] people can be seen competing to compose or cobble together pastoral dramas. Some writers combine two or three whole actions, others stuff in lofty and philosophical conceits; some add on something extra, and others in order to perfect them vainly believe that in these and similar respects they ape the *Pastor fido*.]

Most pastoral drama after Guarini can be seen to have drawn to some extent on the *Pastor fido* and Tasso's *Aminta*. Being readily available in print, these provided a useful source of dramatic situations and character types, as well as an example of the emerging new lyric style that was polemically moving away from Petrarchan formulae. Guarini's complex plot structure, which the dramatist had posed as something of a challenge for future dramatists, was also much imitated in preference to Tasso's simpler *Aminta*.[8] Given the large number of pastoral plays composed during the seventeenth century, often by inexperienced writers, it is not surprising that many were clumsily constructed and repetitive as Malacreta complained. Yet, as with Petrarchist poetry in previous decades, the canonized models could in the right hands be ingeniously and skilfully adapted, and novel variations achieved.

In many cases, such imitation led merely to the rather pedestrian, but sometimes witty manipulation of the canonical models. For example, Ercole Pelliciari's 'tragedy with a happy ending' set in Arcadia, *I figlioli di Aminta e Silvia et di Mirtillo et Amarilli* [The Children of Aminta and Silvia, and Mirtillo and Amarilli] (Venice, 1617) functions as a 'sequel' to *Aminta* and the *Pastor fido*, and also features characters whose names recall those of the male protagonists in Bonarelli's *Filli di Sciro* (Niso and Tirsi).[9] In ideological terms, few touch upon serious issues to the same extent as Tasso and especially Guarini, though many later plays are underpinned by moralizing *sententiae*.

The Vicentine dramatist Pietro Antonio Toniani is very unusual in raising the problematic concept of free will in his *Floriano il fido* (1616), as his compatriot Maddalena Campiglia and the Paduan Cesare Cremonini had done before him.[10] The complex plot of *Floriano* starts with the eponymous hero's beloved (Gerinda) having been picked as the annual sacrificial victim of Berica, where the play is set. Floriano urges her to escape from under the watchful eyes of the city's priests (I. 2, p. 38), reminding her that God may take pity on them, despite their apparent opposition to Divine Will, because he has granted humans 'libertà [...]/ Errante e peregrina/ Dal *libero volere* accompagnata' [freedom [...] wandering like a pilgrim and accompanied by free will] (I. 2, p. 34). However, this plan is not executed. An *antefatto* of a violent family feud is introduced and a complication in the form of a rival to Floriano, and the emphasis falls increasingly on points of honour, leaving aside the earlier hints of religious questioning. Like other seventeenth-century authors of tragicomedies, Toniani ultimately appears anxious to avoid suggestions of non-conformity. A disclaimer, conventional in late sixteenth-century tragedy to establish the author's observance of religious orthodoxy or to disassociate him ambiguously from the design of the preceding work, is added in conclusion to his play.[11] This points out the purely hedonistic end of poetic fiction:

> È cosa omai notoria [...] che 'l senso che si dà a tali parole, cioè Sorte, Fato, Fortuna, Destino e altre simili, s'attribuisce derivato dalla prima causa. E inoltre sono usate da' poeti perché apportano dilettevole lettura [...]: ragione adunque, che qual si sia persona potrà leggere senza alcuno sospetto: sempre intendendo, sano modo, conforme alla volontà di Santa Chiesa Cattolica Romana. (p. 164)

> [It is by now well known [...] that the meaning given to words such as Chance, Fate, Fortune, Destiny and the like is to be understood as deriving from the prime cause. Furthermore, they are used by poets because they are pleasing to read [...]. This means that anybody can read them without suspicion, as long as it is understood that they reasonably conform to the will of the Holy Roman Catholic Church.]

Many pastoral plays after the *Pastor fido* seem to lack an explicit social or political message. Dramatists tended to leave aside such issues, which the Church increasingly sought to monopolize, in order to concentrate on producing the immediately consumable pleasure that audiences of theatre-goers and readers desired. Guarini argued that audiences went to the theatre 'per fine di ricrearsi e non di piagnere o contristarsi' [for the purpose of enjoyment and not to weep or feel sad] to defend the suitability of his pastoral tragicomedy over tragedy and licentious comedy in his times.[12] For the same reason Ingegneri considered pastoral plays, with their pleasing stage-sets, sweet verse and delicate *sententiae*, preferable to tragedies, which are described as 'spettacoli maninconici, alla cui vista malamente s'accomoda l'occhio disioso di dilettazione' [melancholy spectacles, which are very unsuitable for people who wish to see something entertaining]. Tragedies perhaps presented too vividly the destructive force of anti-social, individual passions or, as Ariani suggests, their ambiguous representation and demystification of real political power may have struck too deeply at contemporary anxieties.[13]

Taste was increasingly becoming a determining criterion for drama and poetry, overriding the Platonizing idea of internal, transcendent poetic rules, and heralding a significant change in the conception of poetry at the turn of the seventeenth century. To win popular approval, writers strove to achieve variety and novelty in their subject matter and especially style. They sought surprising effects through unusual and virtuoso combinations of ideas and types of expression; and the leading poet of the day, Giambattista Marino, is famously known as stating: 'E' del poeta il fin la meraviglia' [The poet's end is to create a sense of wonder].[14] For this reason, the dominant trend in Seicento poetry, can be broadly characterized by its recherché use of *concetti* (conceits) and *arguzie* (wit), its daring linguistic experimentation, and its hedonistic sensuality.[15] Many dramatists show similar concerns with creating a rich poetic language — all too often, in the view of Ingegneri, to the detriment of unified invention and plot construction.[16]

Guarini had already indicated ways of achieving the effects of *meraviglia* and pathos to move and delight audiences in his pastoral tragicomedy, while still observing the principles of unity, verisimilitude and decorum. For example, *meraviglia* was achieved through the unexpected happy resolution to the complex plot and the apparently novel combination of selected elements from previously distinct genres (including tragedy, comedy, the ancient tragicomedy, satyr-drama, and eclogues) — a tendency which, as we will see, would later be taken to more daring extremes by dramatists such as Giovan Battista Andreini. Guarini advocated a mixed style to match the form of the tragicomedy, thereby challenging the rigid categorization according to classical genres by ancient rhetoricians like Demetrius of Phaleron. Referring to the authority of rhetors of the second Sophistic, especially Hermogenes, Guarini proposed the use of a range of styles combining the tempered 'dolce' [sweet] and 'grave', and avoiding the more extreme magnificent and humble styles. This poetic effect is explicitly likened to combinations of colours or musical tones, suggesting the intense discussions on music and Greek tragedy which had begun in the 1580s, and contributed to the development of opera.[17] Guarini was in fact one of the foremost lyric experimenters of his day, and had practical experience of writing madrigals for musical setting, as well as of composing texts for ballets and other occasional entertainments.[18] He was aware that the use of a mixed and ornamented lyric style would be pleasing to audiences and justified it as being appropriate to the Arcadian context. Yet others criticized this practice as being intrinsically opposed to dramatic principles. Malacreta for instance described Mirtillo's speeches as 'una dissipita raccolta di madrigali' [a dissipated collection of madrigals].[19]

During the first decades of the seventeenth century, there was a growing tendency to privilege lyrical and descriptive passages in pastoral plays to achieve different pleasing effects, often without the corresponding attention to classical principles of decorum and unity that Guarini and Ingegneri had advocated. Indeed, Zuccolo's spokesman in his dialogue proposes that modern writers of pastoral drama should if necessary leave aside such principles to satisfy the desires of the audience, since: 'il gusto degli uditori [...] deve essere uno scopo onde il poeta non mai, o di rado, levi l'occhio' [the taste of the audience [...] must be an end from which the dramatist never or rarely departs].[20] Though ultimately preferring poets to observe verisimilitude, Guidubaldo Bonarelli also noted in 1612 that the poet should either aim to please or achieve his end through pleasure.[21]

Romance and Pastoral Drama

Another important change in pastoral drama following Guarini's *Pastor fido* is the more noticeable usage of themes, motifs and dramatic scenarios drawn from romance. Pastoral and romance had of course been intimately associated since ancient times. Prose and verse romances often contained pastoral episodes, and could take place entirely within pastoral landscapes, as with Longus' *Daphnis and Chloe* and in Sannazaro's influential *Arcadia*. Regular pastoral drama was from the start clearly influenced by such models, especially in its use of magic, madness, cross-dressing, and interwoven love stories. For instance, in Beccari's *Sacrificio* (1555) a magic potion is given to one of the characters to make her invincible, a satyr makes use of a magic sleeping powder and truth-drug, and Melidia's brother is turned offstage into a wolf. Amongst those dramatists who paid greater attention to Aristotelian principles of verisimilitude and unity such elements were increasingly mediated or removed.

Nonetheless, the complex vicissitudes of the mismatched lovers and sometimes the fortuitous recognitions of identity (typical also of comedy) remained.

Besides the popularity of vernacular romances, there was a market in Italy already from the early sixteenth century for Alexandrian prose romances or novels, whose complex plots, psychological characterization, themes like the testing of sexual fidelity, and emphasis on female figures could likewise be assimilated into regular pastoral drama. Of these, Heliodorus' late example *Aethiopica* (c. 225–50 AD), had become better known in Italy (including Ferrara) from the mid-sixteenth century through translations and commentaries, which had significantly imbued it with Christian symbolism. It influenced both Tasso's *Gerusalemme liberata* and Guarini's *Pastor fido*.[22] Typically, such works portray a pair of lovers who are either married or betrothed, often of noble stock and sometimes of mysterious birth. Separated by accident, they undergo a series of misfortunes, such as kidnapping by pirates, forced slavery, attempted rape or murder, shipwrecks, which bring them into contact with far-flung places and exotic strangers, before being happily reunited, often involving the revelation of their true identity.[23] Those produced in the age of the Second Sophistic, also provided elegant examples of how to integrate flashbacks, tales within tales, switching narrative perspectives and other devices to ensure suspense and the audience's marvel at the ending — the same concerns that faced later writers of romance and increasingly also drama intended for readers.

Tasso's polemical epic-romance *Gerusalemme liberata* (printed 1581) was instrumental in suggesting new directions for pastoral drama, especially following the mediating example of Guarini. The *Liberata* not only explored resonant political and religious themes, as well as presenting more psychologically complex heroes and heroines, but it evoked powerful feelings of horror, pathos and marvel through its richly figured poetic language, and it abounded with theatrical images. Guarini integrated some of the heroic values, the aristocratic figures and the moralizing ideologies of the *Liberata* into his pastoral play to enoble the genre. Notably, he imitates the episode of the noble quarrel between the unjustly condemned lovers Sofronio and Olindo (Canto II), over who should make the ultimate sacrifice for the other (*Pastor fido*, V. 2. 105–25), a situation often repeated in pastoral drama, for example by Bonarelli, Cesana and Toniani.[24] Guarini's Amarilli also dramatizes an inner struggle between love and honour similar to that of Tasso's princess/shepherdess Erminia. This figure, though cut from Tasso's revised version of his epic (*Gerusalemme conquistata*, 1593), remained popular and continued to be drawn on in drama and the visual arts, and to some extent also in opera, during the next two centuries.[25]

However, the assimilation of the dramatic pastoral with the narrated romance (or epic) posed some dramaturgical challenges, notably regarding the unity of structure. In his theory on epic poetry, Tasso recommended the need for episodes and complications as long as they were verisimilar and appropriately integrated into a unified plot, since the variety that they bring is 'dilettevolissima' [most delightful] and 'necessariissima [...] a' nostri tempi' [extremely necessary in our times] (*DAP*, II, 40). As mentioned in chapter 3, the poet did not advocate the similar use of narrated episodes in tragedy.

Guarini seems to have taken Tasso's theory on variety in unity in the epic to heart in composing his *Pastor fido*, though without specific acknowledgement:

> S'egli è vero che la maraviglia ne' poemi nasca dall'irricchire il soggetto con episodi che l'unità non offendano, a me pare che'l *Pastor fido* n'abbia gran parte, essendosi in lui con tanta esquisitezza osservato il precetto dell'unitá che c'insegna il grande Aristotile. (*Compendio*, p. 266)
>
> [If it is true that poems appear marvellous when the subject is enriched with episodes which do not offend unity, then I think that the *Pastor fido* contains much that is marvellous, since it most exquisitely observes the principle of unity that the great Aristotle teaches.]

The commentary to his play adds that no episode, however delightful, could be removed without ruining the plot (*Annotazioni*, fol. 80ᵛ). Thus accounts of portentous dreams or visions, oracles, descriptions of tragic and romance-type *antefatti*, and pleasing spectacular episodes like the *Gioco della cieca*, are all justified as being necessary in terms of the intrinsic plot-structure as well as for creating an effect of *meraviglia*. Nonetheless, they added considerably to the overall length of the play. While *Aminta* is a mere 1996 lines long, the *Pastor fido* consists of 6862 lines, which provoked much criticism from Denores and others. Ingegneri advised generally that such plays ought only to extend to 2500 lines (excluding choruses), so as not to cause discomfort for spectators, though pastorals could perhaps be a little longer 'per la soavità della favella, e per molto numero di versi rotti' [because of their sweet style and the great number of broken [i.e. shorter, usually seven-syllable] lines].[26] For Malacreta, however, the *Pastor fido*'s 'immensa mole' [immense mass] of episodes ruined the dramatic verisimilitude, and made the play's action appear longer than the prescribed twenty-four hours, partly explaining why large cuts were made for the magnificent 1598 performance.[27]

Many subsequent writers of pastoral drama largely ignored such objections about the overall length, as well as Guarini's emphasis on unity. They frequently included long and sometimes unrelated episodes, drawing especially on Tasso and Guarini's plays: accounts of attacks on a nymph by a satyr or other monster, descriptions of attempted suicides, reports of pseudo-tragic oracles, visionary dreams, sacrifices of an innocent victim, the slaying of mythological beasts, and lost children being found. Increasingly, narratives of exotic encounters and travels, and kidnappings by pirates were added, to provide further opportunities for ensuring the necessary novelty and *meraviglia* that could otherwise seem in short supply, given the continual recycling of pastoral ingredients in the plays. For example, in Muzio Manfredi's *Semiramis* (1593), the eponymous heroine is at one point described as being carried off by over twenty bandits ('masnadieri'), against whom she valiantly tried to defend herself (IV. 7), later being rescued by her noble beloved, Mennone. Meanwhile, her companion Tisira has committed suicide, but is cured by three passing 'pilgrim' shepherds, one of whom was Armenian and healed her with magic potions (V. 2). Giovanni Capponi's *Orsilla* (1615), which partly imitates the main plot of Bonarelli's *Filli di Sciro*, features a young lover, kidnapped in infancy by African corsairs from Tuscany and carried off as a slave (I. 2–3). He appears at the start of Act III with a beard and an unusual costume, and later describes the foreign court where he had stayed (III. 2).[28]

Such episodes are often narrated and so rely on the rhetorical device of *energia* which, as Tasso explained: 'con parole pone innanzi a gli occhi la cosa, che pare altrui non di udirla, ma di vederla' [uses words to place the object before someone's eyes, so that they seem not to hear it described but to see it] (*DAP*, III, 55). This allows the restrictions of unified place and time to be overcome, though in Tasso's view it was a device less appropriate for drama than for epic, which lacked the visual power of stage effects. The increased use of narrated episodes in pastoral drama therefore seems to be partly related to the growing popularity of the genre for readers, as attested to by Zuccolo.[29] It also suggests a desire to transcend imaginatively the limitations of the unified, fictional pastoral setting found in the *Pastor fido*, which only occasionally makes reference to an outside or parallel synchronous existence. Many later pastorals suggest more varied geographical vistas. These were sometimes described from within the conventional settings of Arcadia, or transfigured local Italian settings like Orsigna in the Tuscan Apennines in Capponi's *Orsilla*. Plays also began to be located in more exotic, remote contexts like those used in tragedy and romances. For instance, Bonarelli's *Filli* is set on the Greek island of Skyros (Sciro) in the Eastern Mediterranean, while Marc'Antonio Ferretti's *Mirinda* (1612), imitative of this play, is set in Crete.[30] This plausibly allows romance episodes to be introduced, as they were in contemporary tragedy.[31] It also opens up ideological problems, as we shall see, by presenting the pastoral in relation to the greater reality beyond, which had been largely elided in plays that assimilated the pastoral space with that of the court.

In the decades after Guarini's *Pastor fido*, distinctions between dramatic genres and non-dramatic ones were further broken down. This resulted in ever more varied and daring combinations, such as *Roselmina, favola tragisatiricomica* by 'Lauro Settizonio da Castel Sambucco' [Giovanni Battista Leoni] (performed and printed in Venice, 1595), Carlo Fiamma's *Diana vinta overo la pazzia di Florindo, traggisatiricomica* [*The Conquest of Diana, or The Madness of Florindo*] (Venice, 1624), and especially Giovanni Battista Andreini's works for the stage, to which we will return. To some extent, this reflected a process that had already been taking place in contemporary *commedia dell'arte* practices, as well as the influence of Spanish theatre, felt particularly in Naples and Rome where Spanish acting companies performed this repertoire.[32] An interesting parallel development around the same time was the flourishing of the hybrid form of vernacular prose romance in Italy, which peaked in popularity in the mid-seventeenth century when it gained recognition as a new genre. This draws on the lyric, novella and chivalric verse romance tradition, exploring a wider range of themes and in a more loosely structured form than was possible in the neo-classical epic in order to generate public appeal.[33] Yet, perhaps as a result of the great popularity of pastoral drama, surprisingly few pastoral romances were produced in Italy despite the example of Sannazaro's *Arcadia*. The combination of neo-classical pastoral and romance themes however gained great appeal in Spain and France especially as a result of Jorge de Montemayor's *Diana* (1559?) and Honoré D'Urfé's *Astrée* (1607–27), which were along with others adapted for the stage.[34]

Bonarelli's *Filli di sciro*

A pastoral drama between court and academy

Having considered some of the broader trends in post-Guarinian pastoral drama, it will be helpful to focus on some examples, starting with Guidubaldo Bonarelli's *Filli di Sciro* (printed 1607). Even allowing for the hyperbolic praise of editors and promoters, this proved one of the most influential pastoral plays both in Italy and outside. Giambattista Marino described it as: 'l'ottima tra le migliori [pastorali] e l'emula dell'ottime per non dir vincitrice, e per nobiltà e purezza di frase e per arguzia di concetti' [excellent amongst the best [pastorals] and imitating, if not surpassing, the best ones, due to both the nobility and purity of the phrases and the witty conceits].[35] In 1787, it was even published with *Aminta* and *Pastor fido* in Orléans in a volume entitled 'Le tre più celebri pastorali italiani' [The three most celebrated Italian pastoral plays].

Count Guidubaldo Bonarelli della Rovere (1563–1608), to give him his full name, was an aristocratic intellectual who like many of his peers lived most of his life in itinerant service. In his youth, he spent time in the courts of Urbino (until 1575), Ferrara, and Novellara (near Mantua), where his father served as a courtier. He was later sent to France (c. 1579–86) to study philosophy in Paris and theology at a Jesuit college in Pont-à-Mousson, Lorraine.[36] Though a promising student, Bonarelli decided against the ecclesiastical career that his father wanted for him and similarly ended up as a courtier, diplomat and ambassador.[37] During his lifetime he served, amongst others, Cardinal Federico Borromeo in Milan (1592), his relative Count Camillo Gonzaga of Novellara (until 1593), Alfonso II d'Este of Ferrara and the Duke's successor, Cesare.

It was only when not actively engaged in courtly service, and particularly after his reconciliation with Cesare d'Este in 1601, that Bonarelli could dedicate himself more to his literary activities. He became a founder member of the Ferrarese Accademia degli Intrepidi [Academy of the Intrepid Ones], and gave an inaugural oration in 1601.[38] It was in this context that his *Filli di Sciro* was written some four years later and its publication arranged in 1606. The academy was very different from ones that had previously briefly flourished in close association with the Estense court in Ferrara, due to significant political changes at the end of the sixteenth century.[39] After years of difficult relations between Rome and the Estense dynasty, Pope Clement VIII saw Alfonso II's inability to produce an heir, and the dubious legitimacy of his named successor, as a valuable opportunity to seize the strategically important fiefdom of Ferrara thereby realizing an earlier papal objective. For while Emperor Rudolph II, on the payment of a substantial sum, had accepted Cesare d'Este as heir to the cities of Modena and Reggio, Pope Pius V had refused to do so for Ferrara.[40] Cesare began a brief military struggle to keep hold of Ferrara on Alfonso's death in late 1597, backed particularly by Venice which was anxious to curb papal expansion, but he was quickly forced to capitulate. In January 1598, he left Ferrara never to return, transferring his court to Modena and thereby losing much of his territory, wealth and political leverage.

The devolution of Ferrara to the papacy in 1598 meant that its cultural activities were no longer subject to the kind of restrictive and jealous control that Alfonso II d'Este had exercized. Comparatively, the Intrepidi had greater freedom than earlier academicians to select their members and patrons, and were not obliged to celebrate dynastic, aristocratic values. The academy was, however, closely associated with the new ecclesiastical authority, being protected by the Cardinal of San Clemente, the Governor of Ferrara, and financed annually by the Great Council. The academicians were also allowed to meet in rooms (the 'Stanze del Cavallo') of the former ducal palace. Under this authority, they appear to have had greater autonomy in their initiatives, which were especially directed towards grand spectacle under the leadership of the theatrical impresario, Marchese Enzo Bentivoglio.[41] Their activities, like those of many academies, were promoted and commemorated in print by the former ducal printer, Vittorio Baldini (d. 1618), now officially working for the Ferrarese state and the academy.[42]

The first edition of Bonarelli's *Filli di Sciro* clearly appears as an academic work, in quarto format with engravings by Francesco Val(l)egio (or Valesio), the same artist who probably designed those for Ciotti's edition of Guarini's *Pastor fido* (1602), and Baldini's emblem and motto on the title page (see fig. 8). It is specified as such in the dedicatory letter to the Duke of Urbino by the secretary of the Intrepidi, Ottavio Magnanini (Ferrara, 20 September, 1607).[43]

> La nostra Accademia [...] ha giudicato che a lei tocchi di prender cura d'un parto Accademico [...] Onde non solo ha determinato di metterla in scena con quella pompa e magnificenza che a lei sarà conceduta maggiore, ma così ignuda come nacque, di darla eziandio alla stampa. (fols. A2^{r-v})

> [Our Academy [...] has decided that it has the responsibility to take care of an academic work [...]. So it has not only decided to stage it with the greatest possible pomp and magnificence, but also to send it to press in the naked form in which it was conceived.]

The academy had already in 1602 staged Guarini's *Pastor fido*, but for the performance of *Filli* they probably planned to use their new theatre, one of the earliest in Italy. This was designed in 1606 by the Ferrarese engineer and architect Giambattista Aleotti (1546–1636), under the direction of Bentivoglio, by transforming an old ducal granary. It provided the first stable theatre in Ferrara since Ariosto's, though it was destroyed by fire in 1679, and was used mainly for the performance of tragedies and pastorals. The celebrated theatre of the Olimpici in Vicenza (inaugurated 1585), for which Aleotti had been asked to produce stage designs for a performance of a pastoral play in 1595, provided a precedent for this kind of building. However, in realizing it, Aleotti could also draw on his long experience of collaborating in large-scale courtly theatre projects, sometimes with Guarini, which resulted in a more modern design.[44] Yet, it seems that *Filli* did not get beyond the dress rehearsal stage in 1607. It is unclear whether the play had already been performed in Ferrara before that time, but it may have been staged twice with elaborate *intermedi* in Mantua in 1604, or possibly in Bologna in 1606.[45] An undated letter from a fellow academician, Alessandro Guarini (son of Battista), to Bonarelli — therefore before the latter's death in January 1608 — seems to refer to an intended third performance.[46]

After its publication in 1607, *Filli* quickly gained immense popularity with readers, going through over sixteen editions within fifty years and over thirty by 1800.[47] It appeared in an (anonymous) French translation in 1624, the first of several, its great appeal being in large part due to the popularity of Tasso's *Aminta* in France. It was translated into English in 1655, when it was described as a sister play to Guarini's *Pastor fido*.[48] *Filli* also continued to be staged, sometimes with additions by distinguished poets. Marino wrote a prologue ('La Notte' [The Night]), included in Ciotti's Venetian

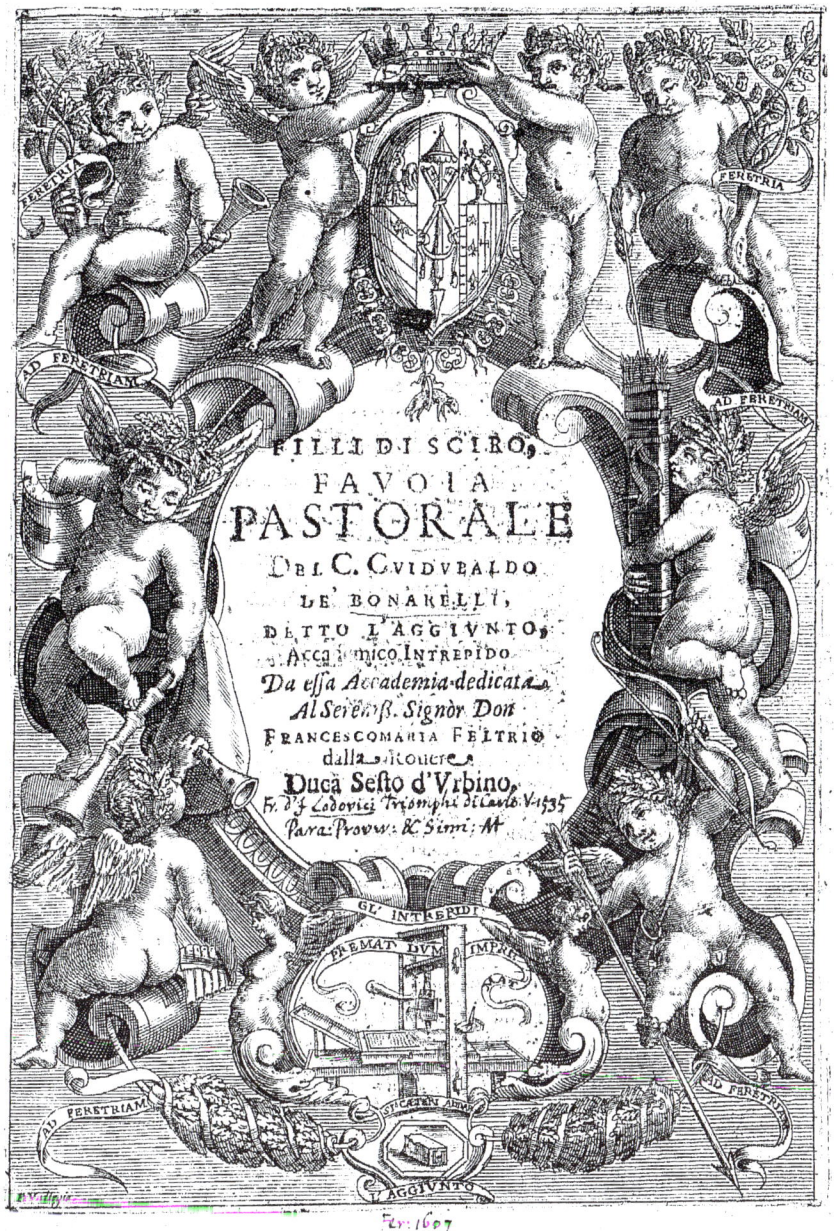

FIGURE 8. Engraving by F. Val(l)egio for the frontispiece of Guidubaldo [de'] Bonarelli, *Filli di Sciro, favola pastorale* (Ferrara: Vittorio Baldini, 1607), with emblem of the printer for the Intrepidi academy.
Reproduced by kind permission of The Warden and Fellows of All Souls College, Oxford (Codrington Library, mm.12.1).

edition of 1607 (see note 43). In 1619 the play was performed in Macerata with a prologue ('La finzione') by Ippolito Aurispa and four visible *intermedi*, which represent the only surviving examples composed for this play. Around 1639 it was performed in Sassuolo, with a prologue by the Ferrarese poet Fulvio Testi (1593–1646).[49] Bonarelli's pastoral apparently also found favour in translation with aristocratic French audiences. On one occasion it seems it was performed by the Duchess of Savoy with her ladies, and it was even praised by Cardinal Richelieu himself. Moreover, *Filli* was regularly performed by French acting troupes, probably using Pichou's translation (1631).[50]

The play evidently quickly roused curiosity and debate because of its peculiar representation of the nymph of the subplot, Celia, who is tormented by being equally in love with two shepherds at the same time. This marked a conscious divergence from the earlier conventional, Petrarchan and neo-Platonic ideal of a lover's single and eternal spiritual love, and affected all the standard ingredients of the pastoral plot — the conversion of the nymph to love, the unreciprocated love entanglements, and even the idea of suicide.[51] Already in 1606 the author was called upon by the academy to defend this novel and paradoxical case of 'double love' over three days before a large audience of *literati*, noblemen and ladies, as is mentioned in the preface to the lengthy printed version (*Discorsi in difesa del doppio amore della sua Celia* [*Discourses in defence of the double love of his Celia*], 1612).[52] The evident ingenuity and bizarre nature of this theme guaranteed sustained interest in the play, as well as demonstrating the play's explicitly academic origins.

The polemical quality of the text was heightened by its association with the emerging Seicento poetic style, which led to the accusation by the French Jesuit critic Dominique Bouhours that it, like other Italian poetry, was affected and artificial. Adrien Baillet in the following century also felt that the erudite *Discorsi* did not excuse the lasciviousness of the play, which he described as 'un piège dressé contre l'innocence et la pureté des moeurs' [a trap set up against the innocence and purity of customs], prompting Italian defences by Giovan Gioseffo Orsi and later by Lodovico Antonio Muratori.[53] Nonetheless, *Filli* proved an important influence on writers of pastoral drama during the earlier part of the seventeenth century, providing a further source for imitation besides the *Aminta* and *Pastor fido*.

Bonarelli's imitation and development of the pastoral 'canon'

Filli provides an interesting instance of alterations to these previous models, in terms of the tragicomic balance, the style, and themes, but there is no sense that it was intended as a critical contribution to the still ongoing debate on pastoral drama. From the start, the play presents a more marked political and tragic dimension, and is heavily influenced by romance-type situations. The action is set not in Arcadia, but on the island of Sciro in the Aegean, which is under foreign domination (see fig. 9). On that day, the Thracian captain, Oronte, is due to arrive with his soldiers to collect a tribute imposed every fifteen years on the islanders, consisting of some of their young children who are to be sent to the King of Thrace as slaves. As in Guarini's *Pastor fido*, there are two closely interwoven plots, where the principal one is determined by a tragic *antefatto*. This concerns Filli and Tirsi, who had been taken away as infants from their fathers (Sireno and Ormino) at the last tribute. Yet, it emerges gradually

FIGURE 9. Engraving preceding Act I of Guidubaldo [de'] Bonarelli, *Filli di Sciro, favola pastorale* (Ferrara: Vittorio Baldini, 1607), depicting the island of Sciro with a pastoral setting and sea-scape, and part of a neo-classical style temple. Reproduced by permission of the Warden and Fellows of All Souls College, Oxford (Codrington Library, mm.12.1, fol. †4^v)

that while in Thrace they won the King's favour at court and fell precociously in love, after which they received his blessing for their future marriage as he lay near to death. A complex series of misfortunes ensued, involving a terrible war and their kidnapping to Smyrna (only fully explained in V. 5), during which time the young lovers were separated and each given to believe that the other was dead. They both however retained one half of a golden necklace given by the King as a pledge of their love. Bonarelli evidently borrows from the romance for his *antefatto*, but also from Francesco Bracciolini's *Amoroso sdegno*, which similarly features a couple who fell in love in infancy but were separated by external events and their names changed, the male shepherd being told his beloved was dead.[54]

At the start of the action, Filli has been living in Sciro for the last few years disguised as Clori, the adoptive daughter of Melisso, to protect her from the supposed threat of the Thracians. Unbeknownst to her, Tirsi (alias Niso) arrived there by chance only few days before. In keeping with romance convention (and the *Pastor fido*), the staged plot depicts the more or less faithful lovers gradually overcoming a series of obstacles so that they can be reunited. The first problem is that, since his arrival, Niso (Tirsi) has fallen in love with Celia, after rescuing the nymph together with another shepherd (Aminta) from the clutches of a centaur. Curiously, Aminta has fallen in love with Celia too, though he is too hesitant to tell his friend Niso, while she equally reciprocates the feelings of the two shepherds. Her consequent guilt and horror at her 'infidelity' and inability to choose between her loves drives her to commit suicide (on stage) by taking poison. Her body is discovered by chance soon after by her lovers who, with the aid of the wise, elderly shepherd, Narete, revive her with their tears. This 'double love' is not resolved until Niso undergoes a change of heart as a result of his recognition of Clori (IV. 7); it is finally clinched by the discovery that Celia is his sister.

The principal lovers are reunited by means of a recognition token: the gold necklace which, when both halves are joined, reveals cryptic lettering and an image of the Thracian ruler. An older intermediary figure (Nerea) persuades Niso that he should persuade his new love (Celia) with a gift and that her close friend Clori should act as go-between. Clori is amazed when he gives her the other half of her necklace and recognizes him as Tirsi, but then despairs on realizing that he now loves another while she had remained faithful to his memory (III. 4). She is later reported to be close to death (IV. 7), at which Niso is handed the complete necklace. He then finally realizes his situation and angrily hurls the necklace into a stream. In Act V he goes to his beloved Filli to beg forgiveness. This is followed by a new twist as the Thracian officers appear in order to punish the sacrilegious act of throwing an image of the king (on the necklace) to the ground. Niso/Tirsi claims full responsibility for the crime before Clori/Filli, who on finally disclosing her real identity offers to die instead. The Thracians seem to recognize the lost children in this 'tenzon d'amore' [love quarrel], but cannot revoke the law. The capital punishment is to take place before the temple (off-stage), where the mothers and children have already gathered for the tribute. Having left this terrible scene, Ormino and Sireno are told by Narete of the worse sacrifice to come and they recognize the condemned lovers to be their lost children. The denouement is somewhat hurried and flat, as the elderly shepherds are informed that the lovers' death was avoided by the timely discovery of a royal decree imprinted on the necklace, which allows them to marry and frees Sciro from Thracian subjugation.

Like other plays of its time, *Filli di Sciro* can be seen to borrow and adapt various aspects from its famous Ferrarese precedents *Aminta* and *Pastor fido*, though this imitation is typically to create effects of surprise or paradox, rather than for the kind of polemical purposes for which Guarini imitated Tasso. Bonarelli paid explicit homage to Tasso especially in the secondary plot featuring the young hunter Aminta and Celia. Nerea, for example, teasingly describes Aminta, newly converted to love, as a 'novello Aminta,/ di grembo alla sua Silvia' [a new Aminta, in the lap of his Silvia] (II. 3. 701–02). Later in the play, Celia, rules out the idea of throwing herself off a cliff to commit suicide, since Tasso's Aminta was saved that way (III. 1. 73–82).[55] A more interesting reworking of *Aminta* is found in the episode of the attempted rape of Celia by the centaur. Bonarelli's version differs by being longer, being related first-hand by the nymph, rather than by an onlooker (a point to which we will return), and for its very different outcome in Celia's 'double love'. Like Tasso's Silvia, Celia is at first bound naked by her hair to a tree, but Bonarelli has his nymph be saved by the timely intervention of not one, but two, shepherds, brought by chance or perhaps destiny rather than being already motivated by love. The episode is also prolonged by a description of how Celia was seized, and of the heroic battle that ensued (I. 3. 473–99; 559–75). Celia's tending of the wounded shepherds with 'medica pietade' [healing pity] (I. 5. 838), leading to their falling in love further alludes to the narrated *antefatto* in Tasso's *Aminta* (I. 2), where Silvia treated Aminta's feigned bee-sting, as well as Erminia healing Tancredi in the *Liberata* (XIX, 112–13), and Angelica with Medoro in Ariosto's *Furioso* (XII and XIX). *Filli* therefore complicates and adds a more pronounced romance dimension to the scenario in Tasso's *Aminta*.

Bonarelli's debt to the *Pastor fido* is clear in his double plot structure, which this time makes use of a staggered mutual recognition by two characters and reversal. However, the recognition in *Filli* is not effected through Sophoclean-style investigation, but primarily through tokens, while the happy resolution is brought about by a sort of *deus ex macchina* (the distant monarch), both typical devices of romance and comedy, and considered less 'artistic' by Aristotle (*Poetics*, 8.1, 8.2).[56] Like Guarini, Bonarelli represents various authoritative father figures mainly of high birth (the principal lovers are descendents of Hercules), which enables the introduction of tragic themes and an elevated style. Yet the cast is explicitly secular, without the priests, oracles or prophets that appear in many other early seventeenth-century pastorals, such as those by Cremonini, Toniani, and Strozzi Cicogna.[57] Divine commandments are replaced with royal decrees, and the 'solenni feste' [solemn festivities] for the 'gran Madre' [great maternal deity] that Celia mentions are notably celebrated outside Sciro on a sacred island (I. 3. 448–49). Compared to Guarini's *Pastor fido*, mythological pastoral elements also play a reduced part, since there is no staged satyr (the centaur episode is narrated). No hunting scenes, festive pastoral songs or dances are dramatized or even alluded to.

Filli also presents a very tempered comic dimension and there is certainly nothing like Guarini's slapstick tussle between Corisca and the satyr. Some comicity is however conferred by Nerea and the young goatherd Filino. Nerea embodies the comedic type of the aging but sensual confidente who nostalgically longs for love like Tasso's Dafne, but lacks the flagrant immorality of Guarini's Corisca. Filino displays none of the violence, drunkenness, or sensuality typical of earlier pastoral goatherds (see chapter 2), but does provide humour through his naivety, forgetfulness, and rhetorical indecorum. For instance, while Celia is contemplating suicide, he appears uttering a hyperbolic, tragic lament that is revealed to be not for his mistress, but for the death of her beloved pet goat, a scene which is described with incongruous pathos and vividness (III. 2. 165–71).

A sense of gentle irony surrounds Celia too. Like Dorinda in *Pastor fido*, this character is excluded from the political agenda of the play, and absorbed in an inwardly focused love experience. But unlike Guarini's character, Celia appears a wholly innocent character, without the suggestive *double entendres* and sensual predatoriness that were criticized in Dorinda (see p. 151). This emerges clearly in the account of her plea to the centaur (Euritone):

> CELIA   […] — Eccomi, dissi,
> a le tue brame acconcia: or vien, satolla
> la scelerata fame. — […]
> Acciocché, divorata,
> nel ventre ingordo almen fussi coperto. (I. 3, 518–20; 522–23)

> [I said, 'Here I am, ready to meet your desires: so come and satisfy your wicked hunger.' […] so that I would be devoured and in this way at least be covered up in his gluttonous belly.]

Clori's amused reaction on hearing this would presumably mirror that of the more knowledgeable audience, reflecting the consistent undercutting of her companion's emotional and moral suffering.

The description of the rape scene by Celia on the whole results in less evident sensual voyeurism compared to Tasso's version, but more pathos and terror. The abducted victim's helplessness is emphasized by using passive tenses and highlighting the visual aspect of the scene:

> CELIA   Già quasi morta,
> non prima in me rinvenni,
> che mi vidi portata in mezzo al bosco;
> vidimi fatta, oimè, d'orribile mostro
> inevitabil preda. (I. 3. 490–94)

> [Already nearly dead, I did not recover my senses until I saw myself carried to the heart of the forest; alas, I then saw that I had unavoidably become the prey of a horrible monster.]

Bonarelli was not alone in his increased emphasis on horrifying and grotesque descriptions at that time. For instance, Bracciolini features a centaur (this time staged) in pursuit of the nymph Clori, described in terms that echo Dante and Tasso's infernal monsters:

> AMINTA   Infuriato schianta
> Di sdegno i rami, e disperato al fine […]
> Spirando foco gl'occhi, il ciel minaccia.
> E si morde per ira ambe le mani.
> (*Amoroso sdegno*, III. 2, fol. 33^v)

[Mad with rage, he breaks the branches, and, finally despairing [...] he threatens the heavens, with his eyes shooting fire, and bites both his hands in rage].[58]

Such depictions appealed to a general taste for monstrous forms of *meraviglia* and for transgressive passions. These could even take a morbidly erotic form, as in Erminia's desire for the seemingly dead Tancredi in Tasso's *Liberata* (XIX, 107) and in Bracciolini's *Amoroso sdegno*: 'Bacerò l'ossa tue spogliate e nude,/ Rotte, sanguigne, e guaste;/ Ma pur reliquie tue' [I will kiss your naked, stripped bones, all broken, bloodied and ruined, but still remains of you] (V. 2, fol. 54^r).

Dramatic procedures of Filli di Sciro

The overall bias towards tragedy in *Filli* may be related to Bonarelli's sense of decorum. As an aristocrat and a literary amateur, he would naturally wish to avoid any hint of an association with professional *comici*. If anything, his play with its strong sentimental quality and concern with moral issues appears to draw on the tradition of *commedia grave* or serious comedy, which became popular in courts and academies from around 1550. This similarly features high-minded protagonists and exploits the use of dramatic irony to create suspense, rather than portray more subversive humour. For example, the tense exchange in *Filli* (III. 4), full of pregnant asides, in which Clori is asked to plead for the love of Celia on behalf of Niso (whom she recognizes as her former childhood sweetheart, while he still believes her to be dead), has some similarities with a scene in the 'serious' comedy *La Pellegrina* [The Pilgrim Woman] (II. 7), composed within the Sienese academy of the Intronati, c. 1564.[59] Aminta's inner conflict between his own feelings for Celia and his friendship with Niso (II. 3, IV. 5–6) also has precedents in this type of comedy, as well as tragedy — and in Barbara Torelli's pastoral drama *Partenia*.

Bonarelli was very likely influenced also by his awareness of the revived theoretical and practical interest in tragedy in various academies (especially in Vicenza, Padua, Florence, and Parma) from the 1580s particularly. Intellectuals around this time were discussing a range of complex issues regarding purgation, characterization, choice of subject matter, the use of choruses, music, and the type of ending. Some, including Guarini and Ingegneri, were also concerned with practical questions of how to represent actions on stage and elicit an appropriate affective response from the audience. In some of these last respects, Bonarelli's approach differs noticeably from that of Guarini in the *Pastor fido*. Indeed, the choices of what is and is not staged in *Filli* may perhaps be read as a polemical response to this model. Most notably, the private *tenzone* between the lovers over who was to die is staged in *Filli* (V. 5), while the sacrifice scene at the temple, which formed the climax to Guarini's *Pastor fido* (V. 3–4) is reported, as is the lovers' union (*Filli*, V. 8–9).[60] Bonarelli thus chooses to represent private pathos over public tragedy. He avoids a choral conclusion too and no inter-act choruses are included. Instead, the play ends with the authoritative Narete alone contemplating the marvels of divine providence which are unknowable on earth.

Bonarelli's practice seems to reflect some of the recommendations of Angelo Ingegneri for pastoral and tragic dramaturgy, which themselves suggest oblique criticism of Guarini's practice.[61] The Venetian discouraged staging sacrifices in his *Della poesia* for dramaturgical reasons, since they are said to 'fare poco bella mostra' [not make very good show] (p. 17) due to the confusion and disorder caused in trying to perform in silence in front of a crowd of onlookers, with the priests sometimes having to turn their back on stage. Furthermore, he considered such executions of justice to be horrifying, especially when they involve human sacrifices. In his view these, like pagan temples and idols, should be avoided out of 'riverenza devuta alla nostra vera e santa religione' [reverence due to our true and holy religion] (ibid.) or rather narrated, as in Euripides' *Iphigenia of Aulis*, which would prevent any indecorum and confer greater *gravitas*.[62] On the other hand, Bonarelli seems to play with Ingegneri's view that staged suicide scenes make a desperate lover appear weak and should be avoided since 'induc[ono] più tosto riso che compassione' [(they) provoke laughter rather than compassion] (p. 16). In Celia's attempted suicide and restoration to life (IV. 4–5), Bonarelli deflates the potentially tragic situation by representing her naïvety as well as the vaguely ridiculous behaviour of her tremulous and tearful lovers. In his theoretical defence, he even suggests that her suicidal thoughts may have arisen 'piú tosto dalla fiacchezza e dalla inesperienza dell'animo che dalla intensione [*sic*] dell'amore' [more because of her weakness and inexperience than from the intensity of this love] (*Discorsi*, IV. 11, 236).

Otherwise, a significant part of the action in *Filli* is reported rather than staged, following Aristotle's preference for tragedy. A sense of drama and pathos is achieved in the descriptions in different ways. The splitting of the accounts of the *antefatti* and offstage events between different characters, and delaying of information creates some suspense. Various metatheatrical hints also punctuate the play, hinting at its providential, tragicomic design, and there is a general fascination with dissimulation especially regarding love, a *topos* in mannerist and especially baroque drama much exploited by Tasso and Guarini.[63] Finally, the descriptions themselves are designed to provoke feelings of horror, pathos and the all-important *meraviglia* through their varied content and virtuoso style, sometimes using complex metaphors, unusual similes and *arguzie*.

Bonarelli frequently delights also in erotic and playful *concetti* that Tasso had described as natural to lyric verse though inappropriate to heroic poetry (see Chapter 3, n. 104), and which had become identified with pastoral drama through Guarini's example. Various lyrical passages display the complex wordplay, assonance, internal rhymes, and *sententiae* that were typical in early seventeenth-century verse and would culminate in Marino's *Adone* (1623). These are particularly evident in the long description of the extraordinary love between the 'fanciullini amanti' [infant lovers] Filli and Tirsi (II. 1), which is marked by some highly artificial conceits, set off by alliteration and chiasmus:

> ORONTE   Con lingua ancor di latte balbettando
> sepper chiamar, prima che mamma, amore. [...]
> Così amoreggiando i pargoletti,
> pargoleggiava Amore. (II. 1. 83–84; 101–02)[64]

[While still suckling, they learnt to lisp 'love' before 'mother'. (...) Thus, as the children were playing at love, Love was playing at being a child.]

Overall, Bonarelli therefore seems to diverge from Guarini by diminishing the contrasts between tragedy and comedy, and by further privileging pathos, *meraviglia*, and idyllic qualities, showing a tendency to move from a madrigalesque to a melodramatic style.[65]

The Politics of the Setting of *Filli di Sciro*

The location of *Filli* on the real island of Sciro, rather than in a largely mythical Arcadia or a transfigured courtly space, explains why the play lacks the universalizing and mythologizing quality of Guarini's pastoral, and reference to related *topoi* like the Golden Age. However, the fairly remote and chronologically indeterminate setting against the broader political backdrop of Thrace and Smyrna provided rich landscapes of the imagination for the dramatist to draw on in descriptions, reconciling the demands of verisimilitude and poetic licence.[66] Exotic elements, including despotic regimes, slavery and strange decrees could justifiably be included in this context, as well as probably 'Eastern' style costumes for Oronte and his officer, Perindo, as depicted in the engravings for acts II and V of the Ferrarese 1607 edition (see fig. 10).[67]

Sciro is presented from the start in political terms, as a subject state of the kingdom of Thrace. As in many a tragedy, this appears as an oppressive, tyrannical regime, a 'barbaro impero' [barbaric domination], which imposes a 'fiero tributo' [cruel tribute] on its subjects (I. I. 116, 119). This consists not of base goods of nature ('parto vil de natura'), but of the inhabitants' infants ('caro dono del cielo' [dear gifts of heaven], I. I. 126), a narrative scenario that draws on the Greek myth of the Minotaur of Crete, and was used also in other pastoral plays.[68] Bonarelli emphasizes the pathos and horror in his wording and through the repetition of the negative 'non di...' on four consecutive lines. Furthermore, Narete later notes, the children are then subjected to such brutal, servile conditions in the seraglio that barely their nurses would recognize them (V. 7. 603–04). The mention of 'il gran signor de' traci' [the great ruler of the Thracians] (I. I. 6) immediately conjures up negative associations to Melisso. The audience would doubtless have shared these, given the classical portrayal of Thracians as rapacious and inhumane. The name of the monarch would also have suggested the much feared contemporary ruler of the Turks, or 'Gran Turco', whose people were known for piracy and taking people captive as slaves.[69]

Bonarelli could plausibly draw on the figure of the tragic tyrant to symbolize the Thracian regime. This figure was popular in the sixteenth century, and is found, for example, in Giraldi's seminal *Orbecche* (which also includes a royal adviser called Oronte and is set in Persia). In seventeenth-century Catholic tragedy the tyrant could further provide a vivid and edifying image of evil, especially when contrasted to the martyr.[70] This is evident in Tasso's presentation of the tyrannical pagan king of Jerusalem (Aladino) persecuting his Christian subjects in the *Liberata* (I-II), which also served to sanction the Church's struggles against the Turks. The motif could be used effectively in a pagan mythological context too, as in Count Pomponio Torelli's *Galatea, tragedia pastorale* (Parma, 1603).[71] This simply structured tragedy draws on the popular Ovidian tale (*Metamorphoses*, XIII) of the monstrous Polifemo's (Polyphemus) jealous lust for Galatea, which leads him to destroy her beloved, Aci (Acis). Polifemo's

Figure 10. Engraving for Act II of Guidubaldo [de'] Bonarelli, *Filli di Sciro, favola pastorale* (Ferrara: Vittorio Baldini, 1607), depicting the Turkish captain Oronte and Perindo in elaborate native costume.
Reproduced by permission of the Warden and Fellows of All Souls College, Oxford (Codrington Library, mm.12.1, p. 38).

rivalry is represented in political and moral terms as a tyrannical abuse of power, driven by violent passions. As described in the prologue by the austere figure of Tragedy, the action shows the destructive effects of love as *furore* and directs the audience to higher spiritual values. For this reason and because of the final ruin predicted for the wicked Polifemo, the play has been described as one of the most moralizing texts inspired by Counter-Reformation sensibilities in the ongoing debate on tragicomedy, and as a strange contamination between tragedy and pastoral.[72]

The king of Thrace in Bonarelli's *Sciro* is not only presented as a political tyrant, but also as the object of a pseudo-religious cult, testifying to his hubristic self-exaltation. Thus Niso's act of throwing to the ground the necklace bearing an image of the king is not only a crime of *lèse majesté*, but an act of sacrilege which is punishable by death:

> PERINDO Oh sacrilegio! In terra
> l' idolo, a cui ogni mortal s'atterra?
> O del mio gran signor, del re de' regi,
> o sacra, o diva imago, ecco i' t'inchino. (V. 1. 1–4)

> [What sacrilege! Is that the idol before which all mortals prostrate themselves lying on the ground? O holy and divine image of my great lord, king of kings, behold; I kneel before you.]

The unmistakeably religious tone used here clearly raises questions about the idolatrous practice of king-worship, which is abhorred by Narete as being barbarous as well as blasphemous, an example of excessive 'alterezza umana' [human pride] (V. 4. 224). Such a stance might suggest Bonarelli's implicit reinforcment of the Church's ideology of its temporal authority, by warning secular princes not to exceed the proper limits of their power — a message that would have had particular resonance in post-devolution Ferrara.[73] At all events, in an age of rising princely and monarchical absolutism in Europe, where rulers were also encouraged to present themselves as divine representatives on earth, such questioning was particularly controversial.

However, in line with Guarini's theoretical ideas on tragicomedy, tragic aspects — including ideas on tyranny — are repeatedly modified or balanced by more idealizing perspectives within the unified pastoral setting of the play. This is evident from the opening conversation between Sireno, the real father of Filli, and her adoptive father, Melisso, in which a tragic perspective on the brutal reality of secular power is contrasted with a providential and tragicomic view of human affairs:

> SIRENO   Nulla vale
> senza scettro real sangue reale.
> E chi vuoi tu che scorga
> sott' umil tetto, in pastorali spoglie,
> fra semplici costumi alma reale?
> MELISSO Se non gli uomini, almeno
> vo' che la scorga il Cielo;
> ché 'l Ciel vede anco ove non splende il sole. (I. 1. 162–69)

> [SIRENO   Royal blood has no authority without a royal sceptre. Who do you think will notice a royal soul dwelling in a humble abode, in pastoral garb, amongst simple folk?

> MELISSO If men do not, then I believe that at least the Heavens will, as they see clearly even those parts that are obscure to the sun.]

The figure who is most clearly identified with the tyrannical order, the Thracian captain Oronte, is also presented from the start in a tragicomic light, by highlighting his humane, emotional side. On arriving in Sciro, he deliberately rejects the formal military mode of conduct in order to enjoy the pleasures of the landscape, which is described in lyric, meta-theatrical terms:

> ORONTE Per sì dolci campagne,
> fra mansuete genti,
> non è d'uopo di gir cinto di squadre.
> Vegno fuor de le tende,
> Perché ristori in questi campi ameni
> La dolcezza del ciel gli orror del mare: [...]
> Oh caro praticello,
> oh leggiadro boschetto,
> mira di che bell'ombre
> incontra'l sole i suoi fioretti ammanta!
> Ecco appunto una scena
> pastorale, a cui fanno
> quinci il mar, quindi i colli, e d'ogn'intorno
> i fior, le piante e l'ombre e l'onde e'l cielo
> un teatro pomposo. (II. 1. 9–14; 18–26)

> [There is no need in such pleasant fields and amongst kindly people to travel surrounded with troops. I am venturing out from the camp so that the sweetness of heaven in these lovely meadows will refresh the horror of the sea voyage: [...] What a sweet little meadow, and delightful wood, see how pleasantly it shades its dear flowers against the sun! Behold a veritable pastoral scene, which the sea and the hills on either side, and the surrounding flowers, plants, shade, waves and sky make into a splendid theatre.]

This representation problematizes Oronte's association with a villainous regime, a situation that is compounded by the fact that Thrace is distant in space (and partly also time), being evoked only through narrated accounts. Moreover, Oronte creates a sympathetic image of the Thracian ruler himself, by revealing the monarch's tenderness towards the infant Filli and Tirsi despite his military and temporal grandeur. He is described as softening his military attitudes towards them so that he seemed to chuck their rosy cheeks ('lusingò lor le vermigli*uzze* gote', II. 1. 51, note the lyric diminutive). On his deathbed many years later, the ruler is even thought to have wept secretly on presenting the lovers with the golden necklace (II. 1. 129–41), which proves to have far-reaching consequences for the future of the lovers as well as for the inhabitants of Sciro. The negative view of his iniquitous domination held by the pseudo-tragic male elders in Sciro (Narete, Melisso, the protagonists' fathers) is thus tempered by this insight into his private emotions. As Guarini observed in defence of the tragicomic character: 'stanno forse i prencipi sempre in maestà? non trattano essi mai di cose private? Per certo sí: perché dunque non può rappresentarsi in favola scenica persona grande, che tratti cose non grandi?' [do princes always live their lives in majesty? Do they never deal with private matters? Of course they do. So why cannot noble characters be represented on stage dealing with more humble subjects?].[74]

Through Oronte's account of the children's vicissitudes, Melisso finally realizes that these were due only to the machinations and lies of a Smyrnian soldier (V. 5). The king emerges as a kind of *deus ex machina*, or a conscious instrument of divine providence, due to his unusual powers of discernment and willingness to act upon them.

> ORONTE   Poscia ver me diss'egli: — Attendi: i' veggio
> in questi duo bambini alme sí belle,
> che a non volgare impresa
> forza è che'l Ciel gli scorga,
> se ne' sembianti umani
> scrive i suoi fati il Cielo, s'io gl'intendo. —
> (Ned uom v'è già, ch'a par di lui gl'intenda). (II. 1. 56–60)

[Then he said to me: 'Wait, I spy such beautiful souls in these two children, that the heavens must destine them for uncommon deeds, if divine fate is written in human appearances and if I rightly understand it.' (And, indeed, no man understands such things as well as he does.)]

However, the apparent failure of the king's plan for their marriage provokes doubts in Oronte about human ability generally to comprehend divine matters (II. 1. 111–12). The king's fallibility seems even more palpable when his idolatrous law apparently necessitates that the newly discovered children be decapitated for sacrilege. Since both Oronte and Perindo have recognized the lovers to be the children lost from Thrace, a tragic conflict develops between divine and royal law. This alters the apparent tension in Guarini's *Pastor fido* between human/divine and natural law in ideological terms, by suppressing the question of whether unguided human nature is sinful. The conflict, though popular in other subsequent pastoral plays, is also shortened here, lacking open discussion or lamentation. The solution comes significantly not from a divinely inspired prophet figure, but from the ruler himself. Oronte's wish for the lovers to come to the temple to fulfil the 'alto voler del gran signor' [supreme wishes of the great lord] (V. 5. 472) — presumed to be their death — paradoxically leads to the revelation that the King had indeed miraculously provided the means (through his command on the necklace) to unite the lovers and liberate Sciro.

The final revelations and reversal occur very suddenly, and are narrated rather than dramatized (as in *Aminta*), which must have left the audience somewhat puzzled. Was the Thracian king, whether alive or dead, instrumental in bringing about the providential design? If so, should his regime should be seen as an enlightened monarchy rather than a tyranny? The overall interpretation is complicated by the fact that the practices of enforced slavery and idolatry do not appear to be universally revoked in the Thracian kingdom, and no further comment is provided by the characters more critical of the regime (Melisso, Sireno and Ormino). Moreover, no satisfactory explanation is given for the tragic disproportion between the cause of the king's war against Smyrna (the children being kidnapped and not returned) and the devastation of 'mille e mille altri' [thousands upon thousands of people] (II. 1. 203).[75] Political critique is therefore avoided. Serpilla merely praises the Thracian ruler as 'autore/ d'ogni lor bene' [creator of all their happiness] (V. 9. 693–94), while Narete marvels at the outcome of events. In the closing lines, the elderly shepherd, now alone on stage, further retreats from commentary on secular matters. He instead relates the past events meta-theatrically to fortune's 'intricati nodi' [intricate knottings] (V. 9. 891), which are suddenly resolved providentially by heaven, commenting: 'A la futura etade/ potran di noi favoleggiar le scene' [In a future age, people will be able to represent our story on stage] (V. 9. 897). Finally, he points to the instability of human affairs, the inscrutability of divine mysteries, and the limitation of human reason, all of which necessitate a blind faith in the divine will:

> NARETE   Deh voi, che troppo arditi
> co' vostri umani ingegni
> sperate di veder fin sovra i cieli,
> quinci imparate omai
> che le cose del ciel sol colui vede
> che serra gli occhi e crede. (V. 9. 902–07)

[Ah you who too daringly hope with human minds to gaze above the heavens themselves, learn then that divine matters may only be perceived by those who close their eyes and believe.]

Bonarelli therefore ends with an unambiguous gesture of religious conformity, withdrawing from questions about temporal and religious authority that were then being intensely debated amongst writers like Cardinal Roberto Bellarmino and Giovanni Botero.

Religious Themes in Bonarelli's Pastoral Play

Godard has argued that Bonarelli represents the human world as being dominated by chance and contingency, which could appeal to the audience's hedonistic tastes, while being stripped of potentially subversive implications.[76] We have noted how, unlike many pastoral plays following Guarini's *Pastor fido*, *Filli* avoids evident contamination between the religious and the secular, and between pagan and Christian rituals, by omitting an overtly religious 'frame' and characters, and by keeping the action at the temple offstage. A suggestion of a christianizing providential design is made in the *lieto fine*, although this was quite common in pastoral plays from after the 1590s and before.[77] Otherwise, he avoids mention of potentially problematic Christian issues, such as free will.

Yet, Godard's view of Bonarelli's generally secularizing perspective in *Filli*, does not take into account the religious elements that are implicitly evoked at various levels of the play: in the plot structure, themes, scenery, imagery, and language. Potentially indecorous pseudo-religious scenes may not be staged, but that does not prevent religious themes being developed in the realm of the imaginary. Indeed, for readers, the descriptions of the offstage action would be as vivid, if not more so, as what was meant to be represented on stage. The temple, for example, appears to be more than just a decorative frame,[78] since it provides a focus for the public and private demonstrations of religiosity and political obedience of the inhabitants of Sciro. Although not required for any of the action, a temple may have figured prominently in the stageset, as in the engravings to Acts I and V of the 1607 Ferrarese edition of *Filli* (see fig. 9), presumably modeled on the 1602 edition of *Pastor fido*. It was also important in terms of the plot. In the very first scene, we learn that Sireno is headed for the temple, and during the course of the play the lovers of Celia are described as having made a splendid vow of thanks there for their recovery (III. 4. 547–49). Later, Oronte wants the condemned lovers escorted there so that his lord's wishes may be executed ''n piú celebre luogo,/ con piú solenne pompa' [in a more celebrated place, with more solemn pomp] (*Filli*, V. 5. 470–71). This suggests the sort of magnificence that was increasingly considered necessary for religion by contemporary political thinkers like Botero, which was enhanced by spectacular religious architecture, rituals, and music.[79]

Finally, the temple also becomes a place for manifestations of pathos and horror. It is described by Sireno as a 'teatro di miserie' [theatre of woes] (V. 7. 518), where the grieving mothers gather with their children for the exacting of the tribute. Though still adopting pastoral imagery, this emotive scene hints at the Biblical episode of the 'Massacre of the Innocents', an immensely popular subject in Counter-Reformation art and literature.[80]

> SIRENO Elle son quivi in un drappello accolte,
> così qual si restringe, attornïata
> da fiero predator, timida greggia.
> Stringonsi i figli al petto,
> rimiranli piangendo, e mentre il pianto
> scorre loro nel seno,
> vanno i bambin suggendo
> da le mamme dolenti
> più lagrime che latte. (*Filli*, V. 7. 533–41)

> [They [the mothers] are gathered there in a group, like a timid flock of sheep huddling together when encircled by a fierce predator. They clutch their children to their breast and gaze upon them weeping; and while their tears run down their breast, the infants suck more tears than milk from their grieving mothers.]

The description of the condemned lovers being led to their execution at the temple where a noisy throng of blood-thirsty Thracians 'mandâro/ sol una voce al ciel per mille bocche,/ gridando: — Mora, mora!' [cried out to the heavens, a thousand voices in unison: Let them die, die!] (V. 9. 725–27) may even hint at Christ's appearance before the crowd for the crucifixion (especially John 19:7).

A more private exploration of religiosity also emerges in *Filli*, particularly through the characters of Clori (Filli) and Celia. As in *Pastor fido*, this takes the form of allusions to confession, penance and absolution.[81] Notably, in the main plot after Niso has finally recognized Clori as his first love (Filli), he acknowledges his betrayal of her fidelity and begs her forgiveness and punishment: 'Errai, misero, errai' [I erred, I erred in my wretchedness] (V. 3. 128). Her response shows her orthodox recognition of her humility, as shepherdess and abandoned lover, and inability to encroach on divine prerogatives:

> CLORI Pastor, s'errasti, il sai;
> sallo Amor, sallo il Cielo:
> ei, che può folgorar, ei ti perdoni. (V. 3. 144–46)

> [Shepherd, you know that you erred, Love and the heavens know too; but let the one who can strike you down forgive you.]

Yet two scenes later, Clori is heroically prepared to assume responsibility for her lover's offence of sacrilege (V. 5). The comedic *balia* figure, Serpilla, closes this episode, though, with the earth-bound perspective that love's power does not extend beyond death. In her view, Niso's 'infidelity' has turned out to be a *felix culpa* ('Felice error'), since he could wash away the blemish ('macchia') with his flowing tears (V. 9. 805).

The secondary plot mixes religious elements with the rhetorical *topoi* of love poetry more ambiguously. For example, Celia's description of the jet of blood that spurted from the wounded Niso to her breast (II. 2. 451–60), which her lover turns into an elaborate conceit of how a man's blood rushes to his heart, may suggest visual images of the crucified Christ. Meanwhile, Aminta's rejoicing at seeing the sun once again, after lying for a symbolic three days in darkness (I. 5. 729–31), is followed by amorous lamentations at not seeing Celia, his 'idolo del sole' [idol of the sun] (I. 4. 644).

Celia's double love allows the introduction of explicitly pagan connotations in the play, and is identified with 'furore' or madness in the *Discorsi*.[82] Since she is unable to imagine any means of absolving her 'mortal error' of loving two shepherds simultaneously (III. 6), Celia attempts suicide, an act that Guarini had defended as noble in tragedy though sinful in Christian religion.[83] The vegetation of 'sterpi' and 'pruni' [thornbushes] (IV. 3. 203; IV. 4. 323) in which her body is later found introduces a non-idyllic pastoral dimension, perhaps with poetic allusions to Dante's wood of suicides. Her torment had been unintentionally aggravated by her confidente, Nerea, who observed that faithless love is a 'spiritel d'inferno' [infernal spirit], that is punished in hell by the 'mostri d'abisso,/ in sembianza de' suoi traditi amanti' [monsters of the abyss in the guise of the betrayed lovers] (II. 2. 308; 316–17). While being restored to life by her own lovers' tears, Celia deliriously (and semi-comically) confuses the surrounding landscape with the Stygian fields of classical hell that she had seen, her lovers with hellish tormentors, and Narete with the aged Charon (IV. 5. 501–21). She herself extravagantly explains her return to life by saying that her soul must have been too horrifying even for hell. Her situation might, however, point more convincingly to the power of love over death (a theme that is developed in a more tragic manner in the main plot), perhaps hinting at and parodying the archetypal pastoral myth of Orpheus and Eurydice.

Celia's horror at her 'infidelity', makes her twin love all the more bizarre and grotesque but, as Bonarelli explains in his *Discorsi*, it is not immoral like the kind proposed in Ovid's *Amores* (II. 10). Unlike the Ovidian narrator, she has no thought of satisfying both lovers (as Serpilla suggested she did), but chooses instead to die. Celia's suicide may be considered a cowardly and imprudent act — which in Aristotle's view made it appropriate for a woman — but it was an understandable if misguided way of ending her torment, and of reacting to her perceived sin, given that she despaired of being able to satisfy her desire (like Phaedra).[84] Thus, Celia remains a tragicomic character, lacking the grander pathos of Clori and some other pastoral suicides. With her conflict resolved, she returns to a decorous feminine modesty:

> SERPILLA Tacque, e chinò le luci
> vergognosette a terra.
> Ma ben per gli occhi al core
> mandò liete e ridenti
> due lagrimette a dire i suoi contenti. (V. 9. 877–81)[85]

[She fell silent and looked down with modest shame; but through her eyes she gladly sent two smiling teardrops to her heart to convey her pleasure.]

To conclude, Celia's 'double love', though somewhat trivialized in the play and the *Discorsi*, challenges conventional Petrarchan views of love and questions the ideological status of pastoral suicides (which Ingegneri had condemned). But most of all, this academic 'case' was used to generate elaborate lyric *concetti* that would produce the novelty and *meraviglia* that was desired by audiences. More generally, the play does suggest some popular Counter-Reformation themes and conventional behavioural ideals, and there is a noticeable reduction of sensuality in the conceits compared to Guarini's model. However, there is less evidence of the latter's moralizing concerns and gestures toward political conformity. Bonarelli tends to avoid direct discussion or staging of problematic political or religious issues, and follows instead Guarini's idea that poetry aims above all to please rather than to teach:

> Il fin del poeta od è il diletto, o non si conseguisce se non col diletto: al diletto due condizioni unitamente si richieggono: il mirabile e'l credibile, perché il credibil senza il mirabile ha del dissipito, il mirabil senza il credibile ha dello stomacoso, l'uno e l'altro congiuntamente del saporito. (*Discorsi*, III, 8, 161)
>
> [The poet either aims to delight, or else he only fulfills his goal through delight. Two conditions together are required to achieve this: the marvellous and the verisimilar, because subjects that are credible but not marvellous are insipid, while those which are marvellous but not credible are nauseating, but with both together they are pleasing to the palate.]

Nonetheless, there is evidence in Bonarelli's *Discorsi* and his dramaturgy that he was not averse to tipping the balance that Guarini proposed between verisimilitude and *meraviglia* in favour of the latter. In this respect, he preluded the artistic licence called for by Marino and his followers.

Further Developments in Seventeenth-Century Pastoral Drama

Changing contexts: Chiabrera and the development of melodramma

A significant number of pastoral plays written after Guarini's *Pastor fido* were, like *Filli*, conceived within academic contexts, as part of a broader experimentation with tragedy and the *tragedia di lieto fine*, for which a variety of solutions were created.[86] Meanwhile, pastoral plays still continued to be produced for courtly or elite performances, both on a private and larger scale, sometimes with a more lyric or comic bias — perhaps depending also on the status of the actors. Such plays could vary considerably in length and complexity of plot, the size of cast, and the degree to which they alluded to the audience. The importance of the context of production to the form of a pastoral play is clearly demonstrated by comparing the two examples by Muzio Manfredi: *La Semiramis, boscareccia* (1594) and *Il Contrasto amoroso, pastorale* (1602, though apparently written in 1591). The *Semiramis* is marked on the title-page as being a work by a writer belonging to academies in Mantua, Parma and Vicenza. The dedicatory letter to the Duke of Parma links it with the author's earlier *Semiramis, tragedia* as well as noting that it was intended for courtly performance. This would explain the use of noble and even divine characters (the mother of Semiramis), an on-stage chorus and one between acts, which closes with a *moresca* [armed dance] and dance to Hymen. The *Contrasto amoroso* is, however, much lighter in tone and lacks a chorus. It is interestingly described in the dedicatory letter as being *pastorale* and therefore different in 'species' and 'manner' from a play that is *boschereccia* (fols A4^{r-v}). In particular, its subject matter is said to be pleasing and decorous for nobleladies, which would make it suitable for its dedicatee, Vittoria Doria Gonzaga, the Genoese wife of Manfredi's patron, Don Ferrante Gonzaga of Guastalla. It not only contains veiled eulogies of the princess and other local ladies, but, as mentioned in chapter 4, p. 106, its nearly exclusively female cast could allow the princess to perform it with her ladies if she so wished (fols A3^r, A5^{r-v}), following an evidently sanctioned practice in courtly society.

The three pastoral plays and 'favolette per musica' [short plays set to music] of Gabriello Chiabrera (1552–1638) further reveal ways in which pastoral drama could be adapted during the early seventeenth century to accommodate audience tastes. He provides an interesting example of the varied experimentation with the genre in his day, so that it further tests generic boundaries — and in different ways from Bonarelli. None of his works can be claimed as truly innovatory or as having a lasting impact on the development of the genre, notwithstanding one critic's assertion to the contrary,[87] though they do show its relationship with the newly emerging form of opera. But the diversity of his production and the author's literary standing justify their mention in an overall assessment of pastoral drama in this period.

Today, Chiabrera is best known for his extensive and varied poetic output, remarkable for its metrical innovations, especially with ancient Greek forms. His general preference for moderate and classicizing styles distinguish him from his more famous contemporary, Giambattista Marino, but secured Chiabrera a longer influence that lasted into the eighteenth century, even after the shift in poetic sensibilities with the Arcadia movement.[88] Chiabrera's activity as a theatre practitioner and dramatist, popular with courtly elites, has only begun to receive greater critical attention relatively recently.[89] Studies have revealed that he worked closely with musicians, painters, and actors during his life in his native Savona and Genoa and beyond. Notably, from the turn of the seventeenth century he was involved in theatrical productions in Florence and Mantua, centres then at the forefront of dramatic experimentation especially with *melodramma*. These experiences left their mark on Chiabrera's dramaturgy. It shows an awareness of new scenographic developments, and the need to respond to audience tastes for drama in which the text was increasingly subordinated to music and the demands of spectacle, as in earlier *intermedi*.[90]

Pieri lists his known dramatic works as including: three tragedies, three *favole pastorali*, seven mythological 'favole "da recitarsi cantando"', the *intermezzi* for Guarini's comedy *Idropica* (performed in Mantua, 1608), and a large number of occasional texts including ballets and 'favolette' to be sung, mostly on mythological and pastoral subjects.[91] Many of these are problematic to date, in terms of composition and performance, unless they are explicitly linked to high-profile courtly occasions. It is likely that, in common with other poets commissioned to produce theatrical pieces, Chiabrera considered most of his dramatic texts to be largely ephemeral and therefore of less serious status. A similar attitude has been noted towards his poetry from the

1590s intended for musical setting.[92] This marks such works off from the same writer's lyric poetry, which was very attentively edited for publication.

All the three surviving regular pastoral dramas by Chiabrera — *La Gelopea*, *Alcippo* and *Meganira* — are termed *favola boschereccia*, and were printed more than once during his lifetime. *Gelopea*, the only one available in a modern edition, seems to have been the first: it appeared in 1603 (Mondovì, Henrietto de Rossi) and was twice reprinted within the next seven years.[93] *Alcippo* was apparently printed in Genoa in 1604, edited by a fellow nobleman of Savona, Pier Girolamo Gentile Ricci, and later appeared in a stylish edition dedicated to Pier Giuseppe Giustiniani in 1614 and in Venice the following year. *Meganira* appeared in a volume of pastoral verse entitled *Alcune poesie boschereccie* (Florence: G. A. Caneo, 1608) and was reprinted with a separate title page in the Venice edition of the *Rime* (1610).[94] The exact dates of composition and performance are more difficult to ascertain, as the plays deliberately lack prologues and no further information is offered in the prefatory material, where given, or in Chiabrera's letters. It has, however, been suggested that *Gelopea* can be identified as the hastily composed 'pastorale' mentioned in a letter of March 1595, and modestly deemed inferior to the two earlier masterpieces of the genre: 'la pastorale fu tumultuosamente composta; né è cosa che si debba vedere dopo molte; e due spetialmente, tanto famose' [the pastoral was composed in a hurry, and is not something that ought to be seen after many famous ones, and two in particular].[95] It was performed in 1603 and 1607 in Sampierdarena, at the aristocratic villa of the dedicatee, Paolo Torriglia, on the Genoese Riviera. This immediately alerts the reader to the possibility of veiled topical allusions, perhaps discernible also in *Alcippo*.[96]

Chiabrera's three pastoral plays are all noticeably on a smaller scale than most of the examples explored so far in this chapter. In common with a few plays that follow Tasso's *Aminta* (Zinano's *Il Caride*, 1590, Torelli's *Galatea*, 1603, and Capponi's *Orsilla*, 1615), they have a simple plot structure with only one set of lovers. There are at most four scenes in every act, and typically only two or three. The cast is very reduced compared to most plays composed after Guarini's *Pastor fido*. Remarkably, Chiabrera does not use a chorus in any of his pastorals, which he explains as being appropriate given the subject matter: 'Ed il Coro rappresentando un popolo, io reputo che non debba luogo avere in azione privata: laonde io mi sono ritenuto di frapporvelo' [and since the Chorus represents a populace, I do not think that it should appear in a private action, and so I have not added one].[97] The choice of this type of action would perhaps account for the absence of a religious or political hierarchy unlike in Guarini's *Pastor fido* or Bonarelli's *Filli*. Authority is rather embodied by private father-figures, and moralistic, pious *sententiae* are liberally sprinkled throughout (as in Barbara Torelli's *Partenia*).

The plays vary considerably in structure, subject matter, and style, which suggests Chiabrera's experimental approach to the genre. In particular, the contemporary, local setting of *Gelopea* immediately sets it apart from *Meganira* and *Alcippo*, which are both set in Arcadia. This explains *Gelopea*'s less evident use of conventional, mythological pastoral elements, though these are limited also in the other two plays — none contain satyrs and other mythological figures, or references to the golden age myth. Some standard pastoral themes are alluded to in *Gelopea* such as an organized hunt (I. 1), and the lover's writing on trees (I. 2). However, the female characters are not presented as typical huntress nymphs (Gelopea is designated as a *pastorella* with a maid) and the male characters are not listed in the cast as shepherds. Rather, the play has a strong comedic emphasis, with its *beffa* and vendetta structure, and urban values.[98] Both lovers for instance appear cross-dressed in order to carry out their revenge following comic (or possibly romance) practices, as opposed to the more erotic pastoral use of this trope in *Alcippo* by the eponymous male protagonist. This perhaps indicates that *Gelopea* reflects documented tastes amongst the Genoese elite for professional actors and comedies.

The somewhat disjointed plot of *Gelopea* starts with Filebo being mutually in love with Gelopea, though it seems they cannot be married, since her wealthy father would disapprove of Filebo's poverty. Meanwhile, the wealthy Berillo is also in love with Gelopea, but despairs of realizing his desires. The complication begins in Act II when an *inganno* is devised by Berillo's friend to set the lovers against each other by stirring up their jealousy, following Corisca's strategy in Guarini's *Pastor fido*. The sly shepherd, Nerino is called upon to tell Filebo of his beloved's secret tryst with a third party in a hayloft. Like Guarini's Mirtillo, the lover is duly inflamed with doubts and desire for revenge (III. 2). Notwithstanding the reasoned scepticism of his sister (Telaira), Filebo decides to go to the barn dressed in female attire to witness and avenge the betrayal, recalling the Polinesso incident in Ariosto's *Furioso*.[99] In Act IV, Gelopea finally appears on stage, devastated by the (false) news of her lover's supposed desire only for her dowry and secret assignation. Despite the dictates of decorum and the fact that it is night-time — something very unusual for pastoral drama but found in comedies such as Machiavelli's *Mandragola*, Ruzante's *La Moscheta*, and later in Flaminio Scala's scenarios and Giovan Battista Andreini's pastoral tragicomedy *Lelio bandito* — she too decides to go to the barn, dressed as a man, to verify the truth, following the model of comic heroines like Fulvia in Bibbiena's *Calandria*.

Act V takes place mostly outside the barn, presumably partly constructed at one side of the stage, from where the hidden Gelopea sees the arrival of the disguised Filebo. Both lovers are at this point planning revenge against their supposed rivals, which very nearly results in death. Fortunately, Gelopea's decision to visit Telaira and explain to her the plan to set alight the hay, and with it Filebo's lover, means that the tragedy can be averted. Telaira attributes this to divine intervention (V. 4, p. 291), a sentiment echoed by her brother, who asserts that God will look after any lover who loves 'drittamente' [properly] (V. 5, p. 296). No further justification or elaboration of a providential underpinning is given to this play. It ends rather abruptly with a swift explanation of the confusion and lies, and Telaira urges the lovers to plead for their apparently divinely sanctioned marriage to Gelopea's father. As in Chiabrera's other two pastorals (following *Aminta*), there is no formal union of the lovers or punishment of the plotters.

Various questions are left unresolved at the end: is the failed *inganno* to be interpreted as a sign of the failure of human ingenuity in the face of divine providence? Or as the victory of chaste love over sexual jealousy, as dramatized in the prologue to the pastoral drama of Chiabrera's friend Gentile Ricci amongst others? Or is it supposed to represent Filebo's disinterested pastoral love for Gelopea triumphing over secular or courtly values (represented by Berillo)? It is unclear if any or all of these underlying messages is intended, but the play evidently shows a preoccupation with moral concerns, which became increasingly important in Chiabrera's verse and his self-representation.[100] In particular, striking emphasis is given in *Gelopea* to the popular baroque theme of anxiety about wealth and social status, understood both as a social and a moral problem. Unlike many earlier Ferrarese and courtly plays, which positively contrast wealthy shepherds to their baser herdsmen, a more critical and unusually realistic dimension is introduced through Nerino. This shepherd, despite his saintly appearances, is said to be ready to commit any crime for money (II. 2, p. 239), like many an unscrupulous comic servant or trickster. However, he himself explains this attitude as the consequence of real poverty and drudgery, which alienate him from the beauties of nature and heaven, and by his hope to avoid famine that year (II. 3, p. 243). He also pragmatically considers that Gelopea will be better off not making this match, since earthly happiness is 'Sol per li possessor delle ricchezze' [only for those who possess wealth] (II. 4, p. 246).

Gelopea also seems to censure the excessive jealousy of the principal lovers, who both risk their honour in different ways in order to exact revenge and take justice into their own hands, and will not be dissuaded by their prudent (female) counsellors. Conflict especially over love affairs was common amongst the quarrelsome nobility in Chiabrera's society, despite severe restrictions on private feuds in Italy following their condemnation by the Council of Trent in 1563. Indeed, the poet had himself been banished from Savona from 1581–88 for having killed a gentleman in a duel.[101] The theme of honour and revenge killings, debated at one point by Guarini's faithful shepherd (*Pastor fido*, III. 8. 45–120), is found also in the *antefatto* of *Meganira* and alluded to in *Alcippo*. It becomes a prominent theme in other pastoral plays from this time too, as in Giovan Battista Andreini's *Lelio bandito* and Toniani's *Floriano il fido*, showing how the earlier emphasis on suicide and self-sacrifice could give way to more aggressive feelings.

Such feelings are particularly striking when expressed by a female protagonist:

> GELOPEA   Non ha loco clemenza
> Nel vendicar Amore;
> Non ti doglia che mora
> Una donna impudica. (V. 3, p. 289)

> [There is no space for mercy in avenging Love: do not be sorry that an unchaste woman will die.]

This statement draws attention to another of Chiabrera's departures from pastoral conventions in this play: namely, in his representation of female characters. Gelopea is no recalcitrant huntress nymph or passive victim to love. Rather, she takes on a semi-heroic or comedic agency, which Vazzoler has tentatively linked with the intention that this part be played by Isabella Andreini, who was noted for her impersonation of masculine roles.[102] However, Gelopea's destructive urges are tempered by a certain amount of comic irony, particularly when she fails to recognize her lover wearing his sister's dress (V. 3) which gives her a tragicomic, though not strictly pastoral, quality. By contrast, the heroine of *Meganira* is represented throughout the staged action as maintaining conventional feminine decorum. Although she had acted daringly beforehand by venturing alone to seek out her lover in Arcadia, she styles herself humbly by the closing scene as 'ancella' [handmaiden] (V. 2, p. 211) to her future father-in-law. Similarly, in *Alcippo* the recalcitrant nymph Clori finally submits meekly to the wish of two authoritative elders for her to marry her lover (Alcippo). Such representations would reflect the more conventional pastoral plots and characters in these two plays.

The simple plot of *Meganira* follows the vicissitudes of the eponymous nymph and her beloved Alcippo and draws noticeably on scenarios from Tasso's *Aminta*, though the overall complication is different. It starts with Meganira having left her homeland secretly after hearing nothing from her beloved Alcippo for over a year since they exchanged promises. She has come to seek him in Arcadia on the occasion of the annual games, but the dictates of feminine modesty make it difficult for her to appear openly in case her brother (Logisto) sees her. Tassian echoes are evident in Alcippo's false inference that he has mistakenly shot the hidden Meganira with a (magic) arrow, after finding her veil in a thicket and seeing blood on the ground (IV. 2) — a situation that also recalls the myth of Cefalo, and Dorinda in *Pastor fido*. Like Tasso's Aminta, Alcippo wants to commmit suicide by jumping off a cliff, then by wounding his breast, but is prevented just in time by Meganira herself. Notably, this encounter takes place on stage rather than being reported as in *Aminta*, which is indicative of Chiabrera's dramaturgical preferences. His lovers also appear together at the end in a scene where Alcippo's father consents to their marriage (V. 1). Some further variation to Tasso's model is provided by two comparatively brief narrated *antefatti* — of the tragic origins of the annual games of Monte Caffio (I. 2); and Logisto's romantic dalliance with an enchantress (III. 1) — which seem to have been included primarily to produce novelty, marvel and horror.

Chiabrera's *Alcippo* draws more noticeably on the other canonical pastoral model, Guarini's *Pastor fido*, with its legal problems and resolution through the recognition of a lost son. The plot is however structured around the theme of persuasion of a chaste nymph (Clori) to love. It is complicated by the fact that her supposed female friend Megilla is in fact a cross-dressed shepherd (Alcippo) secretly in love with Clori (revealed I. 2), following the example of Guarini's Mirtillo, and Jupiter in Groto's *Calisto*. Alcippo rouses suspicion on refusing to bathe with the nymphs after a hunt (obviously for different reasons from Ovid's Callisto) and is described as being literally exposed and nearly killed by them. However, the nymphs appeal to two venerable legislators, Tirsi and Montano, to have Alcippo put to death according to an Arcadian law. The debate that ensues (Acts III-V) between the elders as to how to proceed, and whether to show exemplary justice or mercy, shows a clear debt to Guarini. So too do the circumstantial evidence and recognition tokens used to reveal that Alcippo is Tirsi's son, believed drowned in infancy. Tirsi's conflict of interests between his duty as legislator and natural affection towards his son is only resolved by persuading Clori to pardon Alcippo's offence and marry him, so that *her* pleas allow the law to be amended.[103] As with *Meganira*, there is little direct interaction between the lovers themselves at the end, while the father-figures play a vital mediating role.

Chiabrera's three pastoral plays therefore variously adapt the canonical models of pastoral drama, as well as integrating some comic *topoi*. They place an emphasis on moral concerns associated with the genre and the pastoral mode generally and, perhaps consequently, provide little space for sensuality or the enjoyment of pastoral pleasures. The later two Arcadian plays also seem to present few opportunities for lively stage action. They are all distinguished to some extent, though, by their inclusion of lyrical passages. *Meganira* in particular makes uncommon use of interspersed rhymes. Chiabrera's inclusion of such set pieces, and even auto-citation in the opening scene of *Gelopea* (as in *Aminta*, I. 1), provided an opportunity to showcase his expertise in composing pastoral verse, which was popular also with musicians.[104] While Chiabrera wrote a tragedy (*Angelica in Ebuda*, 1610) and short 'favolette' for musical setting, his lack of dramaturgical explanation for his pastoral plays makes it unclear whether these were meant to be sung even in part. In the dedicatory letter to *Meganira*, where he raises the much debated question about whether drama should be in verse or prose, Chiabrera only notes impartially that, while many consider verse less realistic, it provides 'soavità e forza' [sweetness and force] as well as corresponding 'al debito delle Scene' [to the demands of the stage]. He concludes that this 'favoletta' [*sic*] has been composed 'primieramente perchè voi vi dilettate nella poesia' [above all so that you gain enjoyment from the poetry].[105]

Chiabrera's most high-profile theatrical work, which officially marked the start of his career as a dramatist, is a short mythological pastoral play, *Il Rapimento di Cefalo* [*The abduction of Cephalus*]. This was entirely set to music (now nearly all lost), mostly by the famous court composer in Florence, Giulio Caccini. It was performed 9 October 1600 in the main hall (Salone grande) of the Uffizi, where it topped the bill of the magnificent festivities programmed for the wedding of Maria de' Medici and Henry IV of France. However, this event is today eclipsed in theatre history by the much smaller-scale performance three days earlier of the first surviving opera, also on a mythological pastoral subject: Ottavio Rinuccini's *Euridice* set to music by Jacopo Peri with Caccini.[106] Chiabrera's 'rappresentazione' appears in five acts without scene breaks and tells the extremely simple tale of the love of the goddess Aurora (Dawn), for the hunter Cefalo (Cephalus), whom she subsequently snatches up to heaven. Almost as in a series of tableaux, various deities singly and in chorus reveal the havoc that has been generated within the universe, because of the goddess's descent to earth to seek out her beloved. Order is only finally restored after Jove himself acknowledges the omnipotence of the god of Love, who then enables Aurora to carry Cefalo away from his preferred earthly love (an unseen nymph). This slender and linear plot therefore significantly reverses the Ovidian version (*Metamorphoses* VII), by having Cefalo choose divine love over that for his wife (Procris), which now produces the happy ending appropriate to the royal wedding, an association highlighted especially in the prologue and 'licenza'.

Although the play is limited in poetic invention and dramatic interaction between the characters, the verse style is carefully crafted for musical setting. Irregular mixed lines with interspersed rhymes are used for the recitative, while strophic sections are used for the prologue, some of the many choruses, and the epilogue by Fame. Poesia [Poetry], who delivers the prologue, highlights the importance of the poetic diction from the start, since it is this that will move the affections and inspire the audience. This point brings to mind the heated discussions, especially from the 1580s, on the complex aesthetic construction of tragedy and to some extent on its relationship with music within the Alterati academy of Florence, of which Chiabrera became a member (as did Ottavio Rinuccini in 1586).[107]

The 'favola' of *Cefalo* is mentioned very little in the official Florentine account of the performance by Michelangelo Buonarroti the younger, except to stress its morality and decorum. In his view, the careful crafting of choice words and exquisitely varied music, perfectly adapted for the characters and conceits, 'ne purgava le menti degli uditori, traendoli a giustizia e a dirittura di vero amore' [purged the minds of the listeners, moving them to justice and even true love].[108] The bulk of the description instead focuses on the extremely elaborate costumes, stage sets, and, above all, the marvellous machines that were created for the performance by the virtuoso stage engineer, Bernardo Buontalenti. These transferred the action from one magnificent set to the next: from Mount Helicon (the prologue), to varied pastoral settings, a seascape (Act II), and celestial spheres, using a variety of cloud machines.[109]

Cefalo therefore shows how a pastoral drama (understood in the loosest sense) could be adapted to integrate the most innovative scenotechnic practices, perhaps influenced by the celebrated 1598 performance of Guarini's *Pastor fido* in Mantua (see Chapter 6). Chiabrera's text however clearly appears subordinated to the spectacle and music, following the well-established pattern of large-scale *intermedi* and already indicated by the way that Guarini conceived his *Gioco della cieca* — with the dance steps being composed first, then the music and finally the poetry, which necessitated its unusual metrical structure.[110] Private accounts of the performance, however, suggest that *Cefalo* failed to fulfil the promise suggested by the novelty of musical recitative on this scale: some considered the style tedious, and there were probably difficulties with audibility both for the audience and between the singers and instrumentalists. There also seem to have been some failures with the machines, owing to insufficient rehearsal and poor direction.[111] These problems perhaps partly influenced the choice to return to the earlier formula of a comedy with magnificent *intermedii* in the next cycle of spectacular entertainments in Florence, as Carter suggests.[112] Rinuccini and Peri's much simpler pastoral *melodramma*, *Euridice*, this time in six scenes and requiring only one other set besides the pastoral one, evidently also suffered from under-rehearsal. But it was this model of music drama, which both realized classicizing intellectual experimentation and appealed to private aristocratic tastes, that was taken up by Claudio Monteverdi in Mantua (with his *Orfeo*, 1607) and provided the basis for the emerging genre of opera.[113]

Pastoral drama and the commedia dell'arte

As well as being developed in ways that suited elite tastes for private or public spectacle, pastoral drama was rapidly appropriated and popularized by professional *comici*. Pastoral eclogues and rustic plays had been of course been performed since the early sixteenth century by professional and semi-professional actors like Ruzante (Angelo Beolco), Niccolò Campani ('Lo Strascino') and Sebastiano Clavignano da Montefalco (see Chapter 2). Pastoral ingredients apparently continued to be used in the scenarios of more formally constituted acting companies, and were particularly developed with the rise of actresses, since they could allow performances with a greater emotional range, with more pathos and even tragic tones. Probably for this reason, some of the earliest actresses even specialized in pastoral roles from 1567. Vincenza Armani (d. 1569), was celebrated for her mask as Clori, while her slightly younger rival, Isabella Andreini, adopted the pastoral persona of Filli as part of her repertoire, and was mourned in death under this name in a pastoral elegy (1607) by her husband, Francesco.[114] It is suggestive that the earliest and only published collection of scenarios by Flaminio Scala (*Il teatro delle favole rappresentative, overo la Ricreatione comica, boscareccia, e tragica*, 1611) explicitly signals the presence of pastoral elements in the subtitle. Only one of the fifty scenarios presented is in fact termed 'pastorale' (*L'Arbore incantato* [The Enchanted Tree], XLIX), but several others contain pastoral elements such as an Arcadian setting, magical transformations, a powerful magician, and comic rustics.[115] Eight pastoral scenarios also appear amongst the one hundred and three in the two-part manuscript collection *Della scena de' sogetti comici* by Basilio Locatelli in the Biblioteca Casanatense, Rome (dated 1618, 1622).[116]

Professional troupes frequently performed regular scripted pastoral plays too. As we have seen, Tasso's *Aminta* may have been performed by the Gelosi in 1573 and was popular with *arte* performers subsequently. Despite Guarini's scornful attitude towards professionals, his play was quickly added to their repertoire — perhaps in part because of his undeclared use of their formulae.[117] Given the longstanding and complex interaction between professional and literary forms of pastoral drama, which still merits further exploration besides the valuable studies by Andrews, Henke, Pieri and Vazzoler, it is no surprise that some *comici* began to integrate their experience of using pastoral elements in performance into dramatic compositions for reading audiences. Their 'irregular' pastoral or rustic drama (eclogues and comedies) appeared in print before the publication of Beccari's *Sacrificio* (1555) and continued to be composed into the late seventeenth century, long after the consolidation of the regular genre. For instance, Calmo's popular pastoral eclogues (*Giocose moderne et facetissime egloghe pastorali* [Playful, modern and most witty pastoral eclogues], Venezia, 1553) were followed by ones by M. Flaminio Guarniero da Osimo (*Il Mago*, and *Nova Arcadia*, 1569). The famous Neapolitan comic actor, Silvio Fiorillo known as 'Capitan Mattamoros' also wrote a three-act, comic pastoral eclogue in Tuscan and Neapolitan in *terza rima* (*L'Amor giusto*, Naples 1604; 1625), as well as *La Ghirlanda Pastorale* [The Pastoral Garland] (1609).[118] Francesco Andreini published two pastoral 'egloghe', entitled *L'alterezza di Narciso* [The Pride of Narcissus] and *L'Ingannata Proserpina* [Proserpina Deceived] (both 1611), as well as including pastoral elements in his two volumes of short comic dialogues *Bravure del Capitan Spavento* (printed 1607 and 1618).

At the same time, some actor-dramatists turned their hand to 'regular' pastoral drama, as it was becoming consolidated as a genre. *La Fiammella, pastorale* (printed and performed in Paris, 1584), by the Veronese actor Bartolomeo de' Rossi, represents an early five-act pastoral play, though it still contains many obvious *arte* features, including comic masks (as in Pasqualigo's *Gl'Intricati*, see pp. 32, 34), and mixes mythological gods, furies, a magician, and allegorical personifications alongside the pastoral characters. Isabella Andreini perhaps demonstrates the most ambitious early attempt of a professional to produce a 'literary' pastoral play (*Mirtilla*, 1588; see chapter 4), though this evidently also draws in part on her practical experience. On the other hand, amateur dramatists also experimented with professional type pastoral drama, such as Ercole Cimilotti (*I falsi dei, favola pastorale piacevolissima* [The False Gods, a most delightful pastoral play], 1614 [1599?], in three acts) and Lodovico Riccato (*I Pazzi amanti, comedia pastorale*, 1613).

Probably the most famous and sustained attempt to meld the two traditions is found in the work of Isabella's eldest son, Giovan Battista (Giovambattista) Andreini (1576–1654). Like his parents he sought to consolidate his professional reputation through aristocratic patronage, notably by Duke Vincenzo Gonzaga, the Medici and Louis XIII of France, as well as through academic recognition by the Spensierati in Florence.[119] He was a prolific dramaturge: besides composing critical works defending the acting profession, his oeuvre comprises comedies, tragedies, sacred plays and others of mixed genres. This last category includes two *tragicomedie boschereccie*, *Lelio bandito* (1620; 1624) and *La Rosella* (1632); and *Ismenia, opera reale e pastorale* (1639), which mixes pastoral with magical romance elements and *commedia dell'arte* masks. Many of his other plays involve broadly pastoral settings, which allow for a more pleasing and varied stage-set and action, ranging from wild, realistic forests to fantastical realms and cultivated gardens, though they do not necessarily imply the usually associated pastoral themes. For instance, Andreini's *La Turca, comedia boschereccia e marittima* [*The Turkish Woman, a pastoral and marine comedy*] (Casale 1611; revised Venice 1620), set on the island of Tabarca, is only superficially pastoral or piscatorial. Most of the main characters should be classed as comic or possibly romance types. A few minor parts are however allocated to the native islanders, who are split between 'isolani' (fishermen dwelling on the coast) and 'pastori' (shepherds living in the mountainous mainland). At one point a small group of shepherds perform a dance with some shepherdesses (II. 7–8), and in the last act they are called upon to arm against the Turks who have invaded the island.

The most experimental combination with mixing pastoral forms is probably Andreini's *La Centaura, suggetto diviso in commedia, pastorale e tragedia* [*The Centaur Wife, a play in comic, pastoral and tragic parts*] (Paris, 1622; Venice, 1633), whose three acts — successively comic, pastoral, and tragic — unfold against the simultaneously urban and pastoral setting of the island Crete, marking something of a self-conscious challenge to the Aristotelian unity of place. However, the author claims that his harmonious balance of different genres within this single hybrid work, which also includes musical episodes, is calculated to provide the variety and *meraviglia* that will appeal to modern audiences.[120]

A short exploration of *Lelio bandito, tragicomedia boschereccia* must suffice here to indicate some of the changes to conventional pastoral drama introduced by Andreini, especially given the scarce availability of his plays. The play has little in the way of classic pastoral features and, instead, oscillates between the heroic/romance and the comic/rustic modes. The action takes place deep within a mountainous forest in the Abruzzi, and, rather like the forest of Arden in Shakespeare's *As You Like It*, features a large, mixed cast of characters. These include the exiled Florentine nobleman, Lelio, with his pedant Sofistico and motley group of outlaws (Farinelli). The protagonist is seeking his political rival (Orazio Gelieri) who had previously kidnapped and presumably defiled his sister, but had thereafter evaded Lelio's attempts to avenge his honour. Also living in the forest are a vulgar Tuscan *carbonaro* [charcoal burner] with his beautiful adoptive daughter, who turns out to be Lelio's abandoned sister in disguise. Meanwhile, Lelio's betrothed (Doralice) has come to seek him out, disguised in male attire as Teodoro. This is only discovered by Lelio after he has nearly killed her for supposedly betraying him (III. 10), after which the couple are reconciled.

The main complication to the plot comes from the order by the Viceroy of Naples that the bandits be extirpated by General Riniero (actually another Florentine in disguise). Events take a surprising turn when Riniero's captain comes to court the *carbonaro*'s daughter on his superior's behalf, and on finding out her story reveals himself to be the now repentant Gelieri (V. 3). He requests and gains forgiveness from Lelio's sister, who agrees to marry him (V. 4), and then in a dramatic scene is finally pardoned by Lelio himself (V. 7). A full conclusion is only reached, however, after Riniero has seized Lelio and his family and men in a nocturnal ambush, after which Teodoro/Doralice is discovered as being Riniero's daughter and the 'bandits' are pardoned (V. 10).

The play thus initially proposes a courtly code of honour which demands vendetta, though when Florinda and especially Lelio are given the opportunity to exact revenge upon Gelieri, they are ultimately swayed by nobler, Christian ideals of forgiveness and peace. Such elevated sentiments contrast with the baser instincts of the buffoon Venturino, the *commedia dell'arte* pedant, and to some extent the other bandits and the rustic *carbonaro* (Sandrino). These characters also provide a farsical and sometimes crude linguistic counterpoint to the 'heroic' characters' Tuscan idiom. The fact that this tragicomedy appears in prose — a new development from around 1600 — allows the dramatist great linguistic flexibility.[121] No fewer than nine regional idioms are showcased in the play, and the stylistic register is equally varied. This pastoral drama therefore has almost nothing in common with the mythological, courtly type, and exemplifies a more popular romance/comic kind on the Spanish model, that would find favour with bourgeois audiences.[122] To some extent it still uses the pastoral mode to provide dramatic variety, and to explore sentimental and moralizing themes such as those of (self) sacrifice, and forgiveness in order to restore harmony in the family and society. However, the promise of achieving this is ultimately linked to the prospect of the characters leaving behind the unruly forest and regaining peace in the urban civilization of Florence.

Concluding Thoughts

This exploration of the various tendencies within pastoral drama in the seventeenth century largely supports, though qualifies, Pieri's important argument that the difficult synthesis between neo-classical dramaturgy and more heterogeneous performance (and compositional) modes, achieved especially by Ferrarese dramatists from around 1550 to 1590, did not hold for long (see Chapter 6, n. 13). With the debates still going on over Guarini's *Pastor fido*, no subsequent dramatist engaged to the same degree in formulating a theoretical model to justify their dramaturgical choices or promote their innovations. However, this was far from the end of the pastoral drama's flowering in practice, despite what some accounts of the genre have suggested. After the efforts to consolidate its status from the 1580s-90s as being equal to, yet different from, tragedy and comedy, and more 'modern' than these, dramatists were able to take pastoral drama in increasingly diverse directions, responding to innovations within dramatic culture and broader social and cultural changes. Certain later examples, such as Bonarelli's *Filli di Sciro*, demonstrate significant structural and thematic developments to the genre in this period. However, the addition of music throughout or of recognizable *commedia dell'arte* topoi ultimately stretched the pastoral drama beyond even the loosely defined forms established over the course of the late sixteenth century.

Many of the significant changes within regular pastoral drama in the seventeenth century are attributable to its increased popularization on stage and especially in print following the enormous success of Tasso and Guarini's examples. This meant that, as with vernacular erudite comedies earlier, pastoral drama became more widely available outside its original domain of the courts. Aspiring dramatists of lower social origins would have been attracted to experiment with the genre given its association with exclusive courtly settings, while its highly imitative and often formulaic nature made it accessible even to those without an elite education. Furthermore, the ambiguous degree of verisimilitude of pastoral drama made it a graceful medium for the indirect flattery of friends and existing or would-be patrons, and in some cases to critique covertly more problematic aspects of reality, as had been possible in Petrarchist poetry. The genre's appeal would have been increased by the fact that it could, more easily than tragedy and comedy, integrate other fast-developing forms of spectacle such as dance, music and stage-engineering that were becoming increasingly popular with audiences. It could also be tailored to a variety of performance contexts that had become established in practice, ranging in scale from elaborate court theatre-sets to garden performances or private stagings by nobles and academicians, besides being read aloud as closet drama. Meanwhile, the rapidly expanding readership of pastoral drama, also resulted in more 'literary' plays, designed to display a writer's lyric style, or skilful control of complex plots on the model of the prose romance that was becoming prominent around this time.

Even so, regular pastoral drama continued to be written in academic and elite contexts at least until the late seventeenth century in Italy and elsewhere in Europe. To some extent this flexible form and the related tragicomedy continued to prove useful in testing out new theories on tragedy and mixed genres, as well as for reinterpretations of ancient dramaturgy and experimentation with music drama. Other practitioners chose a more conservative and rarified model of pastoral drama, emphasizing its mythological associations, which added to the possibilities for aristocratic eulogy. Arguably, the last noteworthy examples were written within the Roman Academy of Arcadia (founded in 1690), which grew out of the academy that had formed round Queen Christina of Sweden in Rome (d. 1689). According to anecdote, the group's name arose from the casual remark of one member that they had 'renewed Arcadia' through their poetic endeavours.[123] Though their views were not entirely unanimous, they broadly sought to restore classical ideals of poetic purity, simplicity, and morality, in opposition to what was perceived as baroque excess, by adopting a mixture of archaizing and more modernizing approaches. On the one hand they sought to re-establish earlier didactic conceptions of public literature observing exemplary models; on the other, some tried to claim possibilities for autonomous imaginative freedom. The pastoral idiom once again proved open enough to accommodate conflicting views on poetry and even cultural outlooks.

Pastoral works of various kinds were produced in the context of Arcadia, including plays which typically served celebratory purposes. One of the most famous is Alessandro Guidi's *Endimione, favola boschereccia* (1692), first conceived in 1688 as a tribute to Queen Christina and performed in the academy in 1691, apparently with additions that she had suggested. It was even used by another of the leading academicians (Gianvincenzo Gravina), as an example of the poetic ideals of Arcadia, despite still showing traces of 'baroque' elements, such as the preference for mythological subjects and the theme of transience of human affairs.[124] The five-act play partly recalls Chiabrera's *Cefalo* in representing the simple myth of the love between a powerful goddess (Cintia, or Diana) and a mortal shepherd (Endimione, or Endymion), and thus the conflict between divine and earthly love. However, Guidi alters the usual tale of Diana's desire for the sleeping Endimione so that the mortal man now adores the goddess, a common trope in courtly tributes to a female patron. After initially spurning him, she is vanquished by Amore's deceptive tale of the shepherd being wounded and falls in love, drawing up her beloved to heaven. The play is on a very small scale, featuring only the two lovers and the god Amore, with a chorus of nymphs and one of shepherds. The influence of Tasso's *Aminta* is evident at various levels of the play: in the presentation of the characters to some extent, in the account of the false news of Endimione's wound, but especially in the style, though Guidi uses a greater variety of mixed lines with rhymes, following earlier Seicento patterns. Yet the overall result is rather stilted and one-dimensional.

The taste for this kind of drama persisted in Europe as long as the court system and academies that patronized it survived. Its themes and conventions are more familiar today though from pastoral verse and prose, song, and the visual arts. These continued well into the eighteenth century to explore sentiments of love or personal grief using pastoral names and disguises set against idyllic backgrounds. So while being recognizably 'literary' or artificial, and redolent of elite culture, this mode could allow the author to focus on the inner, imaginative experience, free from temporal limitations and the constraints of 'reality' as presented by social obligations. For this reason, such representations of lamenting or amorous swains and their shepherdesses have had a lasting and deeply entrenched presence in European culture. Regular pastoral drama could appeal to similar emotions and similarly steer a precarious course between conflicting idealizing and realistic/satiric modes, between ancient and modern forms, and high and low styles. Yet it is also noteworthy for marking an important transitional phase in theatre history, by enabling creative experimentation and initiating the questioning of neo-classical dramatic rules. Through its challenge to genre boundaries in the contemporary canon, sanctioned above all by popular appeal and in part by theoretical claims, this essentially hybrid genre may be seen to prepare the way for 'modern' mixed forms, like opera, that could respond more freely still to the demand for new kinds of theatre.

Notes to Chapter 7

1. Zuccolo, fols 10^v, 27^r; Ingegneri, *Della poesia rappresentativa*, pp. 4, 25.
2. See for example Franca Angelini, 'Il *Pastor fido* di Battista Guarini', in *Letteratura italiana*, ed. by Alberto Asor Rosa, *Le Opere*, II: *Dal Cinquecento al Settecento* (Turin: Einaudi, 1993), 705–24 (p. 707); Marzia Pieri, *La Scena boschereccia*, p. 174; Antonio Belloni, *Il Seicento* (Milan: Vallardi, 1952), p. 392. Though for a contrasting view of pastoral drama's continuing development, see Cesare Molinari, *Le nozze degli dèi, un saggio sul grande spettacolo italiano nel Seicento* (Rome: Bulzoni, 1968), p. 120.
3. See Domenico Sella, *Italy in the Seventeenth Century* (London: Longman, 1997), pp. 188–212. For some seminal negative views of poetry from this period, see the Arcadian Gianvincenzo Gravina, who explicitly expressed distaste for modern pastoral drama, *Della Ragion Poetica, libri 2*, in *Scritti*

critici e teorici, ed. by Amedeo Quondam (Rome: Laterza, 1973), II, XXII, 318; Francesco De Sanctis, *Storia della letteratura italiana*, ed. by Benedetto Croce, 2 vols (Bari: Laterza, 1949), II, 181–219; and Benedetto Croce, *Storia dell'età barocca in italia*, 2nd edn (Bari: Laterza, 1946), pp. 22–40.

4. For a more nuanced and revisionist vew, see for example, Alberto Asor Rosa, *Il Seicento, La nuova scienza e la crisi del Barocco* (Bari: Laterza, 1974), pp. 3–10, 15–18, 30–36; Roberto Alonge, 'Letteratura e spettacolo nel Seicento', in *Storia della società italiana*, ed. by Giovanni Cherubini and others, 25 vols (Milan: Teti, 1981–90), XI: *La Controriforma e il Seicento* (1989), 463–85 (on theatre, pp. 475–85); Andrea Battistini, *Il Barocco, cultura, miti, immagini* (Rome: Salerno, 2000).

5. See Pieri, *Scena boscherecchia*, pp. 169–74; on pastoral performances in southern Italy, see Luigi Ammirati, *Una serata di Gala a Nola nel '500. La prima rappresentazione del 'Pastor Fido' con il "Prologo" di G.B. Marino*, intro. by Luigi Vecchione (Basilicata-Nola: Opinione, 1962), pp. 9–11; on Dalmatia, Ivano Cavallini, 'Le accademie venete del cinquecento: la musica nel teatro e nell'attività speculativa', in *I Due volti di Nettuno. Studi su teatro e musica a Venezia e in Dalmazia dal Cinquecento al Settecento* (Lucca: Libreria musicale italiana, 1994), pp. 25–44 (p. 29); on Crete, see Bancroft-Marcus. Nearly all of the many pastoral plays I have found published in Naples are dated after 1599 when Guarini's *Pastor fido* was first performed in southern Italy; exceptions are Carlo Noci, *Cintia* (1596) and two mythological tragicomedies by Anello Paulilli from 1566 (see Chapter 5, n. 12).

6. 213 academies of various kinds were established in Italy in the period 1550–1600, with at least 568 more created in the following century, see Amedeo Quondam, 'L'Accademia', in *Letteratura italiana*, I: *Il Letterato e le istituzioni*, ed. by Alberto Asor Rosa (Turin: Einaudi, 1982), 823–98 (p. 872). On changes in material conditions of culture, Jon R. Snyder, '*Mare magnum*: the arts in the early modern age', *Early Modern Italy, 1550–1796*, ed. by John A. Marino (Oxford: Oxford University Press, 2002), pp. 143–65 (pp. 157–60).

7. *Filli di Sciro* appears in the Ricciardi series of La Letteratura italiana, Storia e testi (*Il Teatro del Seicento*, 39, ed. by Luigi Fassò (Milan, 1956), pp. 325–461). All references to this edition.

8. *Compendio*, p. 287.

9. For other close imitations of *Pastor fido*, see Rossi, pp. 252–57; and Belloni, pp. 393–95, 399.

10. See also the dedicatory letter of Cesana's *La Prova amorosa*, which suggests the political utility for rulers of learning of pastoral loves. The question of free will is raised by the priest in Campiglia's *Flori*, I. 2. 128–33 (see the edition by Cox and Sampson, p. 18).

11. See Louise George Clubb, 'Fate is for Gentiles: The Disclaimer in Baroque Tragedy', in *Italian Drama*, pp. 231–47.

12. Guarini, *Compendio*, pp. 244–45; Ingegneri, *Della poesia*, p. 7. On the prevailing hedonistic view of literature, see Franco Croce, 'Critica e trattatistica del barocco', in *Storia della letteratura italiana. Il Seicento*, ed. by Emilio Cecchi and Natalino Sapegno (Milan: Garzanti, 1988), pp. 495–547 (pp. 497, 505–06).

13. Ariani, 'Introduzione', pp. LXII–LXVIII. Though on the rise of seventeenth-century Italian tragedy with a strong religious dimension, see Alonge, pp. 476–77.

14. Fischiata, XXXIII, line 9, in *La Murtoleide, Fischiate del Cavalier Marino* (Frankfurt [actually Italy]: Giovanni Beyer, 1626), p. 39. For Tasso's view on the necessity of 'maraviglia' in poetry, though combined with verisimilitude, see *DAP*, I, 7–10.

15. On *concettismo*, a key feature linking the various strands of Italian poetry in the early seventeenth century from Marino to Chiabrera, and also poetry in France, England and Spain, see Claudio Varese, 'Teatro, prosa, poesia', in Cecchi and Sapegno, pp. 551–994 (p. 792). For the more moralizing and heroic style practised at the same time by lyric poets like Fulvio Testi, see Marcello Turchi, 'Introduzione' to his edition of *Opere di Gabriello Chiabrera e lirici del classicismo barocco*, 2nd edn (Turin: UTET, 1974), pp. 9–63 (pp. 31–38).

16. *Della poesia*, p. 5. For below, see Guarini, *Compendio*, p. 287–88; Henke, *Pastoral Transformations*, pp. 124–29 (mixed affective responses); Norbert Jonard, 'Le Baroquisme du *Pastor fido*', *Studi secenteschi*, 10 (1969), 3–18 (pp. 6–8).

17. *Compendio*, pp. 248–55; Gianfranco Folena, 'La mistione tragicomica e la metamorfosi dello stile nella poetica del Guarini', in *La Critica stilistica e il Barocco letterario* (Florence: Le Monnier, 1958), 344–49 (pp. 346–47); and Claude V. Palisca, 'The Alterati of Florence, Pioneers in the Theory of Dramatic Music', in *New Looks at Italian Opera: Essays in Honor of Donald J. Grout*, ed. with intro. by William W. Austin (Ithaca: Cornell University Press, 1968), pp. 9–38.

18. See Elisabetta Selmi, 'L'Autore e l'Opera', in her edition of Battista Guarini, *Il Pastor fido* (Venice: Marsilio, 1999), pp. 25–74 (pp. 27–28).
19. Malacreta, *Considerazioni*, p. 101, see also pp. 116–17; Guarini, *Compendio*, pp. 248–55; also Beni, *Risposta*, p. 140.
20. Zuccolo, fol. 8^r; see also fols 17^v–18^r.
21. Bonarelli, *Discorsi in difesa del doppio amore della sua Celia* [Discourses in defence of the double love of his Celia], I, 3, 149 (argument for unrestricted imaginative freedom in poetic invention); I, 8, 161 (for a more restrictive view of good poetry). The *Discorsi* are published in Guidubaldo Bonarelli, *Filli di Sciro, Discorsi e appendice*, ed. by Giovanni Gambarin (Bari: Laterza, 1941), pp. 139–248; all references to this edition.
22. Heliodorus' romance influenced the story of Clorinda in *Liberata*, XII; for an analysis of Tasso's complex rewriting and Christianizing of the Greek text, see Walter Stephens, 'Tasso's Heliodorus and the World of Romance', in *The Search for the Ancient Novel*, ed. by James Tatum (Baltimore: Johns Hopkins Press, 1994), pp. 67–87. On Guarini and Heliodorus, see Selmi, *'Classici' e Moderni*, pp. 96–100, 102; on the early popularity of romance in Italy, see Pieri, *Scena boschereccia*, p. 50.
23. See Niklas Holzberg, *The Ancient Novel. An introduction*, transl. by Christine Jackson-Holzberg (London: Routledge, 1995), especially pp 1–6, 9–11; and 99–105 (Heliodorus).
24. Cesana, *La prova amorosa*, IV. 8, especially p. 128 echoes *Liberata*, II, 33–34. See also Toniani, *Floriano il fido* (V. 1). On Bonarelli's imitation of the *Liberata*, see Alain Godard's excellent 'La *Filli di Sciro* de Guidubaldo Bonarelli: précédents littéraires et nouveaux impératifs idéologiques', in *Réécritures 2: Commentaires, parodies, variations dans la littérature italienne de la renaissance* (Paris: Université de la Sorbonne Nouvelle, 1984), pp. 141–225 (pp. 182–85).
25. See Eugenio Visdomini, *L'Erminia, favola pastorale*, BPP, MS Parmense (folio) 389 [n. d.] (which notes that is based on the *Liberata*, XIX); two other pastorals I have been unable to consult were presumably inspired by the same character: Facconio Ostiaense, *Erminia, favola boschereccia* (1617), Cataldo Antonio Mannarino, *L'Erminia, favola boschereccia* (1610). Tasso's epic also influenced the tragedies of Pietro Bonarelli (*Solimano*, 1620) and Bracciolini (*Evandro*, 1613); and prose romances, which began to flourish c.1630. See Varese, pp. 596, 604; and Albert N. Mancini, 'Narrative prose and theatre' ['The Seicento'], in Brand and Pertile, pp. 318–25 (pp. 318–21, 333). On the *Liberata*'s influence on the musical language of seventeenth-century opera, see Lorenzo Bianconi, 'I Fasti musicali del Tasso, nei secoli XVI e XVII', in *Torquato Tasso tra letteratura, musica, teatro e arti figurative*, ed. by A. Buzzoni (Bologna: Nuova Alfa Editore, 1985), pp. 143–50 (pp. 148–50).
26. Ingegneri, *Della poesia*, p. 28.
27. *Considerazioni*, pp. 68–69; see chapter 6, n. 6.
28. On the use of sumptuous or exotic costumes, see Ingegneri, *Della poesia*, p. 29; Molinari, *Le nozze*, p. 133. For their use in *Filli di Sciro*, see fig. 10; see also n. 67 below.
29. Zuccolo, fol. 6^v. On the increasing tendency for private stagings/readings of tragedy and comedy at the end of the sixteenth century, see Barish, p. 26.
30. On the use of exotic pastoral settings (as in Shakespeare's *Tempest*), see Pieri, *Scena boschereccia*, p. 178; compare the creative possibilities allowed by the Scandinavian settings of the tragedies of Tasso and Shakespeare, see Clubb, *Italian Drama*, pp. 191–94.
31. Compare the tragedies of Federico Della Valle and Ortensio Scammacca, see Michela Sacco Messineo, *Il Martire e il tiranno: Ortensio Scammacca e il teatro tragico barocco* (Rome: Bulzoni, 1988), pp. 24–26; Molinari, *Le Nozze*, pp. 130, 132.
32. Molinari, *Le nozze*, p. 121.
33. Varese, pp. 649–55.
34. Françoise Lavocat, 'Introduzione' to Lucrezia Marinella, *Arcadia felice* (Florence: Olschki, 1998), pp. VII–LX (pp. VII–VIII, XVII).
35. Marino, Letter to Antonio Bruni, secretary of the duke of Urbino, 1624/5, cited in Gambarin, *Filli*, p. 302.
36. See Francesco Ronconi, 'Vita del Conte Guid'Ubaldo Bonarelli della Rovere', in Guidubaldo Bonarelli, *Opere* (Rome: Ludovico Grignani, 1640), pp. 1–12 (p. 5). Another life of Bonarelli by Lorenzo Crasso is included with the edition of his *Filli di Sciro* (Rome: Fabio de Falco, 1670). For further detail, see Franca Angelini Frajese, 'Bonarelli, Guidubaldo', *DBI*, 11 (1969), 583–85; and especially Godard, '*Filli*', pp. 143–50.

37. Letter to Camillo Gonzaga, 30 March, 1591, in Giuseppe Malagoli, 'Studi, amori e lettere inedite di Guidobaldo Bonarelli', *GSLI*, 17 (1891), 177–211, (pp. 197–98; and 189–93 on his amorous relationships).
38. The oration was published by Vittorio Baldini (Ferrara, 1602). On the Intrepidi, see Maylender, III, 342–44.
39. On earlier Ferrarese academies, see chapter 2; Godard, '*Filli*', pp. 154–59.
40. T. Ascari, 'Cesare d'Este', in *DBI*, 24 (1980), 136–41. See ch. 3, n. 9.
41. See Southorn, pp. 80–86; also 110–11 (the Intrepidi); T. Ascari, 'Bentivoglio, Enzo', in *DBI*, 8 (1966), 610–12; Cavicchi, pp. 61–63; and P. Fabbri, A. Farina and others, 'Il Teatro degli Intrepidi di Giovan Battista Aleotti rivive verso le nuove techniche dell'acustica virtuale', http://pcfarina.eng.unipr.it/Public/Papers/070-Ciarm95.pdf (accessed 08/06/2005).
42. On Baldini, see Chapter 3, n. 87.
43. See the recent reproduction of the 1607 edition: *Filli di Sciro*, intro. by Raffaele Manica (Manziana [Rome]:Vecchiarelli, 2001), though the critical intervention is very limited. The Codrington Library, All Souls College, Oxford holds another edition of the work from 1607 with the same preface, in a small format without engravings, printed by G. B. Ciotti (Venice, 1607) (kk.14.24).
44. For detail on the theatre's design, see Fabbri, Farina and others. On Aleotti, see also chapter 6, n. 37.
45. On the Mantuan performance, see Burattelli, pp. 58, 90 (Bonarelli's play is referred to only as a 'pastorale'); for the possible one in Bologna, see Godard, '*Filli* ', p. 160. Cavicchi is unsure whether the play was ever publicly performed (p. 62).
46. Quoted in Godard, '*Filli*', p. 160.
47. Gambarin, pp. 323–31.
48. *Filli di Sciro or Phillis of Scyros: An excellent Pastoral translated into English by J. S. Gent* [Jonathan Sidnam] (London: Printed by F. M. for Andrew Cook, 1655), fol. A3^r. For French translations and imitations, see Daniela Dalla Valle, 'La fortune française de la *Filli di Sciro* au XVIIe siècle', *Revue de littérature comparée*, 4 (1972), 333–59. For details of a Dutch translation (1728), see Gambarin, p. 323. On the reception of *Aminta*, *Pastor fido* and *Filli* (and other Italian pastorals), see also: for France, Jules Marsan, *La pastorale dramatique en France à la fin du XVIe et au commencement du XVIIe siècle* (Paris: Hachette et Cie, 1905; repr. Geneva: Slatkine reprints, 1969), pp. 151–58, 498–501; for England: Henke, *Pastoral Transformations*, pp. 47–50, and Lois Potter, 'Pastoral drama in England and its political implications', in *Sviluppi della Drammaturgia Pastorale nell'Europa del Cinque-Seicento*, ed. by M. Chiabò and F. Doglio (Viterbo: Union Printing, [1992]), pp. 159–79 (pp. 172–73, 175 on the influence of *Filli*); and for Croatia, Cavallini, p. 30.
49. Marino's prologue and sonnet are cited in Gambarin, pp. 251–57, 301–02, see also p. 330; for Testi's prologue, see pp. 258–62. Marino had written a prologue for a performance of Guarini's *Pastor fido* in Nola (1599); Aurispa's prologue and 'Rime de' Quattro Intermedii apparenti cantate nella Filli di Sciro pastorale' appear in Pietro Salvioni's edition of the play (Macerata, 1619).
50. Dalla Valle, 'Fortune', p. 337. For the Savoy performance, see chapter 4, n. 39.
51. Godard, '*Filli*', pp. 174–78; Varese, p. 558, Croce, 'Critica', p. 504.
52. The *Discorsi* were also translated into French in 1707 (Marsan, p. 501).
53. Relevant extracts are cited in Gambarin, pp. 307–08 (Bouhours), pp. 309–10 (p. 310) (Baillet), pp. 311–12 (Orsi), pp. 312–19 (Muratori). For a psychoanalytical interpretation of the French reception of Italian pastoral drama, see Marco Lombardi, '"L'Ombre d'un plaisir" nei sottoboschi della pastorale', in *Teatri barocchi. Tragedie, commedie, pastorali nella drammaturgia europea fra '500 e '600* (Rome: Bulzoni, 2000), pp. 489–507. See also Elena Sala di Felice, 'Il "Pastor fido" e la tragicommedia nella polemica Orsi-Bouhours', in *Dalla tragedia rinascimentale alla tragicommedia barocca. Esperienze teatrali a confronto. In Italia e in Francia*, ed. by E. Mosele (Fasano [Brindisi]: Schena, 1993), pp. 61–91.
54. Francesco Bracciolini, *Amoroso sdegno, favola pastorale* (Milan: Ad istanza di Agostino Tradate libraro, 1597). This imitated Cristoforo Castelletti's *Amarilli, pastorale* (Ascoli: Giuseppe de gl'Angeli, 1580), see Belloni, p. 398.
55. For further examples, see Godard, '*Filli*', pp. 170–75. All references from the edition by Fassò, which follows that of Gambarin (see n. 7 above). They include act, scene and line number(s); line numbering starts afresh each act. There is no known autograph manuscript of the play.
56. Guarini sees his type of recognition as imitating that of Sophocles' *Oedipus*, and following all the

conditions that Aristotle most admired (*Annotationi*, fols 225^{r-v}). The use of tokens for this purpose (as for example in Longus' *Daphnis and Chloe*) was deemed inferior and probably removed from an earlier version of the *Pastor fido*, see Selmi, 'Classici e moderni', p. 84; also p. 35 n. 91 on Guarini's use of this device in competition with Tasso's tragedy *Torrismondo*. More generally, see Terence Cave, *Recognitions. A Study in Poetics* (Oxford: Clarendon Press, 1988), pp. 33–40 (on Aristotle), 55–83 (Renaissance commentaries on this poetic device).

57. Dottore Uno Strozzi Cicogna, *Delia, Tragedia de' Pastori* (Vicenza: Giorgio Greco, ad instanza di Paolo Meietti, 1593). This play is however effectively a tragicomedy.

58. See also the account of the centaur seizing a nymph by her hair and engaging with her lover in violent combat (*Amoroso sdegno*, IV. 1). A terrifying (though ultimately cowardly) satyr also appears in Toniani's *Floriano il fido* (I. 1, pp. 20–22). See also the violent, tyrannical Cylops (Polifemo) in Torelli's mythological pastoral tragedy, *Galatea* (see p. 215).

59. I thank Richard Andrews for drawing my attention to this parallel. On this scene, see his *Scripts and Scenarios*, pp. 228–30; also 239–40 (on Sforza Oddi's *Erofilomachia* [*The Struggle between Love and Friendship*], 1572); and 227–44 (serious comedy in general).

60. For details on the staging of the sacrifice scene, see Guarini, *Annotationi* (fol. 213^v). This scene was imitated closely in Cesana's *La prova amorosa* (V. 2).

61. On relations between Ingegneri and Bonarelli, see Doglio, *Della poesia*, p. 35 n. 9.

62. Though see Paolo Beni's observation that Guarini plausibly represented ancient pagan rites as being imperfect and unjust in comparison to modern religion (*Risposta*, pp. 201, 229, 241).

63. See Jonard, pp. 12–18; Perella, 'Fate', pp. 255–56; Gian Piero Maragoni, 'Il carattere del genere drammatico pastorale e la *Filli di Sciro* di Guidubaldo Bonarelli', *Critica letteraria*, 8 (1980), 559–80 (pp. 567–69); and Godard, '*Filli*', pp. 168–69, 190–96.

64. Compare also Bracciolini's *Amoroso sdegno*, in which Silvia (alias Dafne) notes: 'Già pargoletta, un pargoletto amante' (II. 1, fol. 25^v).

65. Maragoni, pp. 562, 566, 577–79.

66. For the idea of imaginative landscapes in Shakespeare's *The Winter's Tale*, see Henke, *Pastoral Transformations*, p. 101; see also Godard, '*Filli*', pp. 164–65; 202–12 (on the ideological implications of the setting), 221.

67. Eastern costumes were also used in pastoral settings in *commedia dell'arte* scenarios, see Scala, *Favole rappresentative*, Days XLIII and XLV (which features a Persian duke named Oronte).

68. See Toniani's *Floriano* (p. 197 above); also *L'Amorosa fede, tragicommedia pastorale* (Venice: Giacomo Sarzina, 1620) by the Cretan Antonio Pandimo (Bancroft-Marcus, pp. 96–98).

69. See for example the Thracian instigation of the horrifying tragedies of Hecuba and Tereus in Ovid's *Metamorphoses*, IV, XIII. The Thracian kingdom is described as 'una risorta Babilonia' [a new Babylon] and practising child slavery in Toniani's *Floriano* (IV. 4, p. 127). For the difficult relations between the Turks and Venice during the seventeenth century, see Sella, pp. 11–13. On the longstanding tyrannical regime in the East (Turkey), see Guarini, *Trattato*, p. 79; Machiavelli, *Il Principe*, IV.

70. Sacco Messineo, pp. 35–38; Bireley, *Counter-Reformation Prince*, pp. 35–36.

71. On Pomponio Torelli (1539–1608), a leading Farnese courtier, and his family, see Lodovico Gambara, Marco Pellegri, and Mario De Grazia, *Palazzi e casate di Parma* (Parma: La Nazionale, 1971), pp. 275–83. On the Innominati academy, an important centre for dramatic experimentation to which he belonged with Angelo Ingegneri and Muzio Manfredi, see chapter 4, and my '"Drammatica secreta"', pp. 105–06.

72. Lorenzo Perrona, 'Chiabrera e la favola di Galatea', in *La scelta della misura. Gabriello Chiabrera: l'altro fuoco del barocco italiano*, ed. by Fulvio Bianchi and Paolo Russo (Genoa: Costa & Nolan, 1993), pp. 295–317 (pp. 296–97); and V. Guercio, 'Tirannide e machiavellismo in scena pastorale: sulla "Galatea" di Pomponio Torelli', in *GSLI*, 115 (1998), 161–209 (pp. 164, 174–75).

73. On the relations of the post-Tridentine Church with secular rulers, see Bireley, 'Refashioning', pp. 72–81. For the view that Bonarelli was representing the Thracians in political terms, making parallels with the recent Habsburg-Ottoman war (ended 1606), and avoiding potentially problematic religious critique, see Godard, '*Filli*', pp. 220–23.

74. Guarini, *Compendio*, p. 226.

75. Ormino is unconsoled by Oronte's description of this revenge: 'Di lagrime e di sangue/ oh infelice ristoro! [What bitter comfort from tears and blood!]' (*Filli*, II. 1. 204–05).

76. Godard, '*Filli*', pp. 217, also 218–19 (on the use of theatrical metaphors for the illusory nature of worldly existence).
77. See, for example, Lodovico Riccato's *I pazzi amanti, comedia pastorale* (1638), V. 1, p. 132; V. 4, p. 146. Even Torelli's tragic *Galatea* indicates future hope from heaven in the final chorus. For earlier dramatic representations of providential design, see also chapter 2.
78. Godard '*Filli*', p. 202.
79. For Giovanni Botero's approval of princes creating solemn religious spectacles, like those organized by Carlo Borromeo in Milan, see his *Della ragion di Stato*, ed. and intro. by Luigi Firpo (Turin: UTET, 1948), II. 16, 140; III. 1,150.
80. See for example Marino's narrative poem *La Strage degli Innocenti* (1605, published posthum. Venice, 1633), and Guido Reni's painting on the same subject (c. 1610–11). There is a hint of this episode also in the threat of Aladino towards his Christian subjects in Tasso's *Liberata* (I. 87. 3–4).
81. See chapter 5. The concept of repentance and forgiveness is also central to Cesana's *La prova amorosa* (following Guarini's model).
82. See Bonarelli, *Discorsi*, II; especially II. 1, 165–68.
83. Guarini, *Compendio*, p. 240.
84. Bonarelli, *Discorsi*, II, 5, 238–48.
85. Compare Tasso's portrayal of the repentant, suicidal Armida's awakening from her faint, and modestly lowering her eyes from Rinaldo (*Gerusalemme liberata*, XX, 129, 5–8).
86. This was probably the case with the plays of Pomponio Torelli and later perhaps Marc'Antonio Ferretti within the Parman academy of the Innominati (see n. 71 above). For the unsuccessful attempts to stage Fabio Pace's (lost) pastoral drama (*Eugenio*) in the Accademia Olimpica of Vicenza (1596–98), see Mazzoni, pp. 61–64.
87. Mancini, pp. 334–35.
88. See Turchi, pp. 9–30; Franco Croce, 'L'intellettuale Chiabrera', in *La scelta della misura. Gabriello Chiabrera: l'altro fuoco del barocco italiano*, ed. by Fulvio Bianchi and Paolo Russo (Genoa: Costa & Nolan, 1993), pp. 15–50 (p. 32, also p. 18).
89. Various useful essays on Chiabrera, dealing also with his theatrical and musical associations, are found in Bianchi and Russo. See also Gabriello Chiabrera, *Lettere (1585–1638)*, ed. by Simona Morando (Florence: Olschki, 2003), 'Introduzione', and ad indicem.
90. Marzia Pieri, 'La drammaturgia di Chiabrera', in Bianchi and Russo, pp. 401–28, especially pp. 406–07. For Chiabrera's contacts with actors, see in the same volume Franco Vazzoler, 'Chiabrera fra dilettanti e professionisti dello spettacolo', pp. 429–66 (p. 443); and on the taste for theatre in Liguria, Giovanni Farris, 'Gabriello Chiabrera, savonese di nascita e di elezione', pp. 51–74.
91. Pieri, 'Drammaturgia', pp. 402–03. For more recent editions of Chiabrera's *Il Rapimento di Cefalo* (Florence: Marescotti, 1608), his tragedy set to music (*Angelica in Ebuda*, Florence: Pignoni, 1615) and other works, see Angelo Solerti, *Gli albori del melodramma*, 3 vols (Milan: Sandron, 1904; repr. Hildesheim: Georg Olms, 1969), III, 9–240. See also Perrona, pp. 295–317.
92. Antonio Vassalli, 'Chiabrera, la musica e i musicisti: le rime amorose', in Bianchi and Russo, pp. 353–69.
93. Both editions by Sebastiano Combi in Venice, 1607 and 1610 (the latter in Chiabrera's *Rime*, Part III, edited by Pier Girolamo Gentile Ricci). I have not been able to consult the edition of *Gelopea* by Francesco Vazzoler (Genova: Marietti, 1988).
94. For details, see Turchi, 'Nota biografica', pp. 67–75 (pp. 69–71); on the 1614 edition of *Alcippo* as the first, and for later editions, see Valerio Pindozzi, 'Pier Giuseppe Giustiniani e Gabriello Chiabrera', in Bianchi and Russo, pp. 107–25 (p. 107). Throughout, references to *Gelopea* and *Meganira* will be to the editions in *Delle opere di Gabbriello [sic] Chiabrera*, 5 vols (Venice: Presso Angiolo Geremia, 1730–31 [I-IV], 1757 [V]), see bibliography. Pier Girolamo Gentile Ricci(o), a member of the Florentine Accademia degli Spensierati, himself wrote a pastoral play (*I sospetti, favola boschereccia*, Venice, Sebastiano Combi, 1608), set in Albaro, near Genoa. On Gentile Ricci's relations with Chiabrera, see Farris, pp. 56, 59.
95. Letter to Roberto Titi, *Savona*, 18 March 1595, in Chiabrera, *Lettere*, no. 65, pp. 66–67; for performance dates, see p. XXVIII.
96. Gentile (Ricci) links both the setting and the outcome of Filebo's love to that of the dedicatee, Giovanni Paolo Torriglia, in his prefatory letter (Venice, 20 March 1607) to *Delle Rime del Sig.*

Gabriello Chiabrera, Parte terza (Venice: Sebastiano Combi, 1610), pp. 3–4. Some of the pastoral names, especially the capitalized PALLA [...] VICINA (Isabella Pallavicino Lupi?) (I. 1, p. 224), seem to suggest real figures, as does the prefatory *canzone* of 1615.

97. *Meganira*, dedicatory letter to Filippo Salviati, p. 164.
98. Urban/comedic issues of female fidelity and avarice had already been integrated into pastoral in Niccolò di Correggio's eclogue, *Cefalo* (1487).
99. For Luigi Groto's earlier use of this source, see above, p. 35; and Pieri, 'Drammaturgia', p. 428 also for other sources.
100. Gianfranco Formichetti, 'La poetica di Chiabrera e le prospettive della poesia religiosa nell'ambiente romano tra manierismo e barocco', in Bianchi and Russo, pp. 126–38; and Chiabrera, Sermon 20 in Turchi, *Opere*, pp. 480–82. More generally, see Croce, 'L'intellettuale', pp. 37–38; Belloni, pp. 6–8.
101. Farris, p. 53; N. Merola, 'Chiabrera, Gabriello', in *DBI*, 24 (1980), 465–75 (p. 466); see also Vazzoler, 'Chiabrera', p. 431. On duelling generally, see Sella, p. 59.
102. Vazzoler, 'Chiabrera', p. 450. Compare the cross-dressed revenge motif in Flaminio Scala's *Favole rappresentative*, Days X and XI; and on Isabella Andreini, see chapter 4.
103. See Belloni (pp. 394–95) for a slightly different version of *Alcippo*, which includes a further character (Radamante). I have been unable to find this version.
104. Turchi, p. 26; Chiabrera cites from the first lines of his verse included in his *Canzonette* (1591) (pp. 161–62), and *Le Maniere de' versi toscani* (1599) (p. 218). *Alcippo* features a lyrical description of the pleasures of nature by Clori (I. 1, pp. 8–9).
105. *Meganira*, dedication to Filippo di Everardo Salviati, pp. 163–64; on the various forms of *Angelica in Ebuda*, see Pieri, 'Drammaturgia', p. 402.
106. *Il Rapimento di Cefalo* was first published in Florence, by Marescotti, 1600; see the edition in *Delle opere*, IV (1731), pp. 297–335. For a formal account of the festivities, see Michelagnolo (Michelangelo) Buonarroti (the younger), *Descrizione delle felicissime nozze della Christianissima Maestà di Madama Maria Medici Regina di Francia e di Navarra* (Florence: Giorgio Marescotti, 1600); the section describing *Cefalo* is cited in Solerti, *Albori*, III, 11–28. See also A. M. Nagler, *Theatre festivals of the Medici 1539–1637* (New Haven: Yale University Press, 1964), pp. 93–100. For the staging of *Euridice* and *Cefalo*, see Claude V. Palisca, 'The First Performance of *Euridice*', in *Queens College Department of Music: Twenty-fifth Anniversay Festschrift*, ed. by Albert Mell (New York: Queens College Press, 1964), pp. 1–23. Rinuccini's text of *Dafne* (1598) survives, though the musical score is lost. For three earlier (lost) examples of choreographed pastoral drama fully set to music in Florence from the 1590s, see Warren Kirkendale, 'L'Opera in musica prima del Peri: Le pastorali perdute di Laura Guidiccioni ed Emilio de' Cavalieri', in *Firenze e la Toscana dei Medici nell'Europa del '500*, ed. by Giancarlo Garfagnini, 3 vols (Florence: Olschki, 1983), II, 365–95.
107. The Alterati also advised Guarini on his *Pastor fido*. See Palisca, 'The Alterati of Florence', p. 30.
108. Solerti, *Albori*, III, p. 28.
109. See Massimo Ossi, 'Dalle machine ... la maraviglia: Bernardo Buontalenti's *Il rapimento di Cefalo* at the Medici Theater in 1600', in *Opera in Context: Essays on Historical Staging from the Late Renaissance to the Time of Puccini*, ed. by Mark A. Radice (Portland, Oregon: Amadeus Press, 1998), pp. 15–35, 297–305; and Cesare Molinari, *Le nozze*, pp. 35–49 (especially 43–49).
110. Guarini, *Annotazioni*, fol. 91^r.
111. Ossi, pp. 22–23, 26; Palisca, 'Musical Asides in the Correspondence of Emilio de' Cavalieri', *Musical Quarterly*, 49 (1963), 339–55 (pp. 350–51).
112. Tim Carter, 'A Florentine Wedding of 1608', *Acta musicologica*, 55 (1983), 89–107 (pp. 92–93). But for grand pastoral spectacle with music in France, see Daniela Dalla Valle, 'Gabriello Chiabrera tradotto in francese: "Le ravissement de Céphale" di Chretien des Croix', in Bianchi and Russo, pp. 507–17 (p. 510).
113. Though for the view that opera was only fully established as a genre outside the court, see Carter, 'Florentine Wedding', p. 93. The libretto of *Orfeo* was by Alessandro Striggio; *Euridice* featured a female singer (Vittoria Archilei).
114. Franco Vazzoler, 'Le pastorali dei comici dell'arte: La *Mirtilla* di Isabella Andreini', in Chiabò and Doglio, pp. 281–99. On the importance of actresses in the early development of pastoral tragicomedy, see Robert Henke, *Performance and Literature in the Commedia dell'Arte* (Cambridge: Cambridge University Press, 2002), pp. 87–88, and 91–92, 98–100 (on Armani).

115. See for example scenarios II, XLII, XLIII, XLIX. Some of the dedicatory verse (by Claudio Achillini, Cesare Orsino, Pietro Petracci) in the 1611 edition mentions pastoral features, while the preface by Francesco Andreini notes the comic, tragic and pastoral stage-sets required to perform them (fol. b3^v). See also the useful introduction to Marotti's two volume edition.
116. Kathleen Lea, *Italian Popular Comedy: A Study in the Commedia dell'Arte, 1560–1620, with Special Reference to the English Stage*, 2 vols (Oxford: Clarendon Press, 1934), I, 137; Henke, *Pastoral Transformations*, pp. 57–60. Five of Locatelli's pastoral scenarios (from vol. 2) are transcribed with a further one from a Neapolitan manuscript in Ferdinando Neri, *Scenari delle Maschere in Arcadia* (Città di Castello: Lapi, 1913; repr. Turin: Bottega d'Erasmo, 1961), pp. 45–93. For English translations of those by Locatelli and four further Italian pastoral scenarios with translations, see Lea, II, 610–74, see also I, 201–12.
117. Pieri, 'Il "Pastor fido"'.
118. Neri, 'Scenari', pp. 17–19; Pieri, *Scena boschereccia,* pp. 176–78.
119. Maurizio Rebaudengo, *Giovan Battista Andreini tra poetica e drammaturgia* (Turin: Rosenberg & Sellier, 1994), pp. 10–24 (biography and outline of works). See also F. Angelini Frajese, 'Andreini, Giovan Battista', *DBI*, 3 (1961), 133–36.
120. See Rebaudengo, pp. 46–50 (pastoral setting); 51–52, 58–60, 70, 73–76 (*La Centaura*). Compare the similar polemic in the prologue to G. B. Leoni's *Roselmina* (1595), fols †3^r-4^r.
121. For an early example of prose pastoral drama see Cristoforo Sicinio (da Toffia)'s *La fortuna, tragicomedia pastorale* (Rome: Giacomo Mascardi, 1610), written 1600 (Pieri, *Scena boschereccia*, p. 173). See also Rebaudengo, pp. 104–15 (p. 107).
122. Pieri, 'Drammaturgia', p. 412.
123. Anna Laura Bellina and Carlo Caruso, 'Oltre il Barocco: la fondazione dell'Arcadia. Zeno e Metastasio: la riforma del melodramma', in *Storia della letteratura italiana*, ed. by Enrico Malato (Rome: Salerno, 1995-), VI: Il Settecento (1998), pp. 239–312 (p. 248).
124. Gravina, *Discorso sopra l'Endimione* [1692], in *Scritti critici*, pp. 51–73 (see also n. 3). For the text of the play, see Alessandro Guidi, *Poesie approvate: L'Endimione. La Dafne. Rime. Sonetti. Sei Omelie*, ed. by Bruno Maier (Ravenna: Longo, 1981). On this and further examples of pastoral plays by Arcadians, see Bellina and Caruso, pp. 244, 276–79; L. Matt, 'Guidi, Alessandro', *DBI*, 61 (2003), 203–08 (p. 205–06); and Belloni, p. 402.

BIBLIOGRAPHY

Abbreviations

DBI   *Dizionario biografico degli italiani* (Rome: Istituto dell'Enciclopedia Italian, 1960-)
GSLI *Giornale storico della letteratura italiana*
MLR *Modern Language Review*

Primary Sources

Manuscript

Cremona, Biblioteca Statale, Deposito Libreria Civica, Ms. AA. 1. 33
Torelli (Benedetti), Barbara, *Partenia, favola boschereccia della Signora Barbara Torelli Benedetti*, Parma [n.d., catalogued as seventeenth century]
Florence, Archivio di Stato (ASF), Archivio Mediceo
Mantua, Archivio di Stato, (ASM), Archivio Gonzaga
Modena, Archivio di Stato (ASMod)
   Archivio per Materie, 'Comici' (unnumbered)
   Cancelleria ducale, 'Letterati'
Parma, Archivio di Stato (ASP), Epistolario scelto
Parma, Biblioteca Palatina (BPP), MS Parmense (folio) 389.
Visdomini, Eugenio, *L'Erminia, favola pastorale* (n. d.)
Vicenza, Biblioteca Bertoliana (BBV), Atti dell'Accademia Olimpica
Pagello, Livio, *La Cinthia, comedia boscareccia del S.e Livio Pagelo [sic], Academico Olimpico* [n.d.], MS Gonzati, 169

Printed

Andreini, Giovan Battista, *Lelio bandito, tragicomedia boschereccia* (Milan: Giovan Battista Bidelli, 1620)
—— *La Centaura, suggetto diviso in comedia pastorale e tragedia* (Venice: Salvador Sonzonio, 1633) [first edn, Paris: N. della Vigna, 1622]
—— *La Rosella, tragicomedia boschereccia* (Bologna: Clemente Ferroni, 1632)
Andreini, Isabella, *Mirtilla, pastorale* (Verona: Girolamo Discepolo, 1588)
—— *Lettere* (Venice: Sebastiano Combi, 1612)
—— *La Mirtilla*, ed. by Maria Luisa Doglio (Lucca: Maria Pacini Fazzi, 1995) [transcription of the Discepolo edition, 1588]
—— '*La Mirtilla': A Pastoral*, trans. with an intro. and notes by Julie D. Campbell, Medieval and Renaissance Texts and Studies, 242 (Tempe, AZ: Arizona Center for Medieval and Renaissance Studies, 2002)
Anonimo della seconda metà del secolo XVI, *Da Nizza a Torino. I festeggiamenti per il matrimonio di Carlo Emanuele I e Caterina d'Austria 1585*, intro. and notes by Franca Varallo (Turin: Centro Studi Piemontesi, 1992)
Argenti, Agostino, *Lo Sfortunato, favola pastorale* (Venice: Gabriel Giolito de' Ferrari, 1568); transcribed in Agostino Beccari, Alberto Lollio, Agostino Argenti, *Favole*, ed. by Fulvio Pevere (Turin: RES, 1999), pp. 201–350

—— [attrib. to AGOSTINO ARGENTI], *Il Castello di Gorgoferusa et il Monte di Feronia, ne' quali si contengono le cose d'arme fatte in Ferrara nel Carnevale del MDLXI* (Ferrara: Francesco Rossi il Giovane, 1566)

ARISTOTLE, *Poetics*, trans. by Malcolm Heath (Harmondsworth: Penguin, 1996)

BALDINUCCI, FILIPPO, *Notizie dei professori del disegno da Cimabue in qua [...]per le quali si dimostra come, e per chi le belle arti di pittura, scultura e architettura, lasciata la rozzezza delle maniere greca a gotica, si siano in questi secoli ridotte all'antica loro perfezione* [1681 vols I–III; 1728 complete edition], ed. by F. Ranalli, 5 vols (Florence: Batelli e Compagni, 1846)

BATTIFERRI DEGLI AMMANNATI, LAURA, *Il Primo Libro delle Opere Toscane* [Florence, 1560], ed. by Enrico Maria Guidi (Urbino: Accademia Raffaello, 2000)

BECCARI, AGOSTINO, *Il Sacrificio, favola pastorale* (Ferrara: Francesco di Rossi da Valenza, 1555)

—— *Il Sacrificio, favola pastorale* (Ferrara: ad istanza di Alfonso Caraffa appresso Giulio Cesare Cagnacini & fratelli, 1587); transcribed in Agostino Beccari, Alberto Lollio, Agostino Argenti, *Favole*, ed. by Fulvio Pevere (Turin: RES, 1999), pp. 1–130

BENI, PAOLO, *Risposta alle considerazioni o dubbii dell'eccellentissimo signor Dottor Malacreta Accademico Ordito Sopra il Pastorfido, Con altre varie dubitazioni tanto contra detti dubbii e considerazioni, quanto contra l'istesso Pastorfido. Con un discorso nel fine per compendio di tutta l'opera* [1600], in Guarini, *Opere* (Verona: Tumermani, 1737–38), IV (1738), 125–300

BOCCALINI, TRAIANO, *Ragguagli di Parnaso, e scritti minori*, ed. by Luigi Firpo (Bari: Laterza, 1948)

BONARELLI, GUIDUBALDO [GUIDOBALDO], *Filli di Sciro, favola pastorale* (Ferrara: Vittorio Baldini [1607]; Venice: G. B. Ciotti, 1607)

—— *Filli di Sciro or Phillis of Scyros: An excellent Pastoral*, trans. by J. S. Gent [Jonathan Sidnam] (London: Printed by F. M. for Andrew Cook, 1655)

—— *Filli di Sciro, Discorsi e Appendice*, ed. by Giovanni Gambarin (Bari: Laterza, 1941)

—— *Filli di Sciro*, in *Il Teatro del Seicento*, ed. by Luigi Fassò, La Letteratura italiana: Storia e testi, 39 (Milan: Ricciardi, 1956), pp. 325–461

BOTERO, GIOVANNI, *Della ragion di Stato, con tre libri Delle Cause della Grandezza delle città, due Aggiunte e un Discorso sulla popolazione di Roma*, ed. and intro. by Luigi Firpo (Turin: UTET, 1948)

BRACCIOLINI, FRANCESCO, *L'amoroso sdegno, favola pastorale* (Milan: Ad istanza di Agostino Tradate libraro, 1597)

CAMPIGLIA, MADDALENA, *La Flori, favola boscareccia* (Vicenza: gl'heredi di Perin Libraro & Tomaso Brunelli compagni, 1588)

—— *Flori, a pastoral drama. A bilingual edition*, ed. with an introduction and notes by Virginia Cox and Lisa Sampson, trans. by Virginia Cox (Chicago: University of Chicago Press, 2004)

CAPPONI, GIOVANNI, *Orsilla, favola boscareccia* (Venice: Violati, 1615)

CASTELLETTI, CRISTOFORO, *Amarilli, pastorale* (Ascoli: Gioseppe de gl'Angeli, 1580; Venice: Iacomo Berechio, 1582; rev. edn, Venice: Giovanni Battista Sessa e fratelli, 1587)

CASTIGLIONE, BALDASSARRE [BALDESAR], *Tirsi*, in *Il Libro del Cortegiano con scelta di opere minori*, ed. by Bruno Maier (Turin: UTET, 1964), pp. 549–71

—— *Il Cortegiano* [1528], ed. by Ettore Bonora, 2nd edn (Milan: Mursia, 1976)

CESANA, GASPARO, *La prova amorosa, favola pastorale* (Venice: Francesco Ciotti, 1606)

CHIABRERA, GABRIELLO, *Il Rapimento di Cefalo* [Florence, 1600] in *Delle opere* (Venice: Presso Angiolo Geremia, 1730–31), IV (1731), 297–335

—— *La Gelopea, favola boscareccia* [Mondovì, 1603], in *Delle opere*, IV (1731), 213–96

—— *Alcippo, favola boscareccia* [Genoa, 1604], in *Delle opere*, IV (1731), 161–212

—— *Meganira, favola boscareccia* [Florence, 1608], in *Delle opere*, V (1757), 1–42

—— *Delle opere di Gabbriello [sic] Chiabrera*, 5 vols (Venice: Presso Angiolo Geremia, 1730–31 [I–IV]; 1757 [V])

—— *Lettere (1585–1638)*, ed. by Simona Morando, Biblioteca di 'Lettere italiane': studi e testi, 59 (Florence: Olschki, 2003)

—— *Opere di Gabriello Chiabrera e lirici del classicismo barocco*, ed. by Marcello Turchi, 2nd edn (Turin: UTET, 1974)
CICERO, MARCUS TULLIUS, *Rhetorici Libri duo. Qui vocantur de inventione*, trans. by H. M. Hubbell as *Two Books on Rhetoric commonly called On Invention* (London: Heinemann, 1968)
CORREGGIO, NICCOLÒ DA, *Fabula de Cefalo*, in *Teatro del Quattrocento. Le corti padane*, ed. by Antonia Tissoni Benvenuti and Maria Pia Mussini Sacchi (Turin: UTET, 1983), pp. 199–207
CREMONINI (CREMONINO), CESARE, *Le Pompe funebri, overo Aminta, e Clori, favola silvestre* (Ferrara: Per Vittorio Baldini, 1590)
CUCCHETTI, GIOVAN(NI) DONATO, *La Pazzia, favola pastorale* (Ferrara: Vittorio Baldini, 1581; repr. Venice: Presso Bartholomeo Carampello, 1597; rev. edn with prologue and *intermedi*, Ferrara: appresso Giulio Cesare Cagnacini, e fratelli, ad istanza di Francesco Mammarello, Libraro in Parma, 1586)
DELLA VALLE, CAMILLO, *Fillide, egloga pastorale* (Ferrara: Vittorio Baldini, 1584)
DENORES, GIASON, *Discorso [...] intorno a quei principii, cause et accrescimenti che la Commedia, la Tragedia, ed il Poema Eroico ricevono dalla Filosofia Morale e Civile, e da' Governatori delle Repubbliche* [1586], in Guarini, *Opere*, 5 vols (Verona: Tumermani, 1737–38), II (1738), 153–206
—— *Poetica [...] Nella qual per via di Definitione, & Divisione si tratta secondo l'opinion d'Aristotele Della Tragedia, del Poema Heroico, & della Comedia* (Padova: Appresso Paulo Meietto, 1588)
—— *Apologia di Jason Denores, Contra l'Autore del Verato* [1590], in Guarini, *Opere*, 5 vols (Verona: Tumermani, 1737–38), II (1738), 313–75
DE' ROSSI, BARTOLOMEO, *La Fiammella pastorale* (Paris: Abell'Angeliero, 1584)
DE' SOMMI, LEONE, *Quattro dialoghi in materia di rappresentazione scenica*, ed. by Ferruccio Marotti, Archivio del teatro italiano, 1 (Milan: Il Polifilo, 1968)
—— *Irifile* [1555/6?], ed. by Giuseppe Dalla Palma, in 'L'Irifile e la cultura letteraria di Leone de' Sommi (con un'edizione critica del testo)', *Schifanoia*, 9 (1990), 139–225
EPICURO NAPOLITANO, see Marsi
FERRETTI, MARC'ANTONIO, *Mirinda, favola pastorale* (Venice: Domenico Venturati, 1612)
GIRALDI (CINTHIO/CINZIO), GIAMBATTISTA [GIOVAN BATTISTA], *Scritti critici*, ed. by Camillo Guerrieri Crocetti (Milan: Marzorati, 1973)
—— *Egle, Lettera sovra il comporre le Satire atte alla scena, Favola pastorale*, ed. by Carla Molinari (Bologna: Commissione per i testi di lingua, 1985)
—— *Carteggio*, ed. by Susanna Villari (Messina: Sicania, 1996)
GIRALDI, LILIO GREGORIO, *Due dialoghi sui poeti dei nostri tempi*, ed. by Claudia Pandolfi ([Ferrara]: Corbo, 1999)
GRAVINA, GIANVINCENZO, *Scritti critici e teorici*, ed. by Amedeo Quondam (Rome: Laterza, 1973)
GRILLO, GIOVANNI BATTISTA, *Breve trattato di quanto successe alla maestà della regina D. Margarita d'Austria N.S [...]* (Naples: Appresso Costantino Vitale, 1604)
GROTO, LUIGI, *La Calisto, nova favola pastorale* (Venice: Fabio and Agostin Zoppini, 1583)
—— *Il Pentimento amoroso, nova favola pastorale* (Venice: Fabio and Agostin Zoppini, 1592) [first edn, Venice: apresso Bolognino Zaltiero, 1576]
—— *Le Orationi volgari di Luigi Groto Cieco di Hadria. Da lui medesimo recitate in diversi tempi in diversi luoghi, e in diverse occasioni, parte stampate, e ristampate altre volte ad una ad una, e parte non mai piu venute in luce* (Venice: A[press]o li Zoppini, 1598)
—— *Lettere famigliari di Luigi Groto Cieco d'Adria scritte in diversi generi, & in varie occasioni con molta felicità, e di nobilissimi concetti ornate* (Venice: Giovachino Brugnolo, 1601)
GUARINI, BATTISTA, *Il Verato secondo, ovvero Replica dell'Attizzato Accademico Ferrarese in difesa del Pastor fido* (Florence: Per Filippo Giunti, 1593 [1592])
—— *Lettere* (Venice: Giovanni Battista Ciotti, 1598)
—— *Il Pastor Fido, Tragicommedia Pastorale [...]. Ora in questa XXVII impressione di curiose, e dotte Annotationi arricchito, e di bellissime figure in rame ornato. Con un Compendio di Poesia tratto da i*

    duo Verati, con la giunta d'altre cose notabili per opera del medesimo S. Cavaliere (Venice: Giovanni Battista Ciotti, 1602)

—— *Opere*, 5 vols (Verona: Tumermani, 1737–38)

—— *Trattato della politica libertà* [1600], ed. by Gaetano A. Ruggieri (Venice: per Francesco Andreola, 1818)

—— *Compendio della poesia tragicomica tratto dai duo Verati* [1601], in *Il Pastor fido e Compendio della Poesia Tragicomica*, ed. by Gioachino Brognoligo (Bari: Laterza, 1914), pp. 219–88

—— *Opere di Battista Guarini*, ed. by Marziano Guglielminetti (Turin: UTET, 1971)

—— *Il Pastor fido*, in *Il teatro italiano, II: La tragedia del Cinquecento*, ed. by Marco Ariani, 2 vols (Turin: Einaudi, 1977), II, 723–946

—— *Il Pastor fido*, ed. by Elisabetta Selmi with intro. by Guido Baldassarri (Venice: Marsilio, 1999)

GUAZZONI, DIOMISSO, *Andromeda, tragicomedia boscareccia* (Venice: Domenico Imberti, 1587; repr. 1599)

GUIDI, ALESSANDRO, *Poesie approvate: L'Endimione. La Dafne. Rime. Sonetti. Sei Omelie*, ed. by Bruno Maier (Ravenna: Longo, 1981)

INGEGNERI, ANGELO, *Danza di Venere, pastorale* (Vicenza: Nella Stamperia Nova, 1584)

—— *Della Poesia rappresentativa e del modo di rappresentare le favole sceniche* [Ferrara, 1598], ed. by Maria Luisa Doglio (Modena: Panini, 1989)

LEONI, GIO. BATTISTA [pseud. LAURO SETTIZONIO], *Roselmina, favola tragicasatiricomica [...] Recitata in Venetia, l'anno MDXVV [1595] [...]* (Venice: Appresso Gio. Battista Ciotti Senese, 1595)

LOLLIO, ALBERTO, *Aretusa, comedia pastorale* (Ferrara: Valente Panizza Mantoano, 1564); transcribed in Agostino Beccari, Alberto Lollio, Agostino Argenti, *Favole*, ed. by Fulvio Pevere (Turin: RES, 1999), pp. 131–99

—— *Galatea* [incomplete MS, n. d.], in Angelo Solerti, 'La *Galatea* di Alberto Lollio', *Il Propugnatore*, n.s. 4 (1891), 199–212

MALACRETA, GIOVANNI PIETRO, *Considerazioni intorno al Pastor fido* [1600], in Battista Guarini, *Opere*, 5 vols (Verona: Tumermani, 1737–38), IV (1738), 1–222

MANFREDI, MUZIO, *Cento Donne cantate da Mutio Manfredi, Il Fermo Academico Innominato di Parma* (Parma: Nella Stamperia d'Erasmo Viotti, 1580)

—— *Cento Madrigali di Mutio Manfredi, Il Fermo Academico Innominato, Invaghito, e di Ferrara* (Mantova: Francesco Osanna, 1587)

—— *La Semiramis, boscareccia* (Bergamo: Per Comino Ventura, 1593)

—— *Il Contrasto amoroso, pastorale* (Venice: Giacomo Antonio Somascho, 1602)

—— *Lettere brevissime di Mutio Manfredi [...] Scritte tutte in un'Anno [...]* (Venice: Roberto Megietti, 1606)

MANSO, G. B., *Vita di Torquato Tasso*, ed. by Bruno Basile (Rome: Salerno, 1995)

MARSI, ANTONIO, *I Drammi pastorali di Antonio Marsi detto l'Epicuro Napolitano*, Scelta di Curiosità letterarie inedite o rare, ed. by Italo Palmarini (Bologna: Romagnoli-Dall'Acqua, 1888)

MIANI (NEGRI), VALERIA, *Amorosa speranza, favola pastorale* (Venice: Francesco Bolzetta, 1604)

ONGARO, ANTONIO, *Alceo, favola pescatoria* (Venice: Francesco Ziletti, 1582)

—— *Alceo*, in Antonio Ongaro and Girolamo Vida, *Favole*, ed. by Domenico Chiodo, with pref. by Giorgio Bárberi Squarotti (Turin: RES, 1998)

PASQUALIGO, ALVISE, *Gl'Intricati, pastorale* (Venice: Francesco Ziletti, 1581)

PAZZI (DE' MEDICI), ALESSANDRO DE', *Tragedia Cyclope composta per Alexandro Paccio de' Medici secomdo [sic] il contexto d'Euripide poeta greco*, in Alessandro Pazzi de' Medici, *Le tragedie metriche*, ed. by Angelo Solerti (Bologna: Romagnoli dall'Acqua, 1887), pp. 137–200

PELLICIARI, HERCOLE (ERCOLE), *I figliuoli di Aminta, e Silvia et di Mirtillo, et Amarilli, tragedia di lieto fine, nelle selve d'Arcadia seguita* (Venice: Antonio Pinelli, 1617)

PERSIA, FERRANTE, *Relatione de' ricevimenti fatti in Mantova alla Maestà della Regina di Spagna dal Sereniss. Sig. Duca, [L']Anno MDXCVIII del Mese di Novembre [...]* (Mantua; repr. in Ferrara by Vittorio Baldini, [1598])

PIGNA, GIOVANBATTISTA, *La Vita di M. Lodovico Ariosto, Tratta in Compendio dai Romanzi Del S. Giovanbattista Pigna*, in Ludovico Ariosto, *Orlando furioso [...] con le annotationi da Giovan Battista Pigna di Ieronimo Ruscelli, la vita dell'autore descritta* (Venice: Valgrisi, 1565), fols ★4ᵛ-A1ʳ

RICCATO, LODOVICO, *I Pazzi amanti, comedia pastorale* (Treviso: Girolamo Righettini, 1638)

RONCONI, FRANCESCO, 'Vita del Conte Guid'Ubaldo Bonarelli della Rovere', in Guidubaldo Bonarelli dell Rovere, *Opere* (Rome: Ludovico Grignari, 1640), pp. 1–12

ROSSI, BARTOLOMEO, see De' Rossi, Bartolomeo

SANNAZARO, JACOPO, *Opere Volgari di Jacopo Sanazzaro cavaliere napoletano, cioè l'Arcadia, Alla sua vera lezione restituita, colle Annotazioni del Porcacchi, del Sansovino, e del Massarengo; Le Rime, Arricchite di molti Componimenti, tratti da Codici MSS ed impressi [...]* (Padua: Giuseppe Comino, 1723)

SCALA, FLAMINIO, *Il Teatro delle favole rappresentative, overo la Ricreatione comica, boscareccia, e tragica: Divisa in Cinquanta Giornate* (Venice: Gio[van] Battista Pulciani, 1611)

—— *Il teatro delle favole rappresentative*, ed. by Ferruccio Marotti, Archivio del teatro italiano, 7, 2 vols (Milan: Il Polifilo, 1976)

SERLIO, SEBASTIANO, *Il Secondo libro di Prospettiva, di Sebastiano Serlio Bolognese* [Paris, 1545], in *Tutte l'opere* (Venice: Francesco de' Franceschi Senese, 1584)

SPERONI (DEGLI ALVAROTTI), SPERONE, *Dialogo della retorica* [c.1538–40], in *Trattatisti del Cinquecento*, ed. by M. Pozzi (Milan: Ricciardi, 1978), pp. 637–82

—— *Apologia dei dialoghi* [written 1574/5], in *Opere [...] tratte da' MSS. originali*, 5 vols (Venice: Domenico Occhi, 1740), I, 266–425

STROZZI CICOGNA, UNO, *Delia, tragedia de' pastori* (Vicenza: Giorgio Greco, ad istanza di Paolo Meietti, 1593)

SUMMO, FAUSTINO, *Due Discorsi l'uno contra le tragicommedie, e le pastorali, L'altro contra il pastor fido tragicommedia pastorale dell'illustre signor Cavaliere Battista Guarini [...]* [1600], in Guarini, *Opere*, 5 vols (Verona: Tumermani, 1737–38), III (1738), 545–96

TASSO, TORQUATO, *Il Goffredo, overo Gierusalemme Liberata [...] Con l'Allegoria universale dell'istesso & gli Argomenti del Sig. Horatio [Orazio] Ariosti* (Venice: Presso Gio. Battista Combi, 1576)

—— *Aminta, favola pastorale* (Venice: Aldo Manuzio, 1581)

—— *Le Lettere di Torquato Tasso, disposte per ordine di tempo*, ed. by Cesare Guasti, 2nd edn, 5 vols (Naples: Gabriele Rondinella, 1857)

—— *Dialoghi*, ed. by Ezio Raimondi, 3 vols (Florence: Sansoni, 1958)

—— *Prose*, ed. by Ettore Mazzali, with preface by F. Flora (Milan: Ricciardi, 1959)

—— *Opere*, ed. by Bruno Maier, 5 vols (Milan: Rizzoli, 1963–65)

—— *Aminta*, in *Il teatro italiano. II: La tragedia del Cinqucento*, ed. by Marco Ariani, 2 vols (Turin: Einaudi, 1977), II, 641–721

—— *Scritti sull'arte poetica*, ed. by Ettore Mazzali (Turin: Einaudi, 1977)

—— *Jerusalem Delivered*, trans. by Edward Fairfax (New York: Capricorn Books, n.d. [1963])

—— *Gerusalemme liberata*, ed. by Marziano Guglielminetti, 10th edn, 2 vols (Milan: Garzanti, 1996)

—— *Aminta: A Pastoral Play by Torquato Tasso*, ed. and trans. by Charles Jernigan and Irene Marchegiani Jones (New York: Italica Press, 2000)

TONIANI, PIETRO ANTONIO, *Floriano il fido, tragicomedia pastorale* (Vicenza: Dominico Amadio, 1616)

TORELLI, POMPONIO, *Galatea* (Parma: Erasmo Viotti, 1603)

VIDA, GIROLAMO, *Filliria, favola boscareccia* (Padua: Appresso Gioanni Cantoni, 1585), in Antonio Ongaro and Girolamo Vida, *Favole*, ed. by Domenico Chiodo, with pref. by Giorgio Bárberi Squarotti (Turin: RES, 1998)

VIGILIO, G. B., *L'insalata: cronaca Mantovana dal 1561 al 1602*, ed. by D. Ferrari and C. Mozzarelli (Mantua: Arcari, 1992)

VIRGIL, *The Eclogues. The Georgics*, trans. by C. Day Lewis (Oxford: Oxford University Press, 1983)
VITRUVIUS, *Ten Books on Architecture*, ed. by Ingrid D. Rowland and Thomas Noble Howe (Cambridge: Cambridge University Press, 1999)
ZUCCOLO, LODOVICO, *L'Alessandro, overo della pastorale, dialogo* (Venice: Andrea Baba, 1613)

Secondary Literature

AFFÒ, IRENEO, *Memorie degli Scrittori e Letterati Parmigiani*, 7 vols (Parma: Dalla Stamperia Reale, 1793; repr. Bologna: Forni, 1969)
ALBINI, UMBERTO, 'Il dramma satiresco greco', in Chiabò and Doglio, pp. 15–27
ALONGE, ROBERTO, 'Letteratura e spettacolo nel Seicento', in *Storia della società italiana*, ed. by Giovanni Cherubini and others, 25 vols (Milan: Teti, 1981–90), XI: *La Controriforma e il Seicento* (1989), 463–85
ALPERS, PAUL, *What is Pastoral?* (Chicago: Chicago University Press, 1996)
AMMIRATI, LUIGI, *Una serata di Gala a Nola nel '500. La prima rappresentazione del 'Pastor fido' con il 'Prologo' di G. B. Marino*, intro. by Luigi Vecchione (Basilicata, Nola: Opinione, 1962)
ANDRETTA, STEFANO, *La Venerabile Superbia. Ortodossia e trasgressione nella vita di Suor Francesca Farnese (1593–1651)* (Turin: Rosenberg & Sellier, 1994)
ANDREWS, RICHARD, 'Isabella Andreini and others: women on stage in the late Cinquecento', in *Women in Italian Renaissance Culture and Society*, ed. by Letizia Panizza (Oxford: Legenda, 2000), pp. 316–33
—— 'L'attrice e la cantante fra Cinquecento e Seicento: la presenza femminile in palcoscenico', in *Teatro e Musica. Écriture vocale et scénique*, Actes du Colloque, 17–19 February 1998 (Toulouse: Presses Universitaires du Mirail, 1999), pp. 27–43
—— 'Theatre', in Brand and Pertile, pp. 277–335
—— 'The Dilemma of Chastity and Sex in Pastoral Drama', unpublished paper for a Symposium at University College, London (1997)
—— *Scripts and Scenarios: The Performance of Comedy in Renaissance Italy* (Cambridge: Cambridge University Press, 1993)
ANDRISANO, ANGELA, 'Il Satiro dell'*Aminta*', in *Torquato Tasso e l'Università*, ed. by Walter Moretti and Luigi Pepe (Florence: Olschki, 1997), pp. 357–71
ANGELINI, FRANCA, 'Il *Pastor fido* di Battista Guarini', in *Letteratura italiana*, ed. by Alberto Asor Rosa, 6 vols (Turin: Einaudi, 1982-), *Le Opere*, II: *Dal Cinquecento al Settecento* (1993), 705–24
ANGELINI FRAJESE, F., 'Bonarelli, Guidubaldo', in *DBI*, 11 (1969), 583–85
—— 'Andreini, Giovan Battista', *DBI*, 3 (1961), 133–36
ANGLO, SYDNEY, 'Humanism and the Court Arts', in *The Impact of Humanism on Western Europe*, ed. by Anthony Goodman and Angus Mackay (London: Longman, 1990), pp. 66–98
APOLLONIO, M., *Storia del teatro italiano*, 2 vols (Firenze: Sansoni, 1981)
ARIANI, MARCO, 'Introduzione' to *Il teatro italiano*, II: *La tragedia del Cinquecento*, 2 vols (Turin: Einaudi, 1977), I, VII–LXXXII
ASOR ROSA, ALBERTO, *Il Seicento, La nuova scienza e la crisi del Barocco*, La letteratura italiana: Storia e testi, V/I (Bari: Laterza, 1974)
ASCARI, T., 'Cesare d'Este', in *DBI*, 24 (1980), 136–41
—— 'Bentivoglio, Enzo', in *DBI*, 8 (1966), 610–12
ATTOLINI, GIOVANNI, *Teatro e spettacolo nel Rinascimento* (Bari: Laterza, 1988)
AUZZAS, GINETTA, 'La "raccolta" delle "Rime de gli Academici Eterei"', in Borsetto and da Rif, pp. 97–109
AVELLINI, LUISA, 'L'eredità di Castelvetro: Guarini', in *Letteratura italiana*, ed. by Alberto Asor Rosa, 6 vols (Turin: Einaudi, 1982-), II/1: *Storia e geografia. L'età moderna* (1988), 578–82

——'"Pelago" e "Porto": la corte e il cortigiano nell'epistolario del Guarini', in Papagno and Quondam, II, 683–96
BALATA, N., 'Dalla Viola, Alfonso', in *DBI*, 32 (1986), 59–60
BALDASSARRI, GUIDO, 'Introduzione' to Battista Guarini, *Il Pastor fido*, ed. by Elisabetta Selmi (Venice: Marsilio, 1999), pp. 9–24
——'Introduzione ai "Discorsi dell'arte poetica" del Tasso', *Studi tassiani*, 26 (1977), 5–38
BANCROFT-MARCUS, ROSEMARY, 'The Pastoral Mode', in *Literature and Society in Renaissance Crete*, ed. by David Holton (Cambridge: Cambridge University Press, 1991), pp. 79–102
BARISH, JONAS, 'The Problem of Closet Drama in the Italian Renaissance', *Italica*, 71 (1994), 4–31
BAROTTI, GIANNANDREA, *Memorie Istoriche di Letterati Ferraresi, Opera Postuma*, 2nd edn, 3 vols (Ferrara: per gli eredi di Giuseppe Rinaldi, 1792)
BATTISTINI, ANDREA, *Il Barocco, cultura, miti, immagini* (Rome: Salerno, 2000)
BEECHER, DONALD, MASSIMO CIAVOLELLA, and ROBERTO FEDI, eds, *Ariosto Today. Contemporary Perspectives* (Toronto: University of Toronto Press, 2003)
BELKIN, AHUVA, ed., *Leone de' Sommi and the Performing Arts* (Tel Aviv: Yolanda and David Katz Faculty of the Arts, Tel Aviv University, 1997)
BELLINA, ANNA LAURA, and CARLO CARUSO, 'Oltre il Barocco: la fondazione dell'Arcadia. Zeno e Metastasio: la riforma del melodramma', in *Storia della letteratura italiana*, ed. by Enrico Malato (Rome: Salerno, 1995-), VI: *Il Settecento* (1998), 239–312
BELLONI, ANTONIO, *Il Seicento* (Milan: Vallardi, 1952)
BENTINI, JADRANKA and SPEZZAFERRO, LUIGI, eds, *L'Impresa di Alfonso II: Saggi e documenti sulla produzione artistica a Ferrara nel secondo Cinquecento* (Bologna: Nuova Alfa, 1987)
BENZONI, G., 'Gonzaga, Scipione', in *DBI*, 57 (2001), 842–54
——'Ercole II d'Este', in *DBI*, 43 (1993), 107–26
BERGHAUS, GÜNTER, 'Stagecraft in the service of statecraft: political aspects of early Renaissance theatre in Ferrara', in Cairns, pp. 1–38
BERGONZI, ELENA, 'Cesare Cremonini scrittore, il periodo ferrarese e i primi anni padovani, la pastorale *Le Pompe funebri*', *Aevum*, 67 (1993), 571–93
BERTHÉ DI BESAUCÈLE, LOUIS, *G.-B. Giraldi 1504–1573. Étude sur l'Évolution des Théories Littéraires en Italie au XVIe siècle* (Paris: [n. pub.], 1920; repr. Geneva: Slatkine Reprints, 1969)
BIANCHI, FULVIO, and RUSSO, PAOLO, eds, *La scelta della misura. Gabriello Chiabrera: l'altro fuoco del barocco italiano* (Genoa: Costa & Nolan, 1993)
BIANCHI, STEFANO, 'The Theatre of Ariosto' (trans. by Hiroko Fudemoto), in Beecher, Ciavolella and Fedi, pp. 176–94
BIANCONI, LORENZO, 'I Fasti musicali del Tasso, nei secoli XVI e XVII', in *Torquato Tasso tra letteratura, musica, teatro e arti figurative*, ed. by A. Buzzoni, (Bologna: Nuova Alfa Editore, 1985), pp. 143–50
BIGI, EMILIO, 'Il dramma pastorale del Cinquecento', in *Poesia latina e volgare nel Rinascimento italiano* (Naples: Morano, 1989), pp. 341–70
BIRCH, PETER, *The Language of Drama. Critical Theory and Practice* (London: Macmillan, 1991)
BIRELEY, ROBERT, *The Refashioning of Catholicism, 1450–1700. A Reassessment of the Counter Reformation* (London: Macmillan, 1999)
——*The Counter-Reformation Prince. Anti-Machiavellianism or Catholic Statecraft in Early Modern Europe* (Chapel Hill: University of North Carolina Press, 1990)
BOLZONI, MONICA, 'Materiali sullo sviluppo del luogo teatrale ferrarese', in Bentini and Spezzaferro, pp. 225–33
BORSETTO, LUCIANA, and DA RIF, BIANCA MARIA, eds, *Formazione e fortuna del Tasso nella cultura della Serenissima* (Venice: Istituto Veneto di Scienze, Lettere ed arti, 1997)
BRAND, C. P. [PETER], *Torquato Tasso. A Study of the Poet and of his Contribution to English Literature* (Cambridge: Cambridge University Press, 1965)

BRAND, PETER, and PERTILE, LINO, eds, *The Cambridge History of Italian Literature*, 2nd rev. edn (Cambridge: Cambridge University Press, 1999)

BRIZI, BRUNO, 'Le feste e gli spettacoli', in *Storia di Vicenza*, ed. by Girolamo Arnaldi and others, 4 vols. (1990) (Vicenza: Neri Pozza, 1987–93), III/2: *L'Età della repubblica veneta (1404–1797)*, ed. by Franco Barbieri and Paolo Preto, 183–210

BROWN, JUDITH C., 'Lesbian Sexuality in Medieval and early Modern Europe', in *Hidden from History. Reclaiming the Gay and Lesbian Past*, ed. by Martin Duberman and others (New York: Dover, 1989), pp. 67–75

BRUNELLO, GIORGIO and ANTONIO LODO, eds, *Luigi Groto e il suo tempo*, 2 vols (Rovigo: Minelliana, 1987)

BRUSCAGLI, RICCARDO, 'Ancora sulle pastorali ferraresi del Cinquecento: la parte del Lollio', in Chiabò and Doglio, pp. 29–43

—— 'L'*Aminta* del Tasso e le pastorali ferraresi del '500', in *Studi di filologia e critica offerti dagli allievi a Lanfranco Caretti*, 2 vols (Rome: Salerno, 1985), I, 279–318

—— 'G. B. Giraldi: comico, satirico, tragico', in Panizza Lorch, pp. 261–83

BULLEGAS, SERGIO, 'Cultura ed emarginazione in Ruzante', *Rivista Italiana di Drammaturgia*, 11/12 (1979), 3–16

BURATTELLI, CLAUDIA, *Spettacoli di corte a Mantova tra Cinque e Seicento* (Florence: Le Lettere, 1999)

CAIRNS, CHRISTOPHER, ed., *Scenery, Set and Staging in the Italian Renaissance* (Lewiston: Edwin Mellen, 1996)

CALENDOLI, G., *L'attore. Storia di un'arte* (Rome: Edizioni dell'Ateneo, 1959)

CALORE, MARINA, *Pubblico e Spettacolo nel Rinascimento. Indagine sul territorio dell'Emilia Romagna* (Bologna: Forni, 1982)

—— 'Angelo Ingegneri "devotissimo e obbligatissimo servitore". Società, teatro e musica nel tardo rinascimento', *Il Flauto dolce. Rivista per lo Studio della Musica Antica*, 16 (1987), 3–7

—— 'Muzio Manfredi tra polemiche teatrali e crisi del mecenatismo', *Studi romagnoli*, 36 (1985), 27–54

CAMPBELL, JULIE D., 'Introduction' to Isabella Andreini, *'La Mirtilla': A Pastoral*, trans. with an intro. and notes by Julie D. Campbell, Medieval and Renaissance Texts and Studies, 242 (Tempe, Arizona: Arizona Center for Medieval and Renaissance Studies, 2002), pp. xi-xxvii

—— '*Love's Victory* and *La Mirtilla* in the Canon of Renaissance Tragicomedy: an examination of the influence of salon and social debates', *Women's Writing*, 4: 1 (1997), 103–24

CARDUCCI, GIOSUÉ, 'Su l'*Aminta* e il *Torrismondo*. Saggi di Giosué Carducci', in Angelo Solerti, *Torquato Tasso, Opere minori in versi*, 3 vols (Bologna: Zanichelli, 1895), III, iii-xli

CARLSON, MARVIN, *Theories of the Theatre. A Historical and Critical Survey, from the Greeks to the Present* (Ithaca: Cornell University Press, 1984)

CARRARA, ENRICO, *La Poesia pastorale*, Storia dei generi letterari italiani (Milan: Vallardi, 1909)

CARPANÉ, LORENZO, *Edizioni a stampa di Torquato Tasso 1561–1994. Catalogo breve*, 2 vols (Bergamo: Centro di Studi Tassiani, 1998)

—— 'La fortuna editoriale tassiana dal '500 ai giorni nostri', *Italianistica*, 25 (1995), 541–57

CARTER, TIM, *Music in Late Renaissance and Early Baroque Italy* (London: Batsford, 1992)

—— 'A Florentine Wedding of 1608', *Acta musicologica*, 55 (1983), 89–107

CATALANO, MICHELE, *Vita di Ludovico Ariosto, ricostruita su nuovi documenti*, 2 vols (Geneva: Olschki, 1930–31)

CAVALLINA, DIEGO, 'L'editoria ferrarese nei secoli XV e XVI', in *Il Rinascimento nelle corti padane. Società e cultura*, ed. by Paolo Rossi (Bari: De Donato, 1977), pp. 341–62

CAVALLINI, IVANO, 'Le accademie venete del cinquecento: la musica nel teatro e nell'attività speculativa', in *I Due volti di Nettuno. Studi su teatro e musica a Venezia e in Dalmazia dal Cinquecento al Settecento* (Lucca: Libreria Musicale Italiana, 1994), pp. 25–44

CAVAZZINI, GIANCARLO, 'Padova e Guarini: la *Poetica* di Aristotele nella teoria drammaturgica prebarocca', in *Il diletto della scena e dell'armonia. Teatro e musica nelle Venezie dal Cinquecento al Settecento*, ed. by Ivano Cavallini (Rovigo: Minelliana, [1990]), pp. 137–88

CAVE, TERENCE, *Recognitions: A Study in Poetics* (Oxford: Clarendon Press, 1988)

——'Ancients and Moderns: France', in *Cambridge History of Literary Criticism*, ed. by Peter Brooks and others (Cambridge: Cambridge University Press, 1989-), III: *The Renaissance*, ed. by Glyn P. Norton (1999), 417–25

CAVICCHI, ADRIANO, 'Imagini e forme dello spazio scenico nella pastorale ferrarese', in Chiabò and Doglio, pp. 45–86

CECCHI, EMILIO, and SAPEGNO, NATALINO, eds, *Storia della letteratura italiana. Il Seicento* (Milan: Garzanti, 1988)

CERUTI BURGIO, ANNA, 'E' una Torelli l'Hippolita amata da Vincenzo Gonzaga', *Aurea Parma*, 84 (2000), 39–46

CHAMBERS, D. S., and QUIVIGER, F., eds, *Italian Academies of the Sixteenth Century* (London: Warburg Institute, 1995)

CHATER, JAMES, '*Il Pastor fido* and music: A bibliography', in *Guarini, La musica, I musicisti*, ed. by Angelo Pompilio (Lucca: Libreria Musicale Italiana, 1997), pp. 157–84

CHEGAI, ANDREA, *Le Novellette a sei voci di Simone Balsamino. Prime musiche su* Aminta *di Torquato Tasso (1594)* (Florence: Olschki, 1993)

CHEMELLO, ADRIANA, '"Donne a poetar esperte": la "rimatrice dimessa" Maddalena Campiglia', *Versants*, n. s. 46 (2003), 65-101

CHIABÒ, M., and DOGLIO, F., eds, *Sviluppi della drammaturgia pastorale nell'Europa del Cinque-Seicento*, Centro Studi sul teatro medioevale e rinascimentale (Viterbo: Union Printing, [1992])

CHIAPPINI, ALESSANDRA, 'Baldini, Vittorio', in *Dizionario dei tipografi e degli editori italiani. Il Cinquecento*, ed. by Marco Menato, Ennio Sandal, and Giuseppina Zappella (Milan: Editrice Bibliografica, 1997), I, 57–62

CHIAPPINI, LUCIANO, *Gli Estensi* ([Milan]: Dall'Oglio, 1967)

CHIODO, DOMENICO, 'Introduzione' to Antonio Ongaro and Girolamo Vida, *Favole*, ed. by Domenico Chiodo with pref. by Giorgio Bárberi Squarotti (Turin: RES, 1998), pp. VII-XXV

——'Tra l'"Aminta" e il "Pastor fido"', *Italianistica*, 24 (1995), 559–75

——'"Soavi licor" e "succhi amari": Guarini e Baldi emuli del Tasso', *Lettere italiane*, 45 (1993), 116–28

——'Il mito dell'età aurea nell'opera tassiana', *Studi tassiani*, 35 (1987), 31–58

CLUBB, LOUISE GEORGE, *Italian Drama in Shakespeare's Time* (New Haven; London: Yale University Press, 1989)

——'The Pastoral Play: Conflations of Country, Court and City', in Panizza Lorch, pp. 65–73

——'The Making of the Pastoral Play: Some Italian experiments between 1573 and 1590', in *Petrarch to Pirandello, Studies in Italian Literature in honour of Beatrice Corrigan*, ed. by Julius A. Molinaro (Toronto: University of Toronto Press, 1973), pp. 45–73

——*Italian plays, 1500–1700, in the Folger Library* (Florence: Olschki, 1968)

COCHRANE, ERIC, *Italy 1530–1630*, ed. by Julius Kirshner, Longman History of Italy (London: Longman, 1988)

——'Le Accademie', in *Firenze e la Toscana dei Medici nell'Europa del '500*, ed. by Giancarlo Garfagnini (Florence: Olschki, 1983), pp. 3–17

CODY, RICHARD, *The Landscape of the Mind. Pastoralism and Platonic Theory in Tasso's* Aminta *and Shakespeare's Early Comedies* (Oxford: Clarendon Press, 1969)

COGNASSO, FRANCESCO, *I Savoia* ([Milan]: Dall'Oglio, 1971)

COHEN, RALPH, 'History and Genre', *New Literary History*, 17 (1986), 203–18

COLEMAN, JANET, ed., *The Individual in Political Theory and Practice* (Oxford: Clarendon Press, 1996)

COLIE, ROSALIE, 'Genre-Systems and the Functions of Literature', in Duff, pp. 148–66
COMPARATO, VITTOR IVO, 'A Case of Modern Individualism: Politics and the Uneasiness of Intellectuals in the Baroque Age', in Coleman, pp. 149–70
COOPER, HELEN, *Pastoral. Mediaeval into Renaissance* (Ipswich: Brewer, 1977)
CORSO, C., *Carteggio inedito fra Battista Guarini e Belisario Bulgarini* (Siena: Accademia degli Intronati, 1951)
COSTA, GUSTAVO, *La leggenda dei secoli d'oro nella letteratura italiana* (Bari: Laterza, 1972)
COTTINO-JONES, MARGA, 'Literary-critical developments in sixteenth- and seventeenth-century Italy', in *The Cambridge History of Literary Criticism*, ed. by Peter Brooks and others (Cambridge: Cambridge University Press, 1989-), III: *The Renaissance*, ed. by Glyn P. Norton (1999), 566–77
COTTON, NANCY, 'Women playwrights in England: Renaissance noblewomen', in *Readings in Renaissance Women's Drama. Criticism, history, and performance 1594–1998*, ed. by S. P. Cerasano and Marion Wynne-Davies (London: Routledge, 1998), pp. 32–46
COX, VIRGINIA, 'Fiction, 1560–1650', in *A History of Women's Writing in Italy*, ed. by Letizia Panizza and Sharon Wood (Cambridge: Cambridge University Press, 2000), pp. 52–64
—— 'Tasso's *Malpiglio overo de la corte*: *The Courtier* Revisited', *MLR*, 90 (1995), 897–918
—— *The Renaissance Dialogue. Literary dialogue in its social and political contexts, Castiglione to Galileo* (Cambridge: Cambridge University Press, 1992)
COX, VIRGINIA, and SAMPSON, LISA, 'Introduction', to Maddalena Campiglia, *Flori, a pastoral drama*, trans. by Virginia Cox (Chicago: University of Chicago Press, 2004), pp. 1–35
CROCE, BENEDETTO, *Storia dell'età barocca in italia*, 2nd edn (Bari: Laterza, 1946)
CROCE, FRANCO, 'La teatralità dell'*Aminta*', in Chiabò and Doglio, pp. 131–57
—— 'L'intellettuale Chiabrera', in Bianchi and Russo, pp. 15–50
—— 'Critica e trattatistica del barocco', in Cecchi and Sapegno, pp. 495–547
CRUCIANI, FABRIZIO, 'Percorsi critici verso la prima rappresentazione dell'*Aminta*', in *Torquato Tasso tra letteratura, musica, teatro e arti figurative*, ed. by A. Buzzoni (Bologna: Nuova Alfa Editore, 1985), pp. 179–92
—— 'Gli attori e l'attore a Ferrara. Premessa per un catalogo', in Papagno and Quondam, II, 451–66
DALLA PALMA, GIUSEPPE, 'Aminta, Alceo, Tirena: Una serie pastorale', in *La Poesia pastorale nel rinascimento*, ed. by Stefano Carrai (Padua: Antenore, 1998)
—— 'Un capitolo della fortuna dell'*Aminta*: l'*Alceo* di Antonio Ongaro', *Rivista di letteratura italiana*, 12 (1994), 79–128
—— 'L'*Irifile* e la cultura letteraria di Leone de' Sommi (con un'edizione critica del testo)', *Schifanoia*, 9 (1990), 139–225
DALLA VALLE, DANIELA, 'Gabriello Chiabrera tradotto in francese: "Le ravissement de Céphale" di Chretien des Croix', in Bianchi and Russo, pp. 503–17
—— 'La fortune française de la *Filli di Sciro* au XVIIe siècle', *Revue de littérature comparée*, 4 (1972), 333–59
—— 'Il Mito dell'età dell'oro e la concezione dell'amore dall'*Aminta* alla pastorale barocca francese', in *La frattura. Studi sul barocco letterario francese* (Ravenna: Longo, 1970), pp. 21–84
D'ANCONA, ALESSANDRO, *Origini del teatro italiano: libri tre con due appendici sulla rappresentazione drammatica del contado toscano e sul teatro mantovano nel sec. XVI*, 3 vols, 2nd edn (Turin: Loescher, 1891)
DA POZZO, GIOVANNI, *L'Ambigua armonia. Studio sull'*Aminta *del Tasso* (Florence: Olschki, 1983)
DAVI, MARIA ROSA, 'Filosofia e retorica nell'opera di Sperone Speroni', in *Sperone Speroni: Filologia Veneta. Lingua, letteratura, tradizioni*, ed. by A. Daniele and others (Padua: Programma, 1989), pp. 89–112
DAVICO BONINO, G., ed., *Il teatro italiano, II: La Commedia del Cinquecento*, 2 vols (Turin: Einaudi, 1977–78)

DAVIDSON, NICHOLAS, 'Theology, nature and the law: sexual sin and sexual crime in Italy from the fourteenth to the seventeenth century', in *Crime, Society and the Law in Renaissance Italy*, ed. by Trevor Dean and K. J. P. Lowe (Cambridge: Cambridge University Press, 1994), pp. 74–98

DE BELLO, RAFFAELE, 'Bibliografia della Collana Palatina delle Pastorali' (BNF, 12-2-0-3), *Studi Secenteschi*, 5 (1964), 161–74; 6 (1965), 285–98; 7 (1966), 145–54

DE BLASI, JOLANDA, *Le scrittrici italiane dalle origini al 1800* (Florence: 'Nemi', 1930)

DE BLASI, N., 'Ercole Bentivoglio', *DBI*, 8 (1966), 615–18

DE LUCA, ANTONIO, *Il Teatro di Ludovico Ariosto*, with preface by Walter Binni (Rome: Bulzoni, 1981)

DENAROSI, LUCIA, 'Il Principe e il letterato: due carteggi inediti di Muzio Manfredi', *Studi italiani*, 17 (1997), 151–76

DE ROBERTIS, DOMENICO, 'Aspects de la Formation du Genre Pastoral en Italie au XVe siècle', in *Le genre pastoral en Europe du XVe au XVIIe siècle*, ed. by Claude Longeon and others (Université de Saint-Étienne: Centre d'Études de la Renaissance et de l'Âge Classique, 1980), pp. 7–14

DERSOFI, NANCY, 'Isabella Andreini (1562–1604)', in *Italian Women Writers. A Bio-Bibliographical Sourcebook*, ed. by Rinaldina Russell (Westport CT: Greenwood, 1994), pp. 18–25

DE SANCTIS, FRANCESCO, *Storia della letteratura italiana*, ed. by Benedetto Croce, 2 vols (Bari: Laterza, 1949)

DI BENEDETTO, ARNALDO, 'L'*Aminta* e la Pastorale Cinquecentesca in Italia', *GSLI*, 173 (1996), 481–514

DIFFLEY, P. B., *Paolo Beni: A Biographical and Critical Study* (Oxford: Clarendon, 1988)

DIONISOTTI, CARLO, 'La letteratura italiana nell'età del Concilio di Trento' in *Geografia e storia della letteratura* (Turin: Einaudi, 1967), pp. 227–54

DOGLIO, MARIA LUISA, see Ingegneri

DUFF, DAVID, ed., *Modern Genre Theory*, Longman Critical Readers (Harlow: Pearson Education, 2000)

DUPONT-BOUCHAT, MARIE-SYLVIE, 'Guilt and Individual Consciousness: The Individual, the Church and the State in the Modern Era, Sixteenth-Seventeenth Centuries', in Coleman, pp. 123–48

DURANTE, ELIO, and MARTELLOTTI, ANNA, *Cronistoria del Concerto Delle Dame Principalissime di Margherita Gonzaga d'Este* (Florence: SPES, 1979)

EMPSON, WILLIAM, *Some Versions of Pastoral* (London: Chatto and Windus, 1935)

ETTIN, ANDREW, V., *Literature and the Pastoral* (New Haven: Yale University Press, 1984)

FABBRI, P., FARINA, A., and others, 'Il Teatro degli Intrepidi di Giovan Battista Aleotti rivive verso le nuove techniche dell'acustica virtuale', http://pcfarina.eng.unipr.it/Public/Papers/070-Ciarm95.pdf (accessed 08/06/2005)

FACCIOLI, EMILIO, *Mantova. Le Lettere*, with pref. by Lanfranco Caretti, 3 vols (Mantua: Istituto Carlo d'Arco per la Storia di Mantova, 1959–63)

FARRIS, GIOVANNI, 'Gabriello Chiabrera, savonese di nascita e di elezione', in Bianchi and Russo, pp. 51–74

FENLON, IAIN, 'Scipione Gonzaga: A "Poor" Cardinal in Rome', in *Music and Culture in late Renaissance Italy* [first printed 1988] (Oxford: Oxford University Press, 2002), pp. 93–117

——'Guarini, de' Sommi and the Pre-History of the Italian Danced Spectacle', in *Leone de' Sommi and the Performing Arts*, ed. by Ahuva Belkin (Tel Aviv University: The Yolanda and David Katz Faculty of the The Arts, 1997), pp. 49–65

——*Music and Patronage in Sixteenth-Century Mantua*, 2 vols (Cambridge: Cambridge University Press, 1980)

FERGUSON, ARTHUR B., *Utter Antiquity: Perceptions of Prehistory in Renaissance England* (Durham, NC: Duke University Press, 1993)

FERGUSON, MARGARET W., 'Sidney, Cary, Wroth', in Kinney, pp. 482–506
——— *Trials of Desire. Renaissance Defenses of Poetry* (New Haven: Yale University Press, 1983)
FERRARI, G. R. F., 'Plato and Poetry', in *The Cambridge History of Literary Criticism*, ed. by Peter Brooks and others (Cambridge: Cambridge University Press, 1989-), I: *Classical Criticism*, ed. by George A. Kennedy (1989), 92–148
FINDLAY, ALISON, 'Gendering the Stage', in Kinney, pp. 399–415
FINDLAY, ALISON, and STEPHANIE HODGSON-WRIGHT, with GWENO WILLIAMS, *Women and Dramatic Production 1550–1700* (Harlow: Longman, 2000)
FOÀ, S., 'Giraldi, Giovan Battista (Giovan Battista Cinzio)', in *DBI*, 56 (2001), 442–47
——— 'Giraldi, Lilio Gregorio', in *DBI*, 56 (2001), 452–55
FOLENA, GIANFRANCO, 'La mistione tragicomica e la metamorfosi dello stile nella poetica del Guarini', in *La Critica stilistica e il Barocco letterario* (Florence: Le Monnier, 1958), pp. 344–49.
FOSTER, VERNA A. *The Name and Nature of Tragicomedy*, Studies in European Cultural Transition, 18 (Aldershot: Ashgate, 2004)
FORMICHETTI, GIANFRANCO, 'La poetica di Chiabrera e le prospettive della poesia religiosa nell'ambiente romano tra manierismo e barocco', in Bianchi and Russo, pp. 126–38.
FORSTER, LEONARD, *The Icy Fire. Five Studies in European Petrarchism* (Cambridge: Cambridge University Press, 1969)
GALLI STAMPINO, MARIA, *Aminta: Staging the Pastoral: Tasso's* Aminta *and the Emergence of Modern Western Theater* (Tempe: Medieval & Renaissance Texts & Studies, forthcoming)
GALLO, V., 'Groto (Grotto), Luigi (detto il Cieco d'Adria', *DBI*, 60 (2003), 21–24
GAMBARA, LODOVICO, MARCO PELLEGRI, and MARIO DE GRAZIA, *Palazzi e casate di Parma* (Parma: La Nazionale, 1971)
GAMBARIN, GIOVANNI, see Bonarelli
GARIN, E., 'Guarino Veronese e la cultura a Ferrara', in *Ritratti di umanisti* (Florence: Sansoni, 1967), pp. 69–103
GAREFFI, ANDREA, ed., *La questione del "Pastor fido". Giovan Battista Guarini Annotazioni. Faustino Summo. Due Discorsi* (Manziana: Vecchiarelli, 1997)
——— 'Cavallerie ferraresi', in Papagno and Quondam, II, 467–87
GARRAFFO, ORNELLA, 'Il satiro nella pastorale ferrarese del Cinquecento', *Italianistica*, 14 (1985), 185–201
GENETTE, GÉRARD, *Paratexts. Thresholds of interpretation*, trans. by Jane E. Lewin, foreword by Richard Macksey [*Seuils* (Paris: Editions du Seuil, 1987)] (Cambridge University Press, 1997)
GIFFORD, TERRY, *Pastoral*, The New Critical Idiom (London: Routledge, 1999)
GIRARDI, MARIA TERESA, 'Tasso, Speroni e la cultura padovana', in Borsetto and da Rif, pp. 63–77
GODARD, ALAIN, 'La *Filli di Sciro* de Guidubaldo Bonarelli: précédents littéraires et nouveaux impératifs idéologiques', in *Réécritures 2: Commentaires, parodies, variations dans la littérature italienne de la renaissance*, Centre Interuniversitaire de Recherche sur la Renaissance Italienne (Paris: Université de la Sorbonne Nouvelle, 1984), pp. 141–225
——— 'La Première Représentation de l'*Aminta*: La Court de Ferrare et son double', in *Ville et Campagne Dans la Littérature Italienne de la Renaissance*, II: Le Courtisan Travesti, Centre di Recherche sur la Renaissance Italienne (Paris: Université de la Sorbonne Nouvelle, 1977), 187–301
GOMBRICH, E. H., 'Renaissance and Golden Age', in *Norm and Form: Studies in the Art of the Renaissance* (London: Phaidon, 1966), pp. 29–34
GOUGH, MELINDA J., 'Courtly *Comédiantes*: Henrietta Maria and amateur Women's Stage Plays in France and England', in *Women Players in England, 1550–1660. Beyond the All-Male Stage* (Aldershot: Ashgate, 2005), pp. 193–215

GRAFTON, ANTHONY, and JARDINE, LISA, *From Humanism to the Humanities. Education and the Liberal Arts in Fifteenth- and Sixteenth-Century Europe* (London: Duckworth, 1986), pp. 53–56

GRAZIOSI, ELISABETTA, *Aminta 1573–1580. Amore e matrimonio in casa d'Este* (Pisa: Maria Pacini Fazzi, 2001)

GREG, WALTER W., *Pastoral Poetry and Pastoral Drama* (London: Bullen, 1906)

GRENDLER, PAUL F., *The Universities of the Italian Renaissance* (Baltimore and London: Johns Hopkins University Press, 2002)

—— 'The Roman Inquisition and the Venetian Press, 1540–1605', in *Culture and Censorship in Late Renaissance Italy and France* (*Journal of Modern History*, 47 (1975); repr. London: Variorum Reprints, 1981), pp. 48–65

—— *The Roman Inquisition and the Venetian Press, 1540–1605* (Princeton N.J.: Princeton University Press, 1977)

GROSSER, HERMANN, '*Aminta*: lo stile della pastorale', in *Il merito e la cortesia. Torquato Tasso e la Corte dei Della Rovere*, ed. by Guido Arbizzoni and others (Ancona: Il lavoro editorial/Cassa di Risparmio di Pesaro, 1999), pp. 237–71

GUARINO, RAIMONDO, 'Beolco e Ruzante. Tra due élites', in *Il Teatro italiano nel rinascimento*, ed. by Fabrizio Cruciani and Daniele Seragnoli (Bologna: Il Mulino, 1987), pp. 149–75

GUERCIO, V., 'Tirannide e machiavellismo in scena pastorale: sulla "Galatea" di Pomponio Torelli', *GSLI*, 115 (1998), 161–209

GUGLIELMINETTI, MARZIANO, 'Introduzione' to *Opere di Battista Guarini*, ed. by Marziano Guglielminetti (Turin: UTET, 1971), pp. 9–69

HAAR, JAMES, 'Dalla Viola, Alfonso', *The New Grove Dictionary of Music and Musicians*, ed. by Stanley Sadie, 2nd edn (London: Macmillan, 2001), VI, 862

HABER, JUDITH, *Pastoral and the poetics of self-contradiction. Theocritus to Marvell* (Cambridge: Cambridge University Press, 1994)

HARRISON, ROBERT POGUE, *Forests. The Shadow of Civilization* (Chicago: University Press, 1992)

HARTMANN JR., ARNOLD, 'Battista Guarini and Il Pastor fido', *Musical Quarterly*, 39 (1953), 415–25

HATHAWAY, BAXTER, *The Age of Criticism. The Late Renaissance in Italy* (Ithaca, NY: Cornell University Press, 1962)

HAY, DENYS and JOHN LAW, *Italy in the Age of the Renaissance 1380–1530* (London: Longman, 1989)

HENKE, ROBERT, *Performance and Literature in the Commedia dell'Arte* (Cambridge: Cambridge University Press, 2002)

—— *Pastoral Transformations. Italian tragicomedy and Shakespeare's Late Plays* (London: Associated University Presses, 1997)

HERRICK, MARVIN T., *Tragicomedy. Its origins and development in Italy, France and England* (Urbana: University of Illinois Press, 1962)

HOLZBERG, NIKLAS, *The Ancient Novel. An introduction*, trans. by Christine Jackson-Holzberg (London: Routledge, 1995)

HORNE, P[HILIP]. R., ed., G. B. GIRALDI, *Eufimia. An Italian Renaissance Tragedy*, ed. with introduction, notes and glossary by Philip Horne, Medieval and Renaissance Studies, 21 (Lewiston: Edwin Mellen Press. 2003)

—— G. B. GIRALDI, *Gli Eudemoni. An Italian Renaissance Comedy*, ed., with introduction, notes, and glossary by Philip Horne (Lewiston: Edwin Mellen Press, 1999)

—— *The Tragedies of Giambattista Cinthio Giraldi* (Oxford: Oxford University Press, 1962)

—— 'The Three versions of G. B. Giraldi's Satyr-Play *Egle*', *Italian Studies*, 24, (1962), 32–43

—— 'Reformation and Counter-Reformation at Ferrara: Antonio Musa Brasavola and Giambattista Cinthio Giraldi', *Italian Studies*, 13 (1958), 62–82

IVALDI, ARMANDO FABIO, 'L'esordio del dramma pastorale: fra sperimentazione e mimetismo', in Panizza Lorch, pp. 381–86

―― '"Il Sacrificio" di Agostino Beccari. Per l'edizione critica del testo', *Atti e Memorie della Deputazione Provinciale Ferrarese di Storia Patria*, s. 3, 24 (1977), 87–136

―― *Le Nozze Pio-Farnese e gli apparati teatrali di Sassuolo del 1587. Studio su una rappresentazione del primo dramma pastorale italiano, con intermezzi di G. B. Guarini* (Genoa: E.R.G.A., 1974)

JAVITCH, DANIEL, 'The Emergence of Poetic Genre Theory in the Sixteenth Century', *Modern Language Quarterly*, 59 (1998), 139–69

―― *Proclaiming a Classic. The Canonization of 'Orlando Furioso'* (Princeton N. J.: Princeton University Press, 1991)

―― 'Self-justifying Norms in the Genre Theories of Italian Renaissance Poets', *Philological Quarterly*, 67 (1988), 195–217

JEFFERY, VIOLET M., 'Italian and English Pastoral Drama of the Renaissance III: Sources of Daniel's *Queen's Arcadia* and Randolphe's *Amyntas*', *MLR*, 19 (1924), 435–44

JONARD, NORBERT, 'Le Baroquisme du *Pastor fido*', *Studi secenteschi*, 10 (1969), 3–18

JONES, ANN ROSALIND, *The Currency of Eros: Women's Love Lyric in Europe, 1540–1620* (Bloomington and Indianapolis: Indiana University Press, 1990)

KINNEY, ARTHUR F., ed., *A Companion to Renaissance Drama* (Oxford: Blackwell, 2002)

KIRKENDALE, WARREN, 'L'Opera in musica prima del Peri: Le pastorali perdute di Laura Guidiccioni ed Emilio de' Cavalieri', in *Firenze e la Toscana dei Medici nell'Europa del '500*, ed. by Giancarlo Garfagnini, 3 vols (Florence: Olschki, 1983), II, 365–95

KIRKPATRICK, ROBIN, *English and Italian Literature from Dante to Shakespeare. A study of source, analogue and divergence* (London: Longman, 1995)

KOLSKY, STEPHEN, 'Theorizing Pleasure in the Renaissance', *Spunti e ricerche*, 4–5 (1988/9), 33–49

KRAYE, JILL, 'Moral Philosophy', in *The Cambridge History of Renaissance Philosophy*, ed. by Charles Schmitt and others (Cambridge: Cambridge University Press, 1988), pp. 303–86

LACAPRA, DOMINICK, 'Comment', *New Literary History*, 17 (1986), 219–21

LA PENNA, ANTONIO, 'Note all'"Aminta" del Tasso', in *Omaggio a Gianfranco Folena*, ed. by Pier Vincenzo Mengaldo and others, 3 vols (Padua: Programma, 1993), II, 1171–82

LARIVAILLE, PAUL, 'Dall'Ariosto al Tasso. Poeta, principe, pubblico nel "Furioso" e nella "Liberata"', in *Studi in onore di Bortolo Tommaso Sozzi*, ed. by Aldo Agazzi, (Bergamo: Centro di Studi Tassiani, 1991), pp. 169–82

―― *Poesia e ideologia. Letture della 'Gerusalemme Liberata'* (Naples: Liguori, 1987)

LAVOCAT, FRANÇOISE, 'Introduzione' to Lucrezia Marinella, *Arcadia felice* (Florence: Olschki, 1998), pp. VII-LX

LAZZARO, CLAUDIA, *The Italian Renaissance Garden. From the Conventions of Planting, Design, and Ornament to the Grand Gardens of Sixteenth-Century Central Italy* (New Haven; London: Yale University Press, 1990)

LEA, KATHLEEN, *Italian Popular Comedy. A Study in the Commedia dell'Arte, 1560-1620, with Special Reference to the English Stage*, 2 vols (Oxford: Clarendon Press, 1934)

LEVIN, HARRY, *The Myth of the Golden Age in the Renaissance* (London: Faber and Faber, 1969)

LODI, LETIZIA, 'Immagini della genealogia estense', in Bentini and Spezzaferro, pp. 151–62

LOEWENSTEIN, JOSEPH, 'Guarini and the Presence of Genre', in Maguire, pp. 35–55

LOMBARDI, MARCO, '"L'Ombre d'un plaisir" nei sottoboschi della pastorale', in *Teatri barocchi. Tragedie, commedie, pastorali nella drammaturgia europea fra '500 e '600* (Rome: Bulzoni, 2000), pp, 489–507

LOONEY, DENNIS, 'Ariosto and the Classics in Ferrara', in Beecher, Ciavolella and Fedi, pp. 18–31

LOUGHREY BRYAN, ed., *The Pastoral Mode. A Casebook* (London: Macmillan, 1984)

LUEBKE, DAVID M., ed., *The Counter-Reformation* (Oxford: Blackwell, 1999)

LYNE, RAPHAEL, 'English Guarini: Recognition and Reception', *Yearbook of English Studies*, 2006 (forthcoming)

McGowan, Margaret, 'Adventure and theatrical innovation at Ferrara and Mannheim', in *The Renaissance in Ferrara and its European Horizons*, ed. by J. Salmons (Cardiff: University of Wales Press, 1984), pp. 61–81

MacNeil, Anne, *Music and women of the commedia dell'arte in the late sixteenth century* (Oxford: Oxford University Press, 2003)

—— 'The divine madness of Isabella Andreini', *Journal of the Royal Musical Association*, 120 (1995), 193–215

Magliani, Mariella, 'Stampatori veneti del Tasso', in Borsetto and da Rif, pp. 121–39

Maguire, Nancy Klein, ed., *Renaissance Tragicomedy. Explorations in Genre and Politics* (New York: AMS Press, 1987)

Malagoli, Giuseppe, 'Studi, amori e lettere inedite di Guidobaldo Bonarelli', *GSLI*, 17 (1891), 177–211

Mamone, Sara, *Il teatro nella Firenze medicea* (Milan: Mursia, 1981)

Mancini, Albert N., 'Narrative prose and theatre' ['The Seicento'], in Brand and Pertile, pp. 318–25

Manetti, Aldo, '*Le Conclusioni amorose*', *Studi tassiani*, 24 (1974), 33–45

Mangini, Nicola, 'Il teatro veneto al tempo della controriforma', in Brunello and Lodo, pp. 119–37

Mantese, Giovanni, *I mille libri che si leggevano e vendevano a Vicenza alla fine del secolo XVI* (Vicenza: Accademia Olimpica, 1968)

—— 'Per un profilo storico della poetessa vicentina Maddalena Campiglia: aggiunte e rettifiche', *Archivio veneto*, s. 5, 81 (1967), 89–123

Mantese, G. and Nardello, M., *Due processi per eresia. La vicenda religiosa di Luigi Groto, il 'Cieco di Adria', e della nobile vicentina Angelica Pigafetta Piovene* (Vicenza: Officine grafiche Sta, 1974)

Maragoni, Gian Piero, 'Il carattere del genere drammatico pastorale e la *Filli di Sciro* di Guidubaldo Bonarelli', *Critica letteraria*, 8 (1980), 559–80

Marchetti, V. and Patrizi, G., 'Castelvetro, Ludovico', in *DBI*, 22 (1979), 8–21

Marcigliano, Alessandro, 'Giovan Battista Verato: un attore nella Ferrara del Cinquecento', in Cairns, pp. 81–99

—— 'Cavallerie a Ferrara: 1561–1570', in *Italian Renaissance Festivals and their European Influence*, ed. by J. R. Mulryne and Margaret Shewring (Lewiston: Edwin Mellen Press, 1992), pp. 75–94

Marini, Lino, 'Lo stato estense', in *I ducati padani, Trento e Trieste*, ed. by Lino Marini and others, Storia d'Italia, 17 (Turin: UTET, 1979), pp. 3–211

Marotti, Ferruccio, *Storia documentaria del teatro italiano. Lo Spettacolo dall'Umanesimo al Manierismo. Teoria e tecnica* (Milan: Feltrinelli, 1974)

—— 'Introduzione' to *Leone de' Sommi, Quattro dialoghi in materia di rappresentazioni sceniche* (Milan: Il Polifilo, 1968), pp. xv–lxxiii

Marsan, Jules, *La pastorale dramatique en France à la fin du XVIe et au commencement du XVIIe siècle* (Paris: Hachette et Cie, 1905; repr. Geneva: Slatkine reprints, 1969)

Marucci, Valerio, *L'Età della Controriforma e del Barocco* (Palermo: Palumbo, 1978)

Matt, L., 'Guidi, Alessandro', *DBI*, 61 (2003), 203–08

Maylender, Michele, *Storia delle Accademie d'Italia*, 5 vols (Bologna: Licinio Capelli, 1926–30)

Mazzacurati, Giancarlo, *Il Rinascimento dei moderni. La crisi culturale del XVI secolo e la negazione delle origini* (Bologna: Il Mulino, 1985)

—— 'Beni, Paolo', in *DBI*, 8 (1966), 494–501

Mazzoni, Stefano, *L'Olimpico di Vicenza, un teatro e la sua 'perpetua memoria'* (Florence: Le Lettere, 1998)

Mazzali, Ettore, 'Introduzione' to Torquato Tasso, *Prose* (Milan; Naples: Ricciardi, 1959), pp. xvii-xliv [trans. and abridged by Eric Cochrane as 'Literature: Torquato Tasso: An Introduction', in *The Late Italian Renaissance 1525–1630*, ed. by Eric Cochrane (London: Macmillan, 1970), pp. 134–48]

MAZZONI, STEFANO, *L'Olimpico di Vicenza: un teatro e la sua 'perpetua memoria'* (Florence: Le Lettere, 1998)

MEROLA, N., 'Chiabrera, Gabriello', in *DBI*, 24 (1980), 465–75

MIGLIORI, A., 'Beccari, Agostino', in *DBI*, 7 (1965), 426–27

MILANI, MARISA, 'Quattro donne fra i pavani', *Museum Patavinum*, 1 (1983), 387–412

MOLINARI, CARLA, 'La parte del Guarini nel Commento al "Pastor fido"', *Schifanoia*, 15–16 (1995), 141–50

—— 'Introduzione' to *Giambattista Giraldi Cinzio. Egle, Lettera sovra il comporre le Satire atte alla scena, Favola pastorale* (Bologna: Commissione per i testi di lingua, 1985), pp. VII–XXVI

—— 'Per il "Pastorfido" di Battista Guarini', *Studi di filologia italiana*, 43 (1985), 161–238

—— 'Dall'"Arcadia" alla favola pastorale', *Studi e problemi di critica testuale*, 26 (1983), 151–67

MOLINARI, CESARE, 'Premesse cinquecentesche al grande spettacolo dell'età barocca', in *Studi sul teatro veneto fra rinascimento ed età barocca*, ed. by Maria Teresa Muraro (Florence: Olschki, 1971), pp. 97–117

—— *Le nozze degli dèi, un saggio sul grande spettacolo italiano nel Seicento* (Rome: Bulzoni, 1968)

—— 'Scenografia e spettacolo nelle poetiche del cinquecento', *Il Veltro*, 8 (1964), 885–902

MONETA, A., 'Costabili, Rinaldo', in *DBI*, 30 (1984), 262–63

MORSOLIN, BERNARDO, *Maddalena Campiglia, poetessa vicentina del secolo XVI, episodio biografico* (Vicenza: Paroni, 1882)

MUTINI, C. C., 'Cavalcanti, Bartolomeo', *DBI*, 22 (1979), 611–17

NAGLER, A. M., *Theatre festivals of the Medici 1539–1637* (New Haven: Yale University Press, 1964)

NEDERMAN, C. J., 'Nature, sin and the origins of society: the Ciceronian tradition in medieval political thought', *Journal of the History of Ideas*, 49 (1988), 3–26

NERI, FERDINANDO, *Scenari delle Maschere in Arcadia* (Città di Castello: Lapi, 1913; repr. Turin: Bottega d'Erasmo, 1961)

NEWCOMB, ANTHONY, *The Madrigal at Ferrara 1579–1597* (Princeton: Princeton University Press, 1980)

NOLAN, P., 'Free Will', in *New Catholic Encyclopedia* ((New York: McGraw-Hill, 1967-), VI, 89–93

ORGEL, STEPHEN, 'What is a Text?', in *Staging the Renaissance. Reinterpretations of Elizabethan and Jacobean Drama*, ed. by David Scott Kastan and Peter Stallybrass (London: Routledge, 1991), pp. 83–87

OSBORN, PEGGY, ed., *G. B. Giraldi's Altile. The birth of a new dramatic genre in Renaissance Ferrara* (Lewiston: Edwin Mellen, 1992)

OSSI, MASSIMO, 'Dalle machine ... la maraviglia: Bernardo Buontalenti's *Il rapimento di Cefalo* at the Medici Theater in 1600', in *Opera in Context: Essays on Historical Staging from the Late Renaissance to the Time of Puccini*, ed. by Mark A. Radice (Portland, OR: Amadeus Press, 1998), pp. 15–35, 297–305

OSSOLA, CARLO, *Dal Cortegiano all''Uomo di mondo'. Storia di un libro e di un modello sociale* (Turin: Einaudi, 1987)

OWENS, JESSIE ANN, 'Music in the Early Ferrarese Pastoral: A Study of Beccari's *Il Sacrificio*', in Panizza Lorch, pp. 583–601

PADE, M., PETERSEN, L. W., and QUARTA D., eds, *La corte di Ferrara e il suo mecenatismo 1441–1598* (Copenhagen: Forum for Renaessancestudier; Ferrara: L'Istituto di Studi Rinascimentali, 1990)

PAGDEN, ANTHONY, *The Fall of Natural Man. The American Indian and the origins of comparative ethnology* (Cambridge: Cambridge University Press, 1982)

PALISCA, CLAUDE V., 'The Alterati of Florence, Pioneers in the Theory of Dramatic Music', in *New Looks at Italian Opera: Essays in Honor of Donald J. Grout*, ed. with intro. by William W. Austin (Ithaca: Cornell University Press, 1968), pp. 9–38.
—— 'The First Performance of *Euridice*', in *Queens College Department of Music: Twenty-fifth Anniversay Festschrift*, ed. by Albert Mell (New York: Queens College Press, 1964), pp. 1–23
—— 'Musical Asides in the Correspondence of Emilio de' Cavalieri', *Musical Quarterly*, 49 (1963), 339–55
PANIZZA LORCH, MARISTELLA DE, ed., *Il teatro italiano del rinascimento* (Milan: Edizione di Comunità, 1980)
PANOFSKY, ERWIN, 'The Early History of Man in Two Cycles of Paintings by Piero di Cosimo', in *Studies in Iconology: Humanistic Themes In the Art of the Renaissance* (New York: Harper and Row, 1962; repr. 1972), pp. 33–67
PAPAGNO, G. and QUONDAM, A., eds, *La corte e lo spazio, Ferrara estense*, 3 vols (Rome: Bulzoni, 1982)
PASQUAZI, SILVIO, 'Le Annotazioni al *Pastor fido* di Lionardo Salviati', in *Poeti estensi del Rinascimento* (Florence: Le Monnier, 1966), pp. 191–233
PATRIZI, G., 'Denores, Giason', in *DBI*, 38 (1990), 768–73
PATTERSON, ANNABEL, *Pastoral and Ideology. Virgil to Valéry* (Berkeley: University of California Press, 1988)
PERELLA, NICOLAS J., *The Critical Fortune of Battista Guarini's 'Il Pastor Fido'*, Biblioteca dell''Archivium Romanicum', 117 (Florence: Olschki, 1973)
—— 'Fate, Blindness and Illusion in the *Pastor fido*', *Romanic Review*, 49 (1958), 252–68
PERRONA, LORENZO, 'Chiabrera e la favola di Galatea', in Bianchi and Russo, pp. 295–317
PERRONE, CARLACHIARA, '"So che donna ama donna": La *Calisa* di Maddalena Campiglia' (Galatina: Congedo, 1996)
PEVERE, FULVIO, 'Introduzione' to Agostino Beccari, Alberto Lollio, Agostino Argenti, *Favole* (Turin: RES, 1999), pp. VII-XXXII
PIERI, MARZIA, 'La drammaturgia di Chiabrera', in Bianchi and Russo, pp. 401–28
—— '"Il Pastor fido" e i comici dell'arte', *Biblioteca teatrale* 17 (1990), 1–15
—— *La Nascita del teatro moderno tra XV e XVI secolo* (Turin: Bollati Boringhieri, 1989)
—— *La scena boschereccia nel rinascimento italiano* (Padua: Liviana, 1983)
—— 'Il "Laboratorio" Provinciale di Luigi Groto', *Rivista italiana di drammaturgia*, 14 (1979), 3–35
PINDOZZI, VALERIO, 'Pier Giuseppe Giustiniani e Gabriello Chiabrera', in Bianchi and Russo, pp. 107–25
PIRROTTA, NINO, and POVOLEDO, ELENA, *Music and Theatre From Poliziano to Monteverdi*, trans. by Karen Eales [from *Li due Orfei*, Turin: Eri, 1969], Cambridge Studies in Music (Cambridge: Cambridge University Press, 1982)
POPPI, ANTONINO, 'Il prevalere della "vita activa" nella Paidea del Cinquecento', in *Rapporti tra le università di Padova e Bologna, Ricerche di filosofia medicina e scienza*, ed. by Lucia Rossetti, Centro per la storia dell'Università di Padova (Trieste: Lint, 1988), pp. 97–125
POTTER, LOIS, 'Pastoral drama in England and its political implications', in Chiabò and Doglio, pp. 159–79
POVOLEDO, ELENA, 'Ferrara', in *Enciclopedia dello Spettacolo*, V (Rome: Le Maschere, 1958), cols 173–85
PROSPERI, ADRIANO, 'L'cresia in città e a corte', in Pade, Petersen and Quarta, pp. 267–81
PUAUX, ANNE, *La huguenote Renée de France* (Paris: Hermann, 1997)
QUARTA, DANIELA, 'Spazio scenico, spazio cortigiano, spazio cortese. L'*Aminta* e il *Torrismondo* di Torquato Tasso', in Pade, Petersen and Quarta, pp. 301–27
QUATTRUCCI, M., 'Argenti (Arienti), Agostino', *DBI*, 4 (1962), 116–17
QUINTAVALLE, A. O., and POVOLEDO, E., 'Aleotti, Giovan Battista', in *DBI*, 2 (1960), 152–54

QUONDAM, AMADEO, 'L'accademia' in *Letteratura italiana*, ed. by Alberto Asor Rosa, 6 vols (Turin: Einaudi, 1982-), I: *Il letterato e le istituzioni* (1982), 823–98

RADCLIFF-UMSTEAD, DOUGLAS, 'Love in Tasso's *Aminta*: A Reflection of the Este court', in Panizza Lorch, pp. 75–84

—— 'Structures of Conflict in Tasso's Pastoral of Love', in *Studi tassiani*, 22 (1972), 69–83

REBAUDENGO, MAURIZIO, *Giovan Battista Andreini tra poetica e drammaturgia* (Turin: Rosenberg & Sellier, 1994)

REINHARD, WOLFGANG, 'Reformation, Counter-Reformation, and the Early Modern State: A Reassessment', in Luebke, pp. 107–28

Renaissance Drama by Women: Texts and Documents, ed. by S. P. Cerasano and Marion Wynne-Davis (London: Routledge, 1996)

RESIDORI, MATTEO, '"Veder il suo in man d'altri": Note sulla presenza dell'*Aminta* nel *Pastor fido*', *Chroniques italiennes*, 5 (2004), 1–15 (electronic issue: http://www.univ-paris3.fr/recherche/chroniquesitaliennes)

RHODES, D. E., 'The printer of Giraldi's *Egle*', *Italian Studies*, 41 (1986), 82–84

RICCÒ, LAURA, '*Ben mille pastorali*'. *L'itinerario dell'Ingegneri da Tasso a Guarini e oltre* (Rome: Bulzoni, 2004)

—— 'Sassuolo 1587: Viene Imeneo', in *Rime e Lettere di Battista Guarini*, Atti del Convegno internazionale (Padova, 5–6 Dec. 2003), forthcoming

—— 'Testo per la scena — testo per la stampa: Problemi di edizione', *GSLI*, 173 (1996), 210–66

RICHARDSON, BRIAN, *Printing, Writers and Readers in Renaissance Italy* (Cambridge: Cambridge University Press, 1999)

—— *Print Culture in Renaissance Italy. The editor and the vernacular text, 1470-1600* (Cambridge: Cambridge University Press, 1994)

RIZZI, FRANCO, 'Le socialità profonde: la famiglia di Luigi Groto, il Cieco d'Adria', in Brunello and Lodo, I, 23–60

ROAF, CHRISTINA, ed., SPERONE SPERONI, *Canace e Scritti in sua difesa*. GIAMBATTISTA GIRALDI CINZIO, *Scritti contro la Canace, Giudizio ed Epistola latina*, Collezione di opere inedite o rare (Bologna: Commissione per i testi di lingua, 1982)

ROSSI, VITTORIO, *Battista Guarini ed il 'Pastor fido'. Studio biografico-critico con documenti inediti* (Turin: Loescher, 1886)

ROSENBERG, CHARLES M., 'Courtly Decorations and the decorum of interior space', in Papagno and Quondam, II, 529–44

ROTONDÒ, ANTONIO, 'La censura ecclesiastica e la cultura', in *Storia d' Italia*, V/I *Documenti*, **2**, ed. by Asor Rosa, 7 vols (Turin: UTET, 1973), 1399–1492

SACCO MESSINEO, MICHELA, *Il Martire e il tiranno. Ortensio Scammacca e il teatro tragico barocco* (Rome: Bulzoni, 1988)

SALA DI FELICE, ELENA, 'Il "Pastor fido" e la tragicommedia nella polemica Orsi-Bouhours', in *Dalla tragedia rinascimentale alla tragicommedia barocca. Esperienze teatrali a confronto. In Italia e in Francia*, ed. by E. Mosele (Fasano (Brindisi): Schena, 1993), pp. 61–91

SALVI, MARCELLA, '"Il solito è sempre quello, l'insolito è più nuovo:" *Li Buffoni* e le prostitute di Margherita Costa fra tradizione e innovazione', *Forum Italicum*, 38/2 (2004), 376-99

SALZA, ABD-EL-KADER, 'Un dramma pastorale inedito del Cinquecento (L'*Irifile* di Leone De Sommi)', *GSLI*, 54 (1909), 103–19

SAMPSON, LISA, '"Drammatica secreta": Barbara Torelli's *Partenia* (c. 1587) and women in late-sixteenth-century theatre', in *Theatre, Opera, and Performance in Italy from the fifteenth century to the present. Essays in Honour of Richard Andrews*, ed. by Brian Richardson, Simon Gilson, and Catherine Keen (Leeds: The Society for Italian Studies, Occasional Papers, 2004), pp. 99–115

—— 'The Mantuan Performance of Guarini's *Pastor fido* and Representations of Courtly Identity', *MLR*, 98 (2003), 65–83

SAVIOTTI, ALFREDO, 'Torquato Tasso e le feste pesaresi del 1574', *GSLI*, 12 (1888), 404–17

SAXBY, NELIA, 'Amore e Venere nell'*Aminta*', *Studi e problemi di critica testuale*, 36 (1988), 103–14
SCARPATI, CLAUDIO, 'Il nucleo ovidiano dell'*Aminta*', in *Tasso, i classici e i moderni* (Padua: Antenore, 1995), pp. 75–104
—— 'Poetica e retorica in Battista Guarini', in *Studi sul Cinquecento italiano* (Milan: Vita e Pensiero, 1982), pp. 201–38
SCHMITT, C. B., 'Cremonini, Cesare', in *DBI*, 30 (1984), 618–22
SCRIVANO, RICCARDO, 'Tasso e il teatro', in *La norma e lo scarto. Proposte per il cinquecento letterario italiano* (Rome: Bonacci, 1980), pp. 209–48
—— 'Cultura e letteratura in Sperone Speroni', in *Cultura e letteratura nel Cinquecento* (Rome: Edizioni dell'Ateneo, 1966), pp. 119–41
SEGRE, CESARE, 'Il teatro del Rinascimento e la semiotica', in Panizza Lorch, pp. 389–401
SELLA, DOMENICO, *Italy in the Seventeenth Century* (London: Longman, 1997)
SELMI, ELISABETTA, 'Guarini, Battista', in *DBI*, 60 (2003), 345–52
—— *'Classici e Moderni' nell'officina del 'Pastor fido'* (Alessandria: Edizioni dell'Orso, 2001)
—— 'L'Autore e l'Opera', in Battista Guarini, *Il Pastor fido*, ed. by Elisabetta Selmi with intro. by Guido Baldassarri (Venice: Marsilio, 1999), pp. 25–74
SIEKIERA, A., 'Ingegneri, Angelo', in *DBI*, 62 (2004), 358–60
SIMONS, PATRICIA, 'Lesbian (In)visibility in Italian Renaissance Culture: Diana and Other Cases of *Donna con Donna*', *Journal of Homosexuality*, 27 (1994), 81–122
SKINNER, QUENTIN, *The Foundations of Modern Political Thought*, 2 vols (Cambridge: Cambridge University Press, 1978)
SNYDER, JON R., '*Mare magnum*: the arts in the early modern age', in *Early Modern Italy, 1550–1796*, The Short Oxford History of Italy, ed. by John A. Marino (Oxford: Oxford University Press, 2002), pp. 143–65
SOLERTI, ANGELO, *Gli albori del melodramma*, 3 vols (Milan: Sandron, 1904; repr. Hildesheim: Georg Olms, 1969)
—— *Ferrara e la Corte Estense nella seconda metà del secolo decimosesto*, 2nd edn (Città di Castello: Lapi, 1900)
—— *Torquato Tasso, Operi minori in versi*, 3 vols, with two essays by Giosuè Carducci (Bologna: Zanichelli, 1895)
—— *Vita di Torquato Tasso*, 2 vols (Turin: Loescher, 1895)
SOLERTI, ANGELO and LANZA, DOMENICO, 'Il teatro ferrarese nella seconda metà del secolo XVI', *GSLI*, 18 (1891), 148–85
SOUTHORN, JANET, *Power and Display in the Seventeenth Century. The arts and their patrons in Modena and Ferrara* (Cambridge: Cambridge University Press, 1988)
STEPHENS, WALTER, 'Tasso's Heliodorus and the World of Romance', in *The Search for the Ancient Novel*, ed. by James Tatum (Baltimore: Johns Hopkins Press, 1994), pp. 67–87
STRONG, ROY, *Art and Power. Renaissance Festivals 1450–1650* (Bury St. Edmunds: Boydell, 1984)
TATEO, FRANCESCO, 'Guarino Veronese e l'Umanesimo a Ferrara', in *Storia di Ferrara*, ed. by Luciano Chiappini, Walter Moretti, and Antonio Samaritani (Ferrara: Corbo, 1987-), VII: *Il Rinascimento. La letteratura*, ed. by Walter Moretti (1994), 16–57
TAVIANI, FERDINANDO, 'Teatro di voci in tempi bui (riflessioni brade su "*Aminta*" e pastorale)', *Teatro e storia*, 16 (1994), 9–39
—— 'Bella d'Asia. Torquato Tasso, gli attori e l'immortalità', *Paragone letteratura*, 35 (1984), 139–71
TISSONI BENVENUTI, ANTONIA, *L'Orfeo del Poliziano, con il testo critico dell'originale e delle successive forme teatrali* (Padua: Antenore, 1987)
—— 'Introduzione' to Niccolò da Correggio, *Fabula de Cefalo*, in *Teatro del Quattrocento. Le corti padane*, ed. by Antonia Tissoni Benvenuti and Maria Pia Mussini Sacchi (Turin: UTET, 1983), pp. 199–207

TUOHY, THOMAS, *Herculean Ferrara. Ercole d'Este, 1471–1505, and the invention of a ducal capital* (Cambridge: Cambridge University Press, 1996)
TOFFANIN, GIUSEPPE, *Il Tasso e l'età che fu la sua (L'età Classicistica)* (Naples: Libreria Scientifica n.d. [1945/6?])
TROTTI, ANTON FRANCESCO, 'Le delizie di Belvedere Illustrate. Raccolta di documenti editi ed inediti', *Atti della Deputazione Ferrarese di Storia Patria*, 2 (1889), 3–32
TURCHI, MARCELLO, 'Introduzione' to *Opere di Gabriello Chiabrera e lirici del classicismo barocco*, ed. by Marcello Turchi, 2nd edn (Turin: UTET, 1974), pp. 9–63
TYLUS, JANE, 'Colonizing Peasants: The Rape of the Sabines and Renaissance Pastoral', *Renaissance Drama*, n. s., 23 (1992), 113–38
—— 'Purloined Passages: Giraldi, Tasso and the Pastoral Debates', *Modern Language Notes*, 99 (1984), 101–24
ULTSCH, LORI J., 'Maddalena Campiglia, "dimessa nel mondano cospetto"?: Secular Celibacy, Devotional Communities, and Social Identity in Early Modern Vicenza', *Forum Italicum*, 39/2 (2005), 350-77
—— 'Epithalamium Interruptum: Maddalena Campiglia's New Arcadia', *Modern Language Notes*, 120/1 (2005), 70-92
VARALLO, FRANCA, see ANONIMO DELLA SECONDA METÀ DEL SECOLO XVI
VARESE, CLAUDIO, 'Teatro, prosa, poesia', in Cecchi and Sapegno, pp. 551–994
VASSALLI, ANTONIO, 'Chiabrera, la musica e i musicisti: le rime amorose', in Bianchi and Russo, pp. 353–69
—— 'Il Tasso in musica e la trasmissione dei testi: alcuni esempi', in *Tasso, la musica, i musicisti*, ed. by Maria Antonella Balsano and Thomas Walker (Florence: Olschki, 1988), pp. 45–90
VAZZOLER, FRANCO, 'Chiabrera fra dilettanti e professionisti dello spettacolo', in Bianchi and Russo, pp. 429–66
—— 'Le pastorali dei comici dell'arte: La *Mirtilla* di Isabella Andreini', in Chiabò and Doglio, pp. 281–99
VIANELLO, V., *Il Letterato, l'accademia, il libro. Contributi sulla cultura veneta del Cinquecento* (Padua: Antenore, 1988)
VICKERS, BRIAN, *In Defence of Rhetoric* (Oxford: Clarendon Press, 1988)
—— 'Rhetoric and Poetics', in *The Cambridge History of Renaissance Philosophy*, ed. by Charles B. Schmitt and others (Cambridge: Cambridge University Press, 1988), pp. 715–45
VILLARI, SUSANNA, see Giraldi Cinzio
WEAVER, ELISSA, *Convent Theatre in Early Modern Italy. Spiritual Fun and Learning for Women* (Cambridge: Cambridge University Press, 2002)
WEINBERG, BERNARD, *A History of Literary Criticism in the Italian Renaissance*, 2 vols (Chicago: Chicago University Press, 1961)
—— *Trattati di poetica e retorica del Cinquecento*, ed. by Bernard Weinberg, 4 vols (Bari: Laterza, 1970–74)
—— 'Castelvetro's Theory of Poetics', in *Critics and Criticism Ancient and Modern*, ed. by R. S. Crane (Chicago: Chicago University Press, 1952), pp. 349–71
WELLS, ROBERT, 'Introduction' to Theocritus, *The Idylls*, trans. by Robert Wells (Manchester and New York: Carcanet, 1988), pp. 9–52
WOFFORD, SUSANNE L., 'The social aesthetics of rape: closural violence in Boccaccio and Botticelli', in *Creative Imitation. New Essays in honour of Thomas M. Greene*, Medieval and Renaissance texts and studies, 95, ed. by David Quint and others (New York: Binghampton, 1992), pp. 189–238
YOCH, JAMES J., 'The Renaissance Dramatization of Temperance: The Italian Revival of Tragicomedy and *The Faithful Shepherdess*', in Maguire, pp. 114–38
—— 'A Greater Power Than We Can Contradict: The Voice of Authority in the staging of Italian Pastorals', in *The Elizabethan Theatre*, 8, ed. by George R. Hibbard (Ontario: P. D. Meany, 1982), pp. 164–87

—— 'Renaissance Gardening and Pastoral Scenery in Italy and England', *Research Opportunities in Renaissance Drama*, 20 (1977), 35–43
ZACCARIA, VITTORIO, 'Le accademie padane cinquecentesche e il Tasso', in Borsetto and da Rif, pp. 35–61
ZAPPELLA, GIUSEPPINA, *Le marche dei tipografi e degli editori italiani del Cinquecento. Repertorio di figure, simboli e soggetti e dei relativi motti*, 2 vols (Milan: Editrice Bibliografica, 1986)

INDEX

academies 17, 18, 28, 32, 33, 47, 63, 68, 99, 107–08, 113–15, 119, 130, 135, 137, 163 nn. 26 & 30, 172, 184, 187, 196, 203–04, 221, 227, 230, 233, 234 n. 6, 237 n. 71, 238 n. 86
   and comedy 16, 29, 211
   and Guarini 132, 135, 137, 172, 187, 194 n. 78
   and pastoral drama 1, 28, 63, 99, 107–08, 113–15, 126 n. 47, 132, 135, 172, 184, 189, 196, 202–06, 221, 232–33, 238 n. 86
Accademia degli Alterati (Florence) 172, 227, 239 n. 107
Accademia degli Animosi (Padua) 135
Accademia degli Elevati (Ferrara) 17, 135
Accademia degli Eterei (Padua) 68, 130
Accademia degli Infiammati (Padua) 135, 163 nn. 26 & 30
Accademia degli Innominati (Parma) 107–08, 109, 126 nn. 45 & 47, 211, 221, 237 n. 71, 238 n. 86
Accademia degli Intrepidi (Ferrara) 194 n. 78, 203–04, 205
Accademia degli Intronati (Siena) 29, 57 n. 75, 211
Accademia degli Invaghiti (Mantua) 32
Accademia dei Filarmonici (Verona) 184
Accademia dei Ricovrati (Padua) 130
Accademia degli Spensierati (Florence) 230, 238 n. 94
Accademia della Crusca (Florence) 130, 162 n. 7
Accademia dell'Arcadia (Rome) 232–33, 233 n. 3, 240 n. 124; *see also* Arcadia, as literary movement
Accademia ferrarese (Ferrara) 68, 69, 93 n. 41, 132
Accademia Olimpica (Vicenza) 57 n. 84, 113, 115, 127 n. 59, 172, 179, 238 n. 86
actors 15, 16, 32, 81, 119–20, 122, 132, 170, 171, 173, 179–83, 185, 221, 222
   amateur 19, 27, 28, 32, 62, 63, 92 n. 14, 105–06, 179–83, 184
   attitudes towards 102, 119, 132, 181, 186
   female 10 n. 17, 20, 102, 105–06, 119–20, 121, 122, 125 nn. 32, 35 & 37, 126 n. 39, 128 n. 81 & 83, 179, 181, 183, 206, 222, 228–29, 239 n. 114
   Jewish 32, 194 n. 92
   semi-professional 26–27, 32, 63, 113, 179
   professional 2, 14, 19, 32, 55 n. 43, 57 n. 87, 62, 63, 92 n. 14, 119–22, 132, 179, 185–86, 195, 196, 202, 206, 224, 228–31
Aleotti, Giambattista 96 n. 94, 165 n. 52, 177, 178, 186, 187, 194 n. 85, 204
Alpers, Paul 4
Amore, *see* love, god of
Andreini, Francesco 118, 229, 240 n. 115

Andreini, Giovan Battista 119, 196, 199, 202, 224, 225, 230–31
Andreini, Isabella 104, 114, 128 n. 89, 225, 228–29, 230
   Mirtilla 10 n. 17, 100, 103, 104, 110, 114, 115, 118–22, 128 n. 83
   see also actors, female and professional
Andrews, Richard 19, 128 nn. 79 & 89, 229
apparato, see stage-set
Arcadia:
   dramatic representations of 22, 30, 34, 131, 142–48, 150–53, 155, 227
   existence in 5, 28–29, 39–40, 45, 143–47
   as fictional space 3–5, 28–29, 30, 36, 45, 46, 63, 115, 129, 141–53, 189, 199, 202, 213, 223, 229, 232
   as literary movement 195, 222, 232–33, 233 n. 3
   social relations in 30, 35–39, 45, 153
   see also Sannazaro
Argenti, Agostino 15, 28, 55 n. 43, 60 n. 137, 63
   Sfortunato 15, 27–31, 36, 38, 39, 41, 45, 49, 50, 56 n. 70, 59 n. 119, 63, 72, 73, 95 nn. 63 & 71, 117, 174, 178, 179
Ariosto, Ludovico 8, 15–18, 19, 54 n. 25, 59 n. 115, 63, 69, 97 n. 104, 99, 147, 204
   comedies 16, 17–18, 19, 35, 36, 44, 53 nn. 13 & 17, 54 n. 28, 56 n. 65, 63, 165 n. 63, 174
   eclogues 64
   Orlando furioso 7, 8, 11 n. 22, 15, 17, 19, 21, 35, 68, 69, 70, 72, 80, 83, 85, 86, 93 n. 35, 104 n. 97, 138, 139, 154, 164 n. 39, 209, 224
Aristotle:
   Ethics 139, 148, 160
   Poetics 3, 7–8, 9, 17, 24–25, 27, 56 nn. 55 & 59, 70–71, 86, 94 n. 48, 97 n. 101, 107, 114, 129, 131, 137–38, 139, 141, 145, 171, 201, 209, 212, 230, 237 n. 56
   Politics 139, 149, 154
   see also neo-Aristotelianism
Armani, Vincenza 228, 239 n. 114

Baldini, Vittorio 80, 82, 96 n. 87, 123 nn. 6 & 7, 191 n. 15, 192 n. 39, 204, 205, 236 n. 38
Barbara of Austria 62, 63, 92 n. 14, 175
Bardi, Giovanni de', *see* de' Bardi, Giovanni
Bargagli, Girolamo (de'), *Pellegrina* 185
Barotti, Giannandrea 161
Beccari, Agostino, *Sacrificio* 1, 7, 10 n. 16, 14, 15, 21, 27–31, 35, 39, 40, 42, 44–51, 58 nn. 95 & 107, 59 nn. 118 & 120, 70, 71, 91 n. 2, 95 n. 71, 99, 121, 122, 147, 154, 162 n. 10, 194 n. 87, 199, 229

cast 29, 30, 44, 45–47, 77
editions 29, 31, 50, 53 n. 9, 56 n. 70, 58 n. 107
as first pastoral play 1, 6, 14, 21, 37 n. 79, 50
performance 27, 28, 57 n. 73, 59 n. 125, 63, 96 n. 94, 108, 174, 175, 177, 179, 191 n. 31, 183
plot structure 27, 29–30, 31, 35, 48–49, 70, 100, 120, 123, 131
Bellarmino, Roberto, Cardinal (Bellarmine, Robert) 161, 218
Belvedere, *see* Ferrara, court palaces
Bembo, Pietro 17, 39–40
Bendidio, Lucrezia 64, 92 n. 18
Beni, Paolo 97 n. 98, 135, 143–45, 163 n. 23, 165 n. 58, 237 n. 62
Bentivoglio, Enzo 204
Bentivoglio, Ercole 17–18
Bentivoglio family 185, 191 n. 28
Beolco, Angelo, *see* Ruzante
Bibbiena (Bernardo Dovizi), *Calandria* 44, 224
Bigolina, Giulia 114
Boccaccio, Giovanni:
  Decameron 42, 63, 86, 134, 167 n. 90
  eclogues 10 n. 12
  pastoral works/romances 7, 25, 39
Boccalini, Traiano 98, 153
Bonarelli, Guidubaldo (Guidoboldo) 203, 235 n. 36, 237 n. 61
  Discorsi 92 n. 17, 199, 206, 212, 220, 221, 235 n. 21, 236 n. 52
  Filli di Sciro 6, 91 n. 1, 106, 171, 196, 197, 200, 201, 202–21, 222, 223, 231, 234 n. 7, 235 n. 24, 236 nn. 43, 48, 49 & 55, 237 nn. 73 & 75, 238 n. 76
    performance 106, 126 n. 39, 235 n. 28, 236 nn. 45 & 49
Borromeo, Carlo 83, 238 n. 79
Botero, Giovanni 218, 219, 238 n. 79
Bracciolini, Francesco 196, 235 n. 25
  Amoroso sdegno 196, 208, 210–11, 236 n. 54, 237 nn. 58 & 64
Bruscagli, Riccardo 21, 69, 73, 84
Bucolics, *see* Virgil
Buonarroti (the younger), Michelangelo 228, 239 n. 106
Buontalenti, Bernardo 178, 185, 228

Caccini, Giulio 227
Calderón de la Barca, Pedro 2
Calcagnini, Celio 16, 17, 21
Calmo, Andrea 11 n. 20, 31, 229
Campani, Niccolò ('Lo Strascino') 14, 228
Campbell, Julie D. 119, 122, 128 n. 83
Campiglia, Maddalena 99, 103, 112–14, 127 nn. 59 & 74
  Calisa 128 n. 74
  Discorso 112–13, 115, 127 n. 56
  Flori 10 nn. 17 & 18, 45, 99, 103, 104, 105, 110, 112–18, 120, 121, 123, 127 n. 69, 128 n. 86, 166 n. 75, 197, 234 n. 10

Carlo Emanuele I (of Savoy) 107, 142, 143, 185
carnival 7, 16, 17, 28, 31, 32, 40, 57 n. 82, 59 n. 114, 62, 65, 92 n. 14, 101, 173, 181, 184, 185, 187, 192 n. 38
Carrara, Enrico 2, 13
Castelletti, Cristoforo 100, 236 n. 54
Castelvetro, Lodovico 15, 48, 86, 97 n. 101, 139, 164 n. 41
Castiglione, Baldassarre (Baldesar):
  Cortegiano, 18, 19, 30, 39, 40, 44, 64–65, 67, 84, 90, 92 n. 22, 94 nn. 52 & 54, 105
  Tirsi, 13, 29, 38, 64
catharsis 71, 134, 140, 156, 164 n. 46, 165 n. 50, 211
Catherine of Austria 142, 143, 185
Cavalcanti, Bartolomeo 17, 22
cavallerie, *see* torneo
censorship 41, 83–85, 96 n. 80, 97 n. 113, 164 n. 44, 139
Charles V 18, 19
Chiabrera, Gabriello 11 n. 24, 119, 128 n. 77, 196, 222, 234 n. 15, 238 nn. 89–91
  pastoral plays 222, 223–27, 238 nn. 93 & 94, 239 nn. 103 & 104
  Rapimento di Cefalo 227–28, 233
Chiappino, Paolo 113, 127 n. 72
Chiodo, Domenico 89
chorus 14, 24–25, 99–100, 109, 115, 126 n. 51, 130, 176, 211, 223
  as character 26, 30, 41, 46, 47, 73, 74, 76, 84, 156, 158, 222, 227, 233
  end-of-act 14, 29, 72, 76, 79, 80, 84, 99–100, 184, 211, 238 n. 77
  and Golden Age 76–77, 84, 88, 89, 101, 147, 152, 159
  in Guarini's *Pastor fido* 130, 134, 159, 161 n. 5, 166 n. 78
  in performance 25, 26, 46, 80, 176, 183, 222, 223, 227
  satyric 24–26
  in Tasso's *Aminta* 14, 72, 73, 74, 76–77, 79, 80, 84, 88, 89, 99, 101, 152
Christina of Sweden 232
Cicero:
  on mixed genres 137
  on rhetoric 135, 139, 148, 164 n. 42, 166 n. 70
  political thought 148, 166 n. 71
Ciotti, Giovanni Battista:
  and *Filli di Sciro* 205–07, 236 n. 43
  and *Pastor fido* 130, 132, 133, 134, 161, 162 n. 8, 165 n. 52, 179, 204
Clavignano (da Montefalco), Sebastiano, *see* Montefalco
Clubb, Louise George 2, 3, 6, 35, 36, 47, 94 n. 51, 100, 128 n. 75
Colonna, Vittoria 47, 102, 113
comedy 3, 4, 8, 13, 15–18, 19, 25–26, 27, 31, 33, 36, 42–45, 51, 55 n. 43, 71, 81, 93 n. 42, 100, 102–03, 104, 120, 124 n. 22, 131, 141, 199–200, 209, 220, 224–25, 231, 232, 235 n. 29
  attitudes towards 7, 8, 19–20, 29, 53 n. 16, 55 n. 43, 81, 83, 102–03, 195, 198

influence on pastoral drama 5, 14, 15, 26, 27, 29–31,
   34–38, 40, 43, 45, 49, 51, 132, 140, 147, 160,
   166 n. 74, 209, 224–25, 239 n. 98
performance of 16, 19, 53 n. 16, 55 n. 50, 57 n. 87, 62,
   63, 92 n. 12, 102, 104, 174, 176–77, 178, 179, 184,
   185, 194 n. 92, 228–29
professional 2, 32, 34, 57 n. 87, 63, 65, 83, 92 n. 14,
   100, 102, 121–221, 128 n. 81, 224, 225, 229, 230,
   237 n. 67; *see also* actors; *commedia dell'arte*
rustic 2, 7, 14, 15, 36, 38, 70, 228, 229
serious, *see commedia grave*
theory on 2, 19–21, 25, 27, 100, 104, 137, 139, 140,
   145–47, 151, 164 n. 50, 186
commedia dell'arte 2, 19, 20, 32, 34, 55 nn. 37 & 43,
   57 n. 87, 62, 65, 83, 92 n. 14, 106, 119–22, 132, 179,
   181, 196, 202, 211, 224, 237 n. 67
and comedy, *see* comedy, professional
and pastoral drama 2, 14, 46, 63, 100, 102, 118–22,
   128 n. 75, 162 n. 12, 186, 228–31, 239 n. 114,
   240 n. 116
see also actors, professional
commedia grave 20, 29, 104, 111, 131, 211
concetti 77, 80, 89, 98, 186, 197, 198, 203, 212, 221,
   234 n. 15
Coreglia, Isabetta, *Dori* 103
Correggio, Niccolò da, *Cefalo e Procri*, 13, 29, 52 n. 5,
   239 n. 98
costumes 37, 96 n. 96, 173, 178–79, 188, 213, 214,
   237 n. 67
Council of Trent 2, 19, 20, 44, 46, 96 n. 89, 102, 139,
   154, 159, 225
see also Inquisition *and* Index
Counter-Reformation 3, 8, 45, 47, 94 n. 61, 102, 137,
   153, 159, 167 n. 84, 215, 219, 221, 237 n. 73; *see also*
   Council of Trent
convent drama 105, 110, 124 n. 20, 126 n. 54
Cox, Virginia 44, 92 n. 22, 94 n. 61, 97 n. 113, 102, 116
Cremonini, Cesare 100, 101, 124 n. 14, 197, 209
cross-dressing 34, 100, 106, 117, 125 n. 37, 160, 199, 224,
   226, 239 n. 102
Cucchetti, Giovan Donato 99, 101, 105, 109, 121,
   123 n. 6, 126 n. 47, 167 n. 93
Cupid, *see* love, god of

da Correggio, Niccolò, *see* Correggio
Dalla Viola, Alfonso 59 n. 125, 174, 191 n. 25
dance:
   courtly 103, 105–06, 173, 175, 193 n. 57, 199
   in *intermedi* 58 n. 107
   in pastoral drama 2, 29, 38, 55 n. 46, 109, 115, 171,
      175, 181–83, 187, 193 n. 57, 194 n. 92, 209, 222,
      228, 230, 232, 239 n. 106
   in satyr drama 22, 25, 26, 55 n. 46
Dante Alighieri 11 n. 23, 15, 42, 77, 139, 210, 220
de' Bardi, Giovanni 178, 185, 187, 192 n. 37
Denores, Giason 131–34, 135, 137–41, 145, 146, 147, 148,
   162 n. 12, 163 nn. 23 & 33, 164 n. 34, 201

de' Rossi, Bartolomeo 58 n. 106, 100, 229
de' Sanctis, Francesco 1
de' Sommi, Leone 15, 18, 20, 32, 33, 57 n. 87, 58 n. 94,
   179
   Irifile 31, 33, 44, 45, 46, 47, 57 n. 82, 58 nn. 94 & 95,
      59 nn. 110 & 120, 75
   Quattro dialoghi 33, 37, 50–51, 57 n. 87, 177, 179, 184,
      192 n. 35
d'Este, Alfonso I: 16, 17, 63, 92 n. 14
d'Este, Alfonso II: 18, 28, 33, 35, 62, 63, 80, 81, 82,
   91 n. 9, 95 nn.66 & 74, 105, 130, 167 n. 88, 172, 173,
   174, 175, 184, 186, 191 n. 20, 203
d'Este, Cesare 14, 192 n. 40, 203
d'Este, Ercole I: 15, 192 n. 33
d'Este, Ercole II: 18, 19, 21, 47, 54 n. 26, 174
d'Este, Francesco (Don) 28, 174
d'Este, Ippolito (Cardinal) 16
d'Este, Laura Eustochia (Dianti) 50, 92 n. 14
d'Este (Della Rovere), Lucrezia 28, 56 n. 70, 63, 80, 184
d'Este, Luigi (Cardinal) 49, 62, 68, 92 n. 12, 174
Diana (goddess) 4, 30, 34, 42, 45, 84, 110, 111, 131, 133,
   146, 152, 154–55, 157
   and Callisto 58 n. 97
   as dramatic character 13, 34
   and Endymion 233
   and single life 30, 31, 41, 84, 109, 115, 116–17; *see also*
      lesbianism
Doria Gonzaga, Vittoria 106, 108, 222
drammi mescidati (mixed drama) 7, 13, 20, 24, 29, 31

echo 40, 131, 171, 181
eclogue:
   classical 2, 5, 7, 13, 26, 27, 39, 51, 64, 67, 126 n. 52, 137;
      see also Virgil, *Eclogues*
   dramatic 7, 13–14, 15, 24, 26–27, 29, 31, 38, 49, 50–52,
      52 n. 8, 62, 69, 80–81, 120, 137–38, 143, 146, 172,
      176, 228, 229, 239 n. 98
   medieval 5, 10 n. 12, 64
   in verse 104, 125 n. 28, 126 n. 46, 128 n. 76
Empson, William 4, 10 n. 7, 166 n. 79
epic 8, 25, 67, 152; *see also* romance
   classical 5
   modern 15, 17, 81–83, 85–86, 87–90, 184, 200,
      235 n. 25; *see also* Ariosto, *Orlando furioso, and*
      Tasso, *Gerusalemme liberata*
   theory on 17, 27, 68–69, 70, 85, 94 n. 48, 137, 145,
      190 n. 14, 200–01, 202
Epicuro Napolitano, *see* Marsi
epithalamium 40, 59 n. 115
Estense dynasty 14, 18, 21, 28, 44, 59 n. 115, 63, 91 n. 9,
   203 *see also* d'Este
Euripides:
   Cyclops 24–26, 51, 56 n. 63, 95 n. 70
   Hippolytus 71, 91 n. 2, 152
   Iphigenia in Aulis 167 n. 90, 212

Farnese, Clelia 108, 178

Farnese, Ranuccio 105, 172
Ferguson, Arthur B. 148, 166 n. 69
Ferrara 18–19, 43, 54 n. 33, 60 n. 132, 62, 68–69, 91 n. 9, 92 n. 17, 167 n. 86, 188, 191 n. 18, 200, 215
  academies 17, 28, 63, 69, 93 n. 41, 194 n. 78, 203–04; *see also* Accademia degli Elevati, Accademia degli Intrepidi, *and* Accademia ferrarese
  court 15–16, 21, 27, 33, 40, 49–50, 62, 65, 71, 80, 81, 85, 105–06, 130, 147, 172–73, 203; *see also* d'Este
  devolution to papacy 91 n. 9, 92 n. 16, 175, 189, 203
  earthquakes 63, 92 nn. 13 & 14, 175
  palaces: Schifanoia 28, 174, 191 n. 27; Belvedere 63, 92 n. 15
  pastoral drama in 14–15, 17, 20–31, 33, 35, 41, 42–43, 44–52, 52 nn. 3 & 8, 58 n. 102, 63–64, 71, 76, 77, 80, 84, 95 n. 62, 146, 147, 173–75, 179–81, 184, 185, 194 n. 78, 209, 225, 231
  religion in 18, 19, 41, 44, 47–48, 60 n. 132, 203
  Studio 16–17, 20, 24, 28, 33, 47–48, 60 n. 132, 62, 68, 92 n. 14, 174, 175, 179
  theatre in 13, 15–31, 28–29, 49–50, 52 n. 3, 53 n. 13, 55 nn. 37 & 43, 60 nn. 136 & 137, 61–64, 65, 92 n. 14, 105, 125 n. 32, 172–75, 177, 179–81, 184, 185, 191 n. 23, 204
Fiamma, Carlo, *Diana vinta* 202
Florence 7, 17, 56 n. 70, 81, 163 n. 24; *see also* Medici
  academies 130, 211, 227, 230, 238 n. 94, 239 n. 107; *see also* Accademia della Crusca, Accademia degli Spensierati
  theatre in 99, 125 n. 32, 177, 178, 179, 185, 187, 192 nn. 36 & 37, 194 n. 80, 222, 227–28, 230, 231, 239 n. 106
Fonte, Moderata 118, 127 nn. 54 & 64
fortune 41, 48–49, 74, 88, 198, 218
Foster, Verna 147
France 18, 19, 47, 62, 66 n. 131, 92 n. 12, 106, 125 n. 35, 126 n. 39, 173, 192 n. 36, 195, 202, 203, 206, 230, 234 n. 15
  pastoral drama in 2, 57 n. 73, 58 n. 100, 82, 95 n. 72, 99, 106, 124 n. 23, 162 n. 16, 195, 202, 204, 206, 236 n. 48, 239 n. 112

garden 63, 92 n. 16
  in *Gerusalemme liberata* 89–90
  as theatrical space 63, 176–77, 178, 184, 230, 232
Gelosi 63, 92 n. 12, 119, 179, 183, 186, 229; *see also* actors, professional; *commedia dell'arte*
Genoa 108, 114, 222, 223, 238 n. 94
genre:
  and the canon 3, 8–9, 11 n. 22, 103–04, 139, 189, 196, 233
  change over time 5, 8–9, 12–13, 19, 123, 129, 202, 231–32
  and drama 5, 8, 21–22, 24, 47, 52, 103, 113–14, 120, 202
  mixing of 7, 33, 137, 141, 199, 202, 230, 233
  theory on 3, 4, 6, 7, 8, 11 n. 22, 12–14, 20, 24–25, 27, 40, 49, 68–69, 131–32, 137–39, 141, 164 n. 48

women and 42, 45, 102–04, 108, 109, 110, 114
Gentile Ricci(o), Pier Girolamo 223, 224, 238 nn. 93 & 94
georgic 5, 67
Giraldi (Cinthio), Giambattista (Giovan Battista) 7, 15, 17, 18, 21–27
  criticism 19–20, 21–27, 44, 55 nn. 45 & 49, 56 nn. 55 & 58, 68–69, 71, 94 n. 46, 138–39, 175
  Egle 15, 21–27, 29, 35, 36, 41, 42, 44, 45, 48, 49, 51, 52, 55 nn. 45 & 46, 56 nn. 63 & 65, 59 nn. 118 & 120, 71, 73, 77, 91 n. 2, 147, 170, 174, 175, 179, 183
  Favola pastorale 15, 27, 35, 43, 44, 45, 48, 49, 109
  Orbecche 21, 22, 56 nn. 51 & 65, 94 n. 46, 174, 213
  tragedie di lieto fine 18, 20, 21, 24, 25, 52, 56 n. 62, 69
Giraldi, Lilio Gregorio 16, 17
Giuliani (Zugliano), Vespasiano 114, 127 n. 56
Godard, Alain 218
Golden Age 4, 5, 19, 67, 76–79, 88–89, 95 nn. 62 & 66, 101, 142–43, 149, 152, 157, 159, 166 n. 72, 188
Gonzaga dynasty 32, 114, 191 n. 18
Gonzaga, Curzio 113–14, 115, 118, 126 n. 44
Gonzaga, Ferrante 32, 82, 100, 107, 108, 113, 126 n. 44, 181, 222; *see also* Guastalla
Gonzaga (d'Este), Margherita 33, 80, 105
Gonzaga, Scipione 68, 80, 81–82, 85, 93 nn. 32 & 33, 130, 162 n. 7
Gonzaga, Vincenzo 33, 80, 105, 132, 161 n. 5, 162 n. 10, 172–73, 185, 187, 189, 230
Gravina, Gianvincenzo 233
Greg, Walter 1, 4
Groto, Luigi (Il Cieco d'Adria) 15, 32–35, 58 nn. 91 & 92, 100, 113, 121
  Calisto 31, 34–35, 36, 40, 42, 45, 46–47, 57 n. 83, 58 nn. 97 & 99, 59 nn. 110 & 120, 117, 122, 226
  Pentimento 31, 35, 36–37, 45, 47, 57 n. 83, 58 n. 100, 59 n. 120
Guarini, Battista:
  critical theory 8–9, 12–13, 14, 21, 27, 51, 123, 129, 132–34, 138–42, 145–46, 149, 150–52, 160, 164 n. 47, 169, 171, 198–99, 215–16, 221, 231, 236 n. 56
  Idropica 55 n. 43, 131, 162 n. 10, 165 n. 63, 166 n. 74, 222
  life 68, 69, 130, 135, 160–61, 162 n. 7, 177, 191 n. 18
  madrigals 85, 95 n. 64, 199
  Pastor fido 1, 45, 102, 107, 113, 123, 129–31, 142–43, 146–48, 150–52, 154–59, 161 nn. 5 & 6, 165 nn. 53 & 65, 170, 200, 209, 211–12
    performances of 96 nn. 94 & 96, 105, 126 n. 39, 165 n. 52, 170, 172, 180–83, 185–89, 190 n. 6, 193 n. 73, 194 nn. 78, 86 & 92, 204, 228, 229, 234 n. 5, 236 n. 49; editions of 132, 133, 134, 162 n. 8; debate on 131–34, 137–42, 143–45, 151, 160, 190 n. 6; fortunes of 99, 124 n. 11, 129, 195, 197, 201

political works 59 n. 121, 149–50, 153–54, 156, 166 n. 73
Guarino da Verona 15, 16, 20, 59 n. 115, 130
Guastalla 32, 82, 100, 105, 106, 107, 108, 172, 181, 222
Guidi, Alessandro, *Endimione* 232–33
Guidiccioni Lucchesini, Laura 103

Habsburg dynasty 18, 143, 156, 189, 237 n. 73; *see also* Barbara, Catherine *and* Margaret of Austria
Heliodorus 200, 235 n. 22
Henke, Robert 3, 5, 119, 141, 170, 229
Henrietta Maria of England 106, 125 n. 37
Herrick, Marvin T. 10 n. 16, 134
Hesiod 76, 149, 166 n. 72
Horace, *Ars Poetica* 8, 24, 56 n. 58, 68, 138
Horne, P(hilip) R. 19, 41, 48

imitation:
 literary 27, 103; *see also* theatergrams
 of pastoral drama 2, 98–101, 122–23, 129, 134, 195, 197, 206, 209, 232
 theory on 8, 9, 69, 92 n. 24, 137–38, 139–40, 141, 146, 161, 167 n. 96
Index 83, 139; *see also* Inquisition
inganno (trick) 30, 49, 73, 143, 146–47, 224
Ingegneri, Angelo 14, 105, 109, 113, 114, 119, 187
 Danza di Venere 100, 101, 105, 109–10, 113, 131, 183
 Della poesia 14, 21, 99, 100, 104, 160, 169, 176, 178–79, 183, 195, 198, 201, 211–12, 221
 and Tasso 81, 99
Inquisition, 32, 47, 80, 82–83, 96 n. 93, 97 n. 101, 136, 139
intermedi 7, 20, 26, 32, 33, 38, 58 n. 107, 80, 85, 106, 115, 171, 172, 176, 177, 181, 184, 185, 187–89, 192 n. 37, 193 n. 67, 194 nn. 80, 86 & 87, 204, 206, 222, 228, 236 n. 49
Ivaldi, Armando Fabio 28, 29, 170

Javitch, Daniel 27, 68
Jones, Ann Rosalind 103

LaCapra, Dominick 141
Leoni, Giovanni Battista, *Roselmina* 202, 240 n. 120
lesbianism 117–18, 120, 127 n. 74
Ligorio, Pirro 19, 174
Lollio, Alberto 15, 17–18, 27–31, 47–48, 54 n. 30
 Aretusa 15, 18, 27–31, 35, 37, 38, 39, 42, 43, 45, 47, 49, 50, 63, 95 nn. 62 & 71, 109, 117, 131, 165 n. 65, 174, 179
 Galatea 15, 18, 28, 31, 36, 38, 58 n. 102
 orations 17–18, 48
Longus, *Daphnis and Chloe* 7, 38, 94 n. 50, 199, 237 n. 56
love:
 'deviant' forms of 120–21, 206, 220–21; *see also* lesbianism
 discussion on 39, 41, 63, 92 n. 17

god of 65–67, 74–75, 100, 117, 118
neo-Platonic 39–40, 41–42, 46, 116, 118, 121, 206
in pastoral drama 2, 4, 26, 38–43, 45, 77–79, 104, 116, 121, 146, 212, 233
Petrarchan 7, 38, 39–40, 76, 79, 95 n. 70, 116; *see also* Petrarchism
sensual 40–41, 72–73, 76–77, 85, 88–90, 101, 112, 116, 121, 160, 198, 221; *see also* epithalamium *and* marriage
see also single life
Lupi, Pietro, *Sospetti* 99
Lupi, Camilla 105
Lupi, Isabella Pallavicino, *see* Pallavicino Lupi, Isabella

Machiavelli, Niccolò 44, 49, 224
MacNeil, Anne 122, 128 n. 87, 170
magic 7, 29, 30, 45, 46, 51, 87–89, 181, 199, 229
Malacreta, Giovanni Pietro 143, 150, 155, 163 n. 23, 166 n. 78, 170, 190 n. 6, 197, 199, 201
Manfredi, Muzio 106, 107, 108, 109, 113, 114, 126 nn. 42, 44, 46 & 51
 Contrasto amoroso 106, 221–22
 Semiramis 108, 126 n. 47, 201, 221–22
Mantua 33, 82, 107, 114, 130; *see also* Gonzaga
 theatre in 31, 32, 33, 51, 105, 108, 162 n. 10, 170, 172–73, 176–77, 179, 188, 189, 191 n. 18, 192 n. 36, 194 nn. 78, 82 & 92, 204, 222, 228
Manutius, Aldo, *see* Manuzio, Aldo
Manuzio, Aldo (the younger) 66, 80, 82
Margaret of Austria (and Spain) 172, 188
Marinella, Lucrezia 104, 114, 127 n. 64
Marino, Giambattista 11 n. 24, 198, 203, 204, 212, 221, 222, 234 n. 15, 236 n. 49
marriage:
 and pastoral drama 35, 40, 42–43, 44, 59 n. 114, 100, 109–11, 112, 116, 127 n. 69, 159, 186, 188–89, 227
 social and moral status of 43, 105, 112, 125 n. 35, 154, 173
Marsi, Marcantonio ('Epicuro Napolitano') 13, 14, 29, 52 n. 8
 Cecaria 13, 14, 52 n. 7, 162 n. 12
 Mirzia 13–14, 29, 59 n. 110
Medici dynasty 18, 103, 149, 230
Medici, Cosimo de' 18, 166 n. 72
Medici, Ferdinando de' 153, 185
Medici, Lorenzo de' 95 n. 70, 166 n. 72
Medici, Maria de' 106, 125 n. 35, 227
melodramma 2, 46, 99, 199, 222, 227, 228, 233
Miani (Negri), Valeria 103, 114, 128 n. 87
meraviglia (*maraviglia*) 71, 83, 143, 165 n. 53, 198–99, 201, 211, 212–13, 221, 230
mimesis, *see* imitation
mode 4
 pastoral 4–5, 12, 43, 46, 67, 87, 90, 104, 125 n. 28, 131, 137, 141, 145–46, 149, 151, 226, 230, 231, 233
Molinari, Carla 27, 55 n. 45, 56 n. 68, 59 n. 118, 130, 134, 148, 165 n. 68

Montefalco, il (Sebastiano Clavignano) 27, 50, 56 n. 65, 179, 228
Monteverdi, Claudio, *Orfeo* 228
music 190 n. 14, 196, 199, 211, 219, 222–23, 227, 228
   at court 20, 28, 105, 107, 173–75, 191 n. 25
   and pastoral 99, 124 n. 9, 222, 227–28, 231–32, 233, 239 nn. 106 & 112; *see also* melodramma
   in pastoral drama 2, 13, 26, 28, 29, 36, 38, 46, 59 n. 125, 115, 171, 174, 175, 181–83, 185, 227, 232
musica secreta 105

Naples 7, 14, 64, 196, 202, 229, 234 n. 5
neo-Aristotelianism 7–8, 15, 17, 24, 29, 52, 68, 69–70, 86, 97 n. 101, 107, 114, 129, 134, 137–41, 146, 149, 161, 163 n. 33, 196, 199
neo-Platonism 19, 46, 85, 102, 104, 138, 140, 183, 198; *see also* love, neo-Platonic

Ongaro, Antonio, *Alceo* 100, 123 n. 7
opera, *see* melodramma
Orpheus 39, 67, 220; *see also* Poliziano, *Orfeo*
Ovid:
   Amores 220
   Ars Amatoria 40, 77
   Metamorphoses 5, 7, 13, 22, 24, 26, 34, 39, 40, 71, 75, 76, 86, 120, 131, 142, 149, 213, 226, 227, 237 n. 69
Padua:
   academies, *see* Accademia degli Animosi, Accademia degli Eterei *and* Accademia degli Infiammati
   university 24, 68, 130, 131, 134–35, 137, 163 nn. 23, 24 & 26, 172
Pagello, Livio 117
Pallavicino Lupi, Isabella 104–05, 107, 109, 114, 115, 118, 127 n. 74, 239 n. 96
Parma:
   academies, *see* Accademia degli Innominati
   court 105, 107, 114, 126 n. 47, 172, 237 n. 71
   press 81, 82, 126 n. 47
   theatre 105, 107, 109, 114, 126 n. 47, 137, 161 n. 5, 172, 211, 221, 237 n. 71, 238 n. 86
Pasqualigo, Alvise (Luigi):
   Fedele 32, 57 n. 85
   Intricati 15, 31–32, 34, 35, 39, 40, 45, 46, 57 n. 84, 75, 147, 229
Pausanias 58 n. 97, 154
Pazzi (de' Medici), Alessandro 24, 56 nn. 57 & 59
Petrarch:
   eclogues 5, 64
   lyric verse 7, 39, 40, 97 n. 104
   Trionfi 139
Petrarchism 19, 39–40, 102, 166, 197, 232; *see also* love, Petrarchan
Pieri, Marzia 2–3, 6, 13, 29, 35, 57 n. 84, 124 n. 16, 169, 171, 176, 222, 229, 231
Pigna, Giovanbattista (Giambattista Nicolucci) 17, 19, 21, 54 n. 25, 55 n. 49, 64, 68, 69, 92 n. 18, 94 n. 58

Piissimi, Vittoria 122, 128 n. 81, 183
Pino da Cagli, Bernardino 83
Pio (of Savoy), Marco 107, 108, 126 n. 44, 178
Pius V 18, 83, 91 n. 9, 139, 203
Plautus 13, 20, 34, 36, 50
   Amphitryo 34, 50, 56 n. 62
   comedies 13, 15, 17, 53 n. 16
poetics, *see* Aristotle, *Poetics, and* neo-Aristotelianism
Poliziano, Angelo:
   Orfeo, 13, 24, 37, 50, 52. n. 4, 56 n. 51
   Stanze 42, 43, 95 n. 70
Polybius 143
print publication 19, 81, 83, 85, 135–36, 139, 204
   of pastoral drama 1, 15, 50, 61, 63, 80–83, 99, 107, 119, 130, 132, 134, 169, 170, 173, 175, 188, 196, 197, 205, 223, 232
   stigma of 19, 81; *see also* censorship
Providence 9, 47–49, 52, 74–75, 142, 147, 159, 167 n. 95, 212, 215, 217–18

Racan, Honorat de Beuil 2, 106
rape 42, 73, 79, 94 n. 54, 122, 128 n. 87, 209, 210
recognition (agnition) 30–31, 35, 58 n. 102, 70, 71, 108–09, 117, 131, 146, 147, 155, 165 n. 65, 200, 208, 209, 226, 236 n. 56
religion 45–49, 83, 112, 136–37, 149–50, 154, 215, 218, 238 n. 79; *see also* Council of Trent *and* Ferrara, religion in
   and pastoral drama 3–4, 7, 9, 33, 39–40, 41, 44, 45–48, 67, 77, 84, 90, 101–02, 123, 140, 146, 151, 152, 154–59, 161, 181, 197–98, 212, 213–15, 218–21, 223, 231
Renée of France (and Ferrara) 19, 27, 47, 60 n. 131, 174
Residori, Matteo 152
Ricci, Bartolomeo 16, 17
Riccò, Laura 2, 6, 10 n. 4, 109, 170
Rinuccini, Ottavio 227, 228, 239 n. 106
Robortello, Francesco 24, 56 n. 58, 134, 137
romance 89, 102, 114, 173, 190 n. 14
   Hellenistic 200, 235 n. 22
   modern, *see* Ariosto, *Orlando furioso*; Tasso, *Gerusalemme liberata*
   prose 104, 202, 232, 235 n. 25; *see also* Sannazaro, *Arcadia*
   theory on 21, 27, 56 n. 58, 68–70, 138
Rome 18, 80, 82–83, 119, 136, 202, 203, 232
Rossi, Bartolomeo, *see* de' Rossi
Rossi, Vittorio 134, 170
Ruzante (Angelo Beolco) 14, 16, 35, 36, 50, 52 n. 8, 58 n. 103, 224, 228

sacre rappresentazioni (sacred plays) 5, 13, 15, 32, 124 n. 20, 126 n. 54, 230
Salviati, Lionardo 130, 134, 162 n. 7, 172, 190 n. 6
Sannazaro, Jacopo:
   Arcadia 7, 14, 26, 38, 39, 40, 46, 56 n. 68, 59 n. 110, 64, 84, 95 n. 71, 104, 107, 110, 165 n. 55, 199, 202

verse 24, 55 n. 46, 124 n. 16
satira, see satyr-drama
satire 5, 35, 76, 77–79, 95 n. 69, 148, 149, 170
satyr 4, 5, 22, 24, 25, 26, 30, 38, 41, 44, 47, 49, 52, 55 n. 46, 70, 73, 74, 77–79, 84, 90, 94 n. 54, 95 nn. 68 & 69, 101, 108, 109, 112, 121–22, 128 n. 87, 131, 133, 147, 148, 150–51, 166 n. 74, 175, 176, 179, 199, 201, 209, 223, 237 n. 58
satyr-drama/play 5, 18, 21–27, 29, 33, 49, 51, 55 n. 50, 56 nn. 58 & 59, 68, 170, 175–76, 192 n. 33, 199
Savoy court 21, 106, 143, 185; see also Carlo Emanuele I *and* Turin
Scala, Flaminio 120, 224, 229, 237 n. 67, 239 n. 102
Scarpati, Claudio 71, 75, 77
Selmi, Elisabetta 130, 131, 151, 161 n. 6, 165 n. 53, 166 n. 74
Senecan tragedy, *see* Giraldi Cinthio, *Orbecche*
Serlio, Sebastiano 22, 23, 55 n. 50, 176, 178, 184
Shakespeare, William 2, 3, 39, 57 n. 85, 58 n. 106, 59 n. 123, 102, 230, 235 n. 30, 237 n. 66
Siena 7, 14, 29, 36, 58 n. 103, 59 n. 119, 187, 211
single life 42–43, 59 n. 119, 84, 112, 117; *see also* Diana
Sophocles 32, 113, 125 n. 32, 147, 159, 165 n. 65, 167 n. 93, 179
Spain 196, 202, 234
 and Italian theatre 2, 162 n. 16, 188, 195, 196, 202, 231
Speroni, Sperone 68, 113, 135–37, 163 nn. 30–33
 Canace 8, 91 n. 2, 94 nn. 43 & 46, 99, 135
 dialogues 92 n. 24, 94 n. 61, 135, 136–37, 138
 and Tasso 68, 71, 80, 83, 86, 91 n. 2, 93 n. 31, 94 nn. 43 & 49, 99, 135
sprezzatura 64–65, 81, 92 n. 23, 184
stage-set (pastoral) 26, 28, 52 n. 4, 63, 87, 96 n. 94, 108, 143, 165 n. 50, 174–78, 184, 186, 187–89, 192 n. 33, 198, 204, 218, 224, 228, 232, 240 n. 115
Strozzi Cicogna, Uno 209, 237 n. 57
Summo, Faustino 135, 151, 160, 163 n. 23, 186

Tansillo, Luigi, *I due pellegrini* 14, 29
Tasso, Bernardo 59 n. 119, 68, 69, 92 n. 12
Tasso, Torquato:
 Aminta 1, 2, 14, 52, 63–64, 65–67, 71–79, 87, 90, 91 n. 2, 93 n. 43, 98–101, 113, 122, 123, 124 n. 9, 143, 152, 197, 209, 226, 233
  editions 80–82, 95 n. 72, 99; performance 63, 80, 91 n. 12, 179, 180–81, 184–85, 195
 critical theory 68–71, 85–87, 93 nn. 31 & 41, 94 n. 48, 97 nn. 98, 103 & 104, 200, 201–02, 234 n. 14
 dialogues 65, 92 n. 22, 94 n. 61
 Galealto 69, 235 n. 30
 Gerusalemme conquistata 86, 90, 200
 Gerusalemme liberata 8, 69, 82, 83, 85–90, 110, 126 n. 47, 130, 132, 134, 138, 145, 159, 160, 162 n. 18, 165 n. 58, 200, 211, 213, 235 nn. 22 & 25, 238 nn. 80 & 85

life 62–64, 69, 91 nn. 5 & 7, 107, 114, 119, 130, 184, 191 n. 18
 and the press 80–83, 85, 95 nn. 79–81
Terence 18, 20, 36, 44, 48, 51, 54 n. 28, 142
 Andria 54 n. 28, 105, 131, 147
theatergrams 3, 94 n. 51, 36
Theocritus, *Idylls* 4, 40, 79, 137
Toniani, Pietro Antonio, *Floriano* 196, 197–98, 200, 209, 225, 237 nn. 58 & 69
torneo 20, 28, 60 n. 137, 62–63, 173
Torelli, Pomponio 107, 126 n. 47, 237 n. 71, 238 n. 86
 Galatea 196, 213–15, 223, 238 n. 77
Torelli Benedetti, Barbara 106–08, 114
 Partenia 100, 103, 106–12, 115, 116, 123, 126 nn. 42, 44, 51 & 54, 127 n. 70, 211
tragedia di lieto fine 20, 21, 25, 52, 69, 71, 197, 221; *see also* Giraldi Cinthio
tragedy 3, 4, 8–9, 21, 27, 56 n. 51, 92 n. 14, 103–04, 113, 115, 141, 145, 178, 179, 195, 197–98, 215, 234 n. 13, 235 n. 29
 with happy ending, *see tragedia di lieto fine*
 and pastoral drama 5, 33, 71, 73–74, 91 n. 2, 99, 100, 109–10, 113, 131, 137, 152, 184, 202, 211, 213–15, 221, 232
 Senecan, *see* Giraldi Cinthio, *Orbecche*
 theory on 20, 24, 25, 27, 55 n. 50, 56 nn. 55 & 59, 69, 70–71, 113, 140, 141, 171, 211, 220
tragicomedy 1, 5, 8, 21, 25, 33–34, 46, 48, 50, 75, 104, 120, 125 n. 25, 132, 140, 145–47, 151, 156, 160, 162 n. 12, 212, 215–16, 230, 232, 239 n. 114
 theory on 21, 25, 33, 51, 56 n. 62, 123, 129, 132, 137–38, 140, 141, 142, 145–46, 151, 153, 186, 198–99, 215–16
Turin 130, 142, 148, 159, 185, 186, 193 n. 73, 196

Urbino 13, 64, 81, 130, 176, 184, 203, 204

Venice 7, 114, 127 n. 64, 132, 134, 137, 163 n. 32, 203
 and the press 19, 31, 81, 82–83, 135, 139
 and theatre 7, 14, 15, 33, 34, 35, 62, 105, 112, 114, 132, 137
Venus (goddess of love) 45, 46, 65, 71, 84, 100, 110, 133, 185
Verato, Giovan Battista 113, 132, 179
Vicenza 112, 113–15, 117, 137, 163 n. 23, 172, 187, 197, 211, 221
 Teatro Olimpico 32, 113, 204; *see also* Accademia Olimpica
Vida, Girolamo 99–100
Virgil 33, 67
 Aeneid 67, 69, 97 n. 104, 142
 Eclogues (*Bucolics*) 5, 7, 10 nn. 11 & 12, 26 37, 38, 40, 64, 67, 76, 79, 95 n. 70, 101, 107, 122, 126 nn. 46 & 52, 137, 143, 145, 183
 Georgics 5, 67
Vitruvius 5, 22, 176

women:
   see actors, female
   dramatists 42, 103–04, 106–23, 124 nn. 20, 22, & 25, 126 n. 54, 128 n. 81
   as patrons 104–05
   and literature 102, 104, 113, 114, 119

Zabarella, Jacopo 135, 137, 164 n. 47, 172